This Book
Belongs
To

The Girl's Companion

BLACKIE & SON LIMITED
16/18 William IV Street, Charing Cross, LONDON, W.C.2
17 Stanhope Street, GLASGOW

BLACKIE & SON (INDIA) LIMITED
103/5 Fort Street, BOMBAY

BLACKIE & SON (CANADA) LIMITED
TORONTO

POTTERY AND BLOCK-PRINTED TEXTILES

THE
GIRL'S COMPANION

EDITED BY

Mary A. Carson

BLACKIE & SON LIMITED

LONDON AND GLASGOW

First published 1947
Reprinted 1948, 1951
New Edition 1956
Reprinted 1956, 1958, 1959

Printed in Great Britain by Blackie & Son, Ltd., Glasgow

PREFACE

This book is intended to appeal to every girl no matter what her special enthusiasms may be. The outdoor girl and the girl who prefers indoor pastimes are both catered for, while particular attention has also been devoted to social and domestic interests in an attractive as well as practically informative manner. Thus the tennis player will find that her favourite game is competently dealt with; so will the clever-fingered girl interested in such subjects as embroidery, and also she who is anxious to be a " handyman " about the house. Nor are lighter themes such as Party Giving, Dancing and Beauty Culture neglected. In every case instructions have been given as clearly as possible, but there has been no " writing down "—the adult readers also will therefore find the material of real value.

All the subjects have been dealt with by experts, and no pains have been spared to make the work worthy of its title of *The Girl's Companion.*

CONTENTS

Section I.—Indoor Arts, Crafts, and Hobbies

Page

EMBROIDERY, by *Mary Fyffe* - - - - - 17
ITS ANCIENT ORIGIN—A FEW STITCHES—MAKING A DESIGN
—COLOUR EXPERIMENTS — APPLIQUÉ — CROSS STITCH —
DRAWN FABRIC WORK—QUILTING (ENGLISH AND ITALIAN).

CROCHET-WORK, by *Agnes Scott* - - - - - 32
PRINCIPAL STITCHES—SHELL PATTERN—FILET CROCHET—
A SIMPLE INSERTION—LACE FILLING.

KNITTING, by *Agnes Scott* - - - - - - 38
CASTING ON AND OFF, TWO METHODS—PLAIN KNITTING—
STITCHES AND PATTERNS—KNITTING A JUMPER—MAKING
AN ORIGINAL DESIGN—DIAGONAL AND DIAMOND PATTERNS.

LEATHER-WORK, by *Margaret Hurd* - - - - 52
MATERIAL REQUIRED —SKETCHING A DESIGN—CUTTING THE
SKIN—THONGING.

FELT-WORK, by *Mary Fyffe* - - - - - - 58
MOST INEXPENSIVE OF HOBBIES—IMPORTANCE OF NEAT
CUTTING—MAKING FLOWER POSIES—DECORATIVE BELT—
POCHETTE—TOYS.

POTTERY, by *A. Macmorland* - - - - - 64
MATERIALS AND TOOLS — CONDITIONING THE CLAY —
SIMPLE MODELLING — BUILDING UP A BOWL (VARIOUS
METHODS)—GLAZING—FORMS OF DECORATION—WARNING
AGAINST ELABORATION.

PRINTING ON TEXTILES, by *A. Macmorland* - - 76
NECESSARY MATERIALS AND TOOLS—CHOICE OF FABRIC—
MAKING A PRINTING BLOCK—WORKING WITH PRINTING INK
—EXPERIMENTING WITH PRINTS—LIQUID DYES—FIXING
THE DYE.

Page

CANE-WORK, by *Mary Fyffe* - - - - - 84
BUYING THE CANE—HOW TO HOLD IT—FORMS OF WEAVING
—THE PROPER TOOLS—MAKING A TUMBLER HOLDER—WORK
BASKET—TEA TRAY.

STENCILS, by *Dorothea Simpson* - - - - - 91
CHOOSING SUITABLE MATERIALS—NECESSARY EQUIPMENT—
IMPORTANCE OF DESIGN—DIRECTIONS FOR CUTTING A
THISTLE, A ROSE AND A SHIP—PREPARING THE PAINT.

HOW TO MAKE A PLAQUE OR WALL MASK,
by *Charles F. Fisher* - - - - - - 94
MOULDING—MIXING THE PLASTER AND COLOURING—
MAKING THE MOULD—TIME FOR SETTING—REMOVING
MODEL FROM MOULD.

PUTTING ON A PLAY, by *Hal D. Stewart* - - - 101
SELECTING THE PLAY—THE PRODUCER—THE SETTING—
SCALED PLAN OF SET—MOVES—THE ACTORS—REHEARSALS
—PROMPT COPY—IMPORTANCE OF PACE—THE STAGE MAN-
AGER — SCENERY AND STAGE — " PROPS " — LIGHTING—
MAKE-UP.

Section II.—Outdoor Activities

ATHLETICS, by *Mary McGavin* - - - - - 113
PREPARING FOR A SPORTS MEETING—SPRINTING—RELAY
RACE—HIGH JUMP—SCISSOR JUMP—OBJECT RACE—AIMING
CONTEST—SPORTS DAY PROGRAMME.

BIRD-WATCHING AND BIRD-NESTING, by *Seton Gordon* 129
HOW TO STUDY WILD BIRDS—THE VARIOUS SONGS OF BIRDS,
AND HOW TO DISTINGUISH THEM—THE FLIGHT OF BIRDS—
BIRD-NESTING—STRUCTURE OF SOME BIRDS' NESTS.

CAMPING, by *Maimie Keay* - - - - - - 141
NO NEED TO BE SPARTAN—CHOOSING A SITE—PITCHING THE
TENT, VARIOUS TYPES—NECESSARY EQUIPMENT—PLANNING
THE CAMP—BUILDING A FIRE—FOOD PREPARATION—LEAV-
ING BEHIND A GOOD REPUTATION.

CONTENTS

Page

CRICKET, by *Brenda Wrightson* - - - - - 166
CHOOSING A BAT—LAYOUT OF PITCH—STANCE FOR BATTING
—FORWARD AND DEFENSIVE PLAY—MAKING RUNS—BOWL-
ING—FIELDING—WICKET-KEEPING.

CYCLING, by *Alexander Taylor* - - - - - 180
THE PLEASURE OF CYCLING—THE BEST ALL-ROUND MACHINE
—THE SADDLE—HANDLEBARS—ANKLING—BICYCLE MAIN-
TENANCE—CLUB CYCLING—SOME RECORDS—ROAD MANNERS
—SPARE PARTS.

GOLF, by *Leonard G. Crawley* - - - - - 192
MENTAL STRAIN OF GOLF—GOLF STANCE; THE SWING—THE
THREE GRIPS—ARM AND WRIST ACTION—KEEPING THE HEAD
STILL—FOLLOW-THROUGH—DRIVING—WOODEN AND IRON
CLUBS—PUTTING.

GYMNASTICS, by *T. H. Hawtin* - - - - - 206
AIDS TO GOOD STYLE—MOVEMENTS WITH INDIAN CLUBS—
STANDING EXERCISES—ON THE APPARATUS (PARALLEL BARS,
VAULTING HORSE)—HOW TO BECOME A GYMNAST—TAKING
PART IN DISPLAYS AND COMPETITIONS.

HOCKEY, by *Audrey Bell* - - - - - - 234
BEST STICK FOR LEARNER—PROPER CLOTHING—MARKING
THE PITCH—RULES OF GAME—DUTIES OF UMPIRE—WORK
OF PLAYERS—DIFFERENT POSITIONS—CHOOSING A TEAM—
GOOD TEAM MANNERS.

LACROSSE, by *Brenda Wrightson* - - - - - 251
EQUIPMENT—HOW TO HOLD THE CROSSE—CRADLING—
TOSSING AND CATCHING—PICKING UP THE BALL—TO
THROW THE BALL—DODGING—SHOOTING A GOAL.

LAWN TENNIS, by *Dorothy Round* - - - - 258
CORRECT GRIPS—SERVICE STANCE AND PLAY—SPIN TECH-
NIQUE—FOREHAND AND BACKHAND DRIVE—THE VOLLEY—
POSITIONAL PLAY — CHAMPIONSHIP STRATEGY — DOUBLES
TEAM WORK.

Page

MOUNTAINEERING, by *Elizabeth Orr Boyd* -   -   - 280
CLOTHES FOR SUMMER AND WINTER CLIMBING—EQUIP-
MENT—THE ASCENT—WARNINGS—UNNECESSARY ADVEN-
TURES—SOME EASY CLIMBS—ROCK-CLIMBING.

NETBALL, by *Mary McGavin*   -   -   -   -   - 293
THE COURT—THROWING—CATCHING—MARKING—DODG-
ING—FOOTWORK—SOME HINTS—THE BOUNCE—PENALTIES
—TACTICS IN PASSING—GAMES LEADING UP TO NETBALL.

PATHFINDING, by *Dorothy Laird* -   -   -   -   - 308
LEARNING TO READ A MAP—COMPASSES AND HOW TO USE
THEM—WOODCRAFT—POINTS TO REMEMBER.

RIDING, by *Primrose Cumming*   -   -   -   - 314
A WELCOME FOR " BARRY ", THE HORSE—HIS FIRST GROOM-
ING—FITTING THE BRIDLE—THE FIRST LESSON—USING
THE REINS—GROOMING AND CARE—LESSONS IN WALKING,
TROTTING AND CANTERING—THE DOUBLE BRIDLE—JUMPING.

RUNNING A TOURNAMENT, by *Audrey Bell*   -   - 333
HINTS FOR THE ORGANIZERS—VARIOUS SYSTEMS, KNOCK-OUT
AND AMERICAN—METHODS OF THE DRAW—PLANNING A
DAY'S PROGRAMME—SUITABLE GAMES.

SAILING AND MOTOR BOATS, by *M. H. Tew* -   - 344
THE BOAT, ART OF SAILING—MOORING—ANCHORING—
CARE OF BOAT—SAILS—ENGINES—FITTING OUT—GENERAL
HINTS—MOTOR BOATS—GENERAL.

FIRST STEPS IN SKI-ING, by *Dorothy Laird*   -   - 360
BUYING THE SKIS — SUITABLE CLOTHING — BEGINNER'S
LESSON—ACHIEVING BALANCE—TECHNIQUES FOR THE ASCENT
—THE DOWNHILL RUN—SECRETS OF SUCCESS.

SWIMMING, by *Margaret D. Kirkwood* -   -   -   - 368
RECORDS HELD BY SCHOOLGIRLS—THE BEGINNER'S STAGE—
DRY LAND EXERCISES—CRAWL MOVEMENTS—BREAST STROKE
—" AT HOME " IN WATER—FLOATING—DIVING—JOINING A
CLUB.

Page

THE YOUNG NATURALIST, by *B. Webster Smith*   - 383
    EQUIPMENT—INSECTS—BUTTERFLY HUNTING—MOTHS AND
    THEIR HABITS—KILLING AND MOUNTING INSECTS—STORAGE
    CABINETS—THE BREEDING OF BUTTERFLIES AND MOTHS—
    CATERPILLARS— BEETLES— SPIDERS— COLLECTING, DRYING
    AND PRESERVING PLANTS—SEAWEEDS—SEA SHELLS—OTHER
    MARINE OBJECTS—BIRDS' EGGS.

Section III.—The Social Side

DRESS AND BEAUTY, by *Phyllis Jenkins*   -   -   - 396
    FASCINATING HISTORY OF DRESS—FIRST INTRODUCTION OF
    HYGIENIC CLOTHING—ACQUIRING DRESS SENSE—SCHOOL
    UNIFORM— GROOMING FOR GOOD LOOKS—CLOTHES CARE—
    POISE AND POSTURE.

FANCY DRESS, by *Dorothea Simpson*   -   -   -   - 410
    THE GAME OF LET'S PRETEND—ITS ORIGINS—DECIDING
    YOUR TYPE—LIST OF POSSIBLE CHARACTERS—SUITABLE
    MATERIALS AND MAKESHIFTS—FULL DIRECTIONS FOR FIVE
    BASIC COSTUMES.

BALLROOM DANCING, by *Mary McGavin* -   -   - 423
    ETIQUETTE OF THE BALLROOM—THE CORRECT POSTURE—
    DETAILED DIRECTIONS FOR QUICKSTEP—MODERN WALTZ—
    SLOW FOXTROT—QUICK WALTZ.

COUNTRY DANCING, by *Mary E. Davidson*   -   - 438
    SQUARE DANCING—NATIONAL FOLK DANCES—INTRODUC-
    TION WALTZ—PUBLIC DEMONSTRATION—CORRECT COSTUMES
    —FULL DETAILS OF LANCERS.

GIVING A PARTY, by *Emma Menzies* -   -   -   - 451
    MIXING THE GUESTS—MENU FOR SUPPER, WITH RECIPES—
    NOVEL INVITATIONS—PLANNING THE ENTERTAINMENT—
    TEAM GAMES — COMPETITIONS — CHARADES — DANCES —
    PARTING SOUP CUP.

Page

THE PERFECT GUEST, by *Biddy Russell* - - - 468
GOOD MANNERS KEY TO POPULARITY—SIMPLE CONSIDER-
ATION—HOSTESS AND OTHER GUESTS—AVOIDING SHYNESS
—TABLE ETIQUETTE—THE GENTLEMAN'S PART—HOSTESS
DUTIES.

HOUSEKEEPER FOR A WEEK, by *Emma Menzies* - - 474
DOMESTIC EMERGENCY—SIMPLE MEALS AND HOW TO PRE-
PARE THEM—ESSENTIAL HOUSEWORK—" DON'T FORGETS "—
TIMETABLE AND MENU FOR A WEEK.

A ROOM OF YOUR OWN, by *Sheila Stuart* - - 488
PLANNING THE COLOUR SCHEME—MAKE-DO FURNITURE—
THE BED—CHOICE OF CURTAINS—PERSONAL TOUCHES—
NEED FOR SPACE—BOOKCASE—IMPORTANCE OF TIDINESS.

Section IV.—Miscellaneous

REPAIRS ABOUT THE HOUSE, by *Sheila Stuart* - 502
WHAT TO DO IN A CRISIS—MENDING A FUSE—GAS ESCAPES
—DRIPPING TAP—FROZEN PIPES—CARPET CATASTROPHES
—TO WASH WOOLLIES—INVISIBLE MENDING—THE MICE
MENACE.

KEEPING FIT, by a *Woman Doctor* - - - - 523
DAILY ROUTINE FOR GOOD HEALTH—CARE OF SKIN AND
HAIR—THE HAPPY NATURE—SOME HINTS ON FIRST AID—
WHEN ACCIDENTS OCCUR—HOME NURSING.

FORMING A CLUB, by *Biddy Russell* - - - - 531
KNOWLEDGE OF CORRECT PROCEDURE USEFUL EVERYWHERE
—SELECTING OFFICE-BEARERS—THE NOTICE-BOARD—DRAW-
ING UP A CONSTITUTION—VALUE OF CO-OPERATION.

MUSIC CLUB, by *Ethel Langston* - - - - - 536
SUITABLE MEETING PLACE—FIRST RECITAL—CLASSICAL AND
JAZZ—APPARATUS—CATALOGUING RECORDS—PRESENTING A
PROGRAMME.

CONTENTS

YOUR OWN LIBRARY, by *J. R. Third* - - - 543
SUITABLE BOOK SHELVES—SELECTION OF CLASSICS—MODERN
FAVOURITES—WOMEN AUTHORS—GREAT POETS—REFER-
ENCE BOOKS.

KNOTS, by *B. Webster Smith* - - - - - 550
ILLUSTRATIONS AND EXAMPLES OF SOME USEFUL KNOTS.

DOGS AND PETS: THEIR CARE AND MANAGE-
MENT, by *S. H. Benson* - - - - - 552
BUYING A DOG—PEDIGREE DOGS—FEEDING A PUPPY—
TEACHING ONE'S PUPPY—BATHING AND GROOMING DOGS—
EXERCISING DOGS—CATS—RABBITS—GUINEA PIGS—CAGE
BIRDS: BUDGERIGARS—CANARIES.

TAKING AND MAKING PHOTOGRAPHS, by *G. J.
Matson* - - - - - - - - 570
INTRODUCTION—BUYING A CAMERA—THE APERTURES—
CORRECT EXPOSURES—EXPOSURE METER—FOCUSING—
TYPES OF FILM—TAKING THE PHOTOGRAPH—TANKS AND
DEVELOPERS—DEVELOPING—DAYLIGHT PRINTING—GAS-
LIGHT PRINTING—ENLARGING—GLAZING AND DRYING
PRINTS.

DRAWING, WATER-COLOUR PAINTING, ETCHING,
by *Ian Campbell* - - - - - - 587
DRAWING—FUNDAMENTAL FORMS—DRAWING FROM NATURE
—SIGNIFICANCE OF LINES—PAINTING IN WATER COLOURS—
PREPARING THE PAPER—COLOURS—COMBINATIONS OF
COLOURS—WASHES AND HOW APPLIED—ETCHING—THE
TOOLS—DRAWING THE SUBJECT—ACID BATH—HOW T
MAKE PRINTS—DRY-POINT WORK.

STAMP COLLECTING, by *G. J. Matson* - - - 598
SOME RARE STAMPS—A STAMP COLLECTOR'S EQUIPMENT—
PERFORATIONS—WATERMARKS—STAMP CATALOGUES—AL-
BUMS—WRITING UP ONE'S COLLECTION—ERRORS ON STAMPS

Page

—DESIRABILITY OF SPECIALIZING—SOME ATTRACTIVE COUNTRIES—MINT STAMPS VERSUS USED—EXCHANGES—
—STAMP CLUB—BUYING FROM DEALERS—STAMP AUCTIONS.

SWEET-MAKING, by *Jane Andrew* - - - - - 610
A POPULAR ACCOMPLISHMENT—SIMPLE AND ELABORATE RECIPES—BONBONS FOR GIFTS.

CAREER GUIDE, by *Jane Andrew* - - - - - 622
An ALPHABETICAL LIST, WITH DIRECTIONS, OF SOME SIXTY POSSIBLE OCCUPATIONS.

COLOUR PLATES

Facing
page

POTTERY AND BLOCK-PRINTED TEXTILES

Frontis.

SOME BRITISH BIRDS –   –   –   –   – 136

SOME BRITISH BUTTERFLIES –   –   –   – 384

FANCY DRESS   –   –   –   –   –   –   – 416

EMBROIDERY

A poet, it is said, embroiders the truth. That is, he embellishes it, enriches it. This seems to be a good definition of embroidery; embellishment, enrichment; the enriching of a material, the adorning of a background. And may it be said that, as in many things in life, the enriching is twofold: to be an embroiderer is to enrich one's own life.

Like most of our crafts, embroidery is of ancient origin. As soon as man began to sew—and needles of bone were found in the Stone Age—he began to embroider. In the early days embroidery came to us from the East. It is mentioned in the Domesday Book, and it is said that, when William the Conqueror came over in 1066, he was astonished at the beautiful work which he found.

The history of embroidery is an interesting subject and one well worthy of study. In this country we have a wonderful heritage, as a visit to any museum will show. In the thirteenth and fourteenth centuries our ecclesiastical work was famous, but after the Reformation, when church forms became simpler, embroiderers turned their attention to personal attire, and never were we more gorgeously apparelled than in the days of Queen Elizabeth, whose wardrobe was said to run to three thousand dresses.

Perhaps the most noteworthy period was in the reign of Queen Anne, when Jacobean embroidery reached the height of its popularity. At that time there was much trading with the East, and ships brought back samples of eastern work, many of them showing the motif of the " Tree of Life ". This inspired the embroiderers of that time to combine this new motif with their own inherited designs to form what has become known as Jacobean work. In most of the work of that period this motif can be seen rising from a series of small mounds, and branching out on either side into curiously shaped flowers and fruits. Following this period, furnishings became lighter in design and embroidery had to be changed to suit. Floral forms became smaller and more delicate.

Quilting was also at the height of its glory in Stewart times. It then went out of favour, but at the present day our taste for quiet furnishings has brought a renewed delight in this most lovely work.

It has an unobtrusive beauty which fits in well with our modern home decoration. Appliqué, another ancient craft, has had a new vogue for the same reason, and also perhaps because it suits our liking for doing things quickly. It is the type of embroidery which produces the maximum effect with the minimum of effort.

So each epoch becomes identified with a certain type of design, and so also does each country.

Stitches.

The tools required to embark on this craft are: pencil, paper, ruler, and set square for designing; needles, thread, material for sewing; and stitches. It is the mark of the true embroideress that she searches until she finds just the right stitch to give expression to the design on which she is working. What a heritage of stitches we have to choose from is evident from a glance through such a book as Mary Thomas's *Dictionary of Stitches*. On close examination we will see that many of them can readily be classed into families: the flat stitches, the chains, the buttonholes, the knots, the pulled stitches. Let me introduce you to a few of them.

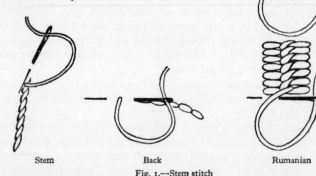

Stem   Back   Rumanian

Fig. 1.—Stem stitch

1. The flat stitches. There is stem stitch or, to give it its old name, crewel stitch, satin stitch, back stitch, and, less well known perhaps, but very useful for filling in leaves and flowers, Rumanian stitch (fig. 1).

2. The chains. Chain stitch, one of the most frequently used of all, deserves a few words to itself. Many of the embroideries of the seventeenth and eighteenth centuries were wrought entirely in this

stitch, and it was a favourite with the peoples of the East. Rows and rows of it worked together make an ideal filling, as can be seen in these embroideries and also in our own period pieces. The rela-

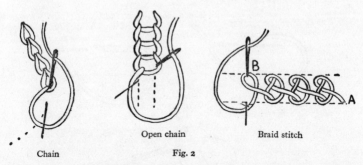

Chain   Open chain   Braid stitch

Fig. 2

tions of chain stitch are numerous. Among them we have double chain, open chain, twisted chain, and a very lovely stitch, braid stitch (fig. 2).

3. The buttonholes. Buttonhole stitch is useful as an edging. It is an amusing exercise for the beginner to see how many different

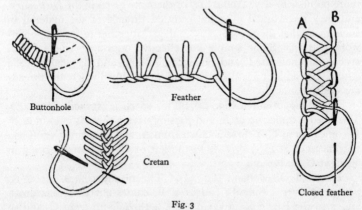

Buttonhole   Feather   A B

Cretan

Closed feather

Fig. 3

ways she can find of grouping the stitches so as to make a neat border or hem. As a filling it gives a pretty lacy effect, and is much used in Jacobean work. Feather stitch, closed feather and Cretan, also good for fillings, are some of the variations of buttonhole stitch (fig. 3).

4. The knots. Most favoured of the knots is perhaps French knot. Bullion knot makes a pretty centre for flowers, and there is also snail trail or, as it is sometimes called, coral stitch (fig. 4).

Button knot

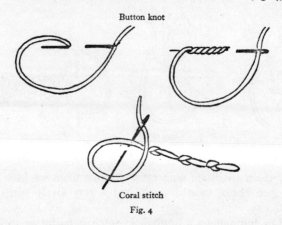

Coral stitch

Fig. 4

5. The pulled stitches. This is a family that is becoming more and more popular to-day. About fifty of them are given in the *Dictionary*, and they are worked over the counted threads of the material in such a way that the threads are " pulled " together to form an open-work pattern. Some simple but effective ones are: single faggot stitch, diagonal raised band, honeycomb filling, and diagonal chevron stitch. Use a blunt needle and a hand-woven linen where the threads are easily counted.

Single faggot stitch (fig. 5a). This stitch is worked diagonally. The needle comes up at A, and passing over 3 threads goes in at B. It comes out at C, 3 threads down from A, and in again at A. Then it comes out at D, 3 threads to the left of C. Repeat by going in again at C, and so on.

Diagonal raised band (fig. 5b). The needle comes out at A, passes up over 4 threads, and in at B, comes out 2 threads down and 2 to the left, goes in again at D, 4 threads up from C, and so on. When the end of the row is reached the needle comes back by crossing over the stitches already made (diagram 2), in at D, out at E, in at B, out at C, &c.

But these are only a few of the numbers of stitches which lie ready to hand waiting to be used, and when we have mastered some

a

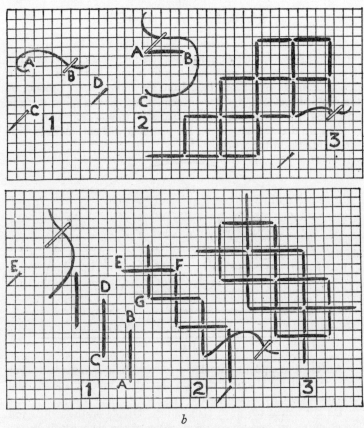

b

Fig. 5.—*a*, Single faggot stitch.   *b*, Diamond raised band

of them, we will find that embroidery has a new interest. It is a
good plan to make a sampler of favourite stitches, and then to finish
it off in the form of a small envelope-shaped bag for holding embroidery threads.   In this way it can always be available for reference.

MAKING A DESIGN

Now we are ready to consider the planning of a design.

Although we are not all born designers there is a creative instinct in each one of us. Far more satisfaction is to be had from a simple design arranged by oneself than from the more perfect product of the professional, and if a few principles are kept in mind there is no reason why we should not be successful in our designing.

Be sure that the design you are planning will not interfere with the usefulness of the article.

Fig. 6

A design should fit the shape for which it is intended. For instance, that for a square cushion should be roughly square, and that for a tea cosy semicircular.

Do not aim at too great elaboration. Decide on the motifs you are going to use and repeat them. One of the elements of design is repetition, and it is a truth that too much variety tires the eye, whereas a motif repeated again and again has a restful effect. This is well illustrated in most borders, where you will find a floral or other form recurring at regular intervals.

Next we come to one of the most important points in building up a design, and that is balance. It is most easily achieved by symmetry, as in a cushion where the four corners are all the same. You will find, however, that you will often get a freer, more interesting result if you do not adhere to symmetry. If you look at fig. 6, which shows a design for a tea cosy, you will see that bands of appliqué divide the tea cosy roughly in half. The rose on one side is balanced by a rose on the other, and two thistles are introduced to fill the space left in the middle. The design is not symmetrical, but it has balance.

This brings us to another principle, that of spacing. Spacing is, generally speaking, the correct placing of objects or floral forms, so that the spaces left will not be too small or too large in any one part, and the general effect will be pleasing.

Thus we see that design is just arrangement, and it is an excellent plan for the beginner to work with coloured paper, and to cut out the shapes, floral forms, or whatever she intends to include in her design, and arrange and rearrange them until she is satisfied that the best possible result has been attained. Then pin them in place and draw in any stems that may be required, being careful to get a rhythmic effect. If you look at any Jacobean design you will see what is meant by rhythm. Invariably the main stem rises from a series of small mounds and flows upwards in undulating curves, branching to right and left, the whole giving a perfect example of rhythm.

There remains one point to be mentioned, and that is contrast. It is contrast that gives life to a design; contrast in tone, contrast in colour; pale shades against a neutral background, glowing colours against a dark one. This strikes a vital note in embroidery.

COLOUR EXPERIMENTS

How we revel in colour in the summer time when the sea is blue and the garden brilliant with flowers of every hue! But in the drab days of winter we must satisfy our need for it in our dress, our curtains, our pictures, and our embroideries, and what a joy it is to come into a room gay with bright colours. There is a theory of colour based on the prismatic spectrum, and a colour circle can be obtained in which the colours are arranged concentrically in the same order as in the spectrum. Those immediately opposite each other are called complementaries, because, when placed together, each becomes more intense. Blue and yellow, red and blue-green, purple and green, orange and green-blue are complementaries. Those which lie side by side are analogous colours, and being near each other in hue, they harmonize, as, for example, orange and yellow.

Experimenting with colour is a fascinating hobby, and a colour circle will be found very helpful in selecting those tints and shades which contrast or combine well. Nature, too, is an inexhaustible source of instruction in the appreciation of colour harmonies. The neutrals, black, white, and the greys, play their part in colour contrast, and an all-neutral scheme can be very beautiful.

One of the most popular types of embroidery to-day offers good practice in design and that is

Appliqué

Appliqué work is the applying of pieces of one material upon another so as to form a pattern. In olden days this form of em-

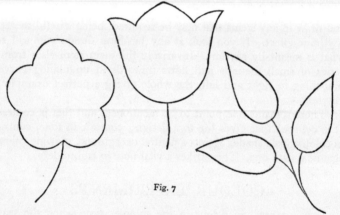

Fig. 7

broidery was largely used for banners and church work. Silks and velvets were employed, and the effect was luxurious. To-day our tastes are simpler, and we prefer to work with linens in their soft clear shades, and cottons in all the range of gay colours obtainable. But any sort of stuff can be used, and it is a good plan to keep a box of oddments to draw upon as occasion requires. Felt, too, is an ideal medium for this type of work, as the edges do not fray and it is easily sewn to the background.

Shapes should be simple in form and of a fair size. Flowers, animals, birds, human figures, as well as geometrical shapes, form suitable subjects (fig. 7). These should be cut out in paper and arranged in various ways until what is considered the most effective design has been achieved. Then tack the pieces to a background, lay tracing paper on top and trace out. The design can then be transferred to the material by means of carbon paper. The pieces forming the design are cut out in the materials to be used, and tacked down in the proper places ready for sewing on to the background. This can be done in various ways. The edge can be turned in all round, and the pieces hem-stitched or herring-boned on. Or they can be buttonholed on or couched down (fig. 8).

Stitchery takes second place in this work, but a few stitches carefully chosen can add considerably to the result. The main interests are in the design and the colour scheme—bright colours on a neutral background or pale shades against a glowing background. On the other hand, a composition entirely in neutral shades, relying on the textures of the various materials for contrast, can be equally delightful.

The tea cosy illustrated in fig. 6 was made in lavender-blue silk. The roses, the tops of the thistles, and the upper bands of appliqué were done in spotted muslin. The leaves, the lower parts of the thistles, and the lower bands of appliqué were

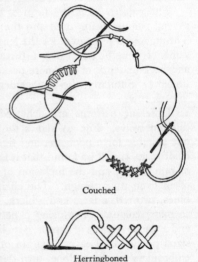

Couched

Herringboned

Fig. 8

in yellow, helio and rose, and green gingham respectively. The stitch used for the stems of the flowers was open chain, and that for the thistles, a cross stitch.

Appliqué is particularly suitable for nursery articles, as amusing designs can be made with animals and birds.

Embroidery by the Counted Thread.

Under this heading we shall group cross stitch and Florentine work, better perhaps classed as canvas work, and the work done on openly woven linen, using the pulled stitches already mentioned, and known as Drawn Fabric Work.

Cross Stitch Work is simple to do and can be very beautiful. Cushion covers and fire screens done in it are always popular, and many beautiful designs can be bought for them. It also makes very dainty borders for tray cloths and towels, and these form good practice for elementary design. They should be worked out on squared paper.

Florentine Work is interesting in that its effectiveness depends largely on the use of colour. It is worked in embroidery wools, which must be thick enough to cover the canvas, and it makes dainty handbags or pochettes and colourful chair seats.

The pattern takes the form of zig-zag lines across the canvas, several colours being used and the shade changing with each row. Throughout a piece of work the length of stitch must always be the same. It may be taken over 6 threads and back under 3, or over 6 and back under 2, or if a more peaked design is desired, over 6 and under 1. Similarly, the arrangement of stitches must be the same in each row.

Different patterns are achieved by grouping the stitches in different ways. Fig. 9A shows the simplest pattern of all, fig. 9B one suitable for a pochette, and fig. 9C a more elaborate one for a chair seat. It will be found that it is best to use two or more shades of one colour, and the inclusion of a black, a grey, or a fawn will often liven up a design. The chair seat might be worked in two blues, two red, a fawn and a black. The pochette will not require so many colours. Try using a petunia, two shades of blue-green and a black. A piece of canvas, 9 in. by 12 in., would make a medium-sized pochette. Leave a margin of $\frac{1}{2}$ in. all round, and after the embroidery has been done, turn this in and line throughout. Fit a lightning fastener—an 8-in. would do for this size—and slip stitch up the sides.

The colours for a pochette can be chosen to match a suit or a dress, and those for a chair seat to go with the colour scheme of a room.

Drawn Fabric Work is best done on hand-woven linen, where the threads are easily counted, and it looks nicest in a one-tone colour scheme. A tea cloth or a set of dinner mats in natural linen sewn with matching thread can be very lovely, for the pulled stitches give a lacy appearance to the work. Floral and geometric designs are both suitable for this work, but they should not be too intricate as the stitches are best used for fillings.

Practise the stitches on an odd piece of linen—it is a good plan

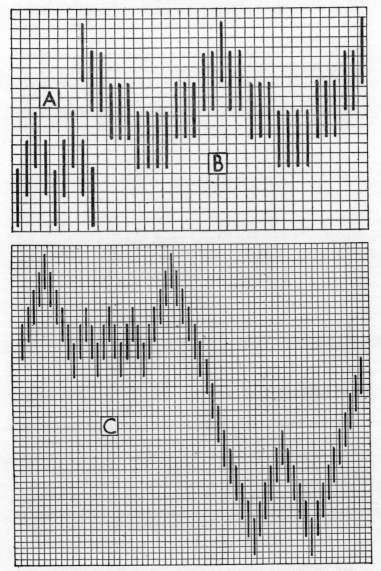

Fig. 9

to make a sampler of pulled stitches alone—and then try making a small tray cloth. You will require a piece of linen about 13 in. by 19 in. See that it is cut by the thread of the material. Turn in a ½-in. hem on the wrong side, taking care to arrange it so that it also lies along the thread. There are several quite simple stitches that can be used for hemming. Mark off a 2-in. square in each corner, about 15 to 20 threads in from the hem. Fill in the squares with your favourite pulled stitches, then join up the innermost corners of each by working a row of an open-work stitch all round (fig. 10).

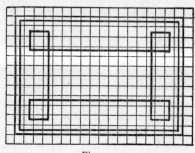

Fig. 10

When you have completed the tray cloth you will be ready to start a set of dinner mats. Try a more ambitious design this time, perhaps a floral spray. And when you have finished them you will have become the slave of the pulled stitches.

English Quilting.

No article on embroidery is complete without mention of quilting, of which we have a legacy of the loveliest of work. It was devised, according to tradition, by the women of the Middle Ages for their menfolk to wear under their coats of mail. Layers of material were sewn together, and this prevented the heavy armour from chafing the skin. Gradually, with woman's tendency to beautify, the sewing developed into pattern. What had first been intended for mere warmth became a thing of beauty, and women themselves began to wear garments made of quilting. During the reign of Queen Anne, embroidery was allied to quilting, and some beautiful pieces of the work of that period still survive.

But quilting, as well as being the adornment of the rich, was

also the province of the poor. If you take a blanket and a sheet
which have seen better days, and some odd pieces of print joined
together, you have the foundation for a warm bed quilt, such as
are made all over England and have been made for generations. For
quilting consists of three layers of material; the topmost layer, on

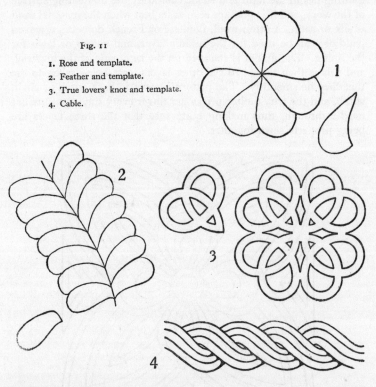

Fig. 11

1. Rose and template.
2. Feather and template.
3. True lovers' knot and template.
4. Cable.

which the pattern is worked, the middle or padding layer, and the
third layer or lining.

Traditional patterns, such as the rose, the feather, the true lovers'
knot, the cable (fig. 11), have been handed down, and homely articles
such as a saucer, a plate, a penny, are used to make them. Super-
stition, too, hangs around them. The true lovers' knot must always
be sewn in the same direction or ill-luck may befall the unhappy
possessor. These quilts are designed as they are being made. With

the help of templates—which are little patterns made of strong paper—the designs are scratched on as the work proceeds. English hand-made quilts are famous the world over.

Besides bed quilts, many delightful articles, such as handkerchief satchets, tea cosies and cushions can be made. The beauty of quilting lies in the light and shade caused by the undulating surface of the work, and it is perhaps seen at its best when the material used is silk or satin. Cotton-wool, domette or French domette, a woven padding, can be used for the middle layer, and cotton or lawn for the lining. The design is stamped on the right side of the material, and this is then tacked to the other layers, care being taken to see that they lie smoothly. The pattern is sewn in back stitch or chain stitch, and the true quilter pricks her finger every time she puts her needle through, thus making quite sure that the three layers are being properly sewn together.

Fig. 12

Italian Quilting.

This is a simpler form, and consists of only two layers of material, one of silk and one of muslin. The design, which is outlined with two rows of stitches, is stamped on the muslin, the two layers are tacked together, and the sewing is done in running stitch on the muslin. Perfection depends on the regularity of the stitches. Wool, which can be bought for the purpose, is threaded through between the rows of stitching, thus giving a raised effect. Use a blunt needle to do this, and see that the lines are well filled with padding. At angles and curves in the design it is necessary to bring the needle out, and then to insert it again at the same place.

When designing for quilting it is a good plan to work over squared paper. Both floral and geometric designs are suitable, and the Celtic type of design looks very nice in Italian quilting. Fig. 12 shows a design for a handkerchief satchet in Italian quilting. It will require a piece of silk 9 in. by 18 in., a piece of material for lining the same size, and a 9-in. square of muslin. After the quilting is done, attach the lining to the silk, fold in two, and slip stitch up the sides.

Shadow Quilting.

This is done in the same way as Italian, but brilliant wools are used in padding. The material must be of organdie or transparent silk, so that the padding will shine through. It then gives the effect of delicate colour, and can be very beautiful.

CROCHET-WORK

Crochet is one of the easiest forms of handicraft to learn, the few simple stitches explained here being the foundation of this work.

Equipment is simple—and cheap. All one needs is a crochet hook and a ball of crochet cotton or rayon. Coarse bone hooks are procurable for work in wool, and steel hooks are used for finer work. Numbers in steel hooks increase with the fineness of the needle, while with bone hooks it is the other way about.

Chain Stitch.

This stitch is the foundation of all crochet-work. Form a slip stitch on the hook, which is held in the right hand as a pencil is

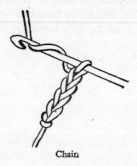

Chain

held, the hook being turned towards you. Hold the thread between the thumb and forefinger of the left hand, so that it is passed over the forefinger and second finger, under the third finger, and out over the little finger. This arrangement lets the thread slip easily through the fingers, but any method which permits of smooth working is satisfactory. With your slip stitch on the hook, place the hook under the thread from left to right and draw the thread through the loop already on the hook. Repeat for the length of chain necessary and try to keep the stitches the same size.

Single-crochet or Slip Stitch.

Place the hook through the edge of the stitch below and draw the loop through the stitch and the loop at the same time. This is principally used for joining and finishing.

Slip Stitch   Double Crotchet

Double Crochet.

Place the hook under the top of the stitch below, taking up both loops, and draw the thread through. Now place the hook under the thread and draw a new loop through the two loops already on the hook. This gives a flat surface.

A ridged surface can be obtained by inserting the hook through the back loop only of the top edge of previous row.

Short Treble or Half Treble.

This is seldom used. Place the hook under the thread, insert it into the stitch below, and draw a loop through this stitch. Place the hook again under the thread and draw a loop through the three loops on the needle.

Treble.

As in the last stitch place the hook under the thread and insert it into the stitch below. Draw a loop through this stitch, making three stitches on the needle. Place the hook again under the thread and draw a loop through the first two loops on the hook. Place the hook under the thread again and draw a loop through the remaining two loops.

2

Long Treble or Double Treble.

Pass the hook twice under the thread before inserting it into the stitch below. Draw a new loop through two loops at a time, three times.

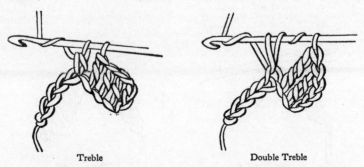

Treble   Double Treble

Increasing.—Merely work two stitches into one loop.

Decreasing.—Simply miss out a stitch of the previous row.

Joining Threads.—The best method is to leave a sufficient length of the old thread to do a few stitches. Work the next six stitches alternately with new and old thread. Ends can be darned in later.

It is also possible, as in knitting, to do three stitches with double thread, the old and the new.

To Finish Off.—Cut your thread and draw it through the loop, pulling it tight. Neaten by slip-stitching the end left for a few stitches, or simply by darning.

Shell Pattern.

This is a good solid surface for woollen pram cover or cosy dressing-jacket.

Abbreviations: ch.—chain; d.c.—double crochet; tr.—treble. Make a length of chain.

1st row: Into 4th chain from hook make 4 tr., miss 2 ch., 1 d.c. into next chain, * miss 2 ch., 5 tr. in next chain, miss 2 ch., 1 d.c. in next ch. Repeat from *.

Shell pattern

Subsequent rows: Make 3 ch., then on first d.c. of previous row make 4 tr., but on subsequent ones 5 tr., and in centre of each group of trebles make 1 d.c.

Filet Crochet.

Filet crochet has as its foundation a square mesh like that of a filet net, hence its name.

Two chain stitches form the top and bottom of each square, and a treble stitch each of its sides. Pattern is shown by filling up certain open meshes, each with two treble stitches. The open meshes are named holes and the filled up meshes blocks.

Filet crotchet

To start a new row if a hole is desired, you work 5 ch., then do a treble into 3rd ch. of previous row.

To start a new row if a block is desired, you work 3 ch., then work three trebles into the first three stitches.

Any pattern or design can first be planned out on squared paper, blocks being shown by crosses, and is quite easily followed, indeed more readily than written instructions.

A Simple Insertion.

1st row: Make a chain of 17 stitches. 1 tr. into 8 ch. st. from hook. * 2 ch., 1 tr. into 3rd ch. st. from last tr. Repeat from * twice, making 4 holes, 5 ch., turn.

2nd row: 1 tr. into the last but 1 tr. of previous row. * 2 tr. into next space, 1 tr. into next tr. Repeat from * once, 2 ch. 1 tr. into 3rd ch. st. at the end of first row, 5 ch., turn.

3rd row: 1 tr. into 1st tr. of previous row. * 2 ch., 1 tr. into 3rd ch. st. from last tr. Repeat from * twice, 5 ch. turn.

INSERTION

Spaces =
2 ch. 1 tr. over 1 tr.
X = 2 treble.

Repeat 2nd and 3rd rows alternately for required length.

A simpler instruction would be: *Odd rows:* 4 holes. *Even rows:* 1 hole, 2 blocks, 1 hole.

Note that in a foundation chain you allow 3 stitches for each block or hole and 5 stitches to turn.

The above insertion is easy enough for a first attempt. As more skill is acquired quite elaborate designs can be plotted out on squared paper, and used for a variety of articles, the ends of a runner, the centre piece of a chair back, or insets in a tea-cloth. If you are joining linen and crochet it is advisable to wash and starch both before sewing in case of later shrinkage.

Motif Crotchet.

This is crochet by the instalment system. As the motifs grow in number, so also grow the number of uses to which they can be put. They can be joined to make cheval sets, luncheon mats, trolley cloths, tray cloths, chair backs, and even a bedspread.

The following design was worked with rayon thread and a No. 2 steel hook. The resulting motif measured 2¾ in., and eight motifs were obtained from one spool. However, the pattern can be used for any kind of thread with a suitable size of hook.

Begin with 6 chain. Join with slip stitch to form a ring.

1st row: 6 ch. * 1 tr. into ring, 3 ch; repeat from * 6 times more, 1 slip stitch into 3rd of 6 ch. (8 spaces).

2nd row: 4 d.c. into each space of 3 chain, 1 slip stitch (s.s.) into first d.c.

3rd row: 1 d.c. into every d.c. of previous row.

4th row: Again d.c. but increase by doing 2 d.c. into every 4th st. (40 st.).

5th row: 1 d.c. into every d.c. of previous row.

6th row: Again d.c. but increase by doing 2 d.c. into every 5th st. (48 st.).

7th row: 7 ch. * 1 tr. into 3rd st., 4 ch.; repeat * from 14 times more, 1 s.s. into 3rd of 6 ch. (16 spaces).

8th row: 5 d.c. in each space. Join with s.s.

9th row: 1 d.c. into each d.c. of previous row.

10th row: * 5 ch., 5 d.c. into next 5 d.c. of previous row; repeat from * 15 times. Join with s.s. and finish off.

Lace Filling.

Make a ring of 8 ch., join with s.s.

1st row: 12 d.c. into ring, join with s.s.

2nd row: Again d.c. but increase by doing 2 d.c. into every 2nd st. (18 st.).

3rd row: Again d.c. but increase by doing 2 d.c. into every 3rd st. (24 st.).

4th row: * 5 ch. 3 d.c. into next three sts.; repeat from * 7 times. Join with s.s. and finish off.

To Sew Motifs Together.

A firm joining is very important. Take a short length of thread and run it in behind the point to be joined for a length of half an inch. Sew the two points with two or three overcast stitches, and

fasten off firmly. The accompanying sketch will show you which points to join, two points of the filling to each motif, then the next two points of the motif to its neighbour.

Another method is to join three motifs to form a triangle, in which case no filling is necessary. This is useful for a cheval set only. The other method builds up better for table mats, and similar articles.

KNITTING

Knitting as a hobby has many advantages. It can be picked up at odd moments; it is so unexacting that it becomes almost mechanical, and is a good accompaniment to the radio; it need not interfere with an evening's gossiping; the materials are cheap, and the resulting garment less expensive and often more durable than the bought article.

In addition, it is comparatively easy to learn to read and knit at the same time, if your pattern is not a complicated one, and I would advise everyone who is fond of reading to keep on trying till she has mastered this worthwhile accomplishment.

EQUIPMENT

Buy good-quality wool, as poor wool makes a less satisfactory garment, and its colours are less likely to be fast. If you are buying needles, choose celluloid or light metal ones which have the number stamped on. If, however, you already possess needles and are not sure of their number, measure them in a gauge, which can be bought quite cheaply, or have them measured in a wool shop. Numbers range from 1 to 24, 1 being the coarsest and 24 the finest. Steel needles are usually made in the finer numbers, an average size for a sock or gloves being 13, while a usual size for a jumper is from 8 to 10, with the ribbed border worked in needles two sizes finer.

WINDING THE WOOL

One of the beginner's commonest errors is to wind the wool too tightly. This destroys the elasticity of wool, but is not so harmful to cotton. To avoid this mistake, wind the wool over four fingers when winding it into a ball. If you wish to wind a skein of wool, and have no one available to hold it for you, just put the skein round the back of a chair, or round the backs of two separate chairs, and you'll find you can wind quite successfully.

HOW TO KNIT

Casting On: First Method.—This is the first thing to learn. Start with a slip knot on your left-hand needle. Pass the point of the right-hand needle from left to right through this loop. With your right hand bring the wool under and over right-hand needle, and draw a new loop through the old. Bring the point of left-hand needle from right to left through the new loop, and slip it on to the left needle. Repeat this process till you have the required number of stitches.

This particular edge is fairly loose and good for edges liable to be stretched a lot, such as the bottom of a vest. To obtain a firmer, neater edge, it is advisable to knit into the back of each stitch at the first row of knitting.

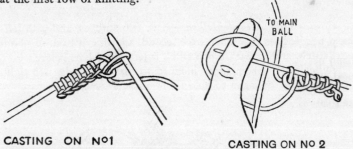

CASTING ON Nº1   CASTING ON Nº 2

Casting On: Second Method.—Using one needle. Make a slip knot, leaving a length of thread sufficient for casting on the stitches. Take the needle in your right hand and pass it through this loop. Put your left thumb under the wool (from cut end), pointing it towards yourself, and turn it up to make a loop. Pass the needle from left to right through this loop. Pass wool (from ball) under and over needle; draw the loop thus made on needle through loop formed on thumb; slip thumb away and pull the thread comfortably close. Your second stitch is made. Cast on number required.

This method is excellent for jumpers, but has not the same stretch, and it is inadvisable for the top of socks or the bottom of vests.

Casting Off: First Method.—Knit two stitches together and pass this stitch back to left-hand needle. Repeat till one stitch only is left. Break off wool and pass the end of it through the loop, pulling tightly. Darn this end into the work. Notice that you must keep the edge pulled out each time to required tension.

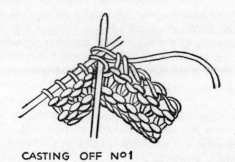

CASTING OFF No 1

Casting Off: Second Method.—Knit two stitches, and with left-hand needle pass first stitch over second, allowing it to drop. Knit next stitch, and repeat till one stitch is left. Finish as before.

A beginner is sometimes inclined to make this edge too tight, and care must be taken to hold the wool fairly slackly.

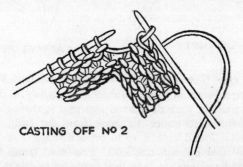

CASTING OFF No 2

Plain Knitting.—Cast on required number of stitches. Hold needle containing stitches in your left hand, the other needle and wool in your right hand. Pass the point of the right-hand needle through the first loop, going from left to right. Pass the wool under and over point of right-hand needle, draw the loop thus formed through the loop on left-hand needle, and slip the first loop off the left-hand needle. Continue to the end of the row. Tension should be such that stitches move easily along the needle.

PLAIN KNITTING

Purling.—In purling, things are done in reverse. You pass your needle into the loop, pointing from right to left (and out to the front). Pass the wool, which is always at the front of the work for purling, over and under the point of the needle. Draw the new loop thus formed through the old and on to right-hand needle.

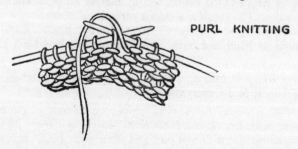

PURL KNITTING

Slip the used loop off the left-hand needle. Continue to the end of the row.

It is important to practise right from the start the proper way of holding the wool in the right hand while knitting. Put the little finger under the wool, pointing from right to left, and towards yourself, and twist it up to make a loop. Put the second and third fingers over the wool and first finger under it. When passing the wool over the point of the needle, move this forefinger only. To use the whole hand is cumbersome and slow. Also push the point of the needle through a very little way, and considerable time and effort are saved.

Plain knitting and purling are the foundations of all patterns in knitting, and should enable you to follow any instructions in a leaflet.

Increasing.—When you need to add to the number of stitches, knit into a stitch in the ordinary way, but before you slip it off, knit also into the back of the loop.

Decreasing.—1. Knit two stitches together, or if it is a purl row purl two stitches together.

2. Slip a stitch, knit a stitch, pass the slipped stitch over the knitted one, letting it drop off the needle.

Joining Wool.—If possible, join at the beginning or end of a row. The simplest method is to knit three stitches with double thread, the old and the new, leaving ends about three inches long. Later these ends are darned into the work.

STITCHES AND PATTERNS

Garter Stitch is the easiest of all. Simply do plain knitting on two needles. The result is a ridged surface.

Stocking Stitch has a smooth effect. On two needles work alternate rows of plain and purl. On four needles knit plain all the time.

Moss Stitch is easiest, with an odd number of stitches, when merely knit 1, purl 1 every row.

Ribbing is useful for tops of socks, the bottom of jumper or cardigan, cuffs, &c. It is a fairly elastic stitch, and keeps its shape. Any repetitive alternation of purl and plain gives a rib. It is rather fun to try out different effects with a scrap of wool and make a rib of your own.

Some Simple Ribs (K.—knit plain. P.—knit purl).

1. K.2 P.2 needs stitches which are a multiple of 4.

2. K.2 P.3 on even rows, K.3 P.2 on odd rows; this stitch needs a multiple of 5.

3. Any type of narrow rib with alternate rows of plain knitting makes a quite effective and slightly quicker stitch, especially good for a vest.

4. A slightly more complicated effect, rather good in cardigan, pull-over or vest, and quite usable in a jumper is this: have stitches a multiple of 5, plus 2 extra. Now K.3 P.2 (ending K.2) every row and await the result, which shows itself after 6 or 7 rows (fig. 1).

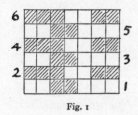

Fig. 1

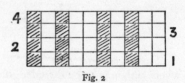

Fig. 2

5. A very effective, rather chic rib (only you can't read when you're doing it) is this—K.2 P.1 K.1 P.1 in odd rows; K.1 P.1 K.1 P.2 in even rows. Stitches should be a multiple of 5. This makes a really smart, tailored jumper with neck, cuffs and basque of one and one rib (fig. 2).

6. K.5 P.1 K.1 P.1 for even rows; K.1 P.1 K.1 P.5 for odd rows. Stitches should be a multiple of 8.

By now I hope you have the hang of this rib business, and can worry out a few for yourself. Remember, any repetitive arrangement of purl and plain will make some kind of pattern.

OPEN-WORK STITCHES

Abbreviations: tog.—together. M.1—Make a stitch. (This is done by bringing the wool forward between the needles to the front of the work, and taking it back over the needle to form an extra stitch if you are working on a plain row. In a purl row you need to take the wool round the needle.)

KEY

▨ Purl	⊞ Purl 2 together
◿ K. 2 together	☐ Knit plain
⊠ K. 2 together through BACK of loops	◯ Wool forward

The simplest open stitch is shown in fig. 3a. Have an odd number of stitches, and K.1 * M.1 K.2 tog., repeat from * to the end of the row.

Fig. 3a

This gives a row of holes. Such holes are useful in any garment where ribbon is to be threaded, or can be used ornamentally, a row of holes every inch or so in a plain stocking stitch garment being quite pretty.

Fig. 3b shows three rows of holes alternating with rows of purl.

Fig. 3c gives a slightly lacier effect, and is obtained as follows:

1st row: K.1 * M.1 K.2 tog., repeat from * to end of row.

2nd row: P.1 * M.1 P.2 tog., repeat from * to end of row.

Repeat these two rows as often as required.

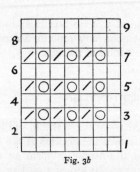

Fig. 3b

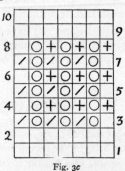

Fig. 3c

A few inches of pattern 3c would give a good top for a vest, or variety could be introduced by alternating narrow bars of 3c with bars of stocking stitch, moss stitch, or reversed stocking stitch.

Simple All-over Design (B.—through the back of the loops). Fig. 4.

Cast on a number of stitches divisible by 8, plus 7 extra stitches.

1st row: K.2 * M.1 K.2 tog. B. K.6, repeat from * till 5 sts. remain. M.1 K.2 tog. B. K.3.

2nd and alternate rows—purl.

3rd row: K.2 * K.1 M.1 K.2 tog. B. K.5, repeat from * till 5 sts. remain. K.1 M.1 K.2 tog. B. K.2.

5th row: K.2 * K.2 M.1 K.2 tog. B. K.4, repeat from * till 5 sts. remain. K.2 M.1 K.2 tog. B. K.1.

7th row: K.2 * K.5 K.2 tog. M.1 K.1, repeat from * till 5 sts. remain. K.5.

9th row: K.2 * K.4 K.2 tog. M.1 K.2, repeat from * till 5 sts. remain. K.5.

11th row: K.2 * K.3 K.2 tog. M.1 K.3, repeat from * till 5 sts. remain. K.5.

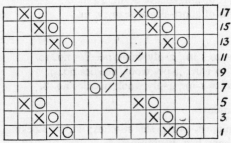

Fig. 4.—Even rows purl

JUMPERS

You can buy a leaflet of a pattern which appeals to you, follow the direction carefully, and keep to the exact tension. If you are a slacker knitter than the designer, use finer needles, and vice versa.

Another method is to find the basic shape which fits you, and create your own jumpers by varying the stitch.

Basic Pattern.

To fit bust 33–35 in.

Materials:

1. 5 to 6 oz. two-ply fingering wool (long sleeves).
   4 to 5 oz. two-ply fingering wool (short sleeves).
   1 pair no. 10 needles.
   1 pair no. 12 needles.

2. 7 oz. three-ply wool (long sleeves).
   6 oz. three-ply wool (short sleeves).
   1 pair no. 9 needles.
   1 pair no. 11 needles.

3. 8 oz. four-ply wool (long sleeves).
   7 oz. four-ply wool (short sleeves).
   1 pair no. 8 needles.
   1 pair no. 10 needles.

Measurements:

Length from top of shoulder, $18\frac{1}{2}$ in.
Length of long-sleeve seam, 18 in.
Length of short-sleeve seam, 5 in.

Tension:

$7\frac{1}{2}$ sts. to 1 in., 2-ply wool, needles no. 10.
7 sts. to 1 in., 3-ply wool, needles no. 9.
$6\frac{1}{2}$ sts. to 1 in., 4-ply wool, needles no. 8.

Abbreviations:

K. knit; P. purl; sts. stitches; st. st. stocking stitch; tog. together; beg. beginning.

The Back.—Using no. 12 (11, 10) needles, and 2 (3, 4) ply wool, cast on 120 (112, 104) sts.
K.1 P.1 till 3 in. ribbing have been worked.
Change to st. st. and no. 10 (9, 8) needles. When work measures 5 in. from start, increase one st. at each end of a row. Do this every 8th (7th, 6th) row till there are 138 (128, 118) sts. on needle.
When work measures $11\frac{1}{2}$ in., shape the arm-holes as follows:
Cast off 6 sts. at beg. of next two rows.
Knit two tog. at beg. and end of next 7 rows. Continue on these 112 (102, 92) sts. till work measures $18\frac{1}{4}$ in.
Shape the Shoulders: Cast off 11 (10, 9) sts. at beg. of each of next 6 rows. Cast off remaining sts.

The Front.—Work exactly as for the back until the work measures 16 in.
Shape the Neck: Knit 45 (41, 37) sts., cast off 22 (20, 18) sts., knit to end of row.

Work on those 45 (41, 37) sts., decreasing once at neck edge in every row until 33 (30, 27) sts. remain. Continue until the arm-hole measures the same as the back arm-hole. Cast off 11 (10, 9) sts. at arm-hole edge thrice. Knit the other shoulder to correspond.

The Neck Band.—Join the right shoulder seam. Using the no. 12 (11, 10) needles, and with the right side of the work facing you, pick up and knit about 120 (112, 104) sts. evenly round the neck. K.1 P.1 for 14 (13, 12) rows. Cast off loosely if you mean to sew up the left shoulder; but if you are going to put on buttons, or a lightning fastener, tighter casting off would be neater.

Long Sleeves.—With no. 12 (11, 10) needles cast on 54 (52, 50) sts. and work 3 in. in K.1 P.1.

Change to no. 10 (9, 8) needles and st. st., increasing one st. at each end of this and every subsequent 7th (6th, 6th) row till there are 96 (90, 84) sts. on the needle. Continue without further shaping till sleeve measures 18 in. (or required length). Cast off 2 sts. at beg. of each row till 20 (18, 16) sts. remain. Cast off all sts.

Short Sleeves.—Using no. 12 (11, 10) needles cast on 88 (82, 76) sts. K.1 P.1 for 14 (13, 12) rows. Change to no. 10 (9, 8) needles and work in st. st., increasing one st. at beg. and end of this and every subsequent 7th (6th, 6th) row till there are 96 (90, 84) sts. When the seam is 5 in. long shape as for long sleeves.

To Make Up.—Press the st. st. parts carefully with a damp cloth.

Sew up all seams.

Press all seams.

Shoulder pads can be stitched in if desired.

Varying the Basic Pattern.—Once you know the basic pattern which fits you, you can ring the changes in any number of ways.

You could use one of the ribs already suggested; or try out a very simple stripe consisting of two rows of st. st. alternating with two rows of reversed st. st. This gives a neat tailored effect if you are slim, and is of course obtained by knitting the first row plain, then two rows purl, two rows plain alternately.

If you decide on stripes of colour, note that the first row of a new colour should be knitted plain, if the right side is towards you, purl if the wrong side is towards you.

Coloured bars knitted in reversed st. st. stand out well on a plain st. st. background; while plain st. st. bars of colour gradually in-

KNITTING WITH
TWO COLOUR WOOLS
BACK OF WORK

creasing in width and ending in a coloured yoke can be very effective.

A two-colour effect, as in the accompanying sketch, is easy and sophisticated.

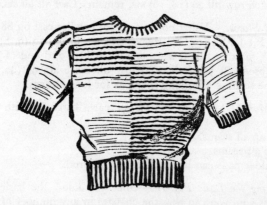

MAKING YOUR OWN DESIGN

When you are on familiar terms with the more ordinary knitting stitches, there may come a time when you wish to knit to a pattern of your own design. This is really quite easy. It requires a piece of squared paper (or a piece ruled by yourself), a little ingenuity, and some careful counting.

Diagonal Pattern.—Fig. 5 shows the design chart for a simple diagonal stripe, the shaded squares showing the stitches which appear purl on the right side. The odd rows are knitted as they appear in the chart, white squares plain, shaded squares purl. To obtain the correct effect you reverse this in the even rows, knitting the shaded squares plain and the white squares purl.

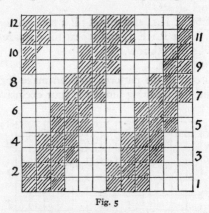

Fig. 5

Cast on a number of stitches divisible by 6.

1st row: K.3 P.3 to end of row.

2nd row: Like the 1st row.

3rd row: K.2 P.3 K.1, and repeat to end of row.

4th row: P.1 K.3 P.2, and repeat to end of row.

5th row: K.1 P.3 K.2, and repeat to end of row.

6th row: P.2 K.3 P.1, and repeat to end of row.

7th row: P.3 K.3, and repeat to end of row.

8th row: Like the 7th row.

9th row: Like the 6th row.

10th row: Like the 5th row.

11th row: Like the 4th row.

12th row: Like the 3rd row.

Diamond Pattern.

This pattern (shown in fig. 6) is very attractive, with perhaps the centre plain stitch embroidered in a slightly darker shade in the yoke, or even in the whole jumper.

Cast on a number of stitches divisible by 8, plus 5 extra stitches. Knit a purl row, then begin pattern.

1st row: K.2 P.1 K.5, and repeat till 5 sts. remain. K.2 P.1 K.2.

2nd row: P.1 K.1 P.1 K.1 P.4, and repeat till 5 sts remain.. P.1 K.1 P.1 K.1 P.1.

3rd row: Like the 1st row.

4th row: Purl all sts.

5th row: K.6 P.1 K.1, and repeat till 5 sts. remain. K.5.

6th row: P.5. K.1 P.1 K.1, and repeat till 5 sts. remain. P.5.

7th row: Like the 5th row.

8th row: Purl all sts.

There is no end to the patterns you can make for yourself. It is good fun—and the resulting jumper is your exclusive model.

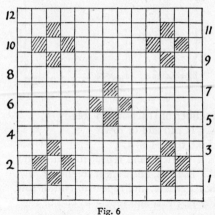

Fig. 6

Pressing.

When the work is finished press all the plain parts, but on no account press a ribbed article whose beauty lies in its elasticity. Stocking stitch responds to a good pressing, but some patterns require only light pressing, as it would destroy their character to do more. Also press carefully the finished seams.

Washing.

Wash out woollies in tepid water. Drying should be carefully carried out. The best way is to keep the garment in shape by laying it flat on a tray, or flat under the living-room carpet is handy if you protect the garment with cloth or paper.

Buttonholes.

The usual method is to cast off a certain number of stitches and cast on the same number again in the next row. Cast on and off again as tightly as you can, as a gaping hole is very unsightly. If it is inclined to stretch run a thread round the back of the hole several times.

General Hints.

If knitting lies aside too long, the row on the needle may be stretched or soiled. Avoid this by knitting a row occasionally if you have no time to do more.

Keep white knitting wrapped in a clean napkin.

Never knit up unravelled wool which has not been washed. To wash, first wind the wool in skeins, and tie them firmly in two places, wash in tepid water, dry quickly, wind into a ball, and it will knit like new wool.

Lastly, if you make a mistake, take it out and correct it.

LEATHER-WORK

Many useful articles are made of leather, and if the skins are carefully selected and carefully worked up the result will confirm the popular saying that " there is nothing like leather " for combining serviceability and beauty.

Such articles as covers for address books, diaries, and any favourite book are fairly easy to make and are very welcome as wedding, birthday, or Christmas presents. It is proposed to describe the processes in detail for making address book covers.

Materials Required.

One carefully selected calf-finished sheep-skin for outsides.

One skiver in brown or fawn for inside.

A few dozen thongs from goat-skin, natural colour or stained brown or orange. Lacquered thongings can also be bought, but the goat-skin thongs are best.

Six address books 6½ in. by 4½ in. from stationery shop.

Colour stains: orange, nigger (dark brown), and Indian red or brown.

Small sponge.

Powder paste bought in small quantities to be fresh.

Drawing pad with good thick paper.

Tube seccotine or quick-drying thick gum.

Tools (in order in which they will be required).

Steel (ruler) straight edge, 2 ft. long by 1½ in. wide, not less than ⅕ in. thick. For beginners an ordinary 12-in. steel ruler would suit.

Set square, about 6 in. by 8 in.

Cutting knife for cutting straight.

Pair scissors, tailor's pattern, for cutting curried edges.

Zinc plate, size 12 in. by 8 in., on which to place the leather when cutting, modelling and stamping.

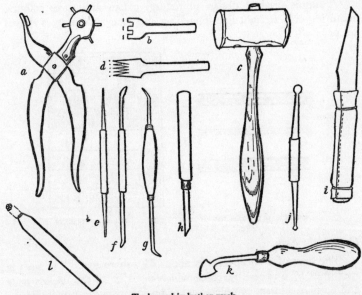

Tools used in leather-work

(*a*) Six-hole punch pliers. (*b*) Thonging tool. (*c*) Mallet. (*d*) Stitch tool for making a line of holes for sewing. (*e*) Tracer, with a fine and coarse end. (*f*) Modeller, with a medium and broad end. (*g*) Dresden modeller, for developing design. (*h*) Incising knife, for cutting in design. (*i*) A paring knife. This is a flexible knife for paring thick leathers. It is wrapped round with a piece of leather to give it a stronger grip. (*j*) Ball-tool. For pushing up the design from the back. (*k*) Plain creaser. To make a burnished line. (*l*) Matting punch.

Hammer.
One or more fancy metal punches for decoration.
Medium modellers.
Straight tracer, for copying the design to the face of the leather.
Single-punch pliers.

ADDRESS BOOK COVER

Design.

Sketch roughly on a plain writing-pad the kind of design wanted, then carefully reproduce the finished design on the drawing-pad. Stiff paper should be used, because it lies flatter on the leather than flimsy paper.

A simple original design in natural colour and three colours, requiring only straight-line modelling and fancy stamping, is shown on page 56.

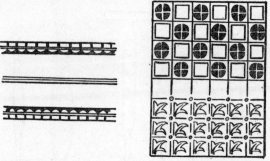

Examples of patterns made from marking punches and border fillets

Cutting the Skin.

The area of a sheep-skin is about $6\frac{1}{2}$ square feet. The area is measured by a special machine which takes in all the useless ends and corners, but six complete sets of book covers can usually be cut out free from any flaws in the skin. Mark the skin off as shown on the sketch on page 55.

It will be seen that the outside covers are from the centre of the skin which is the best part, and are each $9\frac{1}{2}$ in. long by 7 in. wide, the $9\frac{1}{2}$ in. lengths being measured along the length of the skin. These are the length suitable for the size of book given.

The skin should be placed on a flat surface such as a bare floor or kitchen table when being marked off, and also when cutting, which is best done with the knife and straight-edge along the lines, though the scissors may be used for the short ones. The skins are now ready for any design which is to be stamped and modelled on the front cover.

Lay the pieces of leather A smooth side upward on a drawing board and place the design (pattern) over it. Clip down with drawing pins at the corner so that the pin heads hold tightly, then draw smoothly and firmly with the tracer tool over the design so as to transfer it to the face of the leather. Then take out the drawing pins and wipe over the face of the leather with a damp sponge, not using too much water.

Go over the straight lines with the straight modeller; then stamp by hammer the spaces Z with the fancy punch.

Take a No. 6 water-colour brush and paint the parts X with the orange-colour stain and parts Y with the nigger stain (dark brown). Before staining place a newspaper between the leather and the drawing-board, so that the board is kept clean.

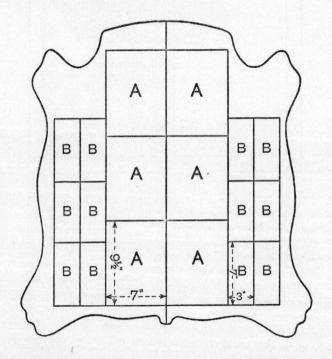

The last stain is Indian red all over. Rub it in with a piece of flannel or old wool undervest. Put very little stain on the flannel and rub with a circular motion. It does not need to be stained the same tone all over.

When the leather is dry it is polished well all over with white wax floor polish.

The skiver lining is then put on. Mix in an old saucer 2 teaspoonfuls of powder paste; add a little water, working it up with a stiff brush until it becomes a smooth paste. Paint the back of the leather all over; place the skiver lining on, pressed close by hand. Then place on flat surface between papers and put a heavy book on top. Leave it in this position for 24 hours.

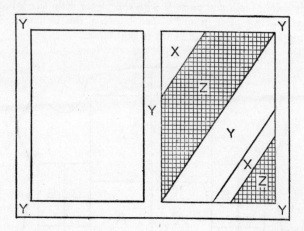

The next process is to place the parts B of the skin in position, one on each side. These will form the flaps into which the covers of the address book are inserted. The parts are to be stained Indian red and well polished first. Put seccotine on the outside edges, place carefully in position, then put under the heavy book again for half an hour. After this the whole cover is ready for thonging.

Thonging.

Examine the cover to see that the edges are even. Use the single-punch pliers and punch holes all round at about the places shown on the sketch.

A light punch mark could be used to make sure that the lines are straight, but it will soon be found, by practice, that the straight line is easily kept.

When completed, hammer the thonging flat on the zinc plate.

The cover is then to be polished all over again and the address book placed inside and kept for a day under the heavy book.

If you do not want so many address books you could make wallets, using the same designs and about the same size.

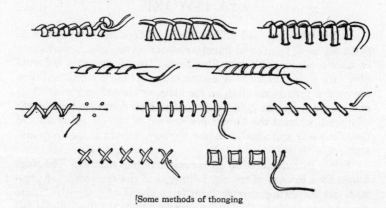

[Some methods of thonging

COMB CASE

The odd pieces of leather left around the side and ends of the skin can be used for comb cases.

For a 1¼ in. by 4¼ in. comb cut two pieces 2 in. wide by 5 in. long and make a similar design on one or both sides to the one shown on the cover, but suitably arranged. No lining skiver is required for these.

I found the bought methylated stain rather expensive, and too difficult to get, so wondered if I could make the stain myself. I took a pint bottle to a chemist shop, but all the methylated spirit they would give me was ¼ pint, and I had to see what I could do with this. I put a small quantity of orange powder in one bottle, Indian red into another, and nigger brown into a third, dividing the ¼ pint of methylated spirit among the three. When trying them a little later I found the colours were more powerful than the bought colours, and instead of a brush, I used a rolled-up flannel, first tipping the bottle up and away again, not soaking it. The stains were applied very lightly. The result was very good.

FELT-WORK

Felt is what is called a fibre fabric. There are three classes of materials made from wool fibres—cloth or woven fabric, stockinette or knitted fabric, and felt or fibre fabric. In the first two, the wool fibres are spun into wool by means of the spinning wheel and then the wool is woven into cloth on the loom, or knitted up into stockinette on the machine. The latter is linked up from one long length of thread, whereas the former has one set of threads going up and down the way and another across the way, known as the warp and weft respectively.

Felt is manufactured in an entirely different manner. The wool fibres, by a process of rolling, beating, and the application of pressure, are forced together to form large sheets of material. These are made in different thicknesses, ranging from the fine, pliable felt suitable for flower-making and for felt hats, to the coarse variety used as under-felts for carpets.

The process of compression leaves the felt with a firm edge that does not fray, and this is one of its greatest advantages. It makes it ideal for using in very many different ways and at the same time easy to work with. No hems are required and articles made of it can be quickly finished. The firmness of the thicker felts renders them suitable for bags and pochettes; no stiffening material is needed. But its most outstanding feature is its reaction to dyes. In no other material do we get more varied and more beautiful colours. Because of this, felt is a joy to work with, and hence also its usefulness for making up into such decorative articles as flowers, bags, cushions, and so on.

Felt-work is an inexpensive hobby. A square of felt can be bought for a few pence, and every scrap of it can be used in some way or another. The only tool required is a pair of sharp scissors. Neat cutting is largely the secret of success. An aid to fast working is a tube of special glue for use with felt, as the felt decorations can be stuck in place with a spot of the glue and then sewn down afterwards.

Anyone who wants to start craftwork at a youth club will find felt-work invaluable. So many useful little articles can be made out of scraps of felt. If you take a circle of felt about two inches in diameter, cut out in a contrasting shade a small flower or a mascot in the shape of a cat or a dog, fix it down in the centre of the circle with glue, and attach a gold safety pin at the back, you will have a dainty brooch which any girl in her 'teens will be glad to wear. Fig. 1 shows a brooch with a basket of flowers for ornament.

Comb cases and powder-puff holders can be cut out in gay-coloured felt, ornamented in front after the same fashion as the brooch, and button-holed round to finish. Little notebooks can be covered in felt, thus giving just that extra decoration that makes for a nice present. Refill notebooks are ideal for this purpose. A piece of felt should be cut out to fit the book, so

Fig. 1

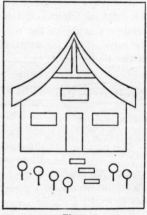

Fig. 2

that it will wrap round and just overlap the edges. Glue down, making sure that it sticks firmly all over. Then ornament the front. An address book could have a little house with roof and windows in contrasting colours. Put a few tiny flowers along the foot to complete, and you will be delighted with the result (fig. 2).

A needle-case could be made in much the same way by folding a piece of felt in two, attaching inside two or more pieces of flannel just a little bit smaller in size than the cover, and decorating in front with a few flowers or some other suitable motif.

Of the many articles than can be made with felt, none perhaps is more popular than a bunch of felt-work flowers, and no gift more appreciated than a dainty posy which will grace a new suit or give just that needed touch to add new life to an old coat. In the lovely colours available, primroses, polyanthus, tulips, chrysanthemums can all be realistically turned out, and many more besides.

FLOWER-MAKING

The method of flower-making consists in cutting out in strong paper or cardboard, little shapes for petals, leaves, &c., placing these on the felt and cutting neatly round them. The various pieces are then assembled to make the individual flowers, and these in turn are formed into a posy. Stems are straight pieces of felt folded over and sewn up the side; stamens are made of a narrow strip of the material fringed and rolled round the end of the stem. The petals are sewn to the top of the stem beneath the stamens, and the calyx, if any, is attached below the petals. Leaves can be fixed to the flower stem or to a stem of their own. Fine wire will be found useful to stiffen the leaves, and can be sewn up the back, where the midrib would be, and concealed by the stitching.

Fig. 3

The simplest flower to start with is, perhaps, the carnation. For this you will require six circles in felt, $2\frac{1}{2}$ in. to 3 in. in diameter, in three matching colours, depending on the colour scheme you wish to suit—two in fawn, two in light blue, and two in dark blue would be a nice combination—also three pieces of green felt $4\frac{1}{2}$ in. by $\frac{1}{2}$ in. for stems, and six long narrow leaves in green in imitation of carnation leaves.

Fold over the felt for the stems lengthways, and stitch on the machine or sew up neatly by hand. Fringe the edge of the circles about $\frac{1}{4}$ of an inch deep all the way round, and fold as shown in fig. 3. Arrange two matching circles together, so as to resemble a carnation; attach a stalk and two of the long narrow leaves and sew in place. Do the same with the other matching circles and finally put all three together and tack to keep in place. Fix a safety pin and your flower is complete.

A bunch of anemones might be your next venture. For these choose felts in purple, petunia and blue. For a single flower you will require five petals, three calyx leaves in green (fig. 4a and b), a piece of black felt 2 in. by $\frac{3}{4}$ in. for stamens, and a piece $4\frac{1}{2}$ in. by $\frac{1}{2}$ in. in either green or black for a stem. Sew up the stem as before.

Fringe the felt for stamens $\frac{1}{2}$ in. deep, sew the end of the strip to
the head of the stalk, roll round, and secure with a few stitches
(fig. 4c). Gather the bases of the petals slightly, attach below the
stamens, curving over and arranging as in an anemone flower. Sew
the calyx leaves to the base of the petals. Make four or five similar
flowers according to the size of posy desired. Cut out three leaves
as in fig. 4d, and sew to the stems. Arrange all into a nice bunch
attaching a safety pin as before.

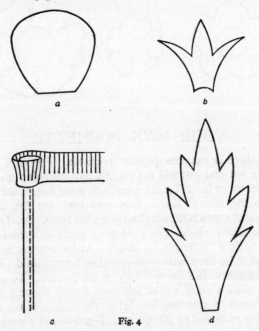

a   *b*

c   Fig. 4   *d*

DECORATIVE BELTS

A pretty and decorative belt can be made in felt, which will give
an added touch of distinction to a dress. Cut a piece of felt of the
required length, and 2 in. to $2\frac{1}{2}$ in. broad. Line throughout with a
piece of petersham ribbon of the same width, stitching along both
top and bottom. The ribbon will keep the felt from stretching.
The belt may then be decorated all round with flowers or other

suitable motifs, and finished off with a buckle in front. Or a side
fastening can be made and the ornamentation massed in front. Fix
the motifs down with a spot of glue, and sew neatly round. A
buttonhole border done in wools to match the colour scheme would
make a nice finish, but this is not necessary. Fig. 5 shows the type
of flower that is suited to this kind of decoration. It has a contrasting circle of felt in the centre.

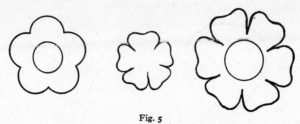

Fig. 5

YOUR OWN POCHETTE

Then there is the ever-popular pochette. For this, choose a
fairly thick felt and you will not require any stiffening material. A
piece 18 in. by 10 in. will make a medium-sized bag. Fold envelope
fashion to the desired shape, then turn back the flap again and
machine-stitch down both sides and along the front. Or, if preferred,
buttonhole neatly round, using coloured wools or threads. Ornament the front with flowers or motifs. As before, the flowers and
leaves should be fixed with glue and then sewn round. Couching
is a good stitch to use for any lines in the pattern. To get a neat
fastening, make a small roll of felt from a strip about ¾ in. broad.
Sew this firmly to your bag just below the middle of the flap. Arrange a loop of thread to slip over it. Fig. 6 shows a simple design
for the corner of a pochette.

TO MAKE TOYS

And now we come to toys. Felt is an ideal medium for toy-
making. It is soft and kindly for a child to hold. It takes stuffing
well. And the edges can be easily and securely sewn together.

Patterns for all sorts of toys, rabbits, elephants, camels, &c., can
be had from a craft-work shop or through a craft magazine, together

with instructions for making up. Be careful to cut out strictly according to directions, baste together, sew firmly and neatly, and stuff tightly, and there is no doubt that your toy will be a success. Old woollen garments when cut into narrow strips make good stuffing material, but if time is a consideration you can use kapok or wood shavings. It is amazing how much can be packed into a toy. Eyes can be bought, but it will often be found that an outer circle of

Fig. 6

white felt and an inner of black will be just as effective. A few stitches in black thread are all that is required for the mouth. Do not be too naturalistic. It is the unusual touch that adds charm to a toy.

These are just a few of the many things one can make with felt. It would be difficult to enumerate them all, but mention might also be made of slippers, which, when ornamented with tiny animals, make an amusing and much appreciated gift for a child, knitting bags, work bags, teapot holders, tea cosies, cushions, and, finally, appliqué and inlay pictures. All are decorative accessories which can be inexpensively turned out in felt.

POTTERY

Pottery, or the making of pots, jars, bowls, tiles, animals and figures, which are to be baked or " fired " in a kiln or oven, is one of the oldest crafts. It dates back to the earliest days of man, when he made his bowls and cups out of clay, and baked them hard in his cooking fire.

The earliest pots were made entirely by hand, and though we still use that method, others have developed. There are three principal methods of making pottery to-day. The one just mentioned, of making a hollow piece of clay with the thumb and fingers and gradually thinning the walls of the pot to be made; the method of building up a pot or jar by coiling long rolls of clay one on top of the other; and the most used method, of " throwing " a pot on the potter's wheel. Those methods will each be dealt with in turn later; meantime, let us consider the material and tools to be used in the making of pottery.

First the clay. This can be got ready prepared from a pottery, and is of two types—stoneware and earthenware clay. The former fires out—i.e. after being baked in the kiln—a pale-grey colour, very beautiful in itself when covered with a transparent glaze; the latter is almost pure white, though, of course, it can be stained buff or terra-cotta.

The only other basic materials required are glazes. Those too can be bought ready made-up to suit the clay being used. Glaze can be got either transparent or coloured, and some quite opaque and solid. All they require is mixing with water and then passing through a sieve (No. 80 phosphor-bronze). A sink brush (" monkey brush "), or ordinary stencil brush, will be useful here to force the glaze powder through the sieve.

Underglaze colours for painting on the design where desired can also be bought in half-ounce packets. Those are best mixed with a little gum tragacanth to make them stick to the surface of the pot.

Next the tools. Those are few, and in fact the fewer the better, as this is a pure hand craft. For the first two methods of making a pot all we shall require are an ordinary pocket-knife and a modeller's flat modelling tool, some rags (flannel, non-hairy), and a few flat pieces of wood to stand our pots on to dry out when they are finished with the first stage.

For the third method (throwing on the wheel) we shall require a potter's wheel. It is a flat revolving metal disk, about 8 in. in dia-meter and 2 in. thick, pro-pelled round and round by a larger disk placed farther down, and attached to the upper by a steel shaft. This lower disk is made to go round by various methods—a treadle or handle arrange-ment or by electric or other power.

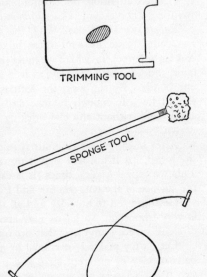

TRIMMING TOOL

SPONGE TOOL

CLAY CUTTING TOOL

Fig. 1

The tools required for this method are also few; the following will be found most useful. Flat pieces of zinc (one will do) for trimming base and so forth. Those can be bought, too, with shapes cut ready for use (fig. 1). Two or three small Turkey sponges, one of which should be fastened firmly to the end of a foot-long piece of stick for going down into the in-terior of pots and taking away the moisture (fig. 1); several pieces of brass wire ($\frac{1}{16}$ in.) for wedging clay and removing the pot from the disk. Each wire should have a piece of wood attached to each end for easy gripping (fig. 1).

In addition to the above tools we shall require several camel-hair paint brushes, a few jam jars for glazes, &c., and a couple or more tin boxes (square biscuit tins) for keeping our pots moist when left over for additions, e.g. handles and knobs. Two zinc buckets or bins for storing clay—one will have a few inches of water in it, and a brick or flat stone at the bottom on which to stand our store of clay free of the water. The clay should be covered with a damp rag or sack with the ends in the water. The other bin will be kept for receiving broken clay from discarded or damaged pots, and any odd pieces of clay.

With regard to the kiln or oven, this may be dispensed with if there is a pottery near at hand, and the owners are willing (as they usually are) to fire your pots. Kilns are expensive to buy and entail very expert attention, but several books on Pottery show methods of building a home-made kiln which is quite efficient.

Before we begin modelling, the clay must be conditioned. It has come to us in semi-moist blocks ready for using, but may contain air pockets, which we must remove or we shall have trouble later. So we knead the clay, as it is required, back and forwards in our hands. By the way, the softness of the clay is important; it should be soft enough to take and keep the impress of a finger easily, and without any clay sticking to the finger when it is withdrawn.

. After kneading we take our wire and make a slanting cut across the lump, lift it up, and slap it down hard on the remaining part. This we repeat several times (it is called " wedging ") until we see the surface of the cuts smooth and free from air holes.

Getting used to our clay and all the marvellous things it can do is very important, so let us play about with it, making things out of small pieces—anything that occurs to us to make.

Let us try making an animal or a man. Begin by rolling some balls of clay of different sizes and pinch them into shapes. Take two balls, a larger and a smaller, and stick them together to make an animal's head and body. By pinching and pressing and adding ears and a tail you have a rabbit (fig. 2). Then try rolling out some pieces shaped like sausages, and using some of the balls already made you can make a man (fig. 2). Try making a hat, boots, birds, and so on.

Do not attempt to be realistic or naturalistic—just aim at the big, simple main shape of things. We can paint those, too, the best of them, with our underglaze paints, after they have been baked once in the kiln, and then dip them in glaze and have them fired again. They will look most interesting and make delightful ornaments.

It is important, if we wish to " fire " those animals and ornaments, that we keep them to a reasonable size (say 6 in. to 8 in.) and thickness of clay (say 1 in.), or they will burst out in the firing.

Great fun and also creative development may be got out of this form of pottery, and frequently very beautiful pieces are made, even by quite young children.

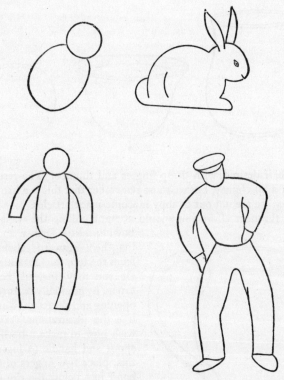

Fig. 2

The Simplest Method.

But now to the more serious forms of pot making. We will begin with the earliest form of pottery, using only the fingers and thumbs to build up our bowl. Take a piece of prepared clay about the size of an orange, and place it firmly on a solid board or table. Push one thumb straight down through the centre of the clay till it reaches about ½ in. from the foot. Now push the other thumb in —having the thumbs back to back—and with the rest of the fingers surrounding the lump of clay gradually open up the inside of the bowl shape, meanwhile turning the whole lump round and round, until the sides are about $\frac{1}{4}$ in. thick. You should now have a shape like a bowl, and to complete it, smooth down the surface inside and

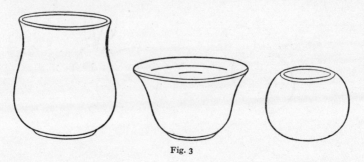

Fig. 3

outside, if desired, with damp fingers and thumbs. The result may appear a bit clumsy, but we must remember that this is a hand craft, and that we are not out to copy machine-made articles.

At the next effort you should attempt pulling the walls of the bowl up a little farther, and bending them outwards about $\frac{1}{2}$ in. from the top, thus forming a rim. Or you may, instead, bend the top in, by gradually narrowing the opening and get results something like the illustrations. You may wish now to make a bowl with a spout and handle (a jug); to do this, place two fingers of the left hand just below the rim of your bowl and about 1 in. apart, and with the middle finger of the right hand depress the rim down between the two fingers holding the clay below. This will make a very fine little spout if done with care.

Fig. 4

To make a handle, roll out a piece of clay to about $\frac{1}{2}$ in. thick, flatten it down to about $\frac{1}{4}$ in., and take off the required length for your handle—mark where the handle is to start and where to finish. Press the top end firmly to the top of the jug, and curve the coil

round, taking the shape you wish, and fasten likewise, by pressure
to the body of the jug (fig. 4).

Building Up.

The second method of making a pot is quite different; it consists in building up a pot from coils of clay laid one on top of another
to the required height.   Start off with a piece of clay about the

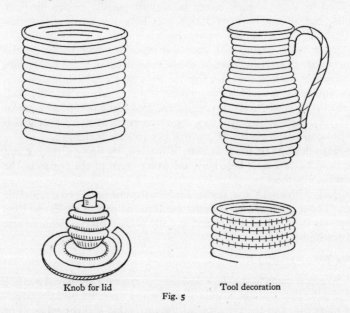

Knob for lid   Tool decoration

Fig. 5

size and shape of a sausage.   With the flat of the fingers of both
hands, roll this back and forth gradually, pulling the hands apart,
and so thinning out the coil till it is about ¼ in. thick and about 12
in. to 18 in. long.   Uniform thickness is desirable, but will take a
little practice to achieve.   To test the proper consistency of the coils
for building a pot take up a coil and twist it round a finger once or
twice—if it does not crack or break it is ready for use.   If it shows
signs of being brittle and cracking, the clay is too dry and requires
re-kneading with more moisture.

To build the pot you begin by pressing out a round flat piece
of clay about ½ in. thick and the size you wish for your base (2 in.

or 3 in. is large enough for your first). Round the top edge of this
base lay on and press down the first coil of clay, and continue round
and round, each circle of clay on top of the one before until the coil
is exhausted (fig. 5). If you wish to continue higher, take the next
coil, flatten its end, and attach it to the end of the one just laid. The
two coils should join firmly in a sloping line. Continue coil after
coil until you have got the height you require. The shape is controlled by using *slightly* larger or slightly smaller circles for your
coils, but always be careful that you have the upper coil firmly
pressed down on the one below (fig. 5).

As the pot grows, take your flat modelling tool and press the
lower edge of each coil over on top of the one below; this will ensure
a smoother surface, and also that the coils are joined firmly together.
An additional way of securing that the coils are sufficiently well
joined is to take the sharp edge of the tool and cut vertically across
the joins outside (fig. 5); this, by the way, adds decoration which
is quite in keeping with the style of pot you are building.

Handles can be fixed to pots, if desired, by using a thicker coil
or twisting two coils together, and fixing them to the pot as in the
previous method.

Lids with knobs, too, can be made to fit your pot, say a marmalade
jar. Those are made by winding a coil round part of itself, and then
carrying it on round and round in a flat surface till the required size
is reached (fig. 5).

The Wheel Method.

We now come to the third and most universally employed method
of making pots—on the wheel. This method was employed thousands
of years ago, and the principle of the method is still the same. The
principle of the wheel has already been described, and now for the
method. The potter sits on a stool or bench, so that she can bend
her head and shoulders right over the wheel and thus have full
power to mould the pot as she desires, and still keep it in the centre
of the revolving disk. She takes a lump of the prepared clay about
the size of a grapefruit. While the wheel is quite still she firmly
places this piece of clay right in the centre of the disk. She has all
the tools required on a shelf nearby (within arm's length), and a
basin of water beside the wheel.

She wets her hands, and also the piece of clay, thoroughly (this
must be done repeatedly), places her hands round the clay with

the little fingers resting on the metal disk, her elbows tucked in firmly to her waist, and resting on her thighs or the edge of the wheel casing. She switches on the power or starts treadling or kicking round the lower disk, and as the speed increases she finds the piece of clay taking shape under her hands—a shape somewhat like a bee-hive (fig. 6); once she is satisfied that the clay is absolutely in the centre of the wheel (and this is vitally necessary if our pot is to be symmetrical), she begins to draw her hands tighter together and to overlap the fingers (fig. 6). This forces the clay up between the hands,

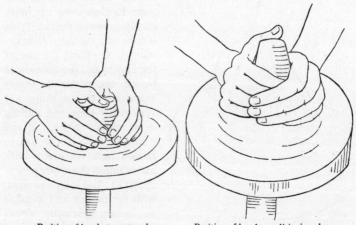

Position of hands to centre clay   Position of hands conditioning clay
Fig. 6

and by gently and slowly raising the hands, and still pressing closer, she gradually forms a cone of clay. She now presses the heel of her right hand down on top of the cone, and, with the left hand supporting the side, presses down slowly and firmly till the beehive shape is once more achieved (fig. 7). This process is repeated several times until the clay seems to be thoroughly plastic.

The next stage is to open up the beehive shape from the top. The potter presses her thumb straight down through the centre of the lump till it is within $\frac{1}{2}$ in. from the base. By moving the thumb now to the right, and with the other hand still supporting the side, she opens up the clay to look like a rather coarse bowl shape. The walls of the pot are, of course, too thick (say about $\frac{1}{2}$ in.), and there is a lot of clay at and round the base. The potter now proceeds to thin down the walls of the pot and to draw up some of the clay from the foot. She puts the fingers of the left hand, flat together, inside the pot, and working out from the centre and up the walls with the knuckle of her right hand presses gently from the outside, and follows up the pressure of the fingers inside (fig. 8). This will have the effect of thinning down the walls, and at the same time raising the height of the pot.

She now has a pot something like an ordinary jam jar, and the

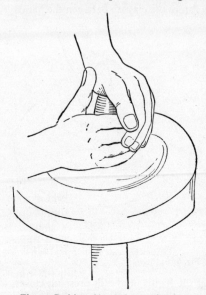

shaping of the real pot now begins. It is better at this stage to clear away any loose clay lying round the base; this is done with the flat, zinc trimming tool. With the flat of the fingers and the knuckle as before, the potter may now shape her jar—pushing out very gently here, and pulling in at another place. If she wants to close in the top to form a neck she places both hands round the upper part of the jar to close it in, and then, with the fingers and knuckle as before, gradually draws up the neck to the required length and shape. The thickness of the walls and base of a pot are important; if we allow them to get too thin

Fig. 7.—Position of hands for pressing down

(under construction) the pot will collapse. The base thickness should be thought of in connexion with the height of the pot, always remembering that part of that thickness will be lost when we take the pot off the wheel.

Well, our pot is finished (we should be content with a very simple shape of bowl or jar to begin with), and to remove it from the wheel we take our piece of brass wire, stretch it tightly across and close to the wheel and behind the pot and pull the wire gently towards us.

The pot can then be lifted carefully from the wheel and put

on to a wooden " bat "—piece of flat wood about 1 in. thick and larger than the base of the pot. It should now be stored in a cool airy shelf for drying out.

Firing the Pot.

The next stage is " firing ", or baking the pot in the kiln (if we intend to do that ourselves). Our pot must be thoroughly dry throughout—you can tell this by the sound of it if you strike it with a pencil—its weight also will indicate whether there is any moisture left inside the walls or base.

The process of baking is to harden the pot and consolidate the particles. This is called " biscuit " firing, and the pot will seldom be watertight after the first firing only. So we shall have to fire it again after putting a glazed surface upon it.

Firing pottery is a very tricky bus-

Fig. 8.—Position of hands for pulling up

iness, and should be undertaken only by those who have seen it done and learnt about the process. It consists of stacking pots on shelves or stilts made of fireclay, inside the kiln, so that the heat passes evenly around them; the heat must gradually increase till it reaches the " firing " point, that is maturity for the special clay being used—usually between 1000° C. and 1500° C. When this has been reached the fire is shut off and the kiln allowed to cool down gradually too; this usually takes about 24 hours, and no cold air should be allowed to reach the pots during this time. All edges of doors " spy holes ", &c., should be sealed up with fireclay before the heat goes off.

The pots are now removed from the kiln, and when quite cold are ready for the next process—glazing.

Before glazing our pots, however, we must decide whether we wish to put on any decoration. This is a very important decision to make from the point of view of Art. If a pot is beautiful in itself, if its shape, proportions and balance satisfy us, no decoration will be required. We must also think of what our vase or pot is to be used for. If to hold flowers, then no decoration is required, the flowers themselves supply the decoration. If, however, the pot is to be an ornament on its own, we may consider decoration. The one point to keep in mind is that any decoration should be part of the pot—it should add to the beauty, strength and purpose of the pot. Something will be said later about forms of decoration.

Meantime, let us get our simple glaze prepared. The glaze may be either transparent or coloured (we can buy both), and one can actually be put on top of the other after the first has dried. We take our glaze powder, put it in a bowl or jar, mix with water to thickness of good milk (the glaze should just adhere to your finger when it is dipped in), then pass through our sieve, using a brush (stencil) to push it through into an open basin.

There are several ways of applying the glaze: by dipping the pot into it, by pouring it over and into the pot, or by spraying with a mouth spray. All are good, but we must see that the inside of the pot has a complete covering of glaze. It is a good idea, both practically and artistically, to leave a part of the pot near the foot free of glaze; this makes for easy handling and also makes a good surface contrast, especially when using coloured glazes.

When the glaze is dry it will lie in a powder form upon the surface of the pot, and should not be handled any more than is necessary, and then only near the base where there is no glaze. The pots are then stacked in the kiln as before—avoiding touching each other—and the firing commenced. It will not be necessary to raise the temperature above 1000° this time; in fact, most glazes mature at from 850° C. to 950° C. The same rules regarding cooling off apply here too.

Decoration.

Now a few words on shapes and decoration. Hand-made pottery is quite different from that made in a factory, and it ought to keep the hand-craft quality throughout, e.g. don't aim at thin metallic edges or highly finished bases, such as we get in fine porcelain ware. We are working with clay, and we must keep the clay feeling.

Make up your mind before you begin what kind of pot you wish to make, draw it, visualize it in your mind, and try to keep your idea of the shape you want all the way through the process of making. Well-proportioned, simple, well-balanced, comely shapes should be your aim. Nothing fancy or extravagant should be attempted. Even spouts, knobs and handles should be simple and in keeping with the material and shape they are to complete.

As to Decoration, this should be thought of as *part of* the original pot from the outset—not something to be added later. There are several ways of decorating pottery. One method is by painting on the design with underglaze colours while the pot is in the biscuit state. All we have to do here is to mix our underglaze colours with water and a little gum tragacanth and paint on the design with a brush, just as one would do on any surface. A warning is necessary here as the colours seldom look what they are said to be, and will become their proper colour only after firing.

Another form of decoration is by " slip "—that is clay thinned down with water and passed through a sieve; it may be coloured, but white " slip " is very attractive for decoration and very beautiful too if used aright. Slip may be put on with a large or small brush, or even poured on, depending on the effect we wish to achieve. There is an instrument made for controlling the slip, somewhat like a cake icing squeezer.

Then there is the method of scratching the surface while the pot is just " leather hard ", i.e. just before it is hard enough for firing. It can also be scratched or scraped to remove the surface after glazing or application of slip decoration. This is called " sgraffito ", and is one of the most interesting forms of decoration because of the way the light catches the edges of the cuts formed. It is very fascinating, and if not overdone can make a very fine finish to our pot.

The kind of decoration is important. It is better to keep to abstract forms: lines (straight and curved), squares, circles, wavy lines, zig-zags, dots, and so forth. If natural forms are used they should conform to the shape of the surface they lie on and emphasize that surface. In any case, don't elaborate! The shape of the pot is the important thing, and this must not be lost though we may enhance it by decoration.

PRINTING ON TEXTILES

This is quite a simple craft, yet at the same time an interesting and a most useful one. There is great joy and satisfaction to be got out of designing and printing our own fabrics, whether for wear or for furnishing; for, besides possessing the charm of the hand-produced article, it provides an outlet for expressing our own personality and creative instincts in the things we have around us. Moreover, it is an inexpensive craft, and the tools are few and easily acquired.

The general principles of the craft are: the cutting out of a pattern (sometimes previously designed on paper) on a piece of plain linoleum, mounting this on a flat block of wood, covering the surface of the linoleum with printing ink or dye, and transferring the design from the block to the fabric by pressure, or by knocking on the reverse side of the block.

The design, if previously drawn on paper, is transferred to the lino, and the parts not intended to print cut away by gouges or knives. In the case of printing with liquid dyes, the surface of the lino would not hold sufficient dye, so we make it absorbent by covering the printing surface with a coat of powdered felt called " flock ", which is made to adhere to the surface of the lino, and so pick up the dye from a pad.

Before beginning the actual details of the process, here is a list of materials and tools required: (1) Ordinary floor linoleum, plain brown and of a good smooth texture (not old or worn). (2) A sheet of ply-wood (5-ply if possible). Ordinary flat $\frac{1}{2}$-in. boarding will do, though it is apt to split when hammered on the back. (3) A set of lino-cutting gouges—three will do—two U-shaped $\frac{1}{8}$ in. and $\frac{3}{8}$ in. and a V-shaped one $\frac{1}{8}$ in., and a beak-shaped knife (fig. 2). (4) A palette knife. (5) A 4-in. rubber-covered roller (squeegee). (6) Two or three slabs of plate glass, 8 in. × 6 in. or larger. (7) A printing mallet (fig. 1); this can be got at the art stores, but an old coal hammer with the handle cut short will do for this. (8) Two or three sheets of felt or old blanket. Newspapers or blotting paper will do here. (9) Fabric inks or liquid dye; those can be bought from the artists' materials stores, specially manufactured for the purpose. (10) Flocking powder and flocking paste; these can be got from the artists' stores too. (11) Clean rags, paraffin or turpentine for cleaning, and, of course, material for printing our design upon.

The choice of fabrics is important, for, while we may print on almost any material, certain types, especially absorbent fabrics, take and retain the printing much better than others. Cottons, if they contain much stiffening, should be washed out first, and the material dried and ironed out again. Linens, not too closely woven, print well.

Silks, though not satins or artificial silks, are good. Wool and silk mixtures and fine woollen cloths and fine velveteens print very well. Avoid all highly polished and lustrous materials, and, of course, only choose unpatterned cloth. The natural weave and mixture of certain types

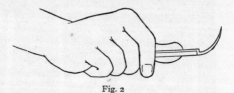

Fig. 1   Fig. 2

supply an excellent background for our patterns, and often suggest the kind of pattern to be used.

Having got all our tools and materials together, we are now ready to begin to make our first printing block; but before commencing on the actual block, take an odd piece of linoleum and try out making cuts with the gouges. Take the V gouge first; this is the one we will use for outlining our design, as it gives a sloping edge to the cut, which helps to support the printing parts left standing. Hold the gouge so that it cuts the lino at an angle of 15° to the flat surface, the butt end of the stem resting in the centre of the palm of the hand. Don't dig down so deeply that the shoulders of the V are below the surface of the lino, or we shall just get a tear, and not a clean cut. Try cutting in all directions—straight and curved, long and short. Now try the U gouges; they will be used mainly for clearing the ground away. Having got used to the tools, now take a small piece of lino, about 2 in. square, and make a few

Fig. 3

cuts on it, using each of the tools, and without further ado try a print of it by smearing it over lightly with printing ink, and pressing it on to a piece of paper or cotton. This will give some idea of how the thing works, and we can now prepare for a serious bit of printing.

Take a piece of lino, say 3 in. square, and draw on it with a pencil or brush a simple design of lines and masses, some strokes and dots and twirls, e.g. (fig. 3) making the lines thick and thin at will, and clearing away pieces where we feel like it. This will not be a consciously constructed design, but it will make a pattern if repeated over and over again on material. Let's try! But before we can start the next stage we must mount our lino on a wooden block. Take a piece of wood, same size as the lino, and glue the lino to fit firmly on top. Put it under pressure till it is firmly attached. (By the way, there is a special adhesive sold for this purpose.)

While the block is sticking down, we can prepare our table for printing. Choose a good solid table that we can stick pins into, cover about a yard square of it with felt or newspapers, or blotting paper, about ⅛ in. thick. A large piece of blotting paper or American cloth should be fixed on top of this padding to take any ink or dye which passes through the cloth. Now fix down the fabric that is to be decorated, with drawing pins. Stretch it quite tight all round so that there are no loose pieces or wrinkles.

Alongside, on another table if possible, lay out the slab of glass, printing ink, roller, cleaning rags and turpentine. Squeeze out some ink from a tube—about a couple of inches of it—on to the slab of glass at the far-away end. Now take the roller, pick up some ink from the slab and roll it back and forth on the glass surface till the roller is covered with ink all round. This layer of ink on the roller should not be too thick—just sufficient to put a thin coating on the lino surface. Now roll the roller back and forward over the surface of the lino until the whole surface is evenly covered with ink. Lift the block with the finger tips, resting them on the wood part, turn it carefully over and place it carefully where we are to make our first print. Having fixed down the block carefully, we take up the mallet, keeping the heavy end upwards, and with the end of the handle sharply strike the back of the block (fig. 4). Do this several times in different places on the block. Now lift the block carefully from the cloth and put it back on the printing table. Let's have a look at our print now. If the inking and printing have been right, we should have a nice flat clear replica of the pattern cut on the block. (It will, of course, be reversed.)

The print should neither be a solid mass of ink, nor yet a pale shadow of our pattern; it should appear as a full-strength granulated surface, showing the texture of the material beneath. If our print is too heavy we must have less ink on the roller, and if too pale, the reverse.

Now we can ink up for our next print and repeat the printing process, being careful to place the block close to our first print.

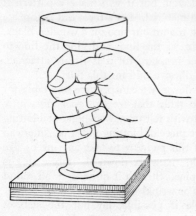

Fig. 4

Hammer down again and lift as before. With regard to our first printing on fabric, it is a good idea to have a piece of odd material to try out our prints upon, and when we have got the right quantities of inking and hammering go ahead with the serious work of printing the large piece of material.

The arrangement of the prints is a matter we must settle before we begin. We may print a whole row of prints, one close below the other right down the edge, or a row along the top. Or we may print a row down the edge and drop the next row half-way down the first. This gives variety and life to the whole all-over effect. Another method is to print the first, then leave a space of equal size and print another, and in our second row, print one opposite the blank space. This will give a blank and a printed space time about (see fig. 5). This can be very bright and decorative.

We should now try out some experiments with our block (on paper), turning it upside down, turning it round in a circle, and so on till we find the best way of arranging the pattern.

From these experiments we have learnt a lot of things—things that work, and others that don't; so for our next attempt we shall plan out our design on paper and arrange the units in the way we wish to print them on the fabric. Having drawn our pattern (which should be a very simple one meantime), we transfer it to the lino

block, either by chalking on the back of it with white chalk, **and,**
after pinning down to the block, trace the pattern through with a
hard pencil, or by first painting over the block with Chinese white

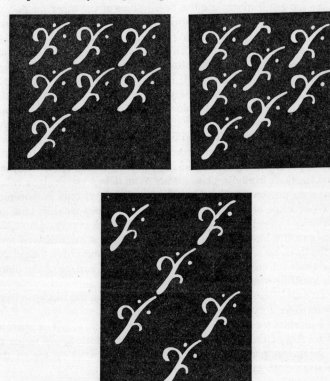

Fig. 5

and then blacking the back of our design with soft lead pencil and
transferring through as before. The latter method is quite good,
as we can now paint in with black the parts that are to remain standing,
leaving the white parts to be cut away. In this way we will be able
to see what our pattern will look like when it is printed, and can set
out to print our scarf or head-gear, or blouse length, or even a pair
of curtains for our own particular room.

When the printing is complete, remove the material from the table and hang it up to dry; this will take about a day, it should then be washed in luke-warm water and ironed.

We have still to explore the possibilities of the other method of printing with dyes. Liquid fabric dyes really print and feel much better on material than printing done with inks, because the dye goes right into the material, and leaves the texture of the cloth undisturbed, edges are softer, and the impression is of the design really belonging to the material, instead of appearing to lie on top.

The method for this way of printing varies somewhat from the last. We cut and mount the block as before, but we must now put a deposit of " flock "—felt powder—on the block to hold the dye, which would otherwise just slip off the smooth surface of the lino.

To put on the flock and make it stick fast we have first to cover the surface of the lino with flocking paste—a strong adhesive which holds the flock firmly in place. This paste is best put on by a roller just as we put on printing ink. A very thin layer only is required. Now put some of the flocking powder into a pepper dish or a tin with holes in the lid, and shake a coating of flock evenly all over the surface of the block. Leave the block aside in some sheltered spot till the flock becomes quite firmly attached—about a day should do. Now shake off any surplus flock, and brush the surface of the block with a stiff brush to remove all loose flock.

To enable us to get an even surface of dye on the block we have now to make a dye-pad. Take a piece of wood about 6 in. × 8 in. and $\frac{1}{2}$ in. thick; cover this with two or three layers of felt or blanket, and on top of those fix a piece of American cloth firmly down to the wood. A piece of felt or blanket is now fixed on top of the American cloth to receive the dye.

We apply the dye to the dye-pad by spreading it evenly all over with a fairly large brush (2-in. hog hair is best). Do not load the pad too heavily with dye, or the block will pick up too much, and it will spread over the material.

We now proceed as before to fix down our fabric on the padded table or board. Now take up the block and press it, face down, on the dye-pad. Do this several times and in several directions, so that the surface of the block gets an even quantity of dye all over; see that it is completely covered with dye, and then carefully place it in position on the fabric. Strike it two or three blows with the fist while holding fast in position with the other; lift up the block and see if the print is satisfactory. If it is not, the block may have been insufficiently charged with dye, or the knocking may not have been strong enough. You may use the mallet for knocking, but excessive hammering should not be necessary.

The surface of a satisfactory print should be a lovely, flat, fine, granulated one, and the pattern should be clean-cut and decisive. If it is not, several things may be wrong; the block may not be cut clean enough, the flocking may have closed up corners and thinner lines of the design, the dye-pad may have too much dye or too little, the block may not have been evenly covered, or the knocking may not have been sufficient. All of these can now be attended to and cured easily, and another print taken.

It is good to have a few odd pieces of the material at hand for trying out our prints before starting on the serious work of printing our main piece of material.

The printing accomplished, there is still a further process to go through with this method; that is, the fixing of the dyes so that our material can be washed easily without the pattern washing out. But, meantime, hang up the material to dry out (a few minutes in this case).

To fix our dyes we have to put the material into a fixing solution of cold water and sulphuric acid—only 2 per cent (i.e. 2 parts of acid to 98 parts of water) should be added to the water. It isn't very strong, and won't injure the hands, though it is always better to use a stick for putting the cloth in and for removing it from the bath. By the way, always add the acid to the water and not the reverse, and use an enamelled or glass basin.

Make up sufficient of the mixture to cover the material when it is pressed down loosely into the solution. Before using the fixing liquid we must heat it in an enamelled pan till it is about 160° F. or 70° C. Pour this into our basin, and immerse the material completely in it for about two minutes. As soon as the material gets soaked in the solution the colours will come up to their true quality of colour and brilliance.

Take the material out of the bath and rinse thoroughly in cold water. When no more dye comes out, put the material into hot soapy water and rinse it round and round. Once again rinse in cold water, wring out and hang up to dry. When nearly dry iron out flat. It will be found that all this process brings up the colour and brightness of the pattern, giving a real thrill of joy at something worthwhile accomplished.

CANE-WORK

When we set out to make a cane-work article we are imitating our earliest ancestors, for primitive woman relied upon her skill in the art of basketry to supply herself with practically all the utensils she required in the home. With the aid of a sharp flint or pointed bone for tool, and with whatever materials lay ready to hand, sedge or willow, tree bark or reeds, she would fashion her plates and bowls; for primitive man ate from a plate made of basket-work, and the vessel he drank from was a basket too. And the weaves used by our ancestors were the same as we use to-day; rand and slew, pair and wale, as they are called.

Though willow is the natural product of these islands for basket-making, cane is a more pliable medium, and therefore easier to work with. Pulp cane, as it is often called, is the inner part of the ratten or cane palm, a trailing plant which runs along the ground and up the trees in the jungles and swamps of Malaya and other tropical parts. It attains great length, and is sometimes as long as 600 feet, yet the average diameter is about 1″. The outer bark is covered with thorns and this makes the cutting and gathering rather difficult work.

When this outer part has been removed, the cane is shown to have an inner glossy covering, and it is this inner bark which is used for chair seating, often seen on bedroom chairs and chair backs. After the inner bark is taken off, there remains the pith or centre part, and this is what we use to make our cane-work articles.

Cane Sizes.

The cane is cut into different sizes, ranging from 1 mm. to 25 mm. in diameter, and graded by numbers from 1 to 18, Nos. 1 to 12 being the most useful to the basket-maker. Nos. 5 to 8 are generally used for stakes of baskets and trays, and Nos. 2 to 4 for weaving.

> I can rand at your command,
> Put on a decent border,
> Upset tight, wale all right,
> And keep my stakes in order.

So runs the rhyme of the basket-maker, and it carries the whole secret of success, for basket-making is just a repetition of a few simple strokes or movements, randing, slewing, pairing and waling or upsetting, and these must be mastered at the outset. Stakes are the upright canes used in the sides of baskets, and the ability to keep these in order is one of the essentials of good work.

Fig. 1

Randing is the simplest form of weaving. The end of the weaving cane is placed behind the first stake. It is then taken in front of the second stake and behind the third, and so on (fig. 1). When a join has to be made the finishing end is left inside and the new cane inserted where the old one would have come out.

Holding the Cane.

In working, the first two fingers of the left hand should be placed one on each side of a stake so that the left thumb can steer the cane between the stakes. The weaving cane should be held between the right thumb and forefinger, as you would hold a pencil, and at a distance of a few inches from the stakes. Move the cane upwards as you push it between the stakes, and pull it down as you take it out. This method should be followed for all the strokes.

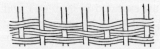

Fig. 2

Fig. 3

Slewing is merely randing with two canes instead of one, using the two canes just as if you were using one, and taking care to keep the top cane on top (fig. 2). The two canes should not be inserted at the same time. Take one stroke with the first cane and then insert the second cane in the place where the first came out. This is a useful weave for making a decorative border in a basket.

Pairing is a variation of randing. Whereas in slewing you use two canes together, in pairing you use first one cane and then the other, and the weave thus formed has the appearance of a twist (fig. 3).

The first pairing cane should be placed between the first and second stakes, and the second pairing cane between the second and third stakes. Take a stroke with the first cane, that is, pass the first cane in front of the second stake, over the second cane and behind the third stake, leaving it at the front. Execute the same movement with the second pairing cane, which has now become the left-hand cane, and continue in this way, always working with the left-hand cane. To finish, draw the end of the cane through to the front beneath both canes.

Waling.

Upsetting or Waling. This is a very firm weave, and is used as a first weave to set the stakes firmly in position, hence the name upsetting. It is worked with three canes. The first is inserted between the first and second stakes, the second between the second and third stakes, and the third between the third and fourth stakes.

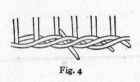

Fig. 4

Starting with the left-hand cane, each cane is now taken in turn in front of two stakes and behind one (fig. 4). Repeat this stroke, always working with the left-hand cane until one row has been completed, that is, until the last used cane comes out on the left of the first stake. Take this cane in front of two stakes and behind one. Do the same stroke with the cane to the left of it, and finally also with the last cane. You will find that the row thus executed is level and complete. Continue in the ordinary way just as when you started.

To finish, draw the end of the cane through from the back beneath the other two as in pairing. To begin a new cane slip the end of the new cane from the front through to the back so that it lies alongside the old one.

Necessary Tools.

Now that we know our strokes, we are ready to begin to make an article, but first we must acquire a few simple tools. They comprise:

1. A short-bladed knife for cutting off ends and sharpening stakes.
2. Side cutters for cutting cane into the required lengths. A pair of garden shears will do quite well for this purpose.

3. A bodkin for clearing a passage for inserting stakes.
4. A pair of round-nosed pliers for bruising stakes to prevent them from breaking when they are to be bent at right angles.
5. A rapping iron for levelling the line of work.

Now we are ready to make an article and will begin with something simple.

TUMBLER HOLDER

Materials required:

> Round plywood base 3″ in diameter.
> Half ounce No. 4 cane.
> 2 lengths of No. 2 cane.
> 2 lengths of coloured cane.

Dip the cane in water and leave for a little. This makes it more pliable and easier to work. This is the first step in making all cane-work articles, and if the cane shows a tendency to break when it is being worked, dip again into water.

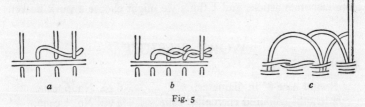

Fig. 5

Cut stakes of No. 4 cane 8″ long and equal in number to the holes in the base which you are going to use—bases bored with holes ready for use are obtainable in a craftwork shop. Insert the stakes through the holes so that they project for a distance of 2″. Take the round-nosed pliers and gently press all the stakes about ¼″ beyond the holes. Now, with the base resting on the table so that the short ends are pointing away from you, bend down the stake nearest to you, passing it in front of the first stake and behind the second. Continue this stroke with the stake immediately to the right of it, and so on until all have been turned down, drawing the last stake under the loop formed by the first stake. This is called a Foot Trac Border (fig. 5a and b).

Turn the base right side up and press all the stakes outwards so as to make them take the shape of a tumbler, and be careful while weaving to see that they retain this shape. Commence to rand, as already directed, by inserting an end of No. 2 cane behind a stake and passing it in front of one and behind one. Continue randing for 24 rows. Then insert a piece of coloured cane and rand 2 rows with it. Do a further 4 or 5 rows with the No. 2 cane, and finish off with one row of pairing by inserting a second cane, and following the directions already given. Pull the ends through to the outside and cut off neatly.

To border, cut off the stakes about 3″ from the last row of weaving, sharpen the ends, dip into water, bend over carefully, and insert each end down the side of the next stake but one (fig. 5c). See that the top of the border is level and finish off all ends neatly inside by cutting off so that they lie against a stake. To give a smooth finish, put a small quantity of methylated spirits in a saucer, set fire to it, and pass the tumbler holder through the flame taking care not to singe it. And be very careful, of course, not to set the house on fire!

Having now gained a little experience we are able to tackle a more elaborate article, and I think we might choose a work basket.

WORK BASKET

Materials required:

Round base 8″ in diameter.   6 oz. No. 6 cane.
2 lengths coloured enamelled cane.   4 oz. No. 3 cane.

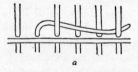 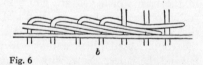

Fig. 6

Cut stakes 15″ long of No. 6 cane equal in number to the holes in the base. Pass them through the holes, allowing them to project for 3½″. Work a Trac Foot Border by turning each stake down in turn, taking it behind the next stake, in front of the two following stakes, and leaving it behind the fourth (fig. 6a and b). The last three stakes will have to be woven through the first three, care being taken to follow the pattern.

Turn right side up, pull the stakes to tighten up the foot border and press outwards. Work 2 rows of upsetting as already described, then rand to a depth of 3″, continuing to press the stakes outwards so as to give the basket its shape. Now work 2 rows of waling, and then introduce the coloured cane in the form of 2 or 3 rows of randing. Add 2 rows of waling, and continue to rand for a further 1½″. Finish off with 2 rows of waling.

Now you are ready to border, and this can take the form of a trac border the same as the foot border. Wet the stakes again if they have become dry, press just above the last row of waling with the pliers, and bend down each in turn, taking it behind one stake and in front of two, and leaving it lying at the back of the fourth. Trim off all ends.

Everyone likes to have a nice tea tray, and to my mind there is no more decorative article than a cane-work tray, especially if worked on a dark, polished oak base.

TEA TRAY

Materials required:

> Oval oak base 20″ × 12″.
> 6 oz. No. 5 cane.
> 2 oz. No. 3 cane.
> Coloured enamelled cane or coloured beads as desired.

The method to begin with is the same as for the work basket, the stakes being cut and inserted in the holes and a Trac Foot Border being worked, but in this case the length of the stakes will have to be 15″. Turn right side up, pull the stakes tight, and work 4 rows of upsetting, or if preferred, 1 row of upsetting and 6 rows of randing. Proceed to decorate with beads or enamelled cane. A bead can be slipped on to each cane all the way round. Or five beads can be placed on five stakes at each end of the tray, thus giving the effect of handles. Or a row of randing with enamelled cane may be worked.

Having completed the decoration, and added a final row of waling, the tray is ready for bordering, and this time we are going to do a Three Rod Plain Border. Squeeze all the stakes immediately above the last row of waling. Take the stake directly opposite to you, which we will call the first stake, and pass it down behind the second stake, pass the second stake down behind the third, and the third down behind the fourth. Now take the first stake, pass it in front of the fourth, over the other two stakes and behind the fifth, leaving it at the front. Bend the fourth stake down alongside so that it lies to the right of it (fig. 7a and b). Do the same with the second and third stakes in turn, the second being taken in front of the fifth and behind the sixth, and the fifth laid down alongside, while

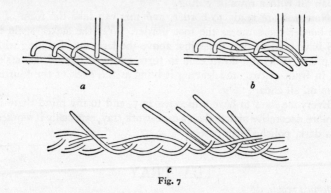

a   *b*

c

Fig. 7

the third is taken in front of the sixth, behind the seventh, and the sixth laid down alongside.

Now you have 3 pairs of canes projecting to the front. Always work with the fifth cane from the right and continue in the same way, taking it in front of the next upright cane, &c., until there is only one cane left standing. Then take the fifth cane from the right as usual, pass it in front of the last standing cane, and bring it through beneath the first stake turned down at the beginning. Bend the last stake down and pass it through beneath the first stake too. The three remaining right-hand canes of the three remaining pairs are threaded through in the same way to complete the pattern (fig. 7c). Trim off all ends.

Now that you can make these articles you can proceed on your own with whatever you fancy.

STENCILS AND HOW TO MAKE THEM

We have all gone through the experience of being kept indoors during a spell of bad weather or, commonest of all, had to stay off school because of a bad cold. Often time has hung rather heavily on our hands, and we have wandered about the house looking for something to pass an hour or so. Here is an idea which is not difficult to do, and can prove most fruitful later on.

Making a stencil is quite easy, and comes in very useful if you are making Christmas presents. It is effective and can be used on paper, cardboard, parchment, and certain materials.

Paper: must not be too thin.

Cardboard: almost any kind except the very coarse surfaces, which are not satisfactory.

Parchment: no trouble at all. Very good.

Materials: linen, sateen, hessian and velvet, but not silks or satins, or any thin material except *voile*.

Stencilling can be carried out on many kinds of articles. Here are a few examples: on a lamp-shade made in buckram; on a parchment or cardboard cover for a telephone directory; or on Christmas cards.

First you require a sheet of parchment—this being the recognized medium for making a stencil—a really sharp knife, two stencil brushes, one a little bigger than the other, a small jar of poster colour, and a bottle of glue. All these can be bought at an art shop.

If you are able to draw your own design, so far so good, but to begin with I advise you to try out the ideas which I have sketched. You see it isn't a case of choosing anything which looks pretty. You have to remember that it is to be drawn in such a way as will cut into a good shape.

We shall take the Thistle design first. Do you see how I have simplified it without taking away its beauty of design? The head is separate from the stem and leaves.

Next we come to the Rose. Study the shape of the petals and you will see how easy it is to cut each one out with a knife. The leaves again are separate from the flowers, and together flower and leaves make a lovely pattern.

Lastly there is the little Ship a-Sailing. The masts, sails, actual body of the ship and the wavy lines to represent the sea are all drawn as separate units.

What I am trying to explain is that in a design for a stencil, which is the first part of the proceedings, you must not choose an

elaborate idea, but rather a simple one, and then again simplify it for cutting purposes.

After you have drawn the design, shade with a pencil the parts to be cut out, so that instinctively, when you look at it, you know exactly where to use the knife. Next take a tracing of the drawing and transfer it on to a piece of parchment. A size four inches square should do you. Again, with a pencil, shade in the parts you want to cut out. Your stencil is now ready for cutting.

To do this it is advisable to have it nailed down with drawing pins in order to keep it stationary. If you have a drawing board on which you can place your stencil, you will find this most satisfactory for working. If not, a piece of strong cardboard will do. I don't want you to use the polished dining-room table, otherwise I shall feel responsible for any scoldings which might take place. A really sharp knife with a small blade is absolutely necessary.

Suppose you have chosen the Thistle design. Cut out the top part first, then the bulbous part, following this with the right leaf, and lastly the left leaf. In cutting, always bear this in mind: work from the top downwards from left to right. When you come to corners press hard, so that the section to be cut out will come away clearly leaving no ragged edges. *This is Important.*

Preparing the paint is the next item, and it should be borne in mind always to use it sparingly. By this I mean not to overload your brush.

Mix your colour in an old saucer. If, when you open the jar of poster colour, you find it soft and creamy, do not use any water. Only use a spoonful of water if the paint has become hard and dry. Place some colour in a saucer and add a teaspoonful of glue. Mix well with your brush. Glue is added to prevent colour from running.

Let us imagine that you have made Mother a compendium for keeping her notepaper and envelopes, and want to complete the effect with a design in the centre.

Lay your stencil where you want it to be, holding it in place with your left hand, and with your right dip the brush into the paint, wiping it against the side of the saucer till all surplus colour is removed, and with a dabbing movement go over all the cut-out parts. You will require to dab fairly hard.

After this is complete put your brush down, and with the forefinger and thumb of each hand lift the stencil quickly. *Leave it to dry.*

The same method is used for the Rose and Ship design.

In stencilling on material use a little more paint on your brush, and when dry iron on the wrong side to remove any stiffness.

If you have any gold or silver paint this will make a very effective stencil.

Until you have become used to working with stencils keep to one-colour designs.

I know of one girl, who on seeing her newly distempered bedroom, decided it needed just that little something extra, and, cutting a star design in parchment, proceeded to stencil a row of stars right under the picture rail, with the result that she had a very charming frieze.

HOW TO MAKE A PLAQUE OR WALL MASK

1. *Material for Modelling*.

Ordinary clay is quite suitable for this purpose, and can be purchased cheaply at any pottery or brick works or from firms dealing in craft workers' material. Fourteen pounds is ample for models of an average size, and you will always have plenty in reserve. Clay keeps better in a tin with a damp cloth covering it, which should be moistened occasionally. At its best it should be neither too wet nor too dry, but just pliable between the fingers without making them messy. Non-drying plastic modelling paste such as plasticine is also suitable, but a little more expensive; it will, however, last almost indefinitely. This type of clay has one or two distinct advantages over common clay—it is much cleaner to use, and is always ready for use after a little squeezing between fingers. Models made from common clay can be baked if a kiln is available.

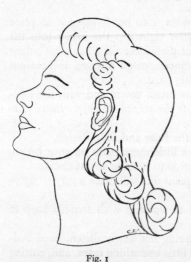

Fig. 1

2. *Making the Model* (fig. 1).

Having decided on the model you wish to make, proceed to build it up, working from the centre. Do not try to model a large lump of clay into the shape you require—the result will be most unsatisfactory. Place a piece of clay about the size of a walnut in the centre of your modelling board, then proceed to build round this with pellets of clay about the size of the end joint of your thumb. These pellets should be made quite soft by rolling and squeezing before being pressed into place. As the model grows you add the projecting darts in the same way. The surface of the finished model will appear like crazy paving. This is smoothed with fingers, then by suitable tools. To save using a lot of clay in larger models, fill the centre with suitable blocks of wood.

3. *Tools for Modelling* (fig. 2).

These can be made quite easily from pieces of wood of a suitable size, such as $\frac{1}{2}''$ dowel rod and some short lengths of wire about $\frac{1}{16}''$ diameter. Various shapes are shown and can be made as re-

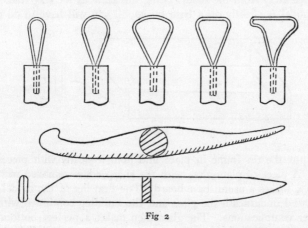

Fig 2

quired. Strips of wood are quite suitable for the all-wood tools, which should be shaped in a similar way to those shown in the diagram. To make the wire tools, cut the dowel rod into pieces about 8″ long and drill a hole in the centre at each end. The wire is bent to shape, then pushed into these holes. A vice to hold the wire when driving the dowel on is useful. Do not make all the tools at once; after a little practice you will soon discover the most useful shapes.

4. *Oil for Coating Surfaces*.

When the model is finished to your satisfaction, you will require some form of lubricant to prevent the clay sticking to the plaster when making the mould. This can be made from a little tallow mixed with paraffin, the tallow being carefully melted in a tin, together with the oil, on the gas ring. Vaseline will do but is messy. A small paint brush is used to paint the oil on the model.

5. *Frame for Moulding* (fig. 3).

A suitable frame can be made by building a clay wall round the model. This should be at least 1″ higher than the model and no nearer than 2″ to the sides. An easier way is to cut two strips of tin of suitable length and width and bend them as shown in diagram, two paper clips being used to hold it together, and the distance away from the model being the same as for clay wall. As the model is already on a base board, all you will have to do now

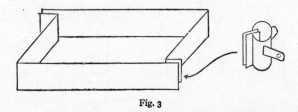

Fig. 3

is to put the tin frame in place and hold it steady with pieces of clay. A piece of plate-glass with the sharp edges removed with an oilstone makes a useful base board. The drawing of the model can be placed underneath the glass and the building continued without further complications. The glass then makes a perfect bottom for the mould. The plaster will come away with a surface like glass.

6. *Mixing the Plaster and Colouring.*

Plaster can be bought from any builder's yard, or a better quality from firms supplying dentists. It is better bought in small quantities as required and must be kept dry. Buy at the same time a little yellow ochre for colouring purposes. To mix the plaster you will require a basin or a tall toffee tin—I favour the latter. The tin should be three-parts filled with water, which is then coloured with the yellow ochre. The plaster is now carefully poured into the water until the cone formed reaches the surface. Place the hand inside the tin with the palm of hand on the bottom and agitate the water until the plaster is thoroughly mixed. Plaster, being quick setting, must be used as soon as it is ready, so see that everything is in order before mixing.

7. *Making the Mould*.

The model is oiled, the tin frame in position, and the plaster ready. Carefully pour a small quantity of plaster on the centre of model and blow it all over the surface, paying particular attention to all crevices. A small brush can be used for this purpose. This priming coat is to prevent air being trapped and so forming hollows in the mould. This should take only a few minutes; then the remainder of the plaster is poured into the mould, working from the centre and letting it flow outwards towards the sides. If you have not mixed enough plaster, leave the surface rough and mix another tinful at once. This must be poured over the first layer within ten minutes, otherwise it will be too dry to bind. If the first layer has dried out, soak it well with water before applying the second layer.

8. *Time for Setting*.

Leave mould for at least an hour before removing the tin frame. Then place mould on its side and leave until the next day.

9. *Removing Clay Model from Mould* (fig. 4).

If ordinary clay has been used, soak it well with water by holding it under the tap. The proprietary brands will not require such treatment. Using one of the modelling tools, remove as much clay as you can from the centre of the model as shown by the shaded portion of diagram. Having done this, grip the clay with your fingers and pull towards the middle, drawing the clay away from the edges of mould. This should be continued all the way round until the clay is quite free, then lifted out, any clay left in crevices being removed with modelling tools. The mould brick should now be allowed to dry out a little longer.

10. *Preparing the Mould for Casting*.

When the mould has dried sufficiently, examine the surface for any discrepancies and make them good with a little " killed " plaster or pellets of clay. To " kill " plaster, you mix as before and stir continually until it has formed a paste; mix only sufficient to fill any holes. Before filling the holes they must be thoroughly soaked with water. After the plaster has dried, smooth the surface with glass-paper. The surface of mould must now be made non-

4

porous. This can be achieved by painting it with french polish
(shellac) or by using a soap solution made with liquid soap and
boiling water. This should be liberally brushed over the surface for
about twenty minutes. The french-polish method is much quicker,
although a little dearer. Two or three coats will be quite sufficient.
When the surface is dry, oil or grease it all over with the tallow and
oil solution, and it is then ready to receive the plaster in the final
stage.

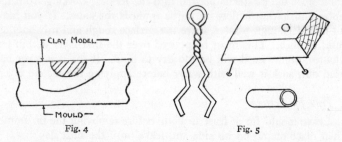

Fig. 4   Fig. 5

11. *Preparing Blocks for Hanging Castings* (fig. 5).

These should be made ready before making the casting. There
are three quite simple but effective methods of doing this. A length
of wire can be twisted as shown, forming an eye at one end and
bending the legs in such a way that they will not pull out of the
casting. This must be inserted after the plaster has been poured
into the mould but before it has had time to set. The second way
is a little more trouble but makes a cleaner job. A suitable sized
block of wood is cut with all its sides tapered as shown, using nails
to act as reinforcement. A $\frac{1}{2}''$ hole is then bored at a slight angle to
the face of the block in an upward direction; thus when it is placed
on a nail driven into the wall at a similar angle the casting will tend
to cling to the wall. This block must also be inserted into the back
of casting while the plaster is still a liquid, the correct level of block
being found by pressing it into place with a rule or straight-edge.
The back of mould can then be easily scraped level by using the
same rule. The third way is to cut a short piece of brass tubing and
insert it instead of the block of wood. Failing a piece of tubing,
a strip of brass can be rolled round a dowel rod and will serve the
same purpose. The back of casting can be cleaned in the same way
as when using a wood block.

12. *The Actual Casting of Model.*

If you can, purchase some white plaster; failing this, use the plaster obtained from the builder's yard. This should be mixed in the same way as when you made the mould, but this time do not colour the water. The tin must be thoroughly cleaned and no hard bits of plaster left in to get mixed up with the new. It is wise to clean the tin out as soon as you have finished with it, while the plaster is still soft. Remember that on no account must plaster be washed down the sink, or it will block up the waste pipe completely. Before mixing the plaster make quite sure everything is ready to hand, the mould greased and the block ready to insert. The plaster is then mixed and a little poured into the mould. This is carefully blown into all crevices, or a small brush used to spread it. When you are quite sure there are no pockets of air, proceed to pour in the remainder until the mould is full. A rubber ball cut in two makes a useful bowl for conveying the plaster from the tin to the mould, and can be easily cleaned by turning it inside out when the plaster has dried. The wire, block or piece of tubing is now inserted in the right position and the cast left for about half an hour. The surplus plaster is then scraped off the back and the casting left until next day to harden.

13. *Removing Mould from Casting.*

When the casting has grown quite hard, rest the mould on a pad of sacking with the back of model facing upwards. You will now see why the plaster used for the mould was coloured. Using a blunt chisel and a mallet, break away the mould carefully, keeping always on the mould side of casting and breaking the pieces off in an outward direction. Once you have broken right through to the casting the rest will come away quite easily because of the grease. It is as well to do this job on some old newspapers; then all the broken bits of plaster can be gathered together and dropped into a bin. When the mould has been removed completely, leave casting to dry out.

14. *Finishing the Casting* (fig. 6).

If the plaster has been poured into mould carefully, the surface will be quite smooth and very little work will be required to make it perfect. Any discrepancies, such as hollows, must be filled in with killed plaster and glass-papered level after it has dried out. Portions of the mould that are still in the crevices must be removed by

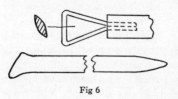

Fig 6

tools made very much like those used in modelling but sharpened as shown in diagram. These are used to scrape away the plaster. For intricate details such as eyes and ears, a suitable tool can be made out of a small file or a piece of mild steel about 6″ long by $\frac{3}{8}$″ wide and $\frac{1}{8}$″ thick, the ends being filed or ground into the shape shown. The file is softened before it is shaped, by heating to a bright red in the fire and letting it cool slowly. After shaping it can be hardened again by heating and cooling quickly in cold water. When everything is to your satisfaction the whole model should be made quite smooth by glass-papering.

15. *Painting the Casting.*

Before you can paint on new plaster the surface must be made non-absorbent. French polish is the most suitable, but size is quite satisfactory. Two or three coats of either should be applied. For the actual painting use oil-bound distemper or artist's oil paint as sold in tubes by the local art dealer. There is, of course, no objection to using oil paint sold for household purposes, but so little is required at a time that the tubes are much more economical. For tube paint you will require a medium ; this is a mixture of varnish, oil and turps which you can buy ready-made, or you can easily make it yourself to the following proportions: one part of varnish, two parts of linseed oil, and four parts of turpentine. A very small quantity is required. You will also need a few small paint brushes and some rags for cleaning. In painting remember that fundamentally all colours are a mixture of red, yellow and blue. The following colours are the most useful: alizarine crimson, vermilion, pale chrome or cadmium yellow, yellow ochre, ultramarine, van dyke brown or burnt umber, together with flake white for toning purposes. Brushes should be cleaned with warm soapy water as soon as you have finished painting and allowed to dry before using again. They can, of course, be washed in turps and used immediately, but do not let them become hard.

PUTTING ON A PLAY

Most people, for some reason or other, fairly early in their existence, feel that they would like to embark on some form of theatrical work. Why this should be I cannot say, but it is none the less a fact. The urge may be only to dress up or it may go to the length of putting on a play. In the latter case, it is well to know how to set about things, and the pitfalls of which you should beware. The play may be quite a small affair in your own drawing-room, and the audience may be your family and friends. It may, on the other hand, be on a bigger scale in some local hall. In either case the same principles apply.

The first problem that will arise will be what play to perform. Well, you have a wide choice, and your final decision will depend on your own taste. But generally speaking, it is wise to start with a play that has a strong plot—that is to say, a good story. It may be either comedy or drama, but, oddly enough, comedy is on the whole more difficult, and if you try it you should certainly avoid the very sophisticated drawing-room comedy, which is hard for amateurs of any age.

The characters in the play must suit reasonably well those who are going to take part. Messrs. Samuel French, Ltd., who publish acting versions of many thousands of plays, also publish a *Guide to Selecting Plays* which is very useful. The Guide gives a short synopsis of the plot and the types of characters required.

It is a good idea to start with a one-act play. It is easier for all concerned, and if you wish to give a full evening's entertainment, it is easier to do three or even four one-act plays than a full-length play. This is because it is easier for the actors to master a character that has to be maintained for only a short time, and it is easier for the producer to map out the moves and generally appreciate a short play where there is one central idea and one scene. If you have a lot of people who wish to act, there will be more good parts available if you do several short plays.

You may have thought of writing a play yourself. A good idea, because there is no better way of learning the technique of playwriting than by producing your first plays in a small way yourself. But do not on any account start with one of your own plays. Get your experience of acting and production first of all with a play that has been tried and proved. Unless you do this, if things go wrong you will never know whether the fault lies in the production or in the actual writing of the play itself. Playwriting is really not a thing that can be taught, although there are several books on the subject, the standard one being Archer's *Playmaking*. To be a successful writer for the stage you must, unless you are a genius, get to know the theatre. There is no better way to start than by producing a play yourself.

Having decided on your play, you must next decide who is going to produce it. The producer is a very important person indeed. It is he who interprets the author's ideas and gives them life. That is to say, he decides how the actors will move, how they will speak their lines, how the scenery shall be designed, where the furniture shall be placed, what sort of furniture it shall be, and so on. In short, he—or she—is in charge of the play until the first performance takes place.

If you can find someone with experience to do this for you, so much the better. If not, and you decide to do it yourself, do not be discouraged. You will make mistakes, of course, and you will come up against many snags, but if you have to sort all this out for yourself you will have learned a lot from your first production. Incidentally, if you go on producing for the rest of your life you will find that you always encounter snags. Your experience, as you go on, will enable you to deal quickly with those you have met before, but fresh ones always appear. No two plays are the same, and neither are the problems they bring with them. It is one of the charms of the theatre that with each production you start afresh with something entirely new. The mastering of fresh problems is a challenge to your ingenuity. If you are anxious to take up the challenge, and if you are alert and have an agile brain, you will always win the battle.

Well then, you have decided on your play, and you have decided to produce it yourself. Your work now falls into two compartments. In the first there is the working out of the play itself and coaching the actors so that they give the sort of performances you wish. In the second there is the material side of the production: the staging, lighting, effects, and all the very necessary things which the audience does not see, but which are essential to the success of the play. The two are not really separate. They overlap. Each obviously affects the other, but it is convenient to deal with them separately here so as to avoid confusion.

You must first of all decide the character and shape of your setting. If your scene is an interior—a room—you must decide where the doors, windows, and fireplace are to be. If you are having the set specially designed, you must at this stage consult the de-

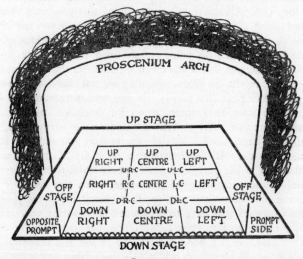

Stage areas

signer and ensure that your ideas are practical and in conformity with the general design of the setting. If, as is more probable, you are going to hire a set, then you must see the firm from whom you are getting it and make sure that you can have the practicabilities (doors, windows, &c.) you want, with the scenery that is available.

Having fixed the set itself, you must then decide on what furniture you require, and where it is to be placed. Again, you must bear in mind what furniture you are likely to be able to get.

The next step is to make a scaled plan of the set, showing the positions of all the furniture, and therefore also showing you what room is left for the characters to move about. The easiest way to do this is to get hold of some squared paper, such as is used for mathematics and science at school, ruled in squares of one inch and one-tenth of an inch. A convenient scale is half an inch to the foot. Then, with your ground plan in front of you, read the play carefully through and mark in pencil on the script (the typed or printed copy of the play) whenever you wish a character to move, and the point to which he or she is to move. At this stage do not worry about small moves such as gestures of the hands or turns of the body, but confine yourself to those that alter the positions of the characters on the stage, including when they seat themselves and when they rise. All the time you are doing this you must visualize the play taking place. You may find that it helps if you use bits of matchstick or small pieces of paper to represent the various characters, and move them on your ground plan as you mark up the moves on the script. But if you do this, remember that whatever it is you use to represent the characters, they are not likely to be to scale.

Avoid making aimless moves. If you wish a character to cross the stage, he must have some reason for doing so, and you may have to invent this. Avoid " fussy " and unnecessary moves, but, on the other hand, do not let the play become too static or it will be dull to watch. All the movements must arise naturally out of the situations in the play, and must appear quite natural, even inevitable, to the audience. At this stage, when you are only preparing the play in general outline, it is almost inevitable that you will put in moves that have to be altered later during rehearsal, so it is wise not to go into great detail but rather to outline the movements broadly. It is a good thing to go to the first rehearsal with your ideas for the play clean cut in your own mind, but a bad thing to force the production to fit these preconceived ideas, if when you come to rehearse, you find, or someone else suggests, a better way of doing things. In short, you must know what you want, but you must keep an open mind on how to achieve it.

This brings us to the actors. Who are you going to have to play the various parts? Obviously it is better to have people who are keen to do it. If your cast (the actors and actresses) have to be overpersuaded to take part, you have a very slender hold over them and they may let you down at the last minute. They may become very keen as the rehearsals progress, but they may not. They may find that the time given to rehearsals interferes with other activities in which they are more interested. So, try to get people who are as interested in the idea as you are yourself. If they have never acted before, you will have to take a chance in your first play as to whether they can act or not. If they are keen and sincere, they will probably put up a good show. It is worth remembering that the converse does not necessarily hold good. I have known extremely good actors who hated acting.

It is as well to make it clear to the cast that from the time you start rehearsals until your play is produced they are going to have to devote most of their spare time to rehearsing and studying their parts. A lot of rehearsals are bound to be necessary, and the less experienced your actors are the more rehearsing they will require. The intensity of rehearsals naturally depends on the period over which you spread them. You may decide to keep them going over the winter months, rehearsing once a week, with more frequent rehearsals when you get near the production date. This is often done. You may rehearse over half the period twice a week, which is better. Or you may rehearse every evening for three or four weeks, which is best of all—but not always practicable. With beginners it is not a bad idea to rehearse only twice a week at the outset, because it gives the actors longer to learn their parts.

As regards learning parts, people vary very much. Some learn them quickly and easily. Others take a long time. But it is surprising how the part comes to you once you start rehearsing. Never let the cast learn their parts before you start rehearsing. In the long run this saves no time. Remember, they have to memorize not only the lines, but also the moves. Once you start rehearsing, and the moves are marked in their scripts, they will automatically learn the two together. If the words are learned first, you will find that the moves come less easily. You may think that this is a small point, but it is one on which you must be firm.

As a producer you must, of course, be firm all the time. You must establish your authority at once, and make it quite clear that what you say goes! This applies to everything connected with the play. A successful production must be a dictatorship and cannot be run on democratic lines. On the other hand, if you are wise you will be tactful. Don't appear to be " bossy ". This irritates people and causes friction. Don't allow arguments. If an actor, or anyone else, for that matter, has a suggestion to make, welcome it. Don't discard a good idea simply because you didn't think of it yourself. You will find that everyone has something to contribute, and that it is the sum of these good ideas that makes a good production, if you control it. Weigh, therefore, every suggestion, and if it is a good one, adopt it. But avoid discussions that become general.

There must be discipline at rehearsals. People must turn up at the right time, and not five minutes late. That, after all, is only ordinary courtesy. The cast must not be allowed to whisper in corners while others are rehearsing. Obviously this is distracting for those who are working.

Whenever you give an actor a move, see that he marks it in pencil on his script and that, at the same time, it is marked in the " prompt copy ". The latter is most important, because the prompt copy is your bible, and must be the final arbiter in any argument. Marking up moves takes a lot of time at the early rehearsals. You may find this irritating and feel that time is being wasted. But that is not so. In the long run, time is being saved. Few people can remember accurately all the moves that are given. If scripts are not marked at the time, there is a grave danger of prolonged argument, particularly if rehearsals are at weekly intervals. In addition to wasting time, such arguments fray tempers and detract from the general smooth running of the production.

Don't take the scripts away from the cast too soon. The actors must, of course, have their scripts until all the moves are finally fixed and parts are memorized. But if you feel it is going to give them confidence, leave the scripts until you are giving gestures and paying attention to individual performances. By that time scripts are a nuisance and parts should have been memorized.

It is better not to ask an actor to copy a gesture or an inflexion which you give him. Rather, try to describe to him the impression you wish him to convey. The reason for this is that no two people ever react in exactly the same way, and an actor may give a perfect imitation of a line spoken by you which sounds stilted and out of key with the rest of his performance.

Pace in the production is most important. Not necessarily speed. But pace suited to the rhythm of the play, quickening towards the climaxes. Start to get this whenever you have got rid of the scripts. Beginners tend to " hang on cues ". This means that instead of answering the previous speaker immediately, there is a split second's delay before the reply. This must be avoided. During the performance, when the audience laugh you must wait until the laugh is dying before you speak, otherwise your line will not be heard. But pausing for laughs can only be thoroughly learned by experience, and laughs do not always come where you expect them, nor always even in the same place at different performances of the same play. Definite pauses for effect must be marked in the prompt copy, so that if in an emergency you have a strange prompter, who does not know the play, he does not prompt in the wrong place. One word about prompters. Remember that when a line is given it must be heard by the actor who requires it. It is better that the audience should hear the line also, than that the actor should not hear it. Prompting is a difficult art. Some people are naturally good prompters. Others are never able to prompt successfully. On the whole, women are better prompters than men, probably because of the quality of their voices.

One final word about production. If you are producing, do not play a part yourself. It is perfectly true that you can point to many cases where famous actors also produced the plays in which they played leading parts. But wait until you are a famous actor before you try this. Even then the wisdom of it is questionable.

And now for the second compartment of which I spoke. So far we have only considered the coaching of the actors in their parts. But there is a great deal more than that, and for these other things you should have various people to help you. First of all, you must have a stage manager. He is your second-in-command. He has authority over all the departments of the production second only to your own. He will control all that goes on upon the stage during the performance. He will arrange with you the scenery, the lighting, and the costumes. He will see that the effects take place at the right time, and that there is always someone there to prompt. He will supervise all the changes of scenery. He will also see that all the properties are there when they are wanted. (Incidentally, properties that are handled by the actors should be used at rehearsals as soon as possible.) He will be extremely busy. As he cannot satisfactorily do all this himself, he will have at least one assistant, called, for short, the A.S.M. Either the stage manager or the A.S.M. should be at every rehearsal. It is they who keep a note of the moves and mark up the prompt copy, and later, when the actors have got rid of their scripts, prompt the play. One or other will prompt the play at the performance—usually the A.S.M., although they may share this task. But the prompter must in any case be someone who has attended rehearsals and knows the play.

You will probably not design and make your own scenery, but you will naturally make every effort to have the sort of scenery you want, probably by hiring it, but perhaps by having something very simple that you can knock together yourselves. Bear in mind the

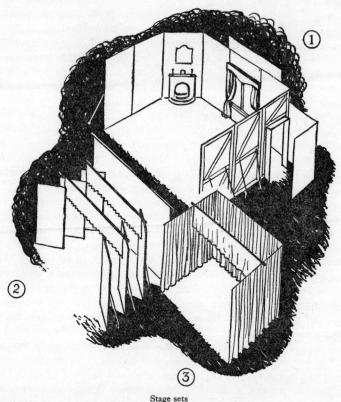

Stage sets
1. Box set. 2. Wing and cloth set. 3. Curtain set

possibility of using draperies. Curtains can make very effective settings. For some plays they are better than flats, as the canvas-covered wooden frames that form the units of normal scenery are called. If you are producing the play in your own house, then draperies are probably the best solution. You should, of course, use the same curtains to surround the whole set, and they should hang in folds and not be stretched taut. If you are depicting an ordinary room, flats containing doors, windows, or fireplace may be used along with the curtains, and these flats can be moved about to indicate a change of scene. This is a convention, but one which the audience will accept.

If you have not got a stage, you should try at least to raise a little the area on which the actors play. A foot would probably be enough in an ordinary drawing-room. This will involve some carpentry, but nothing that is very advanced. You may even be able to borrow the timber and send it back afterwards, if you do not make too many nail holes. It is, of course, much easier if the stage is there already, and if you play in a hall it will be.

The stage manager must, as soon as possible, make a list of the properties required for the play, and set about getting them. Properties contribute enormously to the appearance of a production. They can give the audience the impression of the sort of room in which the play is taking place, and of the people who live in it. The simpler your scenery has to be, the more you should concentrate on getting the right kind of furniture and properties. There are always certain things that the actors handle, or that, although not handled, are mentioned in the play. These you will get as a matter of course. But you must get many other things that are not mentioned. These other properties are called stage dressing, and it is this stage dressing that stamps the character of the set. There are a great many plays that take place in ordinary middle-class living-rooms. If you are doing one of these and the audience sees only the properties that are mentioned in the script, the room will almost certainly look bare. The odds and ends that are always lying about in such a room, the ornaments, the papers, and so on, will all be missed. The stage manager should make a list of what is required, and go round his friends, borrowing what he can. As he must obviously start to do this a long time before you are going to perform the play, he should note against each article where he is going to get it, and arrange for its collection later.

The stage manager must also make out what is called a " property plot ", showing the position of all the " props " on the stage, with a list of those required off for actors to take on. He should also add a list of what are called " personal props ". These are things like cigarette cases, matches, handkerchiefs, &c., with which actors have what is called " business ", and which they carry on their persons.

The actors themselves are responsible for these, but a wise stage manager will make sure that they have them before they go on the stage. All props should be checked by this list before each performance.

Stage lighting

1, 2, 3. Battens.   4, 5. Spots.   6. Foot.   7. Flood.   8. F.O.H. (Front of house) spots

The lighting of the stage is a study in itself, and a very fascinating one. There are many excellent books on this subject. If you have electric light in your house, it is quite a simple matter to rig up footlights with a flex and plug, to plug into one of the lighting points in the room. But you should consult an electrician to make sure that you do not overload the circuit and fuse the lights or perhaps cause a fire. You can buy bulbs and holders and screw the latter on to a light wooden batten. You should, if you can, have three circuits wired in parallel, each third lamp being on the same circuit, and being operated by the same switch. You can use old cocoa tins for reflectors, and buy coloured gelatine to put in front of the light. Remember that the audience must not see any naked light. The reflector must conceal the bulb from them. If you have one colour of gelatine per circuit, and can make or hire dimmers so that each circuit is on a dimmer, then you can get a great variety of light. This all sounds very complicated, but it is quite possible to achieve in a drawing-room if you take a little expert advice and consult one of the books on the subject. You must also have at least one batten which is similar in all respects to the footlights, but hangs from above, being hidden from the audience by a cloth border of some kind.

In the absence of electric light you may have to make do with oil lamps or whatever lighting is available, but the same principles apply. Remember that you can always produce effective stage lighting by using car batteries and lamps of the appropriate voltage. If you do this you must make sure that the batteries are sufficiently charged to last out the performance.

Generally speaking, it is wiser to use gelatines of soft colours. Pale pink gives a warm light, and is good for costumes. Amber gives a sunny effect, and steel blue a cold one.

Stage lighting is unnatural, and casts unnatural shadows on the actors' faces, which must therefore be made up with grease paint. There are various makes of grease paint, sold usually in sticks, numbered according to the colour. The most generally used colours are 5, a yellowish flesh tint, and 9, a reddish flesh tint. The two combined, rubbed on the face, will produce the groundwork necessary for most characters. Older people are usually sallower, therefore you would use more 5 than 9 if you were making up as an elderly man. If you were supposed to be a particularly healthy, wind-blown young sailor, then you might use only 9, using carmine to give the redder colour on and above the cheek bones. You would normally use 9 for that purpose, with a 5 and 9 make-up. The eyes should be outlined with a very narrow line of blue or brown, according to their colour, to make them stand out. Lines on the face are shown by using grease paint liner of a dark shade—brown or dark red—but remember that each line must have the corresponding high light in a light colour (white in the case of a pale make-up) alongside it. It is the high light and shadow together that produces the effect. The one without the other is useless. Try to put your lines where they will eventually come as you grow older, and with your finger blend them into the groundwork of your make-up. Your eyebrows should also be darkened. After you have made up you must powder thoroughly with blending powder, to fix the make-up and prevent the skin glistening. For moustaches and beards you can buy crêpe hair, which is stuck to the face with spirit gum. If you require a wig, the only satisfactory thing is to hire it—and make sure that it fits you.

Remember that you will wish to remove the make-up after the performance! To do this simply rub theatrical cold cream over the face and wipe off with a towel, cotton-wool, or face tissues. On no account attempt to wash before you have removed your make-up.

There are many books on the various subjects I have mentioned, specially written for amateurs. I have mentioned one or two, but there are many others, including a very comprehensive work called *Theatre and Stage* edited by Harold Downs. This is in two large volumes, but it contains all you are likely to wish to know about every aspect of putting on a play.

I hope I have not made the business of play production sound too complicated. It is certainly not easy to achieve perfection, but then it rarely is in anything that is worth while. The golden rule is to refuse to be discouraged. Go ahead! You will be surprised how good the result will be.

ATHLETICS

EVENTS

Most girls like to run, to jump, to throw, and to aim at a target, and events involving these activities are usually included in a sports programme. In schools, the gymnastics, games, and other physical activities carried on throughout the session build up the stamina of the pupils, so that there is no sudden, very intensive training for the sports day. Practice of athletics is part of the scheme of physical education, and is carried out in short spells usually during the weekly games period. Girls should consult their games mistress about practice out of school hours.

The actual athletic sports meeting should not drag on. It is better to have two or three afternoon meetings than one long one which extends into the evening. The number of events in which a competitor may take part should be limited. If the meeting is spread over two afternoons a girl could compete in six events, three each day. For example:

FIRST DAY	SECOND DAY
1. SPRINT.	1. OBJECT RACE.
2. HIGH JUMP.	2. THROWING CONTEST.
3. AIMING CONTEST.	3. RELAY RACE.

If, while practising, a girl feels unduly tired, and feels that she has not the strength to go on to the end of a run, she should not force herself to do so. This does not happen often, and there is no need to feel alarmed about it, but if there is some defect then the sooner it is attended to the better. A doctor should be consulted about the advisability of taking part in athletics. If running and jumping are forbidden, throwing and aiming might be allowed.

The fundamentals of every movement in running, jumping, throwing and aiming must be carefully learned. Each movement should be analysed and mastered; the arms, legs, trunk and head— each should be taken separately. There should be practice of combining the movements, until finally the body is working smoothly and rhythmically as a whole. Beginners will soon gain confidence and appreciate good style if they begin at the beginning, and grasp the fundamentals. After the fundamentals have been mastered, actual practice may be begun.

LIMBERING UP

Limbering up is a means of gradually warming up the muscles, so that there is no sudden strain when the actual track or field events call for the maximum effort. Movements such as marching on the spot with ankle stretching, small running steps in place, skip jumping, and easy jog trotting, are useful preliminaries. These may be followed by knee raising to touch the forehead and trunk bending downward to touch the floor.

LIMBERING DOWN

Limbering down after an event is just as important as limbering up. The body should be kept warm, and on the move, and the slowing down process should be very gradual. There should never be a sudden finish to a run. Warm clothing should be put on after a run.

THE SPRINT

The runner must first of all learn to run in a straight line. This can be tried out walking, then running slowly, then running quickly. White lines in the playground are good practice ground. The ankles must be supple, and so must the joints of the feet and the toes. Ankle-circling exercises and heel-raising exercises are good for suppling the ankles and feet. The foot should point straight forward, because a step taken with the foot turned out is shorter than that with the foot straight forward.

The whole leg should be used in running. The thigh should be pulled forward with a good bending of the knee. The leg should be well stretched forward on each step, so that the foot may be put down in advance of the knee and running from the knee down avoided. This helps to increase the length of the stride, and therefore decreases the number of steps required to cover the distance.

The legs should not be kicked up behind. This action is only a waste of energy and time.

The body should lean forward from the ankles, not from the waist, at an angle of about 75 degrees from the ground (fig. 1). The head and neck should be held still, and at no time turned to see where the other runners are. This slows up the runner and makes her swerve.

There are two methods of arm action, and arm action is extremely important; arms and legs work together in all walking and running.

The Arms. Method 1.

A baton or ruler should be grasped, with one hand at each end, palms towards the body.

Fig. 1

The arms swing backwards and forwards across the body, while each shoulder shrugs as the arms swing to that side (fig. 2).

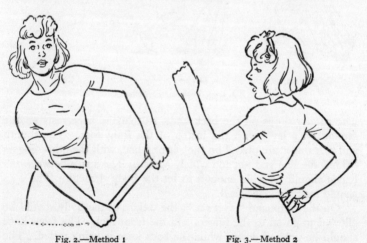

Fig. 2.—Method 1   Fig. 3.—Method 2

Method 2.

The arms should be swung forward and up to chest or shoulder height. The hands may be clenched or held with the fingers straight. The action is straight forward and back with emphasis on the forward swing. The elbows should be bent, and the quicker the action the more the elbows have to be bent.

THE START

There are two ways of starting a race: either the natural standing start or the crouch start, of which there are two methods.

CROUCH START

Method 1.

On the command " On your mark " the front foot is placed on the ground, with the toe about six inches behind the starting line.

On your mark　　　　Get set　　　　　　Go

Fig. 4.—Crouch start.　Method 1

The runner drops on the back knee, so that the knee rests on the ground on a level with the instep of the front foot. The thumb and first finger are placed on the starting line, with the other fingers behind the line and not too widely spread. The space between the hands should be wide enough to let the body through. The eyes should look straight ahead.

On the command " Get set ", the weight of the body should be allowed to go on to the fingers and the front foot. The front knee should be pressed down, while the back knee is being raised. The head should be far enough up for the eyes to look at the spot where the rear foot will come on its first step. The runner should be able just to keep her balance. The fingers should be firmly enough placed on the ground so that the palm does not fall towards the ground.

On " Go ", or on the pistol shot, the rear foot should be pushed strongly off the ground and brought forward for the first step, and a series of short jabbing steps should be taken. Meanwhile the arm on the side of the forward foot swings strongly forward, while the other swings back. The runner should be conscious of a strong arm swinging, and of a jabbing action of the legs as the body gradually rises to its natural running position.

Method 2.

" On your mark "—the runner should drop comfortably on to her heels with the back foot quite close to the front, and the front

On your mark   Get set   Go

Fig. 5.—Crouch start. Method 2

foot twelve inches or so from the line. The hands should rest lightly on the ground.

" Get set "—the hands should be placed on the starting line, far enough apart to let the body through. The weight should be swung forward on to the hands and the front foot. The body should be brought almost parallel to the ground.

" Go "—the rear leg should be pulled forward, and the arms swung vigorously forward and back.

THE FINISH

The runner should practise running through a piece of wool, known as " the tape ". She should run at full speed through this, and only afterwards should she slow down. There should be no throwing up of the arms or throwing back of the head, but the normal running action should be maintained. All other movements

| This way | Not this |
| Fig. 6.—The finish | Fig. 7 |

slow down the pace. Runners should slow down very gradually after passing through the tape and should never pull up with a jerk (figs. 6 and 7).

RELAY RACE

Without doubt relay races are the most popular events at a sports meeting. In a relay race a token is carried by a team of runners. The team covers a set distance, each runner running a part of that distance. The first runner carries the token and hands it on to the next, and so on until the last runner runs with it across the finishing line. A wooden baton is the usual kind of token. It should be about a foot long. The best race is that which is round a track, the left shoulder towards the centre of the track. The runner receives the baton into her right hand and gives it with her left.

The Change Over.

The perfect change of baton is that in which both girls are running at full speed when the baton is changed over. No time is lost

if it is done in this way, but, unfortunately, very few pairs of runners
ever reach this high standard of efficiency (fig. 8).

A popular length for a relay race is 440 yards, each runner running 110 yards. A line is drawn across the track, 100 yards from the
starting line, and another line is drawn 20 yards farther on, 120
yards from the starting line. The baton must be changed over from
the first to the second runner within this 20-yard area.

The second runner stands a little in front of the back line, looking
back over her right shoulder watching the first runner. When she
sees the first runner coming up she gets ready to receive the baton,

Fig. 8.—The change over

and starts running. She looks forward whenever she starts running,
and never looks back again. After having received the baton she runs
on until she has given it to the next runner, or in the case of the last
runner until she has crossed the finishing line.

The outgoing runner starts running holding her right hand as
far back as possible, with her arm fully extended and the palm turned
in the direction of the oncoming runner. The fingers should be
close together, and the space between the thumb and fingers as wide
as possible. The baton is put into this space by the oncoming
runner. The girl who is giving the baton reaches forward with her
arm fully stretched. She holds the baton by the end nearest to her,
and puts the other end into the outgoing runner's hand. Whenever
this runner feels the wood touch her hand, she closes her hand, and
so grasps the baton. The baton must always be *given*, there is no
question of *taking* or *groping* for it.

The outgoing runner must look forward and have perfect confidence that the other girl will give the baton to her. Whenever she receives it she should change it to the left hand in readiness to hand it over. The last runner need not do this. A great deal of practice is needed in baton passing, since it is most important that the baton is not dropped. It has been said that a race can be won by girls who change over well, rather than by a team of speedier runners who have not practised the change over.

Much practice is needed so that an outgoing runner knows when to start running. At the change over both runners should be moving at full speed. If the outgoing girl starts too soon, she may be over the front line before the incoming runner has made up on her, and so her team would be disqualified.

HIGH JUMP

Two upright stands are needed, and these should be placed 12 feet apart. A lath is placed on pegs, which protrude from the stands. The pegs should protrude towards the side of the stands on which the jumper lands. This is most important because then the lath will go with the jumper if she touches it.

In competition each jumper may start jumping at any height. It is better to begin about six or seven holes below the highest height at which she hopes to clear the lath. This gives her time to warm up before she has to make her greatest effort. When a competitor fails three times to clear the lath at any one height, she is out. She is allowed three tries. When a jumper runs up to the lath and does not jump, but stops or runs under it without knocking it off, she " gibs ". Three " gibs " count as one failure to clear the lath.

A sideways jump is the best, because the feet can be as high as the lowest part of the body when the jumper clears the lath.

SCISSOR JUMP

The most popular sideways jump for girls is the scissor jump. The first thing to discover is which is the easier foot to jump from. If it is the left foot then the jumper should run up from the right-hand side, if the right foot, she should run up from the left-hand side. The spring is always taken from the foot farther from the lath (fig. 9).

The Run Up.

The run up should be at an angle of 45°, or even more, from the lath. Even, light, springy steps should be taken with the weight of the body over the front foot.

Fig. 9.—High jump. Diagram at left hand shows straight leading leg. The diagram at right hand shows (*a*) leading leg being pulled down, (*b*) second leg being lifted over, (*c*) body leaning forward.

The Take-off.

The jumper should take-off from the spot which will bring her directly over the lath when she is at the height of her jump. This needs practice, so that it has become practically automatic, by the day of the competition, to take-off from exactly the right place.

The heel should strike the ground on the last step of the run up, that is, on the take-off. The spring travels through the foot to the toe. As one foot strikes the ground, the other leg should be swung vigorously as high as possible with the knee straight. The second leg should then be whipped up with equal vigour, while the leading leg is pulled down sharply after it is over the lath. Each leg should be straight as it crosses the lath. If the knees are not straight, the feet will be lower than the hip, and one of them might knock off the lath before the competitor has reached her maximum height.

To help the leg action, and to prevent the jumper from landing on her back and jarring herself, she should lean forward from her waist while in the air.

As an aid to keeping the body up while it is going over the lath, the arms should be swung strongly forward.

All effort should be towards lifting the body upward and over the lath. The take-off and the landing should be close together to make this possible.

The head should be turned away from the lath while the body is rising, and turned towards it while the body is going over. As the body begins to drop it should be turned round towards the place where the jump was taken. This carries the hips away from the lath.

A sand pit should be prepared for the landing. This need not be an elaborate affair, but it is essential to land on sand. When a pit cannot be provided, then several barrow loads of sand on top of grass may be used. The competitor must do everything possible to prevent any jar when landing. She herself can lessen the shock by relaxing, as she lands, at ankle, knee and hip. She should not rebound as she lands, she must " give ".

OBJECT RACE

In the object race judgment counts as well as speed, and the eye also comes into it. The runners start from behind a line which is drawn through a box about 1 foot square. In front of this box are marked two other boxes, the first 32 feet from the starting box, and the second 42 feet from it. In the second and third boxes are placed objects, such as a square wooden block or a bean bag.

The competitor must complete the following series of runs:

1. Run from box A, lift object from box B, and place it in box A.
2. Run to fetch object from box C, run back to touch the object which is in box A, and return box C's object to its own place.
3. Run to box A and return the object which is there to its own place in box B.
4. Run and finish the race by crossing the finishing line.

The objects must each be in its own box at the finish, otherwise the competitor is disqualified. The actual track is box A to B, B to A, A to C, C to A, A to C, C to A, A to B, B to finishing line.

For this race, the competitor should practise running in a straight line so as to cover the minimum distance. She should reach well out for the object. She need not run right up to the box, she need only run far enough to be able to reach out and lift the object (fig. 10). She can find out where to pull up by first of all standing with the right

This way   Not this

Fig. 10.—Object race: reaching out

hand touching the block, with the body turned to the left, and the right foot forward. The right knee should be well bent, and the body leaning forward. After taking this position she should stand up and see how far back are her feet. By doing this she will know where she should pull up behind each box when she is taking part in the actual race. This is a strenuous race and requires practice.

THROWING FOR DISTANCE

A cricket ball, stool ball, or hockey ball may be used for hard-ball distance throwing. The competitor throws the ball from behind a line marked on the ground. Neither foot may cross the line until the ball has been thrown. The distance is measured from the line to the place at which the ball strikes the ground, not to where it rolls. The throw should be overhand.

The ball should be held in the fingers and should not be sunk in the palm. Both arms should be raised forward to shoulder level. The left arm should remain there, while the right one is swung downwards and then backwards to shoulder level. As it swings back the right elbow should be bent, so that the hand holding the ball is almost touching the shoulder. The arm should now be thrown forward with a good upward thrust. The ball is propelled

into the air by a final turn of the wrist and flick of the fingers (fig. 11).
Some people are naturally good throwers, but everyone can

Fig. 11.—Distance throwing

develop their throwing powers by practice. It is the development
of an easy co-ordinated movement of the feet, the arms, and the body
which helps to add distance to a throw.

If the thrower is right-handed the left foot should be forward, the left shoulder pointing to the direction in which the ball is to travel. After the arm action has been completely mastered, a three-step start may be added. The thrower runs forward for three steps beginning with the left foot, she takes a quarter turn to the right, so that her left shoulder is towards the direction of the flight of the ball. She then changes all her weight to the right foot and hops on to it. She should hop just before she throws. At the same time she should gather all her force into her right arm in preparation for the throw. The practice of these preliminary movements is well worth while. It is best to practise in twos.

When the ball leaves the thrower's fingers the arm should follow-through with the weight of the body behind it. At the same time the thrower spins round on her left foot, and finishes facing the other way. A step should be taken on to the right foot to maintain the balance.

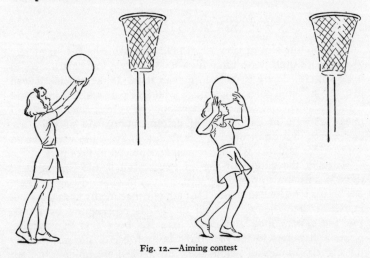

Fig. 12.—Aiming contest

AIMING CONTEST

Netball Shooting.

This is a very popular competition. Shots at goal are taken at different distances from the goal, and points are awarded for each goal shot. Points are sometimes given when the ball hits the ring without going through—fewer points than for a goal.

The competitor should stand with the weight on the left foot, with the right foot back on the toe for support. The ball should be held in the fingers of the right hand, with support from the left. Aim should be taken with the right arm straight and the palm towards the thrower (fig. 12).

For the throw, the knees and ankles should bend simultaneously with the bending of the elbows and wrists, and a slight lowering of the upper arm. As the arm is bent, the back of the hand should be turned towards the thrower. The ball is propelled towards the goal by a straightening of the arms, the knees and the ankles. As the arm is straightened the palm of the hand should be turned again, so that the ball spins as it rises to goal. This spin helps to keep the ball in the ring when it might otherwise bounce off. The ball should always rise above the net and drop in. Aim should therefore be taken for a spot above the ring.

SPORTS DAY

What is the aim in view when practising athletics? Is it merely to run more quickly, to jump higher, to throw a longer distance, to hit a target? There is more to it than that. If the scheme is well planned and well carried out, those who take part will become more mentally alert, and will show development of character on sound lines. Powers of endurance, of determination, and of poise are developed; but unfortunately it is almost always those who have an aptitude for athletics who have been encouraged to take part.

Usually the climax of the athletic season is the Sports Day; there is no point in practising with no aim in view. Recently there has been a tendency to conduct the athletic meeting by a team system in which the " house ", school or club is represented by teams. But the system most commonly used has been that of awarding prizes and points to the first three in each event, the girl gaining the highest number of points being proclaimed champion. In both these systems it is those who have a natural aptitude who take part. What of the others? If they compete at all, they go off without knowing what their standard of achievement is.

Here is a system which has been tried and which has been proved sound. It encourages everyone to take part. The best still give their thrilling performances and the less apt are not merely spectators; they join actively in the fun, and have the satisfaction of knowing that their efforts count. The great advantage of this method is that in it every girl takes part on the Sports Day.

In this system the competitors are graded, not only by age, but by age, height and weight, so that the physique of the girls is taken into account. The grade in which a girl is placed is arrived at by means of the following carefully prepared table, which is an adaptation of that introduced by F. J. Reilly, a New York headmaster. The table was prepared for the Scottish Education Department.

THE CLASSIFICATION TABLES

Points	Age	Height (inches)	Weight (lbs.)
1	9	48	52–56
2	10	49, 50	57–62
3	11	51, 52	63–69
4	12	53, 54, 55	70–76
5	13	56, 57, 58	77–87
6	14	59	88–97
7	15	60	98–106
8	16	61	107–112
9	17	62	113–116
10	18	63 and over	117 and over

From the preceding table the points allowed for each of the factors are read off. These three numbers are added, and the total fixes the girl's physical grade as shown in the following table:

Points Total:	3–6	..	..	Grade A
,,	,,	7–10	..	..	,, B
,,	,,	11–14	..	..	,, C
,,	,,	15–18	..	..	,, D
,,	,,	19–22	..	..	,, E
,,	,,	23–26	..	..	,, F
,,	,,	27–30	..	..	,, G

The events chosen for athletic sports days usually include running, jumping, throwing and aiming. Minimum and maximum standards of performance are fixed for each grade in each event. On the Sports Day points are awarded for individual performances, one point for the minimum standard, and ten points for the maximum. A score book is kept in which are recorded each girl's results. When all the events are over, the points gained by each girl for all the events are totalled.

For example, a girl has taken part in an 80-yard sprint, netball shooting, an object race, throwing, and in high jump. She has gained 9, 8, 6, 10 and 4 points respectively for each event. Her total would be 42 points out of a possible 50 points.

The standards are arrived at by keeping records of performances at practices during the session. The average standard should be found and from that maximum and minimum standards can be fixed.

It is usual to have a school or club divided into teams or houses. A simple way of identifying them is by the use of colours—red, blue, green, orange. On the Sports Day the actual total points gained by every girl in a house are added, the possible total points are added, and a percentage found.

Inter club or school competitions might also be carried out by awarding points for standard achievements. Flat races could be replaced by relay races. Some girls might run, others jump, &c. For example, Grade C might compete in the throwing event, while the girls of Grade A might compete in the high jump. It would not matter if the numbers competing were uneven since the scoring is done on a percentage basis. Take, for example, a competition of five events:

Number in team			12	6	8	10
Possible score ..	..	..	600	300	400	500
Actual score ..	..	..	245	210	250	250
Percentage ..	..	..	$40\frac{5}{8}\%$	70%	$62\frac{1}{2}\%$	50%

BIRD-WATCHING AND BIRD-NESTING

Birds are perhaps the most beautiful living creatures. The study of birds is a joy not only to the young, but to the middle-aged and the old. It is a study which never becomes monotonous or dull. One of the most distinguished admirals of the day wrote to me recently: " I envy the people with knowledge of birds; they need never have a dull moment."

I think most girls have a natural interest in birds. It is important therefore that this instinct should be encouraged and developed.

Britain is fortunate in that it has a large and varied bird population. The people of Britain are more bird-minded than the people of certain continental nations, such as France and Italy, where song birds are shot and netted for food. In Britain, even in towns and great cities, the naturalist can study birds. In London, for example, the parks are full of birds. I do not refer to the sparrow, which is found everywhere, even in the most slum-infested areas, but to real countryside birds, such as blackbird and thrush, starling, wood-pigeon, kestrel, black-headed and common gulls, and many species of duck. Those confiding duck of St. James's Park may be visitors from distant lands. A ring on its leg identified a tufted duck which wintered on the water of St. James's Park. It had been hatched and reared in Novaya Zemlya, two thousand miles to the north-east, in the Arctic.

Each one of us unaided can watch and study birds, but a pair of good binoculars are a help, and good bird books are of course necessary. The approach to bird study can be made through the eye and the ear: the one is the complement of the other.

The song of birds is heard mainly in the spring and early summer of the year, yet there is not a month in the twelve when bird song may not be heard, and it ceases altogether only in days of snow and hard frost, when each bird is striving wholeheartedly to find food sufficient to keep itself alive, and has neither time nor inclination to sing.

Let us start at the New Year. We will suppose that the weather is open, or moderately so, the snowdrops showing white flowers, low on the ground and still unopened, a faint feeling of approaching spring in the air. If we go out into the garden or into the woods we may expect to hear the robin's song in early January. Both robins—cock and hen—sing, but the song of the hen robin is more seldom heard. The robin's song is poured out in a wave—a rush and tumult of liquid notes with a quality of sadness running through them. The wren also sings in January. For so tiny a

For watching distant birds a good field-glass or a good telescope is necessary

bird the wren's song has been described as " shattering ". Watch a wren sing. The singer shakes and quivers, as though scarcely able to bear the torrent of song which it has evoked. Although a winter singer the wren is not really a hardy bird. A friend of mine, who lives in the Perthshire highlands, each spring destroys the old house martins' nests on his house, in order that the sparrows may not commandeer them and nest in them. During one very severe winter, there was prolonged frost and snow from the New Year until well into February. My friend and his wife feed the birds several times each day at a bird table, but the wren does not usually appear at bird tables, for it is particular in its food. As week after week of frost and snow succeeded one another, it was noticed that the wren population were disappearing. The matter was later forgotten, but when the old martins' nests came to be taken down no fewer than five wrens were found dead in one of them. The wee birds, cold and starving, had huddled together for warmth in the cosy nest, and the intense frost had perhaps numbed them there, and the sleep of death had succeeded to the sleep of weariness.

A bird which may be expected to be heard in song before January is over is the missel thrush, sometimes called the storm cock. As its name implies, the storm cock is happy in wild weather. His song is heard when a gale of westerly wind shakes the leafless branches and moans through the canopy of the forest. The missel thrush chooses usually for a singing post the topmost branches of a high tree, from which he flings his song in the teeth of the storm. The song thrush sings steadily and evenly; the missel thrush sings in bursts of song, each burst, consisting of a dozen notes or less, poured out with passionate strength; a brief pause, and the song is repeated in an almost similar form. The missel thrush is the largest British song bird.

In places the song thrush sings throughout the winter, but the winter song is usually that of young birds, tuning themselves in. It is late in January before the song thrush sings his full sweet song. The song thrush's notes are usually calm and serene. You will recall the immortal lines of Robert Browning:

> That's the wise thrush; he sings each song twice over
> Lest you should think he never could recapture
> The first fine careless rapture!

Of the Hebridean song thrush, which sings in the treeless Western Isles, a friend of mine, a bird-lover, wrote the following notes on hearing for the first time, on the north-west wing of the Isle of Skye, the song of a Hebridean thrush:

" A Hebridean song thrush sang every evening on the chimney stack above my room. One glorious evening at midsummer he sang (by Single Summer Time) until almost midnight, gazing (so it seemed) over the sea on to the long line of the Outer Hebrides, and on the gorgeous colouring of the sky after a sunset which, without darkness, would soon change to sunrise. Sometimes he would cease his song, and remain for a time quite still, then again lift his voice in adoration."

The thrush is a mimic, although not so finished a mimic as the starling, which sings under favourable conditions throughout January. The starling is not a great singer, yet he is a great and unrivalled mimic. There was some space of late devoted in the press to a tame starling in the Thames valley, which was able to talk. That is not surprising, and I should say that a tame starling could be taught to speak in human language more easily than a parrot. The beautiful song of the curlew is often imitated with much skill by the starling, and in the Outer Hebrides I have heard a starling give a perfect imitation of the call of a whimbrel, in early May, when these birds were migrating northward over the Hebrides.

In January, sometimes even before it, the song of the dipper or water ousel may be heard. The dipper haunts the clear, fast-flowing burns and rivers of Wales, the north of England and Scotland. The dipper's song is subdued, musical and long-sustained; it might almost be likened to the song of the stream itself.

In February the chaffinch breaks his silence. His cheery song has been likened by a friend of mine to the words: " You-silly-little-bird I'm-going-to-BEAT you!" The chaffinches in each district in Britain vary slightly, but unmistakably in their song. When a boy, I used to note the differences in their song along the valley of the Aberdeenshire Dee. The chaffinches of Banchory had a different pattern of song from the chaffinches of Aboyne; those of Aboyne were unmistakable from those at Ballater, and at Braemar, near the head of the valley, one heard yet another pattern of chaffinch song. In February, when the chaffinch begins to sing, his song is imperfect, and ends when only three-quarters complete. Warde Fowler, in one of his books, compares the song of the chaffinch to a bowler running with fast steps up to the wicket, and with an overhand turn of the arm delivering the ball; he remarks that when the chaffinch begins to sing he reaches the wicket, but is unable to " deliver the ball ".

In February, usually near the end of the month, the blackbird sings. The song of the blackbird, which is said to be the most numerous bird in Britain, exceeding even the house sparrow in numbers, is one of the most beautiful bird songs. It is a liquid, flute-like song, and a phrase which the bird fancies may be repeated time after time. The song is not measured and steadily delivered like the thrush's song. A few liquid notes are sung, there is a pause, and the notes, or perhaps different phrases, follow. The blackbird's song is nearer in construction to the song of the missel thrush than to the song thrush. The blackbird begins to sing comparatively late in the season of bird song and ends early. It is rare to hear a blackbird sing in the country in July. In a town, for some reason, the song continues later, and is heard habitually to the middle, and sometimes to the end, of July.

Another February singer is the skylark. This is a unique singer among birds. The songster mounts on rapidly driven wings against the breeze, higher and higher, becoming smaller and smaller, until at last he is lost to sight in the deep blue heights of the sky. Unseen the singer pours earthward his flood of music; the notes fall in a torrent of rapture, then, after a time, the singer himself is seen, in full song, slowly descending. The last few yards of the descent are made more quickly; the flight is altered so that the bird may see that no enemies are near. In the Western Isles the skylark arrives in February, replacing those of his race which have wintered here, and which now return toward the north-east, some as far as Siberia. In the Western Isles, or Hebrides, the skylark is named the Virgin Mary's Linnet.

The great poets have written of the skylark's song:

> Higher and higher from the cloud thou springest,
> Like a cloud of fire;
> The blue deep thou wingest,
> And singing still dost soar, and soaring
> Ever singest.

Wordsworth wrote of the skylark's song the immortal line

> A privacy of glorious light is thine.

A more humble song is the yellow hammer's, also heard in February. It has been likened to the words, " Little-bit-of-bread-and-no-cheese ", the singer dwelling lovingly on the word " cheese ". Like the chaffinch the yellow hammer has difficulty in finishing his song in the early part of the singing season, before he has, so to speak, thoroughly " tuned up ".

To my mind the curlew, who begins his song in March, has a charm of singing all his own. I should not perhaps refer to the singer as " he ", for both male and female birds sing. The trilling whistle, uttered faster and faster as the singer soars on tremulous wings or glides aerily to earth, has in it a quality of beauty and sadness found in the song of no other bird. My wife and I have lived for most of our lives in curlew-haunted country, and I recall, during the First World War, when I was stationed far from the singing haunts of curlews, we used to go by train and then on push bicycles to a high-lying moor in March and April, where we could be sure of hearing the curlew's song, and in hearing it recapture some of the beauty of earlier days.

By sitting quite still and silent it is often possible to watch birds at close quarters. Movement and sound betrays the watcher and scares the birds.

Another moorland bird, the small and inconspicuously plumaged meadow pipit—called in Scotland the heather lintie—sings in March. Like the skylark, he climbs into the air, but only a little way, and then, still singing, descends to earth like a tiny parachute.

April sees the return of the warblers—small and delicate birds which have wintered far south of Britain. The chiff-chaff indeed is often with us before the end of March, but it is April before the willow warbler arrives. It is a red-letter day in the life of the bird-lover when he or she hears the first willow warbler in song. A small and delicate song it is, and running through it is a quality of sadness and humility. I have listened to it after an early May snow-storm—no uncommon thing in the Highlands—and have heard these mournful, tuneful cadences of song proceeding from birch trees, snow laden and pendulous with that white, delicate covering. A sturdy blackbird, as he alighted to sing, shook the snow from the trees, yet the willow warblers were so delicate that they scarcely disturbed it. Lord Grey of Fallodon, in his book, *The Charm of Birds*, describes the willow warbler's song as a " succession of slender and delicate notes, forming a completed sentence, which is repeated again and again at short intervals ". He says, truly, that the song is entirely without any note of bravado, exultation, or challenge, such as is suggested by many other songs.

The wood warbler is less common than the willow warbler. The song has an elfin quality; it consists of a shivering and quivering succession of notes that are almost an ecstasy. This is usually preceded by a clear, gentle whistle, oft-repeated.

Blackbird and garden warbler, sedge warbler, reed warbler and others, arrive and sing in April, and the common and lesser whitethroat are also heard during this month; the excited, scolding song of the common whitethroat is often heard from roadside hedges.

It is late in April when the king of British songsters tunes and sings—the nightingale. This is usually a secretive bird, but a friend wrote to me to say that a pair of nightingales often fed on his lawn, and when their family were grown they accompanied them, looking like very large robins. The nightingale, like the robin, sees well in twilight, and its song may be heard throughout the night. The song of the nightingale is a repetition of one set of notes, followed by a pause, and then by a succession of other notes, which may resemble the earlier ones or be entirely different. It is sung by moonlight, above a fragrant carpet of wild hyacinths and among the young bursting leaves. You will remember Keats' " Ode to the Nightingale ", and how in immortal words he wrote that the nightingale's song was the same which

> Oft-times hath
> Charm'd magic casements, opening on the foam,
> Of perilous seas in faery lands forlorn.

(In his original MS. Keats wrote " keelless seas "; he later deleted " keelless ", and in its place wrote " perilous ".)

The cuckoo, too, arrives in April. Its song is simple, yet it adds a great charm to the countryside; the soft, double note, tirelessly repeated, seems like the voice of the spirit of spring as she moves northward and awakens the sleeping earth to energy.

I have touched lightly on bird song. I might write more—of the song of the oyster-catcher beside some Highland river at midnight; of the wonderful song, rarely heard, of the elusive greenshank, when the singer pours out a succession of flute-like calls when flying high backwards and forwards overhead. There are few birds which have no song, and it is a delight to him or her, who loves nature and is eager to know these songs, to search out the singers in wood and field, moor and mountain. Lord Grey of Fallodon once told me that he had wished especially to hear the song of the greenshank, but had never heard it. I think, so seldom does the greenshank sing, one must live near greenshank country in order to hear that song.

The best way to learn the ways of the birds that are with us in spring is by listening to their song. But there are birds—for instance, the swallow tribe—which can be identified and recognized by their flight rather than by their song, although our barn-swallow has a charming, warbling song.

There are four swallow-like birds in this country, and it is surprising how few people know one species from another. Let us begin with the largest of them, the swift. It is true that the swift does not really belong to the swallow family, but is nearer to the nightjar, yet its associations are rather with the swallows.

The swift is a dark, sickle-winged bird, tireless in the air. Town dwellers, as well as those who live in villages and in the country, know the swift. I have seen many swifts flying above the streets and houses of Edinburgh and Glasgow, and it is common on the outskirts of London, though not above the city itself. The swift is exceptional, if not unique, among birds in that it drives its wings alternately. This is so remarkable a fact that it has been doubted by some observers, but I believe is well authenticated. In summer warmth, swifts from the low ground fly up to hawk insects above the highest Scottish hills. In June, 1945, when on Ben Wyvis at a height of more than 3000 feet above the sea, I saw a gathering of swifts fly backward and forward above the sun-heated slopes, fly-catching. About the same time, a correspondent told me that he had been watching swifts above the summit of Cairngorm, 4084 feet above the distant sea. Swifts nest in old steeples, in crannies beneath the eaves (always out of sight), in houses. On

SOME BIRDS BRITISH

1. Chaffinch. 2. Kingfisher. 3. Bullfinch. 4. Greenfinch. 5. Song Thrush. 6. Goldfinch. 7. Great Tit. 8. Blue Tit. 9. Yellow Hammer. 10. Ring Dove. 11. Jay. 12. Green Woodpecker. 13. Linnet. 14. Cuckoo. 15. Green Plover. 16. Barn Owl. 17. Pied Wagtail. 18. Sparrow Hawk.

a fine summer evening a company of swifts may fly backwards and forwards past their nesting sites, at tremendous speed, screaming in wild abandon as they fly through the dusk. A swift never deliberately alights on the ground; if it should strike wire netting and fall to earth its legs are so short that it may find it impossible to rise, and I have found one in this plight in the grass. There it crouched, cold and miserable, and undoubtedly would have died had I not taken it into the kitchen, where it recovered in the warmth. I then carried it outside, and threw it into the air, when it flew happily away. The swift drinks, gathers nesting materials, even mates, in the air.

Swallow, house martin, and sand martin—all are smaller than the swift. The sand martin is the least of the three, and is brown on the back. It nests in holes which it digs in gravel banks. The swallow and the house martin nest in, or on, human habitations. The swallow may be known by its long, deeply forked tail, and its red chin and throat. The house martin is a dark-blue bird, with white at the tail base. People often speak about swallows nesting beneath the eaves of a house. They confuse the house martin with the swallow; the swallow nests *inside* outbuildings such as cart sheds, cow byres, and the like. Its nest is small: it is made of mud but is *open at the top*. The house martin builds a much larger nest of mud, beneath the eaves of a house; the narrow entrance is near the top, but permits only just sufficient room for the bird to fly in and out. The enemy of the house martin is the house sparrow, which often takes possession of the house martin's nest when it is finished. It has been said that on occasion the house martin will wall in the opening after the hen sparrow has begun to sit, thus imprisoning her so that she dies of starvation.

My space is nearly filled, and I have written nothing of the birds of prey—the lordly golden eagle, grandest of British birds, the fierce peregrine, the mouse-eating kestrel, the ruthless sparrow hawk and merlin, the hobby, so fast that he is able to catch swifts on the wing. Nor have I mentioned the great army of birds which arrive in Britain at the onset of autumn—the tribe of the whooper and Bewick's swans, the barnacle geese from Greenland and Spitsbergen, the white-fronted geese from Iceland, and smaller brent geese from Novaya Zemlya. Nor have I described the waders from the far north—the knot which circle above an estuary with great wariness, flying, turning and diving through the air as one bird, the gnomish dunlin, the white-breasted sanderling, the godwits and grey plover, the great white glaucous gull from the Arctic, the merciless greater black back, the sharp-winged black-headed gull. Of the duck, too, I have said nothing—the widgeon which fly whistling through the dusk, the golden-eyed and tufted ducks, expert divers both of them, the small and jaunty long-tailed ducks, scoters, smews and goosanders, pochards, pintails, and many others.

Coward's books on birds and the *Practical Handbook of British Birds* will fully describe anything I have omitted.

My last few remarks must be on bird-nesting. Many girls go through a phase of desiring to collect the eggs of as many species of birds as possible. Egg collecting in moderation does no harm; what is harmful is the desire to acquire the eggs of rare birds, and to possess oneself of as many clutches of eggs of the same species as is possible. The desire to collect birds' eggs should be changed as quickly as possible into the desire to study birds at the nest; to photograph them at home. This will give more lasting happiness and profit than the finest collection of eggs. When the nest is found and the eggs are taken the chapter of knowledge is ended; when the nest is found and the hatching and youthful days of the young birds are studied, and the ways of their parents, knowledge is increased without doing harm to the birds. Especially remember rare birds. We have as a nation certain rare and beautiful birds. Through shooting and egg collecting we have lost the osprey and the sea eagle; let us see to it that we have not the shame of exterminating other rare birds which still live in these islands. Some of these rare birds are the golden eagle, the hobby, the dotterel, and, farther to the south-east, the Dartford warbler.

Many birds make nests of great beauty. The nest of the long-tailed tit is a work of art, and may take many weeks to complete. In one nest of a pair of long-tailed tits 1776 feathers were counted. Think of that; the birds—for I think it has been proved that both cock and hen help at the building of the domed nest—must have made 1776 visits with feathers alone. They must have flown several hundred miles. No wonder that the long-tailed tit's nest takes weeks, sometimes months, to complete. What a contrast to the nest-making of the guillemot, or the fulmar! The guillemot lays her large pear-shaped egg on the bare rock; the fulmar scrapes out a shallow depression on a ledge of the cliff. Yet all ocean birds are not so casual. The gannet, for example, makes a nest of considerable size, and brings to it strange articles. The gannets of the Bass Rock, nesting near the classic golf links of North Berwick, sometimes take golf balls to their nests. But it is in land birds, and chiefly in the smaller land birds, that the true art of nest-building is found. The chaffinch's nest is a model of neatness. It is built in a tree or bush, and so well does it harmonize with its surroundings that it is hard to see; each small piece of lichen and bark is placed delicately yet firmly in position. The willow warbler, chiff-chaff, and wood warbler make domed nests. The willow warbler and the chiff-chaff both line their nests deeply with feathers, but the wood warbler

For watching nesting birds a hide made of sacking and poles is useful and often necessary.
The hide should be placed at a distance from the nest in the beginning, then, day by day,
brought gradually nearer the nest.

carries no feathers in the nest. This is perhaps strange, yet not more strange than the difference in the nests of song thrush and blackbird. The blackbird is content with a grass-lined nest; the song thrush, after reaching this stage of completion, adds a layer of mud. It might be thought that it would be less comfortable to brood one's eggs on a layer of hard, dried earth than on a bed of soft grasses. Why, then, add the layer of mud? The bird that builds the largest nest is the golden eagle. The eagle's nest is called an eyrie. A pair of eagles may use the same tree, or rock, for many years. I have known one nest for forty years. It is on an old pine tree, and is now a full fifteen feet deep. Think of this: a man six feet high, standing at the base of the nest, would be unable, by nine feet, to look into it.

Some birds nest on the ground with no shelter or protection; the eggs of these birds are usually protectively coloured, so that they can be seen with difficulty. The oyster-catcher's eggs are like the shingle bed on which they rest; the eggs of the curlew resemble the moorland; the eggs of the terns the sand.

The earliest birds to nest are the crossbill and the heron, which lay in early February. In some districts the raven is as early a nester as the heron; in others he is a few days later. The latest birds to nest are the hobby, the nightjar, and the stormy petrel. The stormy petrel, a bird scarcely larger than a swallow, does not, in the Hebrides, lay her one white glossy egg until July, and I have seen the young still in the nest in November.

The joy of birds, the charm of birds, the beauty of birds; all these things can be seen and felt by the bird-lover, who, wherever he or she may be, is never lonely.

CAMPING

Camping is most definitely an adventure, and in our innermost hearts, lurking under the conventional self which the world sees, there is this longing for adventure. To go off on our own, to stand or fall by our own efforts, and to be responsible to ourselves for ourselves, gives us the feeling that the world is our plaything, and we will play with it, not it with us.

Not only does camping give us a better understanding of, and a greater sympathy with, the country, but we ourselves are strengthened both in health and character. There is a definite satisfaction in being able to live comfortably when there is only a strip of canvas between you and the downpour.

So many people think that to camp or hike means giving up a comfortable way of living for one of acute discomfort, or at best something akin to the Spartan life. It is only the bad camper who is uncomfortable.

If we wish to be good campers, and become better ones, we must

You don't throw your hand in on wet mornings

foster and develop our skill and resourcefulness, must enlarge our powers so that we can meet the challenges of difficulties and enjoy overcoming them. That may sound pretty grim if you have never camped, but really all that it means is that if it is a wet morning and the fire will not light, you won't throw in your hand and go off and buy breakfast in the hotel; that would be a weak thing to do.

If you have the desire to camp then there is almost bound to be a touch of humour in your make-up. One can never have too great a sense of humour, in its true meaning, and especially the ability to laugh at oneself.

Let me make it clear that when I speak of camping I mean every type of outdoor holiday: hiking, cycling, Youth Hostel, as well as living in a tent.

When camping, do try to pull your weight, do not shirk the not so pleasant jobs, but take your turn at them and do them willingly and cheerfully. After all, there are very few of these unpleasant jobs to be done, and a second-rate person, who will not take her share, can spoil the whole holiday. It is better not to take any second-rate people with you on holiday, or, if you do, make up your mind before the holiday starts how you are going to cope with them. For it is no use continually nagging at them; that would make life unbearable for all; you must gently persuade them into doing their share of the work.

Remember that when camping one is living in a very small intimate group, and therefore there must be first-class teamwork, a willingness to give and take. So choose your companions with great care, for the chances are that the holiday will either make, cement, or break friendships. You see, living so close together people get to know each other very well, and it is no longer possible to hide the flaws in our character. But those friendships which are made at camp are grand.

Having decided on an outdoor holiday, the next thing is to choose what form the holiday is going to take. If the decision is hostelling, then you must become a member of the Youth Hostels Association, who will supply membership handbooks of hostels and all other information. The London address is The Youth Hostels Association, 29 John Adam St., London, W.C.2., membership subscription for those over 21 is 10s. 6d., 16 to 21 years of age, 5s. 6d., and for those under 16 years of age, 2s. 6d. In Scotland, application should be made to The Scottish Youth Hostels Association, 108 Renfield St., Glasgow, C.2, and membership subscription for those over 21 is 10s., 16 to 21 years of age, 5s., under 16 years of age, 2s. The subscriptions for both associations are payable on the 1st of January of each year.

CHOOSING A SITE

When hostelling it is not necessary to go over the route beforehand, nor is that necessary if hiking and pitching a tent each night, as one can make-do with an inferior site when it is only for the one night. But for an indoor or canvas camp, where the same site is going to be used for a week or ten days, then it must be inspected before booking to make sure it is suitable.

We once booked a site without having seen it; never again! The site was described in such glowing terms—it had everything that the heart of a camper could desire—that our vaunted camping senses were completely smothered. Then came the day, and the site— and what a sight! It took all our humour to save the situation, for it proved to be all that a site should not be. For one thing, it had a very bad position, and we knew that if it rained we were in for a bad time. It did rain, and continued to rain for most of the fort-

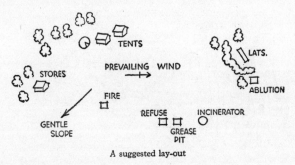

A suggested lay-out

night. Within twenty-four hours that super-site was mud, and the air was being rent with agonized cries as people executed war dances in an effort to keep upright; rarely was the war dance of any avail. Our ingenuity was stretched to the full in an effort to keep our bedding, clothes, and ourselves dry. Still, even that camp was enjoyed.

When looking at a site remember that the holiday is still two or three months ahead, that things will look different then; so make sure that the ground is clean, that you will not come back in the summer to find that you have to cleave your way through nettles and thistles. Make sure that the site is well drained, sheltered from the prevailing wind, near a supply of wood, not too far away from a source of food supply—that is very important for one's appetite is always colossal at camp—and that there is plenty of washing and drinking water near; water is such a heavy, uncontrollable thing to carry.

Be really fussy about the drinking water, actually " old-maidish " about it, because if it is not pure it can cause such a lot of trouble, and painful trouble at that. Try to draw it from a main water tap and most definitely not from a river or burn; there is no saying what dead sheep, &c., may be lying farther up the stream, and running water does not purify itself. That is not a tall story, but a fact. So, if in the slightest doubt about the purity of the water, boil it before using for cooking or drinking.

Water gathers in the hollows or depressions of a field, so never pitch a tent on these spots, because even if, in wet weather, the water does not get to the stage of being a young lake, it is much

Camp near your water supply

better to be about half-way up a gentle slope. Not too steep a slope, or you will either slide out of bed or have water in the head. Ground that is covered with moss or tussocks of coarse grass will probably flood, or at least be very damp, in heavy rain.

Try to have some protection from the prevailing wind, trees or bushes, if possible. These not only give protection, but are a convenient supply of wood and also give cover for the latrines and wash places. The trees will show the prevailing wind as their branches are bent over to leeward, that is, they will be bent over in the opposite direction from which the prevailing wind blows. Of course, there is no guarantee that the wind will be in that direction during the period of the camp. One would almost think that the prevailing wind has only to see a tent being pitched and it becomes perverse and blows in the opposite direction.

If you are camping in a hut, make sure it is clean, that there is no dampness, and that it is in good condition. You do not wish to disappear through the floor and then be charged with the repair, when in reality the floor boards were full of dry-rot and should have been repaired long ago. Go over the hut with the owner the day you arrive, and give him a note of anything that is broken or cracked, and again the day you leave, so that if you have damaged anything you can arrange to pay for the repair, and you do not run the risk of being charged with repairs for which you were not responsible. Check up on the mouse holes. If there are any, lay plans as to how you are going to deal with the mice. I leave that to your

own imagination, but something must be done, either traps or a borrowed cat, or the mice will get in among the food, and that most definitely will not do. They may even get into the beds, and it is a most startling sensation to feel some unknown monster moving at the foot of your bed. The same, only more so, applies to rats. It is almost impossible to avoid mice or rats near a farm; the only hope is that there will be enough food at the steading to keep them there. The snag is that people will not admit that the species is about, and one is left to discover the fact for oneself when the larder door is opened and out dashes a huge mouse. On such occasions the mice are never small.

Go over the hut with the owner

If the hut has indoor sanitation and washing arrangements, try the flushes in the lavatory two or three times to make sure they are working. See that the drains are in order; run the taps and note how quickly the water runs away. You can but hope that all will be well during the period of the camp. Before using the drinking water turn on the taps and allow the water to run for at least ten minutes, in order to run off the water lying in the pipes.

It is wiser not to share the site with sheep, cattle or horses, as their curiosity is so easily aroused; they will come sniffing round the tents, trip on the guy ropes, or take a dainty nibble at the dish cloths, or any other washing hanging up. At night sheep have a fondness for snuggling against the tent brailing, and it is rather disconcerting to be wakened during the night by what feels like a young elephant pushing at one's back. Besides, the animals make a nasty mess of the field—though in the absence of wood I have followed Kipling and made a grand fire of dry cow " pancakes ". Make sure that they are quite dry otherwise they are no use.

Remember to ask permission to lift turf, gather wood, and light fires. Find out about private ground, game preserves, young plantations, &c., remembering that all campers are judged by the individual camper.

When planning the lay-out of the camp, start from the windward

Cows are inquisitive

side with either tents or huts, then, in the following order: store tent, cooking fire, refuse pit, grease pit, incinerator, wash places and latrines. This means that the wind is blowing from the tents towards the latrines. Should there be a burn, " make camp " so that the burn flows past the camp before it comes to the latrines.

Try to choose a nice flat piece of ground on which to pitch the tent. The knobbly bits can be flattened, and a small hollow made for your hip, with a mallet. It is usually the small knobbles not noticed through the day which at night grow into mountains. Do not pitch the tent under trees, as the ground there is invariably damp and the drips from the trees rot the tent canvas. There is also just the chance that lightning or a rotten branch might strike the tent, ripping it and knocking out the occupants, which is not a very pleasant prospect.

CHOICE OF TENTS

Opinion differs as to whether a ridge or bell tent is best for using as a store tent. Personally my vote goes to the ridge, as it usually has a door at either end, which means that one end can be closed, according to which way the wind and/or rain is coming. Also, all the available space can be used, where in the bell tent space is lost because of the slope of the walls. Whichever is used do not have it in line with the fire, as, when the wind changes round, the smoke and sparks will be blown on to and into the tent, either setting it on fire or kippering the contents and occupants.

Make a wood-pile on the opposite side of the fire to the store tent. Next comes the refuse pit, grease pit and incinerator. These should be in line with the wood-pile. The general idea is that the wind reaches them after it has passed over the store tent and cooking fire, also people are not so apt to fall into them when they are out of the direct line of the fire. It is quite a good notion to rope them off as a safety measure.

Now the tent or tents: pitch them on a line running at right angles to the store tent and not nearer than fifteen yards to the fire. Keep the door away from the prevailing wind, otherwise, in wet weather, the rain will come straight in and everything will be soaked.

Last of all come the wash places and latrines, which, if possible, should be hidden because, although they are on the leeward side of the camp, being a different shape from the tents they seem to catch the eye first. So make them as inconspicuous as possible. Do not have them too far away; 50 to 100 yards from the tents is enough.

A ridge tent is very much lighter to handle than a bell, and is more easily ventilated as it has a door at either end, which means that both can be opened in good weather, and in rain one can be opened with no danger of draughts. In a bell there are only three ventilators in the apex, which do not give sufficient ventilation, so the only way to air the tent is to keep the door wide open. This is all right in good weather, but when it is wet it means that a large part of the " floor " becomes sodden. If the door is closed and the brailing raised on the leeward side, one is almost blown up the tent pole by the draught. There is this to be said for a bell, that it stands up to wind better than any other type of tent. I remember, after a stormy night, creeping out to make the breakfast, and beholding our stores being battered by the wind and the rain. The tent, which was a ridge, had been blown far, far away. We eventually retrieved it, not too much the worse of its wandering.

Four, or at a pinch, five, people can live in a bell. That may not seem many, but remember the question of ventilation, which is important; also there is all the gear to be stowed away, and some floor space must be left, otherwise you will be playing hop, skip and jump round the tent.

Of course a bell is far too heavy to carry for hiking. The cost of a bell tent is round about £10, but varies according to quality.

A ridge, 9 feet long by 6 feet wide, will sleep four people comfortably, and that size costs anything from about £6 upwards, according to quality. The winter is the best time to buy a second-hand tent, as at that time the demand is small and therefore the prices are lower. You may be lucky to pick one up fairly cheap, but before you close the deal have the tent pitched so that you can go over it and really see what you are buying.

There are various reliable firms from whom second-hand tents may be bought, or tents hired. These firms advertise in all the leading newspapers. Hiring charges for tents are usually about 15s. per week for bells, and 21s. per week for ridges; these prices vary according to the prices of new tents.

PITCHING A BELL TENT

Pitching a bell tent—that is, putting it up—can be done by six people. It is too heavy for fewer than four, and it is silly to try to

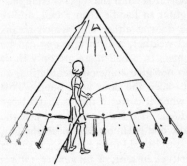

Bell tent secured with storm rope

do the job with less than that number, as someone may strain herself badly.

Take the tent, mallet and pegs out of the bag.

Choose the piece of ground on which the tent is going to stand, and drive in a peg, not too deeply, because it has to come out once the tent is pitched, on the spot where the base of the tent pole will rest when the tent is raised. Decide which way the tent door is going to face, take

the pole and lay it against the centre peg so that the opposite end rests on the spot where the tent door is going to be, drive in a peg at that end of the pole. Now place the pole on the other side of the centre peg, so that the pole and the door peg are in a straight line, again drive in a peg at the end of the pole. Repeat the performance twice more so that the line joining these last two pegs crosses the first line at right angles.

Unroll the tent, so that it is in the form of a triangle, the door on top, the foot of the triangle along the line of the centre peg, with the apex pointing to the peg opposite the door peg. See that the ventilation hoops are open, as sometimes they get bent in packing, and once the tent is pitched nothing can be done about them, short of lowering the tent. The door should be laced across.

The main guys, counting from the door by the left, are the first,

Angle of tent pegs

sixth and thirteenth, and by the right, the second, seventh and thirteenth. Find and undo these guys, slip the sixth on the left and the seventh on the right—that is, the two side guys—over the side pegs, leaving the rope at full length.

Unhook the door brailing, and get the strongest person of the party to act as poleman. Slip the pole into the tent, making sure that the head of the pole fits into the grommet, which is the circle of rope at the apex—it can be reached through the ventilators—and

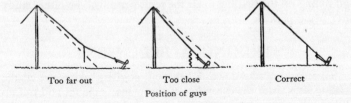

Too far out   Too close   Correct

Position of guys

see that the butt of the pole is placed against the centre peg so that it will give leverage when the pole is being raised.

There should be two people on the side guys, one to each guy, and one person with the pole. A fourth is needed at the back peg to slip on the thirteenth guy as soon as the tent is raised, and a fifth to slip the first and second guys over the door peg. The person on the thirteenth guy can help the poleman by raising the head of the pole. When the pole is half-way up the thirteenth guy is slipped on, and at the same time the person at the door guys takes the strain; the door guys are slipped on when the pole is perpendicular. Tighten the four guys and the tent will stand, but should there be a strong wind hastily drive in extra pegs, one between each of the four main guys.

Having got the tent pitched, hook the door brailing across; undo the remaining guy ropes, and peg them down, starting with the two on either side of the back peg, working round both sides of the tent simultaneously towards the door peg, which can then be removed;

Properly pitched

the centre peg can also be removed. See that the tent seam and the guy rope are in a straight line. Working in this way there is no chance of the door being strained and unable to close properly, also it spreads the tension evenly over the canvas.

Peg down the tent walls, making sure that they are perpendicular to keep them dry, and that the sod cloth is on the inside. Check and make sure that the pole is really perpendicular, that the guys are all of the same tautness, not only for the sake of the appearance of the tent, but that there may be no undue strain on any one part of the canvas. The runner of the guy should be one-third of the way up the rope.

Finish off by undoing the door brailing, opening the door wide, and rolling up the brailing to air the tent, which will be rather stuffy after being packed.

STRIKING A BELL TENT

To strike, or take down, a bell tent, start by taking out all the brailing pegs, with the exception of the mains; take off and roll up all the other guys, taking out each peg as the guy is removed. As in pitching, there is one person as poleman, and another to each of the main guys. The back guy is released, and the canvas pushed in towards the pole, while the people at the side and front guys release their guys and act as anchors. As the poleman lowers the pole towards the back guy, the " anchors " ease off gradually till the tent is lying on the ground once more in the shape of a triangle, with the door uppermost. Whoever is on the back guy has to be pretty nippy to keep out of the way of the pole as it is being lowered. But please do not throw the tent on the ground as the pole may rip the apex. Withdraw the pole, roll up the main guys, remove, scrape and stack the pegs so that they will dry.

The tent door should be in the centre of the triangle; smooth away all creases, and fold back the ventilators. Fold over the apex of the tent till it comes down to the top of the door, fold the sides over to within a few inches of the centre, fold again, lift one side over on top of the other, and roll tightly from the top downwards. Take a firm hold of the tent, or it will work loose, raise one end slightly and draw on the tent bag, when it is half-way on a few good shakes will finish the job. Lay the mallet and pegs on top and lace the bag.

TO PITCH A RIDGE TENT

Three or more people are required to pitch a ridge tent. Choose the direction in which you wish the tent to stand, lay the ridge pole on the ground in that direction, and put in a door peg at either end. Lay the tent on the ground with the bottom edge along the ridge pole. Now take the ridge pole and slip it into place inside the top

Securing four main guys of ridge tent

of the tent, next fit the spike of the door poles into the holes in the ridge pole and roof. The butt of the door poles should be against the door pegs.

Drive in the four main guy pegs, two at each end, at an angle of 45° from the door pegs and about four paces distant from each other and the door pegs.

To avoid damaging the ridge pole or spikes, raise both door poles at the same time. When the poles are perpendicular slip on the four main guys and tighten them evenly, making sure that the door poles are in line with each other, and that they are really perpendicular, otherwise the strain will not be evenly spread over the canvas. The tent will now stand.

Close the door and put in the door brailing peg. Beginning on the windward side, otherwise the tent may blow away, peg out the four corner guys, then the other guys, and lastly put in the brailing pegs.

The main guys are thicker than the others, and are either attached to the roof of the tent or are slipped over the spike of the door pole. If the corner guys are single, peg them out diagonally from the end

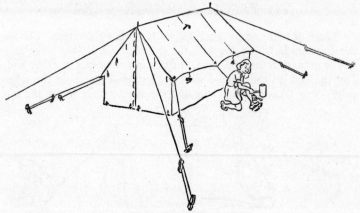

Securing intermediate guys

of the tent. Once the tent is pitched the mains on the same side may be crossed, and so leave the doorway free; this also helps to prevent a jointed ridge pole coming apart.

If the tent is properly pitched, there will be no sagging or wrinkles, it is all a matter of putting the pegs in the proper place.

To strike a ridge tent simply reverse the pitching process. When packing it begin by folding the door over, and continue as for a bell.

When a peg is being driven in, hold it in the hand to steady it at an angle of 25° to the ground. A few knocks with the mallet will give it a start, then place the foot which is farthest from the mallet hand against the peg to act as a guide, and a few more knocks are all that is required. Never knock a peg sideways when taking it out, as this is apt to break it. To loosen, work the peg " fore and aft ", then give a good pull following the line of the peg.

Sometimes bell tents are inadvertently given the wrong length of guy ropes and pole; if the guys are too short and the pole too long it takes a Hercules to raise the tent, as the guys will be at their fullest long before the tent is raised, so move the pegs nearer the centre. If the pole is too short raise it on a good solid flat stone.

If possible do not strike and pack a tent when it is damp or wet. Even if it is going to be packed away only for a short period, first see that it is thoroughly dry, paying special attention to the double pieces, mildew and rot set in so very quickly. If at all possible, do not store it in a bag but hang it out in a loft or other dry place. If it has to be stored in a bag keep the bag off the floor so that the air can get about it and the mice cannot.

Never walk on a tent when it is lying on the ground, and in wet weather, if by mistake you come against the wet canvas, put your finger on the spot and draw it down the canvas to the top of the tent wall. The water, which would otherwise drip down, will follow the course you have traced for it. Keep kit and bedding away from the tent walls, as dampness will come through if they are touched.

COPING WITH WIND AND RAIN

In rain and at night, when there is always dew, slacken the guys, as moisture shrinks the guy rope, and if it is not slackened it will snap. To save someone going out during a very wet night, when the guys have tightened more than usual, make a small hole beside the foot of the tent pole, into which the pole may be slipped, and this will automatically slacken all the guys. One night I was wakened by very heavy rain drumming on the tent. Being afraid that the guys would snap, and not having made an emergency pole hole, I felt around in the darkness for my waterproof, found it, pulled it on, and struggled into my wellingtons. Then panic! Something was moving under my bare instep. All consideration of the others vanished, and yelling like an Indian brave on a scalping expedition, I encouraged all and sundry to come to my aid. When the wellington was at last removed, the Something proved to be a harmless beetle, which no doubt was in a greater panic than I. Moral, have that emergency hole ready, and always shake boots, shoes, &c., before putting them on. It is amazing how one's sense of proportion goes all haywire during the hours of darkness.

Should there be rain and a strong wind at the same time, cope with the wind by seeing that all the pegs are in firmly, and keep the brailing down, ease off the guys as they shrink, keeping the canvas taut.

Examine the pole every day to see that it is straight. It is amazing

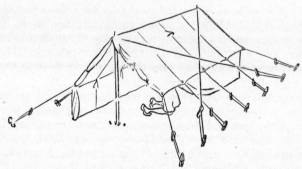

The tent storm set

how drunken it can become overnight, and it must be straight, even if it involves the trouble of slackening and tightening different guys to get it so. Never put nails in the pole or any type of pin in the canvas. All these things help to shorten the life of a tent. The bottom half of a jointed pole is usually the one with the iron socket.

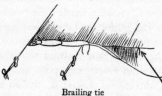

Brailing tie

Sometimes there is difficulty in getting the two parts to fit, in which case if the parts are metal apply some grease; if wooden, blacklead them.

In wet weather the brailing on the leeward side can be looped up on to the inside brailing ties. There is a wooden button or rope knot at the top of every guy line, and if the brailing is wet it can be looped up on to them so that the tent may be aired, and the brailing allowed to dry at the same time.

When the entrance to the tent becomes worn, a bell may be swung to a new entrance. Take a firm hold of the pole, loosen all guys, and move them round two or three pegs. The tent will swing round as the guys are moved. The only way to change the position of a ridge doorway is by repitching.

If there is any danger of the pegs not holding they can be encouraged to stay in the ground by laying a bag of earth against the peg on top of the guy rope, or by driving in another peg so that the notch fits over the back of the first peg. To dry pegs after striking a tent, scrape the earth off them, lay two on the ground about six inches apart, place another two on top, also six inches apart, but at right angles to the first ones, repeat till all the pegs are built up on top of each other. The wind will soon dry them.

When a runner of a guy rope will not stay put, but keeps slipping down, make a loop in the rope on the front of the runner, and slip a piece of stick through the loop.

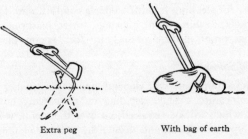

Extra peg   With bag of earth

Danger of pegs not holding

To keep kit and bedding free from dampness raise them off the ground; this also prevents the grass from becoming yellow. Fold blankets in a ground sheet and tie the bundle with a piece of string, lay two pieces of wood, or four flat stones, on the ground, and place the bundle on top. Raise the rest of the kit in the same way. Bedding should be aired daily.

Carelessness is usually the cause of a tent catching fire, but if it is caught in time it can be smothered with a blanket. Should it get a good hold, make sure no one is in the tent, pull out the pole, and the tent will collapse. Throw on water, earth, or stamp on it. If it is impossible to move the pole or get near it, take off the guys and pull the tent over, head to wind, to keep the air out. If oil caused the fire use earth to smother the flames, as water would only spread the burning oil. Strike any other tent to which the fire might spread.

EQUIPMENT

A good deal of thought must be given to the matter of equipment. It is hard to lay down general rules, as the equipment will vary according to climate, size and type of camp; but it will fall under the headings of personal, cooking and general equipment.

Personal kit depends on taste, but a complete change of clothing is essential, and either wellingtons or sandshoes for wet weather. No socks or stockings should be worn with the sandshoes, as it is the body heat drying them that causes colds and other upsets. An extra jersey for sleeping in adds to one's comfort, and do not forget handkerchiefs, washing outfit, pyjamas, towel, hairbrush and comb, mirror, waterproof, electric torch, knife, fork, spoon, plates, &c.

Cooking Equipment.

Cooking equipment will depend upon the number going and the type of camp. When deciding on how many bowls, dixies, pans, &c., which will be required, go over the menu, which should be drawn up beforehand, and decide the number of utensils which will be in use at the same time. Do not burden yourself with too much gear, but on the other hand keep above the safety line so as to avoid the tragedy of having dinner in two parts, because there was no free pan in which to cook the pudding. The pans should not be all the same size, and if possible have aluminium ones as they do not rust or allow the food to burn easily.

Take tins for storing dry groceries. The milk should be kept in a special jug or can which should be scalded daily. Also remember butter muslin for covering food and making into tea bags, dishwashing things, and drying cloths, tin opener, wooden spoons, knives, forks, spoons, plates, &c., frying pan, or if there is a dixie the lid can be used. A marked pint jug is a very useful thing.

General equipment includes tents, groundsheets, screening for latrines and wash places, rope, string, trowel, toilet paper in a tin box to keep it dry, basins, pails, enamel ones for drinking water if it has to be stored, first-aid outfit, axe.

The following can possibly be borrowed near the site: bricks for the fireplace, tin or wire netting to make an incinerator, spade.

The equipment lists can be augmented as necessity and taste

dictate. If any equipment is being hired, place the order in good time; three months' notice is not too long if the camp date falls on a peak holiday period.

As hired dixies and pans are greased for storing make sure they are clean before using them for cooking. All hired or borrowed equipment should be returned in at least as good, if not better, condition than it was received.

Non-stainless knives can be cleaned by working them up and down in the earth, or with sand or wood ash. Wood ash is excellent for cleaning pans, &c. Dry all equipment thoroughly after cleaning, it will save you at a later date having to use " elbow grease " to remove rust.

Ground Sheets.

Treat groundsheets with respect, as otherwise they will cease to fulfil their function. Do not walk or stand.on them; never lay anything hot on them, and if something gets upset over them wipe it off at once. To make sure that a groundsheet is waterproof, hold it up to the light, then any flaw will be apparent. Even the smallest hole should be repaired at once; this can be done by applying a bicycle patch, or if it is a tear, put on a piece of adhesive tape. Never use a groundsheet for carrying wood, or lay one on stony or prickly ground, as it will become punctured and torn. Always lay it rubber side to the ground.

When a groundsheet gets wet hang it up to dry before rolling it up. When rolling several at one time do not place two rubber sides together as they will adhere to each other. It is a wrong idea that one is warmer and drier by having a groundsheet on top of the blankets, because this prevents ventilation, and condensation makes the bedding damp. It may be necessary to lay a groundsheet over the foot of the bed nearest the door in wet weather.

An axe is a necessity in camp, but does not need to be large, provided it is well balanced, sharp, and the head fitting firmly on the handle. When wielding an axe do not let any spectators nearer than two yards, otherwise they may get a black eye from a piece of wood jumping away from the axe. Stand in a position so that, if the wood is missed, the axe will not bury itself in either leg or foot. The edge of the axe is damaged if chopping is done on the ground or on a stone, so use a firm piece of wood as a chopping block. Do not be too fierce; the weight of the falling head will do most of the work, and never attempt to cut through a knot in the wood; it just cannot be done. Refrain from being idiotic enough to fool around with an axe.

Have first-aid kit in camp—enough to cope with minor injuries or accidents; for anything more serious get a doctor. A chemist will supply the articles and give advice on their use.

In camp, with the change of food and living conditions, health habits are sometimes upset. This is important, and must receive attention as the body must get rid of waste products to maintain good health. Should the regular habit not return in two or three days take a tablespoonful of liquid paraffin.

The screening of the wash places and latrines must not be transparent, it can be made of sheeting or hessian. It should be clear of the ground, and high enough to afford shelter to a person when standing upright. The poles require to be longer so that they may be sunk into the ground a little way, and space left at the top to hold the guy lines. The latrine should not be smaller than four feet square with an overlapping door and some method of signifying when it is occupied.

Stake out the length of the trench required; one six feet long by fifteen inches broad and three feet deep will last ten campers for a week: if there are more than ten campers make another cubicle. Remove the turf by cutting it into squares of about one foot, using a spade; ease one edge up, going deep enough to prevent the grass roots from being damaged. Kneel down and take a hold of the edge with one hand; using a knife in the other hand, work the earth away from the turf till the square can be lifted off. Stack the sods earth to earth or grass to grass in a shady spot. When the trench is being dug have the earth thrown to the side opposite the doorway and about a foot away from the lip of the trench.

Slip two guy ropes on the top of the poles; knock the four poles a little way into the ground at a distance of four feet from each other, so that they form a square. After each pole is in the ground peg out the two guy ropes, one parallel with and the other at right angles to the trench. When the four poles are in position run a rope round the top, securing it to each pole in passing. Now take the screening and start by wrapping and securing it round one of the door posts, pass it round the outsides of the other three poles, arriving back at the starting post with enough screening to allow a flap over. Attach the screening by loops of string to the rope running round the top of the poles. The screening of the wash places is the same. A tin of toilet paper and a trowel should be kept in each latrine, and only enough earth to cover should be put into the trench each time. To disinfect the trench, wood ash should be sprinkled on every day, and if flies are bothersome sprinkle a little paraffin round the edge of the trench. A trench should not be opened up again for at least two years.

GREASE AND REFUSE PITS

The grease pit is used by the cooks for the disposal of all used water; dirty greasy water should not be thrown on the ground. To make the pit lift the turf, dig a hole two feet square by two feet deep, loosen the earth on the bottom and sides, half fill the pit with stones. Make a lattice of strong sticks big enough to lay over the hole, lace bracken, brushwood, &c., through the lattice. The greasy water is poured gently over the lattice; do not stand yards away and throw, your aim is not good enough, and the lattice would not stand the strain. The bracken, &c., should be changed every second day, the used bracken being dried and burned in the incinerator.

The incinerator is made by rolling a piece of inch-mesh wire netting into a cylinder, and folding over one end to form a base. Lift two square feet of turf, lay three bricks on the ground to form a triangle, lay another three on top, covering the spaces, then set the incinerator firmly on top. An old oil drum with holes punched in the sides and foot can be used instead of wire netting. Any burnable rubbish is burned in the incinerator, also tins, which are afterwards hammered flat and put into the refuse pit.

The refuse pit can be made the same size as the grease pit, but the size and duration of the camp must be taken into consideration. Only flattened tins, broken jars, and unburnable things should find their way into the refuse pit, which means that there should not be much in it. Each day cover the refuse with earth and a sprinkle of wood ash to disinfect. The pit should be filled in when within ten inches of the surface.

There is always someone near a camp who is grateful for peelings for pigs or poultry. Anything eatable should be put into the pig bucket, but not tea leaves, fruit stones, or inedible fruit skins; they go to the incinerator.

BUILDING THE FIRE

In order to avoid burning the grass round the cooking fire, it is necessary to lift a piece of turf about six feet square. The easiest way to do this is to cut it into four pieces and lift one piece at a time. Lay a double row of six bricks, with a space between each, and a little less than a pan's breadth between the row, so that the prevailing wind will blow down the row; place a second set of bricks on top of the first, so that they cover the spaces. Naturally the length of the fireplace depends on how many pans are going to be over the fire at one time.

The great secret of getting a fire to light quickly is in using the right sticks. Start by making a bed of dry thickish sticks, on top

Building the fire

make a little heap of dry grass, leaves, whin, birch bark, pine or larch needles; round this, building in cone shape, add very thin twigs, then slightly thicker, and so on. See that the layers are self-supporting and not crushing the kindling with their weight. Light the fire from the windward side, so that the wind will act as bellows, and have sufficient wood collected to keep the fire going once it is lit. Should it be necessary to give the fire a bit of encouragement oneself, form the lips as for whistling, blow strongly so that the lips, to retain the shape, have to resist the breath. Listen to the fire, and if there is a roaring sound then the blowing is correct and has found the right spot, if the roaring is absent then instead of the fire being encouraged it is being blown out or the right spot has not been found.

If the wind keeps changing direction when the fire is being encouraged, be ready to get off your mark quickly, otherwise hair, eyebrows and eyelashes are apt to get singed. When a strong wind is blowing, things either take longer to boil or boil over, so to check the wind close the windward end of the fire with either one or two bricks placed on top of each other. Also watch out for flames coming through the spaces between the bricks in case they come in contact with clothing.

The best woods to use for starting a fire are fir, spruce, pine, birch and larch; these burn quickly without giving much heat. Oak, ash and beech are slower to start but give a steady heat and leave glowing ash; they make good cooking fires. Lime and sycamore burn quickly when quite dry, but do not give much heat. The best that can be said of elm is that it makes a good smoke screen. You will, of course, never hew down growing trees or living branches.

A fire should never be left while there is any doubt about it being out. Withdraw the bigger sticks first, rub them together till there is no white ash left, then stack them ready for the next fire. Take a stick and scatter the rest of the fire between the bricks so that it will cool off; but do not be too energetic or some of the fire may land on and burn the grass. Resist the temptation to use water to put out the fire; it certainly puts it out but makes a very wet place for rekindling. When satisfied that the fire is dead, take the top row of bricks and lay them on top of the dead fire; this will help to keep the bed of the fire dry.

Wood can be dried by laying it on the outside of the bricks. Make sure that the morning's kindling will be kept dry overnight, even if it means taking it into the tent. The wood pile should be handy to the fire and should consist of wood chosen for its burning qualities. Have the thin pieces at one end, increasing in size to large bits at the other end. Cover the pile at night or during rain, making sure that no pools of water will collect on the cover, as when the cover is lifted the water has a habit of running on to the wood. It is best to anchor the cover as this keeps it taut and also prevents it from being blown away.

FOOD PREPARATIONS

Food plays an all-important part in camping; one seems to be perpetually hungry. Have definite, regular meal hours. Make out the menus before going to camp, and decide what stores can be bought at camp, and what must be taken.

Try to have a well-balanced but varied diet, using plenty of green vegetables. The best body-building foods are milk, cheese, eggs, meat and fish. Many vegetables such as peas, beans, potatoes, and also bread, help in body-building, but they are not so good as the others. The energy foods which provide fuel for the body are bacon, ham, bread, butter, margarine, cheese, dried fruit, dripping, suet, lard, honey, oatmeal, potatoes, rice, tapioca, sago, sugar. The protective foods which help to protect the body from disease are milk, butter, margarine, cheese, eggs, tinned or fresh herrings and salmon, liver, potatoes, green vegetables and salads, fresh or tinned but not dried fruit, carrots, tomatoes, wholemeal bread.

When making up the menu remember that it is not only the amount of food that matters, but that it is the right food, so see that there is food from each of the groups in the day's menu, and this will give a good balanced diet. Try to have as much variety as possible.

MENUS FOR FOUR PEOPLE

BREAKFAST	LUNCH	SUPPER
Porridge and milk. French toast.	¾ lb. mince. Syboes. Steamed Leicester pudding.	Potatoes and cheese (prepare enough potatoes to do breakfast as well).
Fried potatoes and bacon.	Quick vegetable soup. Steamed fruit pudding.	Fried mince patties (left over mince from day before plus egg, potatoes, parsley).
Toad-in-the-hole. Fried sausage or	Fresh fruit and cream. Cheese leek stew.	from vegetables). Summer salad (made
Cheese and tomato savoury.	Sea pie (peas and beans included).	Shepherd's pie. Bisto gravy (odds and ends bound by a gravy).
Cheese frizzles.	Carrot soup. Steam plum pudding.	Fried lentil cakes.
For cold raw day. Herring. Bacon and egg.	Vegetable soup. Steam suet pudding (6–8 oz. suet pastry, plus cost of fruit).	Cheese pudding.

Quantities for Four People.

Porridge: 2 oz. oatmeal; 1 pint boiling water.

French Toast: 2 thick slices bread; 2 eggs; 1 cup of milk.

Mince and Vegetables: ¾ lb. mince. Buy enough for two days' supply.

Leicester Pudding: Cream 3 oz. fat and 3 oz. sugar. Beat in 1 or 2 eggs, then flour. Steam in greased cups in the soup pot if there is a shortage of pans.

Cheese Potatoes: 6–8 potatoes; 1 oz. fat; 2 oz. grated cheese;

1 gill milk. Cook the potatoes then cream them and add fat and grated cheese.

Vegetable Soup: Make white sauce—1 oz. fat; 1 oz. flour; 1 pint milk. Add vegetables cut finely or grated.

Steamed Fruit Pudding: Suet Pudding: 3 oz. suet; $\frac{1}{2}$ lb. flour; some dried fruit.

Mince Patties: Left over mince; cooked potatoes and parsley with egg to bind.

Sausages: $\frac{1}{2}$–$\frac{3}{4}$ lb.

Cheese Leek Stew: One large pctato per person sliced $\frac{1}{4}$ in. thick. Add a cup of milk. Simmer till almost tender, add 2 oz. cheese, 1 tablespoon chopped syboes and seasoning. Finish cooking —20–30 min. altogether.

Cheese and Tomato Savoury: Toasted bread with tomatoes and cheese grated over it.

Sea Pie: Vegetable stew with pastry steamed on top.

Shepherd's Pie: Add meat essence to any mixture of meat and vegetables, with salt and pepper. Reheat and serve with mashed potatoes.

Cheese Frizzles: One tablespoon flour; 2 of oatmeal, and 3 of grated cheese; 1 teaspoon baking powder, add salt and pepper, cold water. Mix all ingredients to a soft dough. Fry in dessertspoonfuls in a very little fat.

Carrot Soup: $1\frac{1}{2}$ lb. carrots; $1\frac{1}{2}$ pints of water; 1 ham bone; salt and pepper.

Fried Lentil Cakes: 1 oz. cooked split peas; cupful breadcrumbs; grated carrot and turnip; parsley; egg to bind.

Bread Pudding: Three slices thick stale bread, spread with jam; 1 dessertspoon margarine; 1 egg; 1 level dessertspoon sugar; $\frac{1}{4}$ teaspoon cinnamon; 1 pint of milk. Grease pan, lay bread, jam side down, in layers. Mix egg and milk and pour over. Mix sugar and cinnamon and spread on top with margarine. Leave to soak for 15 min. Cook 45 min.

These are simply suggestions in case inspiration ceases. An oven can be made by placing a tin box over the fire.

The porridge can be cooked the night before, and kept warm by placing the pan in a hay box, which is made by digging a hole and lining it with straw to the thickness of about a foot. The pan is covered by a cushion of straw, and the whole covered with a groundsheet. A box can be used instead of digging the hole.

CAMP LARDER

A very good larder can be had by digging a hole two feet square by two feet deep, if possible in a shady spot—in the shade of the store tent will do. Cover the foot of the hole with flat stones and pour water over them to dampen. Make a lattice as for a grease pit. Stand the milk jugs, butter, &c.—all having been covered with butter muslin—on the flat stones and lay the lattice over the top.

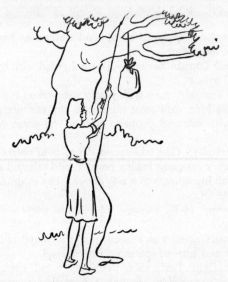

Meat suspended out of harm's way

Water should be poured over the stones every day to keep them cool.

It is unwise to keep meat in an underground larder, as foxes and dogs have a knack of finding it there. Meat is best kept by partly cooking it first, then putting it on a plate inside a butter muslin bag, which can either be suspended inside the store tent, or from the branch of a tree safely out of harm's way.

All sorts of handy gadgets can be made, such as shoe racks, which are made by pushing two forked sticks into the ground in line with each other, and the required distance apart. Push in another two forked sticks about three inches in front of the first ones. Lay a stick on top of the taller forks and another between the shorter forks. Place a pair of shoes on the rack, so that the heels fit over the back stick and the soles rest on the front one.

A short branch lashed to the tent pole makes a good clothes-hanger. The branch should not have too many off-shoots, as that would mean that there would be so much clothing hanging round the pole that the ventilation would be stopped.

If you use your hands, brain and ingenuity there is no need for you to be uncomfortable in camp.

When breaking camp a good deal of the cleaning can be done the day before; have the menu arranged so that as few pans as possible are needed for the final meal and all the stores are eaten up. Do the packing first then strike the tents, take down the screening, and fill in the pits and trenches. These should be filled in to slightly above ground level as the earth will sink when it settles. Water the top layer of earth before relaying the turf, so that the grass roots have every chance of taking. Burn all rubbish and make sure the earth is cold before relaying the fireplace turf. Return all borrowed gear with thanks. Remember to pay any outstanding bills. Leave only your thanks behind.

Try not to rouse the farmer's ire by wandering through fields regardless of crops; climbing over fences instead of slipping through them; barging through hedges instead of using a gate, and then leaving the gate open, so that cattle stray, instead of securing it; frightening sheep, especially in the lambing season, so that they dash all over the place; give them a fairly wide berth and then they will not be upset.

Do not tear up half the countryside so that a few wild flowers may be taken home; they have no lasting powers, and will be dead by the time home is reached.

Be very careful with lighted matches and cigarette ends—by rights there should be no cigarettes—it is so easy to start a woodland fire; so make sure they are extinguished.

And please do not indulge in the passion of carving your mono-gram on every tree, stone and seat that you pass; no one is impressed or cares that you have passed.

All campers and hikers are judged by the standard you set and by your behaviour, so it is up to you not to let your fellow campers down. Good Camping to you.

CRICKET

You will have heard the names of famous cricketers such as Grace, Hobbs. Bradman, Hutton; these of course are all men, but that does not mean that girls cannot play, so why not try to become a player yourself. There is now a Women's Cricket Association, and if you practise hard, and like the game, you may one day be able to play as a representative of your country. In the following article I am going to try to make you interested in the elementary forms of cricket, and to give you ideas of how to practise and enjoy the game.

If you look in the dictionary you will see that cricket is " an outdoor game played with bats, a ball, and wickets, between two sides of eleven players ". It was played as early as 1300, so the game has been going for a very long time.

The above definition sounds a rather grand affair, and not much use if you belong to a small family, or have only a few friends with whom to play; but don't be put off, you can have a lot of fun learning to play, and at school you may be able to play the game properly with full teams.

Perhaps there is a local men's cricket club? If so, go and watch them play, and see if you don't want also to learn to bat and bowl, and possibly play as well as your young brothers; they will probably scorn the idea of you, a mere girl, wanting to play! Don't listen to them; find your own friends and get them to practise with you, and when you have achieved some measure of success, offer to play with the boys. You will probably find you are quite equal to them.

Now let us examine the game in more detail.

THE BAT

This is made of white willow, and the trees are specially grown to make bats. Any good sports shop will advise you on what is the best type of bat. Do not choose one which has too long a handle; this will make you feel uncomfortable when it is in your hands.

It should feel well balanced, light, and easy to lift and swing; a weighty bat does not mean that you will be able to hit the ball farther.

Care of the Bat.

Do not use your bat on gravel; you must find some grass on which to play. If the blade of the bat becomes scratched it will soon be rendered useless. Give it a good oil up with raw linseed oil, about eighteen inches from the bottom; rub it well in, especially up the edges. You must not do this often or it will soak up too much oil and become heavy and unwieldy.

THE BALL

This is much the same as a good hockey ball with an outside cover of leather. Buy a real cricket ball, and start with the correct implement. Do not accept a composition ball; it is not a good substitute; it is light, and will not teach you to bat well.

Having a bat and ball, you are now ready to practise, and need only a friend to play with.

WICKETS AND PITCH

There are six wickets, three at each end of the pitch, placed together so that a ball will just not pass between them. They are joined together by placing two bails on top; these are balanced and not fixed. (It is the aim of the bowler or one of the fielders to get these bails off or to hit the wickets down to get a player out.) The pitch lies between these two sets of wickets and is twenty-two yards in length. (I advise you when beginning to play to have a shorter pitch, say twenty yards.)

You can see the layout of the pitch in the diagram, on p. 168 and the track on which the batsmen have to run.

A run is scored when the batsman, with bat in hand, touches the ground inside the line of the " popping crease " with some part of his person or bat. One batsman is receiving the bowling, and the other is waiting to run when his partner hits the ball to some part of the field, and considers the distance is far enough for himself and his partner both to get to the opposite wickets and over the popping crease. In this case the fielders return the ball as quickly as possible to either the bowler or the wicket-keeper, in order to

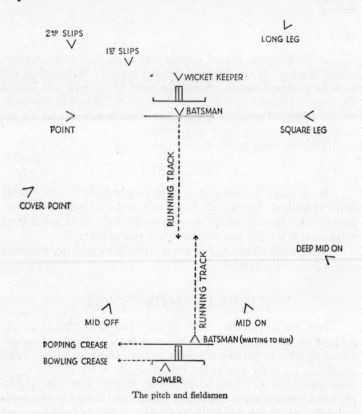

The pitch and fieldsmen

get the bails off. Only the batsman running to the wickets which are hit down or have the bails knocked off, is " out ", the other continues his innings.

THE FIELDERS

These are placed around the pitch, in places which are most likely the best for intercepting the ball when hit by a batsman. I have shown a simple plan of fielding places, although, as you will learn later, there are many other ways of placing them, but you need not worry about them now. They are placed by the bowler so that he can, by clever bowling, make the batsman hit the ball where he wants and more easily get him out, the fielders being in the path of the ball.

The Pitch and Fieldsmen.

Now I think we can go into more detail on how to bat, bowl and field. I shall not attempt to give you the rules; there are a great many and would take up too much space. You can very easily buy a book of rules only, and will find they help you to understand how the game is played.

Batting.

This is important, because if you cannot hit the ball to score runs you will not be a great deal of use to your team. So we will discuss here some of the simple methods you can use to help you to begin the makings of a batsman.

Stance.

Stand easily with your feet slightly apart, your face turned towards the bowler, and with your bat placed *on* or *inside* the popping crease, covering the wickets or at least part of them. (You will make what is called " the block " in which you will place your bat each time, so that you have it in the same part of the crease.) Get quite comfortable in your stance; be able and ready to move your feet to reach the ball with your bat wherever it may pitch. At all costs keep your feet " alive " and make them work with your eyes and brain (just as you have to be quick in your footwork when playing tennis or any other ball game). Your feet should begin to move almost as soon as the ball has left the bowler's hand.

For any straight ball it is better to keep your legs clear of the wickets, because if the ball hits them while they are in front you will be out " leg before wicket ".

Holding the Bat.

It is usual to hold the bat about the middle of the handle, the right hand below the middle and the left above it. In this way you will get the best control over the bat. If you hold the handle too high up, you will find you are slow in making your strokes.

The right hand should grasp the handle firmly with the wrist behind it, and the thumb and fingers towards the ball; the *left* hand grasps with the knuckles forward. Take your bat and feel this; look at your hands and see if they are placed as I suggest. The right hand takes a firmer grip than the left; you will find when you are standing waiting for the bowler that the face of the bat is somewhat turned towards your legs, and your left shoulder will be turned towards the bowler, unless you feel more comfortable standing with your shoulders facing more towards the bowler; in this case do so.

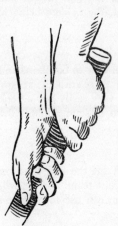

Holding the bat

Hitting the Ball.

There are many and various strokes that can be made in batting:

Attacking strokes stepping forward.
Defensive strokes stepping back.
Drives, cuts, &c.

Whatever way you hit the ball be sure to stick to a few golden rules:

(1) Forget that you have wickets to defend and aim to hit the ball on the face of the bat.

(2) Attack the ball with the bat, and do not let the ball just hit the bat. (This is sometimes called "blocking", and should be used only on rare occasions.)

(3) As the ball leaves the bowler's hand, lift your bat off the ground and slightly backwards in preparation for making your stroke.

(4) Keep your eye on the ball.

(5) Make up your mind quickly what stroke you intend to make and play with decision.

A Straight Bat.

This is a term you must make yourself very conversant with, as most strokes must be played with the bat in this position. (Excep-

tions are " cuts " and " pulls ".) If you cannot play a straight bat
you will never become a good cricketer.

The term means that the toe of the bat faces the ground, and
the bat is held perpendicular to the ground or with a slight slope

A straight bat

forward from handle to toe for a straight ball. In this way the
bat covers the wickets, and nine times out of ten the bowler will be
defeated.

In Forward Play.

Move your left foot with the bat, or move both feet. Keep your
bat low to the ground until after the ball has been hit, then follow
through in the direction in which you have hit the ball. Practise
this stroke slowly without a ball; watch your bat at the time of
meeting the ball (in imagination) and see if your bat is *straight*.

When you begin to play with a ball, try to meet the ball just as
it is leaving the ground. Of course it will depend on how near the
bowler puts the ball to you as to whether you can do this.

Do not be late in getting to it. If your stroke feels good it will probably be correct. Ease and a firm flow are essential.

Playing forward

Defensive Play.

When you realize you cannot play forward to reach near enough to where the ball is going to pitch, then you may have to play back. In this case you move back towards the wickets with your right foot, and at the same time get the face of your bat in line with the flight of the ball. (Remember, your bat will have been lifted from the ground before you make this stroke.)

When the ball leaves the bowler its flight may be outside the wickets, but when it pitches it may come off at an angle towards the wickets (termed a " break "). So you have to be very quick in watching the ball and getting the face of your bat into the right position. You cannot be out " leg before wicket " if the ball hits the ground outside the line of the wickets, and then bounces off your legs, so you can safely move your feet in front of the wickets and they will act as a second line of defence; though it is not advisable to think of using your legs in preference to your bat, because you may be " found out " by a ball which has pitched straight on the wickets and you will be " out ".

In defensive play, if your bat is not straight, the ball is likely to glance off the edge of the bat and go up in the air; you will then be caught out by slips or point.

Do not try to leave your wickets and go out to hit a ball that is wide; leave these alone until you have learnt style in your strokes, otherwise you will become what is known as a " slogger ", which is a player who makes strokes in any way and does not know what he is doing.

Defensive play

Try to keep your ball low to the ground, and place it away from the fielders.

Work on these few simple rules, and when you have mastered them you will be able to add other more advanced strokes. This you can do by reading books on cricket or getting coached by a professional. Keep these possible faults in mind and avoid them:

(1) Bat not straight.
(2) Eye not kept on the ball.

(3) Too late lifting the bat from the ground.

(4) Too late playing to the ball.

(5) Undecided, too late making up your mind what stroke to play.

Making Runs.

There are two players to make runs, and each works with the other, that is the batsman and his partner, who is standing at the bowler's end of the pitch. This partner must move a little forward down the pitch after the ball has left the bowler's hand (not before, or he may be stumped by being outside the popping crease) and be ready to run on the slightest chance. The batsman will be equally ready to move after playing his stroke and to steal as many runs as possible without endangering either player being " run out ". (Refer to the wickets and the pitch!)

The batsman must call " yes " or " come on " to any ball he has hit that he can see himself, but if he hits a ball behind his own wickets he will expect his partner to call if there is a chance of making a run, and if there is not, to call " no " or " wait ". Once the running has started, it is for the batsman facing the ball and with the longest distance to cover to call the second or third run, or on the call " no more " they must cease running. If the ball is hit to the boundary the runs are scored for the batsman without running up and down the pitch.

Runs can also be scored from a ball that goes past the batsman and the wickets without being touched (called a bye), or if it goes off any part of the batsman other than his bat or hand. In this case it is the partner who decides and calls the run. Bad fielding by the wicket-keeper often gives byes to the batting team.

Hints on Running.

(1) Keep on the alert.

(2) Decide quickly and definitely when to run.

(3) Run hard.

(4) Keep your bat low to the ground, especially to slide it over the popping crease.

(5) Combine with your partner; it is very bad play to get your partner run out.

BOWLING

Over Arm.

This needs a lot of practice, and although there are certain good rules to follow, each individual must find his or her own best way of delivering the ball.

The Grip.

Hold the ball for straight forward bowling with the first and second fingers on either side of the seam of the ball, and let the little fingers fall into place lower down, the thumb gripping opposite to the fingers. The ball should lie comfortably between these three fingers and the thumb. (The third finger takes no part in the grip, and the ball does not lie in the palm of the hand as you might expect.) Hold the ball firmly.

The grips vary slightly for putting on breaks and spins, but my advice to you is to learn the footwork, arm and body action first, and when you can pitch the ball just where you like, it will be time to learn to do these more difficult types of bowling.

The Run Up.

Make this any length you like from the wickets, but don't overdo it or you will find you are tired too quickly, and your bowling will flag; make the approach long enough to gain speed for your delivery.

The ball must be bowled with one foot on the ground behind and within the bowling crease (see diagram). It is good to work out the number of steps back from the wickets, and then always bowl from the same distance each time. Make a mark on the ground and this will help you to know where to start from.

It is usual to bowl from the left side of the wickets if you are a right-handed bowler, but you can, if you prefer, bowl from the right side; this is called bowling " round the wicket ".

Delivery.

The arm swings from behind upwards and downwards forward, with a straight elbow. The arm should come up high and close to the head. The left shoulder (for a right-handed bowler) should be towards the wickets at which he is bowling, and as the ball is released from the hand the hips swing round and the delivery is accomplished with plenty of body movement forward. Let the ball " go " just in front of the line of the head. Later, when you want to vary the pitch of the ball, let it go behind the line of the head to get a sharper rise; this variation will make it more difficult for the batsman.

Aim and pitch your ball about one and a half yards in front of the batsman, and go on practising this until you can achieve it each time. This accuracy will make it difficult for the batsman, as a ball pitched short or full is easy to play and will be certain to add runs to the opposing team.

Be content to get a good-length ball; you are out to make it hard for the batsman to know what your ball is going to do, so vary the speed, length of pitch and line on which you are bowling. All these things help to confuse and agitate him.

The stumps are known as leg, middle and off, the leg being the one nearest the batsman's legs, so you can aim for different ones and still take the bails off or get the wicket down.

FIELDING

You will already know how to catch a ball, and how quickly you have to move if you want to reach it. I am going to try to help you to become more efficient, and to be a really useful member of your team, for it is good fielding that counts in shortening a match.

Alertness of *feet*, eye and mind are all essential. Be ready to stop the ball from going past you. Always expect the ball to come to you each time the batsman plays a stroke—never wait for the ball to reach *you* but start running towards it and meet it. You will be surprised at the balls you can reach if you start soon enough. Move across to cover behind a fellow fielder if you can; he may miss the ball, and you will be there to save extra runs being scored.

Picking up the Ball with Two Hands.

Bend your knees out, get *behind* the ball with both hands close together and the fingers pointing down to the ground. As the ball reaches the hands let them " give " very slightly back, then immediately stretch the knees and prepare to throw the ball in to the wickets with a step forward with one foot.

With One Hand: The Right.

Have the left foot forward, the knees bent, and the hand with the fingers pointing down to the ground. Receive the ball with your eye on it, and here you can just stretch your knees and are in a " ready " position to throw the ball in without further steps. This is of course a less safe way of fielding, and I do not advise you to use it until you are proficient in the use of the two-handed method.

Picking up the ball with two hands

Throwing in to the Wickets.

In general, use an overarm throw. Anticipation as to which end to throw the ball in to is essential for getting out a batsman who is running between the wickets. As you are stretching your knees from picking up the ball, look at the pitch, and make up your mind to which end you want to send the ball. This should be to the end from which one of the batsmen is farthest away.

How to Throw.

Use a stance with the left shoulder forward as in bowling, and use your body twist; as you throw, stretch your elbow forcibly. So your arm is bent at the elbow to begin with, and ends stretched, with the weight of the body on the left foot.

A ball full-pitched up to the bowler or wicket-keeper is good; you must judge your own ability to throw the required distance. If you cannot throw very far, send the ball to an intermediate fielder, who is " backing you up " between the ball and the wickets. This is of course slower and should not be used unless necessary; try to give your fellow fielder an easy, accurate ball to catch or field so that he can pass it on quickly.

Practise throwing and fielding with a friend. You can have good fun, and it is a fine feeling to be master of the ball and be able to do what you like with it.

Catching the Ball.

Cup your hands together with the palms facing the downward flight of the ball; let them " give ", as in fielding, as the ball enters them. In going to meet a catch do not get too far under the ball, or you may have to step back. This means your balance is not secure at the moment of receiving. Catches can be made low or high, and a relative change of position of knees and hands will then have to made. Have your hands near your body and in general they should be raised to at least chest level. Keep your eyes on the ball until it is in your hands.

If you have to use a one-handed catch, then " give " in the same way as previously described, as the ball is more likely to bounce out of one hand; for a wide ball reach out well and you will be surprised at the balls you can catch.

When practising with a friend, use a real cricket ball and get used to the feeling of its hardness; it doesn't hurt if you do as I have told you.

Wicket-keeping.

The wicket-keeper wears a pair of padded gloves, and pads on the legs which come up above the knees. These help to stop the ball when the batsman misses it; the gloves soften the catching of the ball, because it is coming very fast at that moment. To be a good wicket-keeper you must have plenty of energy, a very good eye and quick footwork. He has an important part to fill and it often falls to his lot to " stump " the batsman out.

Other Fielders.

Slips, point, mid-on, and mid-off are all placed close to the wickets, and they have to be players of particular speed and accuracy.

There is much that I could go on telling you about cricket, but I hope this will be a beginning and that by now your interest in the game has been stimulated. Has it? If so, good luck to you, and I hope one day I may have the pleasure of seeing you performing in international games.

CYCLING

Nature has been kind to Britain. No one knows that better than the cyclist. And one of the happy features of our land is its compactness. A cyclist has actually ridden from Land's End, in the south, to John O' Groats, in the remotest north, in 2 days and 6 hours. That, of course, is the record for the 865-mile trip. And that is one way of covering the country. But it is not the sort of way you or I would choose. There is always more fun to be hand out of being less energetic. In fact, the happiest cycling day I can recall was one in which I covered only ten miles.

I remember it well. We were on the island of Mull. We fell in with a number of the old worthies of the place and they got started telling us, in their gentle voices, the legends of the district. We couldn't get away. As a matter of fact, I don't think we really wanted to. There was one old chap there, he called himself the bard of Mull, all his stories were in rhyme. It was he who coaxed us, with his winning ways, to climb Ben More. I shall always be grateful to him.

Yes, the easy-going way is the more enjoyable. I could go on telling stories of that tour and of many others. But that would not be very fair. It would be very much better if you mounted your own bicycle and went out and made your own cycling history. I shall content myself by helping you in any way I may.

Record-breaking Syd. Ferris had his solitary eye focused on the Great North Road when he did his epic " End-to-End " ride. But not for us the shortest distance between two points. We would rather follow the fretted coastline of Devon and Cornwall, or linger in the ancient cities on our route as we travel north by, say, the Wye Valley or through the lovely old-world villages of the Cotswolds. We could then have the choice of the ride through Snowdonia or through Warwickshire's and Cheshire's twisty lanes. And then there is the splendour of the English Lake District to greet us, with its passes and its thrilling mile-long free-wheels. That would take us to the once-troubled border country where the sheep can now graze on the rolling hills without fear of " the rievers ", and we would have entered the wonderland which is Scotland. We would pay a visit to the " bonnie banks of Loch Lomond "—probably the most beautiful stretch of cycling country in Britain—and so, northwards, through dark Glencoe; onwards, by the road to the isles: we would look upon Skye and wonder; we would ride by the shores of lonely Loch Maree, on into Ullapool and, ever northwards, into the heart of " Wildest Britain ". Our easy pedalling would take us over the " top " of the land and so to our journey's end, to the last house on the mainland, to Groats.

It can all be done. I have done it. You can do it. Not all at once, perhaps. But one part of the country could be our hostess during one holiday and then we could visit another part in another year. And then, of course, there are the limitless other " beauty spots ". There is the Shakespeare country; the Burns country; our cathedrals; Derbyshire and the Pennines; Yorkshire with its rolling dales; Kent, the garden of England; there is London and the many other places of great historic interest; there are our walled cities of York, Chester; there is Wells, Bath, Stonehenge, Edinburgh. And there are all these pleasant little roads round our own hometown on which we can enjoy an evening's ride, solo or with some of the members in the youth club or friends who live in the neighbourhood.

Well mounted and decently equipped, we have the " open sesame " to happy and healthy hours spent in a wonderful land.

I was a schoolboy when I began real cycling. That was over twenty years ago. I am just as keen now as I was then. For that I have to thank the man who sold me my first machine. He happened to be a regular cyclist as well as being a cycle agent. That meant a lot. It meant that I got the right sort of mount. Had it not been for " old Jock ", I would probably have been burdened with one of those so-called " safety " bicycles which are the regulation bicycles of this country and which account for the popular belief that cycling is hard work.

There are the two types of bicycles, the one with upright handlebars, and the " racer " (fig. 1). The latter, in spite of its bad name, is the safer model, and it is light and strong. Its one serious disadvantage is that it entails the stooping position, which makes for bad posture. The upright—or " sit up and beg "—machine scores on this point but is generally heavier to ride.

I have put some measurements into our sketch. You see that

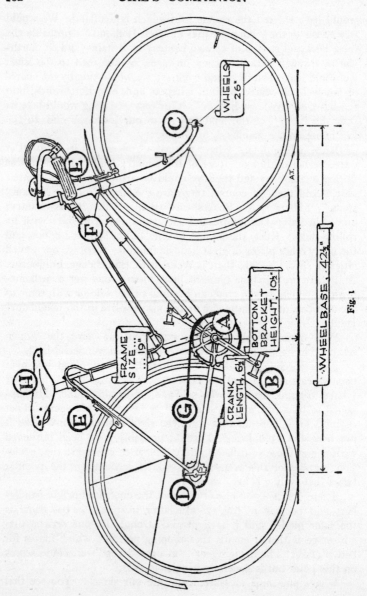

WHEELS
26"

C

E

F

BOTTOM
BRACKET
HEIGHT, 10½"

A

FRAME
SIZE ... 19"

H

CRANK
LENGTH, 6½"

B

E

G

D

WHEELBASE, 42½"

A.T.

Fig. 1

one from the bottom-bracket (A) to the ground—10½ in.—that is low enough to allow the rider to put her foot on the ground when she has to halt, say, in traffic. A girl mounted on the type of machine which was designed in the day of her grandmother has to engage in the dangerous trick of dismounting each time the signals say " Halt ", and then of climbing back on again when the lights change to " Go ". And the low-built bicycle has another advantage: it reduces the amount of wind-resistance with which the rider has to contend.

The frame in our picture is 19 in. in length. That will be about the most suitable size for a young girl. Some years ago, a friend of mine bought his twelve-year-old son a new machine. On the ignorant and almost criminal advice of the salesman, he went home with a 20-in. model. The salesman had explained that the youngster " would grow to fit it. And that, anyway, the 20-in. bicycle cost just the same as a smaller one ". Better to have too small a machine than one which is too big.

Unless a girl knows that she will be using her machine exclusively for club-riding and for touring, she should get an open frame. A " boy's " bicycle prevents the wearing of a skirt.

But here is how to find the size which best suits you. Take your inside-leg measurement, and from this deduct 10 in. If, for instance, the measurement from the ground up the inside of your leg is 29 in., a 19-in. frame is your size. As you grow, of course, the saddle and handlebars can always be raised to keep pace.

The saddle! A tender spot. And, if not properly fitted, a sore spot! Some years ago, I was a judge in a newspaper competition which invited readers to suggest improvements in the bicycle. More than half of the ideas submitted were designed to make the saddle more comfortable, or, rather, should I say, less uncomfortable. All sorts of springing arrangements and pneumatic coverings have been tried out, but still the seat continues to hurt. I am not going to tell you that I can guarantee you armchair comfort. But I do know hundreds of lads and some girls who have ridden over 200 miles in one day—in 12 hours to be precise—and they have not been unduly troubled with saddle-soreness. During these rides, they probably left the saddle for not more than one spell of a few minutes. Those riders, of course, took good care in the first place to buy the best saddle they could afford, and, having got it, they looked after it. And then they were particular to have it fitted in the right position. Those are the three things to be careful about.

If we could specify our dream mount, what sort of saddle would we select? In the first place, we would not need to take the saddle which goes with the standard machine. Too many of the seats fitted in the factories are narrower than they ought to be. A B.10 size is better than a B.17.

If you mean to go in for hard riding with a speedy club, don't be afraid of those springless things—a piece of leather (and, sometimes, pretty hard leather too) stretched over a wire frame. Once they have been treated and " ridden in ", they can be your cycling friend for life. But, mark you, if you feel that something with springs in its chassis would suit you better, then have it. The girl who intends using her machine more for utility purposes, in towns and for easy pottering, could do with some cushioning. But for touring, for club-running, for racing, springs can be done without. The spring has the tendency to keep the leather pressed constantly against the body. This causes sweating.

I would like to tell you the way to position your saddle so that it will be just right. There are two things to watch. The first is the height. What height should we make it? Well, mount your machine and we shall find out. Put the saddle at the height which will allow you to pedal with your *heels* on the pedals. You should be able to do this without undue wobbling. When you have slackened that wee nut behind the seat-pin and slid the saddle up and down until you have got it into this position, then lock it. Now, of course, nobody goes pedalling with the heels. That is the wrong way. The right way to pedal is with the *ball* of your foot. When, therefore, you have positioned your saddle in the way I have suggested, you will find that you have left yourself just enough " play " to give you comfort when you go to ride the right way.

But the saddle can be made to slide backwards and forwards as well as up and down. How do we know how near or how far from the handlebars to fix it? The bicycle in the picture has the peak of the saddle $1\frac{1}{2}$ in. " behind " the bottom-bracket. You should try your seat in this position. Test it by allowing a piece of string, with a weight attached, to hang from your saddle peak. You will be able to see if the distance between the string and the bottom-bracket is $1\frac{1}{2}$ in.

Most girls are far neater cyclists than boys when they are properly positioned on their machines, and it really is worth all the bother you may have in moving your saddle about until you get it to suit. And, if in doubt, make the saddle too low rather than too high.

If you are going in for club or speed cycling you will want dropped handlebars like the bicycle in the picture.

A bar with about $2\frac{1}{2}$ in. of a drop and of about 15 in. in width —take your shoulder measurement—would be best suited for most girls. Champions design handlebars for their own personal use, but ordinary folks can make the best of an extensive range of shapes and sizes. Again, I would whisper, don't necessarily take the machine as it is in the show-case. Talk over all the points I have mentioned with the dealer. If you feel that he knows his business, follow his advice. Show him this article if you care. Make your own adjustments as to handlebar height and the distance you will position it from the saddle peak. As a guide, I would say, start with putting the top of the bar level with your saddle, and be careful that you do not have to over-reach. The more you have to lean forward, the heavier the load you will be placing on your wrists. They'll soon complain if you overdo it. And the higher you raise the bar, the more weight you throw on to that tender spot, the saddle. Try to divide your weight over the pedals, the saddle, and the bar, in that order.

Everything I have said can be made to apply to almost every kind of machine. Even if your machine came to you very much second hand, it can be brought up to date. All the fittings are adjustable. Don't be afraid to experiment. It is not the best and most expensive machines which yield the most; it is those bicycles which are nicely " positioned " and well looked after.

But before I go on to give tips on " looking after " a bicycle, I would like to let you into the secret of easier cycling. We have the kind of bicycle we need, we have made it to our measure, now we are going to find out how to ride it properly. You know the old saying " Brains versus brawn ". This is the brainy way of riding. They call it " ankling ". I know a rider who got himself into a British Olympic team, thanks, not to his physical strength, but to his ankles —and to the way in which he used them.

The whole theory is to keep a constant pressure on the turning pedals rather than to exert a tremendous effort at any one point. I have done a little drawing to show how this is best done (fig. 2).

In position A, the crank is standing straight up. Theoretically, at least, no matter what amount of pressure is applied *directly* on top of this pedal, it will never push it *down*. But if the heel is dropped a little, little effort is wasted in coaxing the pedal *round*. In positions B and C, the foot is still turning on the ankle so that it is always levering the crank round rather than pushing it down. In position D, the foot is now " clawing " the pedal backwards and, in position E, I have fitted a toe-clip and strap and the foot is now able to help

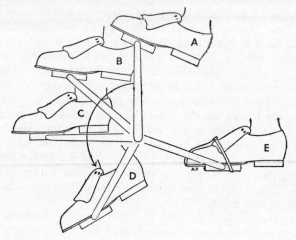

Fig. 2

the pedal on its upward arc. Some riders nail a strip of leather to the sole of the shoe so that it will fit inside the back-plate of the pedal, and thus assist them in this clawing action.

This is a technique worth practising. It is grand exercise, too, for the ankles. Watch someone on the road whom you know to be a good and experienced rider. Watch the ankles. See the heel dropping at the top of the pedal's circumference. Look at the steady, almost effortless riding. Practise on your own. The best way to do it is to ride with a fixed wheel and, by taking one foot off the pedal and " working " solely with the other, you will find that you are, almost automatically, riding like a champion.

So now we have the bicycle, the position, and this ankling-action secret. I shall add a Maintenance Guide, a list of Things to Remember, say a few words about the sporting side of the game, and then wish you " Good cycling ".

The A B C of Bicycle Maintenance.

The letter " A " in our sketch labels the bottom-bracket—the power house of the bicycle. Adjustment is made on the side opposite from the chain-wheel. Release the lock-ring; tighten or slacken the cup until you have the spindle which passes through the bracket free from side-shake, and then fix by screwing up the lock-ring. The cranks should be able to spin about a dozen times. Heavy oil is the best lubricant.

B. Pedals. Adjustment made at end of the spindle under the dust cap. Have them firm, rather than slack. Heavy oil.

C. Hubs. Standard type is adjusted like the pedal—with a lock-ring and cone. Tighten until the weight of the valve can still swing the wheel. Heavy oil. But do not overdo the lubrication. When oil runs down the spokes, it perishes the rubber of the tyres and tubes.

D. Free-wheels and variable gears. Free-wheels require no adjustment. Thin oil. If ratchet is slipping, try injecting paraffin to clean it. The other way of cleaning a free-wheel is to take the whole thing to pieces. This is often a night's work; at least, the reassembling can be. Adjustment of Sturmey-Archer and B.S.A. 3-speed gears is made by releasing lock-nut at the end of the control chain, and by manipulating the milled nipple which you will find there. When the control lever is in the " normal " position, the indicator rod, which passes through the spindle, should be flush with the axle-end. Oil as for free-wheel.

E. Brakes. Adjust until brake-shoes are close enough to wheel rim to allow the wheel to pass without rubbing. Our sketch shows the regular rim-brake (calliper model). Hub brakes are becoming increasingly popular. Although not so quick in action as the best of the rim-brakes, they are smoother and are not so subject to lose some of their efficiency in wet weather. Lubricate according to maker's instructions.

F. Steering-column bearings. Adjustment made by top bearing. Should be tight, although not stiff or binding. Do not allow to be slack or to have any play. Pack with heavy grease when dismantled. Oil as frequently as you do the other parts.

G. Chain. At tightest place, should not be taut. It is dangerous, especially to fixed-wheel riders, to have it slack enough to be wobbly. The handiest way to lubricate, is to trail the oil-can on the inside of the chain while you keep " turning " the pedals.

H. The saddle. Do not let the saddle get wet. An occasional application of Mars oil, of castor oil, or of dubbin is good for the leather. You can, too, give it a polish with brown boot polish. If it is new, be prepared to have to put up with some inconvenience while you are " breaking it in "—getting it to suit your own particular shape. In time, the leather may require tightening up. There is a nut for this purpose under the saddle peak.

If you attend to all these parts, lubricating where required, every 250 miles, there isn't much which should give you trouble.

How to dress: For those who suit them, shorts are best; sometimes a divided skirt can be very neat, and this outfit has the advantage that when the young girl reaches her destination, she is at perfect liberty to walk about, to enter shops and to do her sight-seeing without feeling " out of place ". Some " shortists " carry a light-weight skirt which can be slipped on at the end of the day. Plus-fours are a hindrance and are most uncomfortable when wet and they tend to balloon in the wind; knickers are much more suitable. See that a jumper is made a little longer than usual to avoid that gap which, otherwise, will appear above your skirt band when you reach forward to grip the handlebars. A golf jacket can be tidy, although a proper cycling jacket as made by specialist tailors is the right thing for the enthusiast. Do not appear in high heels. Have your clothes loose-fitting and airy. When dismounted for a rest, slip on something extra. Unless in very cold weather, it is not necessary to put on additional clothing to go cycling. Good-fitting cycling shoes have no real substitutes.

Cycling can be everybody's game. It can be easy-going, it can be strenuous. Most of the 12,000,000 cyclists in this country use their machines for utility purposes and for occasional pleasure trips. But we do have a very keen and active organization of sporting and club cyclists. The younger members go in for racing, while most of the older brigade do the organizing work. There are two distinct types of racing game: road and track, probably the most popular being the road game—time trials, to give the sport its official description. The Road Times Trials Council and the Scottish Amateur Cycling Association look after the interests of time trialists. It is very much a British form of racing. On the Continent, road sport is run, with maximum publicity, on massed-start lines. Here, our riders shun the limelight and do not allow their activities to be fully advertised. There is a reason for this. We do not need to go into it all here. Sufficient is it to say that the authorities would not welcome great crowds obstructing the traffic if the public knew that a road race was to take place at a certain place and at a certain time. To avoid possible inconvenience to other road users, time trialists prefer to have their sport even if it means that they do not, at times, get the publicity their very wonderful athletic feats deserve.

It really is one of the few forms of sporting competition which can be said to be sport for its own sake. Whoever takes part in it, is a real enthusiast. The trial, for instance, starts at about six in the morning. The riders are set off—all alike in inconspicuous dress —not in bunches, but spaced out at intervals of one minute between each. And pacing is not allowed. When one rider catches another, she has to keep well clear of her rival as she passes. In order, too, that there will be no freak records put up in wind-assisted events, all the " races " are promoted on an out-and-home course. All have to return to the timekeeper and have their times recorded.

There was, until the war put a halt to it all, a growing interest on the part of girls in races, and promoters were always willing to add a ladies' race or two to their sports programmes. The National Cyclists' Union, which controls the track game, is hopeful of reviving that interest in the immediate future. The address of the N.C.U. is 35 Doughty Street, London, W.C.1. They will gladly put you in touch with a local club. Membership fees, which include insurance, are very nominal.

The other big national cycling body is the famous Cyclists' Touring Club, of 3 Craven Hill, London, W.2. As the name suggests, the club is interested in touring, and plays no part in running races. They have local branches all over the country. Annual subscription is 10s. And then there is the National Clarion Cycling Club, with some 200 local clubs and a national subscription, which includes insurance, of 6s. 6d. per annum. Write to West View, Hopwood Lane, Halifax, Yorkshire.

One of the most gruelling championship honours which an athlete can aspire to win in the B.B.A.R.—The British Best All-rounder Competition. From April until October, the finest riders in the country are going all out to gain a place among the leaders in this title contest. The riders are tested at distances of 50 miles, 100 miles, and 12 hours. Each person's best performance in these events is taken, and an average worked out.

Although no girls have figured in leading places in the B.B.A.R., there are some very fine speed merchants among the fair sex, and most clubs are glad to cater for lady members. In fact, many champions among the men would not find themselves so well placed in the B.B.A.R. lists were it not for the girls in the club turning out to help feed the various clubs' champions while they are engaged in their non-stop long-distance rides.

One of the handiest cycling guides I have is a well-used slip of paper which I have by me here as I write. It is a list which I made out years ago. It details items I would be likely to need if I were going week-ending, hostelling or camp touring. Before I pack, I gather everything I intend taking. And, so that I shall not find myself stranded in the back of beyond minus a necessary part of my gear, I use this list, ticking off the various articles as I collect them. To guide you in making your own list I give you this copy of mine.

Cash, Youth Hostel card, Hostel booking cards, rail tickets, maps, writing pad, pencil, spectacles, sun-glasses and case, first-aid kit, tooth-brush, soap, towel, sleeping-bag, handkerchief, pyjamas, dish towel, swim-suit, slippers, spare socks or stockings, underwear, comb, nail-brush, boot-brush, polish, duster, camera and spools.

Cape and sou'wester, tools, paraffin stove, stove-parts and prickers, matches.

Tent, pegs, ground-sheet, cooking utensils, salt, sugar, tea, cocoa, fat, bacon, margarine, oatmeal, jam, knife, fork and spoons.

It is surprising how so much can be made to fit into such small bulk and be packed in the panniers.

Road Manners.

Toleration, good manners, consideration for others: necessary as are these conditions in any walk of life, they are absolutely essential to users of the open road.

Although of course those of us who ride the single-track vehicle are not liable to do grievous injury to a third party, there is still much we can do to minimize road accidents. We can learn the Rules of the Road and the Highway Code.

Mechanically, we can make sure that our brakes are in good order, that our reflector is clean and that our rear light is functioning. When riding in company, we can be careful not to monopolize the road. Most clubs have an unwritten code of their own. Some are more precise and have a road drill in black and white in their membership books. For instance: One whistle—" All on "; two whistles—" ease up ", and three whistles—" all off ". The captain, in the lead, and the sub-captains, who take up the rear, are the whistlers.

While it is best when club-riding to keep two-abreast, it is not fair to form one long continuous line. It is safer, in many ways, to allow breaks in the chain. For instance, the club would be well advised to ride thus:

Those gaps in an emergency allow overtaking traffic to " cut in ". In wet weather, too, to avoid the spray from the wheel in front, this formations helps:

The good cyclist, of course, does not stop at being mannerly. She goes further. She is willing to assist a fellow traveller in trouble, and even if one does not require a helping hand, it is encouraging when a comrade of the wheel slows down and inquires, " Is there anything I can do to help?"

GOLF

In my lifetime, many of the best players have written books about golf and how to play this very difficult but most agreeable game. Whilst I always welcome criticism of my views and theories, I hope that those who detect the many omissions in this article will remember that it is but one short chapter, and that the space allotted precludes my dealing at greater length with the many details of playing technique.

Golf differs from other games in many ways. Apart from the games which are played upon a billiard table and a croquet lawn, it is the only game played with a stationary ball; and yet, I believe there is none more difficult, none more agonizing to the mind, and none that requires more self-discipline and patience.

The marked improvement in golf clubs and golf balls is partly responsible for the great advance in the general standard of play during recent years. Men like Braid, Taylor, Jones, Locke, and Cotton, who have given the best part of their lives to the study of the game of golf, have not only popularized it enormously, but their doctrines and methods, aided by the camera and the cinematograph, remain for the benefit of those who come after. In our country Cotton himself is largely responsible for the vogue of *practising* both amongst amateurs and professionals; and it is idle to pretend that serious practice is not beneficial to everyone, whatever his standard.

To my mind, golf has two very distinct sides. There is the mental side and the physical side, and both are of the utmost importance; for both mind and body must be drilled to act automatically and in complete harmony. Let us examine first the importance of drill for the mind.

In his admirable book, *Golf, My Life's Work*, J. H. Taylor says: " To try to play golf really well is far from being a joke, and light-heartedness of endeavour is a sure sign of eventual failure." In that sentence I believe " J.H."—to use his more famous soubriquet —strikes a note which rebounds in the conscience of every golfer. We all want to play well, and however well we play we all want to play better. At his best Henry Cotton believed that he could always have played better. That very fact places each one of us in—as it were—the same struggling atmosphere, whatever our ability, whatever our physical attributes, and with whatever temperament nature has endowed us. I believe that since the game of golf is an entirely individualistic one, its very loneliness during the strain of battle demands greater powers of concentration and greater powers of self-control than any other game. Herein lies much of its fascination. There is but one golfer of our time of whom I have never seen it recorded that he was feeling the strain or that he was unfit. This man is an American, the mighty Hagen. Of others, " J.H." admits that he often felt sick during a championship, but he throve on this horrible feeling. Henry Cotton often looks a ghastly colour in the arena where his name might appropriately be Stalin (man of steel). Bobbie Jones, an incomparable champion, gave up competitive golf that he might better enjoy his life. At the very other end of the ladder, I remember playing in a club foursome competition with a banker friend of mine whose handicap was 19. On the morning of the 36-hole final, I saw him emerge from the cloakroom looking both pale and drawn. He apologized for his ashen appearance and explained that he was always sick before every round of a competition !

I believe it to be a matter of great importance that all young players should be fully aware that golf demands a very great mental effort, and let no young player imagine that her opponent is less highly strung for the occasion than herself. We all feel the strain. Oddly enough, match and medal play seem to require an altogether different outlook. In these days of large fields comprising more than 200 competitors, most of whom can hit the ball a long way with a modicum of accuracy, the 18-hole match has ceased to be a real test of ability. In a short sprint match over 18 holes, luck plays far too big a part in the result of the match. A bad lie here, a bad kick there, and a long putt or two can put out the greatest player. Bobbie Jones himself never overcame his dislike, and indeed his fear, of this form of golf. When at the zenith of his powers, he came from America many times to compete in the British Amateur Championship and yet he was but once successful. Difficult as it is to put into practice, there is only one way to acquire complete peace of mind for a championship match. One must be philosophical and say : " I am going to play par, I am going to ignore my opponent's ball, and if my opponent can beat my par, here's luck to him."

Medal play, on the other hand, even over 18 holes, almost invariably produces the right winner and at any rate the one who plays best on the day generally wins the tournament. Many young players have to wait patiently before winning their first medal competition because, through lack of experience, they have had one disastrous hole. If on quiet reflection that disaster is reconsidered it will nearly always be found that after all it was quite unnecessary. Let us take it for granted that however well we play we are bound to make a slip or two. The correct attitude of mind should be, " Whatever happens I am going to keep the ball in play, and when I make a mistake it is going to cost me the minimum number of strokes." In other words, having, shall we say, driven into the rough, make up your mind that, unless the ball is lying really well, you are going to hit it back on to the course with the easiest and safest club. That is the only way in which sevens, eights and nines can be avoided.

We have neither time nor space here to go thoroughly into the question of the rules of golf, but nevertheless they are of the utmost importance. My advice is, get to know them and, moreover, carry a copy in your pocket when playing an important game. Lest this piece of advice be taken lightheartedly it might be well to record that had Mr. Cyril Tolley, one of the greatest amateur golfers of all time, known the rule concerning a ball touching clothes he would in all probability have won the British Amateur Championship for the third time at Hoylake in 1933.

Having very briefly touched upon the mental side of golf, we now come to the physical side or drill for the body. Since none of us are made alike, it is obviously impossible for all of us to play in exactly the same way; but although this be so, there are certain basic principles which to-day are almost universally employed by the great players of our time. There are, however, two divergent schools of thought upon the question of which hand strikes the ball. (I assume for the moment we are all right-handed.) Having, at one time, been of the company of those who imagine that the blow can be delivered with the back of the left hand, I am now a convert to the school which believes that the right hand delivers the blow and that, if you want to play with the left hand, then you must turn round and play left-handed. The remainder of this chapter is based almost entirely upon this assumption.

To watch a good golfer—man or woman—hit a ball from a distance is to my mind to watch an agreeable and at once a beautifully natural performance; yet I know of no game in which, in order to strike the ball correctly, it is necessary to go through a more complicated and unnatural series of movements. The term " a natural golfer " is erroneously used; in my view, no such people exist to-day, and if they do I am sure that they are not first-class players. On the other hand, there are undoubtedly people who can make the complicated golf swing appear to be a perfectly natural performance.

Let us now get down to the mechanics of the golf swing. What you must remember is that there are many ways of swinging a golf club successfully, and I propose to describe the way which appears to me to produce the most consistent results. All sorts of methods are successful over short periods, but the best player to-day is the one whose off days are fewest and whose off days are not disastrous.

The Grips.

The first question we must study is the all-important grip of the club. The golf club is really rather a difficult implement to grip comfortably and yet properly, and as much patience is required to get accustomed to an orthodox grip as is needed to teach oneself to keep the head down. Before defining what I believe to be the orthodox grips of the modern golfer, I would like once again to emphasize the difficulty of gripping the club comfortably and correctly. It may be beneficial if I here recall my own experience. When starting to play at the age of twenty, I thought I was copying some expert's particular grip, but I was not. I got accustomed to this grip; but later on, when I tried to break myself of it and assume an orthdox grip, I found it extremely difficult to get comfortable. Moreover, it was diabolically difficult to hit a ball with the new grip. The way I got over this difficulty was to carry about a walking-stick, similar in size to the grip of a golf club, and constantly to handle it in the correct fashion. After several days I found that the new grip had become the natural one and I was able then to start hitting a ball. Therefore, make up your mind to get accustomed to a good sound grip before attempting to hit a golf ball, and above all, stick to it.

We may say that there are to-day three good standard grips, and whilst each one is fundamentally the same in regard to the position and angle of the hands on the club, they differ in so far as each one gives a totally different feel to the striker.

The three grips are the overlapping or Vardon grip, the interlocking grip, and the two-handed grip. Taking them in turn: (1) In the overlapping grip, it will be seen that the little finger of the right hand lies in the groove between the first and second fingers of the left hand. (2) In the interlocking grip, the little finger of the right hand and the first finger of the left hand are interlocked. (3) In the two-handed grip, the hands are not joined together, and each rests naturally on the shaft independent of the other. I believe the overlapping grip to be the most popular to-day,

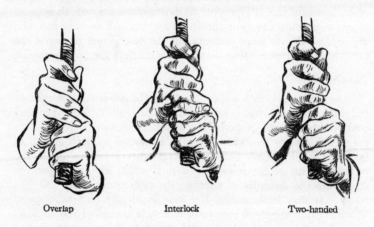

Overlap   Interlock   Two-handed

tor it gives the hands the best chance of working together. People with long fingers often find the interlocking grip most comfortable. Personally, I do not like it, since to me it always creates a tendency to put the left hand too far on top of the shaft. The two-handed grip is the easiest to get accustomed to, but with this grip there is always a risk that the hands will not work smoothly together. Perhaps what commends it most is that it is used both by Cyril Tolley and Dai Rees. Cast your eye back at the illustrations and you will notice that they are fundamentally the same.

Stance.

While a good striker of a golf ball can hit the ball accurately from any stance, no hard-and-fast rule can be laid down as to the best stance to adopt. There are three to choose from: closed, square, and open.

The important point is that the stance must be comfortable and suitable to the particular individual. Leading professional teachers prefer the open to the closed stance but do not object to the square.

From my own experience I heartily recommend the principle of

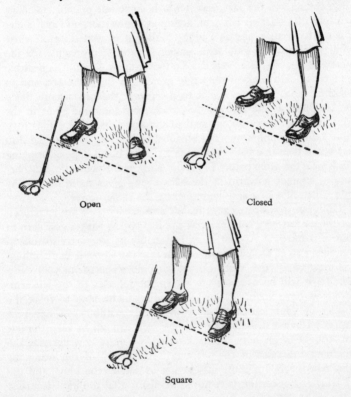

Open

Closed

Square

adopting the most comfortable position. Having found what suits you best, never alter it because you have seen some great player standing very differently. What suits him may not suit you!

One word of warning. If you find the closed stance agreeable, bear in mind that with this stance one is very apt to stand more and more closed. with the ball lying more and more off the back foot. This will cause topping and all manner of trouble.

Lastly, for a normal shot, whatever your stance the ball should lie approximately opposite the left heel.

Arm Action.

The difference between the old and the modern golfer is in my judgment due to the fact that it has been found possible to make great use of a straight left arm, acting as a governor, and at the end of it a left wrist, acting as a hinge. All golfers want to make their swing mechanical. This achievement is utterly impossible for the human being, but, if a basis can be found upon which it is possible to take the club back in the same groove, in the same arc, and to the same point, for every shot to the green, then it is more likely that the blow at the ball can be struck from the same point in the swing, through the same arc and in the same direction. This may sound rather complicated; but obviously, if you do not take the club back along the same path each time there can be no hope of bringing it down on the same path. Try it out and see for yourself. Furthermore, a straight left arm in the back swing gives more or less the same width of swing and consequently the same power.

How can we learn to get this left arm straight? I am convinced that the easiest way is to practise the movement with a golf club in front of a mirror. At first, it will probably be necessary to roll up your sleeve so as to make quite certain that the elbow is not bending. It is most likely, too, that in order to achieve success in your early attempts it will be necessary to stiffen the muscles of the left arm. Once you have acquired the knack you will be able to relax the muscles of your left arm and swing easily without any apparent tension. Having drilled your muscles well enough to keep the left arm straight throughout the back swing, we must now examine the remaining functions of the left arm. At the top of the swing the right hand begins to come into action to deliver the blow, and the left arm, as a governor, is required to ensure that the blow is struck in the right direction. No real difficulty will be found in keeping the left arm straight until the point of impact with the ball, but since we are trying to arrange that the club head shall travel for as long as possible in the intended direction, it is of the utmost importance that the left elbow should not " break " until the club head has travelled at least two feet past the ball. The elbows of both arms should be close together and remain together, thus forcing the club head to travel square in the direction of the target.

Keeping the elbows together after striking the ball is one of the most difficult physical operations in the golf swing and can only be acquired with patience and practice in front of a mirror. I would say that it is utterly impossible to achieve, if in the early stages one is endeavouring to hit a ball at the same time.

There was a time when almost all who aspired to teach golf were inclined to say: " Get the wrists down when addressing the ball." This very bad advice was in some ways quite natural, since if the wrists are down or " cocked " before the swing begins it is more than likely that they will be cocked at the top of the swing. Nevertheless, if the wrists are cocked or partially cocked when addressing the ball the whole back swing tends to become too rigid and the left hand loses its suppleness.

Bobbie Jones once said: " You can tell a golfer's ability from the first ten inches of his swing," and before leaving the back swing we must deal with this most important section, as well as the position of the hands at the top of the swing. It is a matter of the utmost importance that the club head should begin its journey back dead square to the ball; that is, it must continue to " look at " the ball for as long as possible. There must be no outward turning of the club head. The way to acquire a sound initial movement of the club head is to make the hands move first, in the direction in which the club head is about to travel. If the wrists are cocked when the ball is being addressed, as already mentioned, they tend to become rigid, and if there is any sign of rigidity the club head is more than likely to start first instead of the hands. It is a curious physical fact that if the hands and club head start back correctly they will both be in a correct position on the return journey, and there will be no excessive pronation of the wrists.

Modern expert golfers do not take the club back nearly as far as the old-timers, since it has been found that a three-quarter back swing will give as much power as a full swing, and in some cases more. Thus we come to the top of the back swing and how best to prevent taking the club back too far. This is quite simple to achieve, provided that the last two fingers of the left hand retain a firm but not tight grip of the club.

I wish to dismiss the question of " Pivot " very briefly. If you allow the left heel to leave the ground as the club is going back, you will be able to turn the back of your shoulders at the ball. This movement, coupled with the use of the right hand in delivering the blow, will ensure that the ball is hit from inside to out, and consequently fairly and squarely in the back.

Very few golfers keep their heads still enough throughout the swing. The head should remain as motionless as is physically possible until well after the ball is on its way. If the head is allowed to sway back with the club it will have to sway forward again, which will at once lead to disaster. Particular notice should be taken of

Address for drive   Commencing back swing

the position after impact of the heads of all great golfers of our time. And remember that no one can play accurately unless he stands still.

Too much is often made of the follow-through and those who practise it do it to such an extent that they force their eye off the ball at the moment of impact. The great thing to remember at impact and immediately after is to ensure that the left arm does not break until the club head has travelled at least two feet past the ball. On the other hand, a nice easy follow-through looks agreeable and finishes off the job.

Lastly, we come to the Rhythm of the swing. All the great artists to my mind appear to have a beautiful rhythm. It is essentially musical and makes the *tout ensemble* a gentle, easy, natural performance. I am convinced that this can be acquired by almost all who play the game but on the other hand, it is seldom that we

Top of swing with No. 2 iron

Finish of full shot with No. 2

ever see a golfer with a really rhythmic swing. The secret lies in taking the club back slowly and, as it were, winding oneself up quietly into the striking position before letting fly. Oddly enough, from the title of our national anthem " God Save the Queen " the basis of a rhythm can be acquired. If we time our swing so that whilst taking the club back we repeat " God-save-the- ", we shall have wound ourselves up slowly. On the way down we can say " Queen ", with a snap. Try to be smooth. This applies from tee to green.

Driving.

What is the object of the drive? as they say in the army. Clearly, from the tee this should be to hit the ball on to the fairway into such a position as to make the second shot as easy as possible. I once overheard Bobbie Jones say in the clubhouse at Sunningdale: " I cannot understand people in this country calling themselves scratch and plus golfers before they have learned what ought to be the easiest part of the game, namely, to hit the ball down the middle of the course from the tee." How true! Even in these days one comes across very few so-called first-class amateurs whom one could honestly describe as being good sound drivers. One of the reasons for this is that on the whole our courses are too wide and in an enormous number of cases the rough is not nearly heavy enough. Thus one may say that the ideal training ground for a young player is a heather course where, unless tee shots are hit straight, a game of golf is misery.

Generally speaking, one would advise young players to drive with an easy club, that is a fairly lofted brassie, for in so many cases the ordinary driver is a difficult club to use except for the expert player. Secondly, one should never be ashamed of driving the ball high since to hit a low drive is one of the most difficult strokes in the game. Once confidence, through studious practice and experience, has been achieved, then a straight-faced driver may be used. Even so, I have for many years made a practice of using a brassie from the tee whenever driving down-wind. The ball travels just as far as when hit with a driver and is much easier to hit straight. Hit the fairway at all costs from the tee and keep the ball in play.

Whereas the driver and wooden clubs are made with a wide flat sole and are intended to sweep the turf, an iron club is made almost in the shape of a knife and is intended to cut the turf. Even amongst the great—particularly in the case of amateurs; and this applies to Bobbie Jones himself—it is unusual to find in one man a great wooden club player and a great iron player. In the case of Jones, the greatest of all wooden club players, by comparison his irons were poor. Wethered, who is still a miracle of efficiency with an iron club, was generally a deplorable wooden club player, since he invariably took a divot with a club not meant for such a purpose. Cotton, on the other hand, is as good with wooden clubs as he is with irons. His standard of efficiency with both is unbelievably high.

As with wooden clubs, set out to hit the ball straight; up to a point the blow may be a descending one at the back of the ball, with a divot of turf being removed beyond the ball. Stand still, and punch the ball rather than sweep it along. Never overdo the " hitting down ", for it makes the stroke more difficult, especially on heavy turf. I believe the real secret of success with iron clubs is to keep the head down so long after hitting the ball as to have to search for it in the sky. If the head has done its job the ball will be found underneath the club head in the air at the end of the stroke.

Putting.

Having suffered much, and perhaps even more than most players, on the putting greens, and having practised for hours on end with no avail, I have reached the age when big golf is rapidly becoming for me a thing of the past. Nevertheless, I have at last learnt an effective method of putting, which I believe to be sound; and different versions of it are used by American golfers. Before describing the actual method, we must first of all consider the mental aspect of putting, and the short game. Where most of us fail is that at the outset we putt to get the ball into the hole, and as long as the ball drops we are satisfied that all is well. Now unless a ball is properly and scientifically struck with the putter it will not consistently travel on the intended line. When our eye is " in " we may achieve some success; when our eye is " out " results will be deplorable. Thus our one and only concern should be to learn to strike the ball properly and sweetly, just as a billiard player does. Never mind where it goes to begin with, just make it roll. And how are we to make it roll? It should be clear that if we impart top spin a ball is more likely to keep the line than one which has a drag or back spin, or when it is slightly cut or hooked. Thus we must endeavour to hit the ball at least half-way up or even on the top.

As to the mechanics of the putting stroke, we must now examine them. To begin with, a normal grip is as sound as any other, though some prefer the reverse overlap, with the first finger of the left hand overlapping the little finger of the right. It should be clear that unless the club head is taken back straight, that is, on a continuation of an imaginary line between the ball and the hole— assuming that the putt is a straight one—it is not possible consistently to strike the ball in the direction of the hole. The easiest way, and perhaps the only way, to take the putter back straight is with the left hand, bending the left wrist in so doing, in this manner. The right hand then partially takes charge, to strike the ball, but the left hand still has a most important duty to perform, and this to my mind is its most difficult function. As the right hand moves the club head towards the ball the left wrist gradually unwinds until the back of the left hand is in line with the back of the left fore-

Putting

arm. Once this position has been reached the left hand, together with the left forearm, should travel towards the hole, enabling the club head to follow right through the ball and finish low near the ground, as in the illustration. So long as the club head strikes the ball half-way up it will be easy to follow-through, but if the putter head so much as grazes the ground the ball is unlikely to be struck fairly and squarely, and consistent results are most unlikely. Similarly with chip shots and short approaches. One's only consideration should be to strike the ball in the middle of the club and smoothly. Finally, with these short shots one should consider: " Am I going to hit the ball off the ground or am I attempting to make it run all the way?" If the ball is to be hit in the air, we must always make up our minds as to the approximate place on the green, or just in front, upon which it is intended to pitch the ball. It will at first seem extremely difficult to achieve, but so long as we always have this at the back of our minds when playing little pitches or chip shots, accuracy will eventually come; therein lies the secret of the short game.

GYMNASTICS

Having taught recreational gymnastics, by which I mean exercises on the parallel bars, vaulting horse, rings, pyramids, mass free standing exercises to music, skipping, dancing, exercises with hand apparatus, such as Indian clubs, dumb-bells, wands, hoops, small rings, flags, tennis rackets, canes, &c., to children, girls and women, varying in age from six to forty, for more than thirty years, I think I can claim to have had sufficient experience to qualify me to give some advice to those interested in this subject.

Many of my pupils have won open, individual, and team competitions, and one was chosen to represent this country in the Olympic Games.

To begin with, there is a fallacy existing in the minds of a great many people that apparatus exercises are bad for girls. Why the recreational type of apparatus should be harmful, and the educational type, as used in schools, should not be, it is very difficult to understand. Also why gymnastics should be likely to do more harm than hockey, tennis, lacrosse, swimming, &c., is something of a mystery. Throughout my career, I have never known any of my pupils suffer structural malformation or organic injury in any way from exercises on the apparatus mentioned previously. I have known only good to be derived from their use. I have known accidents to occur, but no more than in an educational gymnasium, and far less than in most women's sports. When put to the test by me, not one person I have questioned on the subject has ever been able to produce one single proof of the assertion that recreational apparatus work is harmful.

I trust this statement will allay any fears parents, girls or women may have regarding the use of the apparatus found in a recreational gymnasium. A great deal of pleasure, as well as mental and physical benefit, can be obtained from exercises on the apparatus, taught properly and progressively. So do not hesitate to join a gym, where the instructor or instructress has a sound knowledge of progressive apparatus work and musical exercises.

206

How to Become a Gymnast.

The younger a girl begins, the better chance she has of finally becoming an expert, artistic gymnast. Girls do not need great strength to perform the basic exercises on the apparatus. For the first two or three years, short, brief apparatus exercises, combined with musical mass exercises, will be found sufficient. There are hundreds of attractive apparatus exercises, and a good instructor can put together fascinating musical free exercises and hand apparatus exercises. The fundamental exercises on the apparatus lead gradually to the more advanced exercises.

Every effort should be made to perform the exercises correctly, and in good style, but at first do not worry too much about perfection. This will be attained by regular, consistent practice. If you are keen to become a highly skilled gymnast, to make rapid progress, persuade your instructor to help you over every difficulty you come across in the gym, and there are plenty, no matter whether it be mass exercises or apparatus work. No instructor who has the welfare of his or her pupils at heart will refuse help to a keen and enthusiastic pupil. Regular practice at least once a week all through the year, except for summer holidays, should enable a girl, by the time she is sixteen, to be well on the way towards being a gymnast. For speedy progress, regular attendance, and keen, conscientious practice, with the help and guidance of your instructor, will work wonders.

Exercises.

The mass exercises given are arranged for solo work, which means that the aspiring gymnast can practise them daily at home, and by so doing, materially assist her progress on the apparatus. They are all of a difficult nature, especially for very young girls. Learn them slowly and carefully. By mastering them thoroughly you will be able to learn the exercises set by your instructor very much more quickly than you otherwise would do.

The apparatus exercises are arranged for gradual, steady progress from simple, easy exercises to quite difficult ones. Learn the terminology of the exercises, as this means a saving of time eventually. Exercises that are quite difficult to one gymnast may prove easy to another. Some learn apparatus exercises very rapidly up to a point, but there comes a time to every learner when nothing seems to go right, and you even seem to be slipping backward. Therefore, make a plan to work to, and keep a record of your progress, so that when you come up against this sticky period, which all gymnasts do, a brief glance at your record will reassure you, and enable you to carry on with renewed determination and confidence to succeed in achieving your objective. Know what you want and work to get it. You can do much worse than become a first-class gymnast, or even a gymnastic instructress.

Style.

To perform any exercise in good style means that it must be done in such a manner that it excites the admiration of the onlooker, and that it is done with supreme ease and gracefulness, the latter a special province of girls. To become a stylish, artistic gymnast means much hard work, even to the natural stylist.

Dancing and mass exercises are a great aid to style on the apparatus. If good style is to be attained, the mind must be exclusively concentrated on the performance of the exercise being attempted. The slightest relaxation of mental control means a loss of style. The limbs must be stretched firmly, but not too rigidly, or the exercises will look wooden. It is easy to see now that the mind as well as the body benefits considerably from musical drills and apparatus exercises. Get your instructor to check your style and help you to improve your weak spots.

Displays.

Consider your club's display as you would a play. All the performers are actors and actresses in every sense of the word. Aim at being a star performer. The display is usually the culmination of the year's work, and it is up to every pupil to do her best to make her club's display the best ever. Be sure you know your dances, skipping, mass and apparatus exercises as nearly perfectly as possible. It is usually a nervous ordeal, especially the first display, but steel yourself to forget your surroundings, and if you keep your thoughts entirely on what you are doing, once you get started the nervousness will completely disappear. There is always a thrill and feeling of satisfaction in the applause of the audience for a well-performed drill or apparatus exercise. See that you deserve the applause.

Competitions.

Most gymnastic clubs arrange annual competitions. Some hold team competitions only, some individual competitions in squads, and many arrange both. Team and individual competitions are sometimes arranged to take place together. No matter what your club arranges, take part in it, whether you think you have a chance or not; it is good experience. All competitions are nervous ordeals, but by competing frequently, one gradually learns to control these nervous feelings. Your success or failure in competitions usually indicates your progress in gymnastics. Always ask to see the marks when the competition is over, but never query the judge's decisions, even if you think you have not been treated too kindly. From the marks you will be able to discern your weaknesses, which you should do your utmost to eliminate before the next competition comes along. If successful do not let your success go to your head. Be modest in victory and sportsmanlike in defeat.

Leadership.

By the time a girl is fifteen years of age, she should begin to seek opportunities of helping the instructor by taking apparatus squads occasionally. Learn the art of " standing by ", or assisting on the apparatus, an art at which the adept is made only by years of practice and experimenting. Pupils have no hesitation in attempting difficult exercises if they have confidence in their instructor or leader. Watch your instructor to see how he assists, and follow his methods, which have only been gained by long experience. Once you have acquired a reputation as a good helper, you will never lack big squads, a very sincere form of flattery.

Dress.

The best dress for apparatus work is a blouse, good-fitting dark knickers, and black stockings. The last are a necessity for apparatus work, as if the bare legs come in contact with the bars, the skin tends to get badly rubbed. For drills and skipping, a neat short skirt, or a tunic with a belt, is usually worn. Most clubs have a distinctive dress, which is insisted on for displays and competitions.

PART A. INDIAN CLUBS

Every gymnast should be able to swing clubs sufficiently well to be able to give a solo of her own composition. This needs much practice, which can be obtained in your own home. For this, rise ten minutes earlier than usual every morning, and the skill you will acquire in six months will surprise you. The best book in existence on the subject is Cobbett and Jenkins' *Indian Clubs*. Purchase a pair of clubs, or sceptres, the correct weight and the right length for your arms. The correct grip is with the knob outside the little finger. Do not grip the handle too hard.

There are two kinds of movements—swings and twists. Swings are large circles done with straight arms. Twists are small circles done with hand and wrist, with either bent or straight arms. There are only two directions, inward and outward. If both arms are stretched upward and the clubs are allowed to fall in towards one another, the resulting circles are called inward circles, and vice versa. If one club does inward and the other does outward at the same time, this produces parallel movements. If one club does inward swings or twists half a circle in front of the other, doing outward movements, this produces " windmills ".

Club movements can be combined with leg and trunk exercises and balance exercises, and the exercises given here are of this type.

Music.—Waltz time. Any well-marked waltz.

Starting position.—Arms bent, clubs vertical, feet together (fig. 1).

Exercises.—Two outward, two parallel, and two inward, in that order, each exercise of 16 counts, 8 counts left side, and 8 right.

Exercise 1. Theme: Outward movements.

1. Place left foot sideways to stride stand, and stretch arms upward (fig. 2).
2. One outward swing.
3. Quarter turn left and bend left knee to forward lunge, $\frac{7}{8}$th outward swing right arm, $\frac{5}{8}$th outward swing left arm behind the body (fig. 3).
4. Face front, $\frac{3}{4}$ inward swing right arm, $\frac{1}{2}$ inward swing left arm; arms now diagonally upward (fig. 4).
5. Slightly bend both arms and cross clubs above head (fig. 5).

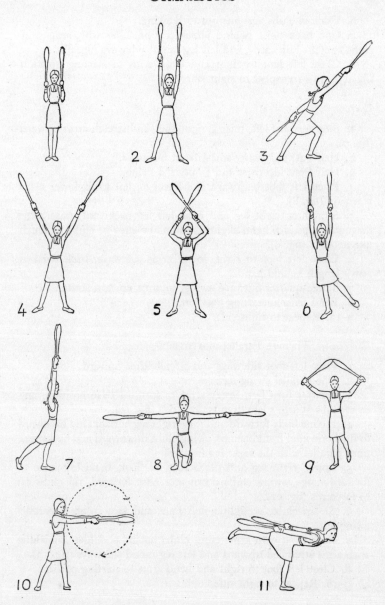

6. Uncross clubs and one outward swing.

7. One back twist behind shoulders, finishing with arms and clubs stretched upwards, and left leg raised sideways (fig. 6).

8. Close left foot to right and bend arms to starting position (fig. 1); 9 to 16 repeat to right side.

Exercise 2.

1. Step forward left, raising right heel, and stretch arms upward (fig. 7).

2. Half outward swing and $\frac{1}{2}$ front hip twist.

3. Half front hip twist and $\frac{1}{2}$ outward swing.

4. Place left foot backward and kneel on left knee, lower arms sideways (fig. 8).

5. Straighten right leg and raise left leg backward, raise arms diagonally upward, bend slightly, and allow ends of clubs to touch one another (fig. 9).

6. Close left foot to right, lower arms sideways, back twist at arm's length behind hands.

7. Three-quarter outward swing, to arms upward stretch.

8. Bend arms to starting position.

9–16. Repeat to right side.

Exercise 3. Theme: Parallel movements.

1. Place left foot sideways and stretch arms upward.

2. One parallel swing left.

3. Quarter turn left, lower arms to forward raise position, and twist clubs at arm's length outside hands (fig. 10).

4. Incline body forward and raise right leg horizontally backward to the horizontal front balance, swing clubs downward and backward, until parallel with the right leg (fig. 11).

5. Lower right leg and place foot on floor, bend left knee to forward lunge, swing clubs down and raise forward, tip clubs on to forearms (fig. 12).

6. Re-tip clubs, straighten left knee and face front, $\frac{3}{4}$ parallel swing left.

7. Back twist with arms bent, clubs behind shoulders, finishing with arms stretched upward and left leg raised sideways (fig. 13).

8. Close left foot to right and bend arms to starting position.

9–16. Repeat to right side.

Exercise 4.

1. Place left foot sideways and stretch arms upward.

2. Seven-eights parallel swing left.

3. Bend left knee to sideways lunge, incline body sideways left in one straight line with right leg, tip clubs on forearms, arms now pointing diagonally upward (fig. 14).

4. Re-tip clubs and ½ parallel swing right, change knee, bending to lunge sideways right, bend body forward and downward and check clubs when they are parallel with left leg (fig. 15).

5. Raise body upright, ⅝th parallel swing left until arms are up--ight.

6. Half parallel swing left and ½ front hip twist.

7. Half front hip twist and ½ parallel swing left, raise left leg sideways.

8. Close left foot to right, and bend arms to starting position.

9-16. Repeat to right side.

Exercise 5. Theme: Inward movements.

1. Place left foot sideways and stretch arms upward.

2. Three-quarter inward swing.

3. Bend left knee to sideways lunge and tip clubs on to forearms (fig. 16).

4. Cross left leg behind right, slightly bending right knee, re-tip clubs, arms remaining sideways (fig. 17).

5. Place left foot sideways to stride stand, one inward swing (fig. 18).

6. One bent arm back twist.

7. One inward swing to arms upward stretch, raise left leg sideways.

8. Close left foot to right and bend arms to starting position.

9-16. Repeat to right side.

Exercise 6.

1. Step forward left, right heel raised, stretch arms upward.

2. Half inward swing both arms and ½ inward twist at hips, all the weight on the front foot.

3. Half front hip twist and raise arms sideways.

4. Place left foot backward, kneel on right knee, slightly bend arms and allow ends of clubs to touch one another, above head (fig. 19).

5. Straighten right leg and raise left leg backward in balance position, straighten arms and stretch arms and clubs sideways (fig. 20).

6. Replace left foot to right and one inward swing, to arms sideways.

7. One inward back twist at arm's length behind hands, and raise arms upward.

8. Bend arms to starting position.

FREE STANDING EXERCISES

The type of free standing exercises that my classes liked most of all were those that incorporated the recognized dancing movements and attitudes, always done to music. The exercise given here has been arranged for waltz time, each movement taking one bar of music, which should be played rather slowly. If the directions are followed carefully with the aid of the diagrams, there should be no difficulty in learning the movements, which should all flow freely one after the other. There is plenty of opportunity to show gracefulness and self-control. Once the exercise has been thoroughly learned, try making up fresh ones on similar lines. It is good fun as well as good exercise. Introduce plenty of balances into your exercises, as they are a great help in cultivating style on the apparatus.

The Exercise. (Illustrations coincide with the following numbers.)

Starting position.—At attention.

1. Raise heels, raise arms sideways upward, and curve overhead, finger tips touching, look upward at hands.

2. Lower heels and point left toe sideways, incline body slightly to the left, lower left arm sideways diagonally downward, palm turned upward, straighten right arm sideways diagonally upward, palm upward, turn head and look down at left hand.

3. Transfer weight on to left foot so that right foot points sideways, incline body slightly to the right, raise left arm sideways and curve overhead, lower right arm and place right hand on hip, look down at right elbow.

4. Raise right arm sideways upward, straighten left arm upward, quarter turn and face left, bend body forward and downward, bend right knee deeply, and swing arms forward, downward, backward,

upward, palms turned upward, at the finish of the movement raise body slightly.

5. Dip body downward and quickly raise upright, swing arms downward, forward, upward, and press slightly backward, bending body slightly backward, palms turned forward, straighten the right leg and raise backward to balance position, weight on the left leg, leg straight.

6. Turn on left foot and face the front, bend left knee to lunge position, place right foot sideways, incline body to the left side, body and right leg in one straight line, swing both arms downward, the left arm being bent finally with the left hand close to the left ear, the right arm being carried sideways, diagonally upward (shot-putting position), look up at the right hand.

7. Straighten the left leg and face right, kick left leg forward and upward, body upright, swing left arm downward and forward until parallel with right arm, raise both arms upward as kick is being finished.

8. Without pause, swing left leg downward, backward and upward to the high horizontal front balance position, bend body forward, as leg is being lowered and raised backward, circle the arms inward, and finish in the sideways raised position (swallow dive position standing on one leg).

9. Lower left leg and kneel on left knee, bend body forward and downward, lower arms sideways and downward, curving arms so that the finger tips are almost touching, as though picking something up, backs of the hands close to the floor.

10. Straighten both legs, face the front, bend the left knee to the sideways lunge position, incline body to the left in line with the right leg, swing arms forward and upward, lower left arm diagonally sideways downward to the left, palm upward, and curve right arm overhead, looking into bend of right arm.

11. Raise trunk upright, raise left arm sideways, straighten right arm and lower sideways.

12. Cross left leg behind right, across bend arms so that the left forearm is above the right forearm, fingers stretched.

13. Rise on toes and complete pirouette to the left, keeping arms in same position.

14. Lunge sideways left, body erect, fling arms sideways, palms downward.

15. Straighten left knee and raise left leg high sideways, lower

arms, cross them, and continue circling them until in the upward stretch position, palms inward.

16. Lower left leg and lower arms sideways downward to attention. 17–32 repeat 1–16 on opposite side.

PART B.   APPARATUS EXERCISES

PARALLEL BARS

From my experience this is the apparatus that girls find most interesting, the variety of exercises being so great. The easy, simple exercises do not require much strength, and are not at all dangerous. The exercises given here are arranged progressively, and are as varied as it is possible to make them in so brief an article. The age groups have been arranged for the budding gymnasts to gauge their progress, which is quite easy if you work to a plan and keep a record of the exercises you learn.

Assistance by the instructor is absolutely necessary for the great majority of the exercises, especially during the first two or three years. All the exercises are arranged for bars at the lowest possible height, usually about 3 ft. 9 in. from the floor. If you can, use bars adjustable for width as well as height. The exercises are described on the left side only, but should always be done both sides. Learn each exercise thoroughly, and when a number have been learned, put them together to form voluntaries, i.e. a series of exercises performed one after the other without pause, usually consisting of about five or six exercises, all following on smoothly. When learning the exercises, aim first of all at becoming familiar with the movements, but as soon as this is accomplished, pay every attention possible to style. You will then find the exercises will become intensely interesting.

The Exercises.

Most exercises for girls are done in the Cross Rest, i.e. with the shoulders crossways or at right angles to the bars. A few exercises are done in the hang below the bars. Exercises may be commenced from a Cross Stand at the near end facing inward, in the centre of the bars, and at the ends facing outward, in between the bars in the side stand (or with shoulders parallel to the bars), or from an outside side stand.

GROUP A

Exercises for Age Group 10–12.

1. From a cross stand, jump to the cross rest at (fig. 1a) the near end, (b) in the centre, or (c) at the far end of the bars.

2. From (fig. 2a) an outside or (b) inside side stand, jump to the front rest of one bar.

3. Jump to the cross rest and (fig. 3a) arch the back; (b) raise one or both heels backward, arching the back; (c) raise one or both knees forward; raise one or both legs with a swing.

4. At the ends facing inward with outer grip, or inside grip, run forward, lowering body below bars until hanging with straight arms, heels on the floor, head, body and legs in one straight line, and return.

5. From a cross stand at the near end facing inward, jump up and swing right leg (a) to inside cross seat on right bar in front of right hand; (b) to riding seat on right bar in front of right hand; (c) to side seat on left bar with right leg over left bar in front of left hand, making a slight turn of the body.

6. From a cross stand at the near end facing inward, jump up and swing both legs forward to (a) outside cross seat on right bar in front of right hand; (b) as (a), with $\frac{1}{4}$ turn right to outside side seat, the left hand changing on to the right bar; (c) as (b), but add another $\frac{1}{4}$ turn right, changing both hands one after the other, coming to the outside cross seat in front of left hand.

7. From an inside cross stand at the far ends facing outward, (a) bend knees and grasp bars with outer grip, raise legs over the face, and hook feet on the bars, slide feet along the bars, turning over backward until (b) hanging face downward on hands and feet, and return.

8. From a cross stand in the centre of the bars, jump up and swing both legs to outside cross seat in front of left hand, and dismount (a) to outside cross stand, left side towards bars; (b) with $\frac{1}{4}$ turn left to outside side stand facing bars; (c) with $\frac{1}{2}$ turn left to outside cross stand with right side toward bars, grasping right bar with right hand as dismount is commenced.

9. From an outside side stand, facing bars, jump up with a $\frac{1}{4}$ turn left to outside cross seat in front of left hand, and dismount as in 8 (a), (b), (c).

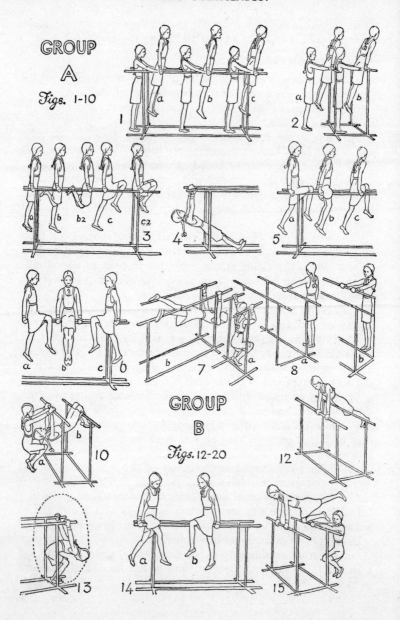

GROUP
A
Figs. 1-10

1   a   b   c

2   a   b

3   a   b   b2   c   c2

4

5   a   b   c

6   a   b   c

7   b   a

8   a   b

10   a   b

GROUP
B
Figs. 12-20

12

13

14   a   b

15

10. From an outside side stand facing bars, grasp bar, (a) bend knees, (b) jump and hook legs on far bar to the hand on legs and hands and return.

GROUP B

Exercises for Age Group 12–14.

11. At the ends facing inward, grasp bars, jump up and swing to outside cross seat in front of right hand, swing legs across both bars to outside cross seat in front of left hand, and dismount.

12. From an inside cross stand jump up and swing to outside cross seat in front of right hand, $\frac{1}{4}$ turn left to front leaning rest across both bars, dismount with a push backward to an outside side stand facing bar.

13. From an inside cross stand at the far end facing outward, bend knees and take outer grip, turn backward and forward somersaults.

14. From an outside cross stand at near ends facing inward, jump up and (a) swing right leg over right bar in front of right hand and with a le t-about turn, changing right hand on to left bar and left hand on to right bar one after the other, and swinging left leg sideways, come to (b) outside cross seat in front of left hand, dismount with right- or left-about turn.

15. Repeat Ex. 2 up to front leaning rest across both bars, then place right knee on the bar and raise left leg high backward, lower left leg, swing it up and dismount by pushing backward, catching rear bar.

16. From a cross stand at the ends facing inward, jump up and swing legs to and fro to outside cross seat in front of right hand, swing legs between bars and swing forward to outside cross seat in front of left hand, dismount.

17. From a cross stand at the ends facing inward, jump up and swing to back leaning rest along the bars, turn on to right hand, raising left arm upward, and jump to the ground.

18. From a cross stand at the far ends facing outward, jump up and swing, and at the end of the backward swing place feet on the bars behind the hands in front leaning rest along the bars, dismount with a jump sideways behind the right hand to the cross stand outside bars.

19. From a cross stand at the ends between the bars facing inward, jump up and swing to outside cross seat in front of right hand, $\frac{1}{4}$

turn left to front leaning rest across the bars, raise right leg and pass it between the bars, and return to front leaning rest, same left leg, dismount.

20. From a cross stand in the centre of the bars, jump up and swing to and fro and rear vault right (over bar in front of right hand) to a cross stand outside bars.

GROUP C

Exercises for Age Group 14–16.

21. From an inside side stand in the centre of the bars, grasp bar and jump up to front rest, (a) raise right leg sideways and place it on the rear bar, same left, to (b) front leaning rest across the bars, dismount backward.

22. From a cross stand at the ends facing inward, jump up and (a) swing left leg over right bar in front of right hand, $\frac{1}{4}$ turn left and place right hand on left bar, pass right leg backward as turn is made, and come to (b) front leaning rest across bars, raise right leg and with another $\frac{1}{4}$ turn left, pass right leg through bars to (c) outside cross seat in front of left hand, dismount with a $\frac{1}{2}$ left turn.

23. From a cross stand at the near ends facing inward, just between the bars, bend forward and downward, (a) raise arms backward and grasp bars with outer grip, turn front somersault (b) to the stand.

24. From a cross stand in the centre of the bars, jump up and swing to and fro, rear vault right with a $\frac{1}{4}$ turn left.

25. From an (a) outside side stand in the centre of the bars, jump up with a $\frac{1}{4}$ turn left to (b) outside cross seat in front of left hand, grasp bars behind, (c) rear vault over both bars to the ground.

26. From a cross stand in the centre of the bars, jump up and swing right leg over right bar in front of right hand, $\frac{1}{4}$ turn left, pass left leg sideways and backward to front leaning rest across bars, place left foot sideways on front bar, and (b) flank vault left over both bars to the ground.

27. Cross stand at the ends facing inward, jump up and swing to (a) outside cross seat in front of right hand, (b) place both hands on bars in front of legs, swing legs off right bar backwards between the bars to (c) outside cross seat left, dismount.

28. Cross stand at the ends facing inward, jump up and swing

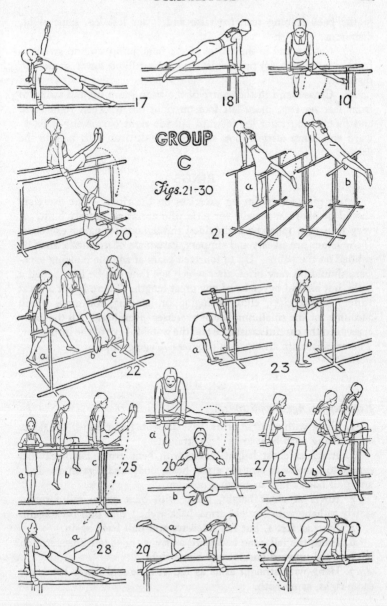

GROUP
C
Figs. 21-30

to the back leaning rest, (*a*) raise and lower left leg, same right, dismount.

29. Cross stand in the centre of the bars, jump up and swing to front leaning rest, (*a*) raise right leg backward and lower, same left, dismount.

30. Cross stand in the centre of the bars, jump up and swing to front leaning rest, place left foot on right bar between right hand and foot, swing right leg forward outside right bar, swing it backward and jump off left foot, and front vault over both bars to the ground.

RINGS

Most girls like swinging exercises on the rings. The exercises should be short, especially for girls who are at all heavily built. A very firm grip must be maintained throughout swinging exercises. If the hands are sweaty and slippery, carbonate of magnesia must be rubbed on the palms. Up to fourteen years of age the hanging exercises should be very brief, after which age they can be lengthened a little, but should never be of any great length. There is not a great variety of exercises, either swinging or hanging, for girls, which accounts for the small number of exercises given here. All the exercises need the careful assistance and the watchful eye of the instructor. The exercises are arranged in progressive age groups.

GROUP A

Exercises for Age Group 10–12.

1. Hang with straight arms, legs straight, feet clear of the floor.
2. Hang with bent arms, legs straight.
3. Rings at chest height, grasp with bent arms, fall backward slowly to hang with straight arms, head, body and legs in one line, and pull back again to starting position.
4. Rings at chest height, grasp with bent arms, fall forward slowly to hang with straight arms, back arched, and pull back again.
5. Start as Ex. 4, but fall sideways and pull back again.
6. From the fall hang backward as Ex. 3, raise left knee, stretch leg forward upward and lower. Same right.
7. Hang with straight arms as Ex. 1, raise and lower left knee, same right, same both.

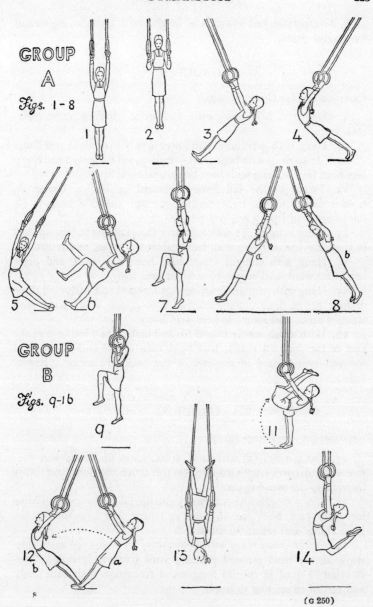

GROUP
A
Figs. 1 - 8

1 2 3 4

5 6 7 8

GROUP
B
Figs. 9-16

9

11

12
b a
13 14

8. Grasp rings just above head height, with a run swing to and fro several times.

GROUP B

Exercises for Age Group 12–14.

9. Hang with bent arms, raise and lower left knee, same right, same both.

10. Hang with bent arms and lower slowly to straight arm hang.

11. Grasp rings with bent arms, jump up, fall backward and bring legs over face to hang with bent body, and return.

12. From (*a*) the fall hang backward as Ex. 3, Group A, revolve slowly to the right, passing through the side hang to (*b*) the hang stand frontways, and return.

13. Hang as in Ex. 11 with legs over face, straighten legs upward to the hang upside down with feet against the ropes, and return.

14. Hang with straight arms, raise heels backward, and press head backward, and return to straight arm hang.

15. Hang with bent arms, swing legs forward and backward three or four times, finally falling backward to upside down hang with straight arms, and return to bent arm hang.

16. With a run, swing to and fro and make a half left turn at the end of the forward swing, half right turn at the end of the next forward swing, drop at the end of the backward swing. Repeat right.

GROUP C

Exercises for Age Group 14–16.

17. Grasp rings (*a*) with bent arms, jump up, bring legs over face and turn over backward until (*b*) feet touch the floor, and return forward to the stand again.

18. Grasp rings with bent arms, jump up, fall backward, and bring legs over face, hook feet in rings and turn over backward to the Nest Hang, and return to the stand.

19. Stand, grasp rings with bent arms, (*a*) straighten arms sideways, slowly bend forward twisting arms (commonly called " dislocation ") until in the (*b*) hang-stand frontways with bent body, and return to starting position.

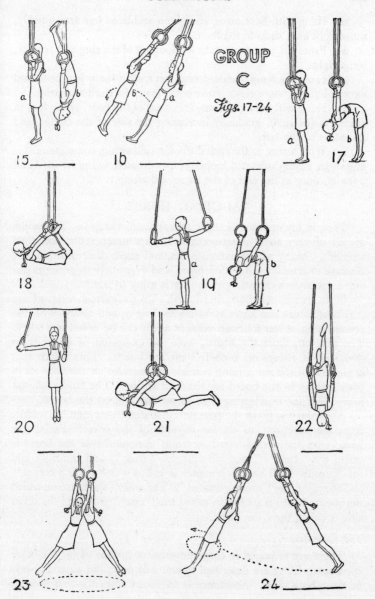

GROUP C

Figs. 17-24

15   16   17

18   19

20   21   22

23   24

20. Hang with bent arms, straighten and bend left arm quickly, same right arm, drop to the floor.

21. From the nest hang, take left foot out of the ring and replace, same right.

22. From the hang upside-down, feet free of the ropes, bend and stretch left leg, same right, same both, lower forward and drop.

33. Hang with straight arms, feet clear of the floor, swing legs in circles to the right, gradually increasing the size of the circles, and the same to the left.

24. With a run, at the end of the forward swing, complete pirouette right, swing backward keeping ropes crossed, swing forward and untwist, drop at the end of the backward swing.

VAULTING HORSE

This, in my opinion, is the ideal apparatus for girls. The vaults are all of very short duration, and require much more skill than strength. Many of the exercises demand great determination and courage to attempt in the first place, and eventually to perform unaided. A stylish, artistic girl vaulter is a joy to watch.

Girls always use the spring-board. Up to fourteen years of age it is best to use the horse at its lowest height, and always with the pommels on. Over fourteen years of age it can be raised one notch. The take-off, from the board, with the exception of about three exercises, is always off both feet off the board. This means that at the end of the run a jump is made off one foot off the floor on to both feet on to the board for the final spring. The single take-off means that the final spring is made off one foot off the board.

Always try to grasp the pommels just slightly beyond the middle from the approach, or on the far side of the horse. Facing the horse with the spring-board in front, the middle of the horse is called the " saddle ", the left end the " neck ", and the right end the " croup ". The left pommel is called the " neck pommel ", and the right, the " croup pommel ". The side of the horse on which the spring-board is placed in called the " near " side, and the other side is called the " far " side.

The Exercises.

These are arranged in three progressive groups as for the other apparatus. They are described to one side only, but should always be done both sides. Assistance is necessary from the first exercise to the last one. Right from the beginning, endeavour to acquire good style. When landing on the floor at the finish of an exercise, always assume the " knees bend " or half squat position.

GROUP A

Exercises for Age Group 10–12.

1. Stand on spring-board, grasp pommels, jump up and down several times (*a*) with and (*b*) without resting legs against the horse, legs straight, back hollow, alighting on the board with (*c*) knees bent for correct landing.

2. From a stand on the board, and from the run, jump and kneel on one or both knees on saddle; dismount backward on the board, or forward by standing on the saddle and jumping forward.

All subsequent exercises are preceded with a run and the take-off is from both feet unless stated to the contrary.

3. Jump to (*a*) the squat (full knees bend) stand; stand upright and (*b*) jump forward to the ground.

4. Grasp pommels and jump to (*a*) the stand, with one foot on the saddle and the other on the neck; (*b*) with one foot on the saddle and the other on the croup; (*c*) with one foot on the croup and the other on the neck in the stride stand—dismount with a jump forward.

5. Jump to the half kneel with the right knee on the saddle and the left foot on the neck, left leg straight, stand up on the horse and jump forward to the ground.

6. Jump and squat legs through the arms to the side seat on the saddle, dismount straight forward, or with a ¼ or a ½ turn, with a push from the hands.

7. Jump to the horizontal, ½ kneel on the right knee, with the left leg extended horizontally backward, body bent forward, place left foot on saddle, stand up and jump forward to ground.

8. Jump to (*a*) the stand on the saddle, jump to (*b*) the stride stand with feet outside the pommels, jump to ground.

9. Jump to (*a*) the stand with right foot on saddle and left foot on neck, astride the neck pommel, jump sideways to the right with (*b*) left foot on saddle and right foot on croup, astride the croup pommel, jump forward to ground.

These jumping exercises standing on the horse may be varied in numerous ways.

GROUP A

Figs. 1-10

GROUP B

Figs. 11-20

10. Jump and squat between arms to the back rest, hollow back, and dismount forward.

GROUP B

Exercises for Age Group 12–14.

11. Jump to (*a*) the half kneel, right knee on saddle, left foot on neck, left leg straight, ¼ turn right to (*b*) the front leaning rest, both hands on croup pommel, head, body and legs in one straight line, dismount (*c*) sideways left.

12. Jump to the stand on the saddle, jump and turn left about on the saddle, (*a*) bend down and grasp pommels, (*b*) raise one leg, throw up backward and (*c*) drop to the ground, holding the pommels.

13. Jump and (*a*) lie on the saddle, release hands and gradually tilt forward until (*b*) hands are on the mat, dismount by walking forward on the hands on the mat, letting the feet drop gently on to the mat; or a (*c*) forward roll may be performed as a finish after the hands reach the mat.

14. Jump and (*a*) squat right foot on the saddle, (*b*) circle left leg over neck pommel, lifting and replacing left hand, raise right foot off saddle and push forward to the ground.

15. Jump and squat right leg between arms to the riding seat on the saddle, then squat left leg through arms to the back rest, raise legs and dismount forward with a push.

16. Jump and (*a*) place both feet on the neck, legs straight, (*b*) raise left arm, and straighten body to side leaning rest, dismount with a jump forward without any turn of the body, alighting with the back to the horse.

17. Jump to the horizontal half kneel on right knee on saddle, left leg horizontally backward, body bent forward, change position of knees and legs, squat right knee on to saddle to (*a*) kneel on both knees, release hands from pommels and raise arms backward, body upright, sitting on heels, swing arms forward and (*b*) jump off both knees forward to ground.

18. Jump and (*a*) with a ¼ turn to the right, place both feet on the neck, knees bent, place left hand on right pommel, and straighten both legs backward to (*b*) the front leaning rest, swing right leg downward and upward and dismount with front vault swing to the left.

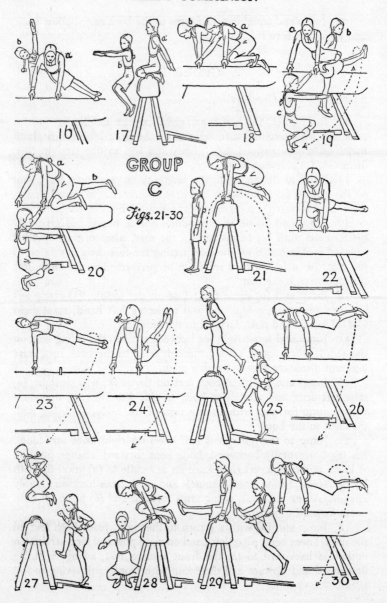

GROUP
C
Figs. 21-30

19. Jump and (a) squat both feet on to the neck, with a $\frac{1}{4}$ turn left and placing right hand on neck pommel, (b) straddle legs to the riding seat on the neck, both hands on neck pommel behind the back, (c) dismount on far side with a rear vault swing.

20. Jump with a $\frac{1}{4}$ turn right and (a) kneel on both knees on the neck, with left hand in reverse grasp, release grasp of right hand and replace on neck pommel beside left hand, (b) stretch right leg backward to the horizontal half kneel, (c) dismount with a right-about turn, retaining hold with left hand while alighting. (Leading up exercise to screw vault.)

GROUP C

Exercises for Age Group 14–16.

With a run, jump and:

21. Squat through the arms.

22. Half straddle (or Woolf vault).

23. Flank vault.

24. Rear vault.

25. Without holding pommels, jump off one foot off the board on to the other foot on the saddle, dismount forward. (Leading up exercise to the clear jump and thief jump.)

26. Front vault.

27. Clear jump over the horse. (One foot take-off.)

28. Squat through the arms with $\frac{1}{4}$ or $\frac{1}{2}$ turn.

29. Thief jump. (One foot take-off.)

30. Screw vault.

HOCKEY

Sports activities are international as well as national, and hockey is in the forefront of international sport. Starting to play while you are still at school (or in your early teens), and continuing after you leave, may one day win an international cap for you. Nowadays everyone hopes for good health, because we all know that healthy lives make happy ones. Playing hockey regularly makes you physically and mentally alert. The fact of enjoying your game with so many others also bears out the saying, " He who true happiness would win must share it ".

A good craftsman cannot turn out the finished article unless he has the proper tools and material, and this applies not only to trades but to games, so the first thing you must do is to buy or borrow the best equipment you can for yourself and your club.

The *stick* for a learner should not be too heavy or too costly, because as you grow older and more experienced you will require a heavier and better one. The length depends on your height and build, and it must not weigh more than 23 oz. Defence players sometimes prefer a heavier stick than forwards, but each player must use the stick she feels suits her best. The width at any point must always allow a 2-in. ring to pass over it, even when tape has been bound round the head of the stick to preserve the surface; but never play with a rubber ring on your stick.

No pointed ends or splinters are permitted, nor insets of hard wood, and only the left side of the stick is flat. If possible, go to a good sports shop and get expert advice when buying your first stick. If your stick begins to splinter, bind it with adhesive tape. Always scrub your stick after playing as it is the dirt drying into the wood that starts the splintering process.

Balls used should be leather, painted white, either seamless or sewn like a cricket ball. They are made of cork and twine, and weigh between $5\frac{1}{2}$ and $5\frac{3}{4}$ oz., and measure round about $8\frac{13}{16}$–$9\frac{1}{4}$ in. As many balls as possible for your club will help stick-work practices, for nothing is more depressing to the keen newcomer than standing about on a cold winter's day waiting for her turn of the ball. One

234

ball between two is ideal, and if you cannot afford leather balls—
except for the actual game—make quite sure that the rubber stick-
work substitutes are quite safe for play; owing to lack of weight
certain composition balls tend to rise and are dangerous. Again,
sound advice from an experienced player or coach will help you to
make a wise purchase. Indoors, all sorts of balls may be used to
practise strokes, e.g. tennis, sorbo, or improvised balls.

Ordinary walking *shoes*, with the addition of studs or bars to
prevent you slipping on a muddy pitch, may be worn, and must be
well laced to give support. Some girls prefer canvas and rubber
lacrosse boots or shoes, which are light and comfortable. No shoes
or boots may have metal spikes or projecting nails.

For the goalkeeper a pair of football boots or strong studded
boots with blocked toe-caps are necessary. These boots should not
fit too closely, because extra socks for warmth and cotton-wool
strips on the insteps for protection when stopping and kicking out
are worn.

Goalkeepers must wear *goalkeeper's pads* which fit snugly next the
limb, but have a wide flat front towards the oncoming ball. They
should reach well up the thigh and down over the instep. At the foot a
pair of kickers—very firmly fixed—fit over the boots. Besides these
protective articles the G.K. should wear plenty of warm *clothing*, e.g.
woollen cap, scarf, jersey, trousers folded neatly under the straps of
the leg-guards, blazer, gloves. It is fatal to feel numb, and you
should stamp your feet and walk about the goal-mouth whenever
play is in the other half of the field, to keep your circulation going.

The other players may wear either tunics, skirts, or divided skirts.
These, when kneeling, should be between $1-4\frac{1}{2}$ in. off the ground.
Either long or three-quarter length stockings must be worn with the
skirts, and long stockings with tunics. All garments should be well
pressed and blouses worn fresh and neat so that the team looks spick
and span. Hair nets are useful, both for appearance and for preventing hair obstructing your view on a windy day. Gloves can be worn,
but most players prefer to do without. Anything which would be
dangerous during play must not be worn, e.g. hard-brimmed eye-
shades, buckled belts with sharp pins.

You will see from (fig. 1) how to mark a pitch, and where the
players should stand at the start of the game (fig. 2). Before beginning
all the players must know at least three things: (1) How to hit the
ball. (2) How to stop it correctly. (3) How to run with it down the

field and pass it to others before being tackled. That is, they should know about driving, fielding and dribbling. Apply to your local education authority for a gymnast, to the local office of the Central

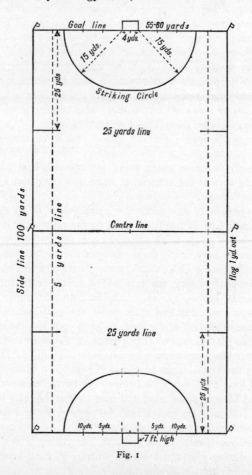

Fig. 1

Council of Physical Recreation for a coach, or to the local secretary of the Senior Hockey Club for an experienced player to help you with these essential but elementary strokes. Even if you can only receive expert assistance occasionally, it will keep you on the right lines, and you can practise the correct methods on your own once you know how to do so.

A grass or blaes pitch may be marked out, and all the club ought to co-operate to keep it in the best possible condition. The grounds-man will appreciate any help in marking and rolling it; many hands make light work, so if you have some spare moments do lend a hand. After rain, too, if drainage is poor some forking will be required, not to mention the inevitable weeds, which grow up on either kind of pitch. Sometimes a wire netting is put around the ground a few yards from the outside lines, and of varying height, to prevent the ball travelling a distance when hit off the pitch, and to keep it private, but this, although ideal, is not essential and is costly.

Each player must know what is expected of her in her own position; what rules she must keep, &c. For a learner, of course, two points and two rules are enough to think about, and then gradually she can learn further coaching hints and more rules as the occasion arises.

Apart from stick-work practices, try to arrange for some short talks indoors, or if the weather breaks, the players might go indoors for a chat on various points, and even in a small space could walk to the positions on the field, or to certain situations showing them the faults, and then the right methods of doing things. If possible have some films with a commentary by either a local or a national " star ", and discussion afterwards on the strokes, play or tactics shown. Films of a game as well as excellent diagrammatic ones are available, and make hockey much clearer to the novice. The All-England Women's Hockey Association Film is excellent. Information may be had from Miss C. E. Pagden, Holmstoun, West Byfleet, Surrey.

START OF THE GAME

Captains of the opposing teams toss for choice of ends, and if there is no umpire must be ready to act as umpire or choose one member of their team to do so. They must point out who is the G.K., if the team has three backs instead of the usual formation of two backs and a G.K., as the third back is allowed the goalkeeper's privileges.

The game starts by the two C.F.s standing facing each other in the centre, astride the line, having left shoulders towards their opponents' goal, and bullying off as soon as the whistle is blown. This bully is taken after every goal and for the start of the second half—usually a school game lasts 50–60 min., senior games 60–70

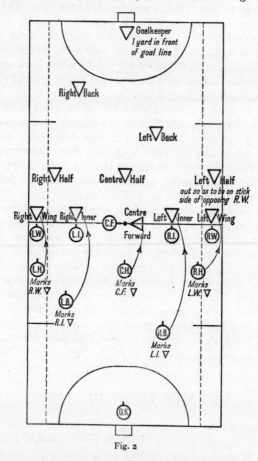

Fig. 2

min., and representative games, i.e. district or international matches, 70 min.—and the teams change ends at half-time.

To bully-off the C.F.s hit the ground on their own side of the ball then their opponents' stick—flat part only—three times alternately, then each tries to get the ball and pass it to one of her own team, and the game has begun. Everyone must be at least 5 yards away from the C.F.s, and nearer her own goal line than the ball.

By passing to one another and travelling towards the opponents' goal line a team tries to score as quickly as possible, therefore the passes are obliquely forward till nearing the circle, when they are centred. No wild hit-and-run methods succeed, but well-placed passes and agile dodges to outwit one's opponent are employed. As soon as the ball is inside the circle the nearest forward shoots at once, and all the others follow up her shot with sticks close to the ground. Thus the G.K., if she stops the shot, has little time to kick it out of danger, and if it deflects from her pads the oncoming forwards have a good chance of pushing it past her into the goal.

A goal is scored when the ball enters the goal, passing under the bar, and having been *hit while in the circle* or glanced off the *stick of an attacker*. If the ball before passing between the goalposts comes in contact with a defender or her stick it is still a goal.

RULES TO REMEMBER

Now for a few rules which players should study and memorize. It is most helpful and much more interesting to illustrate a talk on rules with amusing practical examples of what, and what not to do. Several indoor tests can be thought of, and competitions in short files can be arranged to see who knows the rules most thoroughly, and can give the best and quickest answers.

At the beginning, the main points to remember are: (*a*) keeping to your own place and portion of the field; (*b*) avoiding dangerous hitting; (*c*) two only struggling for possession of the ball at a time; (*d*) when passing the ball to a team mate, angle it so that the ball goes in front of her and not at her heels (fig. 3). Other rules and coaching points come in from time to time as the event arises.

Offside.—A player is penalized if she is gaining an advantage from being in an offside position, or if she is obstructing an opponent. You are offside if nearer to your opponents' goal line than the ball at the moment it is hit or rolled in—*unless* in your own half of the field, or *unless* there are at least three of your opponents nearer their goal line than you are. If this happens (1) *inside the circles*—a free hit is awarded to the opposite team from any spot within the circle; (2) *outside the circles*—a free hit from the spot where the player was offside.

Fouls.—1. Stick must *never* be raised above shoulder height.

2. Must not play the ball with the rounded side of stick.

3. Never undercut the ball; this happens when ball rises from a hit taken with the weight on back foot and stick going under instead of behind ball. The scoop stroke is allowed except as a free hit (or when dangerous), but this is a special stroke, and not faulty hitting.

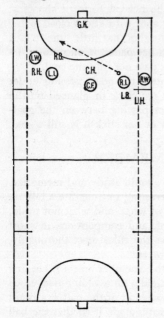 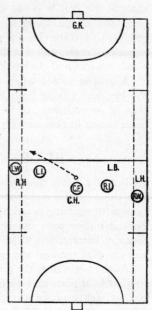

Fig. 3

4. A player must not strike, hook, hold or interfere with an opponent's stick.

5. Never pick up, push or throw the ball with the hands. You may stop the ball with your hand, and it may be caught, but must at once be released to fall perpendicularly.

6. Kicking is not allowed, nor are you permitted to use any part of your person (except for stopping), so that the stick is the only thing which moves the ball in any direction.

7. You cannot hit or pass the ball between your own feet.

8. Do not trip, shove, push, charge, shin, strike at or in any way personally handle your opponent.

9. Never obstruct by running in between your opponent and the ball or getting in her way at all.

10. You cannot take part in the game unless you have your stick in your hand.

Don't be put off by all the " cannots " and " must nots ", but try to play as clean a game as possible, and you'll probably never even realize there are so many fouls. Remember, too, every time you foul your team has a free hit against it, which may set your opponents right on an attacking move for a goal.

If you foul (1) *outside the circles*, a free hit is given to opponents where the foul happened; (2) *inside the circles*, (*a*) if attacking team foul, a free hit to defenders from any point in the circle, (*b*) if defenders foul, either a penalty corner or penalty bully is awarded to the attackers; (3) outside or inside the circles, if two players foul simultaneously a bully-off is taken at that point, and all players must be onside, that is, nearer to their own goal line than the ball.

Free Hit.—This has to be taken with all other players 5 yards away from the striker, and the ball must be hit from the spot where the foul occurred. It must be stationary, and may be hit or pushed along the ground. If the striker hit at, but missed the ball, the stroke is taken again unless she has given " sticks ". If she just taps the ball she must not touch it again until it has been touched or hit by another player.

If the striker fouls *inside the circles*, a penalty corner is given to the opponents; if *outside the circles*, the free hit goes to the opponents.

Penalty Bully.—This is awarded for a wilful breach of a rule by the defence inside the circles, if a player strike at the ball with her stick above her shoulder, or in any case when a goal most probably would have been scored but for the occurrence of the foul. It is therefore generally given against an excited G.K. or back. The bully is taken by the offender, and any player selected by the other team, on a spot 5 yards in front of the centre of the goal line. All the other players must stand beyond the nearer 25-yard line in the field of play, and must not cross this line or take any further part in the game until the bully is completed.

GIRL'S COMPANION

After the completion of the bully the game may be restarted:

1. By a *25 bully* when the ball is sent out of the circle and over

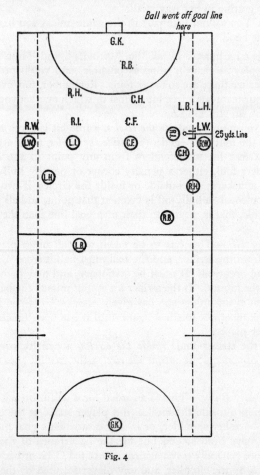

Fig. 4

the goal line by *attacker*, or sent out of the circle over circle line by *defender*, or when *attacker* fouls (fig. 4).

2. By a *centre bully* when the ball is put through goal-posts by *either* player, or when *defender* fouls.

The penalty bully is *retaken* when *defender* sends ball over the goal line except through the goal, and for a simultaneous breach of any rule by both players, or for interference by any other player.

Roll In.—When the ball goes over either side line it is rolled in by a player of the opposite team from that which touched it last. It must be sent into play from the point where it crossed the side line, but may go in any direction (fig. 5). If the ball does not come in to the field the roll is retaken. The ball must not bounce and must touch the ground within one yard of where it went off. The person

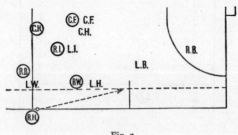

Fig. 5

who rolls it in must have her feet and stick behind the side line, and may only play the ball again after another player. No one must stand within the 5-yard line or outside the side line. A foul by the roller-in gives the roll to the opposite team, otherwise it is taken again.

Twenty-five: Long corner, Short corner.—1. If the ball is sent over the goal line by an *attacker*, or is unintentionally put over by a player of the defending team who is beyond the 25-yard line, a *25 bully* is taken on the 25-yard line at a spot opposite to where the ball crossed the goal line.

2. If the ball glances off, or is unintentionally sent over the goal line by any of the defence behind the 25-yard line, a *corner* is given to the attacking team unless a goal is scored.

3. If the ball is intentionally sent over the goal line by any of the defence, a *penalty, or short corner*, is awarded to the opponents, unless a goal is scored.

Long Corner (fig. 6).—No player can take a flying shot at goal directly from the corner hit, or from a pass from one of her own side

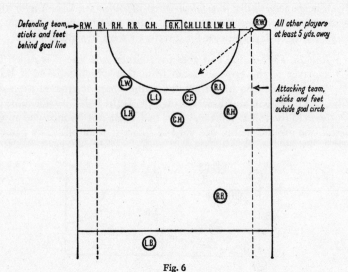

Fig. 6

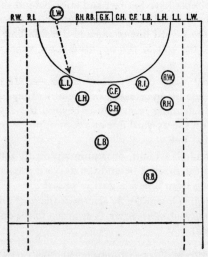

Fig. 7

unless the ball has been stopped or fielded first, or has touched the stick or person of an opponent.

The person hitting the corner stroke cannot play the ball again until it has been touched or hit by another player. If the striker misses the ball she may try again, as long as she has not given " sticks ".

Short or Penalty Corner (fig. 7).—The ruling is the same as for a long corner, except that the ball is hit from a point on the goal line not less than 10 yards from the goal-post on *whichever side* the attacking team prefer.

In either corner, if attackers cross circle, or defence come over goal line before the ball is hit, it is retaken. If the *attackers* break the rules *inside the circle* a free hit is given to the opponents from any spot within the circle—if outside the circle a free hit to the opponents from the spot where the foul occurred.

DUTIES OF UMPIRE

1. Forbid the use of balls which are not safe, or correct size, or weight.

2. Do not allow a player to use a stick which is not regulation type or which endangers other players.

3. If the goal-posts or bar are displaced and the ball pass at a point which in the opinion of the umpires is between where the posts, or below where the bar should have been, she shall give a goal.

4. Have the power to penalize a player who continually raises the ball.

5. If the G.K. in stopping a hit at goal does not make the ball drop perpendicularly from her hand, she must not be penalized if it has merely rebounded off her open hand.

6. A ball touching an umpire or post is in play unless it goes off the ground.

7. If at a free hit or roll-in an umpire considers that a player is standing within 5 yards to delay the hit or roll she shall not stop the game.

8. It is for the umpire to decide whether *intentional* or *unintentional* has happened, and therefore whether a 25, long, or short corner is taken.

9. Umpires do not change ends at half-time, but continue to umpire for the whole of their side line, and in as far as the 5-yard line and the half of the field which is on their right as they face the centre of the pitch.

10. One umpire takes time and the other checks, deducting all wastage (event of accidents or downpour of rain, &c.). Extra time is given if a penalty has been awarded just on time or half-time, and until a decision has been reached the ball is in play.

11. Must not coach during a game, and should write down the goals as scored with name of, or position of scorer if possible.

12. Blow the whistle: (a) start and end each half of the game, also to restart after a goal in their own half of the field; (b) for a penalty or to stop the game for any other reason; (c) signal a goal; (d) when necessary to indicate that the ball has passed over the goal line or side line.

13. For rough play, misconduct, or in the case of the G.K. dangerous kicking, the umpire has discretionary power to warn or penalize the offender or to send her from the field.

14. If an accident occurs the time lost is noted and added to the end of the half during which it occurred. Play is restarted by a bully, on a spot chosen by the umpire in whose half the player was hurt. When the accident is the result of a foul the appropriate penalty is awarded.

15. Umpires should wear clothing of a different colour from the players so as to avoid confusion and should always carry a whistle, copy of current rules, two pencils, small notebook for score, and a watch with second hand.

16. The umpire's decision is final!

The Players.

Forwards: 5 in a row.

Work of Centre Forwards.—Responsible for distributing play.

Be able to pass to right or left with short or long passes equally well.

Pick up and shoot quickly from hard centre drives from the wings.

Centre position in field so must not wander.

Develop skill in obtaining ball from the bully.

Try to throw off opposing centre half who is marking you, and always try to put yourself in a better position to receive the ball than your opponent.

Hold your line of five together, and be full of ideas so as to vary tactics to puzzle your opponents.

Never be a completely selfish and individualistic centre; combine, particularly with inners.

Left and Right Inners.—Pass out to wings diagonally to corner flag in mid-field, and sometimes a hard drive to other inner or wing across the field, but in towards centre near striking circle, where it is easier to shoot.

When tackled and lose ball summon extra energy and tackle back and worry opponent who has got ball till she has to pass hurriedly or have it taken from her.

Move your position to combine with member of your own team who has the ball and avoid crowding on one spot.

For the roll-in move towards the 5-yard line when roll is between the two 25-yard lines, but sometimes draw opponent well off and then rush to it at last moment, or draw opponent off so as to leave space for roll to go to C.F.

Responsible for marking opposing inner at roll-ins.

Converge slightly on centre as you reach shooting circle, and shoot as soon as inside, but not too close to each other as this draws defence in with you too.

Pass on the run with the right drive if you are a L.I. and want to pass right across to opposite inner or wing. Perfect this stroke as well as strong, quick push passes.

Keep ball controlled so as to be able to get rid of it quickly; avoid holding on to it too long or you will be tackled.

Learn variety of bullies for the 25.

Follow up all shots at goal by the other members of your team.

Practise with your own wing running up and down field, using short passes to go behind the marking opponent.

Practise taking corners quickly.

Left and Right Wing.—Learn to place corner hits where you want them to go, and make your first hit successful each time; vary place.

Stay close to side line in mid-field.

When three inside forwards are trying to shoot keep just outside the circle ready to rush if the ball comes in your direction; follow up the other shots.

Try to intercept all clearing shots from opposing defence near their goal circle.

Get rid of the ball before you pass your opponents' 25 line.

Make a tremendous effort to save the ball going out of bounds—reach out, with one hand on stick if necessary, to lengthen your reach.

Try to avoid being offside.

Hit all centre drives hard and place them accurately while running at top speed.

Practise dodges for outwitting opponent when you have the ball.

Learn to roll in quickly without fouling, and with either hand, as wings take roll-in when ball goes off side line opposite goal circle in opponents' half of pitch. This is so that half back can back up own inner, and also be ready to mark opposing wing.

Avoid shooting from impossible angles, rather pass back to own inner or C.F.

Learn to dribble with ball close to stick and at top speed, and practise drives to opposite side line as well as a good push pass. L.W. needs to master the drive to the right, as it is her centring shot and vital that it is accurately placed without loss of speed.

Half Backs.—Three in a line. During play the half line should be a diagonal line.

Centre Half.—Main duty is to mark opposing C.F. and try to get the ball before her, therefore learn to anticipate opponent's tactics.

Do not interchange with another defence unless absolutely necessary.

Feed own centre and both sides of the forward line with passes placed ahead of them so that they do not slacken pace.

When defending, must not wander from centre of field.

Speed in passing the ball on from a backward pass at the bully-off.

At a 25, glues herself to opposing C.F.

Key position on field, so untiring in backing up own forwards, and ready to shoot quickly herself; also quick to dash back and re-mark her C.F. and defend, if ball cleared.

If not well placed for a good clearance, use judgment. A short pass to another of your defence better situated for a long hit to a clear space is far better than hitting at random.

Left and Right Halfs.—Mark opposing wings and place yourself opposite stick side of wing to be marked.

Be able to tackle from either side without fouling.

Take roll-ins quickly, varying them.

Be ready to interchange with own back when necessary, so be on the alert.

In attack may come slightly off wing to back up shooting.

When opposing wing has ball, must never give up the chase.

Pass out to wings when defending inside own circle, and towards centre when nearing opponents' shooting circle.

Be ready to receive clearing hits from other defences.

Try to prevent wings from centring accurately.

Pass well ahead to own wing. In own 25 if the ball is on the other side of the field come in and mark the inner as the back will be covering her partner. If the ball is on your own side of the field mark the wing.

Left and Right Full Backs.—They play forward or back according to the side of the field the play is, so that they stand diagonally ready to cover should one be passed by opposing forwards.

Know how to combine with each other and discuss tactics together before play.

Outside their own circle keep to the oblique positioning already mentioned.

Never pass across own goal when forwards about to shoot, but using diagonal pass across field to opposite inner or wing when well away from own circle.

Be careful not to block the G.K.'s view in defending near goal.

Stop all hits before pass to own team.

When outwitted by opponent dash back to mark another opponent when their marker has gone to tackle your opponent.

Back up bully on 25-yard line.

If G.K. has to leave goal mouth one or other of the backs takes her place till she has time to return.

Never pass the ball straight back to where it has come from, or up and down the field, but pass out to wings or inners or across field and pass into clear spaces.

Goalkeeper.—Mostly use *feet* to clear ball as much quicker, but in a few instances a hard hit with stick, or when there is no time to get across to right, push out stick in right hand to deflect ball over back line.

Stand about a yard in front of goal line nearer left post and hold stick in right hand ready to cover that side of goal, and to have left hand free for stopping high shots.

Try to clear to a space, using inside of opposite foot and having knee bent to start with, then extending it strongly as follow through.

Face the ball squarely as it approaches and be ready to move to either side of the goal as required.

Be able to kick equally well with either foot and *never*, if you have time to stop before kicking out, use a fly kick as this is dangerous and you cannot place it accurately.

Try to stop ball dead close to feet, so let knees bend forward to trap it, keeping legs tightly together.

Study opposing forwards' tactics, and use caution when leaving goal to go out to tackle. If certain you can get there first, don't hesitate—as happens when one forward has outstripped the others and has either not reached the ball passed far ahead or has lost control of the ball. Come out sometimes to smother a forward who has dribbled far into the circle. When you can reach a loose ball in the circle more easily than another defence, shout " Mine !" and go for it. Come out on occasion to vary tactics or as pure bluff. But for a learner I suggest staying by your goal till you gain confidence.

LACROSSE

This game was originally played in Canada. It is a game in which a solid rubber ball, about the size of a tennis ball, is caught

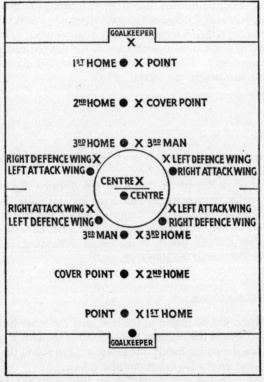

Fig. 1.

in, carried, and thrown by a long-handled racket called a Crosse. It is a game of great speed, and one which is not restricted by too many rules.

The Game is played by two teams of twelve persons in each, who are lined up in the formation in fig. 1 at the start of the game, and reform in the same positions after each goal has been scored.

The idea is to run, passing the ball from crosse to crosse between the players of one team until one of the players is near enough to the goal to shoot the ball between the posts. The opposite team to that which has the ball tries to get it by intercepting it while it is in flight, and so start in turn to attack and shoot a goal for their team.

As you will have seen from the diagram of the field of play, the players are arranged in twos, one from each team, who play against each other, except in the case of the goalkeeper. As in any other game there are tactics which have to be learnt, such as when to leave your own player in order to stop another who has dodged and got away from her opponent. However, when you play this game you will be coached and taught the tactics, which are not at all difficult to understand.

Equipment.

A crosse, a pair of canvas boots or shoes with rubber soles and studs, and a pair of leather gloves.

The Crosse is shaped as shown in the diagram, fig. 2, and is laced by leather thongs which run from top to collar, interlaced with clockgut; these form the " net " in which the ball is caught. You will see in the illustration the different parts to which I shall afterwards refer. The length of the crosse is about 46 in., with a thin handle like a stout walking stick.

How to Hold the Crosse.

Either hand can be placed at the butt, and the other hand holds the collar. (Look at the diagram.) The hand at the butt is the hand which we call the power hand; the grasp is taken round the handle, the other hand grasps loosely round the collar.

When at ease the crosse should be held with the backbone towards the ground, the angle pointing downwards and the guard upwards, the elbow of the butt hand bent, and that of the collar hand hanging straight down by the side of the body. Try this grasp and try to feel no strain in your arms or body

Cradling.

This is the movement used to keep the ball in the crosse when you are running or dodging an opponent. As the word implies, it is a soft rhythmical movement which goes on continuously whenever you have the ball in your crosse. Cradling must be mastered

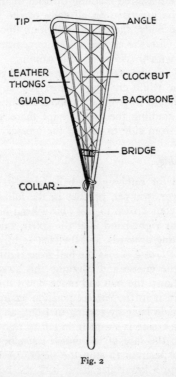

Fig. 2

before you can play the game with any success whatsoever, and you can practise this movement alone indoors or out.

Hold the crosse in front of the body, with the collar hand slightly higher than the butt hand; now swing the arms forward and upward and downward again, as if the action were that of a boat rolling from side to side, the big roll going upwards; make the power hand do the greater amount of work by using the wrist; the movement must be rhythmical.

Now try to do this movement walking forward, the crosse moving up with the first step and back with the next step; this again is rhythmic. It can then be taken whilst skipping forward, and later running slowly, and then at full speed. (Be careful not to stiffen up when running.)

Once you have mastered cradling in front of the body the same movement must be practised on all sides of the body. Keep the crosse close to the body, therefore bend your elbows and twist the top of your body with the crosse, always remembering to move the crosse in rhythm with the steps of your running.

The ball should not be taken in the crosse until you have mastered the feeling of ease while cradling; when you do begin practising with the ball, it should lie five inches above the bridge on the backbone. By good cradling the ball is kept there all the time, and should not rattle from side to side in the crosse.

Tossing and Catching.

In preparation for catching the ball, when it is passed to you from another player, you can practise in the following way. Toss the ball up with your crosse to just above head height, and rather to the right if your right hand is at the collar, then with the head of the crosse pointing upwards, and the face slightly opened towards the ball, sweep the crosse across the ball from right to left, catching it in the top of the crosse and continue this sweeping movement into a cradling action; the ball will move down the crosse, and the cradling will retain it in the correct position against the backbone. Catches can be made later by tossing in front, and to the left. In this latter case the crosse is swept from left to right.

In all catching the face of the crosse must be opened towards the ball, and in a position to stop the flight. A low ball needs a high butt hand and a low collar hand with the head of the crosse down.

Give slightly backwards from the ball as it meets the crosse, this gets rid of the hard impact. Try to get the ball and the crosse to move as one as the ball touches the net.

Picking up the Ball.

This is important. Although in the game you try to keep the ball in the air, there are times when the catch is missed or the crosse is checked by an opponent, and the ball falls out, and then the quickest player in picking it up gains an advantage for her team.

To Pick up a Stationary Ball.—Just before you reach the ball bend well down with the body and knees, brush the whole head of the crosse along the ground, and push under the ball with a quick sharp movement, and immediately raise it and begin cradling and continue running fast.

To Pick up a Moving Ball which is rolling away from you. Adhere to the same rules, but make your speed greater and push more sharply under the ball.

To pick up a ball which is coming towards you, watch the ball very carefully at the moment of picking it up. The head of the crosse is lowered to a right angle to the line of the ball, the butt raised so that the ball runs on to the net. At that moment raise the head, lower the butt and continue cradling at once. Practise this by throwing a ball against a wall, and picking it up as it bounds back.

Remember two golden rules: (1) Run very fast at the moment of pushing the crosse under the ball. (2) Go on cradling as soon as it is in the net.

To Throw the Ball.

Now we must embark on how to throw the ball. To be efficient you must learn to throw the ball from any point at either side of your body, particularly on the side of your collar hand.

The Over-arm Throw. (All descriptions of throwing will apply to a player with the right hand at the collar.)

The crosse is lifted so that the head is over the right shoulder. To do this the right arm is bent and the elbow lifted, the left hand is raised forward. To expel the ball pull down sharply with the left hand, and extend the head of the crosse in the direction you wish to pass the ball; the longer the throw the more you straighten the right arm, and the farther down towards the ground the face of the crosse is brought; also the butt hand is raised higher, and a larger distance gained for it to pull down. The ball can be thrown in any direction by twisting the shoulders.

The Horizontal Throw.

The crosse is held nearly parallel with the ground. This movement is used for short passes, and is carried out in much the same way as the others. The right hand is drawn slightly back, and the butt hand forward, then, with a wrist flick of the power hand and a forward movement with the other hand, the ball is directed forward, leaving the crosse at the angle.

Avoid a long scooping movement of the crosse. Practise short passes aiming to get the ball to travel in a direct line from your crosse to that of the person to whom you are passing. Again, turning the body helps you to send the ball in any direction.

The Under-arm Throw for passing a long distance; this is a useful pass, and is mostly used by defence players; it is also used as a means of taking a quick low shot at goal. The crosse is carried across to the left side with a strong body turn to the left, till the right shoulder is pointing in the direction in which the ball will travel; the head of the crosse is lowered to point down with the butt hand raised; the ball is thrown out of the crosse by a forward movement of both arms combined with a pressing down of the butt hand and lifting of the collar hand.

Try to follow these methods of throwing the ball, and practise until you can do them running at full speed; they are all used for passing the ball to other players in your team, and need to be as accurate as threading the eye of a needle. When passing the ball it should be placed in the space in front of the player to whom you are passing, so that she does not have to lose speed in waiting for it to come to her. If she has an opponent near she must use her speed to reach the ball first. Clever avoidance of an opponent is achieved by good dodging.

Dodging.

A good dodge is one which is unexpected; it is a combination of quick running and sudden turns used in short spurts, to make your opponent wonder which way you are going. When dodging, whilst running towards an opponent, you can swerve to one side, and then with a quick body twist change to the other side. It must be sudden and unexpected to be effective. When dodging, carry your crosse with your body turn, keep it close to you to avoid having it checked by an opponent.

If you are a defence player you will have to *mark* your fellow player even when she has not got the ball, keep close to her, watch her eyes when facing her, to see where she expects the ball to come, follow her crosse with yours, and concentrate on trying to get the ball first.

You will hear the terms *Body Checking* and *Crosse Checking*; the first is merely keeping on the goal side of an opponent, so stopping her from running in the direction she wishes to go. Crosse checking means getting the ball away from her. This is done by a small sharp movement, a wrist flick in an upward or downward direction on the head of an opponent's crosse to dislodge the ball and take possession of it. Avoid a big swing of your crosse as it is dangerous.

Shooting a Goal.

Practise as follows:

1. A high shot from near the goal.

2. A long shot when the ball rebounds from the ground just outside the goal square.

3. The under-arm shot used as for an under-arm throw, keeping the ball close to the ground.

Place your shots. Be quick once you decide to shoot. Be surprising.

Do practise all I have told you on your own, for it is the secret of becoming a good exponent of the game.

The points in favour of lacrosse are: The possibilities of the fun it offers when practising without having to play as a team; the joy of mastering the technique, such as cradling, catching, throwing, &c.; the fact that there are few rules in comparison to most team games. (The rules can be bought in a sports shop.) The speed, the space, the freedom (there are no real boundaries) and exhilaration derived from it are soon apparent to all who play this game.

9

LAWN TENNIS

Many reading this article will have received, while playing tennis at home or at school, advice and coaching from many different people. Some of the things I shall say may well contradict such teaching, so let me make myself clear at the outset.

There is seldom only *one* right method of doing a thing well, and so there are many ways of holding a racket, and of hitting a ball over a net. Some of them are right and others wrong. It will be my endeavour to indicate the methods which I have found most successful in my own experience. Don't be misled by the fact that you can sometimes do the wrong thing and get away with it. If

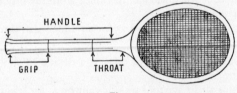

Fig. 1

there is a real fault in your game, it will let you down at every critical moment, and, after all, it is the player who can maintain a steady style under pressure who wins matches. Thus, unless you are prepared to look for, and correct, faults in your game, you will find yourself unable to reach any great heights. If you want to look forward to enjoying your tennis, and at the same time have the satisfaction of knowing that it is steadily improving, then it will be well worth your while to take trouble over cultivating a good style.

Three things, I think, combine to produce the good player. They are: correct grips, good footwork, and what is called, "ball sense". If you start the game young enough, and are well taught, you will probably find that you slip naturally into all three of these; but often those who do not take up games very early find both footwork and ball sense very difficult to acquire. Grips you *can* learn, if only by practising them over and over again, as they are simple and easily described. On the other hand, it is more difficult to describe ball sense and footwork. As a matter of fact, the two are really one, the co-ordination of eye and muscle, which enables you to approach the ball and strike it at exactly the right moment.

Tennis is an excellent game for many reasons, chief among

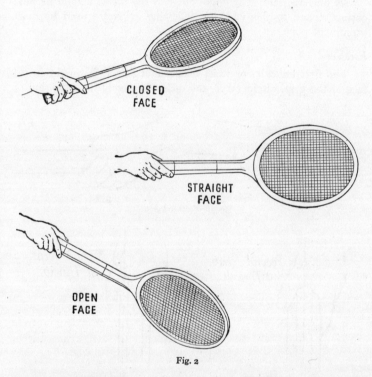

Fig. 2

which is the fact that it is a game you can play and enjoy after you leave school. Also, it is a graceful game—or should be—but can only be so with correct grips and good footwork, for without them players look awkward and lack balance. It is not too strenuous for a girl, can be enjoyed equally by both sexes, and can be a great social asset, both in the holidays and after you leave school.

To begin at the beginning, we will learn first about the racket, as it is important that you should know the names of its various parts, and fig. 1 will show these clearly. Then look at fig. 2, and you will see the different angles and tilts of the face of the racket.

CORRECT GRIPS

As we have said, it is important that the racket should be held correctly, and to this end, the following grips are used by most prominent players:

Forehand.

The first knuckle, or base, of the first finger, is on the broad face of the grip. Remember, the racket is merely the extension of

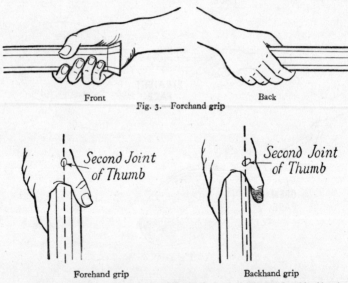

Front   Back

Fig. 3. Forehand grip

Forehand grip   Backhand grip

Fig. 4.—Diagram to illustrate the difference between the forehand and backhand grips. Note how the hand moves round the handle for the backhand, and how the thumb moves so as to give more support. The position of the second joint of the thumb is indicated in order to make the amount of movement of the hand clear.

your hand and arm. If you were going to hit the ball with the palm of your hand, you would do so with your hand in a position perpendicular to the ground at the end of your extended arm. So, to get the correct grip, do just this, place the racket along your hand,

and close your fingers round the grip. The leather end of the grip should not stick out from the hand, but should rest on the fleshy part of the palm. With this grip the wrist is free to give power to your stroke, and it is the only grip that I would teach for the forehand. We will deal with each grip in turn, and then go on to the actual stroke production afterwards.

Backhand.

The backhand drive is a fundamental stroke in the game, and is as important as the forehand. It stands to reason that if you can play only on your forehand, your opponent has only to keep play on your backhand to hold you continually on the defensive; and the purely defensive player wins few matches against anything like good opposition. In spite of this very obvious fact, many players *do* tend to avoid their backhand. You are probably only too familiar with the feeling: " It's coming on my backhand. I must run round it and hit on my forehand." You have probably seen others doing it too, and so the idea has got into your head that the backhand drive is a difficult shot, and to be avoided whenever possible. It is therefore most important that you should get the right grip (it is shown in fig. 4), and be able to change to it quickly and confidently without having to look at your hand every time.

Stretch out your hand in front of you, the palm horizontal, and then imagine you are going to hit something, or someone, a backhanded blow with the side of your hand. You will find that your first action is to bend your arm across your body, and then to fling it out and away from you. Do this several times, looking at yourself in a mirror if possible. Now the grip. Put your hand out again in the horizontal position, place the racket under the palm, the racket lying in the same straight line as the arm, and the face of the racket vertical to the ground. The knuckle at the base of your first finger is on the narrow edge, and on top of the grip.

With the forehand and the backhand, you now know the two grips you will be using nearly all the time.

Service.

The grip is the same as for the *forehand*, except for a slight shift which I will explain when we come to stroke production. Later on, as you grow more sure of yourself, you may change your service grip to one somewhere between your forehand and your backhand, but to begin with, you will find it easier to have just the two grips to concentrate on.

STROKE PLAY

As the game begins with service, we will take this first. I mentioned a slight " shift " in the grip in the last paragraph. Hold the racket as for a forehand, stretch it above the head in a position over

Fig. 5.—Shaded edge represents right side of body. Single leg indicates weight distribution. Note that in *f all* the weight is on left foot, the right having swung forward and round it

the left foot, with the racket face towards the net. Now allow the butt of the racket to move slightly in the palm, so that the wrist is comfortable. After practising this once or twice, you will be able to take this grip automatically. Stand next in a position where you can swing a racket freely, and either draw a line on the ground, or drop a handkerchief, to represent the service or baseline.

Now follow closely the little figures in fig. 5. The first six of these show stages of the swing of the racket during the serve, and the seventh shows the track of the head of the racket from the commencement of the swing to the moment of impact with the ball. The follow-through is shown by the dotted line.

Service Stance.

The first thing you should notice is that you stand, not facing the net, but sideways to it (i.e. with the left shoulder pointing towards the net). The feet should be slightly apart.

To commence the swing, point the racket in the direction you want to send the ball, holding the face of the racket perpendicular to the ground. Now swing the racket down, across your legs, and away from the net, up to the level of your right shoulder, turning the face of the racket outwards as you do so. At this point, your arm and racket should be in the same straight line. Now bend your elbow, so that the head of your racket travels up and behind your head as in fig. 5c, and is then practically touching your opposite shoulder. At this stage the racket face is again perpendicular—see that it is, as it is most important.

From there, you relax the wrist, allowing the racket head to drop down as far as it will go. Now swing it up to a point as high as you can reach, and sweep it forward in the direction in which you want to send the ball, and with the face of the racket also facing there. The ball is hit just as the racket begins its downward swing.

Once you reach the highest point of the swing, your weight is transferred smoothly from the right foot to the left, and as you hit, your body is turned *into* the ball, to enable you to bring all available muscles and weight behind the stroke. In timing with this transference of weight from right foot to left, your right foot is following up the stroke, as it were, and at the moment of impact, *all* your weight is on your left foot, with your right foot coming forward to finish inside the court at the end of your swing.

When this swing is done quickly, it is like the swing of an Indian club, and is one complete movement; I have broken it up only to simplify its explanation.

Throwing up the Ball.

Note that in fig. 5e the ball is hit slightly in front of your left foot. This is very important. Now, you may have found that the swing is easy, but when the ball is thrown up, it is difficult to remember it all; the ball just doesn't seem to be in the right place at the right time. If the ball is thrown up correctly it will go just a *little* higher than you can reach, not way up into the sky. If the ball is allowed to drop to the ground, it will do so inside an imaginary circle of about 18 inches diameter, just in front of, and nearer the net than, your left foot.

I suggest you practise throwing up a ball, remembering these two things; but don't imagine you will perfect it in a day or a week. More double faults are made by a bad " throw up " than by anything else. The swing becomes automatic after a while, but it is where the racket strikes the ball that decides its destination, and if

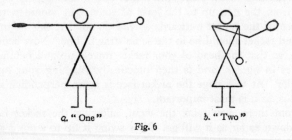

a. " One "   b. " Two "
Fig. 6

the ball is thrown up askew, it means the racket will strike the ball in anything but the right position.

You know the swing, and you know where to throw the ball. Now let us see if we can put the two together. Take up the correct position and do a few practice swings without the ball, counting to yourself, in even time, 1, 2, 3, and see that on three you are on the position in which you should hit the ball. To find out the right time to throw the ball, I suggest this next simple exercise.

Let the hand that is holding the ball hang down at the side of the body, point the racket where you are going to send the ball, and you are ready to start the exercise. Swing your racket back on the first stage of the service, i.e. almost to shoulder level, and *at the same time* swing the arm holding the ball towards the net and up to the height of your left shoulder. As you do this, say " One ". This position is shown in fig. 6a. Now swing back to the original position and say " Two ". Continue doing this until you feel you have the rhythm of it. Now practise throwing the ball up as you say " One ", and when you are learning a service for the first time, it is a great help to do one or two of these preliminary swings each time you serve.

Having thrown up the ball, let your racket continue on its swing, counting this time up to "Three", and striking the ball on "Three".

If you have to hurry through your count, it means that either you haven't thrown the ball high enough, or that your swing is too slow. If you have to wait while the ball comes down, it means you have thrown the ball too high. Remember, it is the position of the face of the racket which directs the ball where you want it to go. In this service, the face of the racket should be flat and facing directly where the ball is intended to go. It is a grand feeling to hit a ball square on the racket, knowing that your swing has been easy and unhurried.

I said a little while back that your service ends with the right foot stepping into the court, and you will find out for yourself that when the ball is thrown up in the correct place, you have to take this step to keep your balance, as the whole idea of each stroke is that you are moving into the ball. In this way, your weight is added to the swing of your racket. You *can* serve, of course, keeping your feet quite still, but if you try it you will realize how much more lifeless it feels.

Follow-through.

The *follow-through* is that part of the swing after the racket has hit the ball. As you will find, it doesn't just stop in mid-air having hit the ball, and it is important that your swing should continue in the right direction. Fig. 5g shows that at the end of your service the racket swings down, and finishes on the *left* side of your body, and not the right.

There are many varieties of service: the spin, the slice, the American twist, &c., but content yourself with learning the flat service first, then you can experiment afterwards.

Forehand Drive.

A sound forehand and backhand game is the foundation of a good player. For the information of beginners, the forehand drive is struck with the left shoulder towards the net, and the backhand with the right. The drive begins with the racket swinging back, and away from the net. The arm should be relaxed, and slightly bent, and the head of the racket held slightly above the level of the wrist. The racket should travel back almost at shoulder height, the body turning away from the net as it does so. That part of the swing is called the back-swing, and there are two types of back-swing for you to choose between. These are, the " detached " and the " continuous ".

The detached back-swing is one where the racket moves back as soon as it is decided that the ball is to be taken on the backhand, and *waits* there until it is time to swing forward to meet the ball. The continuous back-swing calls for better timing, the racket moving backwards and then forward with no pause in its swing. In this the racket moves back on a higher plane than its forward swing; that is, it describes a wide curve at the end of the back-swing. The first of these is the easier to learn, the second looks better. Both are equally effective when played well. So it can be left to you which you decide to use. Try them both and see what you think.

Spin Technique.

A typical forehand drive is hit about waist high with the ball on a line with the middle of the body. The racket face is flat at the moment of impact, but the follow-through ends with the face closed. This is to give the ball a certain amount of " overspin ", to keep it in court. A ball hit with a flat face, and then the face rapidly closed, up and over the ball, is said to have " overspin ", or " top-spin ", if you prefer the term. Such a ball loses speed, as compared with a flat drive, but bounces higher and drops suddenly at the end of its flight, due to the spinning of the ball in mid-air. Thus a ball can be hit harder at a point below the height of the net, rise over it, and still finish inside the court on the opposite side.

A ball hit with the racket face open, and moving under the ball, from top to bottom, is said to have " backspin ". This takes even more pace from the stroke. It is used mainly to alter the pace in a rally, or for a stroke known as the " dropshot ". It should not be used otherwise, because of the loss of pace entailed. One eminent player who used to use the shot effectively as a definite part of her game and characteristic of her style was Miss Helen Jacobs, of U.S.A.

Study fig. 7 to see the relative positions in which the ball should be hit. A low ball is hit in front of you, to lift it, and a high one is hit in front of you to bring it down. Note that at *all* times, " in *front* of you " means nearer the net than you are. As most strokes are played sideways to the net, it will be confusing if you do not get this clear.

When playing a drive, visualize yourself as being on a railway track. You move along one rail, and the ball comes to meet you along the other; the pause is the distance you can stretch with your racket and arm, as the ball should be hit with the arm straight. The wrist is flexed at the commencement of the forward wing, so that the racket head is a little behind the wrist. From there until the moment of impact the racket head starts catching up, and when the ball is struck, the head is level with the wrist, while in the follow-

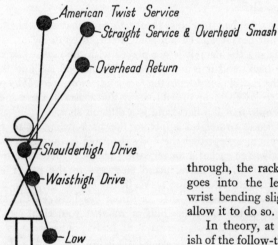

Fig. 7.—Points of impact of ball with racket according to height of bounce

through, the racket head goes into the lead, the wrist bending slightly to allow it to do so.

In theory, at the finish of the follow-through, the racket should point in the direction of the flight of the ball. In actual practice it does that, and then swings a little over towards the left shoulder.

Remembering what I said about using your weight, you advance to the ball, and as you hit it you step on to your left foot. Now, when playing or running quickly, it is impossible to keep your balance if you attempt to maintain that position, so the right foot comes round at the completion of the stroke, to speed your recovery for the next stroke. For a ball struck when it is really low, it will be necessary to bend the knees, and lower the head of the racket. The only time when you should not move to meet the ball with your racket on its back-swing, is when you are running to reach a short shot close to the net, and feel you can only just get there in time. In that case, run with your racket stretched out in front of you, and give the ball a push or a flick with your wrist, to get it over the net.

William Tilden, one of the greatest lawn tennis players in the world, once said that a great tennis player was one with the ability to scramble, that is, one who would discard any piece of form in order to return the seemingly impossible shot, with both hands, if necessary.

Backhand Drive.

It may be bad teaching theory to say what a backhand drive is *not*—but nevertheless I am going to begin by doing so. It is not played facing the net; it is not played with the racket just pushing the ball back, and it is not played with the ball striking the same face of the racket as it does in the forehand. Now, we will be positive, and try to lay for ever the old bogey that exists in the minds of so many people that the backhand is a difficult shot.

The same principles apply to the back-swing as to that for the forehand, except that the body is turned farther away from the net, to give the racket a longer swing before it meets the ball. To get the feel of the drive, stand sideways to the net, the feet a little apart, and holding the racket in the correct grip. (See fig. 4.) Now place the racket so that its throat lies between the shoulder and elbow of the left arm. This means that your right arm is bent at the elbow, and rests across your body. The wrist is slightly " cocked ", so that it is always a little below the head of the racket, and the racket head remains above the wrist until the follow-through. This is very important.

Now swing the racket parallel to the ground, straightening the arm as you do so, until the racket is just in front of your right foot. This is the point at which the ball is struck. You will see at once, that the farther you turn, and swing away from the ball on your back-swing, the longer will be your swing, and the faster your racket can move to meet the ball. It is the speed at which your racket is moving that gives pace to the flight of the ball, not just plain strength. The follow-through finishes with the racket pointing where the ball has gone, and with the face slightly closed. As I said, the wrist is still cocked at the moment of impact, and must not be allowed to sag. If it does so, the head of the racket will drop, and there will be little strength in the shot.

Having got so far with your swing, can you say on to which foot you step to meet the ball? Right? And right it is.

Changing Grip.

One thing you will have to learn, and that is to be able to shift your grip quickly and easily from the forehand to the backhand grip. This will come only with practice. In between strokes, hold your racket either with the forehand or the backhand grip—not half and half—and support the throat of the racket lightly with your left hand. This is known as " cradling " your racket, and in that position it is easy to make a quick change to whatever grip is next required.

There, then, you have your two ground strokes. Now I would like to slip in a few general do's and don'ts before going on to volleys and overhead smashes, where the ball is struck before it bounces.

DON'T: Sit back on your heels, with your racket dangling at your side.

DON'T: Run into the ball; it cramps your shots.

DON'T: Be tense: it makes you awkward and jerky.

DON'T: Just push the ball; hit it crisply and cleanly.

Do: Stand facing the net, racket cradled, and held well up.

Do: Keep the weight on the toes.

Do: Watch the ball all the time.

Do: Move along sideways to the ball.

Do: Follow-through in line with the intended flight of the ball.

Do: Relax, and swing easily.

THE VOLLEY

A large number of players content themselves with playing ground strokes all the time, and have little or no ambition to learn how to volley. If you have seen any first-class players, you will have noticed how frequently they volley, and you may have been sufficiently interested to study just when, and why, they do volley. Ground strokes can be used either in attack or defence, but the volley in its true sense is always an attacking stroke. For that reason, it is a very valuable addition to any player's armoury of attacking strokes.

It is, as you know, a stroke made before the ball has touched the ground. It can be played as high as you can reach, or as low as you can bend, but the easiest position is just above shoulder height, and if you are fortunate enough to have someone to practise with, I suggest you throw balls to one another at that height. Although later on you may volley from as far back as the service court, to begin with stand a little bit farther away from the net than you can reach with your outstretched racket.

Now hold your racket with your backhand grip, and so place it that the head protects your face. If someone then throws a ball as if to hit your face—it needn't be hard—you will find that your first reaction will be to push your racket at the ball. And that is exactly what you *should* do when you volley. If you find it more comfortable you can shorten your grip a little; many players find that gives them added strength.

There are several points to remember when volleying. There is little or no back-swing, because of lack of time, and back-swing adds length to the flight of the ball, and as you are nearer the net you have less distance to cover. Concentrate on direction of return, rather than on speed. There is little or no follow-through, as follow-through adds to the bounce, and most times you want a volley to " die " quickly—that is, to bounce very little. Except in an overhead smash, the shoulder is used very little; in the volley it is the wrist which is used to give both speed and direction.

Backhand Volley.

Now, from that preliminary defensive volley, " to save your face ", try one a little higher than shoulder height, but just far enough away from you to make you step towards it. Which foot? Right for your backhand, and left for your forehand. You will find at once, that a high ball has to be hit down to be kept in court. Let me say here that a high backhand volley is one which many girls find extremely difficult, as in the position in which it is made the arm and wrist seem to have little strength. The importance of having the wrist cocked on a backhand volley cannot be over-estimated, particularly on account of this feeling of weakness. Try it for yourself, and you will see that you can produce a much firmer wrist when it is slightly cocked, than when it is straight. The best way to learn the volley—or, indeed, any shot—is to have someone throw balls to you underarm, just to the spot you want them to; you can take it in turns to do the throwing.

If you want to return the ball close to the net, the racket should be slightly closed, while if you want the ball to go deep to the base-line, the racket should be flat. The low volley has to be hit with the open face to lift it over the net, but it should be remembered that a ball hit up will go out of court unless the power of stroke is controlled.

Forehand Volley.

The same idea of a short, sharp slap is used in the forehand volley, stepping to meet it with the left foot. The wrist and forearm are used, and there should be very little shoulder movement. By moving the position of feet and body, you will find the ball can be directed to different places. The wrist too can direct the ball at unexpected angles. With practice they will be unexpected to your opponent only, so don't be depressed if to begin with they are unexpected to you also. It simply means that you must first master the simple straight volley, and when you have done so you can go on to the more devastating angled volleys. On a low forehand volley, bend the knees, and try to keep the head of the racket up, rather than drop the head and try to lift the ball. The farther away you are from the net, the harder you can afford to hit the ball, but the principle of the stroke remains the same. There are really only two types of volley that are necessary, the flat one described above, and what is known as the " drop volley ". The term is self-explanatory, as " drop " is exactly what the ball does when it hits the ground. It is used when your opponent is on the base-line, and you want to make sure that the ball will not bounce high enough to give her time to reach it. It is played with the open face, and the racket, beginning high, hits down the back of the ball, to finish low. With a great deal of chop, or slice, as it is called, the ball will actually bounce back towards you. Even with this chop volley there is little swing and follow-through. As a general rule, all volleys are short, sharp strokes with little flourish. When able to hit individual shots, like these I have been describing, try hitting them backhand and forehand alternately, remembering the rest position between strokes and the quick, subsequent change of grip. In a tight corner it is as well to know that it is possible to hit a forehand volley with a backhand grip, but very difficult to play a backhand volley with any grip other than the correct one.

Overhead Smash.

This stroke, properly played, should produce a winner nearly every time, and yet, it is a stroke which has resulted in more errors and frank mis-hits than any other, due to trying to hit too hard, mistiming, failing to keep the eye on the ball, and trying to hit the ball too soon. The stroke itself is the same as the service, except that there is no back-swing, or " wind up ". You move to meet the ball with your racket either hanging down the back or on a level with the left shoulder. In other words, in the position half-way through your service swing.

As soon as you realize that you are going to hit an overhead smash, move under the ball as if you were going to catch it like a cricket ball. A lot of beginners seem to think they have an unlimited stretch, and just stand still watching the ball sail over their heads well out of reach. To get into the way of moving backwards, lay down your racket for a moment, and try to catch a few high balls that are going just over your head. This will give you the idea of moving into the correct position, and make you keep your eye on the ball at the same time.

The ball is hit with the arm stretched up as far as you can reach, and a little in front of you. That is to say, as the racket begins its downward swing. If necessary, jump to the ball. After all, the higher the ball at the moment of impact, the harder you can hit it and still keep it in court. If the ball is too far behind the head to make an attacking stroke, then the ball has to be returned high, and placed as deep as possible in your opponent's court.

If you realize that the ball is going right over your head, and yet is going to drop in court, then wheel round and run for the base-line, keeping in mind where you expect the ball to drop, so that you can again turn round and return the ball with a forehand drive. You will find that you can turn, run forwards, and turn again, much more quickly than you could cover the same distance with no turns but running backwards. Besides, you will find that your balance is much better when you actually play the stroke.

Keep on your toes when moving to hit an overhead shot, taking short steps. You will find that by so doing, it is easier to get into the correct position for hitting the ball. The racket face should be flat at impact, but if you are advanced, you can experiment in hitting the ball with a slice, so that it curves in its flight, and changes direction when it bounces.

The actual spot to which you hit the ball depends, of course, on the position of your opponent, but speed is essential; a quick swing of your racket will give you this. One of the commonest mistakes made in the overhead smash is trying to hit the ball too soon. The result is that you miss it altogether, with your racket well into its follow-through by the time the ball has reached the spot where you intended to hit it. This means that you have taken your eye off the ball, and are looking too soon at the place you thought the ball

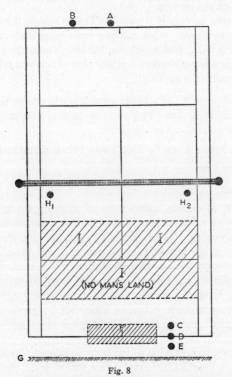

Fig. 8

would go. You must follow the ball right up to your racket. There will be lots of time to see where it has gone once you've made sure of hitting it.

POSITIONAL PLAY

Both in singles and doubles there are certain recognized positions which meet requirements for a good deal of the play. These are best understood by studying fig. 8. Now here are a few explanatory notes which may help you to understand the diagram.

A is the singles serving position.

B is the doubles serving position.

C, D, and E are the positions for receiving service, both in singles and doubles. They vary according to the speed and angle of the service.

F is the area known as " base ". Try to return here after each stroke in singles, when playing from your back court.

G is too far back, and leaves you too much court to cover.

H1 and H2 are positions in doubles play which you take up when your partner is serving.

After your partner has served, move slightly nearer the centre of the court from these last two positions, so that you can more adequately cover your share of the court.

I is " No Man's Land ". Don't stay here a moment longer than you have to.

Singles Tactics.

There are, of course, many ways of working up to a winning point, some easier than others, but all of them should be the result of definite planning. Thus, when you are serving, you have the chance of attacking before your opponent; you should therefore decide before each service what your method of attack is to be. It may be angled across the court, or straight down the middle, or you may rely simply on the speed, plus, of course, placing, of your service. Having served, drop back a little, but be prepared to move to any position quickly, according to your opponent's return of service.

When receiving a service which is straightforward and easy, you can attack with your return and, for that shot at least, your opponent has thrown away the advantage of having service. And a very definite advantage it is, as anyone who has witnessed first-class tennis will agree. One has so often seen sets lost, in effect, by the loss of one service game, and the failure to win one back from the opponent. Your return should either be deep to your opponent's base-line, to force her back and prevent her angling her return and give you more of the court to play with in your next shot; or it should be acutely angled, to draw your opponent out of the court. Should the service be good enough to put you on the defensive, remember that a slow, high return will give you more time to recover, and a better chance of converting defence to attack with your next shot. But remember also that such a return *must* be deep, as otherwise your opponent will be able to run up to the net and " kill " it.

Again, if you can get your opponent on the run by swinging the ball alternately from one corner to the other, and then suddenly break the rhythm by shooting two consecutive shots to the same corner, you will often win the point by catching your opponent hopelessly on the wrong foot. Find out your opponent's weakness— it may be her backhand, in which case you would work her gradually out of position on her forehand, and then swing the ball across the court to her weak spot. If you simply pepper her backhand you will only give her the much-needed practice and confidence she lacks, and at the same time you are deliberately cramping the variety of your own shots. She'll probably finish up by producing a winner off the despised backhand, and that will shatter your own confidence in your plan of campaign more than somewhat. I have seen that happen in important matches, more than once.

The more control you have over your own shots, of course, the more complicated can be your tactics. A combination of deep drives and short, angled shots will draw your opponent out of court, and also make her do a lot of running about. If you know your opponent dislikes playing net, or has a knack of dallying in " No Man's Land ", plan to draw her up to the net with short drives, and then either lob over her head, or pass her with a hard drive down the lines. On the other hand, should she be a good net player, it is essential your drives should be deep; she will show little mercy to the ball that bounces in the middle of the court. Following up your drives to the net is one of the best methods of attack, and so important is net play, that it has a special section of its own.

Net Play.

To anyone who has seen first-class tennis, I shall not have to mention the advantages to be gained from good net play. Almost without exception men of international tennis standing are expert in this field. You have only to see a really first-class men's doubles, and you will see that the vast majority of winners are made at the net. This has been a characteristic of men's play for years. Women, on the other hand, tended to rely rather on the base-line drive, concentrating on accuracy. Later, however, from the beginning of this century, more and more prominent women players began to play at the net. This has spread steadily until now the first-class woman player relies on her volleys to win many points and save her many steps. Maybe this has been done at the cost of some loss of the classic accuracy in driving which used to typify women's play, but the game has gained much more in speed and variety. So you will see that if you intend to get down seriously to improving your game, it will be essential that you do not neglect this most important part of it. You must learn why, how, and, even more important, when, to play at the net.

Why you should play at the net can be answered very simply by saying that it helps you to win points speedily, decisively, and with the minimum expenditure of energy. That doesn't mean that you should play a lazy game, but simply that in many close games, other things being equal, or nearly so, victory will go to the one who is less tired, and consequently more accurate. In other words, expend your energy, but always to the best advantage. Nothing can be more tiring than these endless long rallies, any one of which could have been successfully ended by a little intelligent anticipation, and a crisp cut-off at the net. Now for the " when ", and when you know that and the " why " you will have automatically discovered the " how ".

Generally speaking, you will find out when to advance to the net only by practice and playing. At the same time, you will find it a safe enough rule to say that you advance to the net on a drive which puts your opponent in difficulties, and at the same time gives you time to get right up to the net, and not get stuck half-way. It follows from this that it is a difficult feat to drive a ball from the base-line in such a way that you can reach the net before the ball is back in your court. Thus, most times the advance to the net follows a drive from mid-court. From that position you can more easily force your opponent into difficulties, and also reach the net more quickly.

When you are playing these half-court shots, remember you have less space to hit into, so you can afford to cut down both your back-swing and follow-through. You will find you can reach the net more quickly if you take the shot on the run. Don't run to meet the ball, then stop and hit it, and start to run again. Take it in your stride, and you will be up at the net almost before the ball has left your opponent on its way back to you. It is also a safe rule to say that you run up to the net along the line of flight of the ball you have just hit. In that way, you will find you will be able to follow and cover most of the angles of possible return.

Anticipation of the return is another thing you can learn only with practice. Some players have it developed much more than others, and a slow runner with good anticipation will be more than a match for a fast runner with poor anticipation. Many things help: watching your opponent's racket and feet will often give you an inkling of where the return will be. Study your opponent's methods, you will be surprised how often she does exactly the same thing every time with a certain shot, and that will be your chance for a quick winning volley.

To play net is to play an attacking game, but few players can attack all the time, so everyone has to learn a defensive game as well; what to do, for instance, with the bustling type of player who rushes the net, and hurries you so that your game begins to go to pieces. Remember one thing. Speed begets speed, so if you are being knocked off your feet, try to slow up the game with lofted drives right to the opponent's base-line, and when she comes in to the net, lob high—very high, if you can—as a change from driving. In a long rally, when you feel you are gradually being forced out of position, if you hit back hard you will only give yourself less time to recover, so lob the ball up high and scramble back to your base as quickly as you can.

If you play anyone with a habitual chop or slice, you will find that the ball will have a tendency to skid down your racket, so it must be lifted, and played with a very firm stroke. Any ball with spin must be played firmly, as such a ball played hesitatingly or tentatively has longer on the face of your racket for its spin to take effect, and will shoot off it at an angle dictated by your opponent's spin rather than by your intentions. In addition, the playing of a firm, vigorous stroke, strikes through the spin, as it were, and largely negatives it. So don't forget: play a shot with spin on it firmly and decisively at all costs.

One last point. NEVER change a winning game. I did it once, and it nearly cost me the championship. I had won the first set and thought: " This is fun; I'll try something different." I then proceeded to lose the next set and a good deal of the final one before I came back to my original game, and ultimately scraped home by a narrow margin.

You may find if you play at school that your opportunities for playing singles are very limited, and that you have to play doubles most of the time. This is a pity in many ways, because, although doubles may be great fun, it does not give you nearly so much opportunity for practice. And in many ways, of course, doubles is an entirely different game. However, if you are really keen to practice, I think most of you will find ways and means to do so.

DOUBLES TEAMWORK

Doubles takes teamwork and tact. You must have confidence in your partner. Don't poach—there is nothing more damaging to your partner's confidence. It is advisable for the stronger player to take the left court. When you are both up at the net, watch your side-lines, but don't leave all the central work to your partner. Get back to your own overheads; but if you know the ball is going well over your head, then it may be quicker for your partner to get it, in which case you change to the other side of the court, leaving your partner to look after your side. If a weak lob is put up to your opponents, it is good policy to retreat to the base-line as quickly as possible.

Angled shots are the best for doubles, and a well-angled shot to your opponent's feet as they come up to the net will often give your partner an easy kill. Try to make openings for your partner. Don't play a lone hand, and if she is playing badly, forget it, and try to play better yourself until she finds her game again. Remember that it's hardly fair to take your partner's good shots for granted, and criticize her bad ones.

If you are really keen, and have a secret ambition to be a champion, take lessons, and take care. Nothing should be too much trouble. It will often mean that you will have to give up doing other things to study and practise, but if you really want to do something you will find you can always do it, if you really go all out for it with no reservations. Try to meet different players; enter tournaments, and try to learn something from every defeat. Very few people learn anything from anything but defeat. You'll have many defeats, but if you really try each time to find out exactly what caused the defeat, then they'll have been well worth while.

Develop confidence in yourself, and a will to win. Refuse to accept defeat till the last point has been called. Tennis is no different from anything else in life; you get out of it just exactly what you put into it. It takes many years of play to produce a champion. So don't be unduly depressed if you happen to lose a couple of games to a girl in the form above you. Equally, don't be too much impressed if you happen to beat her. The same will happen to you some day. Just go on working at the game, enjoying it for itself and for what it gives you. Look for your mistakes and put them right. Then test them out and put them right all over again. Each year you will be strengthening your game and widening your experience.

Fight your way to the top in your own circle and then go on to the one above. Each one will be more difficult, and each will give you better value and greater satisfaction, until, finally, I hope, you may attain your ambition, on whatever level it may be. You will then be able to go on to the court knowing you've done some solid work to get there; and that's something which will help you to produce your best game when you need it most.

MOUNTAINEERING

There is no pleasure comparable with that of reaching the summit of a mountain, whether you ascend by the easiest path or by sheer rock faces. The air is exhilarating. The sense of achievement is very strong. The troubles of the lower slopes are forgotten. You have conquered, and the world of mountains is yours as you look around.

A fair amount of preparation precedes this triumph. It is important to plan your climb before you do anything else. Having decided on your mountain, you should study the map for the best route. On the well-known mountains there is usually a well-defined path which is represented on the map by a dotted line. That does not mean that every dotted line running up a mountain on a map is a good path. Some of these paths take a great deal of finding and some exist only on paper, having been lost since the map was printed. Nevertheless their existence on paper is an indication to you on the line to take.

You cannot set out to climb a mountain wearing the same clothes as you would wear to walk in a park, and it is necessary to give some thought to the food you carry and to the gear you pack in your rucksack. It is best to plan beforehand exactly what you will wear. Many girls like shorts for walking on hills and mountains, just as many like a short pleated skirt. Choose which you find the more comfortable, remembering that comfort and freedom of movement should be your aim. For rock-climbing close-fitting breeches or slacks tucked into long hand-knitted socks are essential to keep your knees from being scratched on the rocks and to avoid catching on projecting rocks. A thin silk or cotton blouse worn under a woollen jumper or cardigan and a waterproof wind-jacket on top will keep you snug and warm, and should the snugness and warmth change to oppression you can take off the jumper and put it away in your rucksack, to be put on again later when the air grows thinner near the summit. An oilskin and sou'wester are essential. Mountains can be bathed in strong sunshine, then within a few minutes clouds can roll up and heavy rain set in. If you do not possess oilskins an ordinary raincoat will do, but you are apt to get wet after a certain stage of saturation is reached.

In summer it is preferable to climb without stockings, but if you are not in the habit of going bare-legged it is not wise to do this. Woollen stockings are the only kind which stand up to mountain climbing. Silk stockings tear and ladder. Cotton stockings fire the feet, and should they get wet remain wet for the rest of the day. Woollen socks, hand-knitted for preference, are essential. If there is room enough in your boots, two pairs of socks make for comfort, the upper pair being turned down over the top of your boots. Boots are better than shoes, but if you find boots heavy or unsuited to your feet have no hesitation in wearing shoes. Boots certainly support the ankles in a way shoes do not, but to feel sure-footed in shoes is preferable to feeling uncertain in boots. If you wear shoes they should be heavy and nailed. Avoid rubber soles, which slip on wet rocks. Whatever your footgear, be sure that it is comfortable and well broken-in to the shape of your feet. If ever you climb in new boots or shoes you will ruin your day's pleasure. You can break in new footgear by wearing it in the garden or by taking short walks.

Winter Climbing.

Climbing in winter time demands a heavier type of clothing: woollen stockings and thick socks, two woollen jumpers and a warm skirt, wind-jacket, scarf, pull-on cap and gloves. Mittens, worn below the gloves, make for comfort. Winter-time mountaineering is for the expert, and should never be attempted unless at least one member of the party is an experienced and competent mountaineer. Winter days are short and winter weather can be very severe on the high tops. A hill with snow and ice about it is, remember, always a strange hill, however familiar under summer conditions. Mountains under snow have, in mass and in detail, beauty which may well fascinate you and tempt you to explore. If you yield to this temptation, do so with caution. Never take surfaces for granted till you have tested them. A nice white slope may be an ice-slide only lightly powdered with snow. There is, however, a special pleasure in climbing in snow of the right consistency. Snow varies vastly in quality, and the more you learn of its variations and their causes the more interesting you will find it.

Equipment.

It is up to yourself whether or not you carry a rucksack. It is a useful thing in which to stow your gear, and has the advantage of leaving your hands free. It has weight, however, and weight on a mountain adds to your expenditure of energy. Moreover, a rucksack on your back makes it difficult for you to balance yourself. It is a good idea to take one rucksack and have each member of the party take it in turn to carry it. It holds quite a lot, but the temptation to carry a lot must be resisted. You need a map and a compass. An altimeter, though not strictly necessary, is a useful gadget to carry. It lets you know the height you have attained, and if used with map and compass can give most accurate results. It is always interesting, too, to know exactly how many feet you have climbed and how many more you have yet to climb. Then you may want to carry your camera. If you have any distance to walk on a hard road from the foot of the mountain, a spare pair of socks is a great comfort. Boots or shoes, it is likely that by the time you've made the descent your feet will be wet, and walking in wet socks on a hard road can cause blisters. It is a good thing to carry a small first-aid outfit in your rucksack, in case of possible accidents.

Food.

Of equal importance to clothes for climbing is food. Sandwiches are the simplest and most compact form of lunch. The ideal sandwich for energy is the humble jam sandwich. Cheese sandwiches are concentrated nourishment, but they are dry and unappetizing; a few lettuce leaves added give moisture to them. Grated cheese and raisins make a sustaining filling. I have found that some sandwiches of each kind make the most satisfying lunch. When making them up remember to allow for a sharpened appetite on the mountain. Sweets make a good addition, and even a little sugar in a tiny bag is a help. It is wise to prepare for all emergencies and to keep an " iron ration " tucked away in a corner. A piece of cheese, a bar of plain chocolate, and some raisins make an ideal iron ration. It is best to get into the habit of never touching it to satisfy mere appetite. You carry it so that if by some unlikely mischance you are stranded you will not starve. Do not be tempted to take a vacuum flask of tea. Tea on the summit sounds delightful, but the flask has to be carried up and carried down again, and you find its weight becoming more burdensome with every step. Mountain streams are pure enough to drink.

The Ascent.

To start climbing a mountain on a bright sunny morning is one of life's most enchanting experiences. The freshness of the air, the early morning sun slanting on the hillside, the promise of a fine day to come, all fill you with a sense of anticipation. You tackle the lower slopes with zest, but you have not mounted many hundreds of feet before you grow breathless and hot. That is because you began too quickly. Frequently it happens that the foothills of a mountain are its steepest gradients, and many people, unaware of this, are apt to rush them. On the other hand, it is unwise to linger too long over them lest you begin to feel that a picnic is preferable to a climb and settle down in a sunny spot for hours while the mountain beckons in vain. The best pace is a slow, steady, unhurried one. You will find that after a time climbing becomes automatic. You will think less and less of your fast-beating heart and more and more of the world of nature around you. You will be able to take pleasure in the altering appearance of the surrounding hills and mountains. At first they will look austere and remote and will make you feel you have a long way to climb in order to be on a level with them. You will be surprised how quickly they lose their height as you gain height yourself.

A good average climbing rate is 1000 feet per hour. That allows for three rests of a few minutes in every hour. Some climbers are against frequent rests. They say the more you take the more you have to take. For myself, I like plenty of rests, even if they extend the time. As well as counteracting fatigue, rests are invaluable for letting you look long on the surrounding hills and mountains, fixing them in your memory for days that are spent in towns and cities. With the aid of map and compass check up on your whereabouts now and again. Try to recognize features of the landscape, rivers, streams, lakes and lochs, woods, farms. Your map is a reproduction, on paper, of the countryside. It is for you to relate the printed information to what you see all around you. If you do this regularly on the ascent you will soon become expert at it, and in your mind's eye there will be a picture of the landscape which, in addition to preserving the beauty of the scenery in your memory, will serve you well should mist come down to obscure the view.

Mist can be a menace on a mountain. Sometimes you can see it coming. If it is widespread and the sky is threatening it is wise to turn. There is nothing to be ashamed of in a failure through mist to reach the summit of a mountain. The most experienced of mountaineers have all known such frustrations at times, and it may be braver to turn back than to go on. Never hesitate to suggest to your friends that you think it unsafe to proceed. The chances are that they think the same thing, and they will be relieved if you take the lead. Foolhardy climbers have caused a great deal of anxiety and trouble to other people, as well as discomfort to themselves, by adhering to their intention of getting to the top when it would have been wiser to give up the project. If the mist comes down suddenly, stop at once and put on your oilskins, then sit down on a rock and wait. Such mist often lifts as suddenly as it descends, revealing the sunshine once more. I once watched a little puff of mist float in among our party. We were completely obscured from each other. In two minutes it drifted away again and we were in the clear air once more.

In no circumstances should members of a party separate. You should keep well together, and there should be no disagreement as to the route. That should be decided on before you set out, and adhered to in so far as it is practicable. Especially in mist should people keep close. Check up now and then to see that no one has fallen behind. Mist varies a good deal in density. A thick blanket of mist makes movement impossible, whereas a thin vapour-like mist does not necessarily slow up your pace though it has to be watched with a wary eye.

If the day is bright there is every prospect that you will reach the summit in a clear atmosphere. Some climbers like to have their lunch right on the summit. This is very pleasant on a warm day with little wind, but mountain tops are seldom without wind, and often it is a biting cold one which chills you rapidly after the heat of the climb. What I like to do is to reach the summit, add a few rocks to the cairn which usually stands on it, take snapshots of the members of the party grouped about it, look around and try to identify the peaks, then descend to a sheltered place (there is usually one out of the wind not many feet below the summit), there to produce the sandwiches and have a twenty minutes' rest before starting the descent proper. While sitting put on any extra clothes you have with you, even though you do not feel cold at the time.

A mountain of 3000 feet will normally take three hours to ascend and two hours to descend. If you make a sufficiently early start—and the best start is an early one—you can allow yourself a slower rate. If you start climbing at say ten o'clock, you are perfectly safe allowing yourself four hours instead of the average three for the ascent. The descent can be at the same rate. It is not any easier to descend a mountain than to ascend it, though it is a little quicker owing to the fact that you are using less energy. The constant downward movement is tiring, and if you are inclined to stumble on rough ground now is the time you will do it. Boots have an advantage over shoes here in giving much needed support to the ankles. Sometimes a brief rest will steady you, and a piece of chocolate or a left-over sandwich will counteract the tendency your knees may have to shake as sometimes occurs on a long descent.

Hostelling.

It is rarely possible to climb a mountain without staying in the locality. The time you spend in train, bus or car to where you want to begin climbing cuts off a good deal of your climbing time, and in the case of train and bus makes you time-conscious all day. Here is where youth hostels come in useful. Most are situated at intervals suited to walkers, but there are a number which have been specially placed for climbers. Black Sail in the Lakes, and Snowdon Ranger in Wales, are hostels both well situated for climbing, while in Scotland there are a large number. Glencoe in the Pass of Glencoe, Glen Brittle in the island of Skye (for the Coolins), Glen Nevis at the foot of Ben Nevis, and Ardgartan at Arrochar on Loch Long, are all excellent centres for mountaineering. Unless you are very experienced or are with an experienced party the mountains of Glencoe and the Coolins will be found too difficult. The gradients are steep and ropes and irons are necessary. At Glen Nevis the Ben is at your door, and there is a path which takes you all the way to the summit of 4406 feet.

I have climbed Ben Nevis in the month of February when it was a crisp sunny day in the glen. Our party was a large one, numbering over twenty, and consequently rather slow, the rate of the party being the rate of its slowest member. As we climbed the air became keener, and from 3000 feet upward we were walking on snow and ice. The gradients on the path are very easy. Indeed once a car was driven to the summit, though that was many years ago, and parts of the track have since been washed away. At 3500 feet we went into a blizzard which raged furiously. A party of fewer members would have been wise to turn, but there were many of us and nearly all of us knew the path of old, so we judged it safe to go on. It was exhausting to battle with the high wind and millions of choking, blinding, whirling snowflakes. We paused not once. The icy summit, with its ruined observatory deep in snow, did not tempt us to linger. Naturally there was no view. We did not even stop to eat our sandwiches.

At exactly the same place, 3500 feet, we emerged from the blizzard, temporarily deafened. Our eyebrows, eyelashes, and what hair had escaped from beneath our caps were frozen, each hair having a separate coating of frosting. We were not cold, but we were very hungry. The leader of the party, however, would not let us sit down and eat until we reached the 3000-foot line and gained ground which was free from snow and ice. There we found shelter of a kind and ate our most unappetizing cheese sandwiches, which tasted quite the finest food we had ever eaten.

Such a day's work is not to be contemplated by a party of two, three, or even four people unless they are competent on snow or ice. Numbers make a great difference to the safety of climbing. Lone climbing is to be avoided. It can be a liability to the people of the locality, and can cause a great deal of work and anxiety to other people and sometimes even loss of life. I have climbed Ben Nevis by myself on a calm, sunny October day, keeping strictly to the path and taking no short cuts, risks, or liberties of any kind. The view from the summit was for a hundred miles around an amazing sea of peaks. It should have been one of the finest days I'd ever had and yet I had an uneasy feeling most of the time. The ideal number for summer climbing is four. In winter it should be much larger for safety.

Some Easy Mountains.

A good mountain to make a beginning with in the Lake District is Skiddaw. There is a convenient youth hostel in Keswick, only a few miles away. You ascend by the southern slopes, which are gentle, and there is a path all the way up to Skiddaw's flat summit, where you will have a wide view of the surrounding country. Helvellyn is another easy climb, provided you ascend from Thirlspot or Green Ghyll and Dollywaggon Hill. You will find on most of the lake peaks good rock-climbing, but also an easy way up nearly every one. The eastern approach to Helvellyn is by a picturesque ridge, fairly narrow in places, known as Striding Edge, and it is to be tackled only after some practice in mountain-climbing.

Ben Lomond is an easy mountain in Scotland to begin with. You ascend from Rowardennan by a marshy path, which becomes drier as you gain height. When you grow more adventurous you may like to tackle the Cobbler (Ben Arthur), which is near Arrochar on Loch Long. It is very spectacular and very easy. You follow up the left bank of the Buttermilk Burn, when you will find the Cobbler massif ahead of you and to the left. You cut up a steep grassy slope in the centre and gain a ridge, which runs up to the wide summit of the mountain in a gradual slope. The view of bens and loch, both sea and freshwater, is very grand.

The Cairngorm mountains are for the experienced and toughened mountaineer only, not by reason of the actual ascent, but because they are so difficult of approach. You must cover so many miles before you even begin to climb that the dangers of fatigue and exhaustion are very great.

Adventures are to be avoided on mountains. The easy route is preferable every time—unless you are a rock-climber. A short cut may land you in all sorts of difficulties and be a very long way round in the end. I remember climbing, one lovely sunny day, on Ben Ime in Argyllshire. It was a long, slow climb to the summit. It was not at all steep, though the mountain is well over 3000 feet high. Our party of six became discontented with the route, and we unanimously decided that we would descend by a quicker and more interesting route. Accordingly we set off eastward instead of southward. We got on very well at first. The ground was rougher perhaps than we anticipated but it was not really difficult. It grew a little steeper. Well, that was what we were wanting. No one complained. It grew so steep that we became intent on the exact place to put our feet, and no one noticed mist creeping up on us until we were right in it. We were all so dismayed that we became very cheerful. That phase wore off. Someone suggested we should climb up again to the summit and descend the ordinary route. The majority thought this was sheer defeatism.

While we argued one of the party loosened a small rock with his foot and it went clattering down. Before it could possibly be out of earshot the sounds ceased. We waited, and, seconds after, we heard it dropping far beneath. We were on the edge of a sizeable precipice. The mist now enveloped us in a thick blanket. We decided to wait until it lightened before making the ascent again. For over an hour we clung to rocks, speaking now and again to each other but not seeing a thing, each in his and her little white world, knowing that to loosen hold and overbalance would be to

Mountain features

fall over the precipice. When at last the mist cleared away we saw with our own eyes the full dangers of our situation and climbed to the summit again to come down the sensible way. Peculiarly enough, the glen below had been bathed in sunshine the whole day.

On another occasion we took a short cut across a scree. Screes are patches of rock chips, and are a source of danger to the unwary. Two of our party were over, two were on it, and two, including myself, were just stepping on to it when the scree started moving, a miniature landslide. We drew back at once, and the two who were on it only escaped by some very agile footwork, by which they finished up forty feet below us, still upright, but breathless and taken aback. The most famous screes in Britain are on the mountains sloping down to Wastwater. They are interesting to see from the other side of the lake, but are positively not to be ventured on. Some climbers become quite expert on screes, and can descend a mountain by means of them much more quickly than they would otherwise do. This is hardly to be advised without practical tuition.

If a patch of scree lies across your route and you cannot avoid it, go over it slowly, testing every foothold before you put your weight on it. Sometimes sheep make little tracks through screes, and these can generally be trusted.

You may at some time or other have to cross a river. If it has no bridge near then it will be necessary to ford it. Look for the part where it is broadest. Find a stick and test the depth before every step, and as you cross keep the stick upstream, not downstream from you. If it is downstream and you lose your footing the stick may get mixed up with your legs and completely upset you. As in mist on a mountain, you may have to turn back. A lot depends on the depth and the current of the water. Safety is everything. Unless it is a very small river it is difficult to cross with bare feet. The stones hurt your feet, sometimes they are slippery, and they make you less sure-footed, throwing you off your balance. If your feet are already wet, there is no reason why you should not walk through the river as you are, complete in socks and boots. Should your socks be dry, take them off, put them in your rucksack or pocket and put on your boots again to cross. This gives you a dry pair of socks to put on at the other side.

If you are using youth hostels you will hear around the fire in the evening talk on routes and discussions of the best ways of tackling mountaineering and hill-walking problems. Very often there will be someone who will have climbed the very mountain you propose to climb the next day and who will be delighted to pass on any advice. You can pick up much useful information in this way. Shepherds, gamekeepers, and local people are knowledgeable about tracks and routes and the weather, and if consulted will give you invaluable help.

Rock-climbing.

So far nothing has been said about rock-climbing, which some regard as merely a specialized branch of mountaineering, others as its chief object. Certain items of the advice given above do not apply to serious work with the rope. For instance, the rock-climber would certainly not agree that the best way up a hill is the easiest; she is on the look-out for difficulties. Again, the best number for a roped rock-climbing party is probably not four, but three.

This branch of mountaineering does not appeal to everybody who loves hills; on the other hand a great many who begin by tramping over passes and making use of paths find themselves tempted to try a little scrambling on easy rocks, and by degrees acquire a taste for real cragsmanship.

A famous mountaineer has pointed out that women sometimes make first-rate rock-climbers because, for one thing, they have neater feet and hands than men.   Certainly there are countless examples to prove that this is a sport in which our sex need feel no inferiority complex.

A little experiment will soon prove whether or not yours are the temperament and physique for this strenuous recreation. An important point to bear in mind is that your legs, not your arms, should take most of the strain on a real climb. Push yourself up with your legs instead of pulling with your arms. The more your arms are above your head the more rapidly they tire (fig. 1). What is called " a good head " may develop with practice; and the fact is that when you are climbing rocks you have very little time or attention to waste on wondering what would happen if somebody slipped. Other matters ought

Fig. 1.—Legs, not arms, bear the climber's weight

to keep you busy, for, as one of a roped party, you have an exacting part to play. The object of the rope is often misunderstood by non-climbers, and, if wrongly used, may be a danger. Its purpose is definitely *not* to haul anybody up difficult places—though on occasion it may be used for that. It is, properly managed, a safeguard for all, except perhaps the leader, who must be absolutely sure, and a great moral support. Roughly outlined, the procedure with a roped party of three is this: the leader, who of course is the best climber, and if possible familiar with the route, ascends the first " pitch ", reaching a point where she has a firm stance, and where she hopes for a rock projection round which she can lead or " belay " the rope (fig. 2). She may have to dispense with this; experience soon teaches the good leader how, even without a real rock belay, she can best employ the rope. Only when she says she is ready does No. 2 start; No. 3 moves when No. 2 has reached No. 1 and adjusted the rope in the same

way. Your duty, if you are "bringing up" the climber below you,
is to keep taking in the slack of the rope, round the belay and perhaps round your own shoulders, in such a way that you always have
a "feel" of the climber while never pulling on the rope; in short,
you must be ready to check the very slightest slip. The friction of
the rope round your shoulders and round the rock projection, even

Fig. 2.—The leader well
belayed

Fig. 3. — Second
climber belayed, show-
ing how she helps to
safeguard the leader

over the edge of a rock, should enable you to bear the whole weight
of the climber even if she should come right off. The ideal procedure is for only one of the party to move at a time.

The rope can sometimes be used also to safeguard the one
climbing above; it should still be over a belay, to hold should the
leader slip (fig. 3). The leader may be able to safeguard herself, to
some extent, by judiciously placing the rope as she ascends.

You must of course learn the special knots for the rope; they
must be such as no strain can loosen—and, obviously, not such as
will run!

For rock-climbing specially nailed boots are essential, and a really good pair, if possible made to measure, is worth its weight in gold.

No amount of instruction on paper can make a rock-climber; your best plan, if you feel you want to try this magnificent sport, is to ask a couple of expert friends to take you up something easy. Watching what they do, and obeying their instructions, you will soon learn the elements, and the experience will show whether or not you have the aptitude.

Rock-climbing is a recreation perhaps unrivalled for giving scope for a great variety of qualities, physical and mental; it inspires, in its devotees, an enthusiasm which is quite incomprehensible to others, but which is ample testimony to the reality of its delights.

The long winter evenings, when summer seems far away, offer an opportunity for increasing your mountaineering knowledge. Happy hours can be spent studying maps, planning climbs and walks and holidays. There are good books on place names which add interest to map reading. On mountaineering itself there are a host of excellent publications. Mountaineering club books give technical information with good diagrams and photographs. The Youth Hostel handbooks of England and Wales and of Scotland give practical details of hostels, hostelling, walking and climbing, and there are fascinating books on climbing in different parts of the world from Everest to the Matterhorn, from the Caucasus to the Highlands of Scotland, from the Pyrenees to the Rocky Mountains. By reading such books you will build up a useful knowledge of mountains, their formation, their vegetation, their weather, and their people.

and dressers carry on into the centre-court, but may not enter the
... in their own end court, the way in which ... attack ...
Finally they may not both leave ... perhaps these three ... and
they may not both pass ...

NETBALL

Netball is a splendid game for girls because of the opportunity
it gives of jumping and reaching upward. It is a very fast game,
involving lots of running and dodging. It develops quick mental
reaction, concentration, and control of body movement. Variety is
introduced by the frequent changes from attacking to defending
play.

In match play the number of players in a team is seven, but
nine players could have a game if it meant that by confining the side
to seven some players would be left out. The game could be played
with teams of five if the numbers were small.

The netball court is divided equally into three (fig. 1). In
each end court there is a circle, and in the centre of the goal lines
are placed the netball posts. A net is attached to a ring at the top
of the stands. When the ball passes through the ring and the net
a goal has been scored, provided it has been thrown within the circle.
The ball is the same as a football.

The captains of the teams toss for choice of goal or for the
first centre pass. The game begins by a pass by the centre, who
must get rid of the ball within three seconds of the whistle having
been blown. Both centres stand with the left side towards the goal
which they are attacking, each with one or both feet touching and
at right angles to the return crease. When the whistle blows the
attacking team—that is, the team of the same side as the girl who is
taking the pass—should dodge to get free, while their opponents
should move equally quickly to mark them. The attacking side
should continue to pass towards their goal. Whenever the ball is
inside the circle the players there should shoot for goal. Meantime,
the defending players should try to intercept the passes given by
the attacking side. When the defenders intercept a pass they
immediately become the attackers.

Crowding is prevented by the offside rule, which keeps certain
players to certain courts. Centre-court players—these are centres,
attacking centres and defending centres—may play in any court,
but may not enter the circles. Goalkeepers, goal shooters, attacks

and defences may go into the centre court, but may not enter the court at the opposite end from the one in which they start play.

Players may not hold the ball longer than three seconds and they may move one foot only if they have landed on both feet.

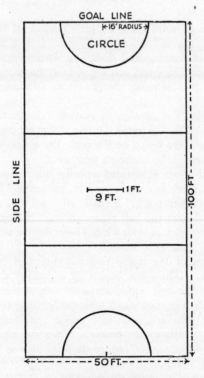

GOAL LINE

←16' RADIUS→

CIRCLE

SIDE LINE

9 FT. ⊢1FT.

100 FT.

←────── 50 FT. ──────→

Fig. 1.—Netball pitch

But should they land on one foot only, then that foot must remain stationary, although the other may be moved in any direction. A player may not take the ball out of the hands of an opponent, and she may not prevent a player from throwing the ball. What she should do is to prevent her opponent from receiving a pass by marking her so well that she intercepts the pass. Copies of the rules may be had from the Ling Physical Education Association, Hamilton House, Bidborough St., London, W.C.1., price 1s. (post 3d.).

Before playing a game of netball it is essential to have practice in throwing, catching, shooting, dodging, intercepting, footwork and jumping.

THROWING

Good accurate passing is needed to keep the game going. The ball should seldom touch the ground. It is therefore imperative to give passes which will reach the player for whom they are intended. In other words, a player must be able to put the ball exactly where she wishes it to go. There should therefore be plenty of throwing practice before the players have a real game of netball.

Fig. 2.—Shoulder pass

Low, quick passes are more useful than long ones, because a long pass is easy to intercept; the opponent has time to see it coming and cuts in to get it.

Shoulder Pass (fig. 2).—The ball is held at shoulder height, the right hand behind the ball with the fingers spread. The left hand should only support the ball. To throw the ball the right arm is stretched forward strongly enough to send the ball the desired distance forward. Meantime the left hand has been taken away. The right arm, wrists and fingers should be straight at the end of the throw, and the weight should be on the left foot, which is ahead of the right. This throw may be used for long passes, too, provided the player puts enough force behind it.

High Shoulder Pass (fig. 3).—The ball is held as it is in the shoulder pass, but the right wrist is bent back so that the ball is propelled upward and travels in a curve. It is a slow pass and is therefore easy to intercept. It tends to slow up the game, and although it is sometimes useful in end-court play it should be avoided in mid-court.

Fig. 3.—High shoulder pass

Shooting (fig. 4).—Some players find the best method of shooting is on the rebound from a catch. They spring to catch the ball, land with a give of the arms, body and knees, then straighten out again, sending the ball into the net.

Another method (fig. 5) is that in which the player stands on one foot with the back foot supported on the toe. The ball is held in the right hand, with the right elbow straight, the player aiming for the centre of the ring and throwing high. After aim has been taken, the right elbow is bent, so that the ball is brought down to the shoulder. The arm is then straightened out again, and the ball is sent up into the ring. The ball should be sent higher than the ring, so that it falls through the net without touching the ring. The chances are that should it hit the ring it will rebound off it.

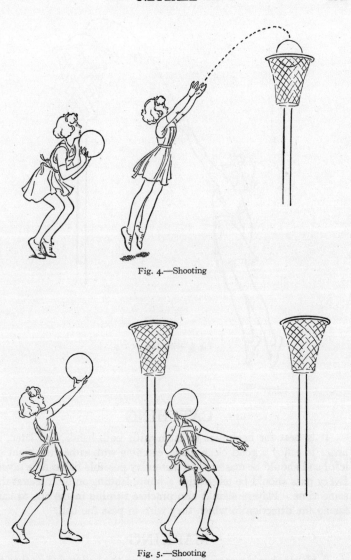

Fig. 4.—Shooting

Fig. 5.—Shooting

Fig. 6.—Shooting

CATCHING

It is best for beginners to catch with both hands, but later, in order to enjoy a good clean game, catching with either the right or left hand should be mastered so that every possible ball can be saved. Every pass should be taken with a jump, landing on both feet at the same time. Players should also practise turning in the air, to land facing the direction in which they wish to pass the ball.

MARKING

A player should try to keep one eye on the ball and the other on her opponent. This can be done if she keeps sideways on to her opponent and not too close.

This way

Not this

Fig. 7.—Marking

DODGING

It is easier to dodge than to mark. Players can dodge forward, backward, or to either side, or they can pretend to dodge to one side then go to the other instead. One of the best dodges is that in which the player darts out to the side (fig. 8). The pass should be sent well

Not this   This way

Fig. 8.—Dodging sideways

out in the direction she is moving. The pass should be made without hesitation, otherwise the marker will have the same chance of catching the ball as the player to whom it was thrown. It is only when the dodger is off her mark before her opponent that she has the advantage.

FOOTWORK

Good footwork is of great importance in all games. The weight should be on the balls of the feet, the feet should be a little apart, and the knees bent a little. From this position it is easy to get quickly off the mark. Supple ankles help a player to spring high to catch a high ball (fig. 9). Light pliable shoes with rubber soles should be worn.

Practices.

1. Sprint in one direction, and at a signal sprint in the other.

2. Continuous high springing.

3. Spring high, with strong arm swinging up. The arms should help the spring.

4. Run to jump over a space marked on the ground, and land, with a give, on both feet.

5. Run, on a signal spring as high as possible, and run on.

6. Run sideways and change direction often.

7. Run quickly, spring into the air, and land with the right foot forward and the knees bent.

Fig. 9.—
Springing for
the ball

SOME HINTS

During play there should be no calling out, clapping hands, or signalling in any way. Besides confusing their own team, players give away their tactics to their opponents. It is also useless to stand still with the arms stretched out towards the ball, waiting for a pass (fig. 10).

Fig. 10.—Waiting for a pass: never be like this

The player who does this is very easily marked, as she has given away her intention to her opponent as well as to her own team.

In the excitement of their first games, beginners are inclined to run to where the ball happens to be, instead of running to a space to which it could be passed. The game becomes a muddle, with everyone trying to gain possession of the ball. Stop when this happens, take up the starting positions, and begin afresh.

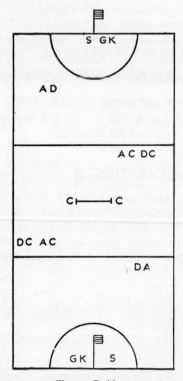

Fig. 11.—Positions

S. Shooter.　A. Attack.　A.C. Attacking Centre.　C. Centre.　D.C. Defending Centre.
D. Defence.　G.K. Goalkeeper.

Goalkeeper and *Defence*.—The goalkeeper and defence should be able to jump and spring high. They must mark the shooter and attack of the opposing side very closely, and so keep them from getting the ball. This is specially important inside the circle, for once the ball is in the hands of either the attack or the shooter inside the circle, she will shoot. When the attack or shooter is shooting, the goalkeeper and defence should still mark closely, in case the ball does not go through the net, but falls into play again instead. When this happens they should try to get possession of the ball, and thus prevent their opponents from having another shot at goal. They should manœuvre to be in a position of advantage without obstructing or touching their opponents.

Goalkeeper and defence should combine to get the ball out of the circle as soon as they can. This is best done by one running outside the circle and the other passing to her (fig. 12). The centre-court players can help by getting free quickly when an attacking move has begun. The goalkeeper and defence have often to change

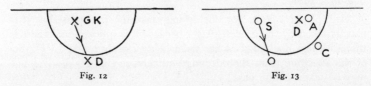

Fig. 12   Fig. 13

quickly from defending to attacking play. When the opponents have the ball, these two are defending, but whenever either intercepts a pass she should start an attacking movement at once and dodge to get free.

Attacking Centre, Centre, Defending Centre.—These players are on the move during most of the game, and are continually changing from defending to attacking play, at one moment dodging away from their opponents, and at the next marking them. They can help the shooter and attack by running to the edge of the circle when these two are too closely marked to be able to receive a pass (fig. 13). It is sometimes difficult to dodge free in the small space of the circle, and it is better for a centre-court player to help than for a circle player to come out.

Goal Shooter and Attack.—Goal shooter and attack must be good accurate shooters. They should also be able to dodge free quickly and cleverly in the limited area of the circle. Whenever either of these players catches the ball within the circle she should shoot at once. Sometimes players show lack of confidence, and instead of shooting they pass to their partner in the circle. It is better to have a shot at goal, although the ball may not go through, than to risk interception. Also, the oftener a player has a shot at goal, the better shooter she will become.

THE BOUNCE

The bounce is taken after two players have held the ball with both hands at the same time, or at the restart of a game at centre after an accident. Both players should stand facing each other with their backs to the side lines and left sides towards the goal they are attacking.

PENALTIES

The Free Pass.

Any player who is not offside may take the free pass, but it is usually taken by the nearest player because it is quicker, and there is therefore less likelihood of her team being closely marked. Players of the attacking team should dodge quickly, so that good advantage may be taken of the pass.

The Throw-in.

(i) *From the Side Line.*—When a ball goes over the line it is thrown in again by an opponent of the side which put it out. The player who throws in must have both feet behind the side line, and must have thrown in within three seconds of taking her position on the side line. The throw should be sent to an unmarked player, and after she has thrown in the thrower should run quickly into the court again (fig. 14). Attacking and defending centres usually take all throws from the side line on their side of the court.

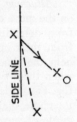

Fig. 14

(ii) *From the Goal Line.*

(*a*) *By the Attacking Side.*—Either the goal shooter or the attack should take the throw-in if the ball has gone over the goal line within the shooting circle. A centre-court player could take the throw-in, if the ball has gone over beyond the circle. She would then have a choice of shooter or attack to throw to.

(*b*) *By the Defending Side.*—Either the goalkeeper or the defence should take the throw-ins, and she should try to get the ball out of the end court or circle into the centre court as soon as she can.

Goal shooter and attack of the opposing team should, of course, try to intercept the throw-in.

Free Shot for Goal.—Only the shooter or attack may take a free shot for goal. It is best to take the throw from either side of the circle, because the ball will likely fall inside the circle if it does not go through the net (fig. 15). The attacking team will therefore get

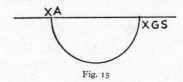

Fig. 15

another shot at goal if they are quick enough. Everyone should be outside the circle when the throw is taken, except when the shooter is fouled within the circle and takes the penalty herself. As soon as the ball leaves the thrower's hands all four circle players should run in to be ready if the ball falls into play. Three seconds only are allowed from the time the shooter takes her place on the edge of the circle to the time she shoots.

TACTICS IN PASSING

1. Whenever a player has passed the ball, she should get free to receive a pass.

2. A player should glance round quickly, or better still be aware, without taking her eye off the approaching ball, of who is free. This will enable her to pass the ball on without hesitation.

3. Although three seconds are allowed for holding the ball, a quick pass prevents the opponents from taking up good marking positions.

4. The ball should never be thrown to anyone who is well marked unless everyone is equally well marked. In any case, it should never be thrown directly at anyone. It should be thrown to either side of the catcher—the side farther from her opponent. That is the side to which she will naturally dodge.

5. All passes should be towards the goal which a player is attacking, and a pass back should be given only when there is no option.

GAMES LEADING UP TO NETBALL

Circle Pass Out.

The player in the centre tries to pass the ball to a player in the outer of the two circles. These outside players should dodge to either side. It is important that the centre player should pass when-

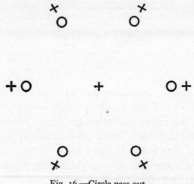

Fig. 16.—Circle pass out

ever she sees to which side the outside player is dodging. It is the outside player who should indicate to which side she is going. The player in the inside circle should try to intercept the pass and should keep in front of and close to her opponent.

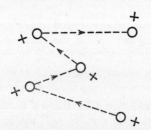

Fig. 17.—Team consecutive passing

Team Consecutive Passing.

In this game the players in the team in possession of the ball try to get as many passes as possible before the ball is intercepted by their opponents. When one's own team has the ball there is opportunity for dodging practice. There is practice in marking and intercepting when the opponents have the ball. This is a most useful as well as an interesting game, because of the many quick changes from attacking to defending play.

The direction of the ball is indicated by arrows.

Useful books on netball and games leading up to netball:

Rules. Ling Assoc., Hamilton House, Bidborough St., London, W.C.1.

Net Ball: Play and Coaching for Clubs and Schools, by R. B. Stratford, Ling Association.

Games and Games Training for Girls and Women, by Central Council of Physical Recreation.

Games Worth Playing, by McGuaig and Clark.

PATHFINDING

Let's go for a walk—not a dull walk along a road, but a free-as-air walk across fields and open land, through dense woods and across streams, never lost, always sure of where we are and where we are going, however confusing the country is around us. For that is what pathfinding teaches us, and turns dull walks into adventures.

There are three keys to this new world, and they must all be used for full enjoyment, though we can get along very well without one or another, if needs be. And the keys are: map reading, compass work, woodcraft.

Mostly you will know the area in which you are going to walk beforehand. In any case, take a map—the largest scale you can get —and pore over it. Get to know it like the face of a friend. From your knowledge of map reading you should be able to visualize the type of country quite well, even if you have never been there.

Map reading is a fascinating study, and can make the farthest spots of the world come to life. On your map you can follow the swoops and curves of your local stream as it descends from the hills behind. " Goodness, I never realized that if I just crossed over the hill from Browns the stream lay there. And how close the contour lines are—there must be a sort of gully—I wonder what it looks like?" And next walk you go and see.

A map is a wonderful friend—both on a dull, wet afternoon at home and when studied in a moment of perplexity far away on a long country walk. If I had one book to take to that mythical desert island we so often hear of, then it would be an atlas, for there is always something new to find in an atlas.

But learn to use your map.

Learn to read latitude and longitude from the figures on the edge. If you are measuring a distance, and there is no scale, always take it from the *side* or latitude of a map. Owing to the orange shape of the earth a degree of longitude is worth 60 miles only on the Equator, and in our latitudes is not worth much more than half of that. While a degree of latitude (though it also varies just slightly) is worth 60 distance minutes or miles everywhere.

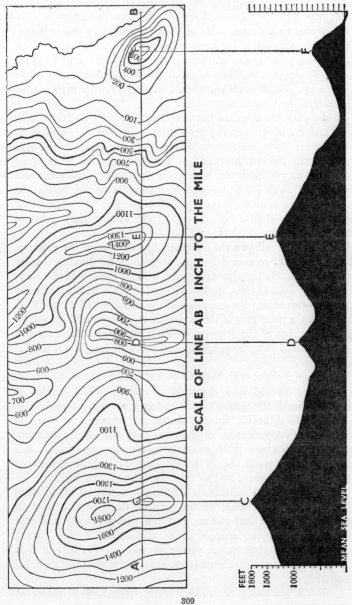

SCALE OF LINE AB 1 INCH TO THE MILE

How to make a section from a contour map
(The vertical scale is enlarged to emphasize the character of the country)

309

Be careful to note the *scale* of your map, and to use as large-scale a map as possible for your tramping, so that as many small landmarks as possible are marked. Note also the year in which it was printed—new motoring roads and spreading suburbs can throw you out a lot. But though you should use as modern a map as possible, natural features change little.

To measure the distance between two places on the map, take a ruler and lay it between the points, then with your compasses or dividers mark off a convenient distance on the scale or the side (remember the *side*) of the map (say 2 miles), and then mark along the ruler until you find you have 5 times 2 miles, plus a fraction which proves to be $\frac{1}{2}$ a mile—that is, a distance of $10\frac{1}{2}$ miles, As the crow flies of course; if the distance is going to be covered by a twisting route it should be measured from intermediary point to intermediary point.

Contour lines tell you the steepness and outline of the country, and you can make section drawings for yourself by drawing a ruler line lightly—always lightly—across the desired section of the map, and dropping lines at right angles to a vertical scale which is usually enlarged to emphasize the character of the country. If there are no contour lines, a good idea of the lie of the country can be gained by watching the path of the streams, which if straight on the map will run swiftly down steep slopes, and curl away in long loops on flat ground.

Woods are marked with little fir or leaf trees to show their type, and bogs are marked with drawings of rushes. Small circles or triangles indicate the summit of hills, and the height in feet is generally marked beside them. Roads are shown less and less boldly as they become more modest and path-like—and remember that the most obscure path generally makes the best walk. Remember, too, that water always makes a desirable objective, whether it be sea, lake or stream, and so does the summit of a hill.

Try to make each walk have a definite reason—to fill in what lies within that blank space on the map, to discover that lake, to follow the course of that stream, and you will gradually find that when you look at your map, a series of pictures of well-known, much-loved places rises before your eyes, whether you look at it at home with that countryside close outside, or years later in a far distant land.

But if we are going to wander freely, especially in forest or

difficult country, we shall require also a compass to tell us where
North lies and therefore in which direction we are heading.

In open country we can fix our eyes on a conspicuous object, and
by making towards it keep our sense of direction and our course.
But in dim weather or at night, or in difficult country with no
conspicuous object to guide us, we can easily get our heads turned
as we turn aside round this rock or that tree or walk up the bank
of a twisting stream to find a better crossing place.

Pathfinders' compasses consist of a small compass mounted on
an oblong of transparent plastic on which there is an arrow. By
placing the compass North-to-South along the latitude lines on our
map, and twisting the base until the arrow lies exactly along the
line of our route, we have our course accurately planned, and have
only to keep the needle on North and walk in the direction indicated by the arrow.

I have used this compass on many occasions in the thick pine
forests of Sweden, up hill and down dale through the roughest of
country in search of a small lake—my most frequent goal—and have
suddenly seen a thinning in the trees, and right in front of me this
lovely little sheet of water, lying cupped and forgotten in a ring of
birches and pines. A wonderful moment, an unforgettable moment
when your own achievement and the beauty of the " objective " blend
to give pure joy.

When using this compass remember to move yourself till you
get the magnetic needle quivering on North. Hold the compass
against yourself, with the course arrow pointing dead ahead, and
then turn as one until the needle is on North.

An ordinary compass will also do very well, but is not quite
so easy to use, for with it we must remember our course.

When we are heading for an unseen destination, all the devices
used by the mariner at sea are ours to use. We use compass, a map
for a chart, course, distance, speed, just as every seaman uses them.
Our course we pick out, as we have seen, from map and compass.
Distance we take from the side of the map, as we have done all
along. Time your speed at your normal walking rate over and over
again, keeping in mind the types of country you are covering, and
soon you will know your average for road-walking—easy open
country, comparatively open woodland, and difficult, hilly, broken
country—the four grades which are used as examples by the Scan-
dinavians, who go in for this kind of thing much more scientifically

and enthusiastically than we do. Short distances you can pace. Here again you want to measure how many natural double strides you take to say 100 yards.

One other point about the compass. Our compass will not point true North, but will be distorted by two factors. One is called variation, and is due to the fact that the earth's magnetic pole is not at the North Pole and, moreover, moves slightly from year to year. The variation, therefore, is slightly different for each place every year, but is the same for every compass at the same spot.

Deviation, on the other hand, is the particular error to be found in our own compass. It is increased by iron in the neighbourhood (such as steel ski sticks), and the error is different for various points of the compass. Finding and correcting deviation is complicated and does not lie within the scope of this article. To correct a westerly variation *add* to the true course, and to correct an easterly variation subtract from the true course when taking out your compass course. Say your map shows that your course from Browns to the gully is 073°, but you know there is a westerly deviation of 8°. Then you must adjust your compass so that your course shows 081°, and you will be cutting out that error caused by the compass needle pointing away up to arctic Canada instead of the North Pole.

Now to the woodcraft part of our wandering.

Learn to know the characteristics of your countryside—the general lie of the country—whether hills and streams run east and west or north and south—which type of vegetation grows on the north and which on the south side of a hill—the type of woods and how they vary in the districts. Soon a hundred small facts cry out at you from the silent countryside, helping you to fix your position and increasing your interest at the same time.

A word of warning about the sun; he is a most treacherous compass, and though, coupled with a watch, he gives the general direction of south (or south-east or south-west), he is not a guide to be relied on too much. He *is* due south at true noon, and the little error involved in keeping Greenwich time all over Great Britain doesn't make much difference—but 'ware summer time!

That moss grows on the north side of trees, according to the legend, can also be misleading, though it does sometimes work.

In Scandinavia there are signposts clearly marked on every rock, as the great Ice Age crashed through the country roughly from N.E. to S.W., grinding smooth the first side of the rock, and leaving the south-west side abrupt and sheer, with broken fragments strewn away from it.

Find out what are the particular characteristics of the country you walk in; a countryman will tell you more in an hour, if he is so minded, than every textbook ever printed.

And now a word or two of warning.

Never go off on a long walk without saying where you are going —and be sure you go there!

Always have someone with you.

If you are going into difficult country on a compass course, note carefully where you will end up if you go wrong, and try to guard against getting lost by having a road or a stream or a lake—some easily recognized natural feature—behind your objective, so that you will know if you have overshot it.

If you are aiming for the end of a lake, shape your course for the middle, and walk up to the end—otherwise you may just miss the lake by a narrow margin.

The shortest distance is seldom the quickest. Learn to make use of paths, ridges, easier ground. wherever they run in the right direction.

Break your distance into sections, from one conspicuous landmark to another, even if this makes the distance a little longer.

Avoid bogs, heavy ploughland and, of course, growing crops. And always shut gates after you.

Always take your map and your compass with you.

And take a warm extra garment and a biscuit or two; they will all pack easily into one of those handy bags on a waist-belt which sports girls wear in Sweden. (If you cannot buy one you can make one with a little canvas bag, the shape of a handbag, fixed to the back of a broad strap belt.)

Schools, Guides and clubs can organize pathfinding competitions—each girl with her map and compass, to make her way from fixed point to fixed point to the goal, perhaps to bring a card or token from each control, perhaps in a more formal competition to be checked in at each objective.

However casually or however seriously you take it up, pathfinding makes a fascinating sport, and one I know you will enjoy.

RIDING

The horse you have dreamed of for months, for years even, is about to become an actual fact. Maybe you have at last badgered your parents or aunt or uncle into buying him, or he may be hired or lent indefinitely for his keep, or given you by someone temporarily bereft of their senses, or he may even have been exchanged for a bicycle and half a dozen hens; never mind how, he is coming to-morrow.

Is everything ready for him?

You have been to the farmer and fixed up about a field and, if it is winter, a daily feed of hay. Just take a last look round and see that there are no gaps through which your precious possession can escape. He must have a good supply of drinking water to which he can get without sinking up to his knees in mud. And make a search for loose strands of barbed wire, upturned harrows and any of that spiky bric-à-brac with which farmers have a curious habit of strewing their fields, and which can easily lame a horse.

I hope the saddle and bridle are coming with the horse, which will save you the task of fitting them, but in case they have to be got from another source I will refer to that subject later. You will also need a leather headcollar with a detachable rope, a dandybrush, a currycomb, a hoofpick, a large duster and a tin of saddle soap.

Then there are your clothes to think of. Don't imagine you will need a complete rig-out suitable for the hunting field; nothing could be more unnecessary. You can even ride in slacks, but a pair of jodhpurs look and feel better. With them a shirt, and in winter a plain jersey or a jacket. The latter needs to be properly cut to go over jodhpurs. A jersey looks much better than the top half of a costume strained round the hips. If you wear gloves choose those knitted from string, as they don't slip on the reins. Ankle boots are preferable to shoes, though either will do, but refrain from sandals, high heels and wellingtons.

If you have to fetch your horse from his former home or from the station, take the headcollar with the rope slip-knotted through the centre one of the three metal rings or loops. Have the buckle undone, slip the nose-band over his nose, and bring the loose end up behind his ears, buckling it on the left side. This strap should be loose enough to allow your hand to be slipped between it and his throat. Lead him along on the right side of the road with yourself on the left of him. This places you between him and the traffic. It gives a horse confidence to have you between him and any likelihood of danger, and if he should shy it would be into the hedge and not on top of you. Very likely he will walk quietly along, particularly if you talk to him, but be on the alert for a sudden tug that might jerk the rope through your hands.

When you get home everyone will gather round to admire, and if he is a normal horse he will enjoy the attention. Do not let there be any doubt in his mind that you are his real mistress. Make a lot of him when you are alone together so that he gets to know your voice, and pay him visits in the field not only when you want him to work. The first time you turn him out leave the headcollar on, minus the rope, as he may be hard to catch until he knows you. It should not be left on permanently as it is liable to rub sore places.

Of course once he has settled into his new home you will be longing to get on his back. By the way, it is quite time this horse had a name, so from now on he will be known as " Barry ". When you go to ride don't carry the saddle and bridle out to the field, for if Barry has any intelligence he will promptly hurry off to the farthest end. Bring him up on the headcollar and tie him in a convenient place. If there is no stable or yard available, choose a strong fence or a wall with a ring in it, and clear the place of tools or wheelbarrows in which he is likely to get his legs entangled.

HIS FIRST GROOMING

Barry is certain to have rolled in his new field, so you will have to get busy with the dandybrush. Start at his head, using firm strokes in the direction that the hair lies, and brush down his neck, shoulder, chest and foreleg, then the back, belly, quarter, flank and hind-leg. Do the other side in the same way, being very careful round the eyes, ears, under the belly and between the legs, as these are ticklish places.

From time to time clean the brush of scurf by drawing it across the currycomb. This is the sole use of the currycomb, and it must never be used on the horse's coat—in spite of the novelists' popular

phrase " a well-curried horse ". That could only mean one thing—
served up on a dish with rice round it !

Brush out the tail and mane; the latter should lie on the " off " or
right side of the neck, and damping the brush will help it to lie flat.
Occasionally horses are foaled with manes that lie naturally on the
left side, in which case they must either be allowed to remain that
way or be clipped right off; hogged is the right term, and it is not
advisable if the horse lives out of doors. You can add a further
bloom to Barry's coat by wiping it over with the duster folded into
a pad.

Now pick up each hoof in turn by sliding the hand down the back
of the leg to the knee, then grasping the hoof with the other hand
and pulling it up. Scrape out mud and any stones with the pick,
and see that the shoes are firm, not worn too thin, or the clinches of
the nails sticking up outside the horn instead of lying flat. If this
is the case an early visit to the blacksmith is indicated. This visit
should be made at least once in six weeks, even if the shoes are not
worn through. They are bound to need refitting, as the horn goes
on growing all the time, and if this is neglected deformity and lame-
ness may be the result.

Now for the saddle and bridle. The saddle is made on a frame
called a tree, the top part covered with leather and the underneath
padded to fit the horse's back. The padding takes the form of two
panels with a deep groove between them. With the saddle are the
irons or metal parts of the stirrups, the leathers which attach them
to the bars under the first and smaller flaps of the saddle, and the
girth which is buckled beneath the lower and larger flaps. Buckle
the girth on the right side, leaving the other end free, then place the
saddle well forward on the shoulders and slide it down on to the
back so that when you do up the girth on the left side it should lie
four inches behind the elbow or top joint of the foreleg. To fit,
the saddle should be well clear of the withers, the bony ridge above
the shoulderblades; in fact, you should be able to get your hand
between them and the arch of the tree, and all the pressure should
come on the panels on each side of the spine, and not on the spine
itself, which is the idea of the groove up the middle. Remember
that when you are sitting on the saddle it will come down closer,
and if it seems too low you must get the saddler to put in more
padding. Draw the girths up slowly until they are tight enough to
keep the saddle from slipping.

FITTING THE BRIDLE

This is how the bridle is made up: the reins and cheeks which are attached to the bit, the nose-band and brow-band which explain themselves, the head-piece which passes behind the ears and through the loops of the brow-band and which is split in two at each end, the broader one of each pair being buckled to the cheek and the narrower, the throatlash, being buckled under the throat. The bit will probably be a snaffle, consisting of two bars of metal jointed together and ending in the rings to which the reins and cheeks are buckled or sewn. It is by no means the best bit, but it is the most satisfactory for beginners to use because you can do the least damage to the horse with it.

To bridle Barry, slip the reins over his head and remove the headcollar. Stand on his left or " near " side with the top of the bridle in your right hand and the bit lying on the palm of your left. Raise the bridle, with nose-band and throatlash undone, up over his forehead until the bit is against his lips. Insert your left thumb in the corner of his mouth where you will be pleased to find he has no teeth, and wriggle it gently. This will cause him to open his mouth and you can slip the bit in, at the same time passing the head-piece over his ears, leaving the brow-band lying smoothly in front. The bit should lie in his mouth without either wrinkling the corners or banging against his lower teeth. You can adjust it by the buckles on the cheeks. Do up the nose-band and throatlash loosely enough to admit two fingers between them and the skin. The nose-band should lie two inches below the cheek bone.

It is important to take care over fitting the bridle, as if it is incorrect it will fidget Barry and also give you less control over him. Once it fits there will be no need to alter it again, except, of course, the throatlash in order to unbridle.

Here, then, is Barry, groomed, saddled and bridled, and yourself booted, perhaps, but definitely not spurred, ready for the first ride. At this point you will need help from a second person. Someone who is fairly active, patient and certainly not nervous of horses. During the first lessons we will assume that this invaluable someone is always on the spot ready to hold, lead and generally control Barry, while you are concentrating on the rudiments of horsemanship.

To mount: stand on the left side just in front of the saddle with the reins in your left hand which, at the same time, rests on the withers. Put your left foot in the stirrup without digging the toe

Mounting, 1

into Barry's side and causing him to move away from you, and grasp the cantle or back of the saddle with your right hand. In theory you spring up lightly, raising your right leg well clear of the

Mounting, 2

cantle, and come down gently in the centre of the saddle, inserting your right foot into the other stirrup all in one smooth movement. In practice you will probably have to make several desperate

heaves before you get anywhere near on top, while your helper has
to put all his weight on the right-hand leather to stop the saddle
being dragged round. After a number of times you will learn the
knack of the spring, unless it is a very tall horse. In the latter case
use a chair or a block, or, failing that, you can let down the left
leather to its last hole, remembering to draw it up again once you
are mounted.

Test the length of your stirrup-leathers by standing upright in

Mounting, 3

the stirrups. The fork of your breeches should just clear the pommel
or front of the saddle. There is no hard-and-fast rule about the
correct length; it is a matter for the individual to decide, and only
after you have ridden for a bit can you find out the most comfortable
length.

Sit easily in the middle of the saddle with your insteps resting on
the bars of the stirrups and thighs and knees against the saddle-
flaps. The legs should hang straight downwards from the knees,
the feet covering the girth. Avoid stooping shoulders, poking chin
and toes pointing down, but do not force yourself into a preconceived notion as to how horsemen should sit. The thing to aim at
is a firm but flexible and balanced seat—balance plays as much part
in riding a horse as in riding a bicycle. So long as you sit rigidly
you will never achieve harmony with the horse's movements.

HOLDING THE REINS

Hold one rein in each hand with Barry's end entering in under the little finger and the loop end coming up over the first finger, against which it is firmly held by the thumb. The hands should be held close together with the knuckles pointing in toward you and nearly touching each other. The reins should just keep contact with the bit when your hands are in line with the pommel.

The non-rigidity rule is even more important with the hands and

Up, and sitting well

arms. The arms should hang loosely from the shoulders with the elbows close to the sides, and controlling the horse should be done as much as possible by curving the wrists inwards, which makes a flexible touch, rather than by drawing the elbows back. If ever you feel your seat to be insecure, never, never hold on by the reins. The front of the saddle or the mane are the places for strap-hanging.

Ask the helper to lead Barry forward at a walk. Avoid the fields, as that is where horses are hardest to control. The best place for a first lesson is a quiet lane or cart-track if it is fairly smooth. The motion of walking is very pleasant, particularly if Barry is striding out freely, which he can only do on a loose—but not flapping—rein. Concentrate on flexibility and balance and keeping an easy position in the saddle.

After a quarter of an hour of walking you will begin to think, oh, there's nothing in this, let's try trotting! So Barry, who has got a

Correct position at the walk

bit bored too, is easily encouraged to trot. At once your assurance vanishes. You are bumped in an unseemly manner all over the saddle, your chin comes forward and most of yourself, and one or

Correct position at the trot

both stirrups slide off your feet. As for Barry, he has his head up and his ears back showing every sign of displeasure.

Let's stop for a minute and reconsider the matter. If only you can keep your toes up a bit the stirrups will stay on, and also your body will be encouraged to keep back in the saddle; and if you can keep your knees even closer to the saddle you won't be thrown about so much. Even so, you will still be bounced up and down in a manner uncomfortable to both horse and rider. To overcome this, someone once invented the sensible plan of rising in the stirrups at the trot. What happens is that you anticipate the jolt of the horse's step by raising yourself and sinking down again in time to the beat.

This hitting the rhythm is important, and if you are a good dancer you will be able to pick it up much more quickly than someone who lacks natural rhythm. Boys and men can ride by muscular control alone, but girls, lacking their strength, need to depend a lot more on balance and rhythm, which is probably why, on an average, they get more pleasure from riding.

Although it has not taken many minutes to explain this trotting business, it may take you several days or weeks to get the hang of it. At first you will find yourself managing the rise for a few steps and then losing the secret again with exasperating recurrence. Do not try to trot for too long at a time. Riding muscles tire very quickly at first, and you will then get worse instead of better.

CONTROLLING THE HORSE

While we have been thus happily occupied, what about the poor helper who has been panting along beside you? It is time he had a rest and you learnt something about controlling Barry for yourself. First find a paddock or a yard where Barry won't be tempted to rush about, and we will consider the matter of " aids ".

These consist of the three things necessary for successfully controlling a horse. The hands, which control the forepart by medium of the bit and reins, the legs, which control the hind-quarters by pressure behind the girth, and the voice, which appeals directly to the horse's mind. Hands and legs must be used in conjunction to get the right results. You should not bring pressure on the reins without using your legs as well. It may sound paradoxical to urge a horse forward when you want him to stop. The explanation is this: by pressure from your legs you have the horse going smartly forward and *up* to his bridle. Only thus is he kept together and alert—collected is the right word—and when you give the signal to stop by pressure on the bit he will respond quickly. You are more or less pushing the horse up against the bit rather than pulling the bit against the horse. If you let him slop along uncollected and

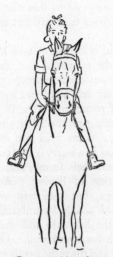

Correct position: front

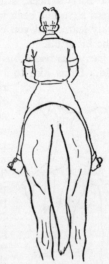

Correct position: rear

behind his bridle, when you do try to stop by pressure on the reins alone, the signal, taking longer to reach his brain, causes him to come to a slovenly halt several paces beyond the place you had intended.

LEFT TURN

Now try turning to the left as you are walking. You will, of course, put pressure on the left rein, and Barry will make a wide turn with his hind-quarters swinging out. Try the same again, this time with a light squeeze from the right leg. This will control his hind-legs as well, preventing his quarters from flying out so that the turn is neatly done in half the area of ground.

Turning to the right, you will reverse the proceedings, using the right rein and the left leg. The use of the legs is even more important when turning at any speed, as a horse turned on its forehand only is liable to side-slip and come down.

When you have the hang of these few facts, you can make your turns even handier by neck-reining. This means moving both hands slightly over in the direction of the turn so that the far rein presses on Barry's neck, still applying the leg pressure as well. Some horses have not been taught to respond to this method, but they quickly learn, and you can make your turn without any pressure on the bit at all.

Well, Barry has had a busy day, and it is time to take him back to his field. Draw him to a halt in the approved way, take your right foot out of the stirrup, put both reins in your left hand and reverse the actions of mounting. (Or, if you feel up to it, swing right off like the girl in the sketch. Some time you may want to dismount in a hurry!) My goodness! The ground feels funny, and there is the sensation of having permanently bowed legs, but this will wear off. Remove the saddle by unbuckling the girth on the left side and drawing it off with a backward pull. Undo the throatlash and draw the bridle and reins gently forward over the ears. Barry will help you by putting down his head and opening his mouth. Once in the field

Dismounting without the stirrup

he will lie down and roll with grunts of satisfaction. This is the best thing he can do, even if it does ruin your grooming, as it will help to dry his coat if he has sweated.

I hope you won't leave the saddle and bridle lying just anywhere. They are valuable things and deserve proper care. A rack is needed for the former, and a U-shaped bracket for the bridle, so that the head fits over it and is not pulled out of shape as it would be by an ordinary peg. Wash the bit well after use, and at least once or twice a week you should sponge all your leather with a damp rag to remove scurf and sweat, and then rub in your saddle-soap, to keep the leather supple and prevent it from cracking. Pay special attention to parts sewn to rings and buckles, as these get the most strain.

The inside of the saddle you must keep clean with a stiff brush unless it is leather-lined, in which case you can treat it like the rest. Once sweat and dust cake on to it there is the danger of giving

Barry a sore back, which will stop your fun for weeks while it is healing. If your girths are leather ones they will need washing and saddle-soaping too; if webbing or string, scrub them occasionally with soap and water and hang them in the sun to dry. Never dry leather by the fire or it will soon lose its natural oils and crack and break. Bits and stirrup iron you can polish up with any kind of metal polish.

While Barry is in the field there is an excellent opportunity for sitting on the gate admiring him and chatting about horses in general. These animals have collected enough facts and terms about themselves to fill a dictionary, and it would probably take you years to learn them all. But for your own convenience it is a good plan to be familiar with the main points of the anatomy.

Let's start at the crest, which is where the head joins the neck and which, if the horse bridles properly, makes the graceful arch of the neck. Where the neck runs down to the shoulder is the wither, which is much more developed in a horse than in a small pony. A fairly high wither topping a long sloping shoulder gives the horse what is called a " good front ", a most desirable addition to a riding horse. The first joint in the foreleg is the elbow, then the forearm and the knee, followed by the cannon-bone. The next joint is the fetlock, and sloping at a slight angle to it a short limb called the pastern, and where this in turn joins the hoof there is a little ridge called the coronet.

Pick up the hoof once again. The outside horn is the wall, the flat part inside the sole; lying across this is a V-shaped pad of rubber-like substance known as the frog. This frog is one of the most important parts of the horse as it acts as a shock-absorber between hard ground and the whole of his frame. If he has good frogs and he has been correctly shod, they should just touch the ground when the hoof is level.

Going back to the body, the barrel is formed by the spring of the ribs from the spine, the flank is the soft part where the ribs cease, the croup is the top of the quarters, and the pin-bone is that projection above the flank. The stifle is the joint on the hind-leg corresponding to the elbow, the thighs are called gaskins, and the hock is equivalent to the knee. The bony part of the tail is the dock. These are just the main points; there are many others, but they chiefly concern breeders and veterinary surgeons.

After experiencing the mess Barry makes of himself when he

rolls in the field, you may want to keep him in the stable, at any rate during the winter. My advice is, don't. Admittedly a stabled horse fed on corn and hay can work harder and faster, and looks smarter too, because you can have his coat clipped in the winter. But apart from costing ten times as much to keep, looking after a stabled horse needs a lot of experience. Out in a field of good grass supplemented by hay in the winter, Nature will keep the horse well and healthy. Directly you bring him in—or up, as the term is— you are going against Nature which means many pitfalls. His meals must be regular and the right quantities for his needs; he will have to be cleaned out, exercised and groomed every day, whether you feel like it or not. And he is prone to all manner of ailments. So for the first year or two be content to go slow and keep Barry at grass, but don't ask him to do the work of a stabled horse—long days hunting or fast galloping.

In really hard weather you would be justified in bringing him into a warm shed or covered yard at night. See that there is drinking water and bedding, and feed him his hay in a rack or a net hung from the wall to prevent it from being trodden on and wasted. The condition of hay varies greatly. Choose hay that is hard rather than soft, but not full of woody weeds like nettles or docks. It should be a nice bright colour and smell delicious. Hay that is musty or dusty is very bad. It has little food value, and if fed in any quantity will ruin a horse's lungs.

From May to October Barry will do well on grass alone; you may have a job to keep him from getting too fat. In a fine mild autumn he may still not be interested in hay till December, but he will certainly need it after that. He will soon let you know when the grass is good again by ignoring the hay. Fourteen pounds of hay a day is supposed to be an average feed, but as so much depends on the climate, the pasture and the size of the horse, you will have to learn by experimenting how much Barry needs. Give him just as much as he will clear up comfortably without any waste.

SECOND RIDING LESSON

After this digression it is time for another riding lesson. I hope that you have been practising walking and trotting, stopping, re-starting and turning about, so that by now you have reasonable command over Barry and the duties of that useful helper have almost dwindled to that of looker-on.

Now for cantering. At this gait the horse moves his legs in a different manner from trotting, so you must be prepared for a change of rhythm. For the first effort choose a soft lane or track, preferably slightly uphill, and start trotting. As soon as you feel Barry going steadily urge him forward with the legs and he will break into a canter. If he has not cantered with you before you may have to give him quite a strong signal before he tumbles to what is wanted, but

Canter

don't " click " to him. That is a bad habit to fall into, as if you are riding with several others you may start the whole bunch off galloping.

At the canter you do not rise in the stirrups. On the contrary, try to sit still by gripping the saddle with your knees and " going " with the stride. It is a very pleasant and easy rhythm to learn, in fact, it is almost too easy. Anyone can canter after a fashion. You can go pelting or lolloping along, according to the nature of your horse, and feel quite happy, even though his head may be in the region of his knees and he rolls like a flat-bottomed boat in a storm. But if, instead of being just a passenger, you apply the aids as you did for trotting, encouraging him to go up to his bridle with his hocks well under him at a steady, collected pace, you will get a feeling of lightness and harmony that only people who really *ride* their horses can achieve.

Incidentally, the best of riders cannot maintain this standard on a grass-fed horse for a great distance, because when he gets blown or tired he begins to sprawl. It is far better to have several short canters with breathing spaces of walking or slow trotting, than to go charging along for a mile or more at a time.

Having got Barry cantering reasonably well on the straight, you can take him into a nice level field and practise turning. Twist about in all directions, leaning your weight slightly the way of each turn to help the balance, and applying the aids as I told you earlier on.

It is best not to stay too long in the same field. Horses get bored and irritable very quickly, and don't give of their best in such a frame of mind.

The weeks have gone on, and by now you must be feeling quite at home in the saddle. Equally important, you and Barry have grown to know each other; in fact, he is almost regarded as one of the family. Bits of his belongings find their way into the house, and the last few pages of the family snap-shot album reveal him in all his aspects. With his co-operation you have found out a lot more about your own countryside; all the green lanes and bridle paths and woodland rides, and probably a good deal of private land too; only you will be wise to ask permission before you ride over it often. It is when you are getting on so famously that things have a knack of going suddenly wrong, and I am afraid it is just that newly-won confidence that is at the bottom of the trouble.

DANGER AHEAD

Along the village street you ride, sitting so easily with several inches of slack rein because Barry is such a steady walker, and your mind busy with interesting thoughts about riding. A cottage door opens suddenly and two mats, heralds of spring-cleaning, come hurtling down the steps. You and Barry are both startled, but Barry gets into action first. There is a lurch and a swerve, and what sounds like a herd of crashing hoofs. Maybe you are on the ground with Barry heading all out for home, or, if you have managed to stay in the saddle, after hauling in your slack reins, you come to a halt fifty yards down the road.

If it is the latter case, don't congratulate yourself too soon that there is no harm done. Going on with your ride you find that something has come over Barry. No more the nice steady walk. He is peeping and shying at every slightly unusual object; stopping with a jerk at the sound of a banging gate or a hen rustling under the hedge, then dashing on several paces with his head up. By the end of a mile you are both in a state of nervous irritability. Most of this could have been avoided if you had not been caught napping on the first occasion. But now that Barry is in this shying mood the best thing to do is literally to talk him out of it; for a familiar voice is one of the most reassuring things a horse knows, provided it is not raised in fear or anger.

Drive him well on with the legs, but do not catch the reins up unnecessarily short, as this will only confirm his suspicions that there really is something to be frightened of. Keep a light contact with his mouth and talk to him in a conversational tone. When a horse is alarmed by an object he tries to pass it with his face towards it and his quarters well away, moving in an ugly crab-like fashion. Apply *both* leg and rein to the side farthest from the object; this should straighten him out and at the same time distract his attention. Never hit or shout at a shying horse, as he will immediately connect the pain or the noise with what he is shying away from and his alarm will be doubled. This is an error on the part of a rider which can turn a quiet horse momentarily alarmed into a confirmed shier.

Barry may take you by surprise in other ways. If you are cantering along sitting a bit slackly and not aiming at that collectedness about which I have been insisting on, Barry decides to add interest to the monotony by putting in a light-hearted buck. Obviously he has been going along behind his bridle or he would not have been able to get his head down. If you are still aboard, sit well down and drive him on up to the bit. If, however, you are flying through the air with the greatest of ease, try to keep a tight hold of the reins; not only to save yourself trudging home on foot, but also because it will prevent you from falling on your head or shoulder.

Soon you will want to go riding in company. Barry will be delighted to go out with other horses. Everything is fine until someone suggests a canter, then away we go with Barry racing for the lead with ominous determination. Don't immediately assume that you are being bolted with. Few horses really bolt blindly, thank goodness. What has happened is that in the excitement of the dash Barry has almost forgotten that you exist. So waste no time in reminding him. Close your legs firmly to bring his hocks under him, lean your weight back and pull the reins with a give and take movement. A dead pull is useless; it only numbs the mouth and reduces the feeling in it. If this has no good results, you can try pulling the reins alternately. If there is some real danger ahead you can stop in a few strides with some hard jabs on the reins, but it is a method to be used only in extreme urgency or you will ruin his mouth for good.

THE DOUBLE BRIDLE

It is possible that the snaffle you have been using up to now is not the best bit for Barry. Few horses go their best in snaffles under all conditions, though most can be ridden on them for ordinary slow hacking. If Barry is consistently hard to stop you could try the double English hunting bridle. This has two bits, a snaffle, rather thinner than your plain one, and a curb with a chain which has a lever action on the jaw. This bridle needs careful fitting, and if possible get an experienced person to do it for you. The snaffle should just touch the corners of the lips, the curb lies beneath it one inch above the tush—the pair of teeth that stand alone in the bottom and top jaws, but which do not exist in the mare's jaws. In the case of the latter it should lie two inches above the corner teeth. The curb chain must lie smoothly along the groove of the chin and loose enough to allow two fingers between it and the jaw.

To hold the double reins, place the curb rein under the little finger, where before you had the single snaffle rein, and the snaffle rein now between the little and third finger, the ends coming out as before between first finger and thumb. The curb rein is left slightly looser than the snaffle, and you must be very careful about applying it, as if used hard the action causes the horse enough pain to make it rear. The best plan is to ride on the snaffle and only bring the curb into play when you need a little more control, by curving your wrists and turning the lower part of your hands in towards you.

I cannot leave you and Barry without a few words on jumping, even though this subject is large enough for a book to itself. First find something suitable to jump; a log in a park is good, or a low pole in a gateway or gap, provided there are no ruts. If you have to make jumps, two hurdles stuck in the ground for wings about twelve feet apart and a pole resting on the bars will do very well. Two to three feet is quite high enough for a start, or lower still if you prefer.

The worst thing you can do when jumping is to pull the horse's mouth as he is going over. It may cause him to refuse the jump next time, or, if he is bold-hearted and does jump again, he will throw up his head to avoid the pain in his mouth, thus causing his hind-legs to drop and hit the jump. Since it is almost impossible to do it right the first time, buckle a strap round Barry's neck under which you can slip two fingers to steady yourself as he takes off. Ride at the jump at a collected trot or slow canter with firm pressure from the legs for the last few strides. As he takes off try to throw your body with his, at the same time letting your hands go forward so that he may have the full stretch of his neck. When he lands your hands come back again, and you should have the same light contact as before.

Of course it won't be as easy as this for the first few times. The art is very much in timing the strides up to the one on which he takes off, so that you can harmonize your forward spring with his. I don't mean that you throw yourself right over his withers in your efforts, though that is better than being left behind; but you do need just that extra impetus at the take-off that makes the difference between going over with the horse and merely being carried over. After you have done a lot of jumping you can teach Barry to take-off at the place selected by yourself by giving him the urge at the right second, but until you are used to the action it is better to give him his freedom on the matter.

WATCH THE EXPERTS

Once you have mastered the main essentials of the different gaits and can jump low jumps smoothly, don't think there is nothing more to learn about riding and horses. In these pages I have only had space to explain the rudiments. Go to a big horse-show one day and watch, not so much the jumping competitors, many of whom have spectacular but completely individual styles, but the classes for show hacks and hunters. Notice how the riders control every movement of their horses with the minimum effort. The better the rider the less he will appear to be doing. Their use of the aids has been brought to such a high standard that their horses are in complete harmony with them; they seem almost to control them by the mind alone. Of course these riders have years of experience behind them, and their horses have been subjected to intensive training before they appeared in the show-ring, so don't expect too much of Barry and yourself next time you go out riding. All the same, keep in your mind what can be achieved by perfect co-ordination between a rider and his horse.

While you are practising and trying to be a little better with each ride, it is easy to lose sight of one important thing. Riding should be a pleasure to you and Barry, and no doubt the better you ride the more happily Barry will go for you and the greater will be that pleasure; but if, when things don't always operate the way you know they should, you become strung up and cross, then you are losing all your fun. After all, it is more a joke than a tragedy if Barry pops you head-first over a jump and then decides to stay on the near side himself. The highlights of riding are not only the thrills of achievement, but also the companionship of a horse, the friends you make, and the possibilities of the beautiful country through which you ride.

RUNNING A TOURNAMENT

Would you like to add to the fun and the thrill of the games you play? One of the best ways is to organize a tournament. This will introduce new members to the others in your club, and soon they will find themselves quite at home. Club members, too, are well mixed, for you do not play with your own particular friends all the time, as you sometimes are apt to do when you arrange to go for an afternoon or evening game.

The competitive element in a tournament gives an added interest to the play, and standards generally improve because better players show an example, and also coach their poorer partners, who otherwise might have gone on for months playing with other " rabbits ", and might never have had a chance of playing with, or against, the " stars ".

If you have a special function arranged, such as a fête, sale of work, bazaar, garden party or dance, that is a good time to think of running a tournament. It may be the means of adding very considerably to your financial gains, when the proceeds are for some charitable cause—national or local—or for the special purposes fund within your own club.

Small events if successful lead to major ones, and often people travel long distances to take part in a tournament, always trying to improve the standard of their game, and also by meeting new people, exchanging ideas, seeing new places, broadening their views on many other subjects as well, e.g. Wimbledon for tennis, St. Andrews for golf.

Duration.

Tournaments may vary according to their duration, as follows:

Day.—Arranged to take place and be completed on a Saturday afternoon and evening.

Month.—Games played with dates agreed to by opponents; each round to be completed by a certain date, and whole tournament finished at end of the month. The challenger is the player or team in top half of bracket (see diagram " Knock-out Tournament "), and usually offers opponent choice of three dates. If unable to play on any of these three occasions, defender may be scratched by referee, and challenger goes forward to next round by a " walk-over ".

Half Year.—When an aggregate is taken of the points awarded to the winners of various events throughout the season and highest total wins.

These three types may be played as singles, couple, or team tournaments, and people who enter for them may be men alone, women alone, or they may play together as mixed couples or teams. Prizes or trophies may be awarded to the winners, or they may play for the honour of being proclaimed " first ".

Some games must necessarily be indoors, and others are played out of doors, while again there are many suitable for either place.

To the novice organizer I would suggest that she start in a small way, and not become involved in tournaments entailing such things as handicapping, with difficulties like " received and owed odds ". Nor does a beginner attempt to cope with large numbers, but limits the entries so as to have reasonable groups, such as 32 for a singles event, 16 for couples, or 6 for teams of seven or eleven players.

The entry may be limited to your own club members, or you may allow each member to bring a friend, or you may decide to organize a tournament open to the general public.

The two kinds I am now going to describe are called " Knock-out " and " American " tournaments. In the former event all the competitors play against each other in twos till the numbers are reduced by half, those winners now compete, and again the victorious 50 per cent move on one round, and so on, until the ultimate winner is found. In an American, however, there are generally one or more sections with perhaps four teams in each section. Here the teams play all other teams in their own section, and are awarded 2 points for a win, 1 point for a draw, and 0 for a loss. At the end the team with the highest total plays the corresponding team in the other section to decide the best all-round team. This latter method of running a tournament is generally more popular as a social event.

You may not know how to work these out, particularly for odd numbers, so here are some diagrams which I hope will help you.

First of all a straightforward draw with eight players or teams entered for a tournament, and all the names entered have been written on slips of paper, folded, and placed in a hat or box. Then, in public, someone draws out the papers one by one to determine in what order the people play each other.

KNOCK-OUT

(When the number of entries is a power of two)

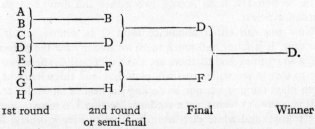

| 1st round | 2nd round or semi-final | Final | Winner |

Here we call, for sake of convenience, the players A, B, C, D, E, F, G, H, the challengers are the upper players in each bracket, i.e. A, C, E, G. In the 1st round B beat A, D beat C, F beat E, and H beat G, so B, D, F, H move forward to the 2nd round. In a small tournament you soon reach the semi-final as our 2nd round is here, and D beats B, F beats H, so in the final D and F have gone forward a round. D beats F and is ultimate winner.

AMERICAN

Entries: 12 teams.
Sections: 3.
Section I score sheet looks like this:

	A	B	C	D	Totals
A	X	2	0	1	3
B	0	X	2	2	4
C	0	0	X	1	1
D	1	0	1	X	2

Teams.

Winner of Section I is Team B, with 4 points.

The X marks the point where a team " plays itself ", if you take the diagram like a graph and run along the horizontal line till vertically beneath the corresponding letter. Do this with B playing A team, and you will see there it gained o points or lost; against C team B won and got 2 points; and against D team B was victorious, and got another 2 points, making the total 4 points for the three games played out of a possible 6 points.

In Section II team C won every game, so got 6 points.

In Section III, team A won two games and drew one, so was awarded 5 points.

Now you can either announce team C as winner, or, if you have time, it is fairer and much more satisfactory for the players to have a short final, and as there are three sectional winners you will have to toss to see which two will play first, and the winner of this match plays the one left out, so finding the best of all twelve teams.

If you have 11 teams, try 2 sections. Section I, 6 teams; Section II, 5 teams; and while each team in I has to play 5 others, those in II play 4 others. The winners of each section play in a final. These must be brief *always* or your tournament becomes long-drawn-out and players are over-tired or lose interest.

Many games need to be slightly adapted, as e.g. in tennis one does not always have time to play a whole set to decide a match, particularly in " American ", but instead every person serves two games in rotation, i.e. if A B play C D, A serves, then opponent C; B then D; A then C; B, and finally D. Eight games in all. In a final, too, a short set may be played, i.e. the first couple to reach 6 games after 5 all, and not going on to a long set, which is the couple to reach 2 more games than opponents after 5 all. Of course, a good couple may win 6–0 or 6–1 right away, and not need the ruling, but it is helpful to have it laid down before play. In a " Knock-out ", the final is usually the best of 3 sets, either 2 short and 1 long, or 3 long, depending on time available.

Adaptations in hockey are that in a tournament if no goals are scored corners count, and those awarded against a team may deprive them of a win, so the defence are particularly careful to clear well, and not to foul in the shooting circle. From the usual eleven a side very often teams are dwarfed to seven a side, and here tactics and rules alter, and each player has to use more initiative and vary her play more.

METHODS OF THE DRAW

Knock-out.

1. When the number of entries is a power of two, e.g. 8, 16, 32, 64, or an even higher power of two, they meet in pairs (as in previous diagram).

2. When the number of entries is not a power of two there are *byes* in the 1st round. The number of byes shall be equal to the difference between the number of entries and the next higher power of two; and the number of pairs that play in the 1st round are equal to the difference between the number of entries and the next lower power of two.

The byes, if even in number, shall be divided equally between the first and last halves of the draw, or, if uneven, there is one more bye in the last half than the first. The byes shall be spread as evenly as possible over the whole of the draw.

Method A.

To draw an event when the number of entries is *not* a power of two, find out and write down:

(*a*) Number of entries.
(*b*) Next higher power of two.
(*c*) Number of requisite byes.

Take a sheet of paper with as many lines as the before-mentioned next higher power of two, and number each line consecutively. Indicate by marks in the margin the divisions of the total number into halves, quarters, eighths, sixteenths, &c. Fix the positions of the byes required by writing the words " a bye " on the lines and in the order mentioned below, until the proper numbers are down, namely:

In a sheet with
    4 lines
        1 Bye, line 4
    8 lines
        3 Byes, lines 8, 4, 6
    16 lines
        6 Byes, lines 16, 8, 12, 4, 14, 6, 10
    32 lines
        15 Byes, lines 32, 16, 24, 8, 28, 12, 20, 4, 30, 14, 22, 6, 26, 10, 18.

The entries as drawn are placed consecutively on the lines unoccupied by the words " a bye ", starting on line 1. Notice that all byes are entered on lines having an even number, and when the entry on each line having an odd number has been connected by a bracket on the right-hand side to the next entry having an even number the draw will be completed.

Here is an example where the number of entries is 17. Next higher power of two and number of lines on sheet of paper 32. Number of required byes 15.

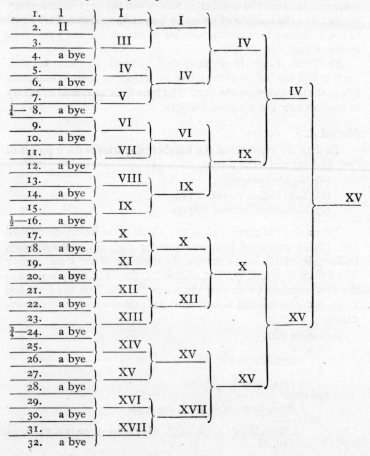

Method B.

From 5–8 competitors.
With 5 there will be 1 bye at the top and 2 byes at the foot:

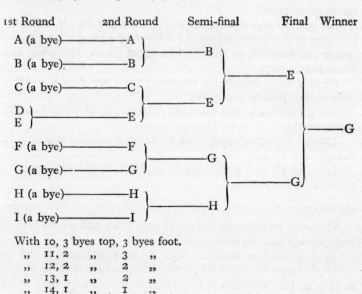

1st Round	2nd Round	Final	Winner
A (a bye) ———— A			
B ⎫		A ⎫	
C ⎬ ———— B			———— A
D (a bye) ———— D		E ⎭	
E (a bye) ———— E			

With 6, 1 bye top, 1 bye foot.
  „ 7, 1 bye at foot.
  „ 8, no byes.

From 9–16 competitors.
With 9, 3 byes at top and 4 at foot.

1st Round	2nd Round	Semi-final	Final	Winner
A (a bye) ———— A		B	E	
B (a bye) ———— B				
C (a bye) ———— C		E		
D ⎫				G
E ⎭ ———— E			G	
F (a bye) ———— F		G		
G (a bye) ———— G				
H (a bye) ———— H		H		
I (a bye) ———— I				

With 10, 3 byes top, 3 byes foot.
  „ 11, 2 „ 3 „
  „ 12, 2 „ 2 „
  „ 13, 1 „ 2 „
  „ 14, 1 „ 1 „
  „ 15, 1 „
  „ 16, no byes.

And so on with larger numbers in like manner.

ORGANIZING A DAY TOURNAMENT

Beforehand.

Decide date, place, and time. This is done by management committee, or one person (and helpers), who run tournament. Referee elected and responsible. All rules and regulations to be adhered to, whatever the game.

Entry names and fees (if any) to be in by certain date, and it to be made known that anyone who has not paid fee will not be entered in draw. A prospectus with information and condition may be issued.

Referee also responsible for conduct of players, and may scratch from tournament those who are late or who may misconduct themselves during play.

Publicity, if an all-in event, may be by use of colourful posters, in shops, clubrooms of all voluntary organizations, &c., announced at meetings, in press.

See ground and arrange for ample hot-water supply, adequate changing rooms, refreshments and helpers for serving. Tea may be indoors, in marquee, on trestle tables out of doors; hire tables and forms if necessary.

Be sure arrangements for cancelling event are clear if weather inclement or pitches unplayable.

Ask groundsman (and check) to mark courts or pitches clearly and correctly.

Arrange for spare equipment to be on hand and someone in charge.

First-aid kit and a Girl Guide or B.R.C.S. member ready to attend to any casualties.

On the Day.

Check up on all arrangements in good time, and see all helpers know exactly what to do and when to do it!

Be at ground at least one hour before tournament is due to begin, and have the draw for partners and matches done in public, so that no later criticism is possible (competitors have right to be present).

The draw to be marked in duplicate. One copy for referee, and one where all can see teams and results.

All must report to referee to be " ticked off " on sheet as they arrive.

When ready to begin remind competitors of main points, also that if short of umpires you may call upon one of the players to act in that capacity. Players may have been informed on prospectus (if one sent out in advance) to be ready to do this, and they are urged in their own interests to umpire if called upon, so long as they remain in the tournament. The umpire's decision is final, and players must not umpire unless (*a*) quite certain of the rules of the game, and (*b*) they know that at the time they umpire they will not be required to play a match.

A blackboard marked with the approximate times of the various matches is useful, and should be in a prominent place as a reminder to the players waiting their turn.

Each pitch or court is clearly numbered, or marked with a coloured flag.

Each umpire has a score sheet, which they mark and report results at once to the referee after each match.

N.B.—Umpires are essential in certain games, such as hockey, lacrosse, but not strictly necessary in games like tennis, where opponents can judge faults for themselves and keep the score.

Stewards—as many as the number of pitches or courts—to direct people to changing rooms, and hurry competitors and umpires to appropriate pitch with necessary equipment, are essential, also see that players have tossed for choice of ends, &c., before others on the pitch have completed their match, thereby avoiding waste of time in the change over. " All Pitches Always Busy " is a good motto.

Create a happy, hard-working atmosphere, as slackness in carrying out organization on the day may ruin all the best and most elaborate prearrangements.

See tea is served either for everyone at set time, or, to save stopping play, as a running buffet. Additional charge may be made for this, or it may be included in fee for the tournament.

It is useful to have train and bus time-tables to hand.

If prizes are to be presented at the end of the afternoon, or at an evening dance, ask someone in an official capacity to hand them over, and the referee must make some brief remarks prior to this, e.g. how pleased to see so many visitors, &c. After ceremony a vote of thanks, e.g. donors of prizes, person who presented them, and to all helpers, e.g. tea-makers and servers, stewards and umpires, &c., is made.

Be sure to either mention a few and say plus all the others, *or* mention everyone who assisted.

If weather breaks and no alternative arrangements possible for that day, be certain all competitors know date and place and time of postponement, or you may decide to cancel complete event.

Follow Up.

Any letters of thanks to firms and individuals to be done at once. If visiting team, then Captain or Secretary writes to thank Organizer of Tournament. Matches in future may or may not be arranged as a result of impressions gained while at your club, so happy spirit, good manners, and genuine sportsmanship matter tremendously. Try to inculcate these if not already present, and your club will thrive; much better relations amongst members and with other people will result.

Any photographs taken may be put in an album, and along with press cuttings make a good record to be seen in the club, or may be sent round or borrowed by members.

Miniature Sports.

A useful suggestion for large numbers in a small space and with improvized equipment, is the miniature sports tournament, where teams move round various events all taking part at same time, and for an equal number of minutes at each event. In this, one caters for all ages and types of individuals, and not necessarily the " games girl ". The activities are simple and varied as to skills, and an energetic one follows a quieter type, and so on. At the end again the team with the highest total of points for all activities is the winner.

The same sort of idea may be worked out with mixed games, where teams play each other for, say, ten minutes, at " Ring the Stick ", then the winners progress in a clockwise direction, the losers the opposite way, and other games such as " Danish Rounders ", " Stoolball adaptation " may be played. All teams are playing something against someone all the time—apart from the two minutes' break to change over.

SUITABLE GAMES

I = Indoors. O = Outdoors.

Hockey, O	Ice hockey, O, I
Golf, O	Tennis, O, I
Swimming, O, I	Lacrosse, O
Skating, O, I	Badminton, O, I
Table tennis, I	Shooting, O, I
Darts, I	Netball, O, I
Cricket, O	Basketball, O, I
Cycling, O	Rowing, O
Canoeing, O	Rounders, O, I
Football, O	Rugby, O
Ski-ing, O	

And all sorts of games such as Longball, Tenniquoit.

Games leaflets may be obtained from the Central Council of Physical Recreation (London Office), 58 Victoria Street, S.W.1, or 21 St. Andrew's Square, Edinburgh.

SAILING AND MOTOR BOATS

Sailing can be the most exciting sport in the world. It can also be very dangerous, so remember—never play the fool in a boat, and always treat the sea with respect.

THE SAILING BOAT

So that you may understand some of the language you hear among yachtsmen, fig. 1 shows a few of the commoner types of craft.

A boat with " round bilges " has a section like fig. 2.

A boat with " hard chines " has a section like fig. 3.

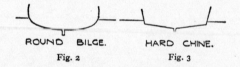

ROUND BILGE.   HARD CHINE.

Fig. 2   Fig. 3

There is an infinite variety of sailing dinghies, from a yacht's 6-ft. pram with a tiny lugsail to the international one—designs probably costing several hundred pounds. We cannot describe them all in detail, so will concentrate on a very popular boat, the 14-ft. sailing dinghy (see fig. 4).

The art of sailing is the art of using the wind to its best advantage. Seamen describe the wind according to where it is blowing relative to the boat.

1. *Sailing before the wind*, i.e. the wind aft.—You sail with your mainsheet well out, so that the sail is nearly at right angles with the ship. If you have a jib you may boom that out on the opposite side, so that you are sailing like this: i.e. goose-winged. Any pole such as the boathook will do, though some ships carry a special sail called the spinnaker, and carry a spinnaker boom for the job. Most beginners think sailing before the wind nice and easy and

344

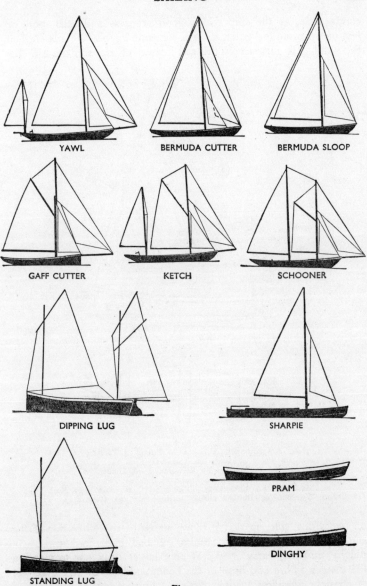

YAWL   BERMUDA CUTTER   BERMUDA SLOOP

GAFF CUTTER   KETCH   SCHOONER

DIPPING LUG   SHARPIE

PRAM

STANDING LUG   DINGHY

Fig. 1

comfortable, as the ship makes good progress and sails more or less on an even keel—that is until someone "gybes". This is when the wind gets forward of the sail instead of aft, and the sail fills

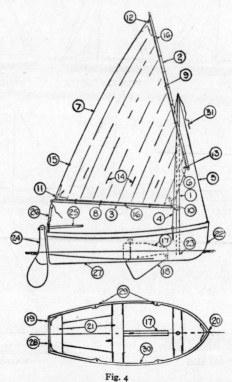

Fig. 4

1. Mast. 2. Yard or gaff. 3. Boom. 4. Shroud. 5. Forestay. 6. Luff. 7. Leech. 8. Foot. 9. Head. 10. Tack. 11. Clew. 12. Head cringle. 13. Throat. 14. Reef points. 15. Reef cringle. 16. Lacing. 17. Centreboard case. 18. Centreboard. 19. Stern. 20. Bow. 21. Thwart. 22. Stem. 23. Mast step. 24. Rudder. 25. Tiller or helm. 26. Sheet. 27. Keel. 28. Transom. 29. Rowlock plates. 30. Gunwale. 31. Halyard.

on the wrong side, so that it blows across to the other side of the ship, sometimes with dire results. A bad gybe may capsize a dinghy, and may carry away gear on a larger boat, not to mention the danger to life and limb of the boom suddenly swinging across, or possible complications if anyone had himself foul of the sheet.

To avoid an accidental gybe, watch your sails carefully, and at the first sign of any lifting put your helm down, i.e. towards the sail, and so bring her head towards the wind. As soon as the sail has steadied, the danger is over and the ship can be brought back on to her proper course. If you have a burgee you are safe so long as it blows out towards the mainsail, but if it starts to blow on the other side, be careful. If you are sailing " goose-winged ", either

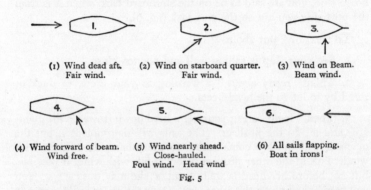

(1) Wind dead aft. Fair wind. (2) Wind on starboard quarter. Fair wind. (3) Wind on Beam. Beam wind.

(4) Wind forward of beam. Wind free. (5) Wind nearly ahead. Close-hauled. Foul wind. Head wind (6) All sails flapping. Boat in irons!

Fig. 5

sail may gybe, but the mainsail is the one likely to do damage. When passage making it is often worth steering a little to one or other side of your course if the wind is dead aft, and so lessen the risk of an accidental gybe. When, due to a shift of wind or change of course, it is necessary to gybe, first haul your sheet well in, then put your helm up, i.e. away from the sail, gently—let the boom come across, and let out the sheet again. With only a little sheet out as the boom comes across, it is under control and will not come crashing over. In rough weather or difficult conditions it is sometimes better to get the wind on the other side of the sail by luffing right up and tacking. (See sailing terms, fig. 6.)

2. *Sailing with the wind on the quarter.*—This is the easiest way : your sheet will be well out, just far enough for the luff not to shake. Your headsails, if any, will be sheeted on the same side as the mainsail, again, just far enough out not to shake.

3 and 4. The more forward the wind becomes, the more sheet you will have to haul in, until finally you are sailing as close as she will go, i.e. you are close-hauled (5). *You are " reaching " for 2, 3, and 4.*

5. *Sailing close-hauled.*—Some boats sail much closer to the wind than others, and most beginners make the mistake, when sailing close-hauled, of hauling in their sheets too far, and so making the boat sail too slowly, and feel dead. It is impossible to sail directly into the wind, so when you cannot sail the course you must zigzag, sailing close-hauled, first with the wind on one side, and then on the other; this is called tacking. When the wind is from the starboard side, you are said to be on the starboard tack, when it is from the port side you are on the port tack (fig. 6).

To tack, or " put about ":

1. See your ship is sailing well and not too close.

2. Then " ready about " a warning to your crew, to duck or stand by to let go the headsheets.

3. Then " lee-o ". Put your helm hard down (towards the mainsail) and let go the jibsheet. The sails will flap violently, but the mainsail will quickly come across to the other side and fill with wind. Pull in the other jibsheet before it fills with wind, if possible, but not before her head is well round or she may miss stays. You will now be sailing on the other tack. Once the sail is refilling steady her by bringing the helm amidships, but don't be in too much of a hurry or you may get the boat in irons, i.e. with all sails flapping, and heading directly into the wind, quite out of control, and probably soon gathering sternway. If this happens, and you want, say, to get on to the starboard tack, put your helm to starboard and pull the aft end of the boom a bit to starboard, in an endeavour to get the mainsail filled with wind. If you have a headsail get the weather (in this case starboard) sheet, and hold it out to starboard, that may make the sail fill with wind and blow her head off to port, and you should be able to get sailing again. If she won't respond then get out an oar and row her head round. A ship " misses stays " if she will not put about—a foul bottom, inexperienced helmsman, rough sea, or sudden squall may be the reason. If in a small ship, and it is urgent to get about, an oar will probably do the trick, but if you have no oar then you must " wear ship ", i.e. get about by gybing, put your helm hard down, and keep it there till the boom comes across—you may have to let out some sheet before she will " pay off " as it is called, but remember to haul it in again as she actually gybes.

Handling.

When you are sailing close-hauled, a sudden gust of wind, i.e. a squall, may heel your ship dangerously; then immediately let out your mainsheet, and this will spill the wind out of the sail and bring her more upright. In an open boat *never*, *never* make your mainsheet fast—always hold it in your hand. You will find experts, even in big yachts, continually " feeling " their sheets—letting them

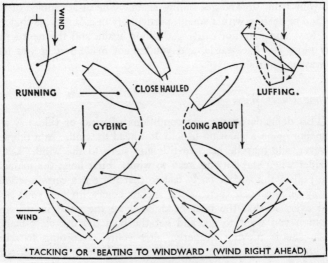

Fig. 6.—Sailing terms

out a little or hauling in a bit, so that they may get the maximum speed from their boats. It is impossible to give detailed instructions about the exact amount of sheet to have in or out, as all boats differ, but the main idea is to get your sheet adjusted till your ship " feels " her best. The general rule is to have out as much sheet as possible, so that the sails are well filled with wind and not flapping, with the ship on her course, or in the case of a foul wind, the ship's head pointing as near the course as possible. A flapping sail usually means you are trying to sail too close to the wind, though if the sail is badly cut, or badly set, it may be difficult to get it properly filled. Sometimes a rope edge will cure a loose leech; adjusting the halyards may help, but do not cut it about without an expert sail-maker's advice. A boat will sail " off the wind " with almost any sort of sail, but to get to windward and sail close-hauled, you do need a reasonably well-setting sail. If you are sailing a decked-in yacht, with the mainsheet made fast, and get caught in a squall, put your helm hard down, i.e. " luff up ", and the ship's head will immediately come up into the wind, and the sails flap, but by so doing the wind is spilled out of them, and the ship will right herself. As soon as the immediate danger of capsizing is over, of course, put your helm up and get sailing again. The disadvantage of this method of dealing with a squall, particularly in a dinghy, is that you lose way, and may not easily get sailing again, and the next squall may blow you backwards, and you cannot manœuvre if you have no way on your ship.

Getting Under Way.

This depends on varying conditions of wind or tide. A ship at anchor or on a mooring usually lies head to wind. In a tideway, however, she may lie head to tide and stern to the wind. Let us consider when she is lying head to wind. First hoist the mainsail, then pull in the anchor fairly fast so that there is a certain amount of way on the boat, then as the anchor comes up put your helm hard over, so that the boat heads well off the wind in whatever direction you want to go, and get the boat moving close-hauled. When she is moving properly, alter course according to where you are bound, let out your sheet if you are bearing away, i.e. going away from the wind, or go about, or carry on as the case may be.

Now consider the case when the ship is lying stern to wind. It is easiest to hoist some sail, and haul in the anchor as she sails up over it, then set your sail properly and sail in the direction wanted. If, however, you don't get the anchor up in time, and it holds her as she sails over it, she will swing round head to wind, and you must proceed as above. These can only be very general instructions as the wind and sea are never the same twice running, and by far the best way to learn is to practise often. Getting under way from a mooring is usually easier, as you can hang on to it until you have got your sails set and the ship heading in the right direction, and then let go and carry on.

Mooring.

When picking up a mooring the ideal is to arrive at the buoy with no way on the ship. This needs a lot of practice, and knowing one's own ship. Generally speaking, try to get to leeward, and then luff up head to wind, putting the ship in irons so that she loses her way as she reaches the buoy. If you try to catch hold of a mooring-buoy with too much way on you, you are likely to miss it or get pulled overboard, and in a big ship you might even drag the mooring. If you do miss the buoy at the first attempt, don't worry, for lots of people do the same, but just get your ship sailing again, and make another attempt.

Anchoring.

When anchoring, the important thing to remember is to have way on—preferably sternway, then the chain will not pull back over the anchor and trip it up. To get sternway on, luff up head to wind, and get the ship in irons, and wait till she begins to blow backwards. If you must anchor with foreward way on, then put your helm hard over one way or another to give her a sheer so that she does not drop back directly over the anchor. If you drop your anchor with no way on, the chain cable just falls in a heap over the anchor, and will almost certainly foul it. As a general rule, let out three times as much cable as you have depth of water. You are liable to drag with less. In strong winds let out more, and if she is snubbing badly a weight of some sort tied to the chain will help. Rope hawsers must be carefully guarded against chafing—tie some rag or cotton waste round chafing spots. If anchored in a tideway, your ship is not safe unless she has a second anchor out—a kedge. The line of your anchors should be parallel to the stream. The kedge warp is made fast to the cable, and the two lowered together till well below the surface of the water. It is best to lay the kedge out from the dinghy, but if you cannot, then let out your anchor cable to its full extent, heave the kedge astern as far as you can, then pull in on your cable, paying out the kedge warp as you do so, but don't pull in your main cable to leave less than three times the depth out.

Care of Boat.

Remember that it is not seamanlike to go to sea in an un-seaworthy boat. So see to it that your boat is as sound as possible.

Also remember that it pays in the end to buy the best you can afford. A cheap boat may prove expensive, as if she is unseaworthy you will spend all your time and money in putting her right. On the other hand, any boat is better than no boat; but if she is in bad condition don't go too far out to sea; keep within swimming distance of help!

To test your boat for rotten wood, get a marlin-spike, or pocket knife, and jab it gently into the wood. If it sinks in easily the wood is rotten and needs renewing. The most likely and dangerous places for rotten wood are, garboard, stem, sternpost. Timbers may often be broken at the turn of the bilge. The bottom of your boat must be sound for safety. To make your boat really sound a competent shipwright is really needed, but quite a lot can be done by patching with tingles, made of copper or lead, tacked over the bad places. These tingles should be well bedded in white lead. Leaky seams need stopping with putty or caulking and painting thoroughly. A well-painted boat is less likely to rot or leak than one whose paintwork has been neglected.

To Paint Your Boat.

First clean her well and give her a good rub down with coarse sand-paper, or water sand-paper, and dry well. Give a good coat of priming, and then fill up any cracks or uneven places with putty or plastic wood. Then give a good coat of paint. When dry, rub down again lightly to get a good surface and give another coat. You should give at least two coats of paint, and if possible three. Again, use the best you can afford, but a coat of tar is better than nothing. Keep your ship's bottom free from weeds or she won't sail or motor if dirty. A good anti-fouling paint is best, but regular scrubbing will keep her clean. Do not paint or varnish in hot sun, rain or frost. Of course, if possible, do it under cover.

To Lay up your Boat.

If possible, keep her in a shed, but if you cannot, try to procure somehow a cover—an old tarpaulin or sail will do. Clean her out. A dinghy is best stored upside down. All boats should be hauled out if not in use in the winter, and protected as much as possible from the weather.

Sails.

Sails should always be dried and never put away damp or they will rot and get mildewed. If their storage place is damp, you must inspect them at least once a week, and hang them up to dry and air. Large sails are of course difficult to hang up, but they can be spread out in the sun on dry grass, or perhaps you might be allowed to spread them out somewhere in the house to get them really dry. Tanned sails keep better than untreated ones. They are heavier and not so suitable for racing or light winds, but if you can find no dry place for storage it would be wise to tan them, though even then they are better kept dry. Sails if not tanned should be mildew proofed.

When you remove your rigging, and all running rigging should be removed when laying up, it will save a lot of trouble later if you label the various halyards, &c. Rotten gear is unseamanlike, so replace rotten rope. To see if the rope is rotten untwist a bit in the middle, and if the centre strand is still looking good and sound, the rope is all right, but if it is the least bit frayed, beware of it and scrap it, if you can possibly manage to buy some new. All rope should be stored in a dry place. Any wire rigging should be rubbed over with an oily rag to check rusting. If the wire rigging has begun to fray, don't trust it.

Engines.

To lay up an engine for the winter, remove the magneto or coil, and keep it at home in a dry place. Before removing the magneto the drive should be marked, so that *when putting it back in the spring the timing will be correct*. All parts of the engine should be well oiled. The engine should be turned over once a week if possible, when a little oil in the upper chamber will check corrosion. If it is to be left for long periods without attention, fill that part of the cylinders above the pistons with lubricating oil. To do this, remove sparking plugs, fill with oil, and then replace them. Batteries, if any, should be removed and kept on a trickle charge.

Fitting Out.

When put in the water after being hauled out for some time a boat will often leak, as the wood may have shrunk. She should,

12 (G 250)

however, take up fairly soon. If she doesn't, try to find the leak and stop it. Seams may need recaulking and stopping in an old boat.

A boat should always start a new season with a new coat of paint—the old saw, " Pity to spoil a boat for a ha'p'orth of tar ", is a true one. As you re-rig your ship, see that your gear is sound. A new thinner rope is stronger than a rotten thicker one. Sheaves and shackles which may have rusted will usually react to oil. All ropes should run freely in the blocks. See that all ends of rope are neatly whipped; a frayed rope's end betrays a slovenly seaman, and incidentally spoils the rope.

Rules of the Road.

Power gives way to sail, but do not expect the *Queen Mary* to give way to you in a sailing dinghy! Courtesy is the keynote of the sea. It is easier for a small ship to manœuvre in narrow waters, so do not get in the way of large steamers. If you are going to alter course, do so in good time so that the other fellow knows. Under sail, ships with the wind behind give way to ships close-hauled. A ship on the port tack gives way to one on the starboard tack. At night a sailing ship carries a green light to starboard and a red one to port, and for large ships, a white light astern.

A steamer or ship under power carries a white light at her masthead as well. The easiest way to memorize the rule of the road is to learn the following rhyme:

> Meeting steamers do not dread,
> When you see three lights ahead,
> Just port your helm and show your red.
> Green to green, or red to red,
> Perfect safety, go ahead.
> If upon your port is seen
> A steamer's starboard light of green,
> There's nothing much for you to do,
> For green to port keeps clear of you.
> If to starboard red appear
> Then 'tis your duty to keep clear.
> Then act as judgment says is proper,
> Port or starboard, back or stop her.

You should study a nautical almanac for fuller details of the rule of the road.

General Hints.

Never go to sea without food and drink in your boat. If possible always carry a vacuum flask with a hot drink in it. You can never be sure what trick the sea may play on you, so be prepared for everything.

Be intelligent about the tide, and always be sure you know what it is doing and where it runs strongest, &c. Get into the habit of studying tide tables and charts. Don't go to strange places without charts of them. An old cancelled one is better than nothing, for the coastline changes very little, though, of course, buoys and lights alter, so you must be up to date with them. Study the buoyage system, so that you know what the various marks mean.

Do not play the fool in a boat, and in an open boat do not stand up more than can be helped, and certainly do not have more than one person standing at a time.

Treat the sea with respect and you will get a tremendous amount of sport and excitement. By all means be adventurous, but not foolhardy. For instance, to sail across the Channel with a well-found little ship, and reasonable knowledge and experience might be adventurous, but to deliberately sail through a notorious tide race " just for the fun of it ", would be foolhardy as well as unseamanlike, quite apart from the fact that someone else might have to stand into danger to rescue you. If you do not believe what the sailing directions, &c., say about tide races, try to watch one from the shore. Good seamen do not have many " narrow shaves ".

Of course, you will learn more from actual practice than any articles or books can teach you, and the way to get to know the sea and your ship is to get afloat and try her, but the written word can direct and help, so buy or borrow all you can that has been written about the sea—the sea is so varied that everyone has his own particular experience and bee in his bonnet, and you will soon find yours once you have got afloat and have had a few seasons in sailing.

MOTOR BOATS

There are many types of motor boats: twin screw, single screw, petrol, paraffin or diesel, &c. Some of these boats are driven with engines of up to 2000 h.p. each. Such high-powered craft are somewhat beyond our scope, so we will consider a small single-screw motor launch of, say, 18 to 20 ft. in length. Once you can handle such a craft efficiently you will soon be able to handle larger craft.

Motor boats can be either of the hard-chine type, with flat bottoms that plane on the surface rather than go through the water, or of the round-bilge type that go through the water. The former are easier to drive at high speeds, but are not such good sea boats as the latter. A hard-chine boat is very awkward to handle at low speeds as she has no grip on the water.

A motor boat is steered either with a tiller or a wheel. Steering with a wheel is like driving a car. The ship's bow moves in the same direction as the wheel. When steering with a tiller remember the ship moves in the opposite direction to the tiller.

The normal gear box fitted to a marine engine consists of forward, neutral, and astern gears. There is no independent clutch as in a car, and no first, second, and third gears, so all you have to remember is that if you push the gear lever forward the boat will go ahead. If it is pulled right aft it will go astern, and if it is left in between these two gears the propeller will not turn, and she is in neutral. Occasionally in an auxiliary yacht there is no reverse gear, in which case very great care is needed when coming alongside or picking up moorings, &c.

When lying alongside a jetty you should move your wheel to steer away from the quayside at the same moment that you put the engine into gear. That is unless you want to move straight ahead at once. If her nose is in between other boats you may have to go into reverse to get her away from the quay, in which case you will have to see that her rudder is pointing in the direction in which you want to go, but this must be done gradually, otherwise the boat swings too quickly and you are liable to hit something. When you are clear of all boats and obstructions you can push the throttle forward so that the boat is moving along as you want.

Anchoring under Power.

Approach your anchorage slowly, allow your boat to lose way just beyond where you want your anchor to lie, then give her a touch astern, and as she gathers sternway drop the anchor and pay out the cable. Always try to approach an anchorage against the tide.

When picking up a mooring under power, again approach slowly. Try to lose way just at the mooring. If you are going too fast and want to slow down by putting into reverse, remember that if the propeller is turning anti-clockwise, the stern of the boat will turn to port and the bows to starboard, and vice versa for a clockwise propeller. So be sure you know in which direction your propeller, and therefore your ship, turns in forward and reverse gears. It is usually easier to err by losing way before the mooring, and giving a touch ahead, than by overshooting the mark and having to go astern. Just how far your boat carries her way depends on her shape, the wind, and the tide. You must find that out by practice. As a general rule, a short stocky boat loses way more quickly than a long lean one.

Getting Away under Power.

When getting under way from a mooring, remember to keep your propeller clear; either give her a good sheer away as you go, or bring the mooring aft before letting go, or else drop astern before getting under way properly.

When getting up the anchor, motor gradually up over the cable, hauling in as you go. When the cable is taut up and down, a touch forward or astern, or a sheer one way or another will usually break out the anchor for you. Remember that when you put the boat into forward gear the ship's head will swing according to the direction in which the propeller turns until she gathers sufficient way to answer the helm. The ship's head goes to port when the screw turns anti-clockwise, and to starboard for a clockwise turning screw. In fact, the opposite to what happens in reverse.

Behaviour.

Do not get the name of " marine hog ". In other words, be courteous afloat. A motor boat must give way to a sailing boat, and let the sailing boat know in good time what you are doing. Remember, a motor boat is usually noisy and fast and leaves a wash. So do not go charging up and down a crowded anchorage at full speed. Always slow down when passing a pier where boats are moored, and go slow past ships at anchor and small dinghies. Your wash might capsize an overloaded dinghy or cause an anchored yacht's meal to land on the cabin floor. By all means go flat out when the channel is clear, but it is not good for any engine to be driven at full speed indefinitely. You will find by experience your most economical and comfortable cruising speeds.

General.

Always carry enough fuel with you and some to spare. Also carry oars, as engines sometimes break down, and a motor boat is quite helpless then. All motor boats should carry a fire extinguisher. Petrol fumes are heavier than air, and so there may be fumes in the bilge, so be careful about naked lights, and use a torch to examine your engine's inside. You cannot be too careful about petrol fumes and lights. Petrol vapour is extremely explosive.

The motion of a motor boat in a seaway is quite different from that of a sailing ship. It is much more violent and rolling. In fact, many motor boats carry a small sail to hoist when passage-making, as it helps to steady them a bit. Do not try to drive your ship into a sea; you will find she will be much easier if you slow down and ride the seas rather than drive through them. If your course is parallel to the waves, you may have to alter course, so that you cross them, as the motion may be so violent that the motor boat might roll under.

Before going to sea you should thoroughly understand the workings of your engine, and where all its various parts are situated. Different makes of engines vary.

Troubles.

If an engine will not go the fault must be either ignition, compression, or fuel supply. Test compression by turning over by hand. Test ignition by taking out the plugs, their leads attached, and turning by hand there should be a spark. The body of the plug must touch some metal part of the engine, and occasionally a plug will spark in the open when it will not under compression. Test the fuel by unscrewing the petrol pipe. When an engine suddenly cuts out it is usually the ignition. If it splutters or races, it is usually the fuel supply. If it misses intermittently, suspect faulty plugs or worn magneto points. Here are a few tips for starting an obstinate engine:

1. Try doping the cylinder with petrol.

2. Try partially stopping the air intake.

3. Take out the plugs and heat them on a stove, or you could fill them with petrol and light them, but that is rather dangerous; be careful not to burn your fingers when replacing the hot plugs.

4. If the engine is hot and will not start, the mixture is probably too rich. Close the throttle, open priming tops if any, and give the engine a dozen or so turns by hand. You will find that all engines have their pet irritations and characteristics, which you will learn about as you know each one in turn.

A common trouble with motor boats is the fouling of the propeller, either by rope or weeds. If you are lucky you may be able to clear it by fiddling about with a boathook, but if not you will have either to go overboard, armed with a sharp knife to cut away the obstructions, or else beach the boat. You will understand, of course, that if the propeller is not clear it cannot rotate, so that if the engine will run in neutral, but stops when put in gear, suspect something round your propeller. Do not try to force a foul propeller by continually putting her into gear, for you will only risk bending it. If you run aground in a motor boat you are likely to damage the propellers, so be sure to examine them after grounding. They are also liable to damage if you hit anything such as floating driftwood.

FIRST STEPS IN SKI-ING

In countries where there is more snow, children begin to ski at the age of four, and climb up and fly down hills as confidently as if they were running. The younger the better—that is the motto for ski-ing.

During the war the Norwegian troops trained in Scotland, and they found the ski terrain much better than it had been considered, though of course ski-ing was becoming increasingly popular in the high parts of Britain before the war. In hard winters this glorious sport will probably become much more common in Britain. Besides, there is a chance of a winter sports holiday in Switzerland or our nearer neighbour, Scandinavia.

There is no sport like it for the freedom and ease and speed of it, the sense of daring, the joys of companionship far out in the wilds, and the great beauties of the winter snow world round about, with changing shadows and sparkling sunlight, trees bowed to the ground by their burden of snow, and far white vistas.

A ski-ing season begins about Christmas time, when the snow is perhaps scanty and generally soft. Then more and more snow falls during January and February. The short days and the heavy snow (which is so pleasant to fall on) gives way to the sun of March and April, when the snow packs hard and icy and the sun bronzes skiers, perhaps in bathing costumes, to a glorious dark brown. Imagine anything more lovely than sunbathing in the snow!

In the evening the skiers gather round great log fires in hotels and cottages. Adventures are relived and tales told of far-off homes —for those bitten by the ski-ing craze will come long distances to satisfy it.

It is possible to ski in the moonlight too, and after work in Stockholm, where I began to ski, we used to change and go out through the woods to a hill lit by arc lights, where young Sweden practised its turns far on into the night.

So, whether you are going abroad to begin in style, or whether there is just a little snow on the ground and someone else's skis available, take the chance and find out why the Norwegians prefer a winter holiday to a summer one.

Buying Skis.

To test whether a pair of skis are the right length for you, stand beside them and reach up. You ought to be just able to grasp their ends comfortably.

Skis are made of birch, hickory or split cane. But your first pair of skis should be made of birch, which is not as strong as hickory, but is much lighter. They must be of equal balance, and, of course, quite straight. Skis are 6 to 7 ft. long and grooved underneath. When you stand them back to back they should be flexed away from each other in a slight bow. You should be able to press them together with finger and thumb.

Skis, light birch skis, are not very expensive, and a full-sized pair can be had for about 25s., and children's skis in a ski-ing country for as little as 4s.

Then you must have bindings to keep the skis on your feet. There are many kinds of bindings; three of the commonest are the standard with spring or leather-strap heels; the rat-trap toe-iron; and the Kandahar, which has a foot-strap. The standard binding, which is easily freed if you have fallen down in such an awkward position you cannot stand up again with your skis on, is probably the safest and best for a beginner.

The commonest kind of ski-sticks are bamboo or steel. Bamboo are lightest and cheapest, steel are strongest. The ski-stick should be arm-pit high; ski-sticks too long or too short are just as bad for learning as the wrong length of skis.

Choosing Clothes.

Here again you can make-do very well with what you have, or you can buy a complete new outfit, just as circumstances demand. Slacks taken in at the ankle and equipped with a broad strap of elastic to wear under the instep to keep them down will do very well. Ski-ing trousers should be made of gaberdine or any other close-woven material. Complete ski-ing suits look very neat, but a windproof jacket worn over a woollen jersey is perhaps more practical. Wool should be worn next the skin, and several layers of thin wool are much warmer than one very thick jersey. Remember woolly or leather gloves; two pairs are essential if you are going on a really long trip in very cold weather. You might lose a glove, and that may mean frost-bite. And you need a cap that protects the ears.

Ski-ing boots are heavy, stiff-soled boots with a groove at the heel round which fits the standard binding. Though they are supposed, strictly speaking, to be kept entirely for ski-ing, I found mine excellent for tramping in.

And you must, of course, remember your sun-glasses. The rays off the snow, especially the ultra-violet rays which are there whether the sun is shining or not, can be very harmful to the eyes. Cream for your face when the sun gets hot is also a necessity; an April sunburn up in the mountains can be as bad and worse than anything you can do to yourself frizzling on the sands in August.

Care of Skis.

A certain amount of care of your skis is essential. At the beginning of the season they will have to be burnt with red tar to get rid of all the wax left from the previous season; this is a professional job and your sports shop will do it for you. They will also put on a foundation of wax. But you yourself will have to wax your skis to keep them in good waterproof condition.

In sticky snow the skis will not glide—or perhaps they glide too much and precipitate you backwards down every hill you want to climb, a most tiring condition. Both can be cut out by judicious use of klister or wax, which are sold in little pots or sticks, ready labelled according to the weather conditions for which they are designed.

To put on an all-over surface, take your ski and apply strips of wax at intervals of four to six inches, then with the flat of your hand sweep it downwards from top to bottom of your ski in long, strong movements, until you have dispersed all the wax into the wood. Whenever your ski begins to look white and worn underneath, that is the time to wax.

When you come in, you must always brush all snow off the face of your skis and leave them upside down, or better still tie them together, top and bottom, with a piece of wood or matchbox between the middles to keep them flexed. Don't put your skis near a fire or radiator or the wood will warp. Skis are always left *outside* a mountain hotel at night.

Your boots, too, must be kept greased and waterproof.

First Attempt.

Now you are ready for your first attempt on skis. Drop the skis on the ground, and kick your toe well into the toe-piece, and fasten the binding round the heel. Remember the clip fastening should be on the outside of the heel. Put your hand through from underneath the loop of leather on the ski-stick, so that you have a

thong of leather over the back of your hand, and your hand is resting in the loop. Now you are ready to begin, though, strictly speaking, you should begin without sticks at all.

Step out, putting your feet down straight and close to each other. Bend your knees—flex them—use them as springs. (If you want to learn quickly begin beforehand with suppling exercises, especially for the knees. Put one foot close in front of the other, bend down, up, ten times. Change to other foot in front, and do it again.)

Correct position for hands

Use the *glide* of the ski. Push off as hard as you can with the back leg. And make it even and rhythmical—count to yourself.

It is really important to learn to ski well on the flat. That is where you have time to get your balance, to learn that controlled speed which looks so unattainable first time out. But the really marvellous thing about ski-ing—for a sport that looks so immensely difficult—is that we can feel ourselves learning right from the very first half-hour.

The most important points in ski-ing on the flat are:

Move naturally, using the glide of the skis.

Push off properly with the back leg.

Transfer your weight smoothly from foot to foot.

Balance. Practise standing, and then gliding, on one ski to gain confidence.

Keep your knees bent and flexed, with hips swung forward, not bottom poked out.

Knees bent

Neat, natural use of the ski-sticks, kept close to your sides, and used like swinging arms, not flung around like flails to your own danger and that of trees and fellow skiers about you.

And, above all, practise, practise, practise.

Commonest faults are:

Not gliding: this is due to bad balance or poor pushing off with the back leg.

Strutting: knees are insufficiently bent, so that the leg cannot take up the correct position.

Lack of rhythm in the stride; practise slowly, counting to keep time, increasing your speed gradually.

At all times the slope of the body should be at right angles to the skis, leaning farther forward the steeper the downslope, straight-bodied, though not straight-kneed on the flat, and with a backward tendency when rushing up a small incline.

Climbing.

Climbing hills can be extremely tiring if you are going the wrong way about it; all the more reason for beginning right from the very start. The method adopted depends on the slope of the hill.

If it is a short or gentle slope *ski* up it. Get up speed before you get there, and, making use of your glide, you will be up and over before your realize it is a hill at all.

Tramp up a steeper hill, using your ski-sticks for extra power. A bit of a stamp as you put down your ski can help to eliminate that nasty slip-back. I found that much the same muscles were used as in climbing a heathery slope.

For very steep slopes the herring-bone step will be necessary. Skis are widely separated, points outwards. The weight is placed on the upper foot—the inside edge—and the position maintained by a firmly placed ski-stick below it. The lower ski is lifted over the upper, weight transferred to it, and stick backing it. And so on, over and over again. You can get up steep slopes at quite a speed, once you gain experience.

Then again you can " tack " up the slopes, keeping the skis parallel, one above the other, bearing the weight in on the inside of the skis, knees bent towards the slope of the hill, and body swung out to balance it. Then, blocking each step with the use of the ski-stick, you can force yourself up practically any slope.

At the end of each " leg " of the tack you turn round, either by a step turn, in which you edge round, ski following ski, until you are facing the other way, or in the infinitely more dashing and quite easy " kick turn ". In this, moving both ski-sticks to one side, you lift one ski until it is at right angles to the ground, swing it right round until it is parallel to the other ski, but facing the other way. Then you bring the remaining leg round to join it.

Downhill.

Now we are at the top of our hill, and we want to go down the other side. Except for jumping (imagine great leaps out into space on skis—I've seen it done, and I'm filled with horrified admiration for those with the nerve to do it), this is the greatest thrill of ski-ing.

Bend your knees, remember to take up a position with your body about right angles to the slope of the hill—that is, weight forward. Keep one ski (either) a little ahead, with weight mostly on the back ski. The leading ski will act as a scout, feeling out the surface. Now we're off—faster, faster—keep your skis parallel. Look out now, they're crossing! Well, that's nice soft snow you've chosen—up you come.

For a short time our downward efforts are moments of sheer joy, finished by minor disaster in one of many forms. Stopping is *the* difficulty for any beginner, that and the mesmeric effect of even one tree. (It's looking at it, even out of the corner of your eye, that leads to your undoing.)

Then it occurs to you that it might be a pleasant change if you learnt to stop, instead of crashing. That is where the snow plough enters your life. I like the snow plough and the stem turn, reliable, unspectacular, slow-speed friends, infinitely more easily acquired than the Telemark or even the Christiania turns.

The snow plough is when you allow the points of your skis to close in a V, while opening your legs and pressing on the inside of your skis, keeping your knees close together. Thus you come gradually to a pleasant stop. And your knees are still bent—or are they?

The stem turn is a development of the snow plough. Get into the position of the snow plough. If you put your weight on one ski you turn in the opposite direction (weight on right ski, left turn, and vice versa). It sounds ridiculously easy—but it works. With a little practice you can use the stem turn to thread in and out of

Telemarks

other skiers, trees, or any other obstacles you may meet on your down path.

Another very useful turn is the skater's turn, generally used on the flat. It is just like a skater's step, and consists in leading out

Christiania

with one ski in the new direction desired, while pushing off vigorously with the other leg. It requires ability to stand on one ski, balance and practice, and can be easily acquired.

The whole secret of ski-ing is rhythm, balance, and maintaining the body atop flexed knees, which act as shock absorbers. One ski—either ski—leads the way, six inches ahead, and acts as guide, taking

Snow plough

up the bumps and unevennesses. Practise changing the leading foot.

All ski-ing is a rhythmic adaptability to constantly changing conditions, so flowing and natural in the old hand—who may be very young indeed. A six-year-old gave me much sound advice in my first

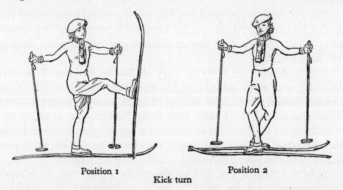

Position 1   Position 2

Kick turn

season, even if he did seem a little pained to discover that such obvious things needed to be explained to anyone not mentally deficient.

Practice gives balance. Balance gives confidence. You will be surprised to find how much you will learn in one week of ski-ing. And how you will love it!

SWIMMING

In the life of a young girl it is very important to take part in all that goes on in your exciting world, and swimming seems to bob up in every sphere. It is included in the School Sports Fixture; it is a badge for the Girl Guides; it is a feature of girls' clubs, keep fit classes or Girls' Training Corps. On holiday the morning and afternoon dips are special attractions with new-found chums. For this young army, with its swim suits, towels and " chittering bites", there is a splashing ground of bathing lakes or pools in most holiday resorts. Each town has its own swimming club where, for a few shillings annually, experienced coaching is given.

Yes, it has become very important to be able to say, " Yes, I swim ", and not to flounder forever at the shallow end, envying the darting fish in the deep water, and growing shivery in the process.

For inspiration you need not fish out the world's records as held by the Japanese, for here are the formidable records of two school-girls, Nancy Riach and Cathie Gibson, of the famous Scottish Motherwell Club.

Nancy Riach held early in 1945 all Ladies Scottish Free Style Records, and even added to this the Scottish Graceful Diving Championship. It was later in 1945 that her young club-mate, Cathie Gibson, captured the 1 mile Free Style Record, and in doing so—swimming on the back crawl—caused a sensation; it never having been heard of before in the annals of swimming. Cathie, at 14 years of age, was the youngest ever to hold a British Record.

Now at school it was, and surely still is, a great maxim to repeat " If they can do it, so can I ". So what about it? It certainly is a tall order, but worth a try, and whether aspiring champions or not, you all like to be in the swim.

Fortunately, the beginners' stage of swimming can be mastered on one's own. You have no horrible feeling of giving your opponent a bad game or letting the team down. In common with every other sport, of course, practice reaps its reward, not in spasms, but regular twice-weekly practices if possible. Don't splash right away into the water and strike out with reckless enthusiasm; a fright of suddenly going under to a beginner or one unused to water will take away all confidence for ever.

Some, but not all, take to the water like ducks, but if you are not one of these, become acclimatized. Get into a swim suit and wander around the edge watching the frolickers, play around in the hot and cold sprays, become thoroughly familiar with the surroundings and, most important of all, note where the shallow end is. This is not time wasted. You must feel perfectly at home in the atmosphere. Then, without any great thought, you will suddenly and quite naturally slip in from the steps. Everyone goes through the stage of bobbing up and down, so don't become disgusted or impatient.

While watching the Motherwell Club at practice one evening, the Superintendent pointed out a tiny tot of 4 years and said, " There's a future champion ". Now all I could see was a plucky little water babe splashing around in great enjoyment and apparently swallowing gallons of water; but the fact that this infant did not gasp, splutter or choke and was indeed entirely at home, I was told, were the first signs of confidence and perfect breathing freedom in water. So take heart and remember that from such frantic gesticulations does the Crawl develop.

In all sports perfect breathing is important. From that you gain the energy for endurance. In swimming, deep-chested, rhythmic breathing is not merely an asset but essential; so start, standing still in the pool, inhale deeply through the mouth and then " duck " your head under the water and exhale. Try this a few times, each time increasing the length of time under the water, but do not endure it until you are blue in the face.

Do you now like the " feel " of the water and want to carry on? The art of swimming, apart from grand sport and good fun, embraces every motion for physical well-being and development. Many cripples have benefited from swimming, and recently I watched a youth who had been in a sanatorium six months previously win a 50 yards race with ease.

Apart from all these pleasures and benefits, I would still impress, " Don't try to swim if you don't like it ". Sport is essentially a pleasure, and if it is forced upon one, all the joy and good are drained from it. Parents who are keen swimmers often make the mistake of

expecting their offspring to be able to swim like fish and force them
to go into the water. This was carried to excess with one swimming
family I knew who even resented their spaniel dog being chary of
water, so flung him into a river to make him swim. Unfortunately,
the dog did not share their enthusiasm, and one member of the
family had an extra dip that day, fully clad, in order to rescue the
spaniel.

At times a little push or encouragement is needed; as I discovered
upon asking Cathie Gibson what, I thought at the time, was an
unnecessary question—if she had always been keen on swimming.
To my astonishment she admitted she actually hated the baths and
nearly wept when dragged there by an enthusiastic and outstandingly
good swimming family. Now her records speak for her ability, and
she herself would tell you she practically lived in the water, practising three times each day and loving it. Cathie, by the way, was
only 5′ 1″ in height, and weighed about 7 st. when she broke her
records, so don't think you are too small to be a champion.

However, you want to swim, having comfortably survived the
first test ducking.

The following exercises are the generally approved strokes, but
don't be discouraged if your every movement is not quite by the
book. Many swimmers develop effective little peculiarities of their
own, and although Nancy Riach was a joy to watch in speed and
style, Cathie Gibson has intrigued spectators and judges alike with
her unorthodox scissor kick. But a swimmer may be disqualified in a
competition for using this kick.

Now we are off. The first sea battle is best fought on dry land, so
lie flat over a chair or table. Thoroughly master the leg movement
first, as this usually causes the greatest difficulty.

CRAWL: *Leg Movement*

Legs straight out and together, with toes well pointed, but
turned inwards (hen-toed); start beating them alternately up and
down about 12 inches, keeping in time to a quick count of 1, 2, 3, 4.
It is important that this movement should operate from the hips
and *not* the knees.

The natural tendency is to flap from the knee joint, so concentrate on the movement operating from the hip. Gradually speed
up the count with slightly more pressure on the downward beat,

but don't lose the rhythm. Even at this early stage, practise the correct breathing. Turn the head left (or right) on beat 1; inhale deeply through the mouth, and turn head back smoothly to exhale on beat 4. All breathing in swimming is done through the mouth.

When this can be maintained without any increasing strain for several minutes, attempt it in the water. Grasp the hand-rail with one hand and use the other, with palm against the wall, to lever the legs to the surface. Don't think of the water as an obstacle. Visualize only the movements, with particular attention to breathing, as wrong timing will result in mouthfuls of water when striking across the baths. The water only adds a little more strain on the muscles, but with diligent and concentrated practice, the legs will become tireless and the action automatic.

After this has been achieved, get hold of a small rubber ring or float, place it in a comfortable position in front and lean hands on it for support. Now propel yourself across the baths—not in any attempt at speed but with even beats, keenly awake to each action and correct breathing, and make sure you are not wasting energy and so losing speed by merely splashing the legs. The heels only must just churn the water. Again practise until achieved with comfort and grace.

Now for the arm action, which is the greater driving force in crawl swimming. This can be practised right away in water, at chest level. With fingers and thumb closed and hand slightly cupped, extend right arm, straight but relaxed, along the surface of the water, and pull through with the determination to master the water—*not* cut it. When the arm is level with the shoulder, recover arm with elbow well up, to surface and extend again to repeat arm drive.

When familiar with the motion and power of the stroke, try it out with the left arm. Practise each arm separately until the stroke is understood. Both arms can then start alternately in full fighting force, the one arm mastering the water as the other arm finishes its pull. Try this engine power by walking across the baths and feel that the arms are pulling their weight. Remember—keep that elbow up and fingers close together.

You have already learned to breathe " on time " with the leg movement; now adapt it to the arm stroke, which is: as the right arm starts to master the water inhale deeply with an easy and

Fig. 1.—The complete crawl
372

not jerky swirl of the head to the left, bringing the mouth clear of the water, and turn head back smoothly to the natural position to breathe out through the water as the left arm is finishing its pull through.

THE COMPLETE CRAWL

Then the great, but alas! often sorrowful moment—the Complete Crawl. Push off from the side, keep the legs going for a little on their own to gain balance, and then introduce the arm stroke and breathing. Do not expect immediate results. But again that Golden Rule—*Practice*—not just carelessly, but knowing exactly what you are doing and why, then progress is achieved slowly but surely. Actually, at its birth, or should I say baptism, the Crawl was only universally accepted as being good for speed over short distances, and it was not until 1926, when an American woman used it to cross the Channel in 14 hours, 34 minutes, that the world sat up and took notice of its full possibilities.

Race records are won and lost in the turn, so pay strict attention to it during your plodding up and down the pond. As you approach the wall, judge the distance and inhale deeply before reaching it. For the left turn (reverse if making right turn) place the right hand flat on the wall with arm bent (left hand should be folded across chest), swing your body (curled) round, and push from wall with right hand. When feet meet the side, legs should be in bend position. Push out strongly till legs are straight and feet together. As momentum slackens start leg movement keeping hands in front and exhaling. Now continue with full stroke.

Some may question the wisdom of starting off as a non-swimmer with the Crawl because friends have progressed through the breast stroke, side stroke, trudgeon, and so to the pinnacle of speed, distance and ambition—the Crawl.

Not so long ago the Breast Stroke was considered almost old-fashioned in Scotland. Now, however, Scotland has a great many outstanding swimmers using it. It is a very graceful stroke and many swimmers find they can cover longer distances on it.

BREAST STROKE

Here are beginners' instructions on the Breast Stroke.

Repeat the breathing or bubbling water exercises as outlined for the Crawl.

Land Drill.—Stand erect. Count or Position (1). Both arms outstretched to shoulder level, fingers close together, thumbs touching and palms downwards, breathe out through mouth.

(2) Sweep arms apart with palms turned outwards to " push " the water aside and pull arms down, mastering the water until arms have reached your side—breathe in deeply through mouth.

(3) With elbows tucked in at side of chest, bring hands together with thumbs touching, in front of chin, at the same time slide one heel up side of other leg to knee level.

(4) Shoot both arms forward to first position and kick right foot out and snap leg together at side of left leg.

Note.—You are now in position (1)—erect and arms outstretched. Repeat until arms, leg and breathing are in harmony. Practise then with left leg.

With no head turning for breathing it is possible to lie across a table or chair before a mirror and watch your movements. To visualize the whole effect is a great help. Another elementary but enjoyable tip is to watch a frog swim. It has a perfect leg kick. I do hope, however, you are more fortunate than I, for my particular frog in its museum case was very " gala " shy, and needed quite a lot of tapping on the glass to provoke it to demonstration.

When land perfect, slip into the water and, by holding the rail in the approved manner, practise the complete leg motion. Make sure power is generated by the swing out and together of the legs. When confident of the stroke, stand a few yards away from the rail and swim towards it, lengthening the distance as confidence and ability grow.

At the beginning at least, repeat the count 1, 2, 3, 4, and don't rush it.

An alternative dodge is to beat it out to the words " take-it-eas-y ". This was once so effective with a youth who so gracefully and effortlessly sailed through the water, that an onlooker was urged to say, " You take it so easy—how do you do it?" the answer being, " Yes, because I am repeating all the time, ' take it easy—

Fig. 2.—Breast stroke

375

take it easy ' ". It also had a humorous sequel, as some time later this youth was careering joyously and recklessly down a water-chute at top speed when he heard a familiar cry from a spectator— " Take it easy—take it easy ".

That is perhaps another advantage of " plodding " a little in the first stages. The quicker you swim with confidence then the sooner you can fearlessly join the fun of 'chutes, water wheels and rafts, between practice.

A practical demonstration of how an easy, graceful glide has greater speed and is not so exhausting, is often a feature of swim-ming galas. The demonstrator first mimes an over-enthusiastic be-ginner, panting up the length of the pond, " snipping " the move-ments and taking 30 strokes in the process. In contrast, with a perfect, easy and complete stroke, the expert covers the same dis-tance in 8 strokes. This is a good test to set yourselves.

Throughout these instructions I have impressed the importance of being " at home " in the water, meaning that you like the sooth-ing lap of the pond or baths and the invigorating breakers of the sea, and have confidence in getting your feet off the bottom.

Now for the sometimes necessary hint of getting your feet on to solid ground again. Mostly this comes naturally to a bather, which is why I have not stressed it before, but there are cases where it has been a decided drawback and panic has resulted from this inability to regain balance, so it is advisable for beginners to test their ability or acquire the simple art. When swimming on the Breast Stroke or Crawl, raise head, sweep the arms, with palms of hands upwards, from well under the water to the surface; this arm action sends the feet down, and to bend the knees breaks the buoyancy.

Whether ambitious or not, it will be well worth spending a little time on floating, and that will complete all the twists and turns and lay a good foundation for the Back Crawl or fancy swimming. Strangely enough, some girls float instinctively even before they swim, while others can never quite master it, and persist in sinking in the middle, thus dragging the feet down. The simplest, if not the most technical way of explaining the position is, as if you were lying flat on your back in bed, comfortable and relaxed and head well back. Wiggle your toes and gently scull with hands and this will maintain a floating balance for any length of time. To this rule there are exceptions; some may require to add the weight of arms outstretched above the head to keep the legs floating, but generally an easy, natural stretched position is sufficient. A good buoyancy for beginning can be achieved by tucking your toes under the rail, getting into position and when comfortably settled, push lightly, with toes, away from the side.

The only agony in swimming has always been the " getting under " for each swim. To wade in, with the water creeping up inch by inch, always reminds me of an Edgar Allan Poe torture, and each time, just before getting over the shoulders I have vowed swimming was an overrated pastime. To dive or even plunge in from the side, however, is a most exhilarating sensation. So dive one must, and more especially is it essential when you have reached the stage or inclination to enter into competitive swimming.

DIVING

Diving has a fascination all its own. To soar through the air like a bird on wing has been most people's ambition from childhood. High Diving, especially the Swallow Dive, is the nearest approach to the fulfilment of this dream. But once again you must take it gradually, literally step by step, as a pleasant side-line or relaxation to the Crawl or Breast Stroke.

Stand in the pond with back to rail, push off with one foot while shooting your arms forward for thumbs to meet, and breathe deeply before pushing off. Lie flat in a front floating position with head between arms and face submerged in water. Keep your eyes open under the water. Hold this position for as long as comfortable. This gives the same sensation as being under the water. Try then from first or second step of pond (*not Diving Dale*) to tumble yourself out into the water with a slight bend of knees and spring from balls of feet. Always remember to shoot arms out and keep head well down between them, otherwise a hearty slap in the face will result. The arms add weight and balance to the head, for it is surprising how the feet become heavy, like lumps of lead, and most reluctant to follow after head and body.

As each plunge becomes easier and you are familiar with the feeling of going under and surfacing, you will find it easier from the height of the edge of the pond. First practise " falling in " head first. With legs together, toes curled round edge of pond,

bend knees and in a crouching position, with head down between
outstretched arm position, allow yourself to lose balance and drop

Fig. 3.—Diving

in. Concentrate on feet leaving side last. Being
completely above water level, you will sink deeper
and have the full feeling of diving. Preferably allow
yourself to float up to surface, but a quick recovery
can be made by pushing off from the bottom with
feet, or if not deep down, a breast stroke leg kick
will hasten the break through for " air ".

Even at this early stage always try to finish up
neatly—a straight line from tip of fingers (arms
being still outstretched beyond head) to toes, which
should be pointed out and not curled up. Practise
until the great unknown underworld conceals no
mystery, then gradually try controlling the legs to
straighten when falling in.

The Dive can now be attempted. Stand erect—
a rigid attention position—and toes curled round
edge of pond. Sway forward and as the balance is
lost, bend knees slightly and spring, from the balls
of feet, up and out, like tracing an arc, and at the
same time shooting arms forward with head tucked
in between them as thumbs meet. As feet leave side, flick up
behind and straighten legs. Curl toes to make ankles taut. This

tends to keep the legs straight. To visualize the flight is of great help.

If the legs still persist in dragging, ask a friend to hold the ankles lightly, and as you spring to flick them up for you. The spring is quite a tricky art, and the tendency is only to shoot out without the upward soar to produce a clean-cut entry into the water. A tip for this is a cane or rod held at suitable height and distance, and over this you must dive in hurdle style. All muscles must be controlled from beginning to end of Dive. A relaxation in mid-air causes the painful " flat flapper ", and to ease up as your head enters the water leaves the legs to bear the crack of the water. Cut the water; do not catch it.

THE PLUNGE

The plunge is throwing yourself as far out and as flat as possible. Used for racing, the advantage of this is easily appreciated; many precious seconds would be lost in sinking and recovering, and to " land " just at the side is a loss of several strokes. Use a crouching position, but keep body relaxed and arms stretched behind, ready for the swing forward on the word " go ". Then breathe deeply, push the feet hard from the side, swing the arms forward, and cover as much distance as you can in the air before you enter the water. The body should submerge about six inches below the surface. As the momentum of your dive lessens, exhale and begin the leg movements to bring the body to the surface, where the full stroke can be used.

To land dead flat slows down the momentum. There must be no hesitation for readjustment between the plunge, landing, and starting the stroke. Some Crawl racers even start the leg thrash in mid-air, but these are exceptional cases, and the main idea is to get away to a flying start.

HIGH DIVING

Being satisfied you can dive neatly from the side, then only is the time to start holding that poise longer for the grace of High Diving. Do it step by step up the dale—thus lessening the giddy feeling often produced by sudden height—and also hold the rigid position longer. Taken in this way, height is sufficiently graded as to be unnoticed.

One warning here—make sure of the depth of the water before diving. With indoor swimming baths, the levels never vary, and the springboards and dales are always at the deep end, but in pools or lakes where the water flow is tidal—beware of low-tide. Also, never run along a springboard taking a flying leap without first testing its flexibility. You can be shot up into the air with calamitous results.

The principles of High Diving are practically the same—to enter the water in a straight line, almost perpendicular. But the flick of the feet at a height must be avoided, as it gives too much force, and is apt to send the legs over the head and slap the water, rather than following through the same " hole".

The position or style is: erect, with toes curled round edge of diving board—hold this until satisfied of firm balance. Smartly raise both arms straight out to shoulder level with palms of hands facing down, eyes looking straight ahead. Swing both arms together, down and beyond hips, and with slight bend of knees, transfer weight to balls of feet. As arms swing forward in continuous motion for thumbs to meet above head, which is again well tucked in, spring from balls of feet, up and out—remembering to straighten and stiffen legs. Hold this position until toes enter water—slide along the bottom and push gently off with feet, still together, and rise to surface at an angle of 45°. Maintain straight position, now horizontal, and face still dipped in pond, for a few seconds before swimming to side.

Fig. 4.—Plain dive

SWALLOW DIVE

The *Swallow Dive* is a thrill to perform and most graceful to watch. The one position, as in the plain dive, is not held, therefore the importance is on timing—with no erratic, jerky changes. Visualize the smooth graceful span of a bird's wing, opening and closing. The same rules for the plain high dive apply until your flight is just clear of the board; with arms outstretched, thumbs touching, then open up arms with palms facing inwards—*smoothly*—like spreading wings until stretched as far beyond shoulders as is comfortable, throw out chest and throw back head. Recover plain dive position just in time to enter water in straight line.

The scope and fun in diving are unlimited; combining grace and excitement are the " Dead Man's Drop ", the " Jack Knife ", the " Somersaults ", the " Double ", and many others. The novel climax to breath-taking diving displays is usually " Charley's Aunt ", which is very simple. From the beginning of a long springboard, run to the edge, giving the impression of about to execute a $2\frac{1}{2}$ somersault, and instead just " keep running " through the air until

Fig. 5.—Swallow dive

you enter the water. This, of course, should be done from a height to get the full effect of " Charley's Aunt " still running.

No champion, or even good swimmer and diver, has been completely self-taught, but there is so much one can do in swimming to make it easier for a coach. That is the main reason I have outlined the foregoing instructions, but I do advise joining a swimming club as soon as possible in your learning days, for practical coaching is essential for polishing off and training.

Another reason for trying out these instructions is that so many persons, both young and old, are very self-conscious about going into a pond and looking " foolish ", as it is so often termed. To be able to slither into the water and start a few practice strokes is very heartening and covers up any embarrassment you may feel. Also, to become familiar with the swimming terms and their meaning makes things easier for you and your instructor. In common with all other sports, swimming has a language all its own. Club atmosphere is definitely friendly and a sure source of progress, and of inspiring and keeping alive enthusiasm.

Thinking, perhaps, with the intensive training required to be undergone in such a championship club as the Motherwell one, that all the fun must have gone out of swimming and it would now be a serious business, I went to the club practice one evening. But no, there were the record breakers, past and present, looking the picture of fitness, happiness and obviously enjoying every minute—which they assured me they did. The very spirit of Mr. Crabb's mass training system promotes friendly rivalry and the enthusiasm or urge to be upsides with your club-mate.

The first period of the evening is " do as you please ", but as I was standing by, talking to the superintendent, I could see his eye and mind were at work, unconsciously perhaps, picking out promising " promotions " to the training period. His interest is not centred only on his " prizes "—every member has his interest.

At the sound of a whistle the pond is cleared, the girls lining up on one side and the boys on the other. Now starts the serious mass training of which the coach strongly approved. Each concentrating on his or her weak point, the one side swims two breadths; then a respite while the other side practised. A spell at this, and they switch to 25 or 50 yards, by this time being sectioned off into stages of ability. A sort of pacing each other. All the time instructors are lined up, catching up weaknesses and suggesting improvements.

One idea for speeding up the Crawl kick is for a swimmer holding the end of a rod to be pulled along the side of the baths, keeping the legs thrashing in time with the " pull ". Some coaches use this method of crawl kick training, but the greater number of swimmers and coaches train with a cork board held in front of the swimmer, arms resting lightly on it, and the legs doing the appropriate kick. This lets the coach see how much power is coming from the leg movement.

This is the general routine of one club, but it is a typical example of the atmosphere, encouragement and friendliness you will encounter if joining any swimming club.

So let it be your turn next to exclaim—" What—you cannot swim!"

THE YOUNG NATURALIST

COLLECTING AND PRESERVING
SPECIMENS

Most of us are collectors at heart. It may be foreign stamps, old coins, models of wooden ships, picture postcards, or even the humble cigarette picture; but we cleave to things of beauty, whether they are valuable or not. The lover of nature finds much pleasure in collecting and preserving such flowers, birds' eggs, butterflies, or perhaps seaweeds, shells, and similar objects as he comes across during his rambles. Of course, he has a second motive in this, the desire to learn more about them; mere aimless collecting for its own sake leads nowhere. The field naturalist will soon learn that he must have available a good working collection of the animals or plants in which he is interested; and these notes are intended to help him, both in collecting his treasures, and in their preservation afterwards.

There are three things which every naturalist, young or old, must possess, and without which he might as well stay at home. The first is a pair of keen eyes, coupled with a large bump of inquisitiveness. The second is patience, willingness to stay silent in a ditch or covert for an hour if need be, watching the birds and animals which are just as closely watching him. The third comprises a notebook and a copying-ink pencil, with which to record *on the spot* all that he observes and collects. Captain Cuttle's dictum, " When found make a note of ", should be engraven on the naturalist's heart. As to the patience requisite, although it is quite good fun to charge through bracken or climb up trees, such methods only frighten away all wild things; if you want to observe these properly you must merge yourself, as it were, into the scenery, so that they take you for granted; and in this way you may learn much which is a mystery to-day even to experts, especially concerning birds.

Certain obvious accessories suggest themselves: a haversack or some other means of carrying one's impedimenta, boxes for insects, jars for live or wet specimens, plenty of pocket room, nets for flying things, a few paper bags, a sharp penknife, a pair of tweezers and some string. Above all, you will require a magnifying glass; one marked " × 10 " will do for most purposes, or a triplet magnifier is quite efficient. With a little ingenuity all these things can be packed up so as to take very little room. Thus equipped, let us sally forth into the woods and along the seashore.

Insects.

Suppose we start with that wonderful insect world, the knowledge of which means so much to farmers, gardeners, and even to doctors. There are many thousands of different kinds of insects in this country. Many of them are quite unsuited to exhibition, and others so minute that they will probably escape notice. It is likely, I imagine, that you will be attracted first to the showy butterflies, then to moths, and possibly also to beetles; but the less attractive members of the winged tribe—the bees, ants, wasps, the various kinds of flies, wood-lice, and the tiny crawling things which scurry away when one disturbs the bark of a decayed tree—should not be overlooked. Many insects are directly harmful to man, by causing disease in food plants, and an enormous amount still has to be discovered about their life-histories.

The butterfly hunter must be armed with two kinds of nets. For the more active species a butterfly net about ten inches in diameter and two feet long, made of mosquito netting, and fastened on a circular wire frame, will suffice; many kinds are available, but one which can be taken off the stick for easy transport is most desirable. A stronger net will also be needed for sweeping along the surface of unmown meadows, ditches and wayside grass verges.

There are about sixty kinds of British butterflies, some of which may be caught in any month from April to October; occasionally one may be seen lazily winging its course through a sheltered garden earlier or later, or even dozing on a sunny wall in January or November. Some of our butterflies are very rare, and as there are usually several broods in a year it preserves the species if you do not attempt to catch rare kinds early in the season; in any event, numbers do not compensate for variety, unless it be the common white Cabbage Butterfly, of which the more you catch the better for everybody. The best place to search for butterflies is in some sunny glade or path beside a wood. The various species have different habits, sipping the nectar of particular plants (plants upon which, a few

SOME BRITISH BUTTERFLIES

1. Purple Emperor.   2. Camberwell Beauty.   3. Red Admiral.   4. Orange-tip.   5. Small Tortoise-shell.   6. White Hairstreak.   7. Common Blue.   8. Brown Hairstreak (also 20).   9. Cabbage White.   10. Grayling.   11. Purple Hairstreak.   12. Peacock.   13. Dark Green Fritillary.   14. Clifton Blue.   15. Swallow-tail.   16. Small Copper.   17. Mazarine Blue.   18. Wood Argus.   19. Marbled White.   20. Brown Hairstreak (also 8).   21. White Admiral.

weeks later, you may find their eggs or brilliantly coloured caterpillars). If, therefore, you see a Red Admiral hovering among a patch of stinging nettles, and at first fail to catch it, do not waste a lot of energy by wildly chasing it; if left alone, there is a fair chance of its returning to the same spot. Some butterflies love the wild hedgerows and grassy verges of our country lanes, visiting vetches and nettles in particular; others (especially some of the beautiful small blues and fritillaries) may be found sailing over open heaths and coarse grassland near the sea, or beside rivulets or ponds, especially on chalkland. The Common Meadow Brown, one of our most familiar species, may be found in almost any field where the herbage is long, throughout the summer. The Cabbage Butterfly haunts market gardens and allotments; it lays its eggs there, and the resultant caterpillars cause an immense amount of destruction. The handsome Purple Emperor frequents willows, poplars and oak trees. Wall butterflies may often be detected asleep on some old brickwork. If you keep your eyes open, you will find more butterflies during a morning's walk in May or June than you had believed possible; but do not kill for the sake of killing. Remember that other people take pleasure in them too.

Butterflies love the light. Most moths, on the other hand, dislike it, although many of them are attracted to lights by a sort of fatal curiosity. There are twelve times as many species of moths as butterflies in Britain, besides hundreds of minute forms which to the untrained eye all look alike (clothes moths and similar small species). Most moths wear sombre brown dress, shot with fawn or pale gold, but the under wings are often brilliantly coloured; a few species, such as the familiar Tiger Moths of our gardens, with their patches of chocolate and white, or the red kinds, or the Hawk Moths, are decidedly handsome. A few moths fly boldly by day, others may be captured during the day on the shady side of fences, walls or trees, or even on the ground or in rooms, asleep. The Old Lady brown moth is often found among the folds of window curtains or resting upon the window ledges. Lappet Moths frequent apple trees and hawthorns, whereas the Oak Eggar haunts hedgerows, heathery tracts, and sand dunes; the hairy caterpillars of both these types are to be handled cautiously, as they can sting. The wild honeysuckle has a strong fascination for several species of Hawk Moths. You can often catch moths at night by hanging up an electric bulb in a dark part of your garden. Many also fall victim to the familiar trick of " sugaring " a fence or a tree trunk. A mixture of beer and molasses or Demerara sugar is painted on the wood with an old paint brush, and the spot then visited regularly, for preference an hour or two after dusk. The results, though good in the aggregate, are apt to be speculative at times, and on some nights the catch may be *nil*. As small moths are very readily damaged, and cannot be handled easily, they should be caught on the end of a camel-hair brush that has been dipped in benzine; they should then be pinned to a cork pad in a collecting box immediately.

Having caught some insects, the next step is to kill them quickly and painlessly, without damaging their appearance too much. You should carry one or two wide-mouthed jars with tight corks (not

Fig. 1
Killing-bottle

glass stoppers) (fig. 1). You may not be permitted the use of the professional's type of killing-bottle, which contains cyanide of potassium—a deadly poison. If, however, you place in the bottom of the jar a layer of crushed and broken laurel leaves, on which a few drops of benzine have been poured, this will do equally well, although it kills more slowly. A small disc of gauze or paper loosely resting above the leaves makes it easier to pick out the specimen when dead. Failing laurel leaves, a piece of flannel on which benzine has been sprinkled (not soaked in benzine) is just as effective, the vapour stupefying the insect and eventually killing it. Ether and chloroform are used in the same way by adults. Do not put too many specimens in one jar; but if you are cramped for storage space, tear up some strips of paper and put them in first, a device which helps to keep insects' legs from getting entangled in one another.

You will find yourself compelled to handle most of your captures. Accustom yourself to the use of tweezers; after ruining a few specimens you will find it the best way, but if you must use fingers, hold the butterfly or moth by the extreme upper edge of the wing, close to the body, and take care not to brush off too many of the scales, for these it is which give the insect its beautiful colours.

The dead specimens should be transferred to collecting boxes. An ordinary cardboard cigarette box will do. It should be lined with wadding; cotton-wool can also be used, but its threads stick to the spiny parts of the insects and take a lot of removing afterwards. Lay your captures upon the lining, keeping them well apart, and noting in your pocket-book their order, appearance, and the details of the place and date of capture as you do so; then add a second layer of wadding, and above that more insects, and so on until the box is filled. Avoid any unnecessary pressure. Moisten the lid of the box before you go out, using a few drops of benzine and carbolic; this keeps pests away, a precaution that is always necessary. As stated above, small moths should always be pinned to a cork lining in your collecting box at the time of capture.

As soon as possible after returning home, and before the insects have hardened, they should be " set " in the conventional manner,

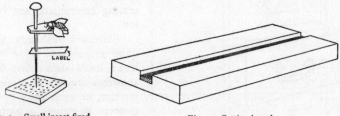

Fig. 2.—Small insect fixed
on cardboard slip

Fig. 3.—Setting board

i.e. by pinning them on to cork at a uniform height above the bottom of the box, and with all four wings expanded. To do this properly requires some patience and skill, but you will soon master it. If the insects have stiffened, they will relax if some damp blotting paper is placed inside the lid of the box, and the lid then closed for a few hours. For setting you will require a supply of special ento-mological pins—you can get these at any natural-history shop—and a setting board (fig. 3). The board should be about 12 in. long, 3 or 4 in. wide, and 1 in. thick. It should have a groove down the middle $\frac{1}{2}$ in. wide and $\frac{1}{2}$ in. deep, which should be lined with a strip of cork $\frac{1}{4}$ in. thick, thus giving a net depression of $\frac{1}{4}$ in. The insect's body rests in this, the wings lying on the surface of the board. The wings are next carefully opened with a needle and then held in position against pins, which must *not* be thrust through them; meanwhile the insect is firmly held down by a pin passing through its thorax into the cork in the groove. Some people keep the wings in position by pasting strips of gummed paper across them, but this requires care in order not to rub off the scales. When the board is filled it should be hung up in a dry place, out of the sun, and forgotten for a few days, when the hardened insects can be removed to your cabinet or storage boxes. When permanently mounted, each insect should have a label stating its name, when and where caught, adding (if possible) a word or two, such as " on a wall ", " on an oak leaf ", &c. You can make suitable labels yourselves by cutting up a sheet of gummed white paper, procurable at any stationer's. It adds to the interest of one's collection if a specimen in the natural state is displayed alongside one that is artificially " set ", and also if the caterpillar and pupa or chrysalis of the species are added. For preserving caterpillars, see below.

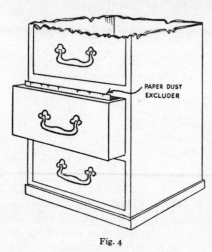

PAPER DUST EXCLUDER

Fig. 4

Expensive cabinets are quite unnecessary. One can make one's own from old showcase drawers of moderate size, or even from open drawers, by nailing or gluing four thin strips of wood round the inside, upon which the glass top may rest. The author of these notes keeps many specimens so displayed, or even in tins, in larger drawers; and to keep out dust he pastes a strip of paper against the inner edge of the large drawer (see fig. 4), so that when the drawer shuts the paper must turn forward and close the slit through which most of the dust finds its way into drawers. In every box or showcase he puts a little powdered naphthalene in one corner, and some in the large storage drawer too. His collection has never been attacked by insect pests, although many of the items are more than twenty years old.

The best specimens of butterflies or moths are usually obtained by rearing them in breeding cages, a method which has the advantage that one learns the life-history of the insect. The eggs, which are of distinctive and sometimes beautiful shapes, are laid as a rule on a particular kind of plant, e.g. the leaves of a vetch, a willow, or a nettle. By transferring a twig with leaves and eggs complete to the cage, and sticking its end in a bottle of water, you may keep it alive till the caterpillar emerges and begins to feed; a fresh supply of the leaves to which it is accustomed must then be provided (fig. 5). You will now enjoy the privilege of observing how a caterpillar, as it grows, is compelled to shed its coat. Eventually it passes to a resting or pupa stage, when, shrivelled up, seemingly immovable and often concealed in a cottony cocoon, it passes through the transition into the full-grown insect or imago; this stage may last a matter of weeks, or it may take an entire winter, depending on the species. You will be well advised to buy or borrow one of the various books which deal with rearing insects, so that you may thoroughly understand what species you are collecting and how to go about it; such a book is W. J. Stokoe's *Caterpillars of the British Butterflies*.

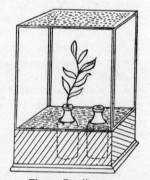

Fig. 5.—Breeding cage

To preserve caterpillars as museum specimens, although a somewhat messy job, becomes quite easy after a little practice. To kill the caterpillar, drop it into methylated spirit, but do not leave it there or it will lose its colours and shrink, for the spirit absorbs water greedily. Benzine will do equally well. Lay the dead caterpillar on a sheet of blotting paper, press lightly on it so that the rear end is pushed out, then cut this end very slightly. Next, run a round pencil over the caterpillar from the head end backwards, so as to press out the juices, but take care not to use much force, or you will damage it irreparably. Most of the green watery stuff being expelled in this way, you now take a straw or a piece of fine glass tubing that has been drawn to a point, and insert the point at the cut end; using a rubber syringe from an old scent spray, blow the caterpillar out. The specimen should then be warmed for a few moments, preferably in an oven, and then mounted, if possible, alongside a specimen of the full-grown species to which it belongs.

Beetles, though much disliked by parents as a rule, are really objects of much interest; apart from bees and wasps, they are perhaps man's best friends in the insect world, being wholesale scavengers. They display not only a wonderful variety of shapes and modes of living, but also a range of brilliant colours which must be seen to be believed. The secret of beetle hunting is to be not too nice where one looks, and always to remember that beetles *hide*. Therefore, turn over stones and fallen branches, especially in woods; look under the rotting bark of some decayed tree; shake out on a sheet of paper or a white cloth some of the moss litter, empty beech-nuts, and whatnot which is always lying between the roots of trees; look under the shadow of walls, or in ditches; even in drains and among manure heaps you will find beetles. In addition, of course, there are numerous water beetles, which have to be fished for with a fine-meshed net. Some beetles can bite one, but the majority of those that you are likely to come across are quite harmless to you. They are best seized with the tweezers and dropped into methylated spirit or (if it be available) boiling water; but they must not be left in the spirit long. Benzine vapour kills them, but some species have great vitality. For preservation, the larger kinds may be mounted with pins driven through the wing case, or neatly stuck on to cards by their legs. A convenient killing-bottle for beetles is a wide-mouthed jar, closed by a cork through the middle of which a corked piece of glass tubing extends (fig. 1); one then has only to take out the smaller cork and drop the unhappy insect into the death chamber.

Spiders.

Spiders, which are not insects, are another very interesting subject well worth studying. The garden species have a regular habit of dropping to the ground and feigning death if attacked, and in that state can quickly be dropped into a killing-bottle containing spirit. You should get into the habit of observing how and where the spider spins its web; you will find that some of the traps are most ingenious. Here again the books in your library must be your help. You will find much curious matter on spiders in R. W. G. Hingston's *Naturalist in British Guiana*.

Plants.

The young botanist will find it essential to collect ferns, mosses, flowers, leaves, if he wishes properly to understand his enormous hobby. Some of these things, and particularly the ferns, make handsome museum specimens; they should be preserved so that they can be referred to and closely examined with a lens whenever necessary. First, they must be absolutely dry. There are two ways of drying a plant, the slow way and the quick one. The slow method does well enough for green parts such as stems and leaves, and for some leaves it is the best. The plant to be dried should be laid out in the desired position on a sheet of thick blotting paper; if very bulky, some of the plant must be trimmed off, so that what remains is reasonably flat. Always arrange leaves so that some show the upper, others the lower surface. If a flower has to be trimmed, cut it open neatly with a razor blade, not quite separating the two halves, and always cut right down to the flower stalk, because parts essential to the identification of the species are contained in the fleshy part of the flower. Take several more sheets of blotting paper, place some above and some below the specimen, and press the whole under two or three heavy books. Of course, a number of plants can be pressed at the same time, but it is desirable to keep each species on a separate sheet. After twelve hours, change the sheets for fresh ones. Repeat this process a day later, and then as may be necessary for the next few days, until the specimens are quite dry. They may then be attached by a spot of fish glue to sheets of cartridge paper, or to a fairly stiff white paper; for neatness, these should be trimmed all the same size, and should be marked in the same place with the name of the plant, date and locality. They can then be stored in trays or in flat boxes; not too many in one container, or the papers will become misshapen.

Always look out for small insects on plants before you dry them. Plants are the natural homes of many insects, some of which live only on particular species. You will usually be able to shake out quite a number from a few flowering grasses which at first sight seemed wholly devoid of them. These insects should be caught with a camel-hair brush dipped in benzine. Preserve them by laying them on wadding in a flat cigarette tin; later, you will find them excellent subjects for your microscope.

To dry flowers satisfactorily has always defied the best skill of the botanist. Sometimes the petals drop off as soon as the plant dies, and invariably the colours change. I prefer on the whole to dry flowers quickly, so as to give some chance of fixing at least part of the original colours. I use a double frame, 12 × 10 in., each half of which is covered with ordinary wire netting of 1-in. mesh. Inside the netting are two layers of cotton-wool. The flower to be dried is placed within the cotton-wool; at this stage both care and patience are needed to ensure that it is in the correct attitude, and it is best to lay it out on a table or board first. The frame is then closed; you may prefer a clip, but I use a piece of string, because it permits more play. I place the frame in front of a gas fire, and in half an hour my plant is perfectly dry. Just to make sure, however, I remove it from the frame, place it between sheets of blotting paper, put a weight on top, and forget it for the next few days. This method fixes yellow hues very well, also some shades of blue and red; some reds, however—e.g. in the common poppy—tend to turn black, whereas some blues fade away altogether, leaving a parchmenty petal. White petals also commonly become semi-transparent and colourless. Brown and violet hues may preserve very well.

Whatever your method, it is always as well, when commencing to dry the specimen, to make a rough sketch of its parts and to note its colours; this, though often difficult at first, soon becomes extremely easy to many people.

Dried plants are most useful when they show the complete life-history of the plant and all its parts. Thus, for a poppy or a rose you should have roots, stem, leaves, flowers and seed; but in gathering wild plants spare them as much as possible, for many of them are scarce. Usually, to gather several stems and flower-heads does no harm; but to tear up more than one root for examination or through mere thoughtlessness is to depopulate the hedgerows.

Seaweeds.

How often have we been compelled by undiscerning seniors to empty our pockets, and throw away some strongly smelling mass of bits of seaweed, cockle shells, coloured pebbles, dead crabs, cuttle-bone, and other flotsam of the seashore! The attraction, however, continues as strong as ever, and our collection can be made to appeal even to people with the most delicate noses. Seaweeds in particular make beautiful objects when properly preserved. They are to be gathered at any level of the strand from high-water mark to extreme low tide. The most delicate and handsome fronds commonly occur among stouter weeds under the rocks at low water, not being able to endure an exposure of several hours to the sun; such species must be gathered from a boat as a rule, but many of them are torn off and thrown ashore during storms. A number of delicate weeds may commonly be found growing on that storehouse of marine life, the root of a tangle; you will find there also objects like small bits of thin string, which should be cut off and carefully preserved. Seen under the microscope, they turn out to be singular and often beautiful colonies of polyp-like animals called hydroids.

As soon as possible after collection, seaweeds should be washed in fresh water, so as to free them from salt and dirt; but do not throw the dirt away, for this also contains many curious things, about which I will speak in another section, to those who possess a microscope. The water should be drained off, and the residue dried, put in a match box or small tin, and labelled; it is certain to afford microscopists hours of entertainment during the winter evenings. To mount seaweeds, a suitable frond should be floated in a bowl of water, and a piece of stoutish white paper, previously cut to size, placed under it, and gently raised from one end. As the water drains off, adjust the weed in the desired attitude, using a camel-hair brush. The plant should then be covered with a layer of coarse muslin, then placed between blotting papers and dried in the same way as other plants; but the papers must be changed more frequently. The majority of seaweeds, but by no means all, will adhere firmly to the paper; when this happens, they can be named, dated and stored away. Remember to remove the muslin early in the drying process, otherwise it may mark the specimens.

On many seaweeds you will notice silvery or furry growths. Do not try to clean these off. They are exquisitely beautiful subjects for the microscope, being the skeletons of tiny colonies of " moss animals " or Bryozoa.

Sea Shells.

Many sea shells may be picked up by examining diligently the lines of dried seaweed which mark the levels of high water and of storms. Others are rolled up by the waves. Many more can be picked out of rock pools or off the broad brown blades of the tangle. A spade swiftly driven underneath the round holes which are so common in wet sea sands may catch a razor-shell or a cockle. The best means of finding sea shells, however, is to make friends with a fisherman, who (for a consideration) will make you a small dredge and will then take you out with it to search the floor of some sandy or not too rocky bay. To kill your captures, merely drop them into fresh water. Shells which are to be preserved should be thoroughly cleaned of sand and weeds, and the animals should be extracted with a pin. Many coiled spiral sea shells (gastropods or marine snails) have a flat, round horny lid, by means of which the animal shuts itself within its shell; these lids must be carefully preserved, cleaned and inserted in their shells with a spot of fish glue. Bivalve shells, after being washed, should be lightly tied together with string or tape, so that the two halves or valves may remain shut when the horny hinge has hardened; otherwise the shell will gape. In mounting bivalves for display, by the way, always show one with the valves closed and one open, for the animal's make-up may be deduced from the lines on the inside. Naming your specimens should not involve you in much difficulty, since the common kinds are displayed in the museums of almost every borough. To house collections of shells, the nests of shallow drawers used for stationery are very convenient. Small shells can be stuck on cards, but the larger ones should be held in place by small nails or gramophone needles.

Other Marine Objects.

To describe here the multitude of other marine objects which anyone with curiosity and industry can acquire would take us too far from our present object; but a few brief notes may help. Starfish should be cleaned in fresh water and laid out to dry in the sun, or in front of a gas fire; this shrivels the soft flesh and destroys the interesting tube feet, but the harder parts remain unharmed. A host of soft or semi-soft creatures, such as Bristle-worms, hydroids, shrimps and their kind, can be killed and temporarily stored in a weak (2 per cent) solution of formalin; one buys 40 per cent formaldehyde at a chemist's, and then to one part of this fluid adds 19 parts of water. Sea urchins can be treated in the same way. All animals with limy shells, however, should be removed from the formalin after a few days, because it eventually dissolves them. The beautiful iridescent worms which burrow in the sand or hide under stones or among tangle roots can be permanently stored in "commercial methylated spirit", which you may obtain specially from a chemist. Jellyfish and other things of that nature cannot ordinarily be preserved at all; you should study them on the spot and throw them away. Beach fleas and other queer crustaceans haunt the dead seaweed, being scavengers of the most voracious kind; and if you have a crab and do not know how to clean it, just turn back its tail, open it, and the beach fleas will, in a single morning, do the job far better than anyone!

Above all, on the shore, as in the wood, do not forget that notebook!

Birds' Eggs.

The collector of birds' eggs should remember the warning given by Mr. Seton Gordon on p. 138. For permanent preservation the shell must, of course, be emptied, cleaned and dried. To blow an egg, you will require either a straw with a sharpened end or a piece of fine glass tubing which has been stretched and broken in a flame. First carefully puncture the shell with a fine needle; then, using an egg-drill, enlarge the hole, but keep it as small as you can. Egg-drills can be bought from any natural-history dealer. Taking the blowpipe in your mouth, with the end close to the hole, blow the contents of the egg out by air. Then blow in some clean warm water, rinse the egg thoroughly, and turn it up on blotting paper (with the hole underneath) to drain and dry. If the egg is " turning "— i.e. if it contains an embryo chick—you may have to sacrifice it after all; but frequently, after the watery part of the contents has been extracted, it is possible to soften the rest by filling the egg with water containing a little caustic potash, and leaving it for a day or two. The embryo will then soften, and by great care can usually be extracted. After using potash, however, pay particular attention to washing it all away, otherwise it will cause the shell to decay. Label the egg with the date, site of nest, and size of clutch, also, of course, the species.

Nothing has been said in these notes about preserving the skins or skeletons of small mammals and birds. This, which comprises the art of the taxidermist, is not beyond the skill of older girls; but it is a very special art, which would require a long article. Information on it can be found, however, in the invaluable *British Museum Instructions to Collectors*. Always exercise caution when handling dead animals, especially if you have any cuts on your fingers, or you may get disease germs into your blood—and that, believe me, is no laughing matter!

DRESS AND BEAUTY

If you of the younger generation really want to come through the later teen years with confidence and charm; if you want your looks to have personality without over-sophistication, youthfulness without childishness; if you want to state by your clothes, your looks and your bearing that you belong, wholeheartedly and intelligently, to a well-defined interim age period, then you have work to do, plans to make. And the first of these is to develop a good, sound, intelligent, modern approach to clothes and beauty.

Make up your mind that they count; that a sound clothes sense is considered an asset nowadays—not a feminine frivolity; that even if you are not " pretty " you can still look " right "; that brawn alone is not enough; that brain alone is not enough; that the modern girl and woman is a balanced product of intelligent co-operation. And it is the part that clothes and beauty play in this team-work plan that I want to present to you.

BABES IN ADULT CLOTHES

The idea of specialized clothes for younger people is, of course, a very recent development. And I think it might be interesting at this point to trace its evolution from the days when even a toddling baby of two wore clothes that were an almost exact replica of its mother's formal gown. I have before me as I write a picture of an Elizabethan family group in which the youngest member—a little girl of perhaps three years old—is wearing the " Mary Stuart " cap, the starched ruff, the long pointed bodice of the period, the spreading farthingale and long, full skirts to the ground.

In Largillière's portrait of the " Old Pretender ", painted in 1695, you have the seven-year-old prince in an ultra-fashionable coat springing out from waist to knee, elaborate gold froggings on fronts and wide, split cuffs, knee-breeches, high-heeled, scarlet-topped buckled shoes, a fall of lace from the throat and, across his little body, the broad ribbon of the Garter. And by his side his little sister (who looks to me about four years old) wears a handsome brocade dress with long satin train, deep round neckline and

a two-tiered lace " frontage " rising inches high on her charming
little head.

Fifteen years later, the same painter—Largillière—painted a
fascinating portrait of King Louis XIV of France with his family,
and there you have a very tiny princess wearing a satin dress with
low-cut bodice, train, and on her head an elaborate head-dress
crowned with curling plumes! This baby-girl—for she is little
more in spite of her formal, grown-up clothes—has leading strings
attached to the shoulders of her tiny gown; and if you can find a
copy of the portrait of the young James Edward I mentioned earlier,
you will see that the little sister by his side has leading strings like
narrow over-sleeves hanging down from the shoulders of her dress.

If, then, tiny children were wearing grown-up clothes in the
seventeenth and eighteenth centuries, how much less chance was
there for teen-age girls and boys to enjoy the slightest respite from
the formal, uncomfortable, unhygienic clothes of their day. There
is a lovely picture of the Infanta Marie Isabelle of Spain painted in
1751 by the famous French painter, Nattier, which shows a very
young girl in a full-span pannier dress and the little lace apron which
was a fashion of those days. And Marie Isabelle reminds me of yet
another Infanta, Queen of France, who at the age of sixteen shocked
the court by running and sliding (and falling!) in all her formal
finery, on the marble floors of the Palace of Versailles.

The first hint of a break with these crushing, adult styles for
young people comes towards the end of the eighteenth century
under King George III. Those of you who know Kate Greenaway's
illustrations (they are considered old-fashioned now, but are still
hard to equal for delicacy of treatment and reliability of costume
detail) will call to mind the boy's high-waisted trousers buttoning
just above the ankle, the frilled blouse, and the little girls in their
Empire dresses with coloured sash and low-cut bodice. They are
still in a sense adult styles, but an obvious effort is being made to
adapt them to younger needs and figures.

VICTORIAN GIRLS

From then on youthful styles developed slowly, very slowly and
not always, I am sorry to say, too surely. Victorian girls were laced
from the age of thirteen or fourteen, and when I say laced, I mean
laced! Twelve, thirteen, fourteen inches were the ideal, the aim,

and an eighteen-inch waist was considered quite a spread. The
crinoline line was in fashion from 1830 to 1870, and while grown-up
skirts swept the floor so that toes peeped out only very occasionally
like " little mice ", young girls were allowed to show their heelless
buttoned ankle-boots (jemimas they were called) and their panta-
lette-covered ankles and calves. These lace and embroidery trimmed
garments were a curious style indeed, and in a day when modesty
was the most highly prized of maidenly virtues! This is what Mr.
James Laver, Keeper at the Victoria and Albert Museum and a
great authority on Victorian fashions, says on the subject: " The
dresses of little girls are probably the most surprising in the mid-
Victorian period. There had been an attempt early in the century
to evolve a free and sensible dress for the young. This attempt was
now abandoned, and little girls were burdened with replicas of their
mother's dresses, some of them even provided with crinolines in
miniature. Fortunately, the skirts were shorter, with the curious
result that the under-linen was allowed to show underneath. So
important did it seem to make a display of fine linen that false
pantalettes were invented—tubes of lace tied on round the knees
and hanging below the skirt."

I myself should like to add that this " invention " made it possible to change the pantalettes which " showed " more frequently
than the drawers which didn't, which seems to me a typically stuffy
Victorian point of view! In the same way Victorian men were
inventing detachable collars, cuffs and shirt fronts, or " dickeys ",
with very much the same object in view—how different from our
modern theories (and I hope practices!) in the matter of underclothes!

By the 'seventies the crinoline has disappeared and the bustle
takes its place. And what a curious line it is! Bunched up rear
draperies overlapping tiered skirts of incredible fussiness. This is
the great era of home-dressmaking. The sewing machine is now
firmly established in the homes (up to this period everything, of
course, had been made by hand), and the ladies of Britain are
happily engaged in turning out these miracles of garish vulgarity,
young girls and even little children following the same involved
and unattractive line. The only advantage I can manage to find
in the 1870 styles is that no two dresses could possibly have been
alike.

With the 'eighties the line simplifies a little, the bustle seems to slip and a smooth, very much corseted hip-line appears for the first time. The interest now is low—well below hip level; and I have fashion plates showing young girls with long corseted cardboard bodies, pleated underskirts and, just where you want most to sit down, a complicated drape and an enormous bow! Try to see some fashion plates of this period—surely one of the least attractive in the whole story of fashion. Followed then a new bustle line—the pert, cock-sparrow bustle of the 'eighties with up-swept hair and giddy little flower-trimmed hats. Then the " Gay 'Nineties " and the glamour of the Edwardian period. Wasp waists, rounded hips, full busts, and the teen-age girl feeling sadly deficient in the fashionable " curves " of the period!

THE NEW LINE

The war came, the first European war, and in the nineteen-twenties that followed a great innovation took place. Skirts overnight were cut to less than knee length, waists slipped twelve inches from normal, heads were bobbed, then shingled, and the " Garçonne "—boyish—line was born. It was hideous, yes, but it was a milestone in the story of clothes. For in that line was expressed for the first time the principles of the rational, comfortable, hygienic clothes we wear to-day. From that moment fashion has steadily looked forward, and I think I am safe in prophesying that never again shall we go back to discomfort, frouziness or lack of essential hygiene in our fashions. (Can you imagine boarding the 8.10 bus in a crinoline!)

It was at this period, too, that rational underclothes, with comfort, support and washability as their main characteristics, came into being. Flesh-coloured stockings also superseded the grey, brown or black horrors that had been our choice up to then. It was then, too, that " sports " clothes, as we understand our pleasant, wearable, practical everyday styles, first appeared, and a new sense of specialized styles for relatively clear-cut age groups. Frenchwomen would seem to have an instinctive gift for this age sense in clothes. American women have brought it to a fine art (teen-age or sub-deb departments are a feature of most American stores, whole magazines cater for the very much younger generation in the matter of health, beauty and styles); only British women are still inclined to drift vaguely from one important stage to another without fully realizing the clear-cut characteristics of each. Clothes, looks, can and should make a definite statement, and I should like to hear yours saying something like this:

" I am sixteen. I am intelligent. I know what I want from life, and I mean to plan and work to get it. I am serious or flippant as the occasion demands. I am free but I am disciplined. I am efficient but not boringly so. I am sensible but round off the corners with a hint of romance. I can be pert . . . and I can be very gentle. I like people, people like me. I have a mind of my own. I know what I like, and I know quite definitely what I dislike. I try to look my best all the time because my good sense tells me that it pays, and, in any case, I feel better able to ' cope ' if I am well turned out. I am not ' clothes mad ', nor do I spend more time or money on them than an intelligent planning of my time and budget demands. And once I have decided what I am going to wear and have put it on in the right way, I try to forget it and my looks, and get down to the job of living. I am glad to be alive, and I am *terribly* glad to be sixteen."

Yes, clothes can say all that and more to anyone who knows how to read their meaning.

Now to brass tacks, or shall we call them steel pins? How can a teen-age girl, who is battling with all the other problems of growing up, manage at the same time to educate herself in the theory and practice of being well and appropriately dressed? Well, of course, the best and most obvious answer is, " let her own mother help and advise her ". Time was when bringing up daughters was a mother's job. She herself understood clothes and handed on the art, just as in the past she it was who handed on the art—so sadly lacking to-day—of house-keeping. And there are still mothers who take this side of their responsibilities seriously. And it goes without saying that the help and direction a clever dress-wise mother can give her daughter from the moment she shows the slightest real interest in clothes, is worth infinitely more than anything I or any other fashion writer, or saleswoman, or woman's magazine can ever hope to offer.

Unfortunately, it is not every mother who has the taste and wisdom to help her daughter to help herself in the early stages and that, of course, is just where and when clothes education should begin. A twelve-year-old girl in a crisp gingham dress with two pigtails tied just in the right way, with scarlet bows, scarlet ankle-socks and well-balanced shoes, freckles maybe on her nose, can show as much fashion sense in her looks as the most glamorous product of Hollywood. And probably more.

SCHOOL UNIFORM

It is a curious and interesting test to look over from the style angle a group of schoolgirls in uniform. The garments are the same, identically the same, and yet how different each girl will look! And it is not simply a question of whether one is pretty and another plain. It is the girl with style (and she is more often than not the plain one) who looks attractive and compels your attention by the way she puts on her clothes, by her grooming, by her sheer *good looks*. Another—pretty maybe—but careless in detail, grooming, careless in the way she stands and walks, lacking essential style, will give just the reverse effect. And you know perfectly well that unless she pulls up and learns something about the importance of looks, she will grow into a careless, untidy woman, and one who will be fighting a big disadvantage all along the line.

The first essential in the business of making the best of yourself (and this applies to any age, anywhere) is to *know yourself thoroughly*. Know yourself honestly and sensibly, acknowledging your good points and planning to play them with intelligent discretion; admitting your poor ones and making up your mind to correct or camouflage these. In this connexion may I please insist that it is much wiser in the long run to admit your knock-knees or your snub nose to the world, to laugh about them with your friends; brooding over them in embarrassment and silence leads nowhere except, perhaps, into silly complexes later on.

Try next to discover your type, and by type I do not mean the current film-star type. I mean the real person that is *You*. Sort out and build up an intelligent personality that truly reflects your mind, and which is reflected just as truly in your looks. But be sure that it is an honest, real personality that emerges—not a pale and silly copy of somebody else.

You may be unusual or you may fall into an everyday group. Colouring, bone-structure, figure, are more important physical factors in the building up of good looks than pretty features. But whether you are going to be spectacular or just pin-neat and efficient-looking in your clothes, tweedy and tough, small and exquisite, whichever way it works out there are certain basic characteristics that belong essentially to your own age group. I made a note from a magazine at the hairdresser's the other day, not only because it summed up to perfection my own ideas on this subject, but also because I like the way it was expressed. Here it is: " It (the younger generation) is confident in the charm of burnished hair, light make-up, flat-heeled but pretty shoes, clear colours and clothes that are crisp, casual and gay. It carries its youth like a banner. . . ."

There you have the whole thing. Clothes that are crisp, casual, gay. Grooming. Poise. *Panache*—the lovely *panache* of youth. (Look up your French dictionary for " panache ".)

Let us go into these points one at a time.

SUITABLE CLOTHES

First the wardrobe. The girl who is 'twixt and between must always remember that her figure is still subject to sudden changes. It is wisest then to avoid tight-fitting clothes. In any case, yours is the age for easy, casual garments that are easy to wear, free to move in, and if you suddenly put on weight your clothes will rise, or rather spread, gladly to the occasion. Have your things very simple, workmanlike. Shirt-waist dresses in gay colours, bright blouses and short flared skirts are always a sound general line to take. Woollies of all kinds, and the chunkier and heavier the better. The heavy coarse texture will make a lovely contrast with your skin. Wear them high-built at the neck, devoid of jewellery.

Loose, easy coats are best, reefers, swaggers, double-breasted ones that go easily and roomily over your heaviest woollies. For town wear particularly trim little suits with crisply tailored jacket and flared skirt. (By the way, make the most of your youth to wear flared and all-pleated skirts; you will find they will not suit you so well later on.) For the country, as well as your tweeds and woollies, be sure to have a practical lumber-jacket in leather and wool, and wear it with a bright scarf tucked into the neck teaming up to your hand-knitted gloves and ankle-socks. Or, if your knitting can stand the test, make yourself gay-coloured wool stockings. Snood your hair on windy days, and be very efficient in the matter of accessories. A battle-dress pocket on the front of your skirt will carry all you need, leaving your hands free for heather and leaves on hiking days.

Don't be afraid of colour; the world needs it, and you, if anyone, should know how to wear it.

For summer days aim at crispness, freshness in your looks, washability in your clothes. Light-hearted linens, gay cottons, ginghams, and don't forget trimmings in bright contrasting braid, or crisp, *broderie anglaise* details for more formal occasions.

Hats may beat you. But if your face is not too round try them small (most school hats are heavy and big; I wonder why?); perch them high and with deliberate straightness on shining, well-groomed hair. Remember that your forehead is a feature at your age and should be seen.

Pinafore dresses are also perfectly suited to your age. It is the most successful of "make-over" styles, and worn with a crisp little washing blouse gives you the maximum assurance of freshness.

WHAT SCHOOLS MIGHT DO

I started this section with mothers. I mean to finish it with schools. I still think that schools could do a lot more than they do to encourage good sound clothes sense. With very few exceptions, school uniform is dull, uninspired, and does absolutely nothing to stimulate a sane and modern attitude to clothes. Make-up and dress sense are both now accepted as factors in ordinary everyday life, and to attempt to stick to back-dated standards in these matters is, to my mind, a very short-sighted policy.

If ever girls needed direction, real intelligent direction in matters of clothes, it is now. Thanks to such factors as the films, the fashion magazines, the wide choice of ready-mades in the shops, the centralizing of fashion, everyone is becoming very fashion-conscious, and unless you are born with natural good taste, or have the good fortune to have a mother with knowledge and good taste to help you out, it is so terribly easy to fall into one or other of the many pitfalls that are yawning to catch you. There is that look of immature sophistication that must be avoided at all costs, and still worse, there are spurious glamour styles that originate in Hollywood and have no place at all over here. If only the schools brought clothes sense, grooming, poise and the rest into line with the other aspects of education, I do feel that they would be making a grand contribution to our British style, but unfortunately the "blue-stocking" attitude of mind still seems to obtain in most of the schools I know.

SECRET OF GOOD LOOKS

Now for the grooming. I sincerely believe that the example of our service girls—W.R.A.C.s, W.R.N.S., W.R.A.F.s—has done a great deal to show what really good grooming can achieve in the matter of looks. It is routine grooming, such as service girls experience, that really makes the difference. For routine grooming is, without any kind of doubt, the biggest single secret of good looks. It does not matter how fine your clothes, how fashionable, how much you paid for your hat, how red your lips, how " permed " your hair—without grooming these things mean just nothing at all.

The groomed look, the fresh look, the pin-neat look, the efficiently turned-out look that gives you confidence in yourself and your job is essentially a product of to-day. And the earlier you learn the trick of routine grooming the more time and energy you will have to put into the exciting and absorbing business of living.

Women who never give themselves the trouble to develop the habit of taking care of themselves seem to me to waste so much time in the end; they always seem to be trying desperately to catch up on themselves, and they are the ones who, when a special occasion turns up, run round in circles saying, " I haven't a thing to wear ". Or else they give you a hopeless look and say that *they* haven't time to fuss with clothes or some other such give-away of inefficiency.

" Habit is a smooth groove in the brain." I remember reading that phrase somewhere, and I can think of no better way of expressing the almost automatic working of a well-schooled mind in the matter of detail. All those everyday things we do to keep ourselves and our clothes fresh, clean, neat, perfect, can and should work on the " smooth-groove " system. The fuller your life and the more you are called upon to fit into every day, the more important it is to plan your grooming habits so that they become an almost unconscious part of yourself and your daily routine. No one fails to clean his teeth when he gets up in the morning, because cleaning teeth has grown into a civilized and accepted habit. And it is just this routine principle that should be brought to hair and skin, hands and clothes.

But what about the time it takes? you ask. " If I set out to do one half they tell me to do in the women's magazines I should never have time for living." Which is perfectly true. But ten minutes a day, could you manage that? I have been into this matter very carefully, I have checked up on my own routine system, and I know that ten intelligently employed minutes a day should see any woman through. Hair brushing (very important), two; skin care, two; hands and nails, two (including washing out the ankle socks or stockings you have been wearing during the day); two for shaking and valeting your clothes, and that leaves two for sewing on a button or taking out a blackhead.

That is, of course, an arbitrary splitting up of your routine grooming time, but it will do as a working basis, and it is up to you to plot it out as best suits yourself.

CLOTHES CARE

Where your clothes are concerned may I please stress the importance of shaking? And I mean by shaking a routine shake every time you take off a garment. It gets rid of dust and dirt, and it helps it to keep in shape. Regular shaking of skirts directly they are taken off helps to correct seating, and reduces bust and elbow bulges in woollies. Air your clothes whenever you get the chance, if only on a hanger in your bedroom or over a chair back by an open window. And when you get the chance put them right out in the garden for a breath of real fresh air.

Shoes should be cleaned at night before you go to bed. And ever so often, when you have ten minutes to spare, give them a thorough wash and clean with leather soap. It is a good idea, too, to make the habit of airing shoes by an open window when you take them off. It helps to keep them fresh and sweet. And to save time and temper (both highly precious commodities these days!) try to organize enough drawer and cupboard space for your things. Have enough hangers too. At all costs, avoid *clutter*. It is a good idea to keep a special drawer or an old suitcase or bandbox for the things you are not actually wearing, so that drawers and shelves are free. Try to be season-minded in the matter of your clothes. When summer is over, wash and put away all the things you will not be wearing. Put them away attractively with layers of tissue paper, so that it will be a real pleasure to look forward to them when the winter is over. And when this happens give your heavy things a sun and air in the garden, beat them, brush them, have them cleaned or washed if necessary, and put them safely away with a careful thought to the moth menace. And to make doubly sure, it is a good idea to take woollen things out from time to time in order to look them over.

Keep yourself washed up during the week—undies, blouses, jumpers, collars. A few things every few days take less than no time, and this system does away with a big weekly wash.

So much for clothes and their care. Now for skin, your hair, your make-up.

If you have a good complexion and an " easy " skin, you will have very little to worry about, and will need practically no make-up. A dusting of powder maybe, but don't, whatever you do, spoil that lovely natural bloom (that an older woman would give anything to have) just because you think it is grown-up to be made-up. If your lips are naturally bright, then use lipstick very sparingly, if at all. You may need a light make-up at night for party wear, but in the day-time with your woollies and your clear skin it should not be necessary. If your skin is normal you should be able to wash it freely with soft water and a good pure soap. If it tends to dryness clean first with a cold cream, then wash. A really dry skin may need an occasional " feed " with some fatty product. A little pure lard is good or olive oil. Simple home remedies like this are often as good as expensive creams. But always have good powder, and if possible good lipstick.

A greasy skin needs lots of water, lots of soapy lather, and if that is not enough you may need a drying lotion of some kind, or even professional advice or help. The same goes for blotches and spots. Don't be self-conscious about blemishes; anyone can have them, and science to-day does help us to face up to almost any condition.

Don't have your hair " permed " unless it is absolutely hopeless. You have plenty of time for that later, and if you start in your teens it is not giving your hair quite a fair chance, is it? A good cut and an occasional set is a wiser way to spend your money. Brushing is important and tends to be neglected in these days of " sets " and " perms ". But go to it. Brushing stimulates the scalp and gives that lovely burnished look to the head.

Hair styles should be very, very simple; far too many girls are going around these days with over-elaborate heads of hair, and however wonderfully contrived, they look sadly out of place with simply tailored suits and woollies. An exception to this rule can, of course, be made on party occasions, when you can sweep it up on top to bring an astonished " oh!" from the family. Or it may be dressed with a single jewel or a posy of real flowers. But be very sure to come back to your simple line the morning after.

POISE TECHNIQUE

Now to poise. Your first aim is self-confidence. Confidence in your looks, in your mind, in your ability to deal with things as they come along. And the secret of self-confidence is poise—moral and physical. And the two are closely associated. Watch the next cat you meet and see how his mind (or whatever a cat thinks with) and his body seem to work together in perfect harmony. Never a wrong line of thought (from the feline point of view, of course!), never a false movement. Perfect co-ordination, perfect rhythm, perfect poise. The cat has it; we, through a process of civilization, seem to have lost the natural thing and have to learn it all over again. One of the secrets is deportment—a stuffy word, but we do not seem to have a better one in our more modern vocabulary.

A woman's walk and the way she holds herself are the foundations of her ultimate appearance, and her charming clothes and her perfect grooming will be as good as lost if she walks with her head poked forward and her rear part out, or if she develops an artificial mincing manner that she thinks " refined ". Teach yourself (for the chances are that they won't teach you at school) how to walk. Tuck in your tail, tuck in your tummy, hold your shoulders easy and straight and your chin in. Head erect, and try to imagine that the top of it is touching the clouds and is anchored there. This is a tip (it was given me years ago by a famous London doctor) that works wonders to your attitude and your manner of moving. With your head held serenely aloft you will find that your movement will come from the hips with a slight swinging motion—like the beautiful Italian peasant women with their pitchers of water on their heads.

Practice this as often as you can until that poised walk becomes part of you. Then concentrate on your extremities. Master your hands—a difficult job. Quiet, restful, well-groomed hands say a lot for a woman, just as restless, self-conscious, fidgety ones say the other thing. And the less said about badly groomed ones the better.

Walk bare-footed and on your toes whenever you can; this will ensure strong arches and strong neat ankles. When you choose your shoes be sure they are big enough to wiggle your toes round in.

To finish, a few words to those who feel they have special figure problems to deal with. The tall girl. The short girl. The fat girl. The gawky girl. We cannot all be perfect, and sometimes an unusual figure means an interesting and unusual type.

If you are over tall then make that your type, gladly, proudly, and don't, please, go around with bent shoulders and a drooping air. Hold yourself all the better, head erect. Wear clean-cut, striking clothes. Stress your shoulder line, wear bold broad belts to cut yourself in two, flaring skirts, big sleeves, big pockets, daring patterns, rough, coarse materials. Wear chuggy shoes, carry big accessories, wear amusing big jewellery, flat hats with stress on the horizontal line.

For the little girl who wishes she were taller, I suggest that little people can be very attractive provided they make a real feature of their petiteness, their daintiness, their exquisite grooming. Or you can help yourself in a dozen ways to create an impression of greater height. Avoid the horizontal line, stress the vertical by throat to hem trims, button-through dresses. Wear your skirt an inch longer and raise your waist a fraction. Wear saucy little pixie hats, and avoid chugginess in accessories and trims. Avoid wide shoulders, and above all, don't make the mistake of wearing ultra-high heels.

The plump girl may always console herself with the hope that it is only a passing phase after all. . . . In the meanwhile be careful of your diet, not too much starch, not too many sweet things, but plenty of wholemeal bread, all the green stuff and fruit you can find—and this goes for every girl who wants to enjoy positive health and to possess a clean and lovely skin. Plenty of exercise and fresh air, special reducing exercises may help too, and be careful how you dress. First give yourself the self-confidence that figure control supplies: good brassiere so that you don't wobble; comfortable but controlling belt; well-cut underclothes that do not get into a bunch round your middle. Avoid very light colours, particularly light blouses; they will make you look very busty. Darker colours suit you best. Straight, roomy coats, flared skirts—and be sure to laugh the whole thing off with your friends.

The thin bony girl can make a fashion feature of her type by wearing rough tweedy garments, ultra-coarse woollies, gay hand-knit stockings to the knee, amusing gloves. All these things will suit, enhance her gawkiness and make her the envy of her plumper friends.

To-day—and this is my closing message—it is not beauty that counts. It is style, personality, and the true elegance that lies not so much in fashion as in being suitably dressed for your type and for the occasion.

FANCY DRESS

I can still recall with the greatest pride the very first time I went to a Fancy Dress Ball. It was held in the school assembly hall which had been decorated for the occasion by a group of my fellow students.

With gaily-coloured distemper, stacks of paper, and lighting, they had achieved an amazing effect without permanently damaging the walls or woodwork. This in itself created a festive atmosphere, and we entered full of anticipation. Everyone wore masks, this being compulsory till a certain hour when they were all whipped off. Wearing an eye-mask adds to the fun and excitement.

Many of the costumes were excellent and completely disguised the wearer. There was a very persistent Chinese Mandarin who kept coming up to me and bowing courteously. This perturbed me, and caused lots of laughter, especially afterwards when I realized it was my Latin teacher.

Not having much money at the time and wondering what would be best to wear, I glanced through the pages of an old history book until I came on the picture of a mediæval princess, complete with high-pointed head-dress, standing on the balcony of a castle looking down at her knight in armour. From that moment I was determined to be like the lady in the picture or die in the attempt. Nothing would stop me. Having been keen on dress-making and actually succeeded in making a petticoat and little summer frock at our sewing class, I felt it would be cheaper making my costume. In any case, there is special satisfaction in creating something like that, for you know it is truly original, and part of the enjoyment is the preparation beforehand.

The dress was semi-fitting, falling just short of an inch from the floor. It had long tight sleeves, a square neck, and a broad three-inch belt which fitted neatly at the waist. Five yards of pale green sateen was sufficient material. Round the neck and belt I stuck on some " pearls " (the remains of a broken string) and gold tinsel ribbon.

The head-dress was of buckram covered with sateen and also ornamented. From the point I sewed pale-green net.

The whole outfit cost not more than ten shillings.

Two of my friends were staying with me, and my parents, in order to give us a send off, ordered a taxi. Our excitement knew no end. At last the great moment arrived, and we all trooped out to the car.

The taxi-driver, a good-natured soul, grinned at me, and looking at my high-pointed head-dress remarked: " Another couple of inches, my lass, and I would have required to cut a hole in the roof for you."

The other two girls were dressed as a Victorian Lady and an Arabian Princess.

Mary, who was the Princess, wanted to stand all the way in case she creased her flowing trousers.

However, amidst all this hilarity, we arrived quite safely, and I swept into the hall feeling like Princess Katherine in the Henry V film, and swept out at the end of the evening with the first prize.

DRESSING UP

The game of " Let's Pretend ", which is really behind all this dressing up, starts when we are tiny tots, and remains with us throughout our lives. As we grow older, of course, it is restrained under a more matured exterior, but it is always there, being part of our nature. Everyone at some time or other has felt a trifle discontented with their general appearance and wanted to change it. Fancy dress gives us an outlet for this feeling, and that is why we enjoy it so much.

Dressing up started centuries ago when bands of strolling players wandered from castle to castle entertaining with music and playlets. Gaily attired, they gave performances to the noble lords and ladies in the evening. I am sure you know the scene in Hamlet where he commands the players to put on a performance of his father's murder. Often at banquets, too, jesters had to fool around in order to amuse the guests.

As the years rolled by people began to have little entertainments among themselves. The various feast days were often used for such occasions.

Later on such famous artists as Inigo Jones began to design

costumes for Queen Elizabeth and her ladies-in-waiting, with the result we had Masques performed for the benefit of the royal court.

So you see, when you take part in fancy dress, you are carrying on a tradition started hundreds of years ago.

There is no doubt that wearing a festive costume changes your whole physical appearance and personality. You do not feel yourself to be the same person, and it is so exciting to feel different.

When the invitation arrives the great problem arises, " Whatever shall I wear?"

The important point to bear in mind is your type. Many hours have been wasted on a costume which is later found not to suit the wearer. Films, nowadays, produce many pictures in technicolour which may give you ideas. But while it is all very well wanting to dress like a certain film star, remember to ask yourself: " Are you the same type?"

Before making a choice study yourself carefully in a mirror, both front and back view.

Then think over the type of party you are to attend. Is it a big affair or just a small gathering?

Is it for any special occasion such as Christmas, Hallowe'en, &c.?

Will you have to walk to it, or will you go in a car?

Will the evening be spent dancing, or will there be energetic games which might prove a strain on your costume?

All these questions are necessary and will guide you along the right lines.

There are many ideas for Fancy Dress which I intend to give and will define them to different types in order to help you. But whatever the costume, simple or elaborate, it must be comfortable and easy to manage. The wearing of fancy dress is as important as its design; no dress can be effective if it is not worn naturally. Never, never be embarrassed; because it is all a game of fun and frolic, and above all, " let's pretend ". It is impossible to enter into the spirit of a party if you are not at ease.

WHICH IS YOUR TYPE?

There are three types into which I am grouping girls—tall, average and small.

Tall Girls are apt to panic at the thought of trying to dress up. They feel they are difficult to suit. How very wrong. Because of their height they can wear men's costumes most successfully. So those of you who have developed long legs through running across the hockey field take heart.

Average Girls are fortunate in being able to wear most styles; the only thing to watch is colouring.

The Small Girl is very lucky, for there are a variety of ideas too

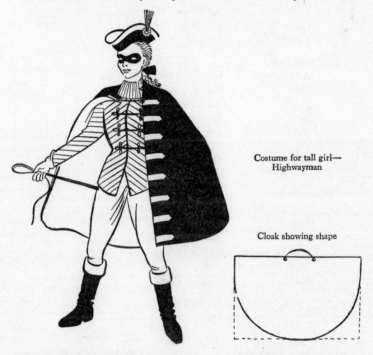

Costume for tall girl—
Highwayman

Cloak showing shape

dainty for our taller friends to wear which are right along her avenue.

I am also including that good sport, the plump girl. She, too, comes into her own, and I have some grand ideas which she alone can carry, and they have proved prize winners before now.

HAIR COLOUR

Now we come to hair colouring. This is quite important, but not nearly so compared with the actual height and build. Grouped together are ideas for the different types.

Tall Girls.

Any colour	Jack and the Beanstalk.
Dark	Chinese Coolie.
Red	Dutch Boy.
Dark	Highwayman (Dick Turpin).
Fair	Tyrolean Boy.
Dark	Chimney Sweep.
Fair or dark	Joan of Arc.

Average Girls.

Any colour	Cherry Seller.
Fair	Skater.
Fair	Mediæval Princess.
Red	Quaker Girl.
Fair	Cinderella.
Dark	Witch.
Dark	Gipsy.

Small Girls.

Any colour	Victorian Schoolgirl.
Fair	Ballet Dancer.
Fair	Alice in Wonderland.
Fair or red	Little Dutch Girl.
Red	Elf.
Dark	Oliver Twist.

Plump Girls.

Dark	Black Mammy.
Any colour	Jolly Wine-keeper.
Red or Dark	Farmer's wife going to market.

Characters out of Hans Andersen, Dickens and Shakespeare afford scope for originality as well.

MATERIALS

Now for a detailed list of suitable materials for inexpensive costumes.

Sateen. Most suitable; cheap, good-wearing but creases easily, and therefore requires ironing.

Hessian. Strong, obtainable in several bright colours, can take paint if you wanted to stencil pattern over it.

Bolton sheeting. Drapes well, and is suitable for cloaks.

Tailor's canvas. Pleats well, and if it is of a fairly soft quality can be used like material. Has a good foundation if you wanted to embroider a bold pattern in gaily coloured wools. To be had only in fawn and grey.

Gauze. Excellent substitute for veils if bought at thirty-six inch width and, incidentally, dyes beautifully.

Butter muslin. Quite good.

Felt. More expensive. Would be too warm to wear as an all-over costume, but is grand for hats, collars, belts and trimming because it does not require hemming.

Furnishing materials. Make excellent costumes because of their pattern.

Plastic materials. Obtainable in many lovely colours with attractive patterns printed all over. Has to be handled with care.

Bed ticking. Very useful, especially because of the bold striped effect. Cheap and good wearing.

Casement cloth. Also cheap and always in self colours.

IMPROVISED MATERIALS

Old curtains. All types have their uses.

Old sheets or table-cloths. Dyed and stencilled or appliqued with bright colours. Very effective.

Old blankets. Excellent for Red Indian costumes.

Suitable trimmings. Coloured ribbons, fringe, tassels, carpet-binding, tinsel ribbon which is used for tying Christmas parcels, feathers, patchwork, buttons and flowers.

Useful tips. Crowns can be made of cardboard, painted silver or gold and ornamented with beads, pearls or blobs of sealing-wax (stuck on with glue) to give the rich effect of jewels.

Paper clips fixed on to material will give the effect of being studded with gold, and incidentally brightens up any drab colour.

Paper doilies glued on to material give the appearance of lace embroidery.

Old-fashioned white lace curtains gathered on to a band and worn over a self-coloured skirt, blue, pink or mauve, give an exquisite appearance for a crinoline.

Navy-blue knitting silk is an excellent substitute for Chinese blue-black hair.

In stencilling or painting on material use poster colour mixed with glue. Place cloth on hard surface and fix down taut with drawing-pins before beginning to paint. When thoroughly dry iron on wrong side to take away any stiffness.

DUTCH GIRL

Various oddments of material or part of an old dress can make up this little costume very effectively.

The simple fitting bodice with elbow-length sleeves is in royal

Dutch Girl

blue, and the bib-like front in white lace is sewn on top. The skirt consists of three pieces of straight material, each about two yards long. First there is red-and-white-checked gingham, then red and last of all royal blue. After stitching the three pieces together gather the skirt on to the bodice.

A novel idea would be to blanket-stitch in bright-green wool along where the red and blue join.

The white cap could be made out of one of those nurses' squares, such as V.A.D.s use. Cut a circle about nine inches in diameter and slice two inches off one side. Run a tacking thread right round the curved part, drawing it into the shape of the head. Fold the straight side (which you remember was cut to make it so) into five pleats so that it fits neatly into the back of the

head. The wings are hemmed in such a way as to allow a fine wire to pass through. This keeps them sitting correctly in shape. If millinery wire is unobtainable the kind which is used for mending

FANCY DRESS: FIVE SUGGESTIONS DESCRIBED IN THE TEXT

electric fuses will do. If your hair is long enough to plait into pig-tails, all to the good. However, all are not in that position. Knitting wool or better knitting silk proves an excellent substitute. Make it into little plaits and sew it on to the inner sides of the cap. This avoids too many bits and pieces.

BLACK MAMMY

This is just the thing for the plump girl, and also quite inexpensive.

Two old table-cloths or sheets dyed primrose yellow and sten-cilled with black or red spots will make into a dress with a fitting bodice and gathering skirt.

Triangular pieces of gaily-coloured oddments make up the scarf and headgear.

A blue-checked patch gives a touch of character to the white apron.

Brass curtain rings act as a substitute for ear-rings.

The important key-note to this costume is the dark make-up. You have probably heard about using such things as soot and olive oil, cocoa and lard and other stratagems. While they may be all right on occasions, I do not think girls will like them. They are dirty and apt to come off on your clothes. My advice is to go to a theatrical shop and buy a bottle of stain. It is not expensive, will not come off on anything you wear, and

Plump girl as Black Mammy

what is most important, will not harm your skin. Soap and water wash it off easily.

CHERRY SELLER

This fancy dress comes from London street criers.

Believe it or not, the dress is made from bed ticking. In case you do not know what type of cloth this is, I will explain. Mattresses, pillows and bolsters are covered with a blue-and-white-striped

Average girl as Cherry Seller

material which is strong, cheap, and for our purpose most effective.

A plain fitting bodice and short blouse on which a full-length skirt is gathered is not difficult to make. White cuffs, apron and fichu, are made next. Deep cherry-red ribbon threaded in and out gives the apron a dainty look.

The hat is made from a circle of cardboard twelve inches across which is covered with red material. Stitch black ribbon on the under-side four inches from each side, as in the sketch. You will be able to keep your hat on quite securely by tying the ribbon under the chin in a demure bow.

If your hair is fairly long brush it into soft curls in order to achieve that old-world charm.

Lastly, you must have cherries in a basket to carry. They can be made of plasticine painted red.

LITTLE VICTORIAN GIRL

A pair of pantaloons, an underskirt with a frilly edge and an old party dress on the lines of the sketch are all you require. A card-

Average or small girl—Little Victorian Miss

board brim shaped like the one in the sketch with lace frilling round the edge is also tied with some gay ribbon.

If you can borrow or beg a pair of lace mittens you will look the real little Victorian.

Some girls have a natural instinct for dressing up, so that they themselves contribute in a decorative way to almost anything they wear.

Others are not quite so fortunate, and I do hope this little article will help them. Successful costumes have been suggested which may cost the wearers very little. It is all a matter of ingenuity. Who knows but that those old bedroom curtains Mother has put away in the attic will enable you to sweep down the hall of your Fancy Dress Party dressed as Mary Queen of Scots with the first prize firmly tucked under your arm—instead of a head.

FIVE COSTUMES SHOWN IN COLOUR

CHINESE COOLIE

An excellent costume for the dark girl and can be worn by almost any age. Pale-green casement cloth, sateen, curtain material or plastic will be suitable.

You will require approximately three and a half yards for a girl of twelve. The jacket is wide and boxy as also are the sleeves, and it has a slight wrap-over fastening at the side. Bind it round the edge with contrasting striped material. Next cut two strips of buckram or cardboard two inches by four, scalloping one side, and cover with red and yellow ribbon or whatever you can manage to obtain, as long as it is a good contrast. Attach to the shoulders like epaulets. The coolie hat is a circle of buckram or cardboard twelve inches in diameter. In order to obtain the correct shape you do exactly what all of us like when we see a lovely new circular cream sponge cake. Cut a piece out, then draw the two sides of the V-cut-out together.

Bedroom slippers to match or sandals will be quite in order.

GRANDMA AS A SCHOOLGIRL

An all-round pleated skirt (probably belonging to an older sister because it will give you just the right length), a lavender blouse with leg-o'-mutton sleeves and ankle-length boots are the main items in the fancy dress. The striped stockings are quite simple—just plain white cotton ones with red bias binding sewn round and round.

Beg, borrow or steal an old-fashioned straw boater, and if you do not care for an umbrella, carry a satchel of books instead.

FANCY DRESS 421

Jack and the Beanstalk

At a first glance one would never dream that all that is required to be bought for this outfit is the material for the tunic and hat. Long black " gym " stockings neatly stitched to fitting gym knickers give the excellent appearance of tights—I know from experience. On one occasion I joined the stockings to a black bathing costume. A white, cream or yellow blouse is the next item on the list.

The tunic may be any vivid colour. Black ribbon sewn criss-cross and little hearts in felt or American cloth stuck on with glue will reproduce the pattern in the picture. Lay your material quite flat and stick the hearts on one by one. When this is done cover with heavy weights and leave for an hour or so.

The pattern can be just as successful if stencilled or painted on. Black poster colour mixed with glue does the trick. When thoroughly dry iron on the wrong side to take out any stiffness.

The only parts of the tunic to be stitched are the sides of the skirt fitting over the hips.

Some curtain materials with delightfully bold designs would be ideal for this costume.

For the hat, a quarter of a yard of buckram and the same of black material are required. The high crown is made in two pieces with a seam right down the centre, front and back. Cover the crown and brim with material before joining them together. Once you have joined the two pieces of the crown and then pinned it on to the brim, you will begin to see the shape in the sketch. A bright green quill stuck in at a jaunty angle gives the necessary amount of dash.

Should this hat be a little difficult to make, a skull cap is just as good.

You will require a broad three-inch belt on which to suspend the little black bag. Jack carried his beans in it, remember!

Black dancing pumps or slippers are the most suitable footwear.

Juliet

This is the fair member of the Capulet family, and those of you who know your Shakespeare will recall with what grace she appeared to be endowed. Two casement curtains (the more faded the better), dyed yellow, should be ample for the princess lines of this dress. The leaf border is quite simple. Cut out in felt or american cloth and stick on with glue. A few bright beads sewn round the hem will enrich the whole appearance.

In order to make the Juliet cap, sew black velvet ribbon criss-cross with a pearl here and there. It will probably take about three yards; and last of all, do not forget the little bag hanging from the belt. No lady of the Renaissance period would have felt her attire complete without one.

Hungarian Peasant Girl

A sort of dream costume which most girls would love to wear.

It consists of a dainty embroidered blouse; a little green bodice in velvet or plastic; a red sateen or plastic skirt over an under-skirt with a frilly hem (again we look to curtains, the net kind this time); and a piece of black-out cloth embroidered in wool and fringed to form an apron.

A tall cane painted black and topped with a bouquet of flowers will not only match the halo head-dress, but will make you the perfect little Hungarian on festive days.

If you cannot obtain the loan of riding boots, do not on any account wear Wellingtons—wear black slippers.

BALLROOM DANCING

Ballroom dancing is one of the favourite amusements of to-day, and is a pastime that can be enjoyed all the year round. As a social asset it is invaluable, for it affords an opportunity of mixing with others. But to attain the highest sense of enjoyment it is necessary to have some knowledge of the fundamentals of the dance.

It is not at all necessary to learn all kinds of intricate steps, but it is necessary to know how to hold oneself well, how to move smoothly, to have good balance, to relax and to keep time with the music. This can be achieved with practice. Once this and the simple fundamental steps set forth on the following pages have been mastered so that they have become almost automatic, then any girl may step on to the ballroom floor with confidence.

It is in the ballroom that a girl may learn most of the social graces. It is the gentleman's privilege to invite the lady to dance with such words as " May I have this dance?" or " Will you dance this with me?" The lady should accept and walk with the gentleman to the floor unless she has already promised to dance with someone else, in which case she should explain why she has had to refuse.

It is customary to applaud when the music stops. If the band gives an encore everyone dances with the same partner again. At the end of the dance it is customary to thank one's partner for the dance. The gentleman should lead the lady back to a seat and remain with her until her next partner comes along. If he himself has another partner for the next dance, he should excuse himself when the music for that dance begins. It is better for everyone that the dancers should mix and that one couple should not dance too many dances together in succession.

THE HOLD

The hold for the Waltz, the Quickstep, and the Foxtrot is the same. Both dancers should stand in an easy, erect position, with the head held well. The elbows should be held well up and away from the body and level with each other. The shoulders should, however, be kept down.

If you are lucky to have a brother to practise with, here are directions for his position. His left forearm should be bent so

that the elbow is at a little more than a right angle, and should have a graceful curve. His hand should be held so that the lady may lay hers between the V made by the thumb and first finger with the palm downwards. The right hand should be placed just below his partner's left shoulder-blade, fingers and thumb together. The man should hold his partner as directly in front of him as to be compatible with comfort. The right hand should guide, the left arm helps balance.

Lady's Position.

The lady should look over her partner's right shoulder. The right elbow should be slightly bent and the right hand should be raised to the same level as the man's. The left arm should be raised and the hand, with the fingers closed, placed on the man's right arm nearer the shoulder than the elbow. The lady should never direct her partner but should follow his lead.

SOME DON'TS

1. Don't shrug the shoulders nor move the arms when dancing.
2. Don't keep the body stiff and taut.
3. Don't stiffen the legs.
4. Don't turn the toes in or out.
5. Don't dance with the feet apart.
6. Don't have conversation with your partner whilst dancing except perhaps when practising.
7. Don't jerk about when dancing, at the same time don't look stiff. Take gliding, smooth steps.

SOME DO'S

1. Keep the arms and shoulders still but not stiff.
2. Relax.
3. Relax the knees, but don't dance all the time with the knees bent.
4. Keep the toes pointing forward.
5. Let the feet brush each other in passing.

THE QUICKSTEP

The Quickstep is one of the most popular dances of to-day. To master it the two fundamental steps, the Walk and the Chassé, should be learned. From these the basic steps are made up: the quarter turns, chassé reverse turn, natural pivot turn, forward and backward lock.

Forward Walk.

1. Stand facing forward (the Line of Dance) with the feet together, the toes pointing forward (not turned out), and the knees a little relaxed.

Forward walk

2. Slide the right foot forward, moving from the hips, till the heel touches the ground at a normal length step forward, now lower the whole foot.

3. As the moving foot passes the other, release the heel of the foot on the ground.

4. The weight at this point is divided evenly between the heel of the front foot and the ball of the back foot, and the knees are straight though not stiff. The weight is now transferred on to the front foot, the toe of the front foot is lowered, and the back foot is drawn up and past the front foot to take a step forward.

5. The ankle of the back foot should be stretched so as to give pressure from the back foot.

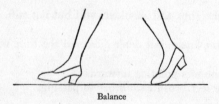

Balance

6. All steps should be taken straight forward and the feet should brush each other in passing.

Backward Walk.

1. Stand with the back to the line of dance, with the feet together, the toes not turned out and the knees a little relaxed.

2. Slide the left foot back, moving from the hips, to a normal length step back. The toe should touch the ground first, then the ball of the foot.

3. As the back foot does this, the toe of the front foot should be released.

Backward walk

4. The weight at this point should be divided between the heel of the front foot and the ball of the back foot, and the knees should be straight though not stiff. The weight is now transferred on to the ball of the back foot, the front foot is drawn up to the back foot, past it, and back to take another step. Care must be taken that the back heel is not lowered until both feet are level.

5. The ankle of the foot moving back should be stretched when the toe is reaching back.

6. All steps should be taken straight back, and care should be taken that the feet brush each other in passing, the toes being neither turned out nor in.

Chassé Step.

This may be taken side, together, side; side, together, back; side, together, forward. It is counted quick, quick, slow (4 beats to the bar). It consists of three steps, a step on to one foot, a close up with the other, and a step with the original foot again.

Quarter Turns.

MAN.

1. Step forward on to right foot, turning to the right .. .. SLOW
2. Step sideways with left foot, still turning .. QUICK
3. Close right foot up to left foot .. .. QUICK
4. Step diagonally back with left foot .. .. SLOW
5. Step back with right foot turning to left .. SLOW
6, 7. Close left foot up to right foot, turning to left on right heel (heel pivot) .. .. QUICK, QUICK
8. Step forward with left foot .. .. .. SLOW

Rise at end of 1, lower at end of 4. Slight rise on 6 and 7.

LADY.

1. Step back on to left foot turning to right .. SLOW
2. Step sideways with right foot, still turning .. QUICK
3. Close left foot up to right foot .. .. QUICK
4. Step diagonally forward with right foot .. SLOW
5. Step forward with left foot, turning to left .. SLOW
6. Step sideways with right foot .. .. .. QUICK
7. Close left foot to right foot .. .. .. QUICK
8. Step back with right foot .. .. .. SLOW

Rise at end of 1, lower at end of 4. Slight rise on 6 and 7.

The following abbreviations will be used hereafter:

R.F.	..	..	..	Right Foot.
L.F.	..	..	..	Left Foot.
fwd.	..	..	..	forward.
bwd.	..	..	..	backward.
R.	..	..	..	Right.
L.	..	..	..	Left.
s.	..	..	..	sideways.
w.	..	..	..	with.

Chassé Reverse Turn.

MAN.

1. Step fwd. on to L.F., turning to L. .. .. SLOW
2. Step s. w. R.F., still turning .. .. .. QUICK
3. Close L.F. up to R.F. .. .. QUICK
4. Step bwd. w. R.F., turning to R. .. .. SLOW
5, 6. Close L.F. back to R.F., turning to L. on
        R. heel (heel pivot) .. .. .. QUICK, QUICK
7. Step fwd. on to L.F. .. .. SLOW

Rise at end of 1 and lower at end of 3. Slight rise on 5 and 6.

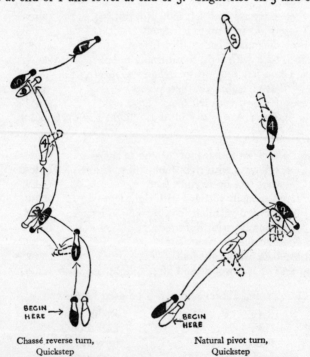

Chassé reverse turn,   Natural pivot turn,
     Quickstep   Quickstep

LADY.

1. Step bwd. on to R.F., turning to L. .. .. SLOW
2. Step s. w. L.F. (short step), still turning .. QUICK
3. Close R.F. up to L.F. .. .. QUICK

4. Step fwd. w. L.F., turning to L. .. .. SLOW
5. Step s. w. R.F., still turning .. .. .. QUICK
6. Close L.F. up to R.F. .. .. QUICK
7. Step bwd. w. R.F. .. .. SLOW

Rise at end of 1 and lower at end of 3. Slight rise on 5 and 6.

Natural Pivot Turn.

MAN.

1. Step fwd. on to R.F., turning to R. .. .. SLOW
2. Step s. w. L.F., still turning .. .. .. QUICK
3. Close R.F. up to L.F. .. .. QUICK
4. Step bwd. on to L.F., pivoting on ball of foot, R.F. in front, for about a ½ turn .. .. SLOW
5. Step fwd. on to R.F., still turning .. .. SLOW

Rise at end of 1 and lower at end of 3.

LADY.

1. Step bwd. on to L.F., turning to R. .. .. SLOW
2. Step s. w. R.F., still turning .. .. .. QUICK
3. Close L.F. up to R.F. .. .. QUICK
4. Step fwd. on to R.F., pivoting to R. .. .. SLOW
5. Step bwd. on to L.F., still turning .. .. SLOW

Rise at end of 1 and lower at end of 3.

Forward Lock.

MAN.

1. Step fwd. on to R.F. outside partner .. .. SLOW
2. Step diagonally fwd. w. L.F. .. .. .. QUICK
3. Cross R.F. up behind L. .. .. .. QUICK
4. Step diagonally fwd. w. L.F. .. .. .. SLOW
5. Step fwd. w. R.F. outside partner .. .. SLOW

Rise at end of 1 and lower at end of 4.

LADY.

1. Step bwd. on to L.F. .. .. SLOW
2. Step diagonally bwd. w. R.F. .. .. .. QUICK
3. Cross L.F. up in front of R. .. .. .. QUICK
4. Step diagonally bwd. w. R.F. .. .. .. SLOW
5. Step bwd. w. L.F. .. .. SLOW

Rise at end of 1 and lower at end of 4.

Backward Lock.

MAN.

1. Step bwd. on to L.F. and lead partner outside   SLOW
2. Step diagonally bwd. w. R.F. ..   ..   ..   QUICK
3. Cross L.F. up in front of R.   ..   ..   ..   QUICK
4. Step diagonally bwd. w. R.F. ..   ..   ..   SLOW
5. Step bwd. w. L.F. and lead partner outside ..   SLOW

Rise at end of 1 and lower at end of 4.

LADY.

1. Step fwd. w. R.F. outside partner   ..   ..   SLOW
2. Step diagonally fwd. w. L.F. ..   ..   ..   QUICK
3. Cross R.F. up behind L.   ..   ..   ..   QUICK
4. Step diagonally fwd. w. L.F. ..   ..   ..   SLOW
5. Step fwd. w. R.F. outside partner   ..   ..   SLOW

Rise at end of 1 and lower at end of 4.

MODERN WALTZ

This is one of the most graceful of all dances and one of the most enjoyable. There are three fundamental figures: the natural turn, the reverse turn and the change.

The waltz step takes three counts, and if you listen to a waltz tune you will be able to count 1, 2, 3; 1, 2, 3; 1, 2, 3; &c. The feet come together on every third count, and the weight is at this point on the toes.

Natural Turn.

Begin facing diagonally to outside wall.

MAN.

1. Step fwd. on to R.F., turning to R.
2. Step s. w. L.F., still turning.
3. Close R.F. to L.F.
4. Step bwd. on to L.F., turning to R.
5. Step s. w. R.F., still turning to R.
6. Close L.F. to R.F. facing diagonally to centre of room.

Rise at end of 1 and lower at end of 3.
   „   „   4   „   „   „   6.

LADY.

    1. Step bwd. on to L.F., turning to R.
    2. Step s. w. R.F., still turning.
    3. Close L.F. up to R.F.
    4. Step fwd. on to R.F., turning to R.
    5. Step s. w. L.F., still turning.
    6. Close R.F. up to L.F.
Rise at end of 1 and lower at end of 3.
      ,,   ,, 4 ,,   ,,   ,, 6.

Reverse Turn.

MAN.

    1. Step fwd. on to L.F., turning to L.
    2. Step s. w. R.F., still turning.
    3. Close L.F. up to R.F.
    4. Step bwd. on to R.F., turning to L.
    5. Step s. w. L.F., still turning.
    6. Close R.F. up to L.F.
Rise at end of 1 and lower at end of 3.
      ,,   ,, 4 ,,   ,,   ,, 6.

LADY.

    1. Step bwd. on to R.F., turning to L.
    2. Step s. w. L.F., still turning.
    3. Close R.F. up to L.F.
    4. Step fwd. on to L.F., turning to L.
    5. Step s. w. R.F., still turning.
    6. Close L.F. up to R.F.
Rise at end of 1 and lower at end of 3.
      ,,   ,, 4 ,,   ,,   ,, 6.

Forward Change after a Natural Turn.

MAN.

    1. Step fwd. on to R.F.
    2. Step s. w. L.F.
    3. Close R.F. up to L.F.
Rise at end of 1 and lower at end of 3.

LADY.

   1. Step bwd. on to L.F.

   2. Step s. w. R.F.

   3. Close L.F. up to R.F.

Rise at end of 1 and lower at end of 3.

Forward Change after a Reverse Turn.

MAN.

   1. Step fwd. on to L.F.

   2. Step s. w. R.F.

   3. Close L.F. up to R.F.

Rise at end of 1 and lower at end of 3.

LADY.

   1. Step fwd. on to R.F.

   2. Step s. w. L.F.

   3. Close R.F. up to L.F.

Rise at end of 1 and lower at end of 3.

Backward Change.

MAN.

   From the Natural to the Reverse Turn.

   Do 1, 2, 3 of Natural Turn, backing diagonally to the centre of the room.

   1. Step bwd. on to L.F., turning to R.

   2. Step bwd. w. R.F.

   3. Step bwd. w. L.F. a very short step, allowing it only just to pass R.F.

   Go straight into 4, 5, 6 of Reverse Turn.

Rise at end of 1 and lower at end of 3.

LADY.

   From the Natural to the Reverse Turn.

   Do 1, 2, 3 of Natural Turn, facing diagonally to the centre of the room.

   1. Step fwd. on to R.F., turning to R.

   2. Step fwd. w. L.F.

   3. Step fwd. w. R.F. a very short step, allowing it only just to pass L.F.

   Go straight into 4, 5, 6 of Reverse Turn.

Rise at end of 1 and lower at end of 3.

SLOW FOXTROT

The fundamental steps in the Slow Foxtrot are the Walk and the Three Step. From these the basic figures are made up—the Feather Step, the Natural Turn, the Reverse Turn.

Walk Forward.

The walk forward is done by long smooth steps from the hips, sliding the feet along the floor. Start with the feet together, the knees slightly bent, and the weight on the front of the feet. The moving foot slides forward on the flat, the weight is transferred to the heel as it passes the other foot, and is continued forward on the heel to the full extent of the stride. Meanwhile, the back heel is lifted and the weight is now between both feet, ball of back and heel of front foot.

This step takes two beats of music and is counted " slow ".

Walk Backward.

Start with the feet together, the knees slightly bent. The moving foot slides backwards on to the toe then on to the ball, keeping the back heel up and at the same time lifting the toes of the front foot. The weight is now between both feet—the ball of the back foot and the heel of the front foot. Draw the front foot back with light pressure on the heel, helping the back heel off the ground until it has passed the other foot.

This step takes two beats of music and is counted " slow ".

Three Step.

The Three Step contains three steps to the bar, and might be termed a run. It is made up of three steps which take four beats of music, so that they are counted Quick, Quick, Slow; each Quick taking one beat each and the slow taking two beats.

MAN.

  1. Step fwd. on to R.F. a medium length step ..   QUICK
  2. Step fwd. on to L.F. a medium length step ..   QUICK
  3. Step fwd. on to R.F. a normal length step   ..   SLOW
Rise at end of 1 and lower at end of 2.

LADY.

1. Step bwd. on to L.F. a medium length step ..   QUICK
2. Step bwd. on to R.F. a medium length step ..   QUICK
3. Step bwd. on to L.F. a normal length step   ..   SLOW

Rise at end of 1 and lower at end of 2.

Feather Step.

MAN.

1. Step fwd. a long step on to R.F.   ..   ..   SLOW
2. Step fwd. on to L.F., turning slightly to wall   QUICK
3. Step fwd. on to R.F. outside partner ..   ..   QUICK
4. Step fwd. on to L.F. in front of partner   ..   SLOW

Rise at end of 1 and lower at end of 3.

LADY.

1. Step bwd. a long step on to L.F.   ..   ..   SLOW
2. Step bwd. on to R.F. ..   ..   QUICK
3. Step bwd. on to L.F., partner stepping outside   QUICK
4. Step bwd. on to R.F. ..   ..   SLOW

Rise at end of 1 and lower at end of 3.

Natural Turn.

MAN.

1. Step fwd. on to R.F., turning to R.   ..   ....   SLOW
2. Step s. w. L.F., still turning   ..   ..   ..   QUICK
3. Step bwd. on to R.F.   ..   ..   ..   QUICK
4. Step bwd. on to L.F., turning to R. ..   ..   SLOW
5. Pull R.F. bwd. to L., still turning on heel and
     finish w. foot parallel and slightly apart ..   SLOW
6. Step fwd. on to L.F.   ..   ..   SLOW

Rise at end of 2 and lower at end of 3.

LADY.

1. Step bwd. on to L.F., turning on it to R.   ..   SLOW
2. Close R.F. bwd to L.F., still turning ..   ..   QUICK
3. Step fwd. on to L.F.   ..   ..   ..   QUICK
4. Step fwd. on to R.F., turning to R.   ..   ..   SLOW
5. Step s. w. L.F. ..   ..   SLOW
6. Step bwd. R.F. brushing L.F.   ..   ..   SLOW

Rise at end of 2 and lower at end of 3.

Reverse Turn.

MAN.

1. Step fwd. on to L.F., turning to L. .. .. SLOW
2. Step s. w. R.F., still turning .. .. .. QUICK
3. Step bwd. on to L.F. .. .. QUICK
4. Step bwd. on to R.F., turning to L. .. .. SLOW
5. Step s. on to L.F. .. .. QUICK
6. Step fwd. on to R.F. outside partner .. .. QUICK
7. Step fwd. on to L.F. in front of partner .. SLOW

Rise at end of 2 and lower at end of 3.
 „ „ 4 „ „ „ 6.

LADY.

1. Step bwd. on to R.F., turning to L.
2. Close L.F. back to R.F., still turning.
3. Step fwd. on to R.F.
4. Step fwd. on to L.F., still turning.
5. Step s. w. R.F.
6. Step bwd. on to L.F.
7. Step bwd. on to R.F.

Rise at end of 2 and lower at end of 3.
 „ „ 4 „ „ „ 6.

QUICK OR VIENNESE WALTZ

The Quick Waltz is always a popular dance, and as in the Slow Waltz the dancer need only know the Natural Turn, the Reverse Turn, and the Balance Step, to enjoy the dance.

Natural Turn.

MAN.

1. Step fwd. on to R.F., turning to R.
2. Step a short step s. w. L.F., still turning,
3. Close R.F. up to L.F.
4. Step bwd. on to L.F., turning R.
5, 6. Close R.F. back to L.F., pivoting on L. heel to complete the turn.

LADY.

1. Step bwd. on to L.F., turning to R.
2, 3. Close R.F. back to L.F., pivoting on L. toe to complete the turn.
4. Step fwd. on to R.F., turning to R.
5. Step short step to s. w. L.F., still turning.
6. Close R.F. to L.F.

Reverse Turn.

MAN.

1. Step fwd. on to L.F., turning to L.
2. Step s. w. R.F., still turning.
3. Cross L.F. in front of R.F.
4. Step bwd. w. R.F., turning to L.
5, 6. Close L.F. bwd. to R.F., pivoting on R. heel to complete the turn.

Make one full turn on steps 1 to 6.

LADY.

1. Step bwd. on to R.F., turning to L.
2, 3. Close L.F. bwd. to R.F., pivoting on R. toe to complete the turn.
4. Step fwd. on to L.F., turning to L.
5. Step s. w. R.F., still turning.
6. Cross L.F. in front of R.F.

Make one full turn on steps 1 to 6.

Balance Step.

MAN.

1. Step fwd. on to L.F., turning a little to L.
2, 3. Cross R.F. behind L.F., weight on L.F.
4. Step bwd. on to R.F., turning a little to L.
5, 6. Cross L.F. in front of R.F., weight on R.F.

LADY.

1. Step bwd. on to R.F., turning a little to L.
2, 3. Cross L.F. in front of R.F., weight on R.F.
4. Step fwd. on to L.F., turning a little to L.
5, 6. Cross R.F. behind L.F., weight on L.F.

or

MAN.

1. Step fwd. on to R.F., turning a little to R.
2, 3. Close R.F. to L.F.
4. Step bwd. on to L.F., turning to R.
5, 6. Close R.F. to L.F.

LADY.

1. Step bwd. on to L.F., turning a little to R.
2, 3. Close R.F. to L.F.
4. Step fwd. on to R.F., turning to R.
5, 6. Close L.F. to R.F.

Once you have mastered these steps you may go off to a dance with complete confidence. And if you want a general maxim as a guide to looking your best—never forget that dancing should be graceful both to perform and to watch.

COUNTRY DANCING

How often the young hostess at a dance has little shivers of anxiety when she sees her friends split up into groups in different corners of the room. The pianist plays a waltz or foxtrot, and one or two couples who have known each other all their lives begin to dance, but as no one joins in they waver to a standstill; the groups close in with low-toned conversation, and somebody nervously lights a cigarette. At this point the hostess begins to feel desperately in need of help, help that is not necessarily conversational, a round dance perhaps; people must be made to mix.

During the war years round dances came into their own again. The Allied soldiers billeted in our towns and villages taught us how every girl could meet and dance with every boy at a party within the first few minutes. Language barriers were forgotten. Some enterprising young man could always find enough English words to form all the dancers into a big circle, then give simple orders such as " All men walk to the right, all girls to the left, stop, dance with the girl facing you ", &c. If a muddle ensued no one worried; arguments and laughter added to the fun and helped to break the ice.

When the American soldiers came to this country they introduced us to a more definite form of the same idea, their own national Square Dances made up of figures with the names such as " Little Yaller Girl ", " Shucking the Corn ", and the " Shoo Fly Swing ". These modern folk dances are so simple that even non-dancers can enjoy taking part. The step, a smooth, lilting walk to any well-known American tune such as " Marching through Georgia " or " Yankee Doodle ", carries the set onwards through arches, circles, and grand chains with a swinging, effortless rhythm.

The most characteristic feature of American Square Dancing is the calling, or giving of orders for change of figure or direction. Those taking part have no need to memorize long sequences of movement; instead, the responsibility lies almost entirely with the caller, who may be one of the dancers or someone standing outside the set. An American who has had long experience can make this a most entertaining part of the performance, sometimes even breaking into spontaneous rhyme or poking fun at a particular couple in the ring.

We in our turn taught them the Eightsome Reel and the Lancers —though to our shame we nearly always forget which figure follows which in the Lancers. To keep you right you will find instructions at the end of this article.

The fact that round dances are popular at informal parties seems to point to a growing interest in the work and play of other countries. Norway is linked to Scotland in a most interesting way by one of her national dances. This " Tritur " is to be found on the west coast of the country, and is a simple little dance for a man and two girls. It begins with a gay circle of skips, but almost immediately opens into a straight line where the man sets to his right and left partners in turn, and all swing into a walking reel of three. For this, one of the favourite tunes is the well-known reel, " The Soldiers' Joy ".

A dance which must have been of Scottish origin is not our only link with Norway. To this day the men of Gudbrandsdal wear waistcoats, and the girls summer dresses, of Sinclair tartan. This part of their national costume has been traditional for over three hundred years. The story is interesting; it goes back to 1612 when a gathering of the Sinclair clan set out to join the mercenary army of Gustavus Adolphus. They landed at the small west-coast town of Andalsnes, but got no farther upon their journey across Norway. The men of Gudbrandsdal set upon them, hurling rocks and tree trunks down the mountainsides. Though the Scots themselves were wiped out, their tartan lived on in the valley to become part of Norwegian dress to-day.

INTRODUCTION WALTZ

Sweden and Denmark are equally rich in national folk dances; Denmark possibly having a larger proportion of the round variety. The following Danish one is sometimes very useful as a form of introduction at a party.

A dance for any number of couples.

Girls stand on the right side of the boys, all hands joined in a large circle facing centre.

FAMILY WALTZ

Danish

FAMILY HOPSA

Part One: Family Waltz.

All dance four soft folk dance Pas de Basque steps, the boy beginning with his left foot, the girl with her right. This causes partners to balance away, towards, away, and towards each other.

Partners now separate, the girl turning to the boy on her right, and the boy to the girl on his left. Take a ballroom hold with the new partner, and in this position waltz round for four bars of music, travelling slightly anti-clockwise. The boy finishes by placing his partner on his right side.

The circle now joins hands as in the beginning, and original partners should find themselves separated by one couple.

Repeat the four balancing steps, and the four bars of waltz turn right round the circle until partners meet and waltz to their proper sides.

At this point the music changes to *Part Two*.

Part Two: Family Hopsa.

Repeat the whole dance as in Family Waltz, but use a light springing Pas de Basque both for the balancing, in the joined circle, and for the turn.

This dance can also be of great use as a guide to the capability of a group of young dancers. A leader may not want to try out each member of a class individually—it is sometimes apt to cause self-consciousness and unnecessary giggling—but in a dance such as the Family Waltz and Hopsa she can join into the ring as a matter of course, and in this way gain much useful knowledge without the reason being obvious.

This common and very trying habit of giggling in an amateur dance group is something which must be dealt with, from a natural common-sense point of view, by both pupils and teacher alike. A young leader can go home at the end of an evening feeling cross and frustrated. She has had a lovely dance to give her girls, but for some reason they did not grasp it as quickly as she had expected. Stupid mistakes kept recurring, left feet were used when it should have been right, arms became entangled, and before long incessant giggling took the place of serious work. If only the leader and the pupils would think the matter over quietly, they might all arrive at some very interesting conclusions.

A straightforward discussion may bring the trouble to the surface at once. After a moment's hesitation a girl may admit that she feels so silly standing waving her arms about when she knows that the others are laughing at her. In one sentence the root of the giggling has been reached—it is almost always nervousness.

It is quite possible that the members of a group have never had the advantage of going to a children's dancing class in their young days, and country dancing in school gives very little practice in the more varied steps and arms movements of Scandinavia or Central Europe. Naturally, it may take two or three weeks before the group can do the dance well enough to appreciate it, but before long grand discussions will take place in the rest periods with pupils gathered round the piano weighing up the merits of the different dances, or talking over the costumes that they would need to make if the dance were to be done in public.

PUBLIC DEMONSTRATION

It is surprising how soon this feeling of wanting to share the interest with the general public begins to simmer in the mind of a folk dance team. It is partly because the work is simple and meant to be done by the amateur rather than by the highly trained product of a ballet school. This does not mean that girls who have studied ballet technique should be excluded; on the contrary, they would probably be a great asset to their group, as they would learn more quickly, their movement would be softer and more controlled, and their footwork neater than that of the inexperienced school or business girls. Their only difficulty might be a slight tendency to over-dance the part, but this could be easily remedied by an occasional reminder that the dancing must be simple, unaffected, and in keeping with the character they represent.

There are many things to be considered before staging a demonstration of national dances. The subject is very wide, as dancing and the kindred arts are fundamental parts of the life of a nation, and it is only by study of such matters that we can begin to understand each other.

Before the war perhaps Scouts and Girl Guides had the greatest opportunity of contact with the young people of other countries. At moots, jamborees, or summer camps international friendships were formed by boys and girls of all nations as they took part in each other's songs and dances round the glowing camp fires. After meetings such as these many a British boy must have realized for the first time that national dancing can be a man's interest just as much as a woman's; in fact, on many occasions he must have watched the Scouts of the Continent demonstrating the intricate steps of their own country, while the girls stood back in an admiring circle.

It is interesting to note that almost all the good solos in Europe are danced by men. The first we think of are naturally our own; the Highland Fling and Sword Dance, though frequently done by highly trained children and girls, are really men's dances, and are seen to the best advantage performed by stalwart Highlanders at a gathering of the clans.

The one solo to be found in Norway is also essentially a man's dance. This " Halling " takes its name from the broad valley of Hallingdal, which runs diagonally across the southern part of the country. Though it is danced by a man his partner has an important part to play. As he dances round in a series of lunging and turning movements she quietly climbs to a standing position on a chair, which has been placed in the middle of the floor, holding in her hand a stick with a hat balanced on the point. After one or two circles round the chair to judge the height and distance, the dancer steadies up underneath the point of the stick, takes aim, and with a flying circular kick sends the hat spinning into the farthest corner of the room, a spectacular ending which is always greeted with a round of spontaneous applause.

From one mountainous country our thoughts turn to another, the Austrian Tyrol. In this fascinating part of Europe, it is again the men who have the lion's share of the fun, their Schuhplattler, or rhythmic clapping figures, being the main feature of nearly every dance. The dancers, dressed in neat home-spun jackets and leather shorts, usually work in groups rather than as soloists, and many of the dances are mimetic in character.

Two men may appear upon the stage engrossed in a most realistic mock fight, an amusing figure being one in which the stronger man swings his partner round until he is directly in front of him and facing the same way. He then grasps him by the waist, and with a well-timed lift turns him in a half somersault through his legs, there the smaller man remains upside down, his feet securely pinned under the arms of his upright partner. In this position the couple circles round the stage, each man beating out rhythmic and hearty slaps on the seat of his opponent's leather shorts. As the phrase of music ends the upright man catches his partner by the belt and heaves him up into a standing position. Now comes the retaliation, the smaller man once more firmly placed upon his feet turns on his partner with what appears to be a resounding slap on the side of his face. In reality it is the other man who makes the noise by clapping his hands on the opposite side from the cheek, which is supposed to have received the blow. This the two men repeat alternately with rising speed and fury until one reels backwards off the stage.

Though the dances just mentioned are for men, there are others of equal charm in which the girls take part, the Miller's Dance being one of the most interesting of the Tyrolean group. This can be done by five or six couples entering in single file, each dancer carrying a sack of flour slung over the shoulder. At a given point the sacks are lowered to the floor to form an outer ring, the men take a firm grasp of their partner's wrists and slide their feet towards the centre of the set. The dance now represents a moving picture of the mill wheel, the men's feet forming the hub, and their taut horizontal bodies with outstretched arms the spokes. In this position the girls almost carry their partners round in a slowly moving circle to portray the grinding of the corn.

It is not only in Austria that we find dances representing a peasant industry or something familiar in the life of the countryside. In Lithuania one of the oldest traditional dances takes the V-shaped formation of a flight of birds. In Sweden the action of a hand loom can be seen with the leading couple as the shuttle flying to and fro. Another equally delightful Swedish dance shows the undulating movement of a windmill's turning sails. Watching this dance, with its brilliant striped costumes, one can almost imagine the passing of sunshine and shadow as the flowing circle moves on.

In many parts of Europe sticks play an important part in the national dances. The swineherds of Hungary lay two sticks on the ground in a crossed position, then dance a sequence of figures nearly as intricate as that of the Scottish Sword Dance. Though the steps are similar, even to the use of the Pas de Basque, the character is different. In Scotland the dancer wears light flexible shoes which enable him to spring with pointed toes, while the swineherd is much less polished in his movement, owing to the fact that he wears heavy-soled-and-heeled top boots, which makes his action slower and more flat-footed.

Shepherds, not to be out-done by those who tend the pigs, have their own special dances, in which they pass their crooks in a figure of eight between their legs as they leap in time to the csárdás music of the gipsy orchestra.

Other stick dances of Hungary go back five hundred years to the time of the Turkish Occupation, when the men had to be content to dance with brooms and brushes as the women were not available as partners.

One of the most charming dances to be seen in Hungary is the Cushion Dance from Szakmár. This district has a beautiful costume, which consists of a short, brilliant-coloured knife-pleated skirt with apron, blouse and waistcoat of pure white cotton embroidered all over with natural wild flowers.

The dance, a traditional part of a Szakmár wedding ceremony, is performed by the bridesmaids, who enter from the sides in single file, each girl carrying a square white cushion embroidered to match her costume. These are held aloft as the lines meet, turn towards the front, or curve outwards into circles with an everlasting rhythm of sharp little heel taps accentuated by the loose mule slippers which clack against the floor.

As the bridesmaids turn their backs to the audience one is struck by the beauty of the stiff skirts. They are rich and satisfying to the eye as they stand out over masses of petticoats, but it is the pleating that is interesting, as it is done by hand. First the material must be arranged in position on a flat surface, then a loaf of bread nearly a yard long is taken straight from the oven and laid upon it, the damp and heat producing the wonderful accordion effect.

Hardened bread dough is also used to make the cone-shaped support for a head-dress in another part of Hungary. Though it is tucked away out of sight under folds of material, it is beautifully ornamented with velvet binding, ribbon, and bead work.

CORRECT COSTUMES

In staging a group of national dances the costumes are just as important as the dances themselves. In this country we are not particular enough about this point; we are far too apt to make a miscellaneous collection of gay skirts and aprons, and in a vague un-thinking way feel that they will do, as they look something like a picture we have once seen of a foreign peasant. This is not good enough, particularly now that there are so many continental societies in Britain to whom we can apply for information. These societies are usually delighted to help anyone who is interested by showing books, pictures or costumes, and they really appreciate even the smallest efforts on our part to further international understanding.

If personal contact of this kind is out of the question, it is sometimes possible to find copies of the American *Geographic Magazine*; the coloured plates are so clear that nearly any costume can be copied down to the smallest detail.

The choice of dance for a newly formed group giving its first performance in public is a little difficult. The round or square dance, which is popular at a party, is usually quite unsuitable for concert work, as the audience has nothing but a back view of the members of the set standing nearest to the edge of the platform. If the dance is square, it is possible to overcome this difficulty to a certain extent by placing it across the four corners of the stage. It may be a little more difficult to dance in this position, but the audience can at least see the formation and the faces of the dancers at the same time.

Perhaps the best dances of all are trios with a boy and his two partners all facing the audience; duets with couples following one another round the stage, or sets in which the dancers can include the audience in their own enjoyment. This sense of giving pleasure and interest to others is the first aim of a national dance group. Light happy work and smiling faces combined with correct detail in dance and costume can do much towards bringing the young people of different countries together.

LANCERS

The dance is arranged in a square set of four couples, the lady standing on the right side of the gentleman, all facing centre.

The top couple stands with its back to the head of the room.

Steps: Walking steps used except where otherwise indicated.

First Figure.

Eight bars of music played for curtsey and bow to own and corner partners.

Top and *Bottom* couples work; *Sides* stand still.

Top Lady and *Bottom Gentleman* advance to meet in centre

(4 walking steps).   Retire (4 walking steps).   Advance to meet again, and turn together with both hands joined (8 walking steps).   Finish back in place.

Top and *Bottom* couples cross the set to change places.

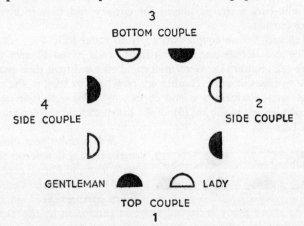

Top couple passing between the dancers of the *Bottom* couple, and turning outwards into place (8).

Top and *Bottom* couples cross back again to own places. *Top* couple dividing and passing on the outside of *Bottom* couple (8).

Corners.

All dancers turn their backs on their own partners, and face their corner partners.

All take four walking steps to the right, repeat to the left.

Take ballroom hold with corner partner and turn with smooth pivoting steps, right foot slightly in advance of left (8).

Repeat the whole figure other three times.

First repeat—*Top Gentleman* and *Bottom Lady* begin.

Second repeat—*Side Lady No. 2*, and *Side Gentleman No. 4* begin.

Third repeat—*Side Lady No. 4* and *Side Gentleman No. 2* begin.

Second Figure.

Eight bars of music played for curtsey and bow to own and corner partners.

Top and *Bottom* couples work; *Sides* stand still.

Top and *Bottom* couples with right hands joined advance to the centre (4). Retire (4). *Gentlemen* stand still and turn their partners round to face them (4). (Ladies are now back to back in the centre of the set.) Partners bow and curtsey (4). All walk four steps to the right, repeat to the left (8). Take ballroom hold with partner and pivot turn (8).

Side couples now divide to make lines of four across the set with *Top* and *Bottom* couples.

All advance (4). Retire (4). Turn partners (8).

The above figure is danced twice in succession by the *Top* and *Bottom* couples, and twice by the *Side* couples.

Third Figure: Ladies to the centre.

Eight bars of music played for curtsey and bow to own and corner partners.

All four ladies advance to the centre (4). Retire (4).

All four gentlemen advance to the centre and join hands in a circle, ladies move in and hold on to their arms with both hands (8). (With rallentando on the first 4.)

All circle round once with sixteen slip steps to the left.

Ladies advance to the centre (4). Retire (4).

Gentlemen advance to the centre and join left hands across in a wheel, taking their partners round the waist with their right arms (8). (With rallentando as before.)

All circle round twice with slip steps forward (16).

Repeat the whole figure.

Fourth Figure: Visiting.

Eight bars of music played for curtsey and bow to own and corner partners.

Top and *Bottom* couples with right hands joined walk to the *Side* couples on their right (4). Bow to them (4).

Top and *Bottom* couples turn to the left and visit the *Side* couples opposite (4). Bow to them (4).

Join right hands across in a wheel and walk round clockwise with eight steps, repeat back with left hands joined.

The two ladies now face each other while the two gentlemen clasp hands behind their backs, and all circle round with slip steps to the left (16).

Top and *Bottom* couples bow to the *Sides*, with whom they have been dancing (4). Turn to the left and visit the *Side* couples opposite (4). Bow to them (4). All join right hands in a wheel (4).

Repeat the wheel clockwise (8). Anti-clock (8). Also the circle of slip steps to the left (16).

Repeat the whole figure with *Side* couples visiting *Top* and *Bottom* couples.

Fifth Figure: Grand Chain.

Single chord played for the curtsey and bow.

All give right hands to partners, and walk right round the circle giving alternate hands. Gentlemen moving anti-clock, and ladies clockwise. When partners meet half-way all set to one another with Pas de Basque step right and left. After this continue chain, and finish with two more Pas de Basque steps (32).

Top couple with right hands joined leads into the centre, makes a half turn to the left and faces outwards in top place; as they arrive in this position the lady moves directly in front of her partner.

The *Second* couple falls in behind the *Top* couple.

The *Fourth* couple falls in behind the *Second* couple.

The *Bottom* couple is already in place when the lady has moved in front of her partner (16).

All ladies move sideways to the left with four walking steps, all gentlemen meanwhile moving to the right. All set with Pas de Basque step right and left (8). Repeat across to the opposite side (8).

Top couple divides, and all cast off down the outsides, and lead up to own places (16). Partners turn (16).

Grand Chain.

15

Repeat whole figure with *Bottom* couple leading into first place facing outwards towards the bottom of the set. *Fourth* and *Second* couples falling in behind.

Grand Chain.

Repeat whole figure with *Second* couple leading into first place facing outwards. *Third* and *First* couples falling in behind.

Grand Chain.

Repeat whole figure with *Fourth* couple leading into first place. *First* and *Third* couples falling in behind.

Grand Chain.

GIVING A PARTY

There are some people who think that if you give your guests a good supper, " that's you done "; all your responsibilities as a hostess are over. I want, at the outset of this section, to assure you that even a hungry schoolboy may vote a party " dud " if it has no more than a supper to recommend it. No, the food at a party is not the one thing needful. It is the thought which we give to the entertainment of our guests that will make the party a success. After all, we can't talk for months afterwards about what we had to eat at Joan's party, but we can and do remember and chuckle over the good fun we had.

Now don't say " Queen Anne's dead!" when I tell you that everybody doesn't think the same things good fun. Some of the boys will probably like games of skill best, some of the girls will think anything but dancing slightly boring, and a few of each will enjoy competitions which require a little intellect, so my advice to the young hostess is, " Have a good mixture of entertainment at your party. If you have a varied programme, everybody is sure to enjoy part of it. So spend plenty of time in planning your programme and in recalling the likes and dislikes of your guests."

LIST OF GUESTS

I have heard young people say that their greatest difficulty in making up the list of guests is the number of people they are obliged to invite.

" If only we could invite just the people we really want, what a jolly party we could have, but it's such a bore—we must ask Mary because she asked us to her party, and we can't omit Jean and Susan because they are relations of ours, and we simply have to invite the boys from next door, and they don't add to the gaiety of any party—indeed, when we see all these names on the list we can't imagine our party being anything but a fiasco."

Well, don't worry about that, for I've a hint to give you about

how to deal with the shy people and the stiff people and the bored
people which I'm sure you will find a success. Divide your party
into *teams* for your games and competitions, and give very careful
thought as to who is to be in each team. For instance, don't put
two bores into one team or two good sports either. Put your shy
guests into separate teams and your intellectuals and your sports
fans; and, if you've had to invite some older people, don't put
them all together. If you do, they're certain to lose interest in the
competition, and you'll likely find them (if men) having a solemn
talk in a quiet corner about the international situation, or (if women)
discussing the best way to get mildew out of linen or some such
utterly unimportant thing like that. So don't on any account let your
birds of a feather flock together. Segregate them (and if you don't
know the meaning of segregate, look it up in the dictionary).

HOW MANY TO INVITE

You will say that this is not a point on which anybody can give
advice, because it depends on the size of your house and on the
number of your friends. But there is one thing I would like to say
on the subject, and that is that I think a party is always much more
fun if everybody can sit down to supper, and incidentally, they
usually get a far better supper if they do. Defend me from the
sandwich-balanced-on-a-saucer variety of supper! I invariably go
home hungry from such a meal. No, make everybody sit down, and,
if you do not have enough chairs, borrow a plank or two from the
joiner and make them into forms by putting a chair under each end
of them, then add to the " comfortableness " by laying a folded
blanket or rug on them. By this plan you will make your two chairs
accommodate six people.

THE MENU FOR SUPPER

As we are talking about the supper table, let us just settle the
menu, though, as I said already, it is really not of first importance
in your preparations. I think you will usually find that the savoury
things at your supper are even more popular than the sweet things,
though the latter make the table look prettier. Sandwiches can be
very varied, but I recommend you to have, in addition to them, hot
sausage rolls. They can be made the day before and heated when

you need them, and you'll find they'll go "like hot cakes". (Don't forget to give your guests paper napkins if you have sausage rolls, because they are messy things to eat, and the girls don't want to leave greasy finger marks on their best frocks.) And, by the way, sausage rolls are much nicer home-made, so here's a recipe, and also a tip for doing a quantity quickly.

SAUSAGE ROLLS

Half a pound of flour;
Quarter of a pound of lard and margarine mixed;
Half a teaspoonful of salt;
Half a teaspoonful of baking powder;
A little lemon juice or lemon essence.

Cut up the fats in the flour with the other dry things, then add water, and mix with your knife to a stiff dough. Roll out, flour and fold in three. Do this three or four times, then roll into a long oblong and cut in four long strips.

Mix three-quarters of a pound of mince with two teaspoonfuls of salt and some mixed herbs or other flavouring. (If you have used lemon juice for your pastry, grate a little lemon rind and add to the meat.) Cut a thick slice of bread and soak it in water; don't squeeze the water out. Mix the wet bread with the meat. Divide into four, and make each quarter into a long sausage, the same length as the strips of pastry. Take a strip of pastry, roll it so as to make it a little broader, place the meat on it, and roll the pastry round it. Cut each of these long rolls into, say, five short lengths. Pinch both ends of each, make two little cuts across the top. Brush over with egg, and bake in a hot oven for full half an hour.

If you prefer to use sausages instead of mince, skin them before placing them in the pastry. You will find this method of making long rolls and cutting them into four or five small rolls much quicker than making each roll separately. Leave the rolls on the baking tin ready to pop into the oven to heat up before supper.

SANDWICH FILLINGS

Egg.—Three hard-boiled eggs. While still hot, peel them and add a good tablespoonful of margarine or butter, a teaspoonful of salt, some pepper, and cut them up with a knife till the whole is a spreadable paste. Then add a good tablespoonful of chopped parsley. This egg mixture might be put into sandwich rolls. If lettuce is available, it could be used instead of parsley.

Sardine.—The great secret of good sardine sandwiches is to add vinegar to the beaten up sardine, so don't forget it.

Tomato.—These do not need a recipe. They might be made with brown bread for a change. Remember to put butter on both sides of the bread; it really is not worth while being economical over sandwiches. (And be sure to put enough of the filling to let the guests know what kind of sandwich they are eating. I once had sardine sandwiches and banana sandwiches at a party, and I never knew which kind I was eating. They both tasted alike—partly because the same knife had been used to prepare them. So, do be careful!)

Cheese.—A very good filling is made with hard-boiled egg beaten up with grated cheese and melted margarine and salt and mustard. But you can make excellent cheese sandwiches with grated cheese alone, made into a spreadable mixture with a little milk, or, better still, cream, if you have it; it is ever so much nicer than grated cheese by itself. If, however, you use grated cheese by itself, put it on little round oatcakes or wheaten biscuits after buttering them. Do not put a moist cheese mixture on them because it makes them soft.

For variety you could have cheese straws instead. You could easily make them after you have made your sausage rolls.

CHEESE STRAWS

> Three ounces of flour;
> One and half ounces of fat (lard and margarine mixed);
> One yolk of egg;
> Salt, pepper and cayenne;
> Three ounces of grated cheese.

Rub the fat into the flour, add the cheese, salt, pepper and cayenne, then mix in the yolk of egg to make a stiff paste. Roll out and cut into straws and cut some into rings. Bake till crisp. Slip the straws through the rings when serving.

Parting Soup Cup.

Another job which must be done the day before the party is to make a pot of good soup. Get a pound of hough (as we say in Scotland, or shin beef, in England), and let it boil and boil and boil with a carrot, a turnip, an onion, and a bit of celery (the little extra flavour that makes all the difference). Next day skim off any fat and add enough meat essence to make it an attractive colour. Then, when your guests go to " put on their things ", run and see that the soup is heating and give them all a cup before they leave, and they will bless you all the way home. As somebody said once, " It's like central heating!"

SWEET THINGS

Here we are talking about going home and the guests have not even arrived yet. But while we are talking about the preparations in the kitchen the day before the party, we may as well decide what sweet things are to be on the supper table. Have one really grand cake in the middle of the table—iced and decorated. It does give a festive air to the supper. If the party is a birthday one, the cake will have candles; when they are lit, turn out all the other lights and sit in the lovely, soft, mysterious candle-light for a minute or two. But, besides the fruity, rich centre cake, have a plain sponge with jam or cream in it, a nice home-made gingerbread, some Empire biscuits, some parkins or shortbread and chocolate biscuits. I never met anyone yet at a party who refused a chocolate biscuit even after they had officially finished their supper.

If you are having trifles and jellies and lemonade, it is quite a good plan to have them after the regular supper is past. That lets you get the table tidied up and the little plates and spoons for the trifles set down with the lemonade and glasses. If you are planning two suppers, you will need to have the first about 9 o'clock and the other about 11.30.

FRUIT CUP

2 oranges;
2 lemons;
½ teacup lime juice;
8 teacups of water;
6 lumps of sugar;
3 tablespoonfuls of castor sugar.

Rub three of the lumps of sugar on to the lemon rinds and three on to the orange rinds. Squeeze and strain the juice of the oranges and lemons through a coarse sieve. Add the lumps of sugar, the castor sugar, the lime juice and the water and stir well till dissolved.

If you have opened a tin of pineapple or raspberries or, in fact, any fruit, for your trifle, keep a little of it and add it to your fruit cup. If pineapple, shred it, but if raspberries just have a few whole ones floating in the cup. And, of course, if you have a refrigerator, chill the cup before serving it.

TRIFLE

Put a large sponge cake into a glass dish after having split it twice across, and spread one of the splits with raspberry jam and the other with lemon curd.

Open a tin of fruit—raspberries or peach slices, or any other you may fancy—and pour it over the sponge cake. Then make a pint of custard according to the directions on the packet, and pour it over and set the whole aside to cool. When cool, spread with whipped cream, and decorate with a few pieces of whatever fruit you may have used for the trifle.

JELLIES

These can be made according to the directions on the packet, but they may be varied in many ways. For instance, a nicely flavoured jelly can be made from a large bottle of kola. Measure the kola into a basin, and allow one tablespoonful of gelatine to every large breakfast cup of the liquid. Heat a little of the liquid and stir in the gelatine till it dissolves, then add it to the rest of the kola. Pour into individual glasses and serve with a dab of whipped cream on the top.

Jelly may be varied by adding some tinned fruit to the liquid jelly or by pouring the hot jelly on to a sponge cake spread with jam.

THE INVITATIONS

Now let us return to the guests. You have now made up your mind whom to invite, and, I suppose, being a modern maid, you may invite them by telephone, though in my young days we were very fond of inviting our guests in poetry (so-called!), and some of them replied in the same form, which made getting the answers very entertaining. When I say " poetry ", I don't mean anything more elaborate than:

> " If you're feeling well and hearty
> Come on Friday to our party ",

and so on, with all the other details and perhaps ending with:

> " We'll have games and dances too,
> Say you'll come dear Mabel (or Johnny, or Jessie) do!"

I remember once getting a reply which began:

> " We have revelled there before
> And your parties we adore ",

which gave us a comfortable feeling of satisfaction and helped to allay that inferiority complex that sometimes assails the hostess as the important date draws near.

PROGRAMME

Now, what about the programme? The idea is to have a competition and a dance alternately, and the competitions must be of two kinds—games of skill and brainy games. At the very beginning, however, we must have a good mixing competition to make the guests move about, to encourage them to talk to each other, and to fill in the awkward half-hour at the outset till everybody arrives. If we are going to work in teams, we must have every team complete if possible at the very beginning of the scoring, so arrange an introductory game for which the score will not count. A familiar one is:

CELEBRITIES

Write names of well-known people on pieces of paper and, as the guests come into the lounge, pin a name on their backs. Their job is to find out who they are and, to do this, they ask questions of all the other guests, who must only answer yes or no. This makes everybody walk about, and it forces the shy folk to talk. When they have guessed, they go back to the door and get another name.

An alternative to this might be to have all the games of skill that you mean to do later in the evening set out in the lounge, and to tell each arrival that he or she may have a practice before the others arrive, so that her team may have good marks. Now let's settle what our games of skill are to be.

QUOITS

This is always popular and, if you cannot get the necessary wooden peg and rope rings, a small box or a hat can be put on the floor with a chalk ring marked round it 12 inches or so away from it. Get six playing cards and mark on the floor with chalk a suitable distance for the competitors to stand. They then throw the cards one by one; if a card goes into the box it counts three, if it lies within the ring it counts one, but if it is touching the ring at any point, it counts nothing. If you have a proper quoit peg, put a ring round it also, and give the same marks—three if on the peg and one if in the ring.

GOLF PUTTING

This can only be done if you can beg, borrow, or steal a " hole " to putt into. They are usually made of tin with sloping sides up which the ball must run to get into the hole. Mark six tees at different distances from the hole. It will be easy enough to provide a putter and a golf ball.

DRIED PEA RACE

Put a pile of dried peas in the middle of a card table. Place empty saucers round the table, one for each member of the team; with a drinking straw at each. The player sits down, puts a straw in his mouth, and, by breathing in, he can hold a pea at the end of the straw. He must then convey the pea to his saucer and place it there by breathing out. A time-keeper gives the players two minutes —by the way, they all do the race at the same time—and then they count how many peas they have managed to collect. You can guess that laughter is the greatest handicap in this race, and that seeing with the corner of your eye that your neighbour is amassing great quantities of peas in his saucer has a most paralysing effect on your own efforts.

DARTS

This is always exciting if you can get hold of a dart board, but a warning is necessary. The board should, if possible, be put in a room by itself, away from all the other competitions, because darts flying from unskilled hands are not at all safe in a room full of people.

WALL QUOITS

Another good game, if you can borrow the necessary rubber rings and a numbered board with hooks on it. The board could very easily be made at home with a few cup hooks screwed into a bit of wood and numbered according to fancy, but the rubber rings would have to be the real thing.

For both wall quoits and darts a bit of chalk will be needed to mark where the competitors are to stand, so don't forget to have it looked out before the party begins. Even though you know exactly where to lay your hands on a bit of chalk, things have a tiresome way of becoming invisible just the very minute they are wanted.

COMPETITIONS

Now we must decide on our competition. It is essential that they should strike the happy medium of being not too brainy and not too simple, because, if they are too difficult, your guests will just give up trying and will begin to talk about something else, and, if they are too simple, everybody will have the same marks and you won't know who has won the prize.

JUMBLES

This is a useful puzzle which anybody can do; the names of towns or animals or birds with the letters mixed will require a little intellignce to guess them, but not too much. Print the names in block capitals like this:

Jumbled Towns. 1. I LOP LOVER (LIVERPOOL). 2. BREW KNIT ROCH (NORTH BERWICK).

Ten would perhaps be enough.

It might be better to have jumbled birds or flowers or animals, because towns are more interesting made into a puzzle like the following:

Scottish Towns. 1. A colour—a Scottish river (Dundee). 2. A relative in good health (Motherwell). You can make up any number in similar fashion, but perhaps in this puzzle also, ten will be sufficient.

IMPS AND KATES AND AGES

There is a big assortment of games which I am grouping under this heading—you know the sort of thing?

Imps. 1. An imp which is cheeky (impertinent). 2. An imp who pretends to be somebody else (impostor), and so on. Look up the dictionary for some more.

Kate. 1. This Kate is not very strong (delicate). This Kate chews her food (masticate).

Age. 1. What age is a vegetable? (cabbage). 2. What age is a game? (cribbage).

GATHERING OF THE CLANS

Every answer must be a name beginning with Mac. 1. Mac—a narrow road (Maclean.) 2. Mac—relatives—not (Mackinnon). 3. Mac—a church dignitary (Macvicar), and so on.

PARTS OF THE BODY

In this puzzle the answer in every case must be a part of the body. 1. Found in a joiner's shop (nails). 2. An animal (heart or hair). 3. A fish (sole).

There is a slightly more difficult form of the same game. Again every answer must be part of the body. The hostess chooses ten quotations, each containing the name of a part of the body. She writes them out, leaving that name blank. For instance:

1. Long —— veiled a light (lashes).
   That had else been all too bright.
2. Her —— is like the snawdrift (brow)
   Her —— is like the swan (neck).

3. He said that Love had curled my —— (hands)
   To cling about his —— (heart).
4. And Beauty draws us with a single —— (hair).

CHRISTIAN NAMES

Make a list of well-known people, either alive or dead, and ask the competitors to tell their Christian names. In the case of people who are always known by their initials, it is surprising how ignorant we often are.

CELEBRITIES

Cut from the illustrated papers photographs of well-known people in the world of art, letters, theatre, cinema and sport. Number them, and get the teams to name them. You will find that you will have to begin preparing for this competition long before the party. There always seems to be a great dearth of photographs just when you are looking for them, and you will want at least ten.

All these games of skill and these competitions should be done by small teams of guests, from four to six in each team. It is a good plan to put the different competitions in different rooms or in different corners. For instance, you might have a brainy competition done in the quietness of the staircase and a game of skill might be arranged in the hall or on the landing or in a bedroom. The Pea Race, which needs a time-keeper, should be kept in the lounge so that the time-keeper may have a comfortable chair at the fire. It is, however, rather nice to do some competitions all together, letting all the teams do the same competition at the same time, but of course keeping their answers strictly to themselves. So let us think of a few such competitions. First in popularity I would place a *Musical Tale*, where the teller of the tale sits at the piano and begins perhaps like this:

Once upon a time a man named (Duncan Gray) loved a girl named (Barbara Allen). They met every evening (On the banks of Allan Water) and he gave her (A Crooked Bawbee), and so on. In each case the teller plays the tune instead of naming it. If, however, a story is too much bother to make up, the pianist might just play ten unconnected tunes for the others to guess. It is wonderful how often we can hum the tune and yet be quite unable to name it.

Warn the teams not to shout out their answers in the excitement of the moment.

Another competition which is better done by the whole party at once is the *Memory Test*. This can be done, either by reading aloud a list of articles twice, and seeing how many the team can remember of them, or twenty articles can be placed on a tray and put in the middle of the floor for a few minutes and then removed before letting the teams write down how many of them they can remember. You will probably find that the members of your team who did not know a single one of the tunes played will shine in the memory test and thus regain their self-respect.

ONE MAN CHARADES

When the company is all assembled in the lounge would be a good time to do some One Man Charades. The hostess herself should do them as they must be thought out beforehand. Here are a few suggestions. First word—*Repeat*. She says, " This is the first syllable ", and then she acts a man wielding a scythe. (She'll certainly need to practise that beforehand!) " This is the second syllable," she says, and proceeds to eat some imaginary food, working her jaws with excessive energy. Then she says, " Whole word ", and recites a nursery rhyme. She might do it twice, but this will probably not be necessary. Here are a few more suitable words. *Sceptic*. 1. Rush about the room after an imaginary swarm of bees, murmuring perhaps, " Of course they *would* choose a Sunday!" then at last confine them in an imaginary hive. This, of course, could not be done outside of Scotland, as I'm afraid the word *Skep* would be quite unknown elsewhere. *Tic* might be acted by holding an imaginary watch to the ear, then shaking it and listening again with a dismal, " Not a sound!" The whole word might be done by simply saying emphatically, " I don't believe it ".

Dozens of words will suggest themselves. I add only one more. *Admire*. With a paper in her hand she adds an imaginary column of figures, " 9*d.* and 4*d.*, 1/1, and 8*d.*, 1/9 and 4*d.*, 2/1 ". The second syllable might be a little more elaborate. With a tea-cosy on her head she might walk in a queenly manner across the room, suddenly stopping and saying, " I cannot put my foot there ". Then, turning to an unseen attendant, she smiles graciously and says, " Thank you ", walks on a few steps, turns again in his direction, and says,

" Rise, Sir Walter Raleigh ". The whole word might be done by talking in a very complimentary way about the dress of one of the guests or enthusing about a flower in a vase. By the way, never actually *say* the word—merely suggest it.

DANCES

Now what about dances, because a dance between games and competitions warms the guests up both physically and spiritually. Well, of course, the dances chosen must be those the hostess likes herself, but she will probably find that old-fashioned or country dances will be much jollier than all ballroom two-somes. Even simple things, which can hardly be called dances at all, such as " Grand Old Duke of York " and " Cumberland Reel ", will be far more of a success than modern gliding measures, and an Eightsome Reel will always be a howling success in more ways than one. If nobody feels competent to play it, there are splendid records to be had of it, and it will be a fine ploy for Daddy to keep the gramophone wound up and to re-start the record when necessary (unless he is the kind of Daddy who wouldn't miss an Eightsome or the Hay-makers for anything, and whose ear-splitting " Hoochs " put the efforts of the young to shame). I think it would be a good plan to keep the dances to Dashing White Sergeant, Strip the Willow, Haymakers and Palais Glide—these will all go well even on a carpeted floor.

PREPARING THE HOUSE

When you clear the lounge for the party, leave as little furniture in it as you possibly can. Put the chairs into bedrooms or into the hall, and remove any of Mother's precious ornaments that may be swept off the mantelpiece or the bureau in the exuberance of the dance. Then do not forget to vacuum the carpet very thoroughly. It is going to be well danced on, so, the cleaner it is the better. Your guests will probably overrun the whole house, so have every room clean and tidy and presentable. During the competitions they may seek a quiet corner, and you want them to feel that they have the freedom of the house.

If you are running the party without domestic help, have plenty of clean dish-towels handy in the scullery. Some of the guests will be sure to offer to wash up after supper. Well, let them do it. It will all be part of the entertainment, and even washing-up can be fun in the right company. Leave the eatables on the dining-room table and, if you are having a second supper with trifles and jellies and lemonade, set these things on the table with the necessary plates and spoons and glasses. Also lay out ready on trays the cups for the soup that you are going to give the party as a nightcap.

You will find after supper No. 1 that the girls who are not helping to wash up will want to powder their noses or tidy their hair, and the men will want to have a smoke and a talk by themselves, so, while the domesticated guests are busy in the scullery, let those others have half an hour to chat before settling down to the programme again.

PROGRAMME

Let us try now to make up a model programme. While the guests are arriving, do some good mixing game such as I suggested at the beginning—"Who am I?" Then, when everybody has arrived, tell each the number of their team and give the captain of each team a notebook and a pencil. You, yourself, had better have a notebook and pencil too, in which you have the correct answers to all the competitions, and in which you will enter the scores of each team as they are made.

You may, of course, want to be in a team yourself, and if you have made up all the competitions yourself that is not very practicable, so here's where Daddy and Mother will come in handy. Let them each make up a competition and not tell you the answers and you will do the same; then one of them can take your place in the team when it comes to the competition that you have made up, and that will let you have the fun of the party as well as your guests. If, for instance, you have made up the Musical Tale yourself, Mother could take your place as the guesser while you play the tunes and tell the tale.

Every house will need a different arrangement of games, but probably there could be four items going on in the lounge: for instance, one table with the Dried Peas Race, two others with competitions on them, and perhaps the Cards in a Hat competition in the middle of the floor. The other competitions and games could be in the bedrooms, hall or stair.

Now let us suppose that you have four guests in each team and six teams. Tell Team 1 to start at Competition 1, Team 2 at Com-

petition 2, and so on, and, when they have finished, the captain is to
come to you (or Daddy; he will almost certainly want to keep the
score) and get his paper corrected and his score entered in the book.
When every team has finished the first competition, have a dance;
then Team 1 goes to Competition 2, and Team 2 to Competition 3,
and so on. The hour of supper No. 1 will depend on circumstances,
but don't make it too late if you are going to attempt to have a
second sit-down meal in the course of the evening.

If you are not going to have a second meal you might produce
ice cream at a certain time, and serve it with a tinned pear or peach
in little individual glasses. It could be handed round in the lounge.
Nobody will mind being interrupted in their games or dances by
such a delectable thing as a Pêche Melba!

PROPOSED PROGRAMME

1. " Who am I?" or, instead, practising the games of skill.
2. Dance—Grand Old Duke of York.
3. Competition—" Jumbles " or " Scottish Towns ".
4. Dance—Dashing White Sergeant.
5. Competition—Quoits or Wall Quoits.
6. Dance—Palais Glide.
7. Competition—" Imps " or " Kates " or " Ages ".
8. Dance—Eightsome Reel.
9. Supper.
10. Dance—Cumberland Reel.
11. Competition—Golf Putting.
12. Dance—Strip the Willow.
13. Competition—Christian Names or Photographs of Celebrities.
14. Dance—Petronella.
15. Competition—Dried Peas Race.
16. Dance—Haymakers.
17. Ice Cream or Second Supper.
18. A Musical Tale.
19. Dance—Eightsome Reel.
20. Competition—" Parts of the Body " or " Quotations ".
21. Dance—Push the Business On.
22. One Man Charades.
23. Prize Giving.
24. Auld Lang Syne.

You will notice that I have suggested the game or dance called " Push the Business On ". Make a big ring with the men keeping their partners on their right-hand side. Dance round, singing:

> " We'll hire a horse and steal a gig,
> And all the world will dance a jig.
> And I'll do all that ever I can
> To push the business on."

For the chorus each man turns to his partner at his right hand and swings her round, singing:

> " To push the business on, to push the business on,
> And I'll do all that ever I can to push the business on."

At the end of the chorus, he places his partner on his *left side*, so at the end of verse two, he finds he has a new partner to swing, and this goes on till everybody is exhausted!

CHARADE WARNING

Now it may be that somebody at the party will be very keen to do a charade, and this can certainly be great fun, but there are dangers connected with it. First, it can ruin a party if the actors take too long to choose a word, or too long to dress up, however funny they may look when they appear, or too long to arrange how they will act the word, however cleverly they do it at length. They *must* remember that the most of the guests are sitting in the lounge waiting for them—doing nothing, not able to begin a conversation because they know that at any minute the door may open and the actors appear. I have known a really hilarious party ruined by a too slowly produced charade, so the hostess should have a list of words ready herself and should also have asked one or two of the guests to have a charade thought out beforehand, and all those who leave the room to do one should realize that the success of the show depends on the speed of its production and the brevity of its pauses.

During the pauses of the charade, Daddy should be adding up the score and finding out the winning teams, and the hostess should have her prizes ready. The prizes should never be expensive. They should bear the mark of the sixpenny store rather than that of Bond Street, but there should be a good deal of fuss over the presentation, and the captain of the winning team should be persuaded to make a speech on behalf of his " men ".

Then the time comes when the wraps must be put on and the slippers taken off and, while that is being done, the hostess should run and put on the soup to heat so that, when the guests reach the dining-room door, booted and spurred, the hot cup may be ready for them. Then off home, not in teams now, but more probably in pairs, and, as the talking and laughing dies away in the distance, the young hostess shuts the front door and tumbles into bed, too sleepy even to dream, but, I hope, feeling that her party has been a huge success.

THE PERFECT GUEST

The happy hostess is she whose guests have obviously appreciated her hospitality and contributed to the pleasure of her party. As a guest, how does one so please one's hostess?

In the first place, by conforming to the rules of conduct indicated in her invitation, and following the lead she gives you. You will frame your reply to her invitation in exactly the same manner as she adopts, casual, or formal. Reply promptly, and in the case of a week-end invitation or a longer visit, let your hostess know the time and manner of your arrival—by train, bus, or whatever it may be—so that she can make her arrangements in time to have you met.

INTRODUCTIONS

According to the type of invitation you receive, you will wear formal or informal dress. You will arrive neither before, nor many minutes after, the time for which you were invited. On introduction to other guests, you will not lapse into a shy silence after the first " How do you do " (which is still more acceptable here than the American " Pleased to meet you "), but you will forget yourself and endeavour to make conversation with your fellow guests. If they are complete strangers, this may seem difficult, but you will find that if you really give your mind to it, concentrating your interest on the other person, casual questions and remarks will lead on until you find some mutual interest upon which you can really talk.

Even if you are not particularly interested in something which obviously fascinates your fellow guest, you should draw her out on the subject and let her do the talking. Strange as it may seem, the art of conversation does not depend on talking, but rather on listening, and if you learn to be a good listener, you may find that you have somehow earned a reputation for being a good conversationalist! That is, you must genuinely listen, with interest and attention, so that your occasional remarks or responses give your fellow guest confidence to continue the conversation. This is an essential requirement in a dinner guest, or at any meal, for you help your hostess immeasurably by keeping the conversational ball rolling.

Avoid the temptation to enclose yourself in a familiar little clique where you need not make any effort to be sociable because you all know each other well and just talk " shop ". If you feel shy, try to remember that your shyness is apt to make other guests uncomfortable, and you have a duty as a guest to spread a sense of enjoyment, not distress.

A further word on the subject of introductions. It is not necessary always to shake hands, and at a dance or any function where you are being introduced to a number of people in succession, it is preferable not to do so. A bow will serve instead, and this simply means a courteous inclination of the head. But whether you decide to bow only, or shake hands, make your decision so definite that it is clear to the other guest what you intend to do and you thus avoid embarrassing confusion. If you happen to be seated when an introduction takes place, you need not rise unless the other guest is a much older person.

HOUSE-GUEST

As a house-guest, you will be treated as a privileged person, however much at home your hostess will make you feel, but more than any other kind of guest civility demands your utmost consideration towards your hostess. Conform to the rules of the household as you know them or learn them.

Avoid giving trouble or making extra work by carelessness or untidiness. Your bedroom and the bathroom should be as orderly when you leave them as when you first entered. Be punctual for meals and appointments. If the household is without maids, offer to help dry dishes, or lay meals, or make your own bed as you would do at home.

You will be encouraged to indulge your own preferences in every form of occupation and entertainment, but your company will be the more agreeable if you choose something you know to be generally acceptable. Try to learn to recognize when your hostess has other matters demanding her attention and would prefer you to amuse yourself. Take sewing or knitting, or a book, or letters to write on your visit, and occupy yourself with these when your hostess is busy, but don't allow yourself to become too absorbed in them!

You may be anxious, as a guest, about certain points of etiquette, and afraid of not doing things in the right way. Nowadays we have a much less rigid code than was observed some years ago, and you can be assured that good manners will carry you a long way. Good manners, remember, are based on consideration for one's neighbour, not on any elaborate set of rules. The story of Queen Victoria accepting tea in a cottage, and drinking it from her saucer, as her host did, is a case in point. This would not have been regarded as " good manners " in the Palace, where drinking tea out of cups was the recognized practice and most agreeable to the majority. But by refraining from emphasizing the difference in their habit, which arose from their differing stations in life, the Queen showed extreme politeness to her host.

The most generally accepted conventions, when you examine them, prove to be quite sensible rules of conduct, designed to simplify living in crowds as we do, not to complicate life. We are taught to eat quietly and inconspicuously; to sit erect; to manipulate our knives and forks in a certain way; to speak in moderate tones not with shrill voices, and not to interrupt other conversations; to show deference to our elders; and a dozen other customs, because by doing so we prevent our natural, selfish, untrained selves turning our social life into the sort of bear-garden you may see and hear in a small boys' school dining hall when they are without supervision.

TABLE MANNERS

If you are at an elaborate meal, and, confronted with a bewildering collection of knives and forks, chance to use the wrong implement, no one will think your manners shockingly bad. If you remember that you work from the outside of the array inwards, in the order of the courses, you will avoid this embarrassment. Don't be nervous of eating unfamiliar food. Your hostess may have provided it as a special attraction, and your timidity will not only disappoint her, but cause you to miss a real experience and pleasure, and certainly diminish the extent of your social knowledge.

Rather than try to cover up uncertainty in the knowledge of procedure at table or in any other respect, be quite frank and simply ask what to do, if you can't find out by quietly watching other guests.

The question of drinks is one which most parents wisely answer in the negative, or prefer to be present when they are dispensed. There is no social distinction whatsoever in drinking cocktails, neither is there any stigma attached to the person who refuses and expresses a preference for a soft drink. Make no mistake about this. An ignorant bravado is foolish and embarrassing to older people looking on. A self-righteous refusal is silly in another way, and equally embarrassing to the onlooker. A politely casual refusal and a request for some other kind of drink is not merely inoffensive but dignified and proper.

THE GENTLEMAN'S PRIVILEGE

There are certain services which a gentleman should perform for a lady, and it is courteous for you to give him the opportunity to do so, such as opening a door for you to precede him, or handing you out of a car, or drawing out your chair from a meal table, or thanking you for a dance and accompanying you to your seat. On the other hand, he sometimes has to take his cue from you, and you must be awake to the fact that if he rises from a chair when you enter a room, he cannot resume his seat if you stand and talk unless you ask him to do so. He may want to smoke, and if you are not a smoker will ask your permission, which you should grant in such a manner that he is not uncomfortable every time he lights a cigarette.

A golden rule for any guest is, " Be yourself ". You may be invited to a party where most of the guests are much older than yourself. Don't attempt to be as sophisticated as you think they are. You will impress no one and only make yourself look foolish. Be natural, and you will find yourself being treated as an equal. Should you be in the company of youngsters, don't be aloof and think you can't enjoy yourself among " such kids ". Throw yourself into the party, just as they do, and let yourself go. There is no doubt you will enjoy it as much as the children, and probably be a great success yourself.

Your hostess will have given a good deal of thought to your entertainment, and you should recognize this and meet her half-way by appreciation of her efforts. Your thanks for her hospitality, at the end of the evening or of your visit, should never be omitted. You should give yourself time to say " thank you ", however simply you may do it, unhurriedly and cordially, as if you really meant it.

A " bread-and-butter letter " is a term sometimes used for a letter of thanks from a house-guest to her hostess after a visit. It is still a very good thing to write, but there is no need to strain yourself over it. Again, be natural and simple, and your hostess will gain real pleasure from your courtesy.

You may begin your visit by bringing your hostess a small gift, of flowers if she lives in town, or of something she cannot easily obtain for herself if she lives in the country, or perhaps sweets for the children. You may leave a tip for the maid before you return home.

HOSTESS DUTIES

If it should happen that you are the hostess, the first service you perform for your guest is to convey to her in the invitation as much as possible concerning the nature of the occasion. A formal invitation—" Miss Mary Smith requests the pleasure of Miss Elizabeth Brown's company "—whether to dinner and the theatre, or to a dance, indicates formal evening dress, and especially in the case of a dance you will also state the time when the function ends, in order that your guest may make her arrangements for getting home.

Your first duty will be to receive your guests, and as soon as possible make introductions. There is nothing alarming in this simple but essential ceremony if you remember that the lady is the important person to whom a gentleman is introduced—if she wishes it. The old formula is, " Miss Brown (or Elizabeth), may I introduce Mr. Jones (or Bill Jones)?" " Mr. Jones (or Bill)—Miss Brown (or Elizabeth)." When you are introducing two ladies, the older, or married one, is the important person, and in that case you say, " Mrs. Green, may I introduce Miss Brown?" " Miss Brown— Mrs. Green."

When the occasion is definitely informal, and you write a friendly note, or even phone, your invitation should still help your friend to know what you plan to do, what to wear, and when to leave. Remember, when you invite a house-guest, that every family doesn't do things in the same way. If you know that in some habits or customs your family differs from your friend's, let her know beforehand, in order that she may not be embarrassed. Here are some points she will want to be assured on: Meal hours; breakfast up, or in bed; grace at meals; changing for dinner; any household duties to be undertaken; church on Sunday; baths; and bedtime.

You need not be afraid of being quite simple on a formal occasion, but informal or formal, you should be quite definite, first in the manner of your invitation, and secondly, in your lead to your guests, showing them what to expect.

All these are not rigid rules of conduct; they are thoughtful gestures, and will help to smooth your path in the social world.

HOUSEKEEPER FOR A WEEK

Can you picture the scene at the breakfast table? Mother reading a letter—a very worried look on her face. Suddenly she says: " Granny is ill and wants me to go to her. How *can* I leave you all? Daddy at work, and John and Mary both at school, and nobody to get you all out in time in the morning, or have a fire and a meal ready for you in the evening. How can I possibly go?"

Then Mary thinks: " Oh, what a good chance for me! I'm certain I could manage to run the house for a week or two and yet not stay away from school. I couldn't miss school with the exams coming so near." And she finds herself saying: " Oh, Mummy, do go. I'm sure I could manage beautifully if Daddy and John would help me. Please don't worry about us, Mummy. I'm certain Granny needs you more than we do."

This section of *The Girl's Companion* might be called " An Open Letter to Mary ". Mother may have had to rush off without having had much time to leave her many instructions. Or perhaps it is Mother herself who has been suddenly taken ill, and whipped off without much warning to a hospital. In any case, whatever the circumstances of the domestic crisis which has left Mary in supreme command of the household, here are a few hints for her how to run the house, go to school, and look after Daddy and John, so that, when Mother comes back, and the household returns to its normal smooth running, Daddy may be able to report that they had all been warm and cheerful and well fed under Mary's management.

Well, Mary, first of all a *warning*. Do not attempt to do too much —just accomplish the essentials, and these are:

1. Good meals.
2. A warm and tidy fireside.
3. Beds made daily.
4. Dishes all washed.

Under unessentials I would class—polishing floors, cleaning brass and windows and silver. I wish I could also say that washing was not essential, and, if Mother is to be away only for a week or even a fortnight, you *could* leave it, but, to let washing accumulate is a major mistake. The dish towel you use, for instance, you should wash out every day. Don't fling it in the dirty clothes basket and take a clean one, however attractive that may be. If you do, you will have half a dozen horrid smelly things waiting for you to wash when Saturday comes round. If I were you, I'd try just to use *one*, and wash it through every day. Pour a little boiling water on it and leave it to soak a few minutes in soap powder, then rub it through and rinse it and hang it up to dry ready for the next day.

We will presume that there is a gas or electric cooker in the house, so that getting the breakfast won't take you very long in the morning. Do not let that entice you to lie so long in bed in the morning that there's only time for breakfast making and for nothing more. There is one job at any rate that you had better do before you go to school, and that is setting the fire ready for the evening. There's nothing will make Daddy miss Mother so much as to come in from his work and find the ashes of yesterday's fire still lying in the grate. Tidy up the fireside in the morning and put the ashes in the bin, and don't forget to put some sticks to dry every day, because damp sticks won't burn, and there's nothing more aggravating than a fire which refuses to " go ". Rake it well out. Lay a sheet of newspaper loosely in the bottom, then three half sheets rolled up separately into long " sausages " and then twisted round and round into tight rings. Three of these rings go on the top of the paper, then a few sticks, then the cinders from the previous evening, then a few small bits of coal. All it needs now is a match from whoever is first home in the evening. There's nothing so welcoming as a cheery fire, so try to have it always lit before Daddy comes home.

Before you set that fire in the morning though, put on the porridge, for I think you'll find porridge and toast the easiest breakfast to have. Many people make porridge " by rule of thumb ", but that's not much use to a novice, so here are some useful quantities to remember.

Porridge.

A teacupful of oatmeal needs four teacups of water and a teaspoonful of salt, and it will make enough porridge for three or four people. Measure the teacup of meal into a bowl, and add to it two teacups of water and a teaspoonful of salt. Put the other two cups of water into a pan and, when it boils, add the meal and water from the bowl, stirring all the time till the whole is boiling. Put the lid on the pan and reduce the heat. While it is simmering away, go and do the fireside and set the fire ready to be lit in the evening. Come back and lay the breakfast table, then light the grill, and turn the heat to go downwards. (The porridge will keep boiling on the top while the toast is doing underneath.) Light a ring and put on the kettle, and, while you are waiting for it to boil, make the toast. Have you ever tried savoury toast for breakfast? Here is the recipe for it.

Savoury Toast.

Cut a thick slice of bread for everybody. Toast it on both sides, and spread it with butter or margarine while it is still hot, then spread it with a thin layer of Bovril or Oxo, and eat it as soon as ever you can.

After you have made the tea for breakfast, fill up the kettle and put it on again for the dishes. Here is where Daddy and John will come in handy! Get them to wash the breakfast dishes while you go and tidy yourself for school, and try to find time, too, to make the beds, for it *is* disheartening to come in in the afternoon and find an unmade bed yawning at you.

Now let us suppose that the whole family can have some lunch at school or in town in the middle of the day, and that the main meal will be in the evening. That meal had better be more of a dinner than a tea, so Mary will have to do a little preparation for it beforehand—for instance, if she wants to have soup. Perhaps she will say: " Oh, I can easily buy a tin of soup and heat it up," but I think she will find it easier in the end to make a good big pot of broth which will last at least three days, and will only take a few minutes to heat up every evening. If you buy tinned soup, you will need a new tin every day and you will have soup only; but, if you make broth, the meat that you have made it with will be delicious eaten cold with beetroot. You can buy the beetroot ready boiled, and, when you get it home, take it in your hand and rub the skin off, holding it under the tap to get it quite clean. Then slice it into a dish and pour vinegar on to it. And there's your vegetable all ready for dinner!

Broth.

Get two pounds of leg of mutton from the butcher, or of mutton which he has boned and rolled. It will be much easier to slice when it is cold if it has been prepared like this beforehand. Put it into a big pot and cover it with three quarts of water and a tablespoonful of salt. When it boils, turn the gas down to a peep to keep it simmering. While it is boiling, take a teacupful of barley, put it in a bowl of water and wash it well in two or three waters, then add it to the soup. Take a bit of turnip, two or three carrots, a few small onions and a few leeks. Peel and clean them, then put them through the mincer (this is far quicker than cutting them up by hand) and add them to the soup. Chopped parsley should be added before serving the broth and after taking it off the heat. If you have the broth for several days, add fresh chopped parsley each day. You may be sure that, if you do, Daddy will remark: " This broth gets better and better every day !"

After the broth is cold on the first day, take out the meat and put it on a clean dish. Also remove the fat which you will find in a hard cake covering the soup. Don't throw it away. It will make a lovely tasty dish which we will call:

Hasty Pudding.

Weigh the fat and make it up to a quarter of a pound with lard or margarine if necessary. Put it in a small pan and, when it is melted, add quarter of a pound of oatmeal. Stir till boiling, then add a teaspoonful of salt, a little pepper, and a small onion cut up roughly, and a breakfastcup of water. Keep stirring till it boils, then empty it into a piedish. When you want to use it, put it in the oven for three-quarters of an hour, and serve it with boiled potatoes. Or, if you have any potatoes left over, mash them and heat them in the oven with the pudding.

Pea Soup.

> Half a pound of split peas;
> Three pints of water;
> Three small onions;
> A bit of turnip and three carrots.

Wash the peas and soak them in the water overnight. Next day put them on to boil with the vegetables, which you have washed and peeled and put through the mincer. Add pepper and salt and a tablespoonful of margarine and a little milk. If you have parsley, add some chopped before serving. Boil for at least two hours.

It is a good plan always to have potatoes with the evening meal. You don't need to spend time peeling them. Just wash them and cover them with cold water and a handful of salt, and let them boil for about twenty minutes. Then pour them and leave them with the lid tight on at the side of the fire for about twenty minutes to steam.

If any of your Hasty Pudding is left, cut it in slices and fry it with bacon. Always serve it with potatoes. If you have any left and don't want to light the oven, mash them and fry them. Put a bit of fat into the frying pan and, when it is smoking hot, press the mashed potatoes in with a wooden spoon, turn the gas low, and leave them for about fifteen minutes. You will then find that they have a lovely brown crisp skin, and that a spoonful of them will go well with your bacon and Hasty Pudding.

I think if Mary is a novice at cooking, it will be safer for her to do most of it by steaming rather than by baking, because a steamed thing is not so easily spoilt, whereas, if you are busy with other things, you may perhaps forget to watch the dish in the oven, and something may be burnt. So let me suggest a steamed meat dish.

Meat Roll.

> Half a pound of mince;
> Quarter of a pound of ham (put through the mincer or cut up small with a knife);
> A very thick slice of bread;
> One egg;
> Pepper and salt;
> A tablespoonful of Worcester sauce or tomato sauce or ketchup.

Cut the crust off the bread and soak it well under the tap. Don't squeeze the water out, but put it into a bowl and add the other ingredients. Mix the whole very thoroughly with your hands, then put it in a bowl and cover it with a greased paper, and steam it for two hours. You need not keep the gas on all that time. It can be steaming at the sitting-room fire while you are at your lessons. Let the water in the pan go about half-way up the bowl, and see that it doesn't boil dry. You can tell by the sound if there is still water in the pan. If you are having it hot, serve it with a tin of beans and tomato sauce, and if it is cold, serve it with beetroot. If your housekeeping experiment is taking place in the summer, serve the roll with lettuce and tomato. In that case it will be much improved with a salad dressing, and here is a splendid one which needs no cooking at all.

Uncooked Salad Dressing.

> One hard-boiled yolk of egg;
> Two tablespoonfuls cream or top of milk;
> Pepper and salt;
> Quarter teaspoonful of made mustard;
> One dessertspoonful of vinegar.

Sieve the yolk of egg. Add the seasonings, then gradually work in the cream. Then add the vinegar. You can garnish the salad with the chopped white of the egg.

Now for one more meat dish which you are almost sure to want to have, and that is mince. Don't just plop the meat into a pan and cover it with water and leave it to stew away, or you will have an unsavoury-looking grey and lumpy substance for dinner, which perhaps may be nourishing enough, but certainly won't be in the least attractive.

Mince.

Put a tablespoonful of lard into a stewpan, and, when it is smoking hot, add the mince, and keep on breaking it up with the back of a wooden spoon. When it is all separated add a few onions peeled and cut up, and keep on stirring and browning. Then add water and salt and pepper, and leave it to stew for about an hour. Before serving, thicken it with a tablespoonful of cornflour rubbed smooth in a little cold water. If it is winter weather, make some " doughboys " and pop them in beside the mince while it is stewing.

" Doughboys ".

> Quarter of a pound of self-raising flour;
> Two ounces of dripping or lard or chopped suet;
> Half a teaspoonful of salt.

Rub the fat into the flour, then add enough water to make a stiff paste (don't dash the water in; add it gradually. It's fatally easy to make your mixture too soft!) Work it with your hands into a big ball. Cut the ball into eight, and roll each section into a small ball with your floury hands. Be sure your mince is boiling when you drop the balls into it. They will need about an hour to cook, and you will probably find that, when you have doughboys in the mince, it won't need any thickening, because they seem to thicken the gravy sufficiently themselves.

Now I expect you are thinking that these meat and savoury recipes are very dull indeed. Perhaps you will think it would be far simpler to fry sausages or bacon or have something out of a tin, and, of course, you will sometimes, but it is handy to know how to cook those other dishes by way of variety. Don't give John the chance to tell his friends that " the tin opener is our Mary's best friend ".

The thing that you will be really interested in producing will be the sweet dish—the pudding. Well, once again I think you'll find steamed puddings the most certain successes for a novice, so let me suggest some.

Seven Cup Pudding.

One teacup each of flour;
,,   ,,   breadcrumbs;
,,   ,,   suet;
,,   ,,   sugar;
,,   ,,   raisins;
,,   ,,   currants;
,,   ,,   milk;
Half a teaspoonful of baking soda;
One teaspoonful of cinnamon;
One egg.

Put all the dry things into a basin and rub them all together, then add the milk and mix well. Before you begin to make the pudding, put some water in a saucepan and let it come to the boil while you are mixing the pudding. When the pudding is well mixed, put it into a bowl which you have greased with a little bit of lard. Tie a cloth over the top and put the bowl carefully into the boiling water, and let it boil for about three hours. You could make any of those steamed puddings one night and then just heat them up the next night. They will need another half-hour's steaming to get them heated through, but remember, you can never steam a thing too long. It doesn't spoil if you cook it for twice the time that the cookery book says.

Roly-poly.

> Half a pound of self-raising flour;
> Quarter of a pound of lard or margarine or suet;
> A pinch of salt.

Rub the dry ingredients together, then add enough water to make a stiff paste. Put a little flour on to the baking board, and roll the paste out thin. Spread it with jam and roll it up (like a Swiss roll). Mother would probably then tie it in a cloth and boil it, but you will find it easier to pop it into a greased bowl (curl it round so as to get it in), and steam it for two hours.

Here is a hint which will save you having to wash the baking board. Don't use it at all! If you have a gas cooker, you will find it has an enamelled plate under the grill. Slip this plate out and roll your pastry on it. It will just need a wipe when you are finished, and can then be slipped back again.

Fig Pudding.

If figs are in season, this is a very simple pudding to make, and it tastes good too.

> Half a pound of flour (self-raising);
> Two ounces of lard or margarine;
> Half a pound of chopped figs (give them a wash before you chop them);
> A teacupful of syrup;
> A pinch of salt;
> A teacupful of milk.

Rub the lard into the flour, add the other ingredients, and pour into a greased bowl. Boil for two hours.

These three puddings are nicer if you serve them with custard, which you should make according to the directions on the packet, but the following quantities are good.

16

Pouring Custard.

Put a breakfastcupful of milk and water mixed on to boil, keeping back a little in the cup. Put in the cup a dessertspoonful of custard powder and a dessertspoonful of sugar. Rub them smooth, and add to the milk when it boils. Stir till it boils up again, then take off the fire.

If it is summer weather, you can open a tin of fruit and serve it with cold custard.

If you have any cakes in your tins which have gone hard, spread them with a little jam or a little tinned fruit which has been left over, then make a pint of table jelly according to the recipe on the packet, and pour it on to the cake.

Another way to make a jelly is to get a bottle of Kola or Orangeade or Lemonade. Measure the amount of liquid in the bottle and allow a tablespoonful of gelatine to each breakfastcupful of liquid. Heat a little of the liquid, and stir in the gelatine till it dissolves, then add the rest of the liquid and pour it into a dish to set. This plain jelly is nicer if served with cold custard.

I have told you how to use up dry cake. I think you are much more likely to land yourself with a lot of dry bread, and I know that if you tell John you are going to make a bread pudding, he will pull a long face and say something rude about it. But here is bread pudding which is quite as good as a dumpling, indeed, if you called it a dumpling, I believe he would ask for a second helping.

Brown Bread Pudding.

Half a pound of scraps of bread (and get the crock tidy!);
Three ounces of sugar;
Three ounces of raisins;
One teaspoonful of ginger;
Half a teaspoonful of cinnamon;
One egg;
Three ounces of suet or lard or margarine;
Three ounces of currants;
One teaspoonful of mixed spice;
A teaspoonful of baking soda;
Milk to mix.

Soak the bread in cold water while you collect the other things and put the pot on to boil, then squeeze it dry and put it in a basin.

Add the other ingredients. If you are using suet, chop it and add, but if you are using lard or margarine, melt it in a little milk. Mix all thoroughly, and pour it into a greased bowl and steam for two hours at least. This mixture could be baked, and, if so, it should be a little softer, so will need a little more milk in it.

Don't let Mother come home to find a bread crock full of hard bread or, worse still, of mouldy bits. Make odd bits into toast, and don't forget to wipe out the crock occasionally to remove any mouldy crumbs.

Now I'm not going to give you recipes for cakes and scones, because you can always buy what you need, and, in any case, I don't think you will have much time for baking if you have home lessons to do. Let me, instead, give you a little list of things to remember when you are the housekeeper. Indeed, we might head the list:

Don't Forget!

1. To put out the ashes and any empty tins or bottles *every day*.

2. To see that all shoes are cleaned in the evening ready for putting on next day. (There's sure to be a rush in the morning, however careful you are.)

3. To remove all scraps of food to the brock pail (if there *is* one in your street). If not, to burn every scrap. You don't want Mother to be greeted by a guard of honour of *mice* when she comes home!

4. If Daddy is away too, don't forget to wind the clocks every day, or every week. You're sure to be late for school if all the clocks in the house stop!

5. If Mother has a favourite plant, don't forget to water it.

6. If Mother is in the habit of sending things to the laundry, don't forget to make up the parcel as usual. You can leave it with a neighbour, and remember to leave her the money for the clean laundry and for the milkman.

7. Don't leave your lessons undone although you are so busy with household duties. It will really be far less worry in the end if you go to school prepared.

8. Always see that there's plenty of bread and potatoes in the house. You'll never starve if you have these two things to fall back on. Try to have a tin or two of meat, fish and fruit ready for emergencies, and, if you use a tin, be sure to get another to replace it the first time you are out shopping.

9. Don't get landed with a lot of odd drops of milk. It is a good plan to use it up each evening if the daily supply comes in time for the porridge in the morning. This is specially true in hot weather.

Here is a very good way of using up any milk that is over— and one that will make you popular with the rest of the family.

Measure what's left in the evening, and put it by cupfuls into a saucepan. Add enough water to make a cupful for everybody. When it boils add a teaspoonful of coffee essence or a teaspoonful of cocoa (made smooth in a little milk). You will, of course, need one spoonful for each person. This will make a nice hot drink for everybody before going to bed, and will also ensure that there will be no milk wasted.

Now what about a weekly time-table?
How would this do?

Saturday: Make broth and a steamed pudding or a meat roll.

Then sweep and dust the whole house if possible. It may have to be just " a lick and a promise ", but try to run the sweeper over all the carpets and dust the surrounds with a mop. If you find dusting a dreary job, switch on the wireless, and you'll be finished before you know where you are. You'll keep time to the music unconsciously, so turn rather to Highland dance music than to a funeral march!

See that there's enough bread, potatoes, and other foodstuffs in the house to last the week-end at any rate.

Sunday: With a pot of broth ready to heat, and a meat roll or cold mutton and a steamed pudding made, the Sunday dinner is ready. Leave the pudding in the basin, and the basin in the pot, and see that there is still plenty of water in the pot. It will heat far better there than in the oven, where it would probably get dry and hard.

You won't need to do any sweeping on Sunday, but the sitting-room may need a run round with a duster. You should have a little leisure in the afternoon or evening to do your lessons, write to Mother, and collect the dirty clothes which you will all have changed that morning, and which would be the better of a soaking before you try to wash them on Monday, so pop them into a tub with some soap powder, and leave them till next day.

Monday: When you come in from school, get the fire lit quickly, arrange what you are going to have for the evening meal, and then, before Daddy comes home, try to get the clothes washed and hung up on the clothes line to dry. If the cuffs of the shirts are dirty, take the scrubbing brush and give them a good scrub on the table.

It is when dirty clothes accumulate that they " get you down ". I remember once knowing a girl who was a " Mother's Help " in a household of six. She was given a month's holiday, and she thought herself very lucky, but when she got back all the month's mending had been left for her, so she was met by forty-eight pairs of socks and stockings in a great heap, not to mention two dozen vests and pants, and other under garments. She could hardly see over it! The sight so disheartened her that she turned and went home again. Now I don't suppose Mother would run away even if she found forty-eight dirty shirts waiting to be washed, but I am sure she would be made very happy if she found that you had at least tried to " keep the washing down " in her absence.

Tuesday: Do the sitting-room extra well, besides doing any necessary cooking.

Wednesday: Iron the things you washed on Monday, after seeing to the evening meal.

Thursday: Give the bedrooms a sweep and a dust.

Friday: Do the hall and front door thoroughly.

On Wednesday, Thursday and Friday, just dust the sitting-room, and, of course, every day, see to the food first. If something has to be left undone let it be the cleaning.

Now I think it would be a good plan to give you a menu for a week in summer, and for one in winter. In both seasons I would have only porridge, or cereal, and toast for breakfast. You will find the morning busy enough without spending time cooking anything extra.

If you must come home for a midday meal, let it be just bread and cheese, but if you have any soup made take it then instead of in the evening. It won't take many minutes to heat. You could have an apple or an orange to finish off this midday meal.

When you come in from school you should make yourself a cup of tea before you set about preparing the evening meal.

Your last meal will be a cup of coffee or cocoa, so that means that the only meal which needs preparation is the evening meal. Here, then, are a few suggested menus for it.

	WINTER	SUMMER
Saturday:	Broth. Hot mutton. Potatoes. Roly-poly and custard.	Mince and onions. Potatoes. Tinned fruit and custard.
Sunday:	Broth. Cold mutton. Beetroot. Fried potatoes. Roly-poly and custard.	Cold meat roll. Salad and dressing. Potatoes. Tinned fruit and custard.
Monday:	Broth. Hot meat roll (made on Saturday). Beans and tomato sauce. Potatoes. Stewed apples and custard.	Sausages. Potatoes. Jelly and sponge pudding.
Tuesday:	Cold meat roll. Beetroot. Fried potatoes. Stewed apples put on to a sponge cake. Pour custard over.	Cold meat roll. Salad. Jelly and sponge pudding. (Make broth.)
Wednesday:	Pea soup. Fried sausages. Potatoes. Fig pudding.	Broth. Hot mutton. Potatoes. Any fruit in season.
Thursday:	Pea soup. Fried bacon. Potatoes. Fig pudding.	Broth. Cold mutton. Tomatoes. Jelly and custard.
Friday:	Mince and onions. Potatoes and cabbage Seven cup pudding.	Fried sausage and bacon. Potatoes. Jelly and custard.

Always make enough soup to last three days. It isn't worth the bother unless you make a good big potful.

If you make a big meat roll, don't serve it every day for three days. Put it in a cool place and have a dinner of sausages or bacon for a change, and then go back to it again.

You will notice that I have suggested cabbage as a vegetable on Friday. Put a little water in a pan with a tablespoonful of salt and a tiny pinch of baking soda. Shred the cabbage with a sharp knife, and put it into the boiling water. Put the lid on the pan, and every now and again turn the cabbage over in the boiling water with a wooden spoon. In fifteen minutes it will be ready. Empty it into a colander and squeeze the water out with the wooden spoon. Get it as dry as you can, then sprinkle a little pepper on it and a few bits of margarine.

Well, Mary, that is the end of my open letter to you. Don't be disheartened if some days you are tired, and your cooking has not been a success and things have, for some reason, gone against you. Even Mother, with all her experience, has days when she feels like that, so don't be discouraged. You will feel more than rewarded for all your efforts when Mother gets home again, and tells you that you did marvellously, and I can assure you of this—you will appreciate in future all she does for you far more than you have ever done before. So, good luck to your housekeeping, Mary!

A ROOM OF YOUR OWN

One of the chief joys of the teen age is when you come into possession of a room of your own, and are able to plan its decoration and furnishing as you would like to have it. If you have hitherto shared a " dorm " at school or a nursery type of bedroom with a younger sister, what a thrill it is to realize that from now on there will be one place in the house which belongs exclusively to yourself, where you can express your own personality, where you can entertain your friends, and where, in moderation at least, you can do as you like.

You are sure to have some ideas on the subject of furnishing it. Maybe your best friend has recently acquired a room of her own and her scheme strikes you as being exactly right. On the other hand, it may serve as a warning to you, what not to do, and make you long to launch out in the opposite direction. In any case, take your time about it. Don't dash pell-mell into the business with more haste than you would bestow on the selection of a new frock. If a frock is a failure you need not wear it all the time, but if you make a mistake with your room you have to go on living with it for a considerable time. Don't spurn advice. A little experience is worth a whole pile of untried ideas. Remember that furnishing and decoration is a specialized job, and it is fatally easy to create an impression far different from what you intended.

The first thing to take into account is colour. By a clever blend of colours you can make an ordinary room appear charming, while colours badly used can wreck a room that is otherwise delightful. Another basic principle is the wise use of space. Your room may not be very large, but by care and skill both in decoration and in the placing of furniture you can make it appear so. Another important pointer is to try to plan your room as a whole so that you avoid any suggestion of " bits and pieces ". Don't clutter it up with little odds and ends that have no special beauty and no usefulness either.

Think of the kind of room you hope to achieve. You do not

want, do you, a room æsthetically pleasing but rather formal; nor a room which is comfortable enough but which has no pretence at a colour scheme; but you do aim at combining beauty and comfort and a welcoming friendliness. The kind of room you are proud to have for your own, a place which, like Barrie's Mary Rose Island, " likes to be visited ".

PLANNING THE COLOUR SCHEME

How to begin? The foundation of all decorating is colour, so you must decide on a double or a triple scheme—one colour for the background and either one or two predominant shades in the furnishings. Neutral tones are best for the background because they blend successfully with any definite colours in the forefront of the room, and for your type of room this neutral tone should be light.

Any of the creamy colours, from off-white to that lovely shade of yellow which makes the room look as if it were flooded in sunshine, are good; and if your room has a cold aspect—that is to say, if it faces north—choose a cream which is faintly tinged with pink for the walls, ceiling and woodwork. This will suggest warmth. If you hanker after such colours as blue, grey or green for the walls, see that the shades are very pale and clear; but these colours are better employed elsewhere in the room, and are not so advisable as a bedroom background as the range of creamy tones. All the woodwork, door, skirting and window, may be painted a shade darker than the walls if you prefer, but the effect is more continuous if they all match up as nearly as possible.

Then there is the question of the wallpaper. Before doing anything drastic consider the paper which is already there. It may be perfectly good but not the shade you want—say a drab grey or fawn. In this case, and if it is not too dark, it can be successfully distempered in any colour that appeals to you. If, however, the paper is quite unsuitable and you must have a new one, choose a paper which is quite plain, or else one that has the design embossed on it in self colours, so that when hung it appears plain. Painters are occasionally partial to panelled effects in wallpaper. You know the kind of thing; a plain paper that has a coloured strip running downwards at intervals round the room dividing it into sections. In a small room the result of this is to make the room seem smaller than it is, and even in a large apartment it is apt to " break up " the walls, and adds to the difficulties of arranging the furniture attractively.

Time spent on deciding the best treatment for the background is not wasted, for in a sense it is the frame which will set off the picture you are about to create. Pay particular attention to the way your friends have treated their walls. And although at this point it is not actually necessary to complete in your mind the colour scheme you mean to have, it is advisable, because if you know what you are striving after you can build up your ideas better as you go on.

ARRANGING THE FURNITURE

Having fixed the background the next step is to take stock of the furniture which is available. Unless you are a very fortunate girl indeed, this is not likely to be brand new. More probably it will be a discarded suite of oak or mahogany not required elsewhere; it may not be a suite at all, merely the overflow from other rooms; or you may be inflicted with the remains of nursery furniture, all painted in a childish immature white.

Suppose you have fallen heir to some unwanted oak or mahogany, not by any means in its first youth, there is no need to be depressed. It is full of possibilities. As soon as it is handed over to you clean it thoroughly. Wash it with a shammy wrung out of tepid water to which a little vinegar has been added, and then polish it with one part polish to three parts elbow grease, till it shines with that well-cared-for look.

Now you can " dress " your room to suit your furniture. Blue, gold and old rose are all good with oak, while delicate pinks and greens and blues bring out the best in mahogany. Chintz or cretonne go well with any kind of wood, using stronger shades with oak and softer sweet-pea colouring with mahogany. If you are not quite certain how to achieve harmony between furniture and furnishings, if you are not yet colour conscious, lay certain colours against the furniture and try out the effect before making up your mind definitely.

But perhaps you are faced with a legacy of some worse-for-the-wear nursery furniture. You feel this is appalling, quite hopeless. You need not despair, for here lies the foundation of a very up-to-the-minute bedroom. As it is, it *is* hopeless, but once you have scrapped the original white and have had it repainted to tone with your general scheme you will be surprised at the result. There is something very fresh and young and at the same time sophisticated about painted furniture if it is treated aright.

By now you will have decided on your colour harmony, and will appreciate the advantage of the neutral background, which enables you to choose any two shades and be sure they will not clash with the walls and woodwork. But, and this is important, you must have

clear colours for painted furniture. You can be rather bold and dashing if you like, but never dingy nor dark. A soft apple green, or shrimp pink, for instance, can be supremely decorative.

Or you may prefer to have the furniture painted to match the walls, and have the detail, such as handles and panelling and the thin lines outlining the drawers, picked out in your prevailing colour note. By thus keeping the actual furniture also neutral, you can use a rich, strong contrasting shade along with it, such as scarlet, green, orange. A point to remember is that when it comes to a vivid colour like red, it is easy to have too much of a good thing. A *dash* of scarlet on a cushion or bordering the window curtains suggests originality and brilliance, but try to imagine a bedspread, cushions and curtains all in an insistent, shrieking red!

Here are one or two ideas from which you might plan a pleasing build up. If you have oak furniture you might choose creamy walls and woodwork, have a counterpane of delphinium blue bordered with purple, these two colours being repeated in the curtains and cushions. Clover colour and larkspur blue make a happy combination, so do varying tones of orange and russet allied to green. If the oak is very dark you might try for a Dutch effect and have dead-white walls, with hangings and bedspread of a strawberry pink appliqued in a fairly strong shade of green.

With mahogany furniture you can make a most charming room. Have the background in pale primrose and link this up with counterpane, curtains and cushions of turquoise blue appliqued in yellow. An alternative suggestion is to use soft-toned chintz for the curtains and bedmat, with self-coloured cushions, each in one of the prevailing colours, say a blue, a lilac and a pink one.

Should you lack a dressing-table or the shape of the existing one not appeal to you, you might scrap it altogether for an ordinary deal table; kidney shape is most effective, and to be really practical there should be drawers down the sides. Cover it in cretonne or chintz, with a deep frill " petticoat " reaching to the floor in the same material. If you cannot get a satisfactory chintz in a small dainty design, use coloured sateen veiled in net. This makes one of the prettiest dressing-tables imaginable, especially with a glass top.

If you have decided to have painted furniture matching the walls and woodwork, try cream colour, and choose a crisp gilt, green, orange, scarlet or even royal blue to pick out the handles and outlining. Blue, however, is one of the less successful shades in painted wood and is apt to appear poor unless it is very carefully chosen. Painted furniture has two distinct practical advantages. When it loses its first freshness a new coat of paint will make it like new again, and finger marks are easily removed by rubbing with a soapy flannel cloth. One disadvantage is that the paint is liable to chip, but if you are careful this need not happen.

A DECORATIVE BED

The bed will, of course, match the furniture. And if the room is to be a bedroom-cum-study-cum-den where you are at home to your pals, and where you will want to subdue as far as possible the bedroom atmosphere, a divan bed is the answer to your worry. During the day, piled attractively with cushions, it is a definite asset to the seating accommodation, while by night it plays its original part. Perhaps, however, the bed in your room is to remain undis-

guised. In planning the furnishings it is necessary to be clear in your mind whether it is to play a single or a dual role, because on this depends the kind of material you will use as covering.

For a bed that is solely a bed you can choose any kind of stuff which may appeal to you, but a divan is a different matter. Its covering must be of sturdy, strong fabric, the kind of stuff you might use for a chesterfield, which will stand up to lots of hard wear and tear. It should be of a colour, too, which will not show the dirt too readily. A counterpane of art silk or linen which would crush as soon as you sat on it would be of no use at all.

All this has to be taken into account when you are choosing your colour scheme. Incidentally, should you have decided on off-white walls, do not repeat the " off-white " in either bedcover or cushions. Off-white curtains are permissible, but while it may sound alluring in a romance, off-white in anything else quickly becomes an unattractive grey. I remember once being shown into an off-white bedroom and certainly the accent was on the " off ". The materials were of superlative quality, but not even the lovely powder-blue carpet and lavender cushions could redeem that slightly soiled look which made you forget everything else.

One of the most attractive assets in a bedroom and in a bed-sitting-room is an air of freshness; therefore, as it is not likely that you will have time to be constantly laundering your curtains and counterpane, choose something that will, at any rate, *look* clean for a reasonable time. Also, before deciding definitely that you must have a divan, better face the fact now that it will entail a good deal more labour than an ordinary bed. Presuming that you will be looking after your room yourself, not only must the bed be trans-formed each morning from bed to day couch, and quilt, &c., tucked out of sight, but the pillows, too, must be dressed up in their day-time cushion covers—and all this process has to be repeated in reverse at bedtime, no matter how tired you are.

CHOOSING THE CURTAINS

Choosing the curtains for your room is rather exciting. Here, as with counterpane and cushions, colour ranks higher than actual fabric. That is to say, you are better to have an inexpensive material in exactly the right colourings than a rich brocade or velvet or silk which is not quite in harmony. As to the kind of curtains you will have, much depends on the shape and nature of the window. It is a matter of taste whether you will have sash curtains or net screens or neither. Unless the room is so overlooked that some sort of pro-tection is advisable, there is just now a preference for unscreened windows. Certainly even fine net curtains help to keep the light out, and it is always pleasanter to sit in a room where the view is un-obstructed.

If you are having a close-to-the-window treatment, net curtains are most successful. Net is dainty and clean looking; it hangs and drapes well, and comes up crisp and fresh every time it is laundered.

Find a net that matches the walls, choosing a fine mesh if the window is small and a larger one for a bigger window. There are some lovely spotted nets with the spots in different colours, and you may like to repeat one of your predominant colours in your screens. If, however, you can only get a plain net, sacrifice the spots, match up with your background, and keep the harmony right.

It is fun to make the curtains yourself. It is not difficult either,

but if this should be your first effort ask someone with experience to help you when taking the measurements of the windows. How disastrous to buy the material and then find you have not ordered sufficient! Some washing fabrics, and notably net, shrink when they are washed, so see that you allow ample hems in case they have to be let down later on. Sash curtains or screens should touch but not lie on the window-sill. By the way, if you are making the cushion covers remember to make these rather tight for the cushion, so that when it is finished it looks nice and fat and " bunchy ". The counterpane is also easy to make. As a I dare say you know, there must not be a seam down the centre, and the bedspread should be wide enough to hang well over the sides.

If you are having long curtains—and I hope you will, they look so cosy when the lamps are lit and they are drawn—you may have to do with some that already exist in the household. And don't

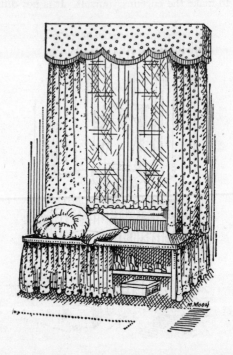

despise these family offerings. Rather use your brains to make them suit your needs. I know a girl who evolved some really marvellous curtains from some old sheets. She bought two packets of dye, one old rose and the other jade green. With the aid of this she made a pair of rose-coloured curtains with a deep hem of jade, and the pink frill also had an edging of green. and these hangings were the envy of every visitor.

If there is a wooden pelmet in your room that saves a lot of trouble, but if you should be tackling the making of curtains and frill on your own, it may help you to know that the depth of the finished frill should be one-eighth of the length of the finished curtains, and if you have a choice of material soft stuff drapes best. Plan your long curtains in art silk, velvet, crash, chintz or cretonne, and providing your colour scheme is right the effect is sure to be satisfactory.

THE PERSONAL TOUCH

Having got this length, having chosen your background and your furniture and linked them both together by skilful treatment of your hangings, your room still seems far from being complete. At this point it might be any room belonging to anybody, got up by a firm of furnishers, if you like, with as yet no soul of its own. It is now up to you to give life to it, to stamp it with your own personality, so that it attains that quality of " differentness " which we all strive after. If you can manage to create a room which is not only pleasing and friendly, but is also distinctive and just a little unusual, you have scaled one of the heights of successful furnishing.

One way of achieving this original effect is by the judicious introduction of one or two pieces of antique furniture. Perhaps the very word " antique " repels you. Perhaps you aim at making your room just as modern as it can be. In that case—for naturally everyone's taste is not the same—you will express your personality in a different way. Do not be persuaded to treat your room in a certain fashion just because someone else admires a certain type of furnishing. It is what *you* like that matters.

For the minute let us consider antiques. Suppose you are mildly curious about the effect they would have against your possessions, how are you to discover whether you will like them or not? Well, frankly, this is where you have to depend on your home people. Buying antiques is a specialized job, and to set off in search of them without some fore-knowledge of the subject is merely asking for trouble. But in many households there are lots of lovely old things which have been handed down in the family from one generation to another, and which may be unused in a lumber room or attic. Have a quiet look round and see whether there are any such pieces in your own home. You may never have thought much of that old chair of Great-aunt Jane's, or the little antique table that stood in a dark corner of the hall, or the quaint old stool in the spare room, but just try them in your room and see how they fit in.

What are the necessities for your room? The stereotyped articles which you must have? I should say a bed, a wardrobe, a dressing-table and a chair or two. These are the minimum, and if your room is small there may not be space for anything else. But if you have

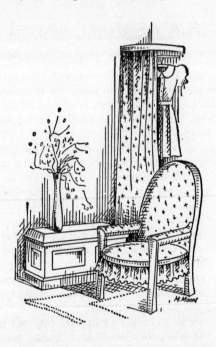

some space to play with, take time some day when you have the house to yourself and do a tour of hopeful inspection.

Probably you feel a trifle vague about what to look for, and are maybe not quite sure what antiques are anyway. To answer the last question first, furniture is not listed as antique until it is at least 100 years old, so that includes many Victorian pieces as well as others of earlier days. What to look for must depend partly on the amount of space available, but chairs and small tables are always an asset, while if you can come on a small unwanted chest of drawers such a thing would be a real find. This might be used with a mirror hung behind as a dressing-table, if you did not already have one, or it might act as surplus storage accommodation.

If it were my room I would also try to scrounge a dressing-stool from somewhere. Not very easy this, I admit, but I would at all events try! Another very attractive piece, if you could come on it, would be a dower chest. These are usually made of oak with panelled sides and a top that is sometimes plain and sometimes carved. As the name suggests, they were originally used to store a bride's trousseau, and if you had one in your room it would not only be a thing of beauty and extremely useful as a spare seat, but it could be used to stow away such awkward articles as a quilt during daytime, sports paraphernalia, an odd rug and the like. Lucky you if a dower chest is waiting for you!

I expect you are thinking how could you possibly put a dower chest, some antique chairs or an old chest beside a modern wardrobe. It doesn't sound right, I know, but strangely enough, if you choose old pieces with care, you will find that they harmonize with twentieth-century furniture astonishingly well. Now please do not misunderstand me: any antique piece will not mix with any modern piece. After all, all modern furniture does not blend. But in the majority of cases the old and the new can be married very successfully. Old things will even tone quite happily with painted furniture, always provided they have been wisely selected. If you do find some antiques which are in keeping with your other things, you will be delighted with the atmosphere of quiet good taste which they will bring to your room.

But whether you have antiques or not you will want a bookcase for your own books. Not only is a room incomplete without books, not only are they decorative, but they do lend an indefinable quality of atmosphere which cannot be gained in any other way. If there is no bookcase available you might get a local carpenter to build in two low shelves alongside the fireplace, and note that one or two longish low shelves are more effective than several narrow high ones.

While on the subject of shelves, if you can arrange to have a fitted cupboard built under the window-ledge, you will find this excellent for housing articles for which there is no special place, and if you place some cushions on top such a cupboard will act as an extra seat.

Another way in which to express your personality is by way of what designers call decor—those added touches here and there, which are not so much necessary as desirable. Happily, the cult for very bare rooms which was in vogue a few years ago is now giving place to a liking for ornaments and pictures and photographs in moderation. Decorators are recognizing that these expressions of personal taste give life and character to the room.

This gives a very wide scope for attractive treatment, but it is easy to be fussy and meaningless in decoration. Try to make some link between the person that is you and the room which is your

own. If you are keen on hockey or tennis there ought to be room for your team photographs. Perhaps you are interested in sewing? Then why not embroider a little sewn picture and hang it above the mantelpiece, or if you have the patience do a tapestry seat for one of your chairs.

Look around for some unusual ornaments. This is the time to do a little mild raiding about the house. Mothers are usually co-operative about this so long as you go about it in reason. Do not worry about such things as expensive crystal vases which may come to grief. Anyhow, these are not nearly so artistic as a piece of pottery or a brass or pewter jug. (Memo.: brass requires a weekly clean;

pewter can be left untouched for months.) If you can lay your hands on one such piece and fill it with beech leaves or red berries or even with some bare twigs and stand it on the mantelpiece, it will make a beautiful picture against your creamy walls.

Be careful about pictures. One pleasing water-colour is better than a jumble of discards from other rooms, and if you cannot find one that appeals to you don't have any at all. You might hang instead an old sampler, if there is one among the family treasures, and if you can place a mirror cleverly so that it catches the light, it not only adds to the decor but creates a desirable effect of increased space.

One last word. This is *your room*. You have designed it, planned it and arranged it, according to your individual taste, and it is as nearly perfect as you can make it. Unfortunately, it will not stay that way without some further effort on your part. No room is charming unless it has two attributes—cleanliness and tidiness. Do not wait for curtains and cushions to become really dirty before washing them, and don't wait either for your mother to take them off to be laundered, for that should be *your* job.

Even if it means getting up earlier in the mornings, see that your room is kept scrupulously clean; an aid to this is to have a duster handy in one of the drawers. And it won't *look* spotless unless it is also tidy—a sad thought if you have a habit of leaving a trail of garments behind you. Speaking from hard experience, the easiest method of attaining tidiness is to clear up as you go, and don't let your room down by walking out on it with things lying all over the place. You could never call a girl smart if her face looked dirty. Neither can a room be really attractive unless it is clean and in order.

REPAIRS ABOUT THE HOUSE

One of the progressive signs of the times is the adaptability of the girls of this generation. They are out to try most things once—not excluding those jobs hitherto labelled masculine with a capital " M ". How often, for instance, do you find a schoolgirl mending a broken fuse while her brother takes his turn with the washing-up. And why not! Brothers no longer shrink from doing their share of the household chores—or if they do, they shouldn't—and girls are now much more mechanically minded than they used to be. Therefore they ought to have a chance to learn something about the technical side of domestic machinery.

Do you feel like that? That if you only knew how to tackle them, there are lots of little repairs about the house that you could do without getting a tradesman in. So often it is a very small fault that can be put right by just a little knowledge. It is merely a matter of learning how. Boys score here; they seem to possess an uncanny instinct regarding mechanical mishaps. Some girls also have this mechanical knack, but mostly they have to get down to it and learn the why and wherefore.

Naturally, there are some household repairs which are beyond anyone but a skilled workman, and in that case do you know which tradesman ought to be called in, in such an emergency? The ordinary jobs you do know about. For electricity trouble you get in touch with the electrician; if the gas supply is erratic you inform the company that supplies the gas; while the plumber deals with all mishaps relating to the water system. But should your ceiling fall—I hope it won't—do you know that the plasterer is your man, and should your roof leak you may need both the slater and the plumber; while the joiner repairs woodwork, mends locks, renews sash cords, and attends to broken windows.

Your job is to learn the ABC of the simpler domestic repairs, enough to carry you through except when something serious occurs Such knowledge may save both time and money, each a very useful commodity. Besides, as a modern girl, this ability to repair and mend ought to be part of your equipment.

MENDING A FUSE

Can you, for instance, mend a fuse? A light fails just when you need it most—what are you going to do about it?

First look out some fuse-wire, a pair of pliers and a candle to work with. *Then switch off the current at the main.* You dare not touch the fuse-boxes till this is done. And, by the way, do you know where the fuse-boxes live in your house? If not, now's the time to make inquiries. You will probably find them in the hall or cloak-

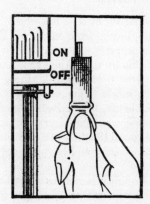
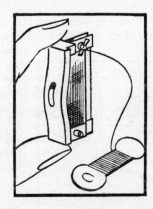

room, attached to the wall high up. *Avoid boxes with lead seals on them.* Inside the one you're looking for you'll see a row of white china holders, each of which is kept in place by a wire. These wires can be detached quite easily, but if you have not done this before, it is wise to examine how they are fixed in position before you remove them. Round each holder is wrapped the fuse-wire, and your job is to find out in which the wire is broken. You will notice that the damaged wire is probably blackened.

Undo the two screws which keep the wire in position and remove the wire, and with a pair of pliers cut sufficient fuse-wire to replace the broken piece. Fasten the new wire to one of the connectors, slip it through the hole in the holder and tighten up the screws again, making sure that the wire fits well without being taut. While you are on the job look over the other fuse-holders to see that they are intact. When this is done close the box and switch on the current at the main to test the mended fuse. I need not remind you that it is not much use trying out the result of your labours while the main current is still off!

In any house fitted with electricity there should always be a supply of fuse-wire kept in some drawer or cupboard known to the family. This wire can be bought in any electrician's shop, and if it should fall to you to renew the existing supply, see that it is of the same thickness as that already in use in the fuse-holders.

FAULTY FLEX

You may suddenly find one day that the electric flex which links up any of the appliances, lamp, radio, heater, iron, &c., is not functioning properly. You may have warning of this by a crackling sound when the current is switched on, there may even be sparks flying, or the only sign of trouble may be the loosening of the protecting covering of braid which is bound round the flex. All of these are danger signals and should not be neglected.

Although it is not necessary to cut off the main current when you go to repair a flex, it is advisable to switch off the local current before you remove the plug and start working on the flex. Having taken the plug from the socket you first unscrew the nails on the wrong side of the plug with a screwdriver. This divides it in two, and at this stage take special note how the parts are linked up. It is nearly always easy enough to take a thing to pieces, but somehow, unless you have a flair that way, all sorts of complications are apt to arise when you go to put it together again.

Now cut off two or three inches of the flex with the pliers, pull back the outer covering of braid and the cotton packing, if there is any, from the first two inches of the cut end of the flex. Get a good strong black reel of cotton or linen thread, and tightly bind the braid and the cotton packing over the flex. This must be done securely, so wind it round about thirty turns, and as neatly as you can. You will see now that the points of wire are quite uncovered and are ready to be fitted back into the plug again. Remove the damaged flex from the plug if you have not already done so. Strip half an inch of the rubber and cotton covering from the cut wires, and fix them in the same way as the damaged wires were previously fixed. Plug fitments vary. If the one you are working on has a hole and set-screw the wires should be doubled and inserted in the hole, but if it has a washer and clamping screw, they are bent into a hook, placed under the washer and the screw tightened.

Serious damage to the middle of a long line of flex calls for expert attention, but if a part of the flex has become so bent that the braid has frayed and the rubber insulators on the wires are exposed, this is a job you can tackle quite well. You needn't renew the whole length of flex. Instead, wind a piece of adhesive insulating tape over the damaged part, overlapping a few inches on either side.

Such accidents to flex are more often the result of careless treatment than of general wear and tear. It is easy to be casual with electric gadgets, so don't think your parents are being fussy when they remind you not to allow a long flex, attached to lamp or radiator, to curl up and form kinks. It mustn't be tramped on either, so don't place it under a rug and then walk cheerfully over it, deluding yourself that it will come to no harm. And when you remove a plug from its socket don't drag it forcibly out by the flex but grasp the plug itself and gently ease it out.

THE VACUUM CLEANER

It pays to be kind to your electric appliances. Treat them as helpful friends, not as slaves that will endure anything and everything. Your vacuum cleaner, for instance. To appreciate its service you've only got to switch a carpet once in a while by hand! But do you remember to empty the bag each time it is used, or at least frequently? And though it must not be washed, do you keep the bag as clean as possible by whisking it out with a hard little brush and so prolong its life?

Don't tell me that emptying the bag is a dusty business. I agree. But because of that don't avoid doing it as often as possible. I suppose you know the best way to go about it? Nothing can be more dust-raising if you turn the dust out on a flat paper. You literally bite the dust, and it hasn't a pleasant taste! But I find that if instead of emptying it flat, you fit a large brown paper bag to the mouth of the vacuum bag, you can do the job with a minimum of flying dust.

Pins, small tacks and minute pieces of coal are very injurious to the machinery of the vacuum cleaner, so before you begin to use it look over the carpet and pick up any such destructive objects. A magnet is a help if you have one. Then there is the business of oiling the cleaner. Usually it does not ask for much but, poor thing, it does require a little at intervals if it is to do its work. Look up the book of words and see what the makers say about the kind of oil to use—as a rule they supply you with a special make suited to the vacuum cleaner's needs—and when and how much.

If you have an electric toaster, do you give it all the care which is its due? You know, of course, never to stand it in hot water, but do you sometimes try to remove crumbs that have gathered with a knife or the prongs of a fork? You are advised not to. If the base can be removed, take it out and brush out the crumbs with a soft brush or even a cloth, and attend to this regularly, for if the crumbs are allowed to accumulate round the heating unit you are quite liable to have a burnt fuse. The toaster is a delicate contraption, and should never be shaken or the wires may loosen.

If the chromium plate becomes stained, as with use it inevitably will, it can be cleaned by sprinkling whiting on a clean soft cloth and rubbing it till it is clean. It is, of course, easier to *keep* it clean than make it clean again, so if milk or tea is spilled on it, or bacon fat stains it, wipe it immediately with a damp cloth and there will be no mark at all. If for any reason you decide to give the toaster a spell off duty, make certain you store it in a dry place. Dampness is injurious to electric apparatus.

THE IRON AND THE 'FRIG

Suppose you are ironing and the heat suddenly goes from the iron, the most likely cause of the trouble is a " blown " fuse. So test for this—and once again do not forget to switch off the current at the main before you begin—and if none of the fuse-holders shows a broken wire you may conclude that it is a job beyond your powers to tackle. With so much movement the iron flex twists very easily, so be careful to keep it straight when using it. If it does bend and become kinky mend it with insulating tape before it gets too bad. Detach the flex as soon as you have stopped ironing, and when the iron is cold lay it away in a drawer or cupboard out of the dust.

It is not necessary to keep the current on all the time you are ironing. If the heat is not automatically controlled keep switching it on and off as you need it. And should you be called away always put off the switch, even though you do not expect to be detained more than a minute. Similarly, never leave the iron resting on a half-ironed garment while the heat is on, while you stop, say, to put coal on the fire. Just as kettles boil over when you cease to watch them, so does an iron scorch the minute your back is turned.

Do you do your share in looking after the " 'frig "? Would you know how to get the best value from it if you were left to cope with it by yourself? It should be de-frosted regularly. *Don't leave the door open.* Moist foods such as milk, fish and meat should be covered in the containers provided, otherwise de-frosting will have to be done more often. Don't put foods in the frigidaire while they are still hot or warm. This wastes current and causes unnecessary condensation.

GAS TROUBLES

Mishaps are not so likely to occur with gas features, but do be careful about turning off taps completely. Some gas fires have two taps; turn them both off. And you do realize, don't you, that to get the best results from a cooker, it must be kept very clean. Wash the burners and rings in hot water once a week or so, and wipe out the oven after you've used it.

Of course gas does escape! What would you do if you returned to the house and were greeted by a strong smell of gas? First try to locate the escape. Perhaps a tap has been left on, or a pot may have boiled over, extinguishing the flame though the pressure has remained on. The one thing you must not do is to strike a light, which might cause an explosion. Common sense indicates the opening of windows to clear the air and turning off the gas at the meter while you explore. If you are far from help and suspect a leak in one of the pipes leading to cooker or fire, you can experiment with soap suds at the probable point of escape, and if they bubble, make a temporary stopping of hard soap. But if possible send for a plumber.

THE TAP THAT DRIPS

Can you think of anything more irritating then a dripping tap? A tap which, turn as you will, refuses to be screwed off, and the drip becomes a trickle, and then a noisy sizzle which tears your nerves to frazzles. To most of us this is a familiar experience at some time or another. All that is wrong is that the tap requires a new washer. In other words, the flat rubber ring which keeps the joints of the tap secure has weakened with wear, is not doing its job, and must be renewed.

Changing a washer is a simple job when you know how. Most households have, or should have, a supply of washers of varying sizes

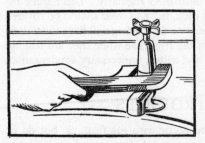

to suit the different taps. Look through the stock before beginning and make reasonably sure that there is one which will fit the damaged tap. Hot-water washers are made of a harder rubber composition than those for cold taps, because the former have to withstand the heat. You will need some tools, too, a spanner and possibly a pair of pliers, depending on the type of tap.

A word in your ear at this point. You are going to be extremely popular with your family if you can undertake such domestic repairs as these, but *only* if you replace your tools and materials where you found them. Nobody wants to clear up after someone else who has had the fun of doing the job proper.

If it is the hot tap that needs a washer, see that the fire in the kitchen, or wherever the hot-water boiler is situated, is kept low. Now turn off the cold water at the main and turn *on* both hot and cold taps till they run dry, when you are ready to proceed in the best plumbing manner. Examine the tap and you will see that it is divided into two parts. The top one includes the part whereby you turn on the water, and the bottom contains the actual tap through which the water runs, the top resting inside the bottom part.

Fit the spanner to the top part and turn to the left. Should it not loosen this way try turning it in the opposite direction. Strange as it may seem, some taps are made to move one way while others go in the opposite direction. Once you have got the spanner started you will find the tap turns quite easily and the top part is easily removed. You will now notice that it is here that the washer is fitted, at the lower end, protected by a small nut. You will now realize why a change of washer is necessary, for the old one will have perished and be partly worn away.

Grip the flange with the pliers and use the spanner to unscrew the nut holding the washer in position. Take off the damaged washer and fix on the new one, verifying the size, and if it is too big cut a small piece off all round, though it is really better to have one that fits exactly. Replace the nut, screw it up tightly, and fit on the tap again. Finish off by reversing the first pro-ceedings. Turn off the taps, turn on the main pressure of

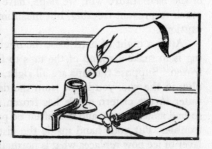

water, and—but you do not have to be told this for it is the expres-sion of the worker's joy—turn on the water, let it gush hard, and finally turn it off completely to ensure that the drip really *has* gone.

FROZEN PIPES

A dripping tap is, however, one of the least of the troubles that can be caused by the domestic water supply. One of the greatest is frozen pipes. The awful thing about burst and frozen pipes is that many households are likewise afflicted at the same time, and it is next to impossible to find a plumber who can come to your imme-diate aid. Therefore it is only common sense to be able to apply first aid to your pipes when they are suffering from an overdose of cold. There is something impish about the way water freezes. It is there one minute, apparently running as hard as Tennyson's brook. You go back to it a minute later and it just isn't there any longer. Or you go to bed leaving everything all right, and wake to a water system that has turned to ice while you slept.

But after all, water obeys Nature's laws, even when it is harnessed for domestic needs, and it freezes in the manner you would expect it to. (Only somehow one never expects one's *own* pipes to freeze!) In short, it is the pipes that are most exposed to the cold which freeze first. A lavatory or cloakroom, occupying an angle of two outside walls, is not likely to survive a bout of really hard frost unless its piping and the apartments themselves are protected by some kind of heating.

Very often a wash-basin or a w.c. is placed close to a window with a pipe running down the wall outside, and this is simply an encouragement to Jack Frost to come and do his worst. The houses of the near future will, we hope, have indoor piping which will do much to prevent freezing, but meantime we must go on taking precautions.

After a night of hard frost the obvious thing to do in the morning is to make a round of the taps to find whether they are fluid or frozen. Suppose the taps are all right, but when you try pulling the plug in the w.c. you know from the dead response it gives that the water in the cistern above has frozen. This, however, may not be so bad as it sounds, and can often be put to rights again with a little trouble. Put your hand inside the cistern and you will find that a layer of ice now replaces what is normally water, and it is just possible that if you melt this ice the water may flow again. Fill a fairly large jug with hot water, adding a handful of salt, and pour over the ice. Continue with this till the ice has gone, and if the freezing has not penetrated to the surrounding pipes this simple treatment may do the trick. At any rate, it is worth trying.

In the old-fashioned type of w.c. where the cistern is placed high on the wall, joined by a pipe to the bowl, this pipe may freeze if it is not lagged. You can do this quite well. Wrap the pipes round with " waste " or with woollen cloths or even with several layers of paper secured with string. Should such a pipe freeze the application of hot cloths will sometimes free it, wringing out one hot cloth after another and laying it on the pipe. This treatment is not convenient to do on a lagged pipe.

It is really a good idea to lag all pipes that can be lagged as soon as a spell of hard frost sets in. I admit that it doesn't make your bathroom look like a magazine illustration, but it all helps the barrage against a freeze-up. Collect all those old rags you've kept for seven years hoping to find a use for, and wind them tightly round all the pipes you can get hold of, and round the ones you can't get hold of as well, for you can manage at least one layer of wool or paper round such pipes as are laid almost flat against the wall. I know, because I've done it!

And while you are about it don't forget the lonely tank up in the attic. Pop up with a woolly jacket to go round it as if it were a precious poodle that didn't like the cold.

The waste pipe of bath, sink or wash-hand basin often freezes. The moment you discover this try to thaw it out, for every second tells. Water freezes in a pipe gradually, a little at a time, and if you act promptly you may avoid a real freeze-up. The warning signal for a frozen waste is the water refusing to run away. If you are lucky you may notice that it is going down very slowly, and by acting immediately you can almost certainly restore it to normal.

Suppose it is the kitchen sink which insists on retaining whatever you pour down, or a wash-hand basin—the treatment is similar for them both. Get some very hot water, make up a very strong salt solution, and pour into the basin. If the basin is porcelain the water must not be hot enough to crack the basin. Allow this to stand for a little, and if it shows no sign of disappearing, ladle out the solution and repeat the process.

An alternative to this is to wind hot-water cloths round the waste pipe beneath the sink, placing a basin under to catch the drips. If this is still unsuccessful put a basin under the U-bend in the waste pipe. Remove the nut there with a spanner, and you will then discover whether the pipe is frozen just after it leaves the basin or beyond the bend. If it is the former, you are much more likely to succeed in removing it, so continue applying wet cloths as hot as you can hold them. A final endeavour is to try thawing the outside pipe with hot cloths, and this treatment, along with the pouring of a salty solution down towards the waste, is the only thing to do when the bath waste is frozen.

Water freezes very quickly once it has left the warmth of the house and encounters the sharp cold outside, hence the freezing of pipes situated on the outside wall. Sometimes you can induce a thaw here by pouring boiling water on to the pipes till the frost succumbs. The difficulty here is that it is not an easy matter to divert water on to a perpendicular pipe, though I have watched a plumber thaw a pipe by this very means, working with what seemed to me misplaced patience with pail after pail of hot water till he freed it in the end, long after most people would have given up.

Then there is the freezing of the taps themselves. Perhaps you know that sinking feeling caused by taps which when turned on refuse to produce a flow of water. If the cold tap is affected apply hot cloths both to the tap itself and to the feeding pipe, and if this has no effect it is safer to turn off the water at the main, so as to lessen the possibilities of a burst pipe when the thaw comes.

The freezing of the hot water, and unfortunately the hot tap freezes more readily than the cold one, is much more of a nuisance because it entails the letting out of the kitchen fire, or the fire by which the boiler is heated—at a time when of all others you want the comfort of a warm fire. Not only is this unpleasant, but a cold house is liable to create more trouble and cause other pipes to freeze as well. Nevertheless, if the hot water goes off the kitchen fire must go off as well, otherwise there may be a serious explosion.

Even worse than a frozen pipe, however, is a burst. Immediately turn off the main supply by shutting off the stopcock so as to empty the supply cistern. If you do this you will save much probable damage to furniture, ceilings, walls, &c. It is not a bad idea to discover, *before* a period of frost sets in, just where the stopcock in your house is.

Worst of all, of course, is for the whole house to freeze up, with neither exits nor entrances for the household water. But to remedy this is a job beyond your powers. You can only turn off the water— this seems a contradiction in terms seeing there is no water to be turned off, but turn it off all the same!—then send an urgent call for the plumber.

Ice in the pipes can cause such a heap of inconvenience that it is worth while taking some trouble to prevent its formation. Some houses " freeze up " more readily than others for a variety of reasons. Houses badly built, and inferior plumbing arrangements, are the chief causes. Some pipes freeze readily on account of their position. Because of a natural desire to have the living and bedrooms of a house facing south, the bathroom and scullery are often on the north side, which is the coldest aspect, and these pipes are more likely to freeze than those with a warmer exposure.

It is only when the heat of the house falls below a certain degree that pipes can freeze. Therefore if you keep a really warm house the chances are that your pipes will escape danger from frost. Unfortunately frost does not go off duty at night, but rather works harder, so this means that a warm temperature must be kept up during the hours while you are asleep as well as by day. This is all right if there is central heating. Where there is not—well, you must do a spot of stoking up before you retire to bed.

Concentrate your energies on those parts of the house where freezing is most likely to occur, places like scullery, cloakroom, bathroom, wash-house and lavatories and also kitchen. Keep the kitchen fire in overnight when the frost is hard. Bank it up with dross last thing. This will keep the tank hot, also the pipes, and as the hot and cold pipes usually run alongside each other, the heat from the hot pipes will do much to prevent the cold pipes from freezing.

For those other parts where there is no fire there is nothing better than a little paraffin lamp. It does not seem to give much heat, but even when turned down very low it somehow does the trick. I have a marvellous one that burns for eight days without attention, and only uses a speck of oil; a very faithful friend in frosty periods. But even a candle may prevent the water crossing the border to iceland. A long one will burn very nearly all through the night. Melt the grease at the bottom so that it stands upright and stick it inside a pail, then there is no danger of fire.

And, of course, electric radiators, the small ones you can fit to a lighting plug, are a boon in very hard frost. The great thing is to have *all* the house comfortably warm, not forgetting the attic which is always perishing in winter. If there isn't a lamp or a heater available, open the trap which leads up to it and allow the warm air to penetrate to those arctic regions. After the door has been open for a very short time you will appreciate just how badly a little heat is needed up there.

But even with all these precautions the last word has not been said. Just before you go to bed make a tour of the house with jugfuls of a strong solution of salt and water. Pour this down all w.c.s, sinks and basins, as a warning to any approaching icicles. And while you are about it, see that every tap is completely turned off. If you leave a tap dripping in hard frost you may as well resign yourself to a frozen waste in the morning, plus an overflow of the water which thus cannot escape. Some people do advise leaving taps running at low pressure all the time during frost, but plumbers are usually against this, and hold that it is better not to leave any flow, large or small.

Another safeguard during frost is to run the water frequently in the pipes. Keep the tank very hot and run it off frequently as well. Then—this may seem a small point, but it is worth heeding—avoid sharp draughts of icy air penetrating into the house. Naturally outer doors must be opened now and again, but they must not be allowed to remain open for any length of time. Not much use going to endless trouble in heating up the house if you are going to chill it again in a matter of minutes.

CARPET ACCIDENTS

Speaking of heat of a different kind, how would you react if a piece of glowing coal fell out and burnt a hole in the rug? I mean, could you tackle the repair of the hearthrug yourself. This sounds rather a fearsome task for the amateur, but in reality it is again just a matter of knowing how. The first thing is to find a piece of carpet similar to the one damaged. Most households have odd scraps of carpet, so have a look round for something which is approximately of the same colour and thickness, and which will do as a patch. Should there be none suitable, if you get in touch with one of the large furnishing warehouses it is likely that they might be able to do something for you. Or you may have some relation willing to oblige.

To make the patch, turn the rug upside down and pull out the pile of the rug all round the hole so that it forms roughly a square. Now take these threads which you have unravelled and turn them back on to the wrong side. Tie them into little bunches of three or four threads, and then fasten down each bundle separately. Use a very strong thread for this and a carpet needle. Take the patch, which should be cut one inch larger all round than the hole, and loosen the pile for one inch on all four sides. This makes it the exact size required. Lay it right side down against the hole with the pile of both rug and patch running the same way, then arrange the loose threads in bundles as you did before, and tack them to the underside of the carpet. Sew the patch on with a stab stitch, which is a kind of back stitch, always working on the wrong side of the rug. When you turn it over the patch will be invisible.

You may have to send the rug to the cleaner's when the repair is completed, especially if new carpet has been used for the patch, but you can quite well clean the rug at home by washing it. Carpet soap is excellent used with hot water, a worn nailbrush, and a clean dry cloth to finish up with. Be careful to wipe away all traces of the soap, none of which should be left in the carpet.

Here is a very good treatment for both carpets and rugs. Mix one ounce of soap flakes and half a pint of boiling water till the flakes are dissolved. Allow to cool, then add two tablespoonfuls of ammonia. When this is stirred it will form a soap jelly which can be used at once. To apply it, wring a cloth out of hot water and rub the soiled parts with it, then brush over with a soft nail brush which has been dipped in the jelly. Rub over again with the damp cloth freshly wrung out, finishing with a clean dry cloth. You will be surprised at the amount of dirt removed during this process, and you may have to renew the hot water several times. For a carpet of pale delicate colours, use rather less ammonia, say one tablespoonful instead of two.

French chalk is a splendid antidote to grease spilled on a rug. Moisten the carpet first with benzine, cover with the chalk, and when the benzine evaporates brush off the chalk and you will find that the grease has also gone. Ink is a more frequent stain than anything almost, but if you treat it the minute it is spilled by rubbing over the stain with a little fresh milk—doing this several times if necessary—it should be easily removed, always remembering to rub with a clean part of the cloth. Salt is another cure for ink stains on the carpet. Sprinkle salt over the stain, then brush off and repeat till the ink no longer shows, and finish off by rubbing a cut lemon on the part, then wipe with warm water.

There is no need to panic if you disastrously spill paint on the carpet, though the sooner you can get to work on it the better. Mix together in a small bottle equal quantities of ammonia and turpentine and shake well. Now apply some of this mixture to the stained part with a clean cloth and leave to soak for about ten minutes. Repeat this several times, and you will then find that the paint will flake off.

If your vacuum cleaner happens to be out of commission and you should have to sweep your carpet by hand, use a firm little switch and brush the way of the pile. If you try to brush against the pile you will brush more dirt back into the carpet than you are taking out.

UPHOLSTERY

Cleaning upholstery, easy chairs, stools, chesterfields and the like, is one of the tasks which you should be able to undertake at home. Not only is it much more convenient to have the chairs cleaned on the spot, and not have the house left bereft of their comfort for weeks while they are sent off to the cleaners, but you get a great kick out of transforming some grimy-looking furniture with a shabby second-hand air about it to a set of pieces that appear new and fresh and very attractive.

The most satisfactory method of home cleaning is to wash the upholstery. This may sound to you a somewhat doubtful proceeding, but if done properly the results are excellent, and it is the way I treat my own chairs. But you must do it on a good day with lots of wind. If you have a garden and the furniture can be carried outside, do so, but if this is not feasible then open all the windows in the room where you propose to work, to admit as much fresh air as possible. For the actual washing use either one of the liquid cleaners that are on the market or else a good carpet soap, and always choose the best brand available. If neither of these is to be had, make up a lather of soap flakes or use soap jelly.

This is how to make soap jelly. Incidentally, it is useful for other tasks besides cleaning upholstery, such as washing delicate fabrics, as well as for washing up. Save all scraps of soap no matter how small they are. The larger pieces may be shredded with a knife or grated if the soap is hard enough. Place the soap in a saucepan with sufficient cold water to cover, then heat it slowly till the liquid is clear, stirring occasionally if necessary. This forms into a jelly which should be poured into an old jam jar and used as required.

Make the upholstery wet with a clean damp cloth, then apply the cleaner with a soft nail brush and rub over till it forms a good soapy lather—treating a smallish area at a time. You will notice from the lather how very soiled the upholstery is. Wipe off the lather with a clean cloth, and if you consider the chair requires further treatment wash it again with a fresh lather. As with the cleaning of a carpet, make sure that all traces of soap are removed, then rub very hard with a clean cloth and leave till dry. When doing any of these "wet treatments", as the professional cleaners term them, see that you have a large supply of clean dusters at hand. It is very poor economy to use a soiled duster.

Perhaps your upholstery does not need so drastic a treatment as washing. In this case you might try a little dry cleaning. With a clean, dry cloth rub some french chalk into the fabric of the upholstery, with special pressure on the soiled parts, then brush off all remains of the chalk with a small hard-bristled brush. It will be advisable to spread a newspaper where you are working to protect the carpet from the chalk.

This method of cleaning does not, however, remove stains. To treat grease stains you should get one of those solvents which have such frightening names, such as carbon tetrachloride or trichlorethylene, and rub a little on the stained parts with a clean cloth. But these chemicals have to be applied carefully, because they are apt to leave a ring round the area which has been cleaned, thus drawing attention to the stained part. Also, these solvents are a trifle "heady" and should be used either in the open air or near to an open window.

From this you will probably agree that where things *can* be washed this is the most satisfactory way of cleaning. Perhaps you did not know that leather upholstery can also be washed. Rub the surface gently with a soft cloth wrung out of soapy lukewarm water, dry with a warmed duster, then polish with furniture cream.

TO WASH WOOLLIES

Do you wash your woolly jumpers and cardigans at home or do you simply make a parcel for the cleaners when they are soiled? If you have always relied on professional cleaning, have a go at washing them next time yourself. It is quite a tricky job. You can't just wash woollies any old way and expect them to look like new, for they won't.

Don't let your jumper get too soiled before laundering it. If you do it will have to be rubbed, and rubbing makes woollies "felty" and hard, makes them shrink, and destroys their cosy softness. Don't use too hot water, just as hot as your hands can comfortably stand, and having made a lather of soap flakes, gently squeeze the jumper till it is clean, keeping it under the water as much as you can. Rinse in water of the same temperature, removing *all* the soap.

Don't wring it. Rather pound the water out between towels. If you can dry it outside choose a fresh day with a good breeze, for woollens should be dried as quickly as possible. Never let them lie about wet, or they'll shrink and never quite recover afterwards.

A jumper should be dried flat. If your garden is free from smoke and smuts, spread a clean towel on the grass, lay the jumper on top, gently pulling it back into shape. You will notice that the washing may have inclined the sleeves to stretch lengthwise; now is the time to persuade them to return to their normal length. Contrariwise the body part tends to stretch out instead of down, and it too should be pulled in the right direction. A jumper that is dried outside needs a good deal of attention. A breeze strong enough to dry

it will also blow it about. One or two clean stones to act as weights are a help if you should have to leave it. As it dries it should be frequently turned, and if you are afraid of fading it is better to dry it on the wrong side.

If you haven't a suitable outdoor drying yard the jumper may be dried just as successfully indoors, and no worry about waiting for a fine day! But you must have a really hot fire, and be prepared to keep it hot for an hour or two. Spread the jumper as before on a clean towel fairly near the fire—not too close in case of sparks or soot. Once again keep your eye on it, not merely turning it over when one side is dry, but turning it round so that it dries equally.

After it is dry you are not finished. It must be pressed, and it is important to do this carefully if you want to restore the attractive tailored look to your jumper. Lay it flat on the ironing board (and for this job the old-fashioned table is better, if you have one), and first press the seams through a clean damp cloth. But *don't* press any ribbing at waist, cuffs, or collar, or you will destroy the elasticity which can never be brought back.

Pressing is almost as important as the actual washing. Iron through a damp cloth, and don't run the iron back and forward as you generally do, but press the iron down on one part, then lift the iron and press another, till you've done it all. Air it thoroughly before putting it away, in a drying cupboard if you have one. This is better than hanging it up. If you do your jumper this way and never let it near cold water—and, of course, you won't dream of soaking it before washing, that's death to any woolly—it should look as good as new when you've finished with it.

WASHING AN EIDERDOWN

Did you know that an eiderdown could be very successfully washed at home? I confess I always had my doubts about this till a guest who was staying with us offered to show how—and even then I had some anxious moments when I saw my quilt, soiled as it was, disappear into the wash tub. But it emerged finally like an old friend who'd renewed her youth.

Here's how to do it. Choose a windy day so as to hasten the drying business—speaking personally, this is not a job I'd like to try indoors, though it can be done. Prepare a tubful of warm soapy water with a good handful of salt in it to keep the colours from running, and wash by kneading and squeezing. Don't rub soap on it unless on very soiled parts. A long-handled vacuum washer might be of help here if you have one. When it is clean rinse thoroughly in warm water, and with the rollers fairly loose put it through the wringer. Carry it outside and shake it before hanging on the line, and continue to shake it at intervals even after it seems dry, so as to separate the down. Air off before the fire, and if the cover is creased take a warm iron—not hot—and smooth it over before it is quite dry.

SPOTS AND STAINS

Are you ever plagued by spots and stains that settle uninvited on your belongings? To most of us they are much more of a menace than straightforward honest dirt. Dirt arrives slowly, imperceptibly, and for a while you are hardly conscious of it, but a stain shrieks aloud, calling attention to itself in an ugly discord. So also when you discover a heat mark on the table—that hideous white discoloration which can be caused by very hot plates or the spilling of scalding liquid. When you catch sight of it you feel that this is here for keeps; but it need not be.

As with most stains immediate treatment is desirable. Indeed, to be Irish, the best way to remove it is before it is there! That is to say, suppose you upset a cup of tea which is only moderately hot, but which will mark the table if it is not attended to, dry the surface with a soft duster, and then polish up hard with a little furniture cream, and the chances are that there will be no trace of the accident.

But should you spill some nearly boiling water from the tea kettle that tell-tale white mark will probably have settled on the table by the time you have fetched a duster. If a very large area is affected it is not likely that you will be able to cure it, but if the mark is comparatively small, try removing it with methylated spirit. Put one or two drops, not more, of the spirit on to a pad of cotton wool. Cover this with two layers of muslin or print, and rub vigorously over the mark in a circular fashion. Follow up immediately with an application of linseed oil well rubbed in. Used like this the methylated spirit will remove sufficient stain and polish from the surrounding wood to smear over the damage caused by the heat.

This treatment is also excellent if, as often happens, you spill some perfume on your dressing-table.

Another cure for heat marks is to rub the stained part with a soft pad which has been dipped into heated olive oil. You may have to continue the rubbing for some time. Finish off by an application of furniture cream rubbed in very well.

Spots and stains which seem to arrive from nowhere and settle on light-coloured walls are a perpetual eyesore, but there are several ways of removing them. One is to rub the stain very gently with a cloth which has been dipped into grease solvent, making a ring round the stain first of all and then rubbing over and beyond it. If the grease mark is not very large or very bad, it will sometimes yield to gentle rubbing with a piece of stale bread or clean india-rubber—but take care you don't make a hole in the paper. Another method is to get someone to hold a clean sheet of blotting-paper over the stain while you pass a warm iron over it.

Nothing makes a book descend to the " second-hand " grade so quickly as an odd spot or two either outside or in. Yet how often this happens, especially if the book belongs to someone else. Perhaps you read while you eat—an enchanting though much-to-be-deplored habit—and some butter leaves its oily trace. Perhaps you have wild thoughts of tearing out the page! But if this is treated with a warm iron and blotting-paper as described above, the blotting-paper will absorb the grease and leave the paper clean. Don't have the iron hot either for wall or book, or the result can be imagined.

Ink stains on walls can sometimes be removed by an " ink-remover " indiarubber, but again go slow with the rubbing. Treat inky stains on books like this also. An alternative idea is to rub the inky page over with a solution of salt and water, then dry it with blotting-paper and a warm iron.

DRAWERS THAT STICK

Do you know what to do if one of the drawers in your dressing-table comes out and in with a grudge, sticking every time you try to shut it? It is such a little thing it seems hardly worth while bother-ing about a tradesman. Scrape the edges of the drawers with a piece of broken glass, then rub these trimmed parts with a piece of candle grease or hard soap, and after that the drawers should run quite smoothly.

Another minor irritation is a squeaking door. You can cure this by oiling each set of hinges, leave for a little to let the oil do its work, then open and shut the door, and if the squeak is still there repeat the process.

INVISIBLE MENDING

A word or two about mending and patching. Does that strike you as a terribly dull subject? Or do you approach it in the light of a mild kind of adventure—which it very often is, and patching particularly can be quite exciting. The other day a girl showed me a frock and asked if I could find out where she had mended it. A cinder had fallen out and burnt a hole right in the front of the dress, and believe it or not, though I searched most carefully I couldn't find it. She was very proud about that invisible mend. You do it like a darn. Pull out some threads from some unseen part of the dress, such as the hem, facings or one of the side seams. Darn on the wrong side with these threads you have pulled out, backward and forward, till the gap is filled.

Have you a hole in your best pair of gloves? Don't just drag it together with an over-seaming stitch, or it will strain the fabric and make it weaken somewhere else. But take a fairly long, strong thread, and button-stitch neatly round the hole. When you've gone round once, repeat the buttonholing, going this time into the stitches you've already made, and keep doing this till there is no hole left.

If a chintz cover or curtain is damaged it is advisable to try to repair it. A simple tear is easily mended. Darn it closely and neatly across and tack in a piece of tape on the wrong side to strengthen the weakened fabric. But if it should have been burned or so destroyed that a piece of the material is completely out, it must be patched. The most effective way of doing this is to take a piece of chintz slightly larger than the gap, sew it in, on the wrong side, and on the right side appliqué round the hole with matching coloured thread. Use a piece of the cover or curtain for the patch, taking it from a part where it will not show, replacing this with new chintz if you have it, and if not, with some material which matches up as nearly as possible.

THE MICE MENACE

But perhaps the household disaster which most scares you is neither burns nor tears, spots nor stains; neither the advent of frozen pipes nor troubles with gas and electricity, but just . . the presence of a small mouse in your home. Say it softly—are you afraid of these silent grey visitors? So afraid perhaps that if you caught a mouse in a trap you could not bear to remove it?

Even if you're not afraid, mice can be very destructive and a great nuisance. One way of removing them is to sprinkle cloths with cayenne pepper and stuff them into the mouse holes. Sprinkle pepper also over shelves which are liable to be visited. Be careful not to leave food lying about. Sweep up every crumb and keep a trap set. If that fails to clear them out, then possess yourself of a lively young pussy with strong hunting instincts. Not only will she kill the mice, but her scent will keep them away.

KEEPING FIT

Every year doctors and scientists make new discoveries which help to cure sick people. New schemes are developed for the care of young children, for better houses, schools, and hospital accommodation, and our chances of living longer, happier, and more useful lives increase. But each one of you can help to prevent illness and its consequent suffering by learning the fundamental rules of preserving health, and trying to keep your bodies healthy.

Between the ages of twelve and twenty, the period we speak of as the " teen age ", many important changes take place in your bodies and minds. It is not so much a period of simple growth as of development. The foundations of a strong frame are laid down before birth and in infancy, but now you are developing from a child to a woman. A rather gawky figure becomes more proportionate, and extra fat collects under the skin to give you a more rounded outline.

Your mind grows and develops also. Problems of the world in which you are living become of interest to you, and taste in music and art is cultivated. You become responsible people with opinions of your own, and begin to take an interest in your personal appearance.

Now the most important thing during this period is to develop a routine of personal hygiene, which will become almost automatic as you grow up, if you begin by understanding the following instructions and conscientiously put them into practice.

SKIN CARE

A daily bath should be taken if possible, or if not, a thorough sponge down, using a good soap. Rinse with warm then cold water, and dry with vigorous rubbing. This removes perspiration and dirt from the pores. A cold bath does not suit everybody, and you should not force yourself to take one just because your friend or brother does.

Pay particular attention to the folds of the body. Excessive perspiration not only has an unpleasant odour, but may cause irritation of the skin and soil clothing. After drying, the folds should be powdered with a little talcum powder. Attention should be paid to cleanliness at the time of the menstrual period. Hands should always be washed before meals, after the daily evacuation of the bowels, and after passing water. Disease often spreads from dirty hands.

A word about make-up: the pores of the skin help it to breathe, and if clogged with perspiration or dirt, they cannot act properly. In the same way, thick creams, rouge and powder, used as beauty aids, interfere with the natural skin action and encourage spots. Healthy young girls have a natural glow in their cheeks which is much more attractive and individual than that obtained from a " box ". This does not mean, of course, that a little foundation cream and powder are harmful for older girls.

Nails should be kept clean and moderately short. Toe nails are best cut straight across.

Eyes.—If you have to work or travel in a dusty atmosphere, bathe your eyes with cold water at night.

Hair.—Your hair will respond to regular brushing. Don't develop a hair style with tight curls or rolls which you are afraid to brush out. Wash the hair every two weeks, or more often if it becomes greasy quickly. Owing to the increased activity of the glands of the body in this developing period, the scalp may produce more oily substances than usual, and make the hair greasy.

Teeth.—Proper cleansing of the teeth is necessary both for health reasons and for appearance. Use a brush with firm bristles, and clean both night and morning. Brush up and down to dislodge the food particles from the grooves between the teeth. Don't eat sweets or biscuits after you have cleaned your teeth for the night. Visit the dentist regularly to have any decay attended to.

There are general principles to be remembered as well. You require *exercise* to keep your circulation active and your muscles firm. Pure blood which has received oxygen from the air when you breathe in, nourishes the body and collects waste substances which are disposed of through the lungs when you breathe out, and also through the kidneys and bowels. Games in the *fresh air* are ideal, but if you have little time for games, exercises, skipping, and a walk daily are good substitutes.

But although your body needs exercise, it also requires *sleep* and *rest* to counterbalance the energy used up the previous day. Nine to ten hours sleep are essential every night, and always remember to keep the bedroom windows wide open.

A well-balanced diet is also necessary to preserve health and prevent disease. The three main components of foodstuffs are:

(a) Protein, which is found in milk, eggs and meat, and helps to build up the body tissues.

(b) Carbohydrates, in sugar and cereals, which give energy.

(c) Fats, in butter and cooking fats, also to give energy and a store of fat in the tissues for warmth.

Some foods, such as milk, contain all three.

Vitamins are extra substances which are naturally found in a well-balanced diet, for example:

Vitamin A in meat and vegetables.
Vitamin B in eggs, yeast and milk.
Vitamin C in green salads and fruit.
Vitamin D in milk and cod-liver oil.

Water is a simple but essential part of our diet. Try to drink a glass of water at least twice a day between meals. Meals should be regular and no snacks should be taken between these times. Do not go out in the morning without breakfast. Regular meals, with plenty of greenstuffs in the diet, water and exercise will prevent constipation.

The choice of clothing is also worth considering. Avoid tight shoulder straps, waistbands, knicker elastic and garters. Apart from irritating the skin locally, they interfere with the circulation to the surrounding parts. Begin to wear a brassiere as your natural development occurs. This is more comfortable, and promotes a good figure. Underclothing should be lightweight and easily washed, and all garments should give freedom of movement. Remember that you are probably still growing. Don't wear tight shoes or stockings, or else your feet will rebel, and corns and other foot troubles so annoying to grown-ups will develop.

Everyone is not gifted with regular features and curly hair, but careful attention to personal hygiene can make you admired and attractive.

It is not always possible to avoid illness. Should you not feel well, tell your mother, or whoever is looking after you, so that you

can be seen by a doctor. Some people say that they don't like
" fussing ", but it is not fussing to seek early treatment, which will
not only shorten your illness, but, should your complaint be an
infectious one, will also prevent it spreading to others.

It is obvious that if your mind is developing too, it deserves
care and attention as much as your body. You cannot literally wash
it and brush it, but you can give it relaxation and rest, and you can
exercise it by reading, talking, learning new things, taking responsibility, and, above all, by using it to create things, either by writing
or composing, or in conjunction with your hands, by sewing, knitting,
cooking, gardening, &c. Whatever your interests are, if they are
different from your school work or your job, they will do you good
and refresh you.

Learn to make friends and to be at ease among both girls and
boys of your own age, and among grown-ups too. Although your
brothers or the boy next door, when younger, probably disliked girls
unless they were tomboys and able to join in their games, now that
they are growing up too they are quite eager to have your company,
and learn to dance with you and play more social games such as
tennis. They begin to admire the way you look and dress and the
things you can do. But boys grow up a little more slowly than girls,
and boys of your own age will probably be much more shy than
you are. If you show off and try to be very grown-up, you will
only embarrass them and spoil a happy friendship. Don't try to be
very grown-up too soon. You have lots of time to enjoy grown-up
activities.

FIRST AID AND HOME NURSING

If you have a chance to attend a course of instruction in First
Aid, either in the Girl Guides or Girls' Guildry, a Red Cross or
similar centre, you will find it both interesting and helpful, but
there are many things which you can easily learn without attending
a class, which will make you a really useful person at home should
an accident occur when there is no one more skilled at hand. Very
often it is just as important to know what not to do as what to do.

Let us consider first of all the simple injuries which occur so
frequently at home, at school, or at play. A knock or fall may cause
a painfully swollen red area. If the skin is not broken this is called
a bruise. Within a few days the part becomes black and blue. Bathing

alternately with hot and cold water helps to ease the pain and reduce the swelling.

If the skin is broken the injury is called a graze. It is important to clean a graze thoroughly, as soon after it has happened as possible, particularly if it was caused by falling on the road or gravel. Washing with soap and warm water, with a drop or two of antiseptic, is the best method. Do not use strong antiseptic on the wound as it may burn the skin. Unless the dirt is removed, germs grow, causing sepsis, and healing is then delayed. A clean piece of lint with a little simple ointment should cover the damaged area, and be kept in place by bandage or adhesive tape.

A cut is caused by a knife or a sharp edge. The edges of the wound gape and bleed. Again, cleansing of the wound is most important. A clean, healthy wound heals quickly; infected ones may take a very long time and leave an ugly scar. If there is much bleeding from the cut, apply the bandage firmly.

A burn is a painful injury. Usually a blister forms quite quickly over the affected part. Don't be tempted to prick the blister as you will probably infect the skin. Greasy ointments or oils should never be applied as first-aid dressings for burns. If you have some baking soda, mix some with a little water into a paste, and apply this to the burn and bandage. If none is available, just cover with a clean dry dressing. Keep the part dry until it has healed. Treatment for scalds by boiling water, fat, or any other liquid is the same. If at all severe, send for a doctor.

A Walking Holiday.

Blisters caused by new shoes on long walks can be very painful. Try to prevent them by wearing your new shoes for a short time each day until they have softened and are comfortable. If you are going for a walking holiday, prepare the skin of your heels and soles by rubbing in methylated spirit every night for a week or two before you start, and rub a little soap on the outside of the heels of your socks or stockings when you start to walk. Once a blister has developed, paint it with tincture of iodine. If it is necessary to prick it, make sure that you use a needle which has been sterilized. This can be done by making the point red hot in a flame and allowing to cool. After the fluid is out of the blister, apply a dry dressing.

Twisted knees, ankles and wrists should be bathed alternately in hot and cold water and bandaged firmly, but not too tightly as the injured joint may swell. If the ankle is very painful, and it is suspected that there may be a broken bone, the patient should not be allowed to walk on it, and skilled help should be sent for. If the wrist is very painful, it should be supported in a sling.

Bleeding from the nose can usually be stopped quite easily. Keep the patient sitting up with the head bent forward, with instructions to breathe through the mouth. With your finger and thumb firmly grasp the front part of the nose on each side and press firmly for about five minutes. The bleeding usually comes from a small blood vessel just inside the nostril, and the pressure described is sufficient to control it.

Some people feel faint easily if they are in a hot room, in a crowd, or often if they are just hungry. They turn very pale and feel dizzy, and if they sit down and put the head between the legs to increase the blood supply to the head, this may be sufficient to prevent them becoming unconscious. If, however, consciousness is lost, make sure that they get as much fresh air as possible by opening the window or carrying them to a cooler room. Keep crowds away, and loosen any tight collar or belt. A little cold water splashed on the face may bring them round, but never try to force any unconscious person to drink, as the fluid may get into the windpipe instead of the gullet.

Young children like to experiment, and often put things into their mouths, nose or ears. If something is thought to be lodging at the back of the throat, turn the child's face downwards, and pass the little finger to the back of the throat in the hope of removing it. If swallowed, give a meal of bread or porridge, as this will form a coating round the object and prevent any sharp edges from damaging the stomach or bowel, and it will probably be safely passed through the bowel and be evacuated in the motion.

Call the Doctor.

If the object swallowed is sharp or large, a doctor's advice should be sought; if some poisonous liquid has been swallowed, send for a doctor immediately, and while waiting, try to make the child vomit by irritating the back of the throat with the finger. Don't poke hairpins into the nose to try to retrieve an object; close up the other nostril and make the child blow through the nose; if this is not successful, refer to the doctor. The doctor should always be consulted about an object in the ear.

When there's an Accident.

There are certain things which you must remember to do for seriously wounded people. Send for the doctor and the ambulance at once. Any injured person, whether burned, bleeding, crushed, or with broken limbs, suffers from a condition known as " shock ". A person who is suffering from shock is cold, very pale and collapsed, and if this condition is not treated promptly the person concerned may die. While waiting for the ambulance to arrive:

1. Keep your patient warm. Cover with rugs or coats. If hot-water bottles are available, place them, wrapped in a rug or scarf, beside the patient. *Never* put hot-water bottles next to the skin of an unconscious person, because he or she is unable to feel, and your good intentions may result in a severe burn which only increases this condition of shock.

2. Move the patient as little and as gently as possible. Cut or tear away clothing to dress a wound, rather than turn your patient from side to side.

3. If your patient is conscious, give a hot, sweet drink, such as tea with plenty of sugar.

4. If the patient is badly injured about the mouth or face, turn him face downwards with the head turned to the side, so that any blood will trickle out of the side of the mouth and not choke him.

5. If a limb is helpless and painful, suspect fracture. Put it in as normal a position as possible very gently. If a leg, bandage or tie above and below the break to the other leg. If an arm, bandage in the same way to the body.

Bleeding.

There are two kinds of bleeding.

1. From the veins. The blood looks dark in colour and trickles out gently.

2. From the arteries. This is much more serious. The blood is bright red in colour and spurts out of the wound. The best first-aid treatment is to cover the wound with a clean dressing or handkerchief and press hard over the bleeding area. If extensive, a bandage is applied tightly over the dressing.

HOME NURSING

If any members of your family are ill in bed, you may have to
act nurse. Try to make their enforced stay in bed as pleasant as
possible, at the same time looking after them and carrying out the
doctor's instructions accurately so as to hasten recovery. A sick-
room should have the windows open day and night, and a coal fire,
if possible, to keep a current of fresh air. A coal fire is also cheerful
for your patient to look at. The patient should be placed out of
the draught, and not directly facing the light.

Warm but light bedclothes and several pillows for support are
necessary. Place a small table at the bedside for a reading lamp,
books, &c. There should be a covered jug of water or fruit drink
kept within reach of the patient, and a drinking glass or mug. Paper
handkerchiefs are ideal for a patient with a heavy cold, as these can
be burnt after use. Any pills or medicines ordered for your patient
should be kept together on a small tray, and given at the times
ordered. Urine and fæces should be flushed down the w.c. as soon
as passed, unless the doctor has asked for a specimen to be kept.

Try to get flowers or a plant to brighten the room, and serve all
meals as daintily as possible on a tray. Sick people are sometimes
rather irritable and despondent, particularly if the illness is a long
one, and a sympathetic, gentle, cheerful nurse can greatly help them

FORMING A CLUB

It may happen in your school, or office, or among the crowd you are friendly with in your district, that there is a proposal to start some kind of club. And it is very probable that, as you grow older, you will still continue to be a member of a club. It is therefore useful right at the beginning to know the correct procedure in forming and running a club, because these are the same no matter what kind of club it may be, or in what part of the country you may find yourself. Also, to be properly organized is an essential of any success-ful club.

Whether your new club is to be a local tennis club, or the kind of sewing bee which raises funds for charity by means of whist drives and snowball teas, or a gramophone club in the church, or a youth club with classes in country dancing, arts and crafts, or a dramatic club at school, the first essential requirement in its organization is that nucleus of enthusiastic people who are not merely interested in the idea, but eager and willing to work for it and to make it work. These are the people who, when you hold that preliminary meeting of all who have said they are interested, will emerge as members of your organizing committee.

CHIEF OFFICE-BEARERS

You may have some experience of committees at school, in which case you will be prepared to meet certain difficulties which sooner or later are likely to arise. The best safeguard, however, against the slings and arrows of outrageous committees is a good chairman, whose chief qualities should be tact, tolerance, and good humour; and the greatest of these is good humour. This does not mean some-one who makes jokes in season and out of season, and dismisses as a triviality some point over which two committee members, or sec-tions of the committee, may be coming almost to blows. The good humour is of that quality which combines sympathetic under-standing with a sense of proportion, and results in an ability to judge impartially between disputants and the cause of their dispute. No, not an easy person to find, this ideal chairman, but among the people available you would be wise to choose the nearest approach to this paragon.

Next in importance to your chairman is your secretary. It is generally recognized that the secretary of any committee does all the donkey work and seldom gets much credit. Whether or not your secretary looks for a due mead of praise (and that may be one of the unconsidered trifles which make or mar the smooth running of your club), she must be the type of enthusiast who will be conscientious at all times. Hers will be the job of notifying members regularly of meetings—and both the notifications and the regularity of meetings are important—of issuing general notices, reports, and recommendations to members or sections of the club, and, of course, of taking precise minutes of the committee meetings.

Co-operation must be the keynote of your committee deliberations, and it is desirable, though not always possible, to have as general committee members people who will honestly endeavour to work together for a common purpose, even when their views differ. It will be the task of the chairman to hold the reins of your committee, guiding the meeting, checking the headstrong members who may want to pull away from or ahead of the others, and encouraging the timid to make their fullest contribution.

I have mentioned difficulties arising from the friction of differing personalities, opposite temperaments, and various points of view, but I hope the mere mentioning of them has not disheartened you, because in working with people, and for them, even for their own good and in their special interest, such difficulties inevitably arise, and must be overcome.

Destructive criticism, and a tendency to hold unofficial committee meetings as it were, to argue over, and carry out post-mortems on business which has already been concluded by common consent at a legitimate meeting, are weaknesses in human nature which the committee chairman will encounter. Prevention being better than cure, it is advisable to give club members an opportunity to air their grievances, or put forward their own views on the best methods of improving the conditions which they criticize. Occasional general club meetings should therefore be held, and a point made of inviting any particular disturbers of the peace to express their opinions.

Sometimes valuable contributions are made by members in this way, but frequently the loudest critic is reduced to silence when she is directly asked for her solution of a problem she may even have thoughtlessly helped to create. Should it be necessary, the most effective way of insisting on constructive criticism and co-operation is to give the chronic grumbler a position of responsibility, even on the committee itself, where she will have to maintain the standard of efficiency she demands of others.

THE NOTICE-BOARD

A frequent source of irritation to club members is " not knowing " or " not being told " of plans or decisions made in committee, and this is a sore point the good secretary will help to eliminate by promptly posting announcements on the club notice-board, and distributing personal notices if necessary. Your notice-board is quite an important feature of your incidental furnishings, and it should be the duty of the secretary to keep this up to date by removing old notices as soon as they have served their purpose. Even then you will come across the member who " never saw the notice ", but you will only encourage this unobservant habit if your board is cluttered with dusty notices everyone has been familiar with for weeks.

The furnishing and decorating of your club, if you have premises or a club room you are free to remodel nearer to the heart's desire, should be used as an opportunity for instilling several recognized club principles into your members at the very beginning of your association together. There is no better way of teaching people a proper sense of personal responsibility than, simply, to make them feel personally responsible. If, under the guidance of someone more knowledgeable and probably with more cultivated taste than yourselves, you clean and paint and decorate these rooms, make curtains and cushion covers, do all the joinery and carpentry and electrical work, beg or borrow furnishings, and so by your own efforts make the place not only habitable but attractive and comfortable, you will not easily be led into future abuse of these amenities and comforts.

CO-OPERATION

This will be the first occasion when co-operation and close team-work are required of your members, and being for such a purpose, you will not find them lacking. Give everybody frequent opportunities for the exercise of this spirit, in some kind of communal undertaking which excites or inspires them, either for the club itself or for an outside cause.

Should your club appear to be so efficiently run and capably led that everything goes smoothly and calmly, you must beware of a comfortable complacency keeping you in a stagnant rut. Even the best-run clubs need a constant stimulus to make them effective and satisfactory to their members. Exchange visits, organize inter-club competitions, have social evenings or joint entertainments, or debates, anything that will help to broaden your horizon.

The specialized club, such as the gramophone club, the dramatic or literary club, may be more confined in its purpose, but there is no reason why its function should not be expressed in various ways, by talks from distinguished speakers, discussions and debates, radio programme nights, and film, theatre, and concert nights, as well as by meetings with other clubs.

GENERAL PROCEDURE

So you are starting a club and you want to get down to brass tacks at once. Call a meeting of the people who are interested, or those who might be, or ought to be. Give them reasonable notice of the date, and a statement of the purpose of the meeting and agenda, e.g. " Formation of Club, Election of Office-bearers and Committee Constitution ". If you are convener of the meeting, you should open the meeting by outlining the object in forming your club, and call upon those present to nominate a committee of management. Someone should act as secretary and make a note of what is said, and of nominations and proposals made, until a secretary is chosen, when she should hand over.

Each nomination for any office should be proposed and seconded. When all the names for that particular post have been given, two people should be appointed as tellers to count the votes for each. The nominee gaining most votes of course takes office. In a large club you may want an Honorary President as a figure-head who need not attend all meetings, but must be the final authority in any controversy, and must at all times be informed of what takes place and of decisions made. A Vice-president who is directly respon-sible to the President may take her place at meetings, and may, if you wish, act as chairman. In a small private club probably only a Chairman will be sufficient. The offices of Secretary and Treasurer may be combined or separate, according to the financial status of your club, or the abilities of your members.

At your preliminary meeting, once the committee has been elected, you should discuss the drawing up of a constitution, including the Objects of Club, Rules of Membership, Subscriptions, Club Meetings, Election of Office-bearers, Committees, Annual General Meeting, Financial Statement. This may be done by the General Committee or a specially appointed Sub-committee, and brought to a general meeting later for discussion, amendment and adoption.

The procedure at any meeting is the same when business of this kind takes place. After discussion of a point, the Chairman should ask a committee member to make a formal motion, proposing that such and such be done. Another should second this, and the Chairman, repeating the proposal, should ask for any amendments. If none is forthcoming, she will assume that the motion is acceptable to all, and is to be carried unanimously. Should an amendment be made, however, and duly seconded, the amendment and the motion must be put to the vote, taking the amendment first. You should, in your constitution, lay down the numbers to form quorums at meetings, and whether or not the President or Chairman will have a casting or deliberative vote, or both, at meetings of Sub-committees or General Committee.

The usual agenda of a committee meeting reads thus:

Minute of last meeting. (Beginning with those present and apologies.)

Matters arising. (Action taken on proposals made; subsequent correspondence, &c.)

Treasurer's Report.

Business. (Items under separate headings, such as Section Reports.)

Any other competent business. (Relevant matters not already covered, new suggestions, complaints, &c.)

An agenda of the business should be sent if possible to members as part of their notice to attend the meeting; otherwise, one should be provided for each member at the meeting.

MUSIC CLUBS

Most of us have belonged to some club or other, a dramatic club, or a camera club, clubs for hockey, tennis or badminton, and so naturally we shall want to belong to a music club. However, unless our own particular school, factory, or youth centre already has one, we may need to form a music club for ourselves. It is surprising how many friends will want to join, once somebody starts the ball rolling. And it is astonishing how many local musicians will come forward to give their services once they see you are keen. Don't be afraid of the responsibility; I know at first it involves a lot of work arranging, collecting money, putting up notices, and buying gramophone records and music, but you will soon find kind helpers, and that half the fun is electing your own " officials ", who share the organizing.

Forming a music club is exciting, because music covers a vast field of varied interests from jazz to opera, and ballet to symphonies and concertos. Music is rather like painting and dancing, it doesn't matter what country you live in, or district, town, or county, nor does it matter what language you speak—everyone old or young, boy or girl, can enjoy a good tune. And music mixes so well with other activities. A drama club I know asked the music group to sing some Scots songs in between the acts of a Highland tragedy. Very effective the singers looked, too, in their kilts.

However, it is not everyone who can act or sing, but they may enjoy listening. Good concerts are often expensive, few and far between, so that it is useful to collect your own concerts as it were, and control them as you wish. So now let us set about forming a gramophone club or a music appreciation group. We will talk about records first, and then see them in relationship to a fuller enjoyment and appreciation of music.

The room in which your group meets is important, and it is best to use the same one each time. If you can't, try and have a cupboard in it that is definitely yours. See that the room is warm, and the chairs as comfortable as possible. To encourage a friendly atmosphere (music groups flourish better in a friendly atmosphere) put the chairs in a circle. Have flowers if you can, and pictures of modern conductors, orchestras, and concert artists. The B.B.C. publications dept. have some fine reproductions for sale. Copies of the *Radio Times*, *Listener*, and other topical magazines finish your setting. Encourage members to bring along any pictures or magazines that they think would be useful.

Don't be disappointed if you have to start in a much humbler way. Many a group of W.R.A.F.s, W.R.A.C.s, or W.R.N.S. derive hours of enjoyment from a portable gramophone on a box, with beds for seating accommodation. A gramophone is your first essential with the right needles, speed, &c., details of which we will look into later. But before you can get your group together remember to put up a very distinct notice giving date, time and place. It is amazing how many people forget to state all three. An arresting poster by an artist friend attracts most attention. After all, concert parties and plays are often most attractively advertised, so see that from the start music is *not* treated as a Cinderella, and your music group gets a fair beginning.

Make your first " recital " as varied as you can; if you do not happen to know very much about your friends' tastes, then include both highbrow and jazz. See that what you select is good of its kind. In fact, aim at quality and variety.

Do not present only symphonies; there are lots of lovely overtures such as Fingal's Cave, light orchestral pieces such as the Strauss Waltzes, instrumental works of all kinds, and your favourite songs from Bing to Caruso. Start very simply. Begin where your group is. There is no use giving a string quartet recording to Chopin fans. The whole of Chopin's Revolutionary study is worth listening to over and over. Remember that Chopin wrote a good deal of other lovely music, so explore his other scherzos, waltzes, polonaises and preludes for yourself. Get up a party to the next piano recital where the pianist includes some Chopin.

I take it that your group is showing a nucleus of enthusiasts one of whom could undertake to make friends of the local librarian. Tell him or her about your new venture, and ask to see the music section in your public library. Borrow a book on the life of Chopin. If you have a piano available, preferably in your gramophone club room, invite a pianist friend to play over again your favourites, persuade her to play over other works by the great Polish composer and tell you about them. Then go on to compare Chopin's piano writing with others. See if you like Debussy's " Clair de Lune ", or his " Golliwog's Cake Walk ".

Get someone to tell you about the kind of music that was popular several hundred years ago and played on instruments with keyboards like a piano. These instruments are different in style, and have such names as virginal, harpsichord, spinet. If you visit your local museum you can see some of these early pianos. Also you can buy gramophone records to hear what they sounded like; then realize what a wonderful invention is the modern pianoforte. I expect by now you are thinking, " Goodness! Imagine playing the ' Warsaw Concerto ' on a harpsichord." So here is where your records really become valuable.

Do this investigating with other instruments : saxophones, violins, clarinets and trumpets have all changed tremendously. Jeremiah Clark's "Trumpet Voluntary" can be compared with Harry James's arrangement and recording of " Flight of the Bumble Bee " (originally written by a Russian named Rimsky-Korsakov).

Listen to B.B.C. programmes and note the names of leading orchestras and conductors. Find out what is on in your own town. You see, your music group does not necessarily have to confine itself to listening to gramophone records and nothing more. The records are a means to an end, and that end is the discovery of wonderful music which you have never yet had the opportunity to hear. Many people had no idea about the lovely music the Norwegian composer Grieg had written until a musical show called " Song of Norway " was produced, then they discovered for themselves the beauty of these Norwegian melodies.

The gramophone club will soon become a Musical Appreciation club. I use the term "musical appreciation" in its best sense. I use it to mean real enjoyment of the greatest music played by the greatest musicians, and I include jazz. I can enjoy a swing session if it is played by as great a clarinettist as Benny Goodman. Some of us have unhappy memories of a youth spent in singing lots of sol-fa, listening to long and complicated lessons on a very difficult subject called " theory ", and the whole uninspiring business labelled " Musical Appreciation "!

Jazz.

Before we leave the subject of musical appreciation just a few words on jazz, swing and dance music. There is no reason why we should not appreciate the best in these provided we take the trouble to understand them. There are several excellent books in shilling editions explaining the difference between real jazz and imitation dance tunes. Any book which talks of the New Orleans jazzmen way back before 1800, and tells you the stories about Duke Ellington, Louis Armstrong, Artie Shaw, and Benny Goodman will do. You will find the life story of Bix Beiderbecke, Pine Top Smith, Buddy Featherstonhaugh, or Jelly Roll Morton and many others all bound up with the history of jazz. Read about Paul Whiteman's betrayal. A good record to have in your collection to take you back to the very beginning, as it were, is Jelly Roll Morton's New Orleans Jazzmen playing " I thought I heard Buddy Bolden Say ", H.M.V. B9216. In fact, any of H.M.V.'s swing series is excellent and includes Pine Top Smith, some good " blues ", and beginnings of Boogie Woogie as in Pete Johnson's and Albert Ammons' two-piano effort on H.M.V. B9251. We must leave the enthusiasts to work out the rest.

Equipment.

I should like to pass on some advice about equipment from different groups I have known. Having launched out successfully in this business of forming a gramophone club, you feel you want the best apparatus available, but at not too high a cost. You may have started humbly with a portable, or perhaps you managed to borrow something better. Anyway, the aim you have in mind is always quality, and so you are very concerned about the reproduction of your loud-speaker. Time spent in attending to this is never wasted. The loud-speaker is the focal point as it were. It does not matter how the sounds get into the speaker, provided that the resultant sounds issuing forth are as near to the original orchestra, instrumentalist or singer as possible.

Appearance will not matter. It is very tempting to have a beautiful radiogram in a nicely polished cabinet, but the price is prohibitive, added to which you do not require the radio part. The most successful loud-speakers are frequently those enormous, ugly-looking, wooden squares. They are scientifically constructed and reproduce the highest notes from the piercing top notes of the piccolo down to the lowest notes of the bassoon. The reason why an ordinary wireless set never sounds quite like the real thing is because it is usually only producing the middle sounds. Worse still, some sets only give out the low notes, which produce the booming tone beloved by the uninitiated.

Briefly, you need an electric motor, a pick-up, an amplifier and a loud-speaker. It is cheaper to buy separate parts, on the advice of a kind father or brother who knows all about electrical equipment, and on the advice of this same kind relative or friend assemble the parts. An old portable antediluvian sort of gramophone of the wind-up type does for a motor, if you can't afford an electric one and can persuade someone to do all the winding. The secret lies in the pick-up; this costs about £1. Next you need an amplifier, which looks like a wireless set in itself and contains lots of valves and things which are connected to the loud-speaker. These items bought separately cost half the price of a shining new radiogram.

Having discussed the true essentials of your equipment, be sure to attend to such details as needles and dusters, record carriers, and so forth. Remember that quite an important way of keeping any group alive is by exchange of ideas, so you may want to borrow records from other societies, individuals, or libraries. Small carriers built to hold twenty-five records, which are easily carried, can be bought for £1. Twelve-inch boxes used to pack records in from the manufacturer to the local dealer are good substitutes, with a cardboard between each record. Records can also be sent by post provided a firm wooden box, well padded, is used; but get an expert to show you how to prepare it.

People have different ideas about needles. Learn how to deal with fibre ones, because some folk will only allow these to be used on their discs; they say that steel needles wear them out more quickly. Personally I feel it is most important to avoid long gaps in a programme, and if you have to wait patiently while the fibre needle is being sharpened before you can hear the rest of your beloved Bing Crosby, then it is most irritating. So I use long-life needles guaranteed to do forty sides, and I change the needle every twenty or so. Have a little brush fixed on to the arm to keep the grooves free from dust, and put on a special speed tester before a recital; watch some lines until they stop moving then you know all is well.

Buying Records.

When you are buying records remember that there is a fifteen per cent discount for educational purposes. If you are forming a club in school one of the teachers will advise you about filling forms to obtain the discount. If you have left school you can do this through a youth club, run either by a voluntary organization or the local education authority. Dance music is excluded.

Finance.

When you have elected an honorary secretary and hon. treasurer at your first business meeting decide how much subscription you can afford towards general funds; 1s. 6d. to 2s. 6d. a month might do for a start, depending entirely upon how much outside help you can get. This will be determined by your own keenness.

Storing and Cataloguing.

As your collection of records grows, you will need to keep a list and have some system of storing. I once spent an interesting morning in the B.B.C., where whole rooms have walls covered with shelves to house their quarter million records; it is the largest collection in the world after the one at Washington, D.C. It is best to store records upright. Laid flat they are apt to get bent; don't place in a warm atmosphere. Ordinary albums stood upright as in a bookcase will do to start.

As your collection increases find a handy man to build you a cupboard with shelves deep enough to take a twelve-inch disc, and have cardboard partitions made every nine inches or so. A ledge along the front prevents them rolling forward on to the floor.

Now for classification; I advise you to use your own system and keep it simple. Put all of the same type of music together and have a loose-leaf file to enter them in under the following useful headings: symphonies, concertos, overtures, orchestral, instrumental (ballets and suites), opera, vocal. Subdivide these into composers. Keep a note of the artist, orchestra and conductor, number of sides, size of record, its number and the length of time each side takes to play. Roughly, allow four minutes each side. Incidentally it is worth while having one of the records with markings on to test speed. When the lines become steady your speed is correct.

To illustrate this cataloguing business; suppose you have the " Warsaw Concerto ". Turn to page marked " Concertos "; on the left-hand side, under "A", put Addinsell, Richard, then Warsaw (for the name of piece), two sides. Suppose, too, that you have acquired a record of José Iturbi playing the " Mazurka in A " by Chopin, then you turn to your page marked instrumental and under " C " write Chopin, the name of the piece, perhaps a "Mazurka", Op. 100, No. 1, piano, &c. Op. is short for a Latin word " opus " which means " work ". Many composers have written so much music that we need to have a system of cataloguing them.

Presentation.

Finally, a few words on presenting your programme. It is a good idea to have a rota, and let each member take it in turn to be responsible for an evening's choice of records. Remember people get fidgety if there is too much talking, leaving insufficient time for music. On the other hand, avoid nervously sticking on a string of pieces with no explanation. Just a few words—explaining, for instance, that this piece of music represents a storm, its title is such and such, the name of the orchestra and conductor—are sufficient. If it is Toscanini, you might mention that he left Italy because he disapproved of Mussolini. Avoid further comment at the time, and probably during the tea interval you will find quite a discussion on the influence of the war on European conductors and their fates.

Earlier I mentioned enlisting the help of a local musician. You might do it this way. Suppose you have bought Reginald Kell's recording of the Mozart clarinet quintet. Then invite a good clarinettist along with his instrument. Get him to play the main tunes from the Mozart work before each record is played. Follow this up with parts of the Rachmaninoff 2nd piano concerto (the music which ran through a film called " Brief Encounter "), where in the slow part you hear the clarinet alternating with a flute in a succession of lovely melodies.

I have said enough for you to go ahead on your own now with other theme programmes, such as opera and ballet. (Remember Tschaikovsky's " Nutcracker Suite ", which is from a ballet.)

Good luck to your music club and remember the golden rule is friendliness. Never let the gramophone concert become an end in itself. It is a substitute, the guide book and map for your journey, but not the journey itself. The journey is through endless paths of lovely music of all kinds still to be explored.

YOUR OWN LIBRARY

There are few pleasures in life so lasting and so satisfying as the pleasure to be obtained from books. How lucky we are too! To those of us who are reflective and discerning, it must be a cause for self-congratulation that we were born, not English or Scottish or American, but English-speaking, and consequently have easy access to the greatest and most voluminous literature in the world. We have merely to learn to read, and we have opened to us an unrivalled storehouse of poetry, drama, essays, novels and history, to say nothing of more technical and recondite types of literature. In short, to enrich our minds and increase our happiness, we have only to read—and, if we are real lovers of books, to form a library, however small.

" Yes," you say, " I should love to have my own library, but while I want to collect books, I should like a little guidance so that I can be sure that I am collecting something worth while. I think my judgment is good, but I'd like some confirmation. How can I know that I am choosing good books? What ought I to read?"

BOOK SHELVES

Before we go on to discuss books, however, it would be better to say a little about keeping them. If you are going to build a library, you must have some kind of shelf-space. If you are lucky enough to possess a good bookcase of your own, well and good, but few young folks are so fortunate. Most of us have little enough room for shelves, and alas! books have a habit of multiplying and overflowing their accommodation.

On the whole, the best kind of bookcase, for most of us, is the sectional type which can be added to as required. The sections are not unduly expensive, and if you can afford them—or if you can persuade an adoring aunt or uncle to make you a present of one at Christmas—you will not regret your choice. On the other hand, open shelves and racks are not to be despised, although they involve much dusting. They are cheaper, perhaps, and may even be made easily enough by a tool-conscious brother or father or uncle.

CLASSICS

The important thing, however, is the choice of the books themselves. Luckily, in these days, there are excellent, cheap series of books that make collecting easy in so far as the classics are concerned. I need mention only the tremendous " Everyman's Library ", so varied and catholic in its scope, and the dainty and pleasantly bound little " World's Classics ". The former runs to nearly a thousand volumes, and the latter to five hundred, the catalogues of both series being in themselves a concise and reliable guide to literature. There are other collections too, both cheap and attractive, which are too numerous to mention. These, and the various cheap editions of modern copyright books issued by many publishers, have not only the advantage of being cheap, but also the additional one of taking up little space.

" That's all very well," you say, a little impatiently, " but what about recommending some books to begin with?" Well, I expect that if you are going to form a library, you are already a book-lover, and will have a nucleus to begin with, old favourites such as *Little Women*, *Good Wives*, *The Swiss Family Robinson*, *The Water Babies*, *Alice in Wonderland*, Grimm and Andersen, and perhaps *The Pilgrim's Progress* and *The Wind in the Willows*. Do not despise old friends now you are growing up; they will often repay your forbearance by giving you a good deal of pleasure in later life. Louisa M. Alcott's *Little Women*, for example, is not merely a child's book, but contains a wealth of characterization and truth to life that give it a permanent value as a picture of middle-class American life of its period, while *Alice in Wonderland* has enough humour and crazy logic in it to provide food for a lifetime.

In discussing additions to this nucleus, let us begin with the older books and work on to more modern ones. I expect that most people are led to books through the medium of the novel, and luckily, English literature is rich in this class of book. We all have our early favourites among authors, and Dickens stands high in the list. No collection of novels could be complete without, at least, *The Pickwick Papers* and what is perhaps his masterpiece, *David Copperfield*. When you have read these you will probably want to go on, and you can allow your own taste and enjoyment to guide your choice. His contemporary, Thackeray, in on no account to be neglected; be sure to add *Vanity Fair* and *Henry Esmond* to your collection. You will never regret meeting Becky Sharp in the first, and you will probably discover that *Esmond* grows greater and more enjoyable with each re-reading.

Of recent years, Anthony Trollope has had a great vogue, and you would do well to sample *Barchester Towers* to find if it suits you. Trollope is hardly one of the greatest novelists; he is a more than competent craftsman, whose novels give an unsurpassed picture of life in Victorian church circles. If you like him, he has many other works to offer you, many of them to be obtained in the " World's Classics ".

Now, before we leave the older novelists, let me put in a plea for Scott. Please do not forget him, or look down on him because, perhaps, you had him forced on you in school. If you do, you are ignoring one of the very greatest novelists. As he did not write for children, it takes a fairly mature mind to appreciate him. So, now, or in the future, read *Guy Mannering* (again if necessary!), or *The Bride of Lammermoor*, or *Rob Roy*, or the best of them all, *The Antiquary*. They are well worth it. Scott's style is not of the best—he wrote too hurriedly for that—but among many other virtues, he could create magnificent characters and tell a tale. No one who wishes to be familiar with the best can afford to ignore him.

Among more modern writers it is difficult to make a choice, not from lack of quality but rather from a surfeit. Stevenson needs no recommendation, and Thomas Hardy and George Meredith have both become " classics ". Of Hardy, I would suggest that you first read *Under the Greenwood Tree*, a charming pastoral story, next, *Far from the Madding Crowd*, a much " meatier " tale, and then what is perhaps his masterpiece, the moving and tragical *Tess of the D'Urbervilles*.

Of Meredith, who has a difficult and very mannered style, but who possessed wit in abundance and a good sense of character, you will probably most appreciate *The Ordeal of Richard Feverel*. His finest work is generally thought to be in *The Egoist*, a book full of psychological niceties, and which is only for a really mature and hardened reader.

You will have read and loved, I expect, Jane Austen's *Pride and Prejudice*, but do not forget her other novels, especially *Mansfield*

18   (G 250)

Park and *Emma*, both of which, in the present writer's opinion, are even better. Perhaps, however, you are, like Sir Walter Scott and Rudyard Kipling, a " Janeite " already, in which event, you may like to sample *The Mysteries of Udolpho* by Anne Radcliffe (" Everyman's "), the horrific tale that inspired Miss Austen to write *Northanger Abbey.*

In addition, if you are wise, you will acquire Fanny Burney's *Evelina*, a delightful story, whose style and delicacy carry off a rather improbable plot. No wonder Dr. Johnson enthused over it when it was published. Another delightful book, off the beaten track, is Susan Ferrier's *Marriage.* The author was a very lively lady whose work was highly esteemed by Sir Walter Scott. Her story is a rich comedy adorned by equally rich characterization. In addition, the " Everyman " edition includes a selection from her racy and humorous letters.

There are many other standard novelists of whose work you have probably read or heard something. You would be unwise to neglect George Eliot and her *Mill on the Floss* and *Silas Marner,* or Charlotte Brontë's *Jane Eyre,* while it would be folly indeed to miss Emily Brontë's thrilling and gripping *Wuthering Heights,* which is melodramatic enough, but which is written with a force and compelling power that few novelists, either men or women, have achieved.

OTHER FAVOURITES

Of Kipling, you may have read the delightful *Jungle Books, Puck of Pook's Hill* and the *Just So Stories.* Add to them on your shelves, *Kim,* a glowing description of Indian life and an excellent adventure story. In addition, Kipling was one of our most notable short-story writers, and naturally a brilliant stylist. Any of his volumes of short stories will be worth adding to your collection.

Another beautiful writer you cannot afford to miss is the naturalist, W. H. Hudson. Read his strange, haunting novel of the South American forests, *Green Mansions,* and meet the lovely heroine Rima. Of his other works, though they are not novels, his autobiography *Far Away and Long Ago* and his *A Shepherd's Life* are not to be missed.

J. M. Barrie may delight you with his *Little Minister,* but his *Sentimental Tommy* is better worth reading. John Galsworthy's *Forsyte Saga* is also well worth possessing, as is also Arnold Bennett's

Old Wives' Tale, one of the finest novels of the century. Of H. G. Wells's enormous and unequal output, you will probably like best the delightful *History of Mr. Polly*, the equally delightful *Kipps*, and the social satire *Tono-Bungay*, which is well worth reading and re-reading.

Do not fail to obtain a copy of James Stephens's charming Irish tale, *The Crock of Gold*, and, in an entirely different genre, of Mary Skrine's beautiful and truly religious story, *Shepherd Easton's Daughter* (" Kingfisher Library "), which is not half so well known as it deserves to be.

Enid Bagnold's *National Velvet* has only to be read to become a favourite: it depicts a family nearly as charming as the Marshes. Other books worth reading are Compton Mackenzie's *Guy and Pauline*, R. H. Mottram's *The English Miss*, Francis Brett Young's *Portrait of Clare*, and J. B. Priestley's entertaining best-seller, *The Good Companions*. Charles Morgan deserves much more than a passing mention. His exceedingly beautiful novels *Portrait in a Mirror* and *The Fountain* are genuine contributions to English literature as well as being absorbing stories.

THE GREAT POETS

It would be a mistake, of course, to confine your reading to prose fiction; there is so much else in English that is first-rate. The glory of English literature has always lain in its poets. No nation, except perhaps the ancient Greeks, has produced such a noble company as Chaucer, Spenser, Shakespeare, Milton, Wordsworth, Shelley and Keats, to mention only a few. You will be familiar with some of their work, I expect; perhaps you read them in school, but do not forget them in later life; they have so much to offer. You will have your own favourites, no doubt, and no list is required here.

To the more modern poets, however, the best approach is through the anthology. To your *Golden Treasury* do not fail to add *The Oxford Book of English Verse*, and do not forget that there are many other " Oxford books " all worth having. Of more modern verse, I should like to recommend three collections, *Poems of To-day* (The English Association: Sidgwick and Jackson), *The Golden Book of Modern English Poetry* (ed. Thomas Caldwell), and *Poems of Our Time* (edited by Richard Church and M. M. Bozman). These are all good.

SHORT STORIES

If you are a lover of short stories, I should recommend as a starting-point, in addition to Kipling, H. G. Wells's *Collected Short Stories*, Katherine Mansfield's *Bliss* and *The Garden Party*, and " Saki's " (H. H. Munro's) *Collected Short Stories*. Begin with his *Tobermory*, and I think you will read on. You can obtain more guidance from the anthologies of short stories to be found in " Everyman's " and the " World's Classics " series. Further, if you are interested in the detective story, there is a good collection, *Tales of Detection*, edited by Dorothy L. Sayers, which will introduce you to many worth-while writers of this branch of fiction.

* * * * * * * * * * *

If you are fond of essays, add to your *Essays of Elia* and *Sir Roger de Coverley*, Hazlitt's essays and some of the volumes of E. V. Lucas, Robert Lynd, Hilaire Belloc and G. K. Chesterton. Above all, if you really love the essay, be sure to obtain Max Beerbohm's *Works* and *More*. You may like also to possess Virginia Woolf's *The Common Reader* and *The Second Common Reader*, which contain good, if rather " highbrow ", literary criticism.

And now—what else? History, the Drama, Biography? If you are interested in history, which can be an absorbing art, bearing no relation to school textbooks, acquire H. G. Wells's *Outline of History* (but do not believe everything he tells you) and H. A. L. Fisher's splendid *History of Europe*.

Biography presents no problem; you will naturally read the lives of those in whom you are interested. As an introduction to modern play-writing, you cannot do better than begin with Barrie's *The Admirable Crichton*, *What Every Woman Knows* and *Quality Street*, and G. B. Shaw's *You Never Can Tell* and *Arms and the Man*. You will soon find more plays to read.

One word of warning: do not fall into a rut in your reading. By that, I mean do not read one type of book only. Your interests and knowledge as well as your judgment will widen and strengthen as you take a wider sweep. There are good books of all classes— even cookery books—and much interest to be derived from reading specialized books as far apart as F. Marian McNeill's *The Scots Kitchen* and Dr. Joad's *Guide to Philosophy*. Have your favourites by all means, but do not confine yourself to them. Try everything once.

REFERENCE BOOKS

Finally, no library is complete without some books of reference. Here are a few: *The Oxford Dictionary of Quotations* (a delightful bedside anthology and an excellent present to receive!), *A Smaller Classical Dictionary* ("Everyman's"), *The Oxford Companion to English Literature* or its smaller brother, *The Concise Oxford Dictionary of English Literature*, and (to be dipped into, not read continuously) *The Concise Cambridge History of English Literature*.

In addition, you should obtain the best dictionary you can buy. Of the good, cheaper ones, Chambers's and the *Concise Oxford Dictionary* are to be recommended. Any or all of these books will prove useful.

So, off you go, building up your library. The more you read, the greater will your appetite and your critical powers grow, and yours will be the unfailing pleasure of always having at hand faithful friends that will entertain, instruct and console you throughout your life.

SOME SIMPLE KNOTS WHICH EXPLAIN THEMSELVES

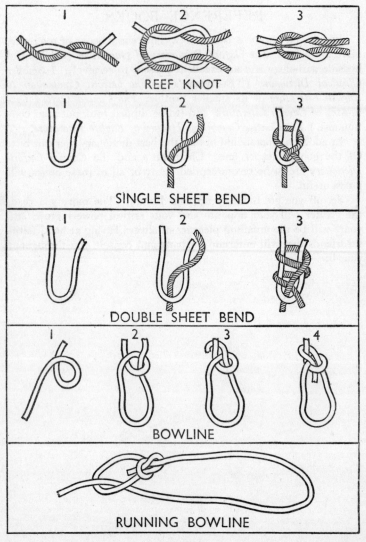

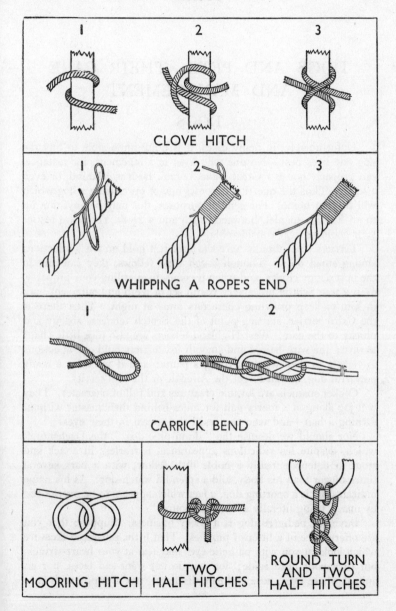

CLOVE HITCH

WHIPPING A ROPE'S END

CARRICK BEND

MOORING HITCH

TWO HALF HITCHES

ROUND TURN AND TWO HALF HITCHES

DOGS AND PETS: THEIR CARE AND MANAGEMENT

DOGS

Unfortunately, in many cases, it is quite impossible to buy the dog one likes best. No one who lives in a tenement, for instance, can properly house a Great Dane, borzoi, Irish wolfhound, or even a setter. Thus the question becomes one of purchasing a dog which will fit your home. For general purposes, this may be anything up to an English spaniel, between which and a $2\frac{1}{2}$-lb. Yorkshire terrier your choice is very considerable.

Terriers undoubtedly have the strongest hold on one's affections among small dogs. Though tough little fellows, they can mix in the best doggy circles, and when it comes to guarding your property, even a wee Scottie has a very useful set of teeth and sufficient bark in him to keep prowling characters away at night. Then there is the Cairn terrier, starting-point of the Scotch terriers, shaggy and plucky to the core. West Highland terriers are also nice little chaps to own; the wire-haired and smooth fox terriers hold our affections as tightly as they would a tramp's pants; and if we want a really powerful dog, do not forget the Airedale or the bull terrier.

Cocker spaniels are lovable creatures and full of character. They will jog along at a merry gait for miles behind their master without turning a hair—and who can resist the appeal in their eyes?

Nor should we despise the " drain-pipe dog ", the Dachshund, which, despite his ridiculous appearance, is fearless in attack and stout in defence; really a noble little fellow, with a bark several times bigger than his body, and a splendid watch-dog. As his name indicates, he is a sporting dog, a fact which appears to be overlooked by many, being literally a " badger hound ".

Buying a pedigree dog is a tricky business. Suppose that you are offered one of a litter of puppies. That little, sad-faced creature which looks at you with pathetic eyes may tear at your heart-strings, but turn your head aside; for you do not want sad faces, nor an animal whose eyes, nose and ears discharge, nor a puppy with bare

BREEDS OF DOGS

St. Bernard	Greyhound
Collie	Airedale
Bloodhound	Fox terrier

patches on its body, however good its pedigree. Rather select the little chap which toddles about and barks cheekily at you, and is ready to bite your fingers. Feeding your puppy is also a problem. Find out what the breeder has been giving it, and carry on in the same way. A puppy whose age can be counted in weeks requires five meals per day. Roughly, the idea is to feed little and often; but as the dog gets older reduce the number of meals and increase the quantity, until the mature dog is having two meals per day. I will come back to this question of feeding later on.

When you buy a puppy you buy trouble, but be tolerant at first. It is quite impossible for him to be clean until he has learned how, and it is sheer stupidity on anyone's part to expect a puppy to have good manners. Give him a comfortable bed, free from draught and damp. When he has been unclean, rebuke him. After each meal, put him out. If he behaves well, praise him. All dogs are extremely sensitive to our tones and soon learn to distinguish when we are pleased or angry; as a rule, they can be taught without thrashing. If you thrash a puppy severely, you will soon thrash all the spirit out of him, confuse his mind, and make both him and yourself very unhappy. Watch your dog. He soon learns to remember, and even when he cannot help misbehaving, is conscious of his fault.

You may desire to have a dog which can compete at shows. If so, you should either be accompanied by someone who is " doggy-minded " when making your purchase, or you should visit several shows beforehand, so as to learn by inspection the principal points of the breed that you have in mind. Whatever the type chosen, when buying, always look for a dog which is not rickety, pot-bellied or spotty-bodied. Look at his mouth. If the upper dentures come too far forward, and the canine teeth do not fit as they should, then he is " overshot ", a bad fault. If the lower line of teeth projects, then he is " undershot ", which is even worse.

Of course, one can only get what one pays for. A two-guinea pup will not set the grass on fire at a dog show. A fair price for a pedigree pup which has a reasonable chance of developing into a prize-winning dog is five guineas; that is, for a dog from six to ten weeks old. This brings me to the question of the age at which the puppy should be when bought. In most cases, it is comparatively safe to take a puppy from its mother at about six weeks, but if possible eight or nine weeks is much better.

BREEDS OF DOGS

Old English sheepdog
Flat-coated retriever

Bull terrier
Foxhound

Setter

Scotch terrier

Labrador

Puppyhood is a hazardous time, particularly during the teething period. From about four months, such things as shoes, legs of chairs or tables, and even carpets, appear very attractive to a playful puppy; really, of course, he desires to ease his mouth, just as a baby does when teething. Give him a bone, and change it for another every three or four days. These bones act on the teeth and gums, allowing the milk teeth to come out, and they assist in cutting the permanent dentures. Bones should be chosen with discrimination. Splintery bones are altogether wrong, particularly rabbit bones, poultry bones, or fish bones. Big juicy shin bones, fresh and clean, are correct for dogs—when one can get them.

Accustoming the puppy to a collar and lead is another troublesome stage in his training. Before your puppy makes his début in public, allow him to walk about the house for a few days with his collar on. Tie a piece of thick string to it. At first there will be a kind of all-in wrestling match; but he will soon get over that. When you do sally forth with him, keep on the move. He may sit down, pull in the opposite direction, or attempt to run round you. Gentle tugs on the lead will invariably keep him on the move, besides teaching him to walk on the proper side. Then he may pull to get in front of you, a common experience. Do not start to walk fast, in order to suit the puppy. Bring him back with " heel ", and keep saying "heel " until he fully understands what you require of him. Of course, if he is particularly dour, pulling him along may result in injury, which should never occur; but even if beaten once or twice, you can master him by patience. Some puppies, as they get on to five or six months, become quite overbearing. Temper on their part must never be overlooked, and if you nip it in the bud you will save yourself a heap of trouble later. An inclination to fight with other dogs in the street must also be discouraged right away; while running and barking at people, or at motor cars, is another undesirable fault.

A folded newspaper makes an excellent correcting weapon. Remember, the quality of obedience must be drummed into your dog. Do not run on to the road after him when he is challenging a Rolls Royce to a race. Keep walking and calling him, and when he does come back, try the folded newspaper and put him on the lead.

Feeding is one of the most important questions in successful dog management. Experienced breeders pay great attention to feeding, and it is hardly necessary to say that incorrect methods cause more trouble than anything else.

Let us start from the very beginning. When puppies are three weeks old I commence to supplement the mother's rations. A teaspoonful of mince every other day can be tried, and at the fourth week of life keep the mother away for periods. During that time give one of the well-advertised dog milks in a saucer. Soon the puppies will learn to lap, and when they can do this nicely, you can increase the period of the mother's absence. By the time they are six weeks old, they should be independent of her.

Avoid drastic changes of diet in puppy feeding; equally important, never over-feed. Because the puppy eats with avidity, do not say: " Oh, it says so much on the tin, but really he can eat more "; just adhere to what is specified on the tin. One must resist the temptation to yield to a whimper and two pleading eyes . . . and close the door!

After seven weeks or so, when the puppy is eating, say, a tablespoonful of mince, put some breadcrumbs into the milk. Wholemeal bread is all right, nor need you throw crusts away.

At eight or nine weeks comes another important stage—" worming ". Worms and dogs are almost inseparable. Because you do not see them, it does not mean that worms are absent. If you get rid of these internal parasites at the age of nine weeks or so you have done well, and will have set a seal of safety on your dog's life. Once again, stick to the regulations printed on the packet; an overdose of worm medicine can have serious results. There are excellent proprietary medicines on the market for treating worms; but in difficult cases, where a dog is inclined to be constipated, medicinal paraffin for three or four days before worming is advised. A fast of about eighteen hours is essential to the success of worming a dog.

At nine weeks four meals per day are sufficient, but the quantities must now be increased. Introduce such novelties as a little gravy and soup, with which you can give puppy biscuits. Incidentally, if you can induce the puppy to eat these biscuits dry, all the better; an excess of sloppy food is injurious to the health of all dogs. As the weeks go on you can slowly get rid of the patent milk and give cow's milk; with this it is a good idea to add a teaspoonful of lime-water or calcium lactate, both of which are excellent media for making bone, and they are also good for the teeth. For rickety puppies they are essential. A teaspoonful of cod-liver oil daily is also a great help in rickets. Buy veterinary cod-liver oil; it is much cheaper and lasts a long time. I have found cod-liver oil good for all dogs. Besides the help it gives in bone forming it is a great tonic for the general health, and it goes a long way to promote a good coat.

We come now to the question of meat. "I never give meat," some people say; "it makes the dog savage." This is rubbish. A dog must have meat to be healthy. The question of quantity is determined by the type of dog; but, as a rough rule, he needs half an ounce for each pound of his own weight. Raw meat is better, because cooked meat loses a certain amount of nourishment. Compromise by giving both; in order to break the monotony I would advise breaking away from meat now and again, and giving boned fish for a day or two. Try a herring, from which you have cut off the head and extracted the chief bones, and feed it either cooked or raw. You will be surprised how much your dog will enjoy it.

Fruit and vegetables can also be given to dogs with advantage, either cooked or raw, this depending on individual taste. Potatoes I am opposed to. No matter how fond your dog may be of them, do not give them because they have a definite heating effect, which can lead to eczema. Porridge too should be left out of the menu for the same reason.

If the mature dog has two meals per day, you are pretty safe; nothing between meals! Give the first meal in the late forenoon and the main meal in the evening; both should be followed by an outing.

When you wish to be kind, give him some liver or tripe, while orange juice will be like a cocktail to him.

"How often should I bath my dog?" is a question I have been asked countless times. Many people who show dogs never give them a tub. Soaking in a bath would soon play havoc with the coat of a Scotch or a fox terrier, while a chow's coat would become like that of a Yorkshire terrier if it were over-bathed.

If the animal smells "doggy", then a bath once a month is advisable, but not more. Just have the water lukewarm, and not deeper than the top of the dog's legs. Wash him over the body first (not forgetting that it has an under-side), and work up to the head. It is quite unnecessary to splash all over his face and frighten him. When you reach the ears work easily and get inside the ears with the cloth, because if you keep them clean canker is not likely to develop. A most important point about bathing is the soap. Carbolic soap should never be used, nor any strong soda soap. Buy a cake of soap which is intended for dogs and use nothing else. Sheep-dip, lysol, and other strong antiseptics are often advised, but my advice is to leave them severely alone. Old and ailing dogs should never be bathed, nor should a dog be allowed out in wintertime just after a bath.

Old fellows which are faltering in their stride, and dogs recovering from illness, may appear to need a thorough cleanse. Here is what to do. Give them a shampoo. For two shillings you can buy a dog shampoo. For some breeds it will do twice, for others, thrice. all depending on the dog's size and on how you use it.

Dry the dog thoroughly with a dry, coarse towel, and then get the brush or comb on him. Very soon he will learn to love this attention, and will probably leap on to the table when he sees you preparing to attend to his comfort and adornment.

In my experience, grooming is much more important than baths; regular grooming can make baths quite unnecessary. Five minutes daily are quite sufficient; and your dog, instead of looking like the Old Man of the Mountains, or a Polar explorer returning after six months without a shave, becomes a dapper little fellow. A metal comb and a stout brush are all you need. In short-coated breeds the comb is better with close teeth; long-coated dogs require combs with wider teeth. Go over the coat carefully with the comb, behind the ears, in below, and over the tail and back, of course. Then the brush. Get " elbow grease " into it.

Dogs like cocker spaniels can be effectively groomed in parts by the finger and thumb. This may seem crude if you have not tried it, but dull hair behind the ears, or even the feathering on the legs, can be well attended to in this way without causing the dog any discomfort. If you can spend ten minutes on grooming your dog, so much the better.

Terriers require special attention. Is there anything more untidy than a terrier which has been allowed to become scraggy? His coat should be plushed or stripped. You can try your hand with the stripping instrument, which costs only a shilling or so, but it is better to leave this job to a professional. Very often proper stripping makes all the difference between a first prize and a reserve card at a show. Twice a year is quite sufficient for the companion dog to be stripped, in April and September; but you should carry on with the comb and brush daily at all times.

Sometimes a dog's coat becomes " stary " and its hair falls out. This may be due to several causes. In cases where there is no skin trouble, mix paraffin with olive oil in equal proportions and rub it well into the dog's coat three times a week. It is undoubtedly an effective hair stimulant; but should the dog be suffering from some more serious trouble the first thing is to get rid of this and to build up his system. A sick dog is almost certain to have a poor coat.

In order to keep a dog healthy, exercise is most essential. To open the front door and turn him loose is no exercise; if he comes back in a frightful state, do not scold him but rather blame yourself. The dog which is allowed out to do as he pleases makes more dog haters than anything else. It also causes road accidents, a matter which dog owners of to-day should never forget. Exercise means taking the dog out with you, walking him on hard roads, so as to keep his feet in good order, and then giving him a scamper in a vacant piece of ground. On the other hand, avoid over-exercise, a thing quite likely to happen with puppies. To have him run after your car or bicycle is cruel. Go out in wet weather or dry; but if it be wet, remember to rub him down thoroughly with a coarse towel when you come in. A damp coat can cause chills, colds, bronchitis and rheumatism.

CATS

Although few dog lovers will admit it, there is something very appealing about a cat; on the other hand, cats are never wholly tamed, and self-interest plays a much greater part in their liking for us than in the faithful friendship of our dog.

While most of us may be contented with a cat of low degree and mixed origin, many people now want a pedigree cat, a Siamese, Persian or Manx. Cats are such independent creatures, and will forage for themselves when other domestic pets are demanding one's attention in no uncertain manner, that I think we take the cat too much for granted; but a country without cats would be unbearable. It is too terrifying to contemplate what would become of us if the rat and mice population were allowed to multiply uncontrolled by the cat.

There is a sad lack of knowledge on cat management; I refer of course to the usual nondescript "tabby", for I know the great care and attention which are justifiably lavished on show cats. Feeding the cat requires careful attention. Puppy biscuits broken up in milk make a pleasant meal, while fish is always acceptable. Cats vary very much, however, acquire special tastes or "fads" in food, and will starve for days rather than eat anything to which they object, even though it be good for them. A cat, like a dog, needs meat, but not too much; and milk and cats are always associated in our minds. A dish of clean water should also be at hand, and should be renewed twice or thrice each day.

A dish of clean water should always be at hand

A cat's coat should be brushed regularly, as it is essential to the pet's health, as well as enhancing its beauty; never use a comb, as it spoils the coat. By neglecting to brush a cat regularly, you are exposing it to the risk of a nasty complaint, known as fur-balling or balling-up. You have all seen a cat lick its coat. At the moulting period there is a lot of loose hair about, and the cat licks this up. Literally a ball of fur enters the cat's stomach, and unless the cat is sick illness may follow. But prevention being better than cure, groom your cat regularly and keep fur-balling away.

Cats are just as liable to worms as dogs, and the best advice I can give is to purchase one of the well-known proprietary medicines from the chemist's or pet shop. Always give medicines to animals in strict accordance with the instructions on the packet. One must, for instance, be very careful about dosing a kitten for worms. An overdose can easily kill a kitten, so it might be wise with a very young kitten to treat it first of all with liquid paraffin.

How often should we feed a cat? An adult cat—one over nine months—should do well on three meals per day. A kitten needs more meals than two each day, but of course the quantity must not be too great, although cats on the whole are not so greedy as dogs, and will often stop feeding when the plate is still half-filled.

RABBITS

Housing is your first problem if you desire to keep rabbits. It may be possible to keep them indoors, but most people prefer to have them outside, and I think that is best. I prefer hutches which

are raised from the ground, and which do not face north or east. The size depends of course on the number of rabbits you intend to keep, but a single rabbit should have a floor space at least two feet square. Excellent hutches can be constructed cheaply from the wood of a provision case, or from an orange box, with wire mesh on one side, and a small door cut into the partition to admit to the rabbit's " bedroom ".

Rabbits will frequently gnaw at the wood of their hutch, especially if a piece is projecting; this annoying habit can be discouraged by occasionally rubbing a paraffined rag over the wood.

In the matter of feeding rabbits, one should aim at variety. Many items of house food are suitable for pet rabbits. Vegetables are always good, as are grass, hay and oats. It is difficult to say just how much food you should provide, because rabbits seem to be happiest when they are nibbling all the time. In a general way, two meals per day are suitable, with something to chew in between.

One of the commonest ailments of rabbits is snuffles. There is a sneezing and coughing, with discharge from the nostrils. You can relieve the rabbit by placing a drop or two of eucalyptus oil and glycerine on the nostrils twice daily. If you have more than one rabbit you should always isolate the invalid in a hutch away from the healthy ones.

GUINEA PIGS

Since the guinea pig was elevated to the dignity of a show animal, it has rejoiced in the name of " cavy ". The cavy section is always an important one at small livestock exhibitions. Guinea pigs are

See how short they can cut the grass

very pleasing and attractive pets, and I have still to hear of one biting a child, or anyone else for that matter. As with rabbits, the question of accommodation depends a great deal on our ingenuity. In a general way, a hutch is built, but avoid draught, cold and damp. I prefer to see all pet animals have adequate space. For three guinea pigs a hutch nearly 3 ft. long should be built, about 18 in wide, and say 2 ft. high. Sawdust or peat moss can be used to cover the floor, and this should be changed regularly. Always bear in mind that cleanliness is an essential duty if one intends to keep one's pets healthy.

No doubt you will be anxious to have your guinea pigs outdoors in summer-time. A concrete run is good, but no matter where you put them, be sure that they are not exposed to attack from dogs, cats, or even rats. If you allow them on to the lawn, you will be amused to see how short they can cut your grass; in fact, guinea pigs are quite the perfect mowing machine. The three varieties of guinea pigs are Peruvian, or long-haired, Abyssinian, and English short-haired.

Guinea pigs are among the hardiest of pets, and do not suffer from many ailments. If kept well fed in nice clean hutches, they will live happily for a long time.

CAGE BIRDS.   BUDGERIGARS

Many good books have been written about cage birds, which are often the hobby of a lifetime, not merely of boys; adults and children alike take pleasure in keeping and rearing these most attractive and responsive little animals. Shortage of space prevents us from noticing here more than two kinds, the budgerigar and the canary.

Let me tell you how I bred my first pair of budgerigars from a blue cock and a green hen. My cage, a wooden one, the front only of which was covered with wire, was about 3 ft. long, 2 ft. deep, and 30 in. high. At the top left-hand corner I placed a nesting box. This was of the usual pattern, with concave bottom and a small hole, large enough for the birds to enter, high up in the corner of the box.

No nesting material was provided. Previous experience had taught me that success can only be achieved with cage birds if one keeps them clean, feeds them regularly, and disturbs them as little as possible. Cleanliness is impossible in a cage unless it has an easily sliding tray at the foot, which can be covered with grit.

In due course there was a great deal of coming and going in the nest box. The cere at the base of the hen's upper mandible or beak had become a deep brown and was rough; the cock's was a bright blue. Incidentally, that is how one sexes budgerigars. In a general way, the top of the hen's beak is brown (very pale blue in a young bird), whereas the same part of a cock bird is always blue.

The hen finally stopped her comings and goings, and spent almost all her time in the nesting box. The cock was most attentive. Immediately her ladyship showed her face at the hole in the nest box, up he would go and feed her, chortling a merry song between times. At this stage one must be less curious than ever. There is naturally a great urge to look inside the box and see how many

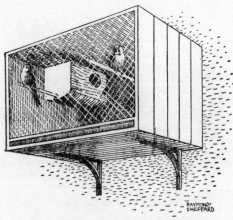

My cage, a wooden one, the front covered with wire, was about 3 ft. long, 2 ft. deep and 2 ft. 6 in. high

eggs there are; and although an experienced breeder of birds may do this with impunity, the beginner is advised to curb his curiosity. There were five eggs in my particular hen's clutch. In due course all hatched out. As one bird was green (a pure colour), and another blue, by what is known as Mendel's law the remaining birds were bound to be all green in appearance; and so they were. I say " in appearance " advisedly, because every one of these green chicks was capable of breeding blue birds. If you mated light greens and blues some of their youngsters would be green, but others blue. This is barely scratching at the great laws of inheritance, but once you have bred birds in this way you will want to proceed much farther, and will learn a great deal about the mysteries of biology by the best of all routes, that of experience.

My first attempt was not the best way of breeding budgerigars. They do much better if there are several pairs. They do not require to be all in the same compartment, as for the purposes of control one pair to one cage is necessary, but so long as they can see and hear each other they are happier. Budgerigars can be bred all the year round, and are likely to assume domestic responsibilities as soon as they have a nest box; but for maintaining their vigour it is best to confine breeding to the late spring. I need hardly add that there is no more suitable bird for an outside aviary. Hardy in the

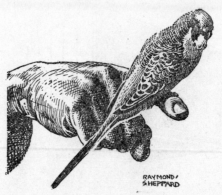

RAYMOND/
SHEPPARD

Teach it to stand on your finger

coldest weather, they can even be kept outside when there is snow on the ground; but in such conditions a comfortable roosting house is necessary. The aviary should face south or south-west, so that the birds get the maximum of sunshine and are protected in the rear from cold north and east winds.

A note on budgerigars would be quite incomplete were I to omit the subject of the talking bird. While in general it can be agreed that cocks make the better talkers, I have also heard some very fluent and loquacious hens. One sometimes hears people speaking about a bird as " coming from a great talking strain ". Such statements are nonsense. Almost every budgerigar can be taught to talk if one sets about teaching it in the right way. A great deal depends on the age of the bird; the earlier one takes it from its mother the better. A good time to begin is just when it has learned to crack seed for itself. Take the bird away from the sound of other budgerigars and start by winning its confidence. Put your hand in its cage, quietly and without fuss. If the bird dashes about then leave it, but go back again soon. In a little while you will be able to stroke it lightly. From this stage teach it to stand on your finger.

All members of the household should agree to use the same words when they talk to the bird; a bird, like a young child, learns to repeat sounds that it has heard sufficiently often for them to be stamped on its mind. Give the bird a name and keep calling it by that name. Once it has mastered this, advance to two words—for instance, " Hullo, Joey !" and repeat them until they too are mastered Thus you can increase its vocabulary by easy stages. A friendly, talking budgerigar is indeed a valued pet.

CANARIES

There are many varieties to choose from among canaries, but I think the beginner would be well advised to stick to the Border Fancy breed until he has gained some experience. Breeding canaries is not so easy as breeding budgerigars, and canaries require more attention. The Border Fancy is probably the hardiest of them, besides being a fine little songster. (Only cock canaries sing.)

The best type of breeding cage is a box, rather smaller than the one advised for budgerigars; I also prefer a cage with a partition, say a sliding wooden one and also a wire one. In the spring, when the cock is in full song and full of vigour, and the hen is fussing about with the small pieces of nesting material that one can buy for her in pet shops, they should be introduced to each other. Previous to this the birds should have been able to see each other through the wire partition. Canaries require a nesting pan, in which the hen will build her nest with the material that you have provided.

When the first egg is laid take it away, and do the same with the first three, keeping them together in a small box—a matchbox will do—but return them at the end of the third day. The reason for this is to ensure that all the chicks hatch on the same day. In about two weeks the young can be expected. You will then require to feed your birds on soft food—grated egg, powdery biscuit food, and the excellent proprietary foods which can be bought at the shop. This must be fed morning and night to the family.

After acquiring some experience, you might want to keep some of the lovely big canaries that may be seen at cage-bird shows. There are Yorkshire, Norwich, Crest, and several others. You might also want to try your hand at blue, white or cinnamon birds, or canaries with pink eyes; but it is best to start at the beginning, as advised above.

Keeping a cage bird in good condition is something which we all strive to do. Regular feeding, fresh water, and a clean cage are essential conditions for good health. At least once every week the cage bottom should be covered with grit. While grit makes the cleaning of the cage an easy matter it is also essential to the bird's digestion. Cuttlefish bone, too, when obtainable, is also advised. Canaries like their bath, but give it only in the morning. If you do so in the evening, the canary will go to sleep with damp plumage, and that is very bad for the bird.

A Norwich canary

A healthy canary is one in tight plumage, and active. When you see him all puffed up (except at night, when he is going to roost) look out for trouble. Get him away from draught and move him into a warm, even temperature. I have found that birds recover their good health through heat sooner than by any other remedy.

You will need to cut a canary's claws periodically. Take the bird in the left hand, its wings to the palm, and with the forefinger and thumb of your left hand hold out the claw which requires to be cut; but before you use the scissors hold the claw up to the light. You will see a thin shadow extending down the claw, and stopping just short of its end. You must not cut back to the shadow, as this is a vein; if you do cut it you will cause the bird pain and the claw will bleed.

For a bird which seems a bit off colour a course of cod liver is helpful. A drop or two mixed among the seed is the best way of administering the oil. For a bird which seems really ill you may put a drop or two of sherry, whisky, or even brandy in the drinking water. But always remember to give heat.

I might go on to talk about cage birds to the end of the book. The brightly coloured and inquisitive, friendly chaffinch thrives

Showing how to hold canary for cutting claws

quite well in confinement, and in the spring his song is charming. Other finches of many kinds make good pets; then there is the linnet; and last of all the raucous-voiced but never tedious parrot. The parrot, in particular, may have been a grandfather before you were born, and he may still be going strong after you are dead. But parrots are a study in themselves, the pursuit of which you will have to follow elsewhere.

TAKING AND MAKING PHOTOGRAPHS

Have you ever heard of Joseph Nicephore Niepce or L. C. M. Daguerre? If not, think of them the next time you handle a camera, for it was these two noted scientists who first discovered how to produce a photograph.

Strangely enough, they both began working on the same idea at about the same time, but it was not until they had been experimenting individually for a long time that each learned of the other's existence, and of their kindred interest. They joined forces in 1829, and soon afterwards perfected what is known as the daguerreotype process.

Photography in those very early days, however, was rather tiresome and exacting, and after a great deal of experimenting it still needed an exposure of three-quarters of an hour to get a decent negative. Compare this with present-day photography, when it is possible to get a perfectly defined picture of a fast-moving object in a thousandth part of a second!

Nowadays anyone can get a good negative with almost any kind of camera and, what is more, can learn quickly how to develop negatives and then make either contact prints, or attractive enlargements many times the size of the original.

Photography is an extremely fascinating hobby, but to get the best out of it, you have got to carry out all the several processes yourself. That this is not at all difficult you will shortly learn, but in the meantime let us consider, for a minute, the different kinds of cameras and how they work.

Choosing a Camera.

If you look in the window of a well-stocked photographic dealer's shop, you will doubtless be amazed at the variety of instruments displayed there. These will probably range from a box camera costing only about two pounds, to a very small but compact-looking camera—known as a " miniature "—costing anything from £50 upwards. In between you will see folding cameras of various sizes and at various prices; large, cumbersome-looking ¼-plate, ½-plate, or even whole-plate instruments used for press work, field work, or studio work; cameras known as reflex cameras, having a large sheet of frosted glass in which you can see the subject plainly while you are pressing the trigger, and so on.

If you have never possessed a camera before and you contemplate buying one, you might well be worried by this varied assortment of instruments. Which shall you buy? Which will give the best results? You may say, " I expect the more expensive the camera, the better the results." This may be true, but like so many truths it is only a half truth, for an expensive camera will give better

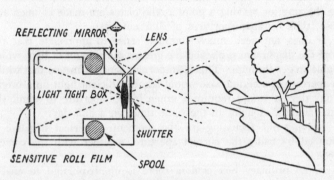

Fig. 1.—Essentials of a simple camera

results than a cheaper one, provided that you know how to use it. This is an important point, and if you have had no experience you will not know how to use it, and it is then ten to one that you will get better results with a cheap camera. That is why beginners are best advised to start off with an ordinary box camera, or a cheap folding camera. When you can handle these properly, *then* is the time to go in for something more elaborate.

All cameras, of course, have the same common characteristics, and in order to start right we must know what these characteristics are. In the first place, then, the camera itself is a box which is perfectly light-tight. At the back we fit a glass negative or a celluloid film which is coated on one side with a special emulsion made sensitive to light. All the time this is kept in the dark nothing happens to it, but immediately it is exposed to light it takes on the light and shadows which it " sees ". Thus the front of the camera is fitted with a lens covered by a specially designed shutter. All the time the shutter is kept closed no light can get through the lens, but immediately it is opened, by the action of pressing the trigger, light goes through the lens and on to the plate or film (fig. 1).

Apertures and Times.

Better-class cameras have, in addition to the shutter, a specially designed diaphragm which can be opened or closed to give different-sized apertures. This diaphragm is a very clever arrangement and consists of a series of curved metal plates fitted inside the lens tube and attached to a ring on the outside of the lens mount. By revolving the ring, or moving a pointer, the plates are made to open and close, thus forming apertures of different sizes.

It does not need much common sense to appreciate that the more the diaphragm is opened the greater the amount of light which is able to get through. This is important, since it means that whilst an aperture of a certain size would admit sufficient light on a bright sunny day, it would require a much bigger aperture to admit the same amount of light, in the same time, on a dull day.

Leaving out focussing for the moment, a perfect negative is obtained by using the correct aperture, together with the correct speed.

In an ordinary box camera there is no diaphragm to enable different apertures to be made, but there are slight variations in respect of time. Many box cameras have three letters on them— T B I.—standing, respectively, for Time, Brief and Instantaneous. These enable the user to expose the film for several seconds or even minutes—known as a Time exposure; or for one or two seconds— known as a Brief exposure; or for a very rapid exposure (actually $\frac{1}{25}$ of a second)—known as an Instantaneous exposure. These differences are obtained by different methods on different models, and it would take considerable space to deal with them all. Always, however, they are simple to understand, and any dealer will explain them in a couple of minutes.

Getting out of the box-camera class, we have instruments with wider ranges of apertures and speeds, and, generally speaking, the more expensive the camera the wider are these ranges. A comparatively cheap folding camera will have three or four different apertures, and probably four or five different speeds (fig. 2).

The apertures will probably be labelled " f 16 ", " f 11 " and

" f 8 ". All apertures are numbered in this way, and the great thing to remember about them is that the bigger the number the smaller the opening. Thus, when you set a camera at f 16 you have a much smaller aperture (admitting much less light) than when you have it set at f 11. Similarly, at f 11 you have a smaller opening than at f 8. Generally speaking, the duller the weather the bigger the aperture, and you will therefore use your apertures—or " stops " as they are called—to suit the conditions. On a dull day you may have to use f 8 in order to get a good picture of a certain subject, whereas on a bright day you will get a perfect picture of the same subject, with the same speed, by using f 11 or even f 16.

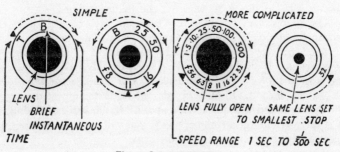

Fig. 2.—Lens and Shutters

This small letter f simply means the proportion of the diameter of the stop to the focal length of the lens. Thus f 8, for example, is of a diameter ⅛ the " focus " of the lens. It would take considerable space to describe this relationship fully, nor would it serve any useful purpose here. It is important to note, however, that the stops are so arranged that each aperture requires double the exposure required by the preceding aperture, and half of that required by the following aperture. Thus, for example, twice the exposure is required for f 11 as for f 8, and half the exposure for f 11 as for f 16, all other things being equal.

Time variations on an average folding camera may be marked something like this—" T, 1/10, 1/25, 1/50, 1/100 ". " T ", of course, stands for " Time " again, and enables you to expose for several seconds or minutes. The figures represent fractions of a second. If, therefore, you place the indicator on " 1/25 ", your shutter will open and close in $\frac{1}{25}$ of a second; if you place it on " 1/50 ", it will open and close in $\frac{1}{50}$ of a second, and so on.

The success of your negatives depends upon the correct use of your stops in relation to times. This relationship can always be obtained very accurately by using an exposure meter, and the possession of one means a very big saving in spoilt and inferior negatives. Exposure meters vary in price from three or four pounds up to about £10, and all are very simple to use. You merely point them at the object to be photographed and take off a reading on a special scale. This reading tells you what speeds to use for various stops.

Until you are lucky enough to own an exposure meter you will have to learn to use your stops and times intelligently, and the best way to do this is to work on the following lines.

On an ordinary summer day between, say, 10 o'clock in the morning and 3 o'clock in the afternoon, you will get perfect pictures of fixed or very slow-moving objects, using f 11 and giving $\frac{1}{25}$ of a second. If a subject is moving fairly quickly, you will increase the stop to f 8 (or f 5·6 if you have it) and decrease the time to $\frac{1}{50}$ or $\frac{1}{100}$ of a second. In other words, the faster the object the bigger the aperture and the quicker the speed. If the weather is dull, or it is early or late on a summer's day, you will increase the aperture accordingly, but keep the time the same.

Using f 11 and $\frac{1}{25}$ second as a basis, you can reckon, as already pointed out, that one stop larger (f 8) will double the exposure and one stop smaller (f 16) will lessen it by half. Similarly, keeping the stop unchanged, but altering the time, an exposure of $\frac{1}{25}$ second will be twice as long as an exposure of $\frac{1}{50}$ second.

This may all seem a bit complicated, but a little experimenting, using different stops and different times, will quickly teach you what to do under varying conditions. Take a whole roll of film of the same subject, altering the stop and time for each exposure, and keep a careful note of what you have done. Then compare the results, and you will learn more than you can learn from reading a thousand words on the subject.

The other important thing connected with a camera is the question of focussing. This is where a reflex camera scores over most others. You will remember that it has a frosted glass screen in which you can see the subject while you are photographing it. The bellows on a reflex can be extended or brought back by the turning of a knob, and you proceed to work this knob until your picture is perfectly sharp on the glass screen. You then know that your picture is in focus.

On cheaper cameras, which do not have this screen, you will probably find a scale of distances round the lens of the camera. These are distances of, say, 5, 10, 15, 20 feet, and so on. In order to focus these cameras correctly, you must judge the distance of the subject from the lens, and set the distance scale at this figure.

Selecting Film.

One other thing to be considered, in connexion with the camera itself, is the choice of film or plate. Considerable progress has been made, in recent years, in the manufacture of plates and films, and the majority have reached a high degree of perfection. Moreover, they are manufactured in scores of different grades and speeds, and the average amateur would be amazed if he were able to see a complete range. The professional, of course, finds this extensive range of great service, but it would merely confuse the novice. All the amateur needs to know is that there are three main divisions of plates and films, known, respectively, as ordinary, chrome and panchromatic.

All the well-known makes of films and plates can be purchased in these three classes, and the variations in price amount to only a few pence.

Ordinary film is now rapidly going out of favour, and for all general work it is advisable to use chrome film. This is more sensitive to some colours than ordinary film and therefore gives better results. It is rather better for greens, for example, but since it will only photograph part of yellow and none of red, it is of little use where bright colours are concerned.

Panchromatic film is sensitive to all colours—even to red—and thus it is of great service in giving true tone renderings in pictures where the variations in colour are very marked.

You will find it a very interesting experiment to arrange a vase of flowers, covering as many colours as possible, and photographing it first with ordinary film, then with chrome film, and then with panchromatic film. Compare the results after development, and you will doubtless be struck by the amount of detail in the last-named, compared with that in the other two.

Apart from its ability to separate colours, panchromatic film has another big advantage in that it is much faster than ordinary film or chrome film. It is therefore very useful for indoor work and for work on dull days. It is ideal, too, for portraits, and gives fine renderings of landscape scenes.

When handling panchromatic material, both before and during development, great care must be taken to keep it away from all light. Remember that it is sensitive to red light, and you therefore cannot use a red lamp in the dark room. The best lamp to use is a green one, and it should be kept at least six or eight feet away from the film.

Taking the Picture.

So much for the actual working of the camera. It may now be worth while considering a few important points which are essential if you are to be certain of getting good pictures at almost every attempt.

In the first place, then, always make sure that your camera is steady. This is important, and it is worth bearing in mind that, providing you have focussed correctly, the steadier the camera the sharper the picture. For anything over $\frac{1}{25}$ second, try to stand your camera on a firm object so that fear of movement is lessened; for $\frac{1}{25}$ and less, hug the camera tightly to the body and try to hold the breath at the moment the shutter is released. Press the trigger firmly but gently. If you jerk it, you may easily move the camera and spoil the negative.

The second thing to be careful about is the light. Never point your lens in the direction of the sun. If you do, you will almost certainly get a failure. The golden rule is—sun almost behind you, if possible; if not possible, then well to one side of you.

In the third place, pay very special attention to backgrounds. So many otherwise very good pictures are completely spoilt through lack of attention to this detail. How many times, for example, have you seen a picture of a friend, posed against the wall of a house or a shed, and looking for all the world as though a drainpipe is growing out of the top of his head! Or, again, you may have seen an otherwise good portrait study—but with the subject standing next to a dustbin! It needs only a little thought and attention, before pressing the trigger, to see that all these ugly things are kept out of the picture. A good idea, when taking a portrait, is to stand the subject as far away from all backgrounds as possible. Failing this,

try to get a shrub or a hedge or a flower border as a background
—in short, something attractive.

Another important thing to study is viewpoint. If, for example,
you are taking a building or a bridge or a monument, do not just
lift the camera and snap it without first studying the subject in
relation to its surroundings. There are always one or two views of
anything which are more attractive than others. Your business as
a photographer is to look for these viewpoints and not to expose

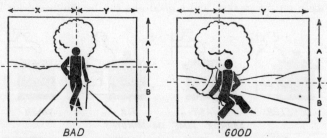

BAD   GOOD

① BEWARE OF SPLITTING THE PICTURE INTO EQUAL PARTS
② TRY AND USE A HIGH OR LOW HORIZON LINE
③ CAMERA USED HORIZONTALLY OR VERTICALLY TO SUIT SUBJECT

Fig. 3.—Composition

your film until you are satisfied that you have found the best viewpoint possible (fig. 3).

When taking moving objects snap them as they come towards
the camera or are going away from it. You will get far better results
in this way than if you try to take them as they flash across the
front of the camera. The same principle applies when you are
photographing from a moving object—a train, for example. Either
photograph your scene as it comes towards you or as you are leaving
it.

Developing.

Earlier on in this article I said that a lot of the fun in photography
came from developing and enlarging one's own negatives. That
more amateurs do not do this is probably due to the fact that the
majority of them believe the work to call for a special dark room,
a good knowledge of chemicals, and more than average skill. Such,

however, is not the case. It is true that the making of exhibition prints may call for specialized knowledge, but it is equally true that it is well within the power of any girl to develop any film satisfactorily and to make creditable enlargements up to whole-plate size.

Let us, then, consider developing first. As far as this is concerned, the days of the old dark room, with a smelly oil lamp and the use of messy chemicals, is a thing of the past. The modern amateur does nearly all his developing in daylight! This is made possible by the use of special developing tanks. There are a number of these on the market, and a good one can be purchased for less

DEVELOP   WASH   FIX   WASH

APPROX TIME IN MINUTES

Fig. 4.—Daylight tank development

than £1. The majority will, of course, only accommodate films, but most of them will take films of varying sizes.

A developing tank is quite a simple affair, and consists of a special spool on to which the film can be wound and which is then placed in a light-tight tank. Developer is poured into the tank and is allowed to remain there for a certain time, depending upon the temperature of the developer.

Assuming you have a tank, the first thing to do is to get the film wound on to the spool. This is done by shutting oneself up in a light-proof cupboard, separating the film from its red-paper cover, and winding it carefully on to the spool. The spool is then placed into the tank and the lid put on tightly. You can now come into the daylight and do the rest without resorting to a dark room at all.

The next thing to do is to prepare the developer, and here you may use either a powder developer, a liquid developer, or a tablet developer. Whichever it is, full instructions will be given with it for tank development.

One of the best developers is undoubtedly an M. and Q. de-veloper (Metol and Quinol), made up in powder form at a few pence a packet. You mix the powders, as directed, in a given quantity of water and take the temperature. Reference to a time-and-tempera-ture chart, supplied with the developer, will then tell you how many minutes to keep the solution in the tank (fig. 4). Note the time when you pour it in, find out from the chart how long to keep it in accord-ing to the temperature, and at the expiration of the time pour it away.

Meantime, you will have prepared an acid fixing bath. Tins of acid fixing salts—usually containing one pound—can be obtained from any chemist, and the instructions on the tin will tell you what proportion of salts to mix with a given quantity of water.

As soon as you have emptied the developer from the tank, fill the latter up two or three times with cold water and so give the film a good rinsing. Then unfasten the tank, take the film out and place it immediately in the fixing solution. It is best to do this in sub-dued light, but this only means going to a corner of the room where there is no direct light from a window.

When the film is taken from the tank you will probably notice that it has a thick white coating on one side. After it has been in the fixing bath a few minutes, however, this coating will begin to dis-appear. You must leave the film in the fixing bath until the coating has totally disappeared—a process which usually takes about 10 minutes. You will help the fixing solution to do its work better by taking one end of the film in each hand and gently passing it to and fro through the solution.

As soon as a film is fixed it must be thoroughly washed, and then left in running water for about half an hour. After this it can be hung up to dry in a clean, airy spot. A shelf in a warm room or a shelf in a greenhouse make ideal drying places, and the great thing to guard against is specks of dust getting on the film and drying into it.

And that is all there is in modern developing—nothing to worry about at all, and if you follow the developer instructions carefully you will never get a failure.

Printing.

There are two ways in which you can get finished pictures from your negatives—either by contact prints or by enlarging. In the first way you can only get pictures the size of the negative; in the second you can make pictures several times the size of the negative.

Contact printing can be done either on daylight paper or on gaslight paper. The two methods differ in operation, and the results are different. The former gives a sepia-looking finish; the latter gives a black-and-white finish.

For either method of contact printing you will require a printing frame, and one of these can be purchased from any chemist for a shilling or two. It has a glass front and a special wooden back which is kept in position by a metal strip. Negative and paper are placed on the glass, and the back is then clamped down to prevent them from moving.

At this point it may be well to mention that there is a right and a wrong side to both negative and paper. A negative has one side shiny and the other side rough. Paper has one side shiny and the other side plain. The rough surface of the film must always be placed against the shiny side of the paper, and the shiny side of the film must be placed face downwards on the glass.

Apart from the resulting tones (sepia against black-and-white), the main differences between daylight printing and gaslight printing are these. Daylight printing requires no developing, only fixing; gaslight prints require both developing and fixing. In daylight printing you can watch the image forming on the paper; in gaslight printing no image can be seen until the paper is placed in the developer.

For daylight printing you must use what is called self-toning paper. This can be bought very cheaply and in various sizes. Be careful not to open it in sunlight but open it instead where the light is very subdued. Place the negative against a sheet of this and put it in the printing frame. Place the frame in the light of the sun, and the picture on the negative will quickly begin to form on the paper. The process can be watched by letting down the small hinged portion at the back of the frame and taking a careful peep at a corner of the paper. Leave the paper in the frame until the image is beginning to get a little on the dark side, and then take the paper out and immerse it in a bath of hypo. This chemical, in the form of crystals, can be purchased very cheaply, and the directions on the box will show how to mix it with water and make a solution. Keep the print in the hypo bath for about 10 minutes and then rinse it in running water for 20 minutes and put it out to dry.

For gaslight printing you will need a dark room, but one can easily be made by pinning a large sheet of brown paper over the window of a bathroom or kitchen. It is best to work in one of these rooms, since then you will have a supply of running water handy.

As mentioned before, gaslight printing is a little more complicated than daylight printing, but it is, nonetheless, quite easy to carry out. This time you will need a developer and fixer as you did for film development. M. and Q. Developer, in powder form, will be perfectly satisfactory, and the directions on the packet will show you how to use it—generally the contents of the packet dissolved in 4 oz. of water. The directions on the tin of acid fixing salts will also show you in what proportion to mix these with water.

After the print is taken from the printing frame it is first placed in the developer, then rinsed in cold water, and then put into the fixing solution. You will therefore require three dishes, and you can either purchase proper dishes for the job—costing no more than a shilling or two each—or you can use ordinary pie dishes. Arrange the dishes in a row and into the first pour the developer. Half fill the second with water and put the fixing solution into the third.

You will need a red lamp, and a good idea here is to get an electric rear light as used on bicycles. It is merely required to give sufficient light to enable you to see how to put the printing paper in the frame properly. Gaslight paper is naturally very sensitive to artificial light, and you must therefore be careful to keep it away from all light, except during the actual exposure.

Prints can be made either by gaslight or electric light. The latter is by far the more convenient, since it can easily be switched on and off. If you are forced to use gas, you must work in one room and make your exposures in another.

Place the negative and paper in the printing frame by the aid of the light from the red lamp, and then hold the frame tightly to the body (to keep out all light) while you switch on the electric light or go into another room where there is gaslight.

Printing is done by holding the frame about a foot away from the light. The time it should be held there varies considerably, according to the density of the negative and the kind of paper being used. An average negative will probably need about 6 seconds, but you will find the correct times only by experimenting. You are bound to waste a few sheets of paper while doing this, but you will quickly know, simply by glancing at a negative, roughly how long it will take.

As soon as you have made the exposure, press the frame tightly to the body again and switch off the light. Then take the paper from the frame and immerse it quickly in the developer. By the light of the red lamp you will see that the paper is perfectly white, but after it has been in the developer a few seconds the image will begin to appear. Gently rock the dish until development is complete, and then take the print out and wash it in the dish of cold water. Then place it in the fixing solution and leave it there for about 10 minutes. After this time place it in a bowl of running water for about half an hour and finally lay it out to dry.

You can, of course, go ahead and make your next print as soon as the first is in the fixing bath, but if you do this put the print face downwards in the solution so that the light does not get at it.

Enlarging.

Enlarging is carried out in very much the same way as gaslight printing, except that different paper is used. That used for enlarging is known as bromide paper.

At this point it might be well to consider, for a moment, printing papers in general—both for gaslight and enlarging. Actually there is a very extensive range to choose from, and papers are manufactured to suit every kind of negative. There are, for example, a large number of different surfaces, and one can get a matt finish, a velvet finish, a smooth finish, a rough finish, a glossy finish, and so on. There are also a number of tints, among which buff and cream are the most popular for certain types of work. The choice of paper depends upon the type of subject. Thus a piece of furniture looks best on a smooth or glossy surface, whereas a country scene is probably more attractive on a matt or a velvet surface.

Apart from different surfaces, however, papers have different grades. Generally speaking, there are three of these—soft, medium or normal, and vigorous. It is possible to obtain nearly all surfaces in any one of these grades, and thus one can get a good contact print, or a good enlargement, from almost any negative.

The grade of paper to use is governed by the nature and quality of the negative, and all negatives should be studied carefully before the paper is chosen. Experience is a good teacher here—as with the times necessary for gaslight printing—but the following principles act as a useful guide.

A negative which has been slightly over-exposed or over-developed, or which contains strongly defined contrasts, will need a soft paper. On the other hand, an under-exposed or under-developed negative, or one with poor contrasts, will require a vigorous paper. More or less perfect negatives, coming between

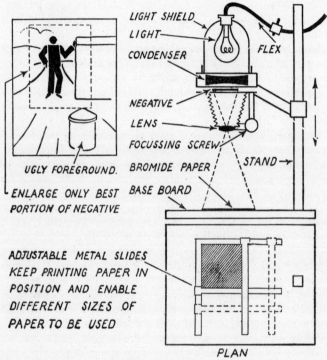

UGLY FOREGROUND.

ENLARGE ONLY BEST PORTION OF NEGATIVE

LIGHT SHIELD
LIGHT
CONDENSER
FLEX
NEGATIVE
LENS
FOCUSSING SCREW
BROMIDE PAPER
STAND
BASE BOARD

ADJUSTABLE METAL SLIDES KEEP PRINTING PAPER IN POSITION AND ENABLE DIFFERENT SIZES OF PAPER TO BE USED

PLAN

Fig. 5.—Enlarging

these two extremes, will print best on a medium or normal paper. The thing to remember is that vigorous paper will bring out and sharpen the details, whereas soft paper will tend to thin them and tone them down.

We return now to enlarging, and it can be said that this is un-doubtedly the most fascinating of all processes connected with photography (fig. 5). Not only can you make a picture several times larger than the negative, but by so doing you often bring out much beauty and detail which are hidden in a small contact print. Apart from this, however, you can change a picture considerably by enlarging that part of it which appeals to you. For example, you may have a very pleasing portrait study, as far as the head and shoulders go, but totally spoilt by ugly things standing near the feet of the subject. With an enlarger, however, you can make a picture of the head and shoulders only and get a remarkably attractive result.

Again, you may have a very fine picture of a country scene showing a typical old country shepherd driving a flock of sheep along a narrow, picturesque lane, but spoilt by a modern car just making its appearance in the background. When enlarging, however, it is quite easy to cut out this car and so get a truly rural scene with every detail in keeping.

Yet again, you may have a good picture with all the details in keeping, but which is badly balanced—too much foreground or background, or too much uninteresting detail on one side. By careful arrangement you can alter the shape of the enlargement considerably and so make the picture far more pleasing.

Enlargers are sold in two styles—horizontal and vertical. The former, however, is rapidly going out of favour altogether, and the latter is undoubtedly the better to work with. In a vertical enlarger the apparatus is mounted on a steel or wooden upright and is made to slide up and down. It consists of a lamp chamber (housing an ordinary electric bulb), a condenser, a glass slide into which the negative is placed, and expanding bellows which terminate in a lens. The steel or wooden upright is fixed to one end of a large wooden base, usually covered with something white.

Before you start to use paper for enlarging, place the negative in the holder and slide the enlarger up, or down, the upright until you have roughly the size of picture you require. You then focus accurately by moving the bellows up or down. Focussing is done by watching the picture on the white base. This picture is always interesting when you see it for the first time, since it shows clearly what your picture is like. By studying it carefully you can decide both what to cut out—if anything—and what shape to make it if it is not satisfactory as a whole. The best way of doing this is to use pieces of cardboard cut in the shape of a letter L. By placing one across the other and moving them about, you can frame the picture to the best advantage and thus plan how to enlarge it.

The base of some enlargers is ruled off in sections so that you know exactly where to place the paper when you are ready to make the enlargements. If there is no such arrangement, you can use one of your L pieces and place it in such a position that it will form a boundary for two sides of the paper.

Bromide paper is generally more expensive than gaslight paper, and since you are using it in large sheets it is obviously not wise to waste it in trying it out for the correct exposure. The best way of finding out the correct time for a particular negative is to carry out what is called a " strip exposure ". Some makers of printing paper include a few strips—usually about an inch wide—in every packet, but if no such slips are provided you can make a few by cutting up a sheet of paper.

To make a " strip exposure ", proceed as follows. Place the strip on the base of the enlarger so that it occupies a position roughly across the centre of the picture. Then cover three-quarters of the strip with a thick piece of cardboard and expose the odd quarter for 3 seconds. Move the cardboard along to the centre and expose the next quarter for a further 3 seconds. Move again and expose the third quarter for another 3 seconds. Finally, remove the cardboard altogether and expose for another 3 seconds. You will now have a strip with four exposure times—12 seconds, 9 seconds, 6 seconds and 3 seconds. Develop it and examine it and you will then have a very good idea of the correct exposure to give. You can now arrange a whole sheet of paper on the base of the enlarger and expose for the correct time.

Developing and fixing are carried out in exactly the same way as for gaslight prints. First put the paper into the developer until the image appears and full development is complete, then a rinse in the cold water, then in the fixing bath for 10 minutes. Finally, a good wash in running water for about 30 minutes, and then careful drying in a warm, clean place.

Glazing Prints.

Some amateur photographers admire the highly glazed prints which are always delivered when one has a film developed and printed at a chemist's. Many imagine that a special paper is used in order to get this finish. Such, however, is not really the case, and glazing is a separate operation performed after the prints have been washed.

Actually it is a simple process, costs little or nothing to carry out, and apart from leaving prints with a high polish it flattens them out nicely.

All that is necessary is to place wet prints firmly on to a glazing surface and leave them to dry. When dry they peel off and are found with a highly polished surface. Several materials are suitable for glazing; they include glass, ferrotype plates, enamel and celluloid sheets, and chromium-plated brass boards. The latter are the most desirable, and they give perfect results. They are, however, rather expensive to buy. Perfect results can also be obtained with any of the other surfaces mentioned, however, provided care is taken to see that they are perfectly clean. This is not always easy, but the difficulty can be overcome by using a glazing solution. Such a solution can be made up from crystals or liquid sold for the purpose and obtainable very cheaply from any photographic dealer.

Ferrotype plates cost a shilling or two each, and will take up to four half-plate prints at a time. Enamel and celluloid sheets are also reasonable in price but are not easy to obtain.

Whichever surface is used, wash it thoroughly with soap and water and give a thorough rinsing with clean water. Then place the wet prints face downwards on the surface, cover them with blotting paper and roll them firmly with a rubber squeegee. It is very important to remove all moisture, and if there are any air bubbles under the print the latter will not take the glazing perfectly.

If using a flexible surface—such as, for example, a ferrotype plate—a better plan is to run the plate and prints through a household mangle; always provided, of course, that it is fitted with rubber rollers.

Prints should be left to dry slowly, and if you attempt to hasten them—by putting them in front of a fire, for example—you will almost certainly get cracks and drying marks. Stand them in a warm place, away from draughts, and leave for about 12 hours. They should then peel off easily and reveal a perfect glaze.

DRAWING, WATER-COLOUR PAINTING, ETCHING

DRAWING

When one comes to think of it, drawing in line is a curious convention. Lines, it is said, do not exist in nature. Every object seen is visible as areas of light and shade, contrasted with a lighter or darker background. But one must accept the line idea; it is almost instinctive to run a line round the form. There is a world of difference, however, in the manifold ways in which this may be done.

When a young child draws a head, it is not visualizing the head so much as cataloguing it, and "entering" symbols for the various parts which the child knows are "necessary".

Child's drawing

Egyptian art

Drawing necessitates seeing intelligently, and the representational drawing which " goes wrong " does so through wrong thinking, for wrong thinking makes untrue seeing. Mankind has been learning to see in this way for thousands of years, and as his knowledge accumulated, so did his power to represent nature—seen in three dimensions — upon a plane surface of two dimensions.

In ancient Egypt, sculpture in the round attained quite a high level of accuracy to nature's forms, sometimes even a very high level indeed, in some portrait sculpture; but in the mural paintings and sculpture in low relief, the figures present such anomalies as the eye-form of the front view imposed upon a head in profile, and the bodies swung round from the hips in the familiar Egyptian convention. Apparently the Egyptian was satisfied with this. Knowledge

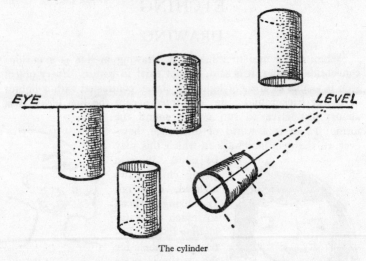

The cylinder

of perspective and foreshortening was yet to come, so the problems were not yet apparent, or were evaded as impracticable.

We have no such limitation of knowledge; it is all available to

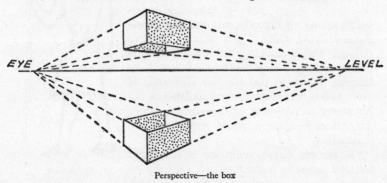

Perspective—the box

us. The highest precision of representation on the flat is possible with study and practice.

The fundamental forms in nature which must first be thoroughly understood are the cylinder, the cube, and the sphere. The cylinder gives us the difficult and ever-recurring ellipse-form, opening more and more as it rises above or sinks below the eye-level. The cube contains the mysteries of linear perspective, and the sphere presents the problems of light and the tones of shadow that render " roundness ".

These fundamentals may be rather quickly passed over in this article, as the reader is likely to have some knowledge of them already, but the importance of practice with these forms cannot be exaggerated. They should be used in imaginative drawings constantly, as the basis of the forms of houses, carts, fences, haystacks, tree-stumps, roads, tunnel-openings, or what you will, until these fall into their relationship with each other in a convincing manner, by knowledge and intelligent observation.

Light and shade—roundness   Drawing in mass and " shapes left "

After this foundation, the mind must be trained to draw from nature with a broader way of seeing—studying the relation in size and position of the main shapes in view, the arrangement that makes the drawing true. There are only general rules for this—every acute mind will find a different plan of campaign, for that is what it is, for each problem. Some key-shape will be found, and from it the solution of the next. It is well to point out the value of the " shapes left ", as these are of great assistance. It is practically impossible to draw a hand with extended fingers, for instance, unless the shapes between the fingers are as carefully observed as the fingers themselves. The shape between two objects gives the outlines of part of both. Tree-forms studied by the shapes left between the branches are rendered with comparative ease.

If the student could truly draw the forms of the objects and the shapes between them, all would be well—his troubles would be over; but it takes a great deal of practice to attain this quick reduction of three-dimensional nature to a two-dimensional drawing. One of the methods of plotting-in the main proportions of a drawing is by checking it with what we may call the " levels and perpendiculars " method. We have one point, we select another to be drawn—we must find our way to it by thinking of a line straight down from the first, or along from it on a level line, and then so much at right angles. Find out where each point would cut the neighbouring form, if produced horizontally or vertically. We must find our way about the drawing by reason and initiative, not by guess.

Another thing to be noted is a quotation from a certain art teacher, who said: " If you can't count them, don't put them in " —referring to leaves and grass, figures in a dense crowd, and so on; they must be " put in " with regard to their appearance in the mass effect.

The kind of line used must be considered. The stiff movements of writing must be forgotten. The hands are not sufficient to control the pencil—the whole arm must be free, and the movements flowing. A pencil is capable of an ugly line or a beautiful one. The quality it produces belongs to the student and to his idea of beauty. Cleanliness is usually to be fostered, a light touch can at least be altered successfully, though a bold attack by a sure hand is perhaps the ideal before us. A wise draughtsman will draw very warily at first; he is aware of the pitfalls before him, and the careful thought and the concentration he must bring to the problems, and he will put his stronger accents in when he knows that he has brought his campaign within sight of victory.

Books suggested:

Drawing, Design and Craft-work. Frederick J. Glass. (Batsford.)
Drawing. Harold Speed. (Seeley, Service & Co.)

PAINTING IN WATER-COLOUR

The first consideration is the paper on which the painting is to be done. To those who have never painted on a stretched paper, this level surface which will not bulge or " cockle " brings new encouragement and hope.

Although there is a great variety of surfaces to exploit later, a medium-grained hand-made water-colour paper, with what is called a " Not " surface, should be used at first. The sheet is cut somewhat bigger than the required painting—about 2 inches each way being allowed for the pasted edges—and is put into a bath of water for about five minutes. It is then placed face down on a towel and the edges dried all round with the same or another towel, but the centre area left very moist. A line of vegetable glue or other adhesive is applied, about half an inch wide all round the edges, and the sheet is then reversed on to its drawing-board, and stuck down. Again the edges are dried by dabbing with the towel, leaving the centre alone. In this way the edges will dry first, and when the contraction takes place in the centre, the edges are ready to take it without slipping. The paper may, of course, be brought over the edges of a board, the corners suitably cut, and the overlap pasted down at the back of the board.

The drawing must be done either before stretching, or after the paper is thoroughly dry, and stretched firmly.

The colours should be as good in quality as possible, and there should not be too many of them, especially at first. It is better to discover the possibilities of a few when exploited thoroughly, than to trust to made-up mixtures which will tempt the student to garishness and vulgarity of colour.

The secret of painting lies in the control of the grey qualities—what looks very green in nature is probably, on keen observation, perceived to verge slightly towards grey—perhaps a bluish, perhaps a yellowish grey, and so on. Nor is it easy to conquer the superficial assessment of colour values.

The colours suggested for a beginner in the excellent book on *Watercolour Painting* by Mr. Alfred Rich (Seeley, Service & Co.) are light red, yellow ochre, cyanine blue, ivory black and burnt sienna. Cyanine blue is used in preference to Prussian blue, which is not a permanent pigment. This is an interesting list, and crimson is cut out to encourage the mixing of quieter purples than would perhaps be used otherwise. The yellow ochre and blue will give soft greens, and the light red, blue and yellow together, a whole series of beautiful greys. Mr. Rich advises the use of ivory black, and suggests that the student should experiment with ivory black in all its tones, and then in combination with each of the other four colours separately.

The student should endeavour not to be quickly tempted to add to the restricted list, but to try to appreciate the greyish beauties that the intermixture of these few should produce. Gradually brighter colours may be added—ultramarine, viridian, raw sienna, aureolin (a clean bright yellow, to be used sparingly), vermilion, crimson lake, or better still, rose madder, and emerald green—the last a colour which cannot be obtained by mixture of blue and yellow, but which should only be used in pure washes, unmixed with other colours.

The manner in which the colour is applied to the paper is of the greatest importance, and must be the outcome of painstaking experiment and personal experience, but it is desirable to know some general rules that painters of experience have learned to follow in their search for beauty in this medium. The most inflexible of these is that the beauty of water-colour is the transparency of the method. The paper must be allowed to shine through the paint; even in the darkest passages there should be a feeling of transparency, however slight. Not only is transparency essential, but this quality is marred by painting several times over on the same area, even when each wash is thoroughly transparent, and even when each wash is correctly applied on a thoroughly dry surface each time. Disaster, of course, is certain if the next wash follows before the last is properly dry. So that the paint will have beauty and glow, the colour of each area must be prepared, the tone of the colour carefully adjusted, and then the colour must be floated on with a big, full brush, taking care not to touch the paper but once in every part, if possible, and then the wash must be left alone, for better or for worse, to dry, except for the removal of the excess at the bottom of the area.

In times past much was made of the method of keeping the paper moist throughout the painting, even to the extent of using such a stretcher as would allow wet cloths to be inserted behind the paper, and such a method may be correct enough in the painting of a misty seascape, or similar subject, but in general the paint should be applied to dry paper, and each area of tone applied on the principle of a series of blots, large and small, which have been allowed to dry without interference.

If the true tone and colour are struck in one painting, the result will have beauty. If certain areas need two paintings, the colour may still be beautiful in surface, but each correction is a danger, and eventually, repeated alteration will dispel the charm of the medium. Because of this, a painting in water-colour must be planned beforehand, not only in composition, and the essentials sought out, but planned in method in advance as well. This done, the execution must be swift, for water-colour is a " shorthand " method of painting, at its best.

To make clear that no method is or can be altogether adequate, we may consider the painting of skies, where an exception to the " dried blot " ideal may readily be found, and where foresight, ingenuity and speed are urgently called for. On a summer day, the blue sky will be rapidly painted from the more intense blue in the upper part, changing to the lighter, greener blue nearer the horizon, in a graduated wash. The shadowed sides of the large clouds which may be necessary to the composition are observed to merge slightly into the blue, while the upper edges are sharply defined. The painter will rapidly float in the greys of the shadows and reflections on the clouds while the blue wash is still wet, and so obtain the softened contour he requires. Now the whole sky is wet together except the brightly lit parts of the clouds, which will be left sharply dry against the blue.

Each painter in water-colour may find his own methods in infinite variety. Some painters get certain effects by exaggerating the colour considerably and then reducing the tone by sponging the over-brilliant colour, and even brushing with the finger-tips in one direction very lightly on the wet surface, making the grain of the paper emerge through the wash, obtaining a mottled tranparency of considerable beauty, but this is not our system of the dried blot, nor is it getting the colour and the tone down at once and untroubled.

Book suggested:

Watercolour Painting. Alfred Rich. (Seeley, Service & Co.)

ETCHING

The name of Etching has been given to a peculiarly fascinating art—a compound of drawing and chemistry, wholly engrossing, whereby prints are made from inked lines inscribed by acid action upon the surface of a metal plate. The word " etching " comes from the Dutch *etzen*, to eat, and etching is an eating-away process.

The first requirement is an etching-plate of suitable material—copper or zinc—its surface absolutely smooth and free from dirt and scratches. The plate obtained, its surface is further cleaned and polished with Brasso, or some such metal polish. The next step is to obtain a " ground ", which when spread thinly on the metal will defy the acid which we are going to use to do the biting for us. This substance is usually composed of two parts of white wax to one part of gum mastic, the wax melted first and the ground gum added little by little. It is readily obtainable made ready for use, as a wax-resinous ball known as Etching Ground. The clean and polished plate is heated on an iron stand or " hot-plate " over a gas-jet, and when the ball of ground will melt readily on trial at the edge of the plate, it is passed over the surface quickly and sparingly. A ball of cotton wool, wrapped in kid or silk, is dabbed over the plate, spreading and thinning the wax. The ground should be bright when the plate is cold. If not, it may be reheated and some more of the ground removed, as dullness is an indication that the deposit is too thickly laid.

When the process of grounding the plate has been successfully completed, the back of the plate must be protected also from the acid; the best and cheapest way to do this is to paint this area with Jet Glaze stove polish, or straw-hat varnish, or a mixture of equal parts of shellac and methylated spirit.

When this coating is dry we come to the stage of making the drawing upon the plate, and for this we need an etching needle, and an excellent one may be made in a few minutes by jamming a new gramophone needle into a wooden handle, and perhaps reinforcing it with sealing wax. It is presumed that the etcher has a drawing ready to transfer to his plate. This drawing is now traced on tracing paper, and it must be noted at this point that the *print* from the plate will be the reverse of the *drawing* we put upon the plate. The tracing should be concerned with the main lines of the design only. Having considered this point, one side or the other of the tracing becomes the " back " of the drawing, and this side is rubbed evenly with white chalk, the excess dusted off carefully. Putting the chalk side down on the grounded side of the plate, the needle is drawn over the lines *very, very* lightly, hardly marking the paper, and the drawing will be found transferred in exceedingly fine chalk lines upon the wax ground. It will not easily come off, even in the acid bath.

The needle is now used to cut through the ground. This will be found to be a free, velvety action; it is not necessary to do more than lay the metal bare with the needle point. The success of the etching depends now upon the way in which this is done—the surfaces are treated in various ways to give the differing textures desired, and the needle will render these according to the invention and experience of the etcher. At this stage the design is seen in negative form, its lines showing up brightly against a darker background.

Now, if the whole work were finished in this manner, with all its texture and shading, and the plate " bitten " in the acid-bath correctly, an etching would be produced, but one with every line almost the same in width and strength. This might be very successful, but as a rule it is desirable to consider how one area may be exposed to the acid longer than another, and so to obtain a variety of thin lines and thick, of distance and nearness, light and shade.

The acid-bath must now be considered. The acid or mordant used is nitric acid, and the strength for copper may be $33\frac{1}{3}$ per cent nitric acid mixed with $66\frac{2}{3}$ per cent of water, and for a zinc plate, which is attacked by acid much more readily, 25 per cent nitric acid in 75 per cent of water. The water must be put into the bottle first and the acid added, otherwise the heat generated may break the bottle. These solutions are not dangerous, with reasonable care, but they must not of course be allowed to get on to the clothes or any valuable surface likely to be burned by their action. Ammonia counters the acid in case of accident.

The acid is poured into a porcelain photographic bath, and the plate carefully inserted. Almost immediately the exposed lines will begin to etch, or bite, the acid forming little greenish bubbles where it is working. A feather may be used to brush the bubbles from the lines, for it is now necessary to judge when the lightest-toned area of the design is sufficiently bitten, so that it may be " stopped out ", or shielded from further acid action. If the plate is put at such an angle that the light gleams from it into the eyes, the bitten lines will appear dark, and an approximate idea of their strength obtained. When this area of lightest tone in the design is considered to be sufficiently bitten, the plate is removed from the bath and washed thoroughly under a tap. The plate may be lifted from this strength of acid with the fingers, provided the acid is washed off immediately, when rinsing the plate. A piece of blotting-paper may be used to dry the plate, and if the light area proves on careful inspection to be adequately bitten, this portion is stopped out with Jet Glaze or similar varnish, and when this is dry the plate is bitten again, until the next area is sufficiently darker than the first, when it is stopped out in its turn. In this way, in careful stages, the etching is built up, and the final darkest areas will be composed of strong well-bitten lines.

The biting completed, the stopping-out varnish is cleaned off with a piece of soft stockinet and methylated spirit. Turpentine will remove the ground from the plate. A few drops of ether will remove the stopping-out varnish more speedily, and the back of the plate must now be cleaned. The plate is now polished once more and the etching will be clearly seen upon it, particularly with the plate-polish showing up in the lines.

The edges of the plate must now be bevelled outwards from the face with a medium file. If this is not done, there may be damage to the printing paper and to the blankets of the etching-press, as the sharp edges of the plate may cut right through them.

The whole process up to this point has been concerned with materials and substances normally easily obtainable; the etching press, however, presents a different problem. It consists of an iron tray passing between steel rollers, rather like a mangle. Indeed, prints may be obtained by passing the etching plate on a board through the rollers of a mangle, if the top levers can be adjusted to allow the board to travel. If a press is unobtainable, the nearest art dealer will undertake to have the prints pulled by a professional art printer.

If we have a press, or access to one, the plate, cleaned and bright, is heated again, and the etching ink applied to its surface with a composition roller faced with blanket, or with a dabber, similar to that used for laying the ground, but faced with cloth or even an old stocking. The ink may be obtained in tubes, and one of Frankfurt black and another of burnt sienna or burnt umber will suffice for a beginner. If only a first proof is required, the ink may be applied in little dabs all over the plate, and then rolled up, or dabbed hard and evenly until there is a good dark colour over all, and the ink well driven down into the lines.

The plate is then allowed to cool. A pad of book-muslin, coarse in texture, a little bigger than the palm of the hand, is now made ready, and the plate is wiped with this, using a circular motion. A second wiping with a second pad of finer texture, and the plate is in condition for heating once more. This heating makes the ink in the lines rise up slightly, more ready to be taken up by the printing paper. The paper we are going to use has already been selected—and there is an infinite variety upon which to experiment—and is thoroughly wetted on both sides, then slipped between sheets of blotting-paper.

The press is prepared. The pressure of the rollers is tested perhaps by running an old plate of the same gauge through, and examining the pressure-marks upon a dry sheet of blotting-paper which takes the place of the printing paper. The hot, wiped plate is placed upon the travelling bed of the press, the damp printing paper on top, a sheet of fresh blotting-paper superimposed on that, and over all the two blankets, first the close-textured " fronting ", and then the more woolly " swan-cloth ". The press is now put into action, the plate is carried under the roller once only, and when the blankets are lifted the print is found, perhaps more satisfactory than the etcher has dared to expect.

A " dry-point " is executed on metal, and printed in an identical manner, but in this case there is no ground, and no acid action on the plate. With a point strong enough to furrow the plate, the lines are impressed by force into the metal, casting up a burr upon either side of the line. The relative strength of the line is therefore a matter of muscular force. Mistakes can be corrected by a scraper for removing the burr, and a burnisher to close up a mistaken line. The characteristic dry-point print is strong and beautiful.

Engraving is similar to dry-point, in that the metal is incised by hand, but the engraver does not furrow the plate—but by using a burin of diamond section, he removes a slip of metal with the stroke of the tool.

There are many excellent books on Etching. One that can confidently be recommended is *The Art of Etching*, by E. S. Lumsden (Seeley, Service & Co.).

STAMP COLLECTING

Stamp collecting is a fascinating and tantalizing hobby; for it matters little whether you have thousands of pounds to spend on it, or merely coppers—there are stamps to be collected by people of all tastes and with pockets of all depths. That is why it is as popular with millionaires and kings as with so many ordinary folk like ourselves.

If you collect for a lifetime you will probably never come into possession of any of the very early stamps of British Guiana, or of the penny and twopenny stamps issued by Mauritius in 1847; but there is just as much fun in hunting for a perfect copy of the Great Britain penny black, or in completing sets of the many fine pictorial stamps to be found in various issues of so many foreign countries.

In passing, you may be interested to know that one of the British Guiana stamps is the rarest stamp in the world. This is the 1 cent stamp issued in 1856. It is not the earliest stamp of this particular colony—the first was issued six years before—but it has become valuable because only one known copy has survived. At the present time this is in an American collection and is valued at £10,000. The owner gave £7343 for it several years ago, and not long afterwards refused £7500 for it. One of the most interesting things about this stamp, however, is that it was once in the collection of a schoolboy. This particular boy was Vernon Vaughan, of British Guiana, and he discovered the stamp on an old envelope in his father's attic. He stuck it in his collection but liked it so little—for it is really only a dirty scrap of paper—that he sold it to a dealer for six shillings. Later it changed hands for £25 and so started on its road to fame.

The early stamps of Mauritius have a history almost as romantic. Only thirty of the first two are now known to exist, and all are in well-known collections. At one time they were bought and sold at about £4 apiece, but now it would take nearly as many thousands to buy one. One of the stamps which King George V prized most was a 2d. Mauritius added to his collection in 1904. It cost £1400 then, but is probably worth nearer three times this amount now.

Although it is not wise to stress the commercial side of stamp collecting too much—for I, like many others, believe that one should collect for the sheer joy of collecting and not with an eye always set on eventual profit—the fact cannot be overlooked that this is an advantage which stamp collecting has over almost every other hobby. If you collect wisely you not only have the pleasure of collecting, but you find, as the years go by, that you have something appreciating in value, and worth more than the money (however much or however little) which you have spent on it.

I have said *if you collect wisely*, and one of the first things I want to emphasize, if you are taking up stamp collecting seriously, is that you *should* collect wisely. But more about this later. In the meantime, let us see what is required, in the way of accessories, before one can start collecting at all. Fortunately, the requirements are not large and the expense is comparatively small.

The very first requirement is a pair of tweezers, and I have put these first because you cannot handle stamps too carefully. If you handle them too often with your bare fingers they begin to get grubby, and, if you are not very careful, it is not long either before they start to show creases or lose a few of their perforations. Stamps which are not perfect are little better than useless scraps of paper. The serious collector—and if you are going to be a collector at all, please do be a serious one—will have nothing to do with stamps which are not perfect in every respect. Your collection will look very ordinary if you half fill it with a lot of damaged and dirty specimens. It is much better to have half the number and have them looking bright and undamaged. So to begin with get a pair of tweezers. A shilling will buy a good pair at any stamp shop, or you can get a pair of nail tweezers from any chemist.

Next, I would advise you to try to get a new or second-hand stock book in which to put your stamps until you are able to mount them up, and a small stock card in which to carry " swaps " in your pocket. Stock books or stock cards are made up of pieces of card across which strips of paper are pasted at reasonable intervals. These strips are pasted only half their depth, so that stamps can be slipped in between the unfastened portion and the back of the card. They are quite easy to make yourself, since all you require is a few sheets of cardboard, some strips of brown paper and a pot of paste.

Three other useful accessories are a perforation gauge, a water-mark detector and a magnifying-glass. The latter is the least important of the three and need not be purchased straight away.

The perforation gauge is very important, and you will be able to get a good one from any stamp shop for a few coppers. Buy as good a one as you can afford, since the very cheap ones are not always accurate and they are often difficult to read.

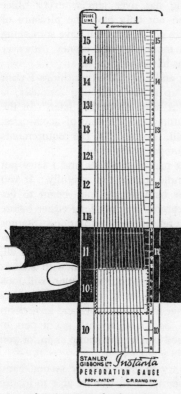

A transparent perforation gauge

(Reproduced by permission of Messrs. Stanley Gibbons, Ltd.)

You may wonder why this gauge is so important, and it may be advisable, at this point, to explain its working to you.

The early stamps of a good many countries were not perforated at all. They were simply printed in large sheets, with small spaces between each stamp, and when the stamps were sold or used they were cut out of the sheets with scissors. In 1854, however, this country adopted a perforation patent brought out by a certain Mr. Archer, and from then on stamps were perforated so that they could be removed easily from sheets and without resorting to the tiresome business of cutting them.

Throughout the years all countries have varied the perforations of their stamps considerably, and a gauge shows to which of these variations a particular stamp belongs.

When you get a gauge you will probably find that it is numbered from 7 to $16\frac{1}{2}$, and the figures represent the number of perforations in each 2 cm. space of the stamp. This 2 cm. is a standard on which every gauge is spaced. In order to find the perforation of a particular stamp, therefore, all you have to do is to place it on the gauge and move it until the perforation fits one of the numbered lines on the scale. The figure against the line is then the number of the perforation.

In passing, it is interesting to note that a perforation will sometimes increase the value of a stamp considerably. Take, for example, the 1½d. George V stamp issued by St. Lucia in 1936. You can have two copies of this stamp and both will look alike. When you test them on the perforation gauge, however, one may measure 14 on all sides while the other measures 12 on one side and 13 on the other. If you have one with the latter perforations you are lucky, since this is worth about twelve times the price of the former. Or you may have two copies of the 6d. deep orange issued by New South Wales in 1905. One is perforated 12 by 11½, where the other is perforated 11 all round. The value of the latter is over two hundred times that of the former.

A watermark detector reveals differences equally as interesting. You will know, of course, what a watermark is, and you may have seen one in all good-quality notepaper. The majority of stamps have been given a watermark in order to make it more difficult to forge them. Often you can see it by holding the stamp up to the light or holding it, face down, a few inches from something black. When the printing of the design is very dense, however, or the paper used is rather thick, it is not at all easy to pick the watermark out properly. It is then that a watermark detector comes in useful. Actually it is only a shallow black tin and its cost is seldom more than a shilling. Used stamps can be soaked in water and laid flat down in the tin, when the watermark will show up clearly. Obviously you cannot do this with unused stamps or you will spoil the gum and thus ruin the stamp. In their case, however, you can put them face downwards in the tin and pour a few drops of benzine on them. Stamp dealers sell special dropper bottles for this purpose, and these can usually be purchased for about eighteenpence or two shillings.

Just as perforations vary considerably, so do watermarks. They take the form of designs or letters—sometimes both. The most common of the Great Britain and British Colonial watermarks is a crown with the letters CA above or below it. The CA may take the form of ordinary capital letters, or of script letters—*CA*. Sometimes the letters CC are found instead of CA. The watermark of some stamps is just one crown and one set of letters. Of others it is parts of more than one crown and more than one set of letters. In these cases it is described as being " multiple crown CA " or " multiple script CA ". In the majority of stamps the watermark is upright, but in a few it is found sideways. " CA ", by the way, means " Crown Agents ", the government department responsible for such stamps.

Stamps are often exactly alike in appearance but differ in watermark, and when this is the case one is almost invariably worth more than the other. Take, for example, some of the values issued in 1922–7 by Gambia. The 1s. purple-yellow may be found either with an ordinary CA or with a script CA. The latter is worth only about half the former. Again, the 5s. green-yellow of the same issue differs in the same way, but here again the ordinary CA is worth about twice as much as the other. You can see, therefore, how essential it is to be able to detect the watermarks of your stamps in order to place them correctly.

The next thing you require is a good catalogue, and you cannot do better here than get one of those published by Messrs. Stanley Gibbons. There are other catalogues of almost equal merit, but the Gibbons catalogue is recognized by almost every person who collects stamps, or who deals in them, and whenever you see a number attached to a stamp as a reference, preceded by the latters " S.G.", you can be certain it is the number of that stamp in the Gibbons catalogue.

The general catalogues are brought up to date every year and are published in two parts—Part I being stamps of the British Empire and Part II those of Foreign Countries. If you cannot afford to buy new catalogues, and cannot persuade a friend to buy them for you, you can sometimes pick up good copies on second-hand bookstalls. Or frequently one may borrow the latest issue from the Public Library.

A catalogue lists all the known stamps and gives prices at which Messrs. Stanley Gibbons are prepared to sell them if they have them in stock. These prices give a very fair idea of current values, and if you set out to do much buying you should try to buy as much below these prices as possible. Sometimes, of course, current prices are above those in the catalogue, since a catalogue goes to press some months before it is issued. Generally speaking, however, these fluctuating prices usually apply to recent issues or popular commemorative issues only.

Having acquired tweezers, stock books, perforation gauge, watermark detector and catalogue, you are now ready to start collecting seriously; and the last consideration is a suitable album and hinges with which to mount the stamps. The latter can be obtained from any stationer's shop, and a thousand cost no more than 1s. 6d. to 2s. Always, however, get the very best you can. A good hinge will keep a stamp tightly fixed to an album leaf but will peel off both stamp and leaf, if required, and leave hardly any mark. Cheap hinges stick well—far too well, in fact—but when you try to pull them off they either refuse to budge altogether or do some irretrievable damage in the process.

Regarding albums, there are scores of different types on the market, but they all fall roughly into three main groups.

The first is the printed album. This is bound tight in book form, and the countries are arranged in alphabetical order. Pictures of many of the stamps are featured, and the various pages are ruled off to accommodate stamps in the order in which they appear in the catalogue. The second is also a printed album, bound tight, but in this case the pages are ruled off in squares and pictures of stamps appear only at the top, together with the name of the country. Both kinds of album are useful, and they certainly help in the arrangement of the stamps. They are, however, more for the lazy collector and give no scope for individuality. Moreover, they possess the one great disadvantage that if a page is spoilt it cannot be taken out without upsetting the whole album.

By far the best idea is to use loose-leaf albums. These are made up of plain loose leaves—plain, that is, except for a very faint ruling into tiny squares to make mounting accurate—which are housed in a stiff-covered binder. The advantages of an album such as this are many. You can, for example, work on each leaf separately, and as your collection grows you can keep rearranging the leaves to suit your convenience. If you spoil a leaf you can easily separate it from the rest of the album without in any way spoiling the collection as a whole.

What to my mind, however, is a bigger advantage is that you can " write up a collection " properly, and my own experience has been that this writing-up business is more than half the fun of collecting.

A collection seldom looks attractive when every page is the same —just covered with stamps all in rows and about the same distances apart. By using loose leaves you can vary the appearance considerably. Some pages will have several stamps on them; others may have only two or three. On some pages a few of your best specimens will be arranged neatly in the centre; on others a whole set will perhaps be spread out to fill the complete page. You can make the stamps on different pages form scores of attractive designs, and the more you vary the layouts the more attractive will the whole collection become.

A generous use of black Indian ink (if you are using white leaves), or of white Indian ink (if you are using black leaves), will help to make your stamps stand out and give the pages an attractive appearance. Ruled, as they are, into small squares, there is practically no limit to the way in which the different pages can be varied. You can, for example, draw one, two, or three lines around a stamp and thus make it appear in a frame. You can join one frame to another; you can vary the thicknesses of the lines; and so on. For your best stamps you can make a black background on which to mount them. First of all fix the position and then paint the leaf black, with Indian ink and a fine brush, over an area a little larger than the stamp. Then mount the stamp in the centre. This always looks effective. Another attractive method of framing is to paint a line all round the stamp, the thickness of a square and one square away from each side.

Using a brush, you may get a few untidy edges, but if you are careful these are not serious, and if you afterwards line them all out with a pen you will soon obtain a very neat finish indeed. To begin with, take a few old leaves and experiment. Work out a number of different layouts, and when you are satisfied incorporate them into your collection proper.

This, however, is only a part of writing up. To make your collection really interesting you should add a few notes regarding the stamps on each page. Above each stamp, for example, write the catalogue number, and if the stamp is a pictorial one write below it the subject of the design. If there is anything especially interesting about a particular stamp add that also. For example, you may have a stamp with a First Day postmark—that is, the first day of issue—or you may have one containing an error, or one with an uncommon perforation. All these points are worth noting.

There are quite a few stamps, by the way, with minor errors, and these are always worth looking for. There is a big thrill when you find one unexpectedly, and it is in this connexion that a magnifying-glass comes in handy, for it enables you to study a stamp more easily. One fairly common error to look for is on the 1 cent green stamp issued by Newfoundland in 1910. Now and then you may find the stamp with an F instead of an E in NEWFOUNDLAND. Such a stamp is worth nearly fifty times as much as the ordinary one. In the Hong Kong Jubilee stamps of 1891 there are several minor errors—such as a short J or a short U in JUBILEE—and all such stamps are worth two or three times the price of the ordinary stamp. Another example is found in the 1936 issue of Turkish stamps. These were the same as stamps issued in 1929 and 1930, except that they were surcharged with some wording, and the date 20/7/1936. On some of the stamps the date is 1926, instead of 1936, and these are catalogued at about twenty times as much as the normal ones.

One other piece of information to put on each page is the year of issue and details of the watermark and perforation. The best place for this is in the top left-hand corner, just below where the ruling begins.

We have covered now all the preliminaries connected with collecting and are ready to get down seriously to the business of collecting itself. There are two things you will want to consider here. The first is what to collect, and the second is how and where to obtain specimens.

In connection with the first—what to collect—you have probably answered, " Why, obviously, stamps!" But it is not as simple as that, and few worthwhile collections have been built up by collectors who have just collected anything and everything in the stamp line. Neither do you often find such a collector remain keen for very long. The reason for this is not far to seek. There are so many hundreds of thousands of stamps issued that, if you collect generally, you have nothing but gaps all over the album. Moreover, you never seem to complete anything.

If you are starting to collect, make up your mind to confine your attention, for the time being, to certain sections. You can, for example, collect only Great Britain, or only British Colonials, or only Foreign. A better plan, however, is to pick out a dozen or two popular countries and concentrate on these. Build them up as far as you can, and when you find it increasingly difficult to fill spaces —because the stamps are either too scarce or too expensive—start on another dozen or so. You can still fill up your main collections as opportunities present themselves.

For your guidance, here are what I consider the twelve most attractive countries among British Colonials, and the twelve most attractive among Foreign.

Among Colonials, then, I would suggest Bahamas, Barbados (from 1875 onwards), Cayman Islands, Cyprus, Egypt, Gold Coast, Hong Kong, Kenya, Leeward Islands, Malta, St. Lucia and South Africa.

My selection of Foreign is Belgium, Czechoslovakia, Denmark, France, Germany, Holland, Italy, Jugoslavia, Poland, Portugal, Spain and Switzerland.

I have selected all these with care as being countries in which it is possible to build up a fairly extensive collection quite cheaply and one which, when built up, should be very attractive to look through. Also, it is not difficult to place the various stamps in the correct issues and catalogue numbers.

Except of the very cheap stamps—say those catalogued under sixpence—do not hesitate to collect more than one copy, provided the copies are all perfect. When you come across pairs, or strips (more than two in a row), or blocks (four or more all together), do not separate the stamps but mount the piece as it is. Pairs, strips and blocks, particularly of some issues, are generally worth a little more than separated stamps. Apart from this, however, if they are dotted about a collection they give it a better appearance than if the collection is made up of all single stamps.

Some collectors confine themselves to the collecting either of all mint stamps or all used. There is something to be said for this practice, but there is no reason why a beginner should not collect both and then decide later on whether he will carry on with both or confine his collecting to one or the other. If you do collect both, however, try not to mix them up in the different sets. Get together a set of all used, or of all mint. If you can get a set of each, so much the better. Sets are more attractive if they are not mixed but, apart from this, they are easier to dispose of, if you ever wish to part with them, and they are invariably worth more.

I advised you earlier on to collect none but perfect stamps and referred then to those which are perforated. When you start to collect the earlier issues—and there is no reason why you should not start straight away—you will not find it at all easy to get perfect copies. In fact, they are very few and far between. You may like to know, however, that a good early copy is one that has been so cut that four margins of white show clearly all round the stamp. Do not despise those with only one, two or three borders, but remember that, as a general rule, those with the most borders, and the widest borders, are the best—and therefore most valuable—stamps.

Having now made up your mind what you intend to collect, you can begin to build up your collection, and if you are going to set about this in the right way there are many points to consider.

Stamps one requires can be acquired in one or more of three different ways. Some you can get from friends for nothing, some you can obtain by exchanging unwanted duplicates, and others you will have to purchase.

Never be afraid to talk about stamps whenever you get the chance. Almost everyone in these days gets stamps at different times, chiefly by correspondence. Let all your friends know that you collect and many of them will be only too pleased to save for you all the colonial and foreign stamps that come their way. Whether you require them or not for your own collection matters little. You can always exchange unwanted ones with your collecting friends.

Try to find out who collects stamps in your town or district, and then endeavour to get an introduction to these people. Stamp collectors, as a body, are a very nice set of people, and nine times out of ten an advanced collector is always pleased to see the album of a beginner and more often than not is willing to give him a few of his own unwanted duplicates.

You can get to know a wide circle of collectors by joining a Philatelic Society. There is one of these in most towns and the annual subscription is very low. Moreover, some societies have special sections to encourage the beginner.

By becoming a member of a society you get far more than an introduction to a number of collectors. Among other things you can attend meetings at which many points connected with collecting are discussed, and at every meeting you will be able to exchange unwanted stamps with other collectors who may have just what you require. Most societies also hold occasional sales at which members can sell small lots which they do not need and can purchase other lots which they do need.

It is a good plan always to have with you a small selection of swaps in a special slip-in pocket-book. You never know when you are going to meet another interested collector, and it is surprising how often you will come across a chance of improving your collection in this way.

So much for the first two methods of acquiring stamps. The third, you will remember, is by purchasing. The limit of your purchases will depend, of course, upon the cash you are able to spare, and I will briefly outline the three best ways in which this can be spent.

The first of these is through a Postal Exchange Club. If you obtain a copy of one of the leading stamp magazines—*Stamp Collecting*, *Philatelic Magazine* or *Stamp Lover*—you will find advertisements of several well-known clubs, and you can safely send for particulars of any of them. Some charge a small entrance fee— ranging from 1s. to 5s.—and others charge no fee at all.

The way in which a club works is as follows. At monthly intervals the secretary makes up a parcel of stamps consisting of anything up to 30 small books, and these are circulated to all members on a mailing list. If you are one of these members the parcel reaches you in due course, and you are at liberty to take out any stamps which interest you, at the prices marked, and when you have been right through the parcel you do it up again and send it on to the next person on the list. The money for the stamps taken you post direct to the secretary.

The books of stamps of which the parcel consists are mounted up and sent in by members. These are usually duplicates and unwanted stamps which a member wishes to sell. You, as a member, are at liberty to send in as many books as you like, and these are included in parcels and circulated. When a parcel has been right round and is returned to the secretary, he breaks it up and returns the books to the several members who have contributed them, together with the money for the stamps taken by other members. All that he deducts to cover his own expenses is 10 per cent or $12\frac{1}{2}$ per cent of the total sales.

There is also a lot of fun to be had in going through club packets, and they afford an excellent way of getting rid of unwanted material.

The second way is to buy stamps from dealers. You will find the advertisements of several reliable firms in the magazines mentioned, as well as in papers like *Meccano Magazine* and *Boy's Own Paper*. Most dealers send out approval sheets of stamps, and you are allowed to have these at frequent intervals, take out what you want, and remit for the stamps taken. There are many dealers who cater for the beginner and who issue approvals at as little as $\frac{1}{4}d$. or $\frac{1}{2}d$. per stamp. Some, too, specialize in low-priced sets and useful assorted packets.

The third way is to buy lots at auction sales. There are several of these sales held in London, from September to July, and you will find these, too, advertised in the stamp magazines. Anyone can visit a sale and look through as many lots as he finds interesting. You can then bid for a lot at the sale or, if you cannot attend, you can tell the auctioneer how much you are prepared to pay for a particular lot, and he will endeavour to get it for you as reasonably as possible. Auctions are made up of all kinds of lots, and you can buy as cheap as 5s. or as dear as a thousand pounds. But whether you buy or not it is an interesting experience to visit a sale.

We have now considered carefully all the main points connected with collecting, and all that remains is to remind ourselves of the three golden rules. These are : to collect only perfect specimens, not to attempt to collect too widely, and, if you spend money, to buy as cheaply and as wisely as possible.

SWEET-MAKING

Even if it is much simpler to go to the confectioners to buy sweets when you want them, there is a special satisfaction in being able to make your own. And perhaps your home, or where you live when you are on holiday, may be far from a sweet-shop; then you will be very popular if you can make candy or fudge. You may be even more ambitious and want to try your hand at bon-bons. With a little experience you will be able to make them look as good as professionally made ones, and then you can do them up in dainty boxes and use them for birthday or Christmas presents. Such a gift, which is your own handiwork, will be doubly appreciated.

Since the supply of ingredients available varies greatly from household to household, and even from time to time, the recipes which follow include both those which use a good deal of sugar, butter and sometimes eggs, and others which we learned to adopt during times of shortage, using alternative ingredients, or much smaller quantities. After surveying your household larder and store-cupboard—and consulting Mother also—you will know what is at your disposal, and then choose a suitable recipe.

As when baking, it is advisable to gather together at the beginning all the utensils and ingredients you will require. Be sure that the utensils are absolutely clean. For sweet-making a long-handled wooden spoon is advisable for stirring, and a marble slab is the best surface to work on.

HANDY MEASURES

16 ounces: 2 level breakfastcupfuls, or 3 teacupfuls.
8 ounces: 1 level breakfastcupful.
4 ounces: 1 level teacupful.
1 ounce: 2 level tablespoonfuls.
$\frac{1}{4}$ ounce: 1 level dessertspoonful.
1 ounce butter: 2 dessertspoonfuls or 1 tablespoonful.

LIQUIDS

1 pint: 2 breakfastcupfuls.   1 gill: 1 small teacupful.

Here are some general directions which you should note carefully before you begin.

Be very particular when measuring ingredients to do so accurately.

The method of testing when candy or toffee is ready is to take a spoon and drop a little into a cup of cold water. Note that this testing water should be really cold. If the mixture is ready it will immediately harden when dropped in the water. If it does not, then you must continue boiling a little longer, and use fresh water when testing again.

If you are adding flavourings to candy, allow it to cool a little before doing so.

When you come to cut toffee, use a sharp and greased knife, and you will find you make a much better job of it.

In some of the recipes an exact temperature is stated; for this purpose a sugar thermometer is best.

BUTTERSCOTCH

One pound Demerara sugar;
Four ounces butter or margarine;
One and a quarter teacups milk;
A little lemon essence.

Dissolve the sugar in the milk and simmer gently for five minutes. Add the butter in tiny pats, mixing well, then continue boiling for about ten minutes or until a drop will harden in cold water. Add the essence, allow to settle, then pour into a buttered tin. When sufficiently cool mark into squares and leave to harden.

BUTTERSCOTCH
(old recipe taken from *The Scots Kitchen*)

One pound brown sugar;
Four ounces butter;
Quarter ounce powdered ginger;
Lemon essence.

Put a pound of brown sugar into an enamelled saucepan and let it dissolve on the range. Beat four ounces of butter to a cream, add it to the sugar when dissolved, and stir over the fire until it has boiled sufficiently to harden when dropped into cold water. Take off fire and then add a quarter ounce of powdered ginger dissolved in a little water or a little essence of lemon. Beat with a fork quickly for a few minutes. Pour on to a buttered slab or dish, and when sufficiently cool mark into squares. When cold, a slight tap will break them off separately.

LEMON BARLEY SUGAR

Half pound sugar;   Pinch cream of tartar;
Half teacup water;   A few drops lemon essence.

Dissolve sugar in water in a strong-lined pan over a slow heat. Add cream of tartar. Boil for a few minutes without stirring until the mixture turns syrupy and a pale golden colour.

Pour into a greased tin and cool for a minute or two. Now sprinkle with lemon flavouring, and with a knife fold the corners of the toffee to the centre. Cut into strips about three-quarters of an inch thick; take each strip by the ends and twist. Replace on tray and leave to harden.

CANDY

Two rounded tablespoons sugar;
One rounded tablespoon syrup;
One level teaspoon baking soda.

Put sugar and syrup into a lined pan and stir until boiling. Boil about ten minutes over moderate heat and stir all the time, otherwise it will burn. Free the soda from any lumps. Remove the candy from heat, add the soda, and beat for a minute or two until the mixture begins to thicken. Turn into a greased tin, cool, mark and leave to harden. Use a much larger saucepan than you think you will need because the mixture froths up when soda is added.

DATE CANDIES

Three cupfuls sugar;
Half pound stoned, chopped dates.

Melt the sugar in a saucepan, being very careful that it does not burn. When it turns to a brown syrup add the dates and pour into a greased tin. When cool, mark in strips, which can be broken up when it is quite set.

CHOCOLATE CARAMELS

Half teacupful golden syrup;
Half teacupful milk;
Half teacupful powdered chocolate;

Half teacupful brown sugar;
One teaspoonful glycerine;
Half ounce butter.

Put syrup, sugar, milk and butter into a saucepan. Let the mixture come to the boil, stirring briskly all the time, then add the glycerine. Remove pan to the side, stir in chocolate gradually, then boil up again, still stirring carefully. Test by dropping a little of the mixture in cold water—when it forms a hard ball it is ready. Pour into a greased tin and cut into squares before it is quite cold. If the caramels are not going to be eaten up at once, they should be wrapped in waxed paper.

SALTED ALMONDS

Put enough butter in a small pan to have it one inch deep when melted. Heat it to boiling-point—test by putting a piece of bread in to brown.

After blanching the almonds, throw them all in at once to brown them.

Mix some salt and a little cayenne pepper on a paper. Take the almonds from the pan and roll them in it, shaking them well until they are nearly cold.

Fudge is a first favourite; here are one or two variations.

CHOCOLATE FUDGE

Two large bars plain chocolate;
One cupful sugar (white);

One teaspoonful butter;
Small cupful milk.

Grate the chocolate and mix it with the cupful of white sugar and the cupful of milk, stirring all the time until the mixture leaves the sides of the pan—from ten to fifteen minutes. Take the pan from the heat and lightly stir in the teaspoonful of butter. Put the pan aside until the mixture is quite cold. It should then be very sticky and thick. Beat with a wooden spoon until it is smooth and flexible. When it no longer clings to the spoon or pan turn on to a greased tin and mark into squares. Let the squares dry off first before handing them round to be eaten.

VANILLA FUDGE

Three cupfuls sugar;
One cupful milk;

One tablespoonful butter;
A few drops vanilla essence.

Melt the ingredients together and cook until a little dropped into cold water forms a soft ball. Then take the mixture off the heat until creamy.

Pour on to a buttered dish, and when nearly cold roll into balls.

COFFEE FUDGE

Three cupfuls sugar;
One cupful strong coffee;

One tablespoonful butter;
Pinch of salt.

Melt the ingredients together and cook until a little dropped into cold water forms a soft ball. Then take mixture off the heat and beat until creamy. Pour on to a buttered dish and when nearly cold roll into balls.

GUNDY (economy recipe)

Two ounces sugar;
Two rounded tablespoons syrup or treacle;
Two level teaspoons baking soda.

Put sugar and syrup into a strong saucepan and dissolve thoroughly over a gentle heat, stirring well. Bring to boil and boil for five minutes; stir in baking soda, having it quite smooth and free from lumps. While still boiling pour at once into a greased tin, leave until cold and set, then break into pieces.

GUNDY (special recipe from *The Scots Kitchen*)

One pound brown sugar;   Two ounces butter;
Teaspoonful syrup or treacle;   Aniseed or cinnamon.

Put into a saucepan a pound of brown sugar, a teaspoonful of syrup or treacle and two ounces of butter. Boil it until it becomes quite hard when a little is put into cold water. Flavour with aniseed or cinnamon. Pour out very thinly on a buttered tin or slab, and when it is cold and hard break up roughly with a small hammer; or when cool enough to handle form into thin round sticks.

HONEYCOMB TOFFEE

Two rounded tablespoons sugar (Demerara preferred);
Two rounded tablespoons syrup;
Two tablespoons water;
One teaspoon (rounded) baking soda.

A fairly large pan is required as the toffee fluffs up to about double its quantity.

Boil sugar, syrup and water together for about seven minutes —or until it is a rich brown colour—stirring carefully. While boiling, stir in the baking soda quickly, then pour at once into a greased sandwich tin and leave to cool. When almost set, loosen edges with a knife and turn on to a wire tray. Leave until cold.

WALNUT TABLET

One pound sugar;   One teacupful milk;
One tablespoonful syrup;
Three ounces shelled and chopped walnuts;
One tablespoonful butter;   One teaspoonful vanilla.

Put sugar, butter, milk, and syrup into a pan. Bring slowly to the boil. Boil until it forms a soft ball—about twenty-five minutes (240 degrees F.). Remove from heat, add walnuts and vanilla. Beat with a wooden spoon till creamy.

Pour into a tin which has been greased and lined with grease-proof paper.

MARZIPAN

One pound sugar;
Twelve ounces ground almonds;
Teacupful water;
Two whites of eggs;
Three tablespoons sifted icing sugar.

Boil sugar and water to 232 degrees F. Take the pan from the heat, stir a little until it begins to form grains, then stir in ground almonds and white of egg. Cook slightly over a low heat. Turn on to a slab, add about three tablespoonfuls sifted icing sugar. Work with a wooden spoon until cool enough to handle then knead it smooth. Divide into sections. These can be coloured and flavoured with different essences and shaped into different forms—fruit, logs, &c.

CARAMEL WALNUT

Marzipan;   Walnuts;   Syrup

Form marzipan into balls, place halved shelled walnut on either side. Allow to dry for about twelve hours. Coat with syrup and when set place in fancy paper cases.

Syrup

To make the syrup dissolve one pound sugar slowly in about a teacupful of water, keeping lid on saucepan. Add a pinch of cream of tartar, bring to boiling-point, skim, boil till a drop will turn hard in water—about 300 degrees F.

MOCK MARZIPAN ALMONDS OR NUTS

Four ounces soya flour (or potato powder);
One tablespoon finely chopped nuts;
Three to four tablespoons sugar;
Two ounces margarine;
Two small teaspoons almond essence;
Two tablespoons water;
A few shelled and blanched almonds or nuts.

Melt the margarine, add the sugar, water and essence, and stir over a gentle heat for a minute. Remove from heat and beat in the soya and nuts, then beat over a gentle heat for another minute. Roll into balls, place an almond on each side. Place on a greased ashet to harden.

STUFFED DATES

Put a small ball of marzipan inside each date. Toss in sugar, and place in paper cases.

MOCK MARZIPAN (second recipe)

Two ounces margarine;
Two ounces castor sugar;
One packet of four (or equivalent) small plain sponge cakes;
One small teaspoonful almond essence.

Cream margarine and sugar; crumb or finely grate cake and add to creamed margarine; add almond essence, then work with hands until a smooth paste.

MARZIPAN POTATOES

Form the marzipan into oval-shaped pieces, then dust with powdered cocoa or chocolate. Place in paper cases.

NOUGAT

Six ounces blanched almonds;   One tablespoon lemon juice;
Six ounces castor sugar;   One tablespoon water.

Bake almonds in a slow oven until they turn a pale yellow. Put sugar, water and lemon in a small pan and heat slowly without boiling until the sugar has completely dissolved; then boil until it is a light brown. Add the almonds. Turn the nougat on to an oiled slab or toffee tin.

One of the ways of using this nougat is to shape it into little baskets. First oil the fingers and basket-shaped moulds; flatten a piece of the nougat big enough to line the mould, work it in with the fingers, tidy the edges, and then take it out of the mould. The baskets are then filled with crystallized fruit, and can be decorated with a handle of angelica and pistachio nuts.

TREACLE TOFFEE

One pound brown sugar;   One pound treacle;
Quarter pound butter;   A few drops lemon essence.

Melt the butter in a pan. Then put in the treacle, brown sugar and lemon essence. Boil the mixture, stirring carefully until a little forms a hard ball when dropped in cold water.

Pour into a greased tin and leave until almost firm. Mark into squares and leave until cold, then break up into pieces.

PEPPERMINT CREAMS

One pound sugar;   One teacupful water;
Pinch cream of tartar; One teaspoonful essence of peppermint.

Boil all the ingredients (except the peppermint) together until on trying one or two drops in cold water a soft ball can be made— in about ten minutes. Pour into a basin, and when cool beat with a wooden spoon until white and creamy. Now add peppermint. Turn mixture on board and knead till soft and smooth—use icing sugar to prevent it sticking. Roll out and cut in rounds.

PEPPERMINT CREAMS (second method)

In this recipe the whites of two eggs are needed, with as much icing sugar as will form a stiff paste. Mix the whites with the sugar and a few drops peppermint, mixing well. Roll out to a quarter inch thick. Cut in small moulds and spread on paper to set. Leave until next day.

TABLET

Four teacupfuls sugar;
Two tablespoonfuls syrup;
One teacupful water.

Boil the above ingredients for about twenty minutes, then add two tablespoonfuls butter and stir until it is ready—that is, when it becomes sugary. Take it off the heat, add one teaspoonful of flavouring just before pouring—essence of lemon, vanilla or ginger may be used.

GINGER TABLET

One pound Demerara sugar;
One gill cold water;
Half ounce ground ginger.

Put the sugar and water into a lined saucepan and stir until they come to the boil. Remove any scum, and then boil until a little dropped in water will form a soft ball—about 245 degrees F. Take the saucepan off the heat, add the ginger, and keep stirring until the mixture begins to turn thick. Have a flat oven tin lined with greased paper, pour the mixture into this and leave it until cold. Cut into neat pieces of equal size.

PEPPERMINT TABLET

Two teacupfuls granulated sugar;
Half teacupful milk;
One tablespoonful syrup;
Few drops peppermint essence.

Dissolve sugar in milk and add the syrup. Bring to the boil and boil exactly three minutes. Remove from fire, add essence and stir till sugary. Pour into a greased tin.

TOFFEE

Two rounded tablespoons syrup.
One tin condensed milk;
Two ounces margarine.

Put the ingredients into a strong pan. Stir until boiling, and boil about fifteen minutes, stirring carefully all the time. Test a drop in cold water; when it forms into a hard ball it is ready. Pour into a greased tin and leave until almost firm. Cut into squares and leave until cold.

RUSSIAN TOFFEE

First Recipe.

One tin condensed milk, sweetened;
Two tablespoons syrup (rounded);
Two ounces margarine.

Put all the ingredients into a saucepan. Stir till boiling and boil for about fifteen minutes, being careful to stir all the time or it will burn. Turn into a greased tin, mark in squares, and when firm roll in grease-proof paper.

RUSSIAN TOFFEE

Second Recipe.

Two teacups sugar;
Two tablespoonfuls syrup;
Three ounces fresh butter;
One tin condensed milk;
Small teacupful water, little vanilla essence.

Melt half the butter, add sugar, syrup, condensed milk, water, vanilla essence. When boiling put in the rest of the butter gradually, broken up into small pieces. Boil until a spoonful tried in water forms a small hard ball—about one hour. Pour into a greased tin and, before quite cold, cut into blocks. Roll in grease-proof paper.

WALNUT MOLASSES

One pound brown sugar;
One teacup water;
Two ounces shelled and chopped walnuts;
One ounce butter;
Pinch of cream of tartar.

(This recipe calls for more experience and skill in making.)

Toast the walnuts in the oven for a few minutes, and then chop them up roughly.

Put water, sugar and cream of tartar into a lined saucepan and boil with the thermometer to 280 degrees F., adding the butter just before reaching this head.

Pour on to a marble slab in a long flat shape; sprinkle with walnuts and fold over with a wooden spoon.

When slightly cool roll with the hands and pull out until about the thickness of a fountain pen—say half an inch in diameter. Then cut quickly in two-inch lengths. Allow the pieces to cool and wrap them in waxed paper.

CAREER GUIDE — What will you be?

Some girls are in the fortunate position that they have always known exactly what they wanted to do with their lives, what career they wanted to take up. For them there may be no problem except finding the means to do what they want. Other girls, perhaps the majority, find this business of choosing and deciding both puzzling and worrying. It is wise to consult a headmistress or elder person and to discuss possibilities in view of your own capabilities; but do not allow them to make up your mind for you. It is your life and you should decide.

There is one point which I, as the older person, would dare to emphasize. Whatever you are going to do, train for it, and secure the final necessary qualifications. Even if you are not going to take up a professional career and are just going to " be at home " —take a domestic science course and win your diploma. You never know what you may be called upon to do in the future, and with accepted qualifications you need never be at a loss for an occupation. But in these days the unqualified person has very little chance of finding interesting work. To help you in your choice, here below is an A.B.C. Career Guide; it shows the varied range available for young women nowadays. So go ahead, and make your choice.

ACCOUNTANCY

As the work of an accountant is concerned with the preparation of accounts, costing, taxation, and almost everything to do with figures, only those who are good at mathematics need consider this occupation. The work is well paid and may lead to highly remunerative posts in commerce. There is a preliminary examination, unless you can produce the General Certificate of Education (with certain specified subjects) or its equivalent.

The length of training usually consists of five years' practical experience in an accountant's office, or three years if a university graduate. Combined with that there is the essential part-time study to pass the professional examinations in order to be accepted as a member of the principal bodies. For the latest regulations write to the Secretary, the Society of Incorporated Accountants, Victoria Embankment, London, W.C.2, or the Association of Certified and Corporate Accountants, 22 Bedford Square, London, W.C.1.

ADVERTISING

The advertising field offers variety and scope to those considering a business career, and who have the necessary self-confidence and initiative. Those who write good English and have a flair for words may specialize as copywriters, or you may specialize in layout—the most striking methods of presenting an advertisement. Some secretarial training is advisable, followed by a practical course at a training school. But actual experience is the best training here, and as soon as possible a post in some advertising office or department should be secured.

AGRICULTURE

There are various branches of agriculture which may appeal to the open-air girl and provide her with a satisfying occupation. Market gardening and fruit farming require capital, but offer openings for assistants; in dairying there is a wide field of employment; and there is also poultry keeping, though it is liable to be more precarious as a source of steady income.

In dairying there are now openings for women assistants on dairy farms, while girls who take the necessary scientific training may work in the laboratories under the Milk Marketing Board; also, many County Education Committees employ dairy instructresses. Those who wish to take it up scientifically should go to one of the universities or agricultural colleges that have dairy departments. The University of Reading, and the British Dairy Institute have a three years' course for the B.Sc. in dairying.

For general purposes, a college diploma in dairying should be taken. The National Diploma requires a two years' course. There are also elementary courses, and also a year's course enabling the student to take the butter and cheese-making certificate of the British Dairy Farmers' Association. Some scholarships are available from the Ministry of Agriculture and the Department of Agriculture for Scotland.

ARCHITECTURE

The first elementary qualification for this is skill in drawing, and along with it a good general education of General Certificate standard. The most satisfactory training is obtained by taking a five years' full-time course at a university or school of architecture. But it is also possible to take a three years' full-time course followed by part-time study for the final examination. A third but slow method is to train by part-time study for seven to nine years. Subjects to specialize in beforehand are mathematics, science, drawing and a language. All information from the Royal Institute of British Architects, 66 Portland Place, London, W.1.

ART

Training usually consists of a three or four years' course at municipal schools of art or at the Royal College of Art, London. Intending teachers usually require to take a further year's course in the principles of teaching.

Commercial Art and Fashion Drawing.

This is a highly competitive sphere, and changing fashions in public taste may render it precarious. The advance in fashion photography has greatly reduced the scope of the fashion artist. For those who fancy it a three years' course in drawing, painting and design is necessary, followed by a period of specialization in print designing.

Designing for Industry

There is increasing opportunity here for the girl with good artistic sense and creative power. Some business acumen is also required. There is also a specialized sphere for those with outstanding talent—perhaps in textile printing, stained glass, jewellery, furniture designing, &c.

AVIATION

There is a variety of occupations under this heading, from pilot to aero club secretary, and airport receptionist. There is also the air hostess, who must combine hostess, waitress and nurse all rolled into one. In most airlines some nursing qualifications are necessary. Applicants usually have to submit to medical examination.

BANKING

Openings for ambitious girls in banking are few. Generally they are restricted to mechanized bookkeeping, shorthand and typing, and the salary range is limited.

BARRISTER

It should be made quite clear that although a few women have made satisfactory careers in Law, it has been in the face of considerable difficulties. The Inns of Court, of which there are four, and to whom admission must be sought, have absolute discretion as to whom they admit to membership. Fees payable on admission amount to about £58, and deposits are required of £50 and £100. Particulars regarding the examinations and other conditions may be had from the Secretary to the Council of Legal Education, 7 Stone Buildings, London, W.C.2.

BEAUTY CULTURE

Those who wish to take up beauty culture should attend one of the schools for this purpose, or go into a salon training centre. Training fees vary, as does also the length of the course.

CHIROPODY

There are various forms of this work which may appeal: private practice, assistant to a chiropodist, or in industrial or municipal foot hospitals. Training is taken at schools attached to foot clinics which most of the bigger towns now possess. The course usually is for two years. This is suitable and remunerative occupation for the girl who may have home ties—provided she has been able to take the approved training. Particulars from local foot hospitals, or from the Society of Chiropodists, 21 Cavendish Square, London, W.1.

CHILD GUIDANCE

This generally involves specialist training in mental health: in psychology at a university, or as provided by the mental health course of the London School of Economics. On becoming qualified, the student should become attached to a child guidance clinic in order to gain experience.

CHILD WELFARE

There are various aspects of child welfare, each of which requires specialization: staffs of nursery schools, clinics, day nurseries, &c.

CHURCH WORK

Candidates for Holy Orders will know that women are not accepted in all denominations; it is mostly in the Non-conformist churches that they may become ministers. They are accepted as missionaries in most churches, and as church sisters or deaconesses —these last are mainly concerned with social work in congregational areas.

CIVIL SERVICE

Posts under the civil service demand high educational standards and are well paid. There are clerical grades, typists and telephonists, Inland Revenue, and Ministry of Labour posts. There are also openings for women in the Diplomatic Corps, and many opportunities in the lesser ranks for foreign service. Entrance to the Civil Service is highly competitive; particulars of the competitions are advertised from time to time. Applications should be addressed to the Secretary, Civil Service Commission, Burlington Gardens, London, W.1, who will give information about the latest regulations.

COMMERCIAL PHOTOGRAPHY

This ranges from portraiture to still-life photography for advertising. Women often do well by specializing in child studies. The way into this occupation is through apprenticeship after one year's training at a school. Competition is keen.

DENTISTRY

There are openings here for young women not only in private practice but under education authorities and public authorities for attending patients in hospitals and elsewhere. Training consists of a short course for the first M.B. or pre-medical examination, followed by four years' study at a recognized dental school, to secure the L.D.S. (Licence in Dental Surgery). A further qualification, the Higher Dental Diploma, is obtainable from the Royal College of Surgeons of Edinburgh and the Royal Faculty of Physicians and Surgeons of Glasgow. Degrees in dental surgery are conferred in several British universities and at Belfast and Dublin.

DOMESTIC SCIENCE

There is a wide field of opportunity here.

Demonstrating.

A domestic science course followed by, or including, specialized training in demonstrating is necessary. Demonstrators may be used either to publicize some domestic cooking appliance, or certain food products.

Dietetics.

Most dietitians are employed in hospitals, but there are openings in industrial catering. Candidates must have a university degree, or qualification in domestic science or be State Registered Nurses. Training takes from one to two years for a diploma recognized by the British Dietetic Association.

Hotel and Catering.

Generally there are no recognized standards, and the best training is by entering the industry and gaining experience. But a few schools of hotel management have been opened in recent years.

Institutional Management.

This involves being responsible for the domestic arrangements of hostels, schools, colleges and similar institutions.

Teaching.

Three-year course at a recognized college.

DRAMA

There are numerous methods of entry to the profession; for example, by way of the amateur company, or by the school of dramatic art. Training at one of the latter, followed by experience with a repertory company, is generally accepted to be the best highway to a successful career. The Royal Academy of Dramatic Art, Gower Street, London, and the Old Vic, are among the best-known schools. All would-be actresses are warned that the life is most arduous.

The theatre also offers some opportunities to women in stage décor, dress designing, producing, and—more rarely—as managers.

DRESS DESIGNING

To make any success as a dress designer, a girl will require to study practical dressmaking, anatomy, drawing from life and fashion drawing. The designer may work for individual clients or for a firm, and the best training is to be apprenticed to a leading designer.

ENGINEERING

The scope of engineering is very wide, and it is only possible to indicate very briefly some of the possible spheres of employment. Among posts open to women are: instructor in a technical or training school, draughtswoman, inspector, assistant in production or planning department, electrical technician, laboratory assistant, &c. For employment in skilled work it is necessary to have the General Certificate with mathematics, physics, chemistry, and for the highest posts a university degree. All particulars from the Ministry of Labour, the nearest technical college, or from the Women's Engineering Society, Ltd., 35 Grosvenor Place, London, S.W.1.

FILM WORK

The way to film stardom is generally by way of the stage. But apart from the players, there are many other occupations available. One is in the dress department, and there is a lucrative role for whoever becomes its chief. It involves expert knowledge of dress and costume in every age, and technical knowledge about colour. The same department employs dress designers, wardrobe mistress and needlewomen. The film studios also use women in the photography department as retouchers, in the joining and cutting of negatives, in scenario writing, in publicity, and occasionally as producers.

FLORISTRY

The florist sells flowers, must know all about them, have good colour sense, and be able to make up bouquets, buttonholes, &c. There is also the flower decorator who may build up a connexion going out to public halls or to private houses to arrange floral decorations. She must learn the business thoroughly to achieve success, and the only way is to begin very modestly in a well-established shop and there learn all the " tricks of the trade ".

HEALTH VISITOR

The health visitor, or Public Health nurse, is concerned with preventive medicine—her job is to keep people, mainly women and children, well. She may also have to assist in school medical services, and the many branches of work for which the Public Health authority is responsible. The nature of her work gives her a varied life. State registered nurses are preferred, and for these training consists of a six months' course for the first examination of the Central Midwives Board followed by a six months' course in health visiting. It is also possible for those who have not trained as nurses to take a two years' Public Health training course at an approved school. All particulars, in England, from the Royal Sanitary Institutes, 90 Buckingham Palace Road, London, S.W.1, or from the Royal Sanitary Association of Scotland, Edinburgh.

HORTICULTURE

If gardening, or market gardening, or fruit farming, appeal to you, this can be one of the most pleasant occupations though it may not bring a fortune; at the same time there is no reason why it should not provide a quite adequate livelihood. You may set up business for yourself as a jobbing gardener in suburbia, or get a post as gardener, or, to begin with, under-gardener, on a private estate, or with a parks committee in a city; or you may go in for market gardening, or specialize in one particular item, or produce, or you may become a horticultural lecturer or inspector under a county council. Here again training is essential, and various degrees, diplomas and certificates are awarded. Full information may be obtained from the secretaries of the agricultural colleges at Edinburgh, Glasgow and Aberdeen, or from the Women's Farm and Garden Association, Courtauld House, Byng Place, London, W.C.1.

HOSPITAL ALMONER

This is one of the more recent occupations which have opened up for girls, and opens wide horizons for a useful and satisfying life. Her chief job is to call on hospital patients after they go home to see that the treatment recommended by the doctor is being carried out—otherwise the person may soon fall ill again—or if she finds that it is not, to discover what is preventing it, perhaps lack of money. Thus, she gets to know a tremendous number of all sorts of people, and is accepted as their friend. For all this the Institute of Hospital Almoners insists on a course of training which includes generally two years at a university to obtain a diploma or certificate in social science, and then about fifteen months practical training.

HOTEL WORK

The hotel industry offers wide scope for young women. From the office typist, manager's secretary to cook, housekeeper, store-keeper, receptionist, to management herself, there are many grades of opportunity. A domestic science training is advisable, and will lead to the post of cook or junior housekeeper, but after that the best training is experience in varied hotels until the trainee decides which type she wishes to specialize in with a view to management herself. The Hotels and Restaurants Association, 88 Brook Street, London, W.C.1, will supply information.

HOUSING MANAGEMENT

Housing management combines the business side of rent collecting and administration with the social aspects of the work. It is useful first to have a university degree or social science diploma. After that the Society of Women Housing Estate Managers arranges training, which consists of practical work on housing estates combined with part-time study for the Women Housing Managers' Certificate. Octavia Hill was the pioneer of this work, and women housing estate managers are increasingly in demand. Physical fitness is essential, as the manager has to be out in all weathers on the long round of visits. All particulars from the above society at 13 Suffolk Street, Pall Mall, London, S.W.1.

HOUSE OR INTERIOR DECORATION

A house decorator must know all about the practical side of decorating—the distempering of ceilings, trimming and hanging of wallpapers, staining and polishing of floors. In addition, she must know about upholstery, how to draw plans of rooms in order to fit them with carpets and curtains, and so on. For expert training there is a course of decoration in the Bartlett School of Architecture at University College, London. In other parts of the country established firms of decorators take pupils to train as assistants.

JOURNALISM

This is one possible career for which an expensive training is not necessary; but it must be emphasized that the widest possible education is advisable, and many of the more responsible papers expect applicants for a post to hold a good university degree. Entrance to the profession for a girl is generally first of all through secretarial work in a newspaper office, where she picks up all sorts of information about editorial work. So a secretarial training with shorthand and typewriting may be a useful stepping-stone to journalistic work. An alert mind, shrewd observation of people, and good health are vital attributes. The work commands a high standard of payment for those who can secure posts.

KENNEL WORK

There are not so very many openings here for girls, but those who are particularly keen on dogs and good at working with them may find an occupation as kennel maid, or higher up as kennel manageress. The latter must know all about canine hygiene, be able to attend sick dogs, and assist with the birth of puppies. She must know about the different breeds of dogs, and how to prepare them for the show ring. A good kennel maid is generally resident.

For those who aspire to running a kennel of their own several hundred pounds' capital is necessary.

LAUNDRY WORK

This sphere of occupation can provide many openings for energetic girls, and lead to a post as manageress commanding a very good salary. It may not always be required, but in general, trainees should have the General Certificate of Education or the equivalent before they are accepted for apprenticeship, during which the apprentice will work in each department of a laundry. The Institution of British Launderers, Ltd., 17 Lancaster Gate, London, W.2, arranges such a course. During the second and third years pupils may go out to various laundries and earn a small weekly wage. Evening classes are also available in many places.

LIBRARIANSHIP

This may appeal to the girl who is not only a " book-worm " but who has the knack of getting others to share her enthusiasm for books. Library work, it is sometimes forgotten, calls for physical fitness, as it involves much standing and walking and carrying of heavy bundles of books. Junior assistants in public libraries do not earn much. It is advisable to study for the professional examination of the Library Association; for the highest posts a university degree is necessary. It is also possible to take correspondence courses. There is a school of librarianship in connexion with University College, London. For all information apply to the Secretary, The Library Association, Chaucer House, Malet Place, London, W.C.1.

MASSAGE

This interesting and remunerative branch of medical work may appeal to those who are not able to give up the longer period of years necessary for medicine. The full massage course takes about two years, and should also include the course in electrotherapy. The General Certificate of Education (with certain specified subjects) or its equivalent is essential. Training is given at many city hospitals and infirmaries, as well as at certain physical training colleges. There are many openings for masseuses in voluntary and municipal hospitals; the alternative is private practice. Particulars from the Secretary, The Chartered Society of Physiotherapy, Tavistock House (South), Tavistock Square, London, W.C.1.

MEDICINE

Students are not encouraged to enter a medical course before they are eighteen years of age. It is as well to be forewarned that the course is lengthy—it may take up to six years—and costly. But the prospects indicate that this profession offers increasing openings for women. There are medical schools in connexion with most of the universities of Great Britain and Ireland, but it is important to find out what facilities there are in local hospitals and infirmaries for post-graduate training. The other important point to remember is that some medical schools admit only a small proportion of women each year. These matters should be fully investigated before embarking on a course.

MISSIONARY WORK

The girl who would like to become a missionary must first of all have religious conviction, and then take steps to acquire professional training and practice for the type of mission work she wishes to do, whether medical, nursing, or teaching. She should apply for entrance to the church or society of the faith to which she belongs. Generally, the missionary training is taken last after the candidate has already qualified for teaching or medicine. Any church will be able to supply information, but further particulars may be had from the Conference of British Missionary Societies, Edinburgh House, 2 Eaton Gate, Sloane Square, London, S.W.1.

MUSEUM WORK

The big national museums employ a large staff of specialists, most of whom hold university degrees, but there is also much less highly specialized work done, such as cataloguing, card indexing, and so on. There are not very many openings here for girls. The Secretary, Museums Association, Chaucer House, Malet Place, London, W.C.1, will be able to advise.

MUSIC

Only those with outstanding talent, plus an infinite capacity for hard work, can hope to make a career from music; but this warning made, there is considerable scope for the enthusiast with more modest ambitions. And of course there are excellent posts as music mistress in good schools. To get anywhere some recognized diploma or certificate is essential, and training is within reach of most parts of the country at schools and academies of music. At the principal schools there are many scholarships open to girls. It should be noted that candidates are usually required to have some certificate of education or to pass a preliminary examination in general English subjects.

NURSING

This is the outstanding profession in which there are at present, and likely to be for very many years, unlimited opportunities for girls. Conditions have greatly improved, and remuneration is satisfactory from the beginning, and may lead eventually to a matronship at the £1000 income level—though these posts naturally are few. It is hard and testing work, but where a girl enters into it with her whole heart it is a most satisfying career. A good general education is essential, and if the applicant does not have her General Certificate she will have to pass an educational test. Training for qualification as a State registered nurse consists of three years' practical hospital experience combined with theoretical instruction. The nurse, it should be noted, is in the rare position of being paid during training.

There are many branches of nursing—child nursing, midwifery, school matron, sister tutor (the teaching of nursing), industrial nursing. State registered nurses are frequently appointed to factory medical departments. There are bursaries and grants in connexion with the industrial training course, which generally lasts three months.

Navy, Army, and Air Force Nursing gives opportunities for seeing the world.

DISTRICT NURSING

The work of the district nurse includes midwifery, maternity and general nursing, and also the free nursing of Public Assistance cases. In some large towns there is a municipal service of district nurses; in rural areas the Queen's Institute of District Nursing is the responsible body. As a rule these nurses are fully trained and State registered; they also receive a special six months' training in home nursing. Nowadays very often the district nurse has a car provided for her and participates in a pensions scheme.

OCCUPATIONAL THERAPY

This is the art of healing through occupational activities. The doctor prescribes the form of activity which may help the patient to recovery, and the therapist chooses a suitable craft and instructs the patient in it. There has been a tremendous development in this work in all kinds of hospitals and homes in recent years. Training consists of a two and a half to three years' course for the examinations of the Association of Occupational Therapists. Craft subjects include basketry, bookbinding, design, joinery, weaving, toy-making, metal and leather work, and so on, but in addition to practical knowledge of craft work the therapist must have the real interest in people which will enable her to win their co-operation towards their own cure.

PERSONNEL MANAGEMENT

Big businesses, factories and warehouses are making increasing use of personnel managers, whose duties include the recruitment and training of staff and the maintenance of good working and welfare conditions. This work comes under the category of social service and the training is similar—a two years' university course in social science, followed by some months' practical experience.

PHARMACY

Chemists' shops have a fascination for many girls, and also the making up of prescriptions. Not only do shops employ women assistant pharmacists, and doctors have women dispensers, they are also required in hospitals. Some may, with special qualifications, become public analysists. A degree in pharmacy is recommended, but as there are many regulations under the Pharmacy Acts, and also regarding the appointments open to women, it is advisable to approach in the first place the Pharmaceutical Society of Great

Britain, 17 Bloomsbury Square, London, W.C.1. A training in
pharmacy takes five to six years; but to become a doctor's dispenser
there is a nine months' course for assistants in dispensing—particulars from the Registrar, Society of Apothecaries, Blackfriars
Lane, Queen Victoria Street, London, E.C.4.

PHYSIOTHERAPY

This includes massage, medical gymnastics and electrotherapy.
Training consists of a two to two and a half years' course for the
examinations of the Chartered Society of Physiotherapy. See particulars under Massage.

POLICE WORK

Women are employed in the police force mainly in matters
concerning women and girls, and previous social work is an advantage. There is a stiff medical examination, and candidates have to
be a required height. Good educational qualifications are expected,
and there is an intelligence test to be passed. Women may become
police sergeants and there are a few who reach the rank of inspector.
Conditions vary in different parts of the country, and information
should be sought from the local constabulary.

POULTRY KEEPING

Because you may have at some time kept half a dozen hens,
do not assume this to be sufficient experience on which to build a
career. At least a year's training should be taken on a poultry farm.
For those wishing to specialize further, there is a National Diploma
in Poultry Husbandry, the training for which includes a year's
practical experience on an approved poultry farm, with at least
two years at an agricultural college. This diploma is essential for
the girl wishing to secure a post as a poultry instructor.

RADIOGRAPHY

There is scope in X-ray work for the girl who has the same
qualities as are required in a nurse—cheerful and pleasant manner
in dealing with patients, and good health herself. Sometimes nurses
graduate into the X-ray department, but the most reliable way to
reach good posts is by taking the Diploma of the Society of Radio-

graphers, either after qualifying as a nurse or acquiring a First Aid or Home Nursing Certificate or similar qualification. Posts available are assistantships to a radiologist in private practice, or in a hospital. Duties include operating the X-ray machine, developing the films, and directing the patient.

SALESMANSHIP

From humble jobs at a shop counter many women have risen to make for themselves very lucrative careers, for a good saleswoman is readily given opportunities to advance. In time she will pass from counter assistant to under-buyer, then buyer, or else manager and superviser. A university education is often an asset towards reaching the higher posts, provided the other business qualifications are also there; but it is not necessary, though General Certificate standard should be reached. Most big firms give their staff some training in salesmanship; and in many cities the commercial colleges have day and evening classes.

SANITARY INSPECTION

The routine work of the Public Health Department in any town or country district falls largly on the sanitary inspectors. Mostly they are men, but in London and in some of the other cities one or more women are employed on the staff. Women undertake inspection of factories where women and girls are employed. To become a sanitary officer it is necessary to hold the certificate of the Royal Sanitary Institute and Sanitary Inspectors Examination Joint Board, for which there is an examination to be passed. Training is given in technical colleges, with a practical course to be undertaken in a health department.

SCIENCE (Chemistry, Physics)

Industry is making use more and more of the chemist, physicist and biologist, but though there are occasional good posts for women they are not numerous. Subjects in which the candidate should be proficient are mathematics, science, and French and German. A university degree in science is necessary. Students sometimes are able to be employed as laboratory assistants while taking their course.

SECRETARIAL WORK

This work ranges from the shorthand typist to the company secretary, from the part-time secretary to, say, a doctor, to the highly responsible post of Parliamentary Private Secretary. Once again, the better the education, the better the possibilities. After that, a good secretarial training, which includes shorthand, typing, card indexing, filing, duplicating, is necessary. But a warning is advisable: too many girls take the shortest, quickest way to get into an office, and then find they are in a dead-end job which can offer no advancement because of their limited qualifications. The enterprising girl, once fully trained, should move from office to office to gain as much experience as possible.

SOCIAL WORK

Under this heading come such posts as hospital almoner, nursery school workers, which are dealt with elsewhere. In addition, there are the wardens of settlements, juvenile employment officers, probation officers, welfare supervisors, &c. Training normally consists of a two years' university course for a diploma or certificate in social science, followed by some months' specialized training for the service in view. The sphere of social service is widening, salary standards improving, so that there is promise here not only of a vocation for the girl who cares how other people live, but also one which may provide a satisfactory livelihood.

SOLICITOR

To qualify to practise as a solicitor it is necessary—in England —to have the consent of the Law Society and to serve for a time as an articled clerk to a solicitor. The usual period is five years, in the course of which various examinations have to be passed. There are numerous fees and expenses, but all particulars may be obtained from the Secretary, the Law Society, Chancery Lane, London, W.C.2.

SPEECH THERAPY

This may appeal to the girl who is a good elocutionist but does not aspire to the stage or even to public engagements. It is the treatment of defects and disorders of speech which make life miserable to those afflicted by them. While good openings are so far few, there are posts for women under certain educational authorities and other public bodies. Training consists of a two to three years' full-time course at a recognized training school. Application to the local Public Health Department will elicit particulars.

TEACHING

This has always been a popular, and one of the principal, occupations for educated women, and it is not necessary to give detailed information about it here. Any teacher or headmistress is able to advise on training and on the various branches of the work which may be undertaken. Under the latest Education Acts it has become one of the best professions available for women, but it is very much to be hoped that only those who *like* the idea of teaching will take it up. Otherwise if they perform their duties without interest, they are doing a grave disservice to the children who come under their care.

VETERINARY SURGERY

This of course is the sort of work for the girl who is fond of animals and good at handling them. It is also one of the occupations which is developing, and in which women are increasingly welcome. If interested in research the woman " vet " may tackle the urgent problems of diseases among farm animals. Training consists of a course of at least five years at a recognized veterinary school.

YOUTH LEADERSHIP

The function of a youth leader is to organize the programme and activities of a club for girls under twenty, and to be interested in their general welfare. This again comes under Social Service (see Training), but it is also possible to take a two and a half years' full-time course provided by the National Association of Girls' Clubs. The Carnegie United Kingdom Trust Bursary Fund awards bursaries for youth leadership training. All information from the National Association of Girls' Clubs, Hamilton House, Bidborough Street, London, W.C.1

If you want to know more about any of the careers mentioned, the Women's Employment Federation, 251 Brompton Road, London, S.W.3, can supply more detailed information. They will also answer inquiries about careers by letter and interview, on payment of a small fee. They also know a great deal about scholarships and may be able to help an inquirer in this way.

If you do not live in or near a big town and want to know what educational facilities and evening classes are available in your area, you can obtain this information by writing to the Director of Education for your district, or to the Town Clerk in the nearest town.